Kaplan GRE® Exam Subject Test: Psychology

Third Edition

Other Kaplan titles related to Graduate School Admissions include:

Get Into Graduate School: A Strategic Approach
GRE Exam 2007 Edition: Comprehensive Program
GRE Exam 2007 Edition: Premier Program (CD-ROM)
Kaplan GRE Exam Subject Test: Biology, 2007–2008 Edition
GRE Exam Vocabulary Flashcards Flip-O-Matic, Second Edition
GRE Exam Verbal Workbook, Fourth Edition
GMAT Math Workbook, Fifth Edition
GRE & GMAT Exams Writing Workbook, Second Edition
GRE Exam Math Workbook

Kaplan GRE® Exam Subject Test: Psychology

Third Edition

This publication is designed to provide accurate and authoritative information in regard to the subject matter covered. It is sold with the understanding that the publisher is not engaged in rendering legal, accounting, or other professional service. If legal advice or other expert assistance is required, the services of a competent professional should be sought.

Contributing Editors: Susan Kaplan, Matt Fidler
Editorial Director: Jennifer Farthing
Editor: Megan Gilbert
Production Editor: Caitlin Ostrow
Production Artist: Joe Budenholzer
Cover Designer: Carly Schnur

© 2006 by Kaplan, Inc.

Published by Kaplan Publishing, a division of Kaplan, Inc.
888 Seventh Ave.
New York, NY 10106

Printed in the United States of America

August 2006
10 9 8 7 6 5 4 3 2 1

ISBN-13: 978-1-4195-5142-0
ISBN-10:   1-4195-5142-6

Kaplan Publishing books are available at special quantity discounts to use for sales promotions, employee premiums, or educational purposes. Please call our Special Sales Department to order or for more information at 800-621-9621, ext. 4444, e-mail kaplanpubsales@kaplan.com, or write to Kaplan Publishing, 30 South Wacker Drive, Suite 2500, Chicago, IL 60606-7481.

TABLE OF CONTENTS

Available Online

FOR ANY TEST CHANGES OR LATE-BREAKING DEVELOPMENTS

kaptest.com/publishing

The material in this book is up-to-date at the time of publication. However, the Educational Testing Service may have instituted changes in the test or test-registration process after this book was published. Be sure to carefully read the materials you receive when you register for the test. If there are any important late-breaking developments—or any changes or corrections to the Kaplan test preparation materials in this book—we will post that information online at **kaptest.com/publishing**.

FEEDBACK AND COMMENTS

kaplansurveys.com/books

We'd love to hear your comments and suggestions about this book. We invite you to fill out our online survey form at **kaplansurveys.com/books**. Your feedback is extremely helpful as we continue to develop high-quality resources to meet your needs.

HOW TO USE THIS BOOK

This book provides you with everything you need to ace the GRE Psychology Exam. This section includes some tips on how to make the most of your prep time.

STEP 1: FAMILIARIZE YOURSELF WITH THE GRE PSYCHOLOGY EXAM

The first chapter, "Inside the GRE Psychology Exam," covers the basics of the test and how it's scored. Once you get a sense of the test, you're ready to get a sense of yourself as a test-taker. Next read Chapter 2, "Test-Taking Strategies," to learn Kaplan's proven methods for increasing your score on this challenging exam.

STEP 2: TAKE THE DIAGNOSTIC TEST

This book contains two simulated full-length GRE Psychology tests with answer explanations. Take one of these tests early in your preparation to get a sense of where you're scoring now, and what score you're shooting for on Test Day.

As you work through your exam, pay attention to the areas in which you perform best. These areas of strength will provide you with the bulk of your points on the actual exam. Also make note of your problem areas. You will need to shore up your knowledge in your problem areas to maximize your performance on the test.

With a clear sense of your strengths and weaknesses, you will be ready to tackle the content chapters that form the bulk of this book.

STEP 3: WORK THROUGH THE PSYCHOLOGY REVIEW, REINFORCING STRENGTHS AND SHORING UP WEAKNESSES

Each content chapter focuses on a specific aspect of psychology that is tested on the GRE Psychology Exam. Based on your performance on the diagnostic test, you should have a good sense of which areas you are strongest in, and which areas need the most reinforcement.

For the best and most efficient review, each chapter includes an outline of the topics covered, at-a-glance charts of important concepts you need to know, plus listings of important figures in psychology and their contributions to the field. Throughout the book, key terminology is highlighted for you. The chapters also include quizzes to help you test yourself on the content covered.

Develop a study plan that devotes roughly the same amount of time to each of the chapters as you go through the entire book. Aim to complete all the content two weeks prior to your exam date. The last two weeks should be spent working through the second practice test and reviewing your notes.

STEP 4: CONCLUDE YOUR PREPARATION WITH THE PRACTICE TEST

Your preparation with this book should conclude with the second simulated full-length GRE Psychology test. After completing this exam, work through the explanations that follow it. Be sure to review the explanations for questions you got right as well as for those you got wrong. This will serve as a good review of the wide range of topics covered on the exam.

After completing the second exam, continue to refer to the content chapters and the diagnostic test to make sure you are familiar with everything we cover in this book.

Use this game plan and then, right before the exam, you can relax. You're ready—you're going to get a great score!

Section One:
THE BASICS

CHAPTER ONE

Inside the GRE Psychology Exam

WHAT IS THE GRE PSYCHOLOGY EXAM?

The GRE Psychology Subject Test is a 2 hour and 50 minute exam designed to test advanced knowledge that a student applying to graduate school in psychology is expected to understand. The test requires knowledge of psychological vocabulary, names, and facts across a variety of psychological fields at the equivalent of an upper-level college class.

The GRE Psychology Exam is a traditional paper-and-pencil test consisting of approximately 215–220 multiple-choice questions with five answer choices, (A) through (E). For each question, you are to select the one correct or best answer from among the choices provided. There are no essay questions.

WHO WRITES THE TEST?

The GRE Psychology Exam is written by Educational Testing Service (ETS)—the same folks who write the GRE General Test, the GMAT, the SAT, and the LSAT. Academic faculty are consulted as the test is generated, but ultimately, the test is written by ETS.

Since these test makers write these tests over and over again, they begin to follow certain patterns that we at Kaplan can unlock for you. More on that later.

HOW DO I REGISTER FOR THE EXAM?

Go to **gre.org** for official ETS information about the GRE Psychology Subject Test. To sign up for the Psychology Subject Test, you can register online at the **gre.org** website, or you can contact ETS directly.

ETS Contact Information

By regular mail at:
GRE-ETS
P.O. Box 6000
Princeton, NJ 08541–6000

By overnight mail at:
GRE
Distribution and Receiving Center
225 Phillips Boulevard
Ewing, NJ 08628-7435

Or by phone at:
866-473-4373
609-771-7670
Monday through Friday, 8:00 A.M. to 7:45 P.M.
Fax: 609-771-7906

Test Dates

The GRE Psychology Subject Test is offered in April, November, and December. The test is normally given on a Saturday, but students claiming special circumstances may request to take the test on the Monday following a testing date.

Be sure to register for a test well ahead of your application deadlines, since you will need to take both the Subject Test and the General Test, and you want to leave some time to retake the exam if necessary.

Testing Fee

At the time of the publication of this book, the fee is $130 if you are taking the exam in the United States and $150 everywhere else in the world. Testing fees have steadily increased by $5 to $10 each year.

On the Day of the Test

ETS recommends that you arrive at the testing center no later than 8:30 AM. You should plan on being at the testing center for a total of 3 hours and 30 minutes. It is a good idea to scout out the test location prior to the day of your test, so you arrive on Test Day well prepared and with time to spare.

Required Items

You will need to bring the following items to the testing center on the day of your test:

- Several (3 to 5) sharpened No. 2 pencils and several good erasers
- The admission ticket provided to you by ETS
- Photo identification with your signature (e.g., passport, driver's license, military ID)

Don't Bring...

Testing aids are not permitted at the testing center. These include but are not limited to: mechanical pencils, pens, pagers, beepers, calculators, watch calculators, books, pamphlets, notes, rulers, highlighter pens, stereos or radios with headphones, telephones, cell phones, watch alarms, stop watches, dictionaries, translators, and any electronic or photographic devices.

You may not eat, drink, or use tobacco during the testing time.

Paper of any kind is not permitted in the testing room.

Sending off Scores

Scores on the GRE Psychology Exam are good for five years. When you sign up for the exam, and again on day of the test, you will be given the opportunity to list up to four schools that you would like ETS to send your scores to for no additional charge. You can also have your scores sent to other schools for an additional charge of $15 per school. Your scores normally arrive by mail six weeks after your test date.

Canceling Scores

If you wish, you may cancel your scores at the end of the test. No record of you taking the test that day will be reported to you or any graduate programs. While this may be a tempting offer when confronted with the frustrations of a tough exam, you should void your score only if something extraordinary has interfered with your performance on the exam. A serious illness is a good example of the kind of extraordinary circumstances that might make canceling your score a wise choice.

Taking the Test More Than Once

You are permitted to take the GRE Psychology Exam as often as you like. We recommend taking the test once and taking your preparation for that test seriously. All previous scores will appear on the score report that is sent to schools, so you should plan on taking the test once and knocking their socks off with a top-notch score. While schools may focus on your most recent score or your highest score, you simplify their task when your report includes only one high-end score.

WHAT DOES THE TEST MEASURE?

The GRE Psychology Exam measures your knowledge of a wide range of undergraduate psychology content as well as your general test-taking skills. This does not mean you have to have taken numerous undergraduate psychology courses to do well on the exam. Instead, you need to master the material that appears on the test and understand the structure of the test and how it's scored to perform at the highest level.

What Material Appears on the Test?

Although the exam tests a wide range of psychology content, it does not require in-depth knowledge of specific psychological concepts or theories. A wide breadth of relatively superficial knowledge of psychological theories, names, and terms is what it takes to achieve a high score. A deep, nuanced understanding of a certain specific school of thought or theory may help in some instances, but in general, such a level of understanding is more than you will need to perform well.

According to ETS, questions fall into one of three content categories:

- Experimental or natural science-oriented (about 40 percent of the questions), including learning, language, memory, thinking, sensation and perception, physiological psychology, ethology, and comparative psychology. They contribute to the experimental psychology subscore and the total score.
- Social or social science-oriented (about 43 percent of the questions). These questions are distributed among the fields of clinical and abnormal, developmental, personality, and social psychology. They contribute to the social psychology subscore and the total score.
- General (about 17 percent of the questions), including the history of psychology, applied psychology, measurement, research designs, and statistics. They contribute to the total score only.

These three categories cover a great deal of material. The bulk of this book is devoted to reviewing the key concepts and names in the categories described above.

How Is the Test Scored?

Your performance on the exam is used to generate a raw score, a scaled score, a percentile rank, and two subscores. Graduate programs weigh the scaled score and percentile rank most heavily.

Raw Score

Your raw score is determined by taking the number of questions you answered correctly and subtracting one quarter of the number of questions you answered incorrectly. Unanswered questions have no impact on your raw score.

For example, if a student answered 155 questions correctly, 20 questions incorrectly, and left the remaining 40 questions unanswered, we could determine her raw score on the GRE Psychology Exam. In this case, her raw score would be $155 - \frac{1}{4}(20) = 155 - 5 = 150$.

Scaled Score

Your raw score is compared to a conversion chart to yield a scaled score between 200 and 990. Conversion charts vary slightly from test to test. The scaled score is supposed to reflect how you would perform relative to a standard distribution of test-takers. Based on your scaled score, ETS also provides a *percentile rank,* which states what percentage of test-takers scored at or below your level of performance.

Subscores

You receive two subscores in addition to your scaled score. Subscore I corresponds to your performance in the Experimental and Natural Sciences category. Subscore II corresponds to your performance in the Social and Social Sciences category. Subscores range from 20–99. Most graduate programs focus on your scaled score rather than your subscores.

What Does My Score Mean?

The scoring information on your score report will look something like this:

MO.	11
YR.	02
TYPE	N
CODE	25
SCORE	800
% BELOW	84
SS1	62
SS2	59
CORRECT	155
INCORRECT	20
OMITS	40

The score report will show your total (scaled) score (in this student's case, an 800) as well as the percentile rank (84th percentile) and subscores for the two subsections. It will also indicate how many questions you answered correctly and incorrectly, as well as how many questions you did not answer at all.

The two numbers that are of most significance to you (and to the schools you are applying to) are the scaled score and percentile ranking. These scores reflect your performance relative to your fellow test-takers.

To use the psychological lingo, the GRE Psychology Exam is a norm-referenced test that requires a broad and general understanding of psychological figures and terms. *Norm-referenced* means that your score reflects your performance *relative to a standard distribution of test-takers*. It is not a test of whether you can simply demonstrate mastery of basic psychological concepts. So get your competitive juices flowing, and remember that preparation is the key. That's where we can help.

CHAPTER TWO

Test-Taking Strategies

GETTING READY FOR TEST DAY

The GRE Psychology Subject Test is a serious exam. Treat it with respect and dedication, and it can reward you with a top-notch score. Take it lightly, and it can ruin your chances of being accepted into graduate school.

Doctoral programs in psychology are extremely competitive, and fellowships are given only to the cream of the crop. Graduate schools need to whittle the field of quality candidates down to a select few. As a result, they prefer to use objective measures wherever possible. That's where the GRE Psychology Exam comes in.

Kaplan has been preparing test-takers for high-stakes exams for over 50 years. Our focus is always on how to make the most of each individual's performance on Test Day. In order to perform at the highest level, you'll need to know the content that appears on the exam and have a clear sense of how the test is structured and scored.

In this book, we'll cover everything you are expected to know on the GRE Psychology Subject Test. Each of the key content areas will be covered in its own chapter, allowing you to target one aspect of your psychological knowledge at a time. As you proceed, pay special attention to the subject areas you know best. Come Test Day, these areas of strength will provide you with the lion's share of your points.

Although the exam tests a wide range of psychology content, it does not require in-depth knowledge of any psychological concepts or theories. A wide breadth of relatively superficial knowledge of psychological theories, names, and terms is what it takes to achieve a high score.

Consequently, we've tried to do a quick survey of all the major ideas and names that appear on the GRE Psychology Exam. We cover all the important schools of psychology that appear on the test, and pay special attention to the key names and terms that are tested most frequently. Simply linking an important name to a related psychological theory or term is one of the key skills to master for this exam. Making connections quickly and confidently will help you rack up points fast.

In addition to reviewing basic psychology content in a clear and straightforward fashion, we'll address how this exam is a timed test of your performance. Each question is equally valued and every correct and incorrect answer is scored in the same way. Understanding the nuts and bolts of the test and how it's scored will help focus your plan of attack come Test Day.

Good strategic guessing, quick decision-making, and careful time management will ensure that you edge out less prepared test takers and arrive at the top-tier score you are shooting for. We'll cover these kinds of tips in detail in the remainder of this chapter.

How to Organize Your Time

Begin with a Diagnostic Test

Most likely, the GRE Psychology Exam is unlike any other psychology test you've ever taken. While you may have taken a survey course or two as an undergraduate, it is unlikely that you took as lengthy or exhaustive a test of your psychological knowledge.

The best way to get a sense of what you're up against is to take a practice test. In the back of this book, we've provided you with two full-length practice GRE Psychology tests with full answer explanations.

Take your first test early on in your preparation for the exam. Taking a diagnostic test will give you a good sense of how you will perform on Test Day. Perhaps more importantly, your performance will highlight your strengths and weaknesses and allow you to develop your study plan accordingly.

Generally speaking, you want to address your weaknesses early on in your preparation, and then move on to your strengths as Test Day approaches. You can get a good sense of where you are on any given subject by taking the Practice Sets at the end of each chapter.

Create a Study Plan and Stick to It

Abraham Lincoln once said, "If I was given eight hours to chop down a tree, I would spend seven hours sharpening my ax." The same sort of reasoning applies to the GRE Psychology Exam. Once you know when you are going to take the exam, create a plan that allows you to work through each of the eight content chapters that follow. Be sure to leave at least two weeks for your final review.

Know Your Strengths

One of the keys to success on this exam is to understand what you know best. As you take the practice tests and read through the review chapters that follow, pay special attention to those areas you've mastered. As we've said before, once Test Day rolls around, these subject areas will provide you with the bulk of your points. While your natural tendency to focus on problem areas and weaknesses, as your test date approaches it is essential that you know where you can bank points and build confidence.

Finish Strong

With two weeks remaining, you should begin your final review. At this point you can review all of the content chapters you've already worked through and prepare for your final practice exam.

Your final review should include taking a second practice test. In addition to the tests in this book, the best simulation of what you'll encounter on Test Day is the released exam available at **gre.org**. This is the same exam that you receive with your registration booklet in the mail.

Taking this practice test under timed, testlike conditions will give you the best sense of what you're up against and how you can expect to perform on the exam. While taking your final practice test, and the real exam that soon follows, remember to apply the tips outlined in the next section.

TEST-TAKING TIPS

You have 170 minutes to complete about 215 questions, some of which will involve reading short passages and examining data or graphs. You will need to carefully budget your time to perform at your highest level on this exam. Here are some strategies to maximize your score.

Answer the Easier Questions First

Easy questions are worth as many points as hard questions. On your first pass through the test, answer all the questions that are easiest for you. Understand which areas you know best, and seek out these questions right from the start. Skip questions that are tough or time-consuming during your first pass through the test.

Make (At Least) Two Passes Through the Test

This means making the quick decision to skip those questions that give you trouble. When you come across a tough question, circle it in your test booklet, and move on. Don't waste valuable time on hard questions early in the exam, especially when there may be easier questions ahead that you have not seen yet. The time you waste on one tough or confusing question could be better spent answering three or four easy questions that appear later in the test. Once you've knocked down all the easy questions and banked those points, you can return to the trickier questions on your second pass through the test.

Mark Up Your Test Booklet

As a student, you may be used to teachers telling you not to write in your books. But when taking the GRE Psychology Exam, it is to your advantage to mark up your test booklet. Circle questions you will return to, cross out incorrect answers, and write down key notes. Just remember that no credit is given for work you do in your test booklet. Make sure you transfer your final answers to your answer grid.

Guess Strategically

There is a $\frac{1}{4}$ point deduction for incorrect answer choices. So random guessing will probably hurt and not help your score. Strategic guessing, however, is essential to a top-notch performance. If you can eliminate one or two clearly wrong answer choices, you should guess. With practice, you can get better and better at guessing on tough questions. Making quick, effective guesses on your second pass through the test will pay off with a higher score.

Be Careful with Your Answer Sheet

It's easy to forget to skip a row on your answer sheet when you skip a question. Make sure you skip the necessary spaces when skipping questions. Also make sure to erase fully when changing your answers. Taking extra care of your answer grid will ensure that you don't give any points away.

Pace Yourself

The GRE Psychology Exam is almost three hours long. It is essential that you maintain your focus throughout. Stay on task and actively work your way through the exam. Don't get frustrated or discouraged when you encounter tough questions. Remember that you don't need to answer every question correctly to get a good score.

The Evening Before the Exam, Relax!

It's tempting to spend the last few hours cramming, but this tends to be counterproductive. Rather than an all-night cram session, do something low-stress, and be sure to get a good night's sleep.

MANAGING STRESS

You will feel stress between now and Test Day. It's up to you to learn to manage your stress effectively. A little stress is good. Stress can be harnessed and turned into positive energy if you follow some simple rules of thumb.

Take Control

Lack of control is a prime cause of stress. Research shows that if you don't have a sense of control over what is happening in your life, you can easily end up feeling stressed and helpless. Focus on those causes of your stress that you can exercise some control over.

Focus on Your Strengths

Make a list of your areas of strength that will help you do well on the test. We all have strengths, and recognizing your strengths can give you the confidence and resolve necessary to conquer stress. Your strengths will help you solve tough questions, maintain confidence, and keep test stress and anxiety at a distance. And every time you recognize a new area of strength, solve a challenging problem, or score well on a practice test, you'll build your confidence. Confidence feeds off itself, and is the cornerstone of a top-notch score.

Imagine Yourself Succeeding

Close your eyes and imagine yourself in a relaxing situation. Breathe easily and naturally. Now, think of a real-life situation in which you scored well on a test or did well on an assignment. Focus on this success. Now turn your thoughts to the GRE Psychology Exam, and keep your thoughts in line with that successful experience. Imagine yourself taking the upcoming test with the same feelings of confidence and relaxed control.

Set Realistic Goals

Facing your problem areas gives you some distinct advantages. What do you want to accomplish in the time remaining? Make a list of realistic goals. You can't help but feel more confident as you see yourself taking the steps necessary to earn a higher test score.

Exercise Your Frustrations Away

Whether it's jogging, biking, pushups, or a pickup basketball game, physical exercise will stimulate your mind and body, improving your ability to think and concentrate. Falling out of regular exercise routines while preparing for a test may wind up hurting your performance. A little physical exertion will help keep your mind and body in sync and help you sleep better at night.

Eat Well

Good nutrition will help you focus and think clearly. Eat plenty of fruits and vegetables, low-fat proteins such as fish, skinless poultry, beans and legumes, and whole grains such as brown rice, whole wheat bread, and pasta. Try to avoid high-sugar and high-fat snacks and overly salty foods.

Work at Your Own Pace

Don't be thrown by other test-takers furiously bubbling in answers nearby. Spend your time working through your answers in your own style; it will lead to better results. Don't mistake other's sheer activity with genuine progress and higher scores.

Keep Breathing

Conscious attention to breathing is an excellent way to keep anxiety down while you take the test. Most people who get into trouble during tests take shallow breaths using only their upper chests and shoulders. Some test-takers may unknowingly hold their breath for long periods of time. Conversely, those test-takers who breathe deeply in a slow, relaxed manner are likely to remain in better control throughout the testing session.

Stretch

If you find yourself getting spaced out or brain-fried as you're taking the test, stop for a moment and stretch. Even though you'll be pausing for a moment, it's a moment well spent. Stretching will help to refresh you and refocus your thoughts.

Section Two:
PSYCHOLOGY REVIEW

CHAPTER THREE

Social Psychology

OUTLINE

Historical Perspective

Attitudes

- Fritz Heider's Balance Theory
- Leon Festinger's Cognitive Dissonance Theory
- Daryl Bem's Self-Perception Theory
- Carl Hovland's Model
- Petty and Cacioppo's Elaboration Likelihood Model of Persuasion
- William McGuire's Analogy of Inoculation

Affiliation

- Leon Festinger's Social Comparison Theory
- Reciprocity Gypothesis and Gain-Loss Theory
- Social Exchange Theory and Equity Theory
- Individual Characteristics

Prosocial Behavior

- Bystander Intervention
- Empathy and Helping Behavior

Antisocial and Aggressive Behavior

- Frustration-Aggression Hypothesis
- Albert Bandura's Social Learning Theory

Conformity, Obedience, and Compliance

- Muzafer Sherif's Conformity Study
- Solomon Asch's Conformity Study
- Stanley Milgram's Study
- Foot-in-the-Door Effect
- Door-in-the-Face Effect

Self Perception

- Clark and Clark Doll Preference Study
- Dimensions of Personal Identity

Social Perception

- Primacy/Recency Effects
- Attribution Theory
- Halo Effect

Groups

- Theodore Newcomb's Study
- Edward Hall and Proxemics
- Zajonc's Theory
- Social Loafing
- Anonymity
- Group Decision-Making

Leadership

- Leadership and Communication
- Kurt Lewin's Study

Cooperation and Competition

- Prisoner's Dilemma
- Robber's Cave Experiment

Social Psychology

Social psychology is concerned with social behavior including the ways people influence each other's attitudes and behavior, the impact that individuals have on one another, the impact that social groups have on individual group members, the impact that individual group members have upon the social group, and the impact that social groups have on other social groups. In this chapter, we will discuss the history of social psychology and its close relationship to sociology and other fields within psychology, theoretical perspectives on human behavior within the social environment, and key concepts and classic studies in the field of social psychology.

HISTORICAL PERSPECTIVE

Although the field of social psychology is relatively young, the scientific study of behavior within the social environment can be traced to 19th century European thought. In 1898, for instance, **Norman Triplett** published what is thought to be the first study of social psychology: he investigated the effect of competition on performance. He found that people perform better on familiar tasks when in the presence of others than when alone. It was not until 1908 that **William McDougall** (a psychologist) and **E. H. Ross** (a sociologist) each independently published the first textbooks on social psychology. Since the 1950s the field has developed rapidly, with an expansion in both the theoretical foundation and scientific study in the area.

Early experiments, such as the important work by **Verplank** in the 1950s, suggested that social approval influences behavior. In his study, he showed that the course of a conversation changes dramatically based upon the feedback (approval) from others. Verplank, together with **Pavlov, Thorndike, Hull**, and **Skinner** (covered in detail in the chapter on learning and ethology), helped to establish **reinforcement theory** as an important perspective in studying social behavior. This theory holds that behavior is motivated by anticipated rewards. The **social learning theorists** eventually challenged early reinforcement theorists. **Albert Bandura** is the main figure in social learning theory (covered in detail in this chapter); he basically proposed that behavior is learned through imitation.

Role theory (Bindle, 1979) is the perspective that people are aware of the social roles they are expected to fill, and much of their observable behavior can be attributed to adopting those roles. **Cognitive theory**, covered in the chapter on cognition, has also been extremely influential in social psychological theory and research. Perception, judgment, memories, and decision making are all examples of cognitive concepts that have influenced our understanding of social behavior.

ATTITUDES

Attitudes have been called the keystone in the edifice of modern social psychology because the subject of attitudes resounds throughout the field. Attitudes include the following components: cognition or beliefs, feelings, and behavioral predisposition. "I love Chinese food," is a simple example of an attitude—I have knowledge or hold certain beliefs about Chinese food, I have strong positive feelings towards it, and I tend to eat Chinese food relatively frequently. Attitudes are typically expressed in opinion statements. Attitudes are likes and dislikes, affinities for and aversion to things, people, ideas, etc.

Consistency Theories

Social psychologists have devoted much attention to the subject of how attitudes change. **Consistency theories** hold that people prefer consistency, and will change or resist changing attitudes based upon this preference. If a person hates cigarette smoking, but falls in love with a cigarette smoker, there would be an inconsistency. If the person is aware of this inconsistency, then, according to consistency theories, the person will try to resolve it. Inconsistencies are viewed as stimuli or irritants, and are often resolved by changing attitudes. This will become clearer as we progress.

Fritz Heider's Balance Theory

The first consistency theory we will talk about is **Fritz Heider's balance theory.** Balance theory is concerned with the way three elements are related: the person whom we're talking about (symbolized by Heider as P), some other person (symbolized by O), and a thing, idea or some other person (symbolized by X). Balance exists when all three fit together harmoniously. When there isn't balance, there will be stress, and a tendency to remove this stress by achieving balance.

In the examples that follow, we have the following elements: Patrick (P), the person whose processes we are considering, Olivia (O), the other person, and Chinese food (X), the thing. The type of relationship between elements considered in the example is liking and disliking. We depicted liking by + and disliking by −.

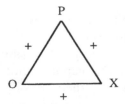
Figure 1: Balance

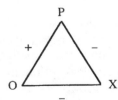
Figure 2: Balance

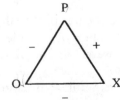
Figure 3: Balance

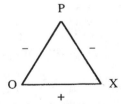
Figure 4: Balance

In the situations depicted in Figures 1–4, there is balance between all of the elements. In figure 1, Patrick likes Olivia, Patrick likes Chinese food, and Olivia likes Chinese food. This triad will not cause stress for Patrick. Balance also exists in Figure 2. Patrick likes Olivia, Patrick doesn't like Chinese food, and Olivia doesn't like Chinese food. Once again, Patrick is agreeing with someone he likes, and the situation is in balance.

Suppose that Patrick doesn't like Olivia. Balance can still exist, if Patrick likes Chinese food and Olivia doesn't, as in Figure 3. Balance also exists in Figure 4. Patrick doesn't like Olivia, Patrick doesn't like Chinese food, but Olivia does like it. Both are examples of Patrick disagreeing with someone he dislikes, and are examples of balance. In general, balance will exist in a triad if there are one or three positives. But balance is only part of the story.

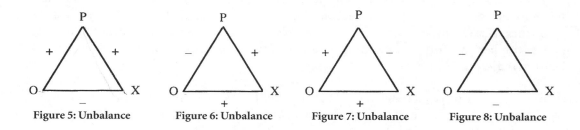

Figure 5: Unbalance   Figure 6: Unbalance   Figure 7: Unbalance   Figure 8: Unbalance

Figures 5–8 are examples of imbalance. In Figure 5, Patrick likes Olivia, but they disagree about Chinese food. There is also imbalance in Figure 6. Here, Patrick dislikes Olivia, but they both agree about liking Chinese food. Imbalance is also evident in Figures 7 and 8. In general, imbalance occurs when someone agrees with someone he or she dislikes, or disagrees with someone he or she likes. If there are zero or two positive signs, the triad is unbalanced.

Balance can be achieved in a number of ways. In Figure 5, where Patrick likes Olivia, but they disagree about Chinese food, Patrick can either change his attitude about Chinese food or his attitude about Olivia. Alternatively, Olivia can change her attitude about Chinese food.

If you found Heider's theory to be a bit simplistic, you're not alone. His original theory has been modified, but that is beyond the scope of this lesson.

Leon Festinger's Cognitive Dissonance Theory

Our second consistency theory of attitude change is **Leon Festinger's cognitive dissonance theory**, a major influence on social psychology. Cognitive dissonance is the conflict that you feel when your attitudes are not in synch with your behaviors. Engaging in behavior that conflicts with an attitude may result in changing one's attitude so that it is consistent with the behavior. This is the most proactive of cognitive dissonance theory predictions.

Here is an example: 1) Joe believes that cigarettes cause cancer; 2) Joe smokes cigarettes. Now, if Joe believes that cigarettes cause cancer, it would be consistent for him not to smoke. But he does smoke. Therefore, these two elements are dissonant. The greater the dissonance, the greater the pressure to reduce dissonance. Dissonance can be reduced by changing dissonant elements or by adding consonant elements. For example, Joe can stop smoking, smoke low-tar cigarettes, avoid reports on the dangers of smoking, criticize reports on the dangers of smoking, or convince himself that the enjoyment is worth the risk.

There are two types of dissonant situations that have been at the forefront of experimentation. They are **free-choice** and **forced-compliance dissonance**. Free-choice dissonance occurs in a situation where a person makes a choice between several desirable alternatives. For example, Scott is involved with two women: Betty and Donna. He is equally fond of both but feels that he should decide between them. He selects Betty and tells Donna that he can't see her anymore. After the decision, according to Festinger, there will be dissonance. Here's why. His cognition that he likes Donna is dissonant with his choice not to go out with her anymore. Since the dissonance emerges after his choice, it is known as **post-decisional dissonance**.

There are several ways of reducing his dissonance. He can tell himself that Betty is more intelligent, more fun, more successful, or kinder than Donna. By accentuating the positive in Betty, he is in effect reducing the inconsistency that emerged from his not choosing Donna, even though he was fond of her. He can also reduce dissonance by accentuating the negative in Donna. These two approaches to reducing dissonance are known as the **spreading of alternatives**, meaning the relative worth of the two alternatives is spread apart.

Forced-compliance dissonance occurs when an individual is forced into behaving in a manner that is inconsistent with his or her beliefs or attitudes. The force may come from either anticipated punishment or reward. For example, if a child is told that she can have ice cream for dessert only if she finishes her spinach, there may be forced-compliance dissonance. This dissonance is created by the fact that she is being forced into a behavior (eating spinach) that is at odds with her attitude (that she doesn't like spinach).

In a classic experiment by **Festinger and Carlsmith** (1959), subjects were asked to perform extremely boring tasks, such as putting 12 spools in a tray, emptying the tray, refilling it and emptying it again, and so on. After one hour of this, subjects were asked to tell the "next subject" (who was actually an assistant to the experimenter) that the experiment was enjoyable and interesting. Some subjects were paid $1 and others were paid $20 to mislead the "next subject." In 1959, $20 was a lot of money. Most of the subjects complied with the experimenter's request. After complying, they were taken to another room and asked to give ratings of the experiment, the real purpose of the experiment. It might be though that the subjects who received the $20 would have reported that they enjoyed the experiment more —after all, they were given $20. However, the $1 group actually reported that they enjoyed the experiment more than the $20 group.

This might seem strange, but the results are actually consistent with cognitive dissonance theory. For subjects in both groups, there is dissonance between the cognition (the task is boring) and the action (telling the "next subject" that the task is interesting). The subjects who received $20 were able to explain away the dissonance by saying to themselves that "yes, the task was boring, but for $20 who wouldn't tell a little lie to the next subject?" Therefore, they experienced little dissonance and they did not have to change their attitudes. On the other hand, the subjects receiving only $1 were not able to easily justify their lies. Therefore, there was much dissonance between the action and the cognition, so to reduce the dissonance between these two elements, the individuals had to change one of the two elements. Obviously, the subjects couldn't change the action because it had already happened. Accordingly, they had to change the cognition, perhaps by thinking that the task was really a nice break from studying. The dissonance was reduced by believing that they actually enjoyed the task. Hence, the $1 subjects rated the task as more enjoyable than the $20 group.

When behavior can be justified by means of external inducements (e.g., $20), there is no need to change internal cognitions. However, when the external justification is minimal, you will reduce your dissonance by changing internal cognitions (e.g., from thinking that the task was boring to thinking that it wasn't really so bad). This is called the **minimal justification effect** (sometimes called the *insufficient justification effect*).

Based upon this experiment, and many others, there are two main principles of cognitive dissonance theory that you should remember:

1. If a person is pressured to say or do something contrary to his or her privately held attitudes, there will be a tendency for him or her to change those attitudes.

2. The greater the pressure to comply, the less this attitude change. Ultimately, attitude change generally occurs when the behavior is induced with minimum pressure.

Daryl Bem's Self-Perception Theory

Cognitive dissonance theory is not the only way to explain the results of the Festinger and Carlsmith (1959) experiment. **Daryl Bem's self-perception theory** has also been used to explain forced-compliance dissonance.

Bem's basic idea is that when your attitudes about something are weak or ambiguous, you observe your own behavior and attribute an attitude to yourself. If you ask a woman if her husband likes brown bread, she might answer, "I guess he does, he's always eating it." In other words, based upon the evidence of his behavior, his wife concludes that he likes brown bread. Suppose you ask the husband if he likes brown bread. According to Bem, the man uses the same type of reasoning about himself. The man might say, "I guess I do, because I'm always eating it." The crux of this theory is essentially that people infer what their attitudes are based upon observation of their own behavior.

How does this explain Festinger and Carlsmith's results on forced-compliance dissonance? According to self-perception theory, why was there a difference between the $1 and the $20 group? The $20 subject looks at his own behavior and the $20 and reasons to this effect: "I said the experiment was fun because of the $20." The $1 subject looks at his behavior and reasons, "One dollar is not enough money to get me to lie about the experiment so I must have had some fun in the experiment." So the $1 subject looks at his or her own behavior and attributes a liking of the experiment to him or herself, while the $20 subject attributes his or her behavior to the monetary compensation. The key difference between Bem's and Festinger's theories is that Bem doesn't hypothesize a state of discomfort or dissonance; therefore in self-perception theory, a person's initial attitude is irrelevant and there is no discomfort produced by behavior.

One interesting implication of self-perception theory is that if you reward people for something they already like doing, they may stop liking it. This effect has been called the **overjustification effect**. So, for instance, if your child likes doing the dishes, and all of a sudden you decide to start giving your child a weekly allowance for doing the dishes, your child may start attributing doing the dishes to being paid, rather than to the fact that he or she likes doing the dishes. Hence, the child will start to like doing the dishes less. Your child mistakenly attributes the behavior now to external causes, rather than to dispositional causes.

Carl Hovland's Model

Carl Hovland's model deals with attitude change as a process of communicating a message with the intent to persuade someone. Hovland broke down the communication of persuasion into three components: the communicator, the communication, and the situation. The communicator, or source, is someone who has taken a position on an issue and is trying to persuade someone to adopt his or her position. The communicator produces a communication (presentation of argument) that is designed with the intent to persuade others. The situation is the surroundings in which the communication takes place.

In terms of the communicator, it has been found that the more credible the source is perceived to be, the greater the persuasive impact. Credibility, the degree to which he or she can be believed, depends on how expert and how trustworthy a source appears to be. Carl Hovland and Walter Weiss (1952) conducted a classic study on source credibility. In this study, they prepared articles on some controversial topics of that era. For example, one topic was: "Can a practical, atomic-powered submarine be built at the present time?" These articles were then presented to American subjects. In some cases the article was said to be written by the physicist J. Robert Oppenheimer, while in other cases it was said to be written by the Russian newspaper *Pravda*. (Oppenheimer, as you might have guessed, was the trustworthy and highly credible source.) The opinions of subjects were ascertained before, immediately after, and four weeks after reading the articles. This process provided the experimenters with a measure of opinion change that could be attributed to reading the articles.

Not surprisingly, the conclusions were that communications by highly credible sources were more effective in changing attitudes than were communications by low credibility sources. For example, in measurements taken immediately after the subjects read the articles on submarines, the "Oppenheimer" article altered the opinion of 36 percent of the subjects, whereas "*Pravda*" altered the opinion of no one. Additionally, over time, the persuasive impact of the high credibility source decreased while the persuasive impact of the low credibility source increased. This unusual effect has become known as the sleeper effect.

Another important finding related to sources is that they can increase their credibility by arguing against their own self-interest. For example, drug addicts who argue against drugs or criminals who argue for greater police power can be very persuasive—much more so than drug addicts who condone drug use or criminals who condemn police brutality. This makes sense in light of the concept that we generally expect someone to argue in his or her own self-interest. Therefore, by arguing in a manner that appears to be against self-interest, an individual produces significant attitude change.

Two-sided messages, which contain arguments for and against a position, are often used for persuasion since such seems "balanced" communication. News reporting has frequent instances of two-sided messages.

Petty and Cacioppo's Elaboration Likelihood Model of Persuasion

A more recent theory about persuasion is **Petty and Cacioppo's elaboration likelihood model of persuasion**. This model suggests that there are two routes to persuasion: the central route and peripheral route. If the issue is very important to us, we're dealing with the central route to persuasion. If the issue is not very important to us or if we cannot clearly hear the message, we're dealing with the peripheral route to persuasion.

Imagine a situation where the persuader is trying to change our minds about something. In the central route (where we care about the issue being discussed), we follow the persuader's argument closely and mentally evaluate the persuader's arguments by generating counterarguments of our own. As you might imagine, in this route to persuasion, strong arguments will change our minds more often than weak messages.

In the peripheral route (where we don't care very much about the issue, can't clearly hear the message, or are otherwise distracted), we either aren't paying attention, or can't pay attention to the persuader's message. Therefore, the strength of the persuader's argument really doesn't matter. What will matter is how, by whom, or in what surroundings the argument is being presented.

Resistance to Persuasion

On the other side of the coin is research into how people are able to resist persuasion. **William McGuire** uses the analogy of inoculation against diseases. In physiological inoculation against disease, an active disease-producing organism, or pathogen, is injected into the body. This pathogen is in a weakened form or strain. In response, the body will ultimately develop a resistance to stronger forms of the pathogen.

McGuire theorized that the inoculation process in the body is analogous to the mind—that people can be inoculated against the attack of persuasive communications. McGuire tested this theory by using what he called **cultural truisms;**—beliefs that are seldom questioned. For instance, "It's a good idea to brush your teeth after every meal if at all possible." Since these beliefs are seldom attacked, they are vulnerable to attack. This is analogous to the vulnerability of people to smallpox if they have never been vaccinated. The cultural truism, however, is vulnerable because the individual has never had practice defending it.

According to McGuire, people can be psychologically inoculated against an oncoming attack by first exposing them to a weakened attack. McGuire inoculated people against attacks on cultural truisms by first presenting arguments against the truisms and then refuting the arguments. These are known as **refuted counterarguments.** For example, you could present the argument that brushing wears away the tooth enamel and then refute it with information that this amount of wear is insignificant. Presenting refuted counterarguments motivates people to practice defending their beliefs. Therefore, when there is an actual unalloyed attack, people will be better able to resist it. In experimental tests, McGuire found that inoculation can be quite effective in developing the resistance of cultural truisms to subsequent attacks. You might expect that cultural truisms inoculated or not would be steadfast, but this is not what McGuire found. Cultural truisms that were not inoculated were actually quite susceptible to attack.

Social psychologists have also found that under certain conditions, people will hold beliefs even after they have been shown to be false. This is referred to as **belief perseverance**. If you are induced to believe a statement and then provide your own explanation for it, you will tend to continue to believe the statement, even when the statement is shown to be false. So, for instance, if you are told that eating chocolate causes acne and asked to try to explain why this is true (by, for instance, explaining that the fat in the chocolate clogs your pores), then you will still tend to believe that it is true even after being told that it is false (and research indicates that it *is* false).

When social pressure to behave in a particular way becomes so blatant that the person's sense of freedom is threatened, the person will tend to act in a way to reassert a sense of freedom. This is referred to as **reactance**. If you try too hard to persuade someone of something, that person will choose to believe the opposite of your position.

AFFILIATION AND ATTRACTION

Leon Festinger's Social Comparison Theory

Leon Festinger's social comparison theory (the same Festinger of cognitive dissonance theory) suggests that we are drawn to affiliate because of a tendency to evaluate ourselves in relationship to other people. Festinger's theory has three principles. First of all, people prefer to evaluate themselves by objective, nonsocial means. However, when this is not possible, people evaluate their opinions and abilities by comparing them to those of other people.

Secondly, the less the similarity of opinions and abilities between two people, the less the tendency to make these comparisons. And finally, when a discrepancy exists with respect to opinions and abilities, there is a tendency to change one's position so as to move it in line with the group. Notice how the need for self-evaluation becomes linked to the need to affiliate.

If affiliation provides a way of comparing one's opinions and abilities, you might expect that the greater the need to compare one's abilities or opinions, the greater the desire to affiliate. **Stanley Schachter's** research found that greater anxiety does lead to greater desire to affiliate. A situation that provokes little anxiety typically does not lead to a desire to affiliate. However, Schachter discovered that anxious people prefer the company of other anxious people. Therefore, the perceived similarity of other anxious people is a factor in the affiliation. Both anxiety and a need to compare oneself with other people may play roles in determining both when and with whom we affiliate.

Reciprocity Hypothesis

Other theorists have concerned themselves with the reasons we affiliate with or are attracted to some people, but not others. According to the **reciprocity hypothesis**, we tend to like people who indicate that they like us. The inverse is also hypothesized: we tend to dislike those who dislike us. Reciprocity suggests that our attractions are a two-way street. We don't merely evaluate a person's qualities and arrive at a like or a dislike: we take into account the other person's evaluation of us.

Gain-Loss Principle

Aronson and Linder hypothesized a twist to the reciprocity hypothesis known as the **gain-loss principle**. The principle states that an evaluation that changes will have more of an impact than an evaluation that remains constant. Therefore we will like someone more if their liking for us has increased (shown a gain) than someone who has consistently liked us. Similarly, we will generally dislike a person more whose liking for us has decreased (shown a loss) than someone who has consistently disliked us.

Social Exchange Theory/Equity Theory

Social exchange theory assumes that a person weighs the rewards and costs of interacting with another. The more the rewards outweigh the costs, the greater the attraction to the other person. This simply means that people attempt to maximize rewards and minimize costs. **Equity theory** proposes that we consider not only our own costs and rewards, but the costs and rewards of the other person. We prefer that our ratio of costs to rewards be equal to the other person's ratio. If one person feels that he or she is getting less, or more, out of the relationship than the other, there'll be an instability due to the perceived inequity.

[handwritten margin note: opposites attract]

Individual Characteristics

Researchers have found that certain individual characteristics tend to play a role in affiliation and attraction. Correlations have been found between affiliation and **similarity** of intelligence, attitudes, education, height, age, religion, socioeconomic status, drinking habits, and mental health. So what about the proverb that says that opposites attract? This is referred to as **need complementarity**, which claims that people choose relationships so that they mutually satisfy each other's needs. In need complementarity, the person who likes to talk is complemented by the person who likes to listen; the dominant is attracted to the submissive; the person seeking nurturing is complemented by the nurturing person. It is possible that similarity is a more powerful predictor on some dimensions and complementarity is more powerful on others. However, even successful complementary relationships have fundamental similarities in some attitudes that favor the dissimilarity.

Research has repeatedly documented the potency of **physical attractiveness** as a determinant of attraction. The **attractiveness stereotype**, or the tendency to attribute positive qualities and desirable characteristics to attractive people, is a likely explanation.

Another factor in attraction is **spatial proximity**. It may not be surprising that people will generally develop a greater liking for someone who lives within a few blocks than for someone who lives in a different neighborhood. What is surprising is that even small differences in proximity can have an effect. One possibility is that the closer people live to each other, the more accessible they are to each other, so potential friendships have a better opportunity to develop. Additionally, proximity may also increase the intensity of initial interactions. Another possibility is the **mere exposure hypothesis**, based on familiarity. This states that mere repeated exposure to a stimulus leads to enhanced liking for it. In other words, the more you see something, the more you like it. **Robert Zajonc** is a key figure in **mere exposure** research.

PROSOCIAL BEHAVIOR

Social psychologists are interested in understanding the determinants of prosocial behavior, or behaviors that benefit other individuals or groups of people, called **helping behavior** and **altruism.** Altruism is a form of helping behavior in which the person's intent is to benefit someone else at some cost to himself or herself. Helping behavior includes altruistic motivations, but also includes behaviors that may be motivated by egoism or selfishness.

Bystander Intervention

The most celebrated line of research in the area of helping behavior is the work of **John Darley and Bibb Latané** on **bystander intervention**. Darley and Latané's research can be traced to a single event. In March of 1964 in Kew Gardens, New York, a woman named Kitty Genovese was stabbed to death in three separate attacks by the same man. Because she resisted, the killing took more than a half-hour. Thirty-eight people were identified as having witnessed the attack and having heard her scream for help. Twice, their apartment lights threatened away the would-be killer. Twice, he returned. None of the witnesses intervened, or even called the police. After the killing there was talk of the dehumanization of people and what was initially termed "bystanders apathy." Mention was made of a new kind of creature, *Homo urbanis*, a city dweller whose only interest is in himself. The apathy of the bystanders was blamed on their personality flaws.

Several days after the killing, Darley and Latané developed a very different interpretation. The bystanders, they thought, were not monsters. They were not even apathetic. Rather, they were engaged in the normal problem-solving process—trying to figure out what was going on and what to do about it. Unfortunately, their problem-solving process, which included evaluation of deterrents, led to not helping. However, it was interpreted that anyone in any emergency might decide not to help, largely because of two situational factors, **social influence** and **diffusion of responsibility** (and diffusion of responsibility was the most significant factor at Kew Gardens that night).

Latané and Darley decided to test for social influence factors by staging emergencies in laboratory settings, since many emergencies are ambiguous (smoke does not necessarily mean fire). Bystanders must first define the situation—a person's judgment will be influenced by past experiences, desires, what the person actually sees, and the influence of other people present (social influence). Indeed, the presence of others may lead to the interpretation of an event as a nonemergency.

Latané and Darley tested for the social influence process in bystander intervention by studying the behavior of students who witnessed an ambiguous event. The students thought that they were taking part in an interview on urban environments. While they were completing a questionnaire, an acrid white smoke was piped into the room. The situation was ambiguous. The smoke could have come from a fire, or it could have been steam from a radiator. Subjects experienced one of two conditions: the subject was either alone or with two confederates. The confederates were trained to notice the smoke, ensure that the subject saw them notice, and then return to the questionnaire. Latané and Darley hypothesized that the two nonresponsive confederates would inhibit the response of the subject. They would influence the subject to define the smoke as a nonemergency. This hypothesis was confirmed. In postexperimental interviews, those who did not respond said that they thought it was not a fire. This concept is known as **pluralistic ignorance**: leading others to a definition of an event as a nonemergency.

The second process Latané and Darley studied was diffusion of responsibility. Once an individual interprets that a situation constitutes an emergency, the person has to decide whether or not to help. If there is only one bystander at an emergency, the bystander knows that the responsibility for assisting falls on his or her shoulders. That individual has one hundred percent of the responsibility to help, will receive one hundred percent of the blame, and will feel one hundred percent of the guilt for not helping. If others are present, however, then the responsibility, blame, and guilt can be shared. As the person weighs the costs and rewards of helping and attempts to resolve the conflict between helping and not helping, the fact that others are in a position to help may sway the person towards not helping.

Latané and Darley conducted another classic experiment to test for the diffusion of responsibility factor in an experiment that would not be affected by the social influence process. The researchers led the subjects in the experiment to believe that they were participating in a discussion on college life. A subject was placed alone in a booth and told that the discussion would take place by intercom. Each person was allowed two minutes to speak. During those two minutes, only the microphone of the person speaking would be turned on. So it was not a discussion in the interactive sense. The test subject was not aware that he or she was the only live participant and that no one was actually listening to him speak. The other speeches were prerecorded. The subjects believed that there were one, two, or five other participants. One of the prerecorded participants spoke about a tendency toward epileptic seizures. Later he pretended to have a seizure (prerecorded, of course). The emergency, then, was not ambiguous and the subject could not tell how other "bystanders" were reacting.

Since subjects were not aware of anyone else's reaction in this experiment, the social influence process was not a factor. Darley and Latané found that when subjects thought that they were the only ones listening, one hundred percent reported the seizure. When subjects thought that two others were listening, 85 percent reported the seizure. When subjects thought that four others were listening, the seizure was reported only 62 percent of the time. The results supported the diffusion of responsibility hypothesis. The more people present, the less the likelihood that any individual will offer help.

Empathy and Helping Behavior

Empathy is the ability to vicariously experience the emotions of another, and it is thought by some social psychologists to be a strong influence on helping behavior. **Batson's empathy-altruism** model is one explanation for the relationship between empathy and helping behavior. According to this model, when faced with situations in which others may need help, people might feel distress (mental pain or anguish), and/or they might feel empathy. According to the model, both of these states are important, since either can determine helping behavior. (Some social psychologists disagree fundamentally, and, instead, believe that helping behavior occurs only when there is some benefit to the individual offering help.)

Batson's model was tested in a series of experiments in which subjects witnessing a person in distress are given a choice to either help or not help that person. (In this context, distress can also include physical pain.) In a typical experiment, subjects watched a closed-circuit television displaying a person needing help (e.g., appearing to receive painful electric shocks). Some of the subjects were given a choice to leave after the first two electric shocks (the easy-escape condition), and others were asked to stay to witness ten electric shocks (the difficult-escape condition). After the second shock, all of the subjects completed a questionnaire that measured the degree to which they felt distress and empathy for the person experiencing the shocks. The subjects were then told that the person being shocked also experienced traumatic shocks as a child, and they were given the opportunity to take that person's place to receive the remaining eight shocks. Subjects in the easy-escape condition who reported more distress than empathy, tended to leave rather than help. Subjects who reported more empathy than distress were more likely to help regardless of whether they were in the easy or the difficult-escape conditions.

AGGRESSIVE AND ANTISOCIAL BEHAVIOR

Frustration-Aggression Hypothesis

The **frustration-aggression hypothesis** is one possible explanation social psychologists have found for aggressive behavior. According to this perspective, when people are frustrated, they act aggressively. In fact, researchers have found that the strength of the frustration experienced is correlated with the level of aggression observed.

Bandura's Social Learning Theory

Bandura's social learning theory is perhaps the most influential theory on aggression that is also focused on social context. Bandura's theory holds that aggression is learned through **modeling** (direct observation), or through **reinforcement** (covered in detail in the chapter on learning and ethology). In his famous study on the effect of modeling, Bandura had two groups of young children aged 3–5 observe either an adult playing with tinker toys, or an adult committing aggressive acts on an inflated rubber "Bobo" doll. In the next phase of the experiment, each child was made to feel frustrated and then left alone in a room full of toys, including the rubber doll. Children who had observed the aggressive model were more likely to behave aggressively towards the doll, similarly to the adult, than the children who had not observed the aggressive model. In some cases, the children copied the aggression on the rubber doll blow for blow. Bandura also believed that aggressive behavior is selectively reinforced—that people act aggressively because they expect some sort of reward (material benefit, social approval, attention) for doing so.

CONFORMITY, OBEDIENCE, AND COMPLIANCE

Muzafer Sherif's Conformity Study

If you stare at a point of light in a room that is otherwise completely dark, the light will appear to move. This illusory movement is known as the **autokinetic effect. Muzafer Sherif** used this effect in a classic study on conformity in which he evaluated the concept of norm formation: Sherif had subjects, when alone, estimate the amount of movement of a point of light in an otherwise completely dark room. Remember, any movement reported is an illusion. He then brought a group of subjects together and had them, as a group, estimate the amount of movement. He found that the subject's solitary estimates changed so that the group agreed upon the amount of movement. Put another way, individuals conformed to the group; their judgments converged on some group norm.

Solomon Asch's Conformity Study

Conformity has been defined as yielding to group pressure. Some define it more specifically as yielding to group pressure when no explicit demand has been made to do so. This is seen in a classic experiment by Solomon Asch. In this experiment, a subject was gathered in a classroom with seven to nine college men and informed that they would be comparing the lengths of lines. Two large white cards were shown. On one of the cards was a single black line (the comparison line). On the other card were three lines of differing lengths. The subjects were asked to choose which of the three lines was the same length as the comparison line.

The comparisons were easy and obvious. Students were told to announce their answers in the order they were seated. The order was not accidental. The next to the last seat was always reserved for the one student in the experiment who was the genuine subject (the others were confederates of the experimenters). On the first two rounds, everyone, including the subject, would agree on the correct answer. On the third round, one after another of the confederates agreed, but on the wrong answer. The genuine subject's response at this point was the heart of the experiment. It was noted that in control conditions, without the misleading confederates present, subjects selected the wrong line less than one percent of the time. Any error greater than this when confederates were present could logically be attributed to yielding to group pressures or conformity.

The researchers found a strong tendency for subjects to conform to the incorrect responses of the confederates. In fact, subjects gave the wrong answer approximately 37 percent of the time. Furthermore, more than 75 percent of the subjects gave the wrong answer at least once. Notice that in this experiment, there was no explicit pressure to conform. What if there were pressure?

Stanley Milgram's Obedience Experiment

Stanley Milgram's experiment is one of the most well-known experiments in social psychology—one that often appears on the GRE Psychology test. Milgram looked at pressure to conform and obedience behavior. In interviews, Milgram said that he had been thinking about Asch's experiments on conformity when he designed his studies. Asch's use of lines, Milgram thought, had a manifestly trivial content.

In Milgram's classic experiment, subjects would arrive at a Yale University laboratory believing that he or she was taking part in an experiment on the effects of punishment on learning. The subject would be introduced to someone called Mr. Wallace, who was 47 years old and described by most observers as mild-mannered and likable. Mr. Wallace was actually a confederate. The subject was asked to draw one of two slips of paper, to determine who would be the teacher and who would be the learner. Both slips said teacher. The learner, Mr. Wallace, was then strapped to a chair. The subject was then taken to another room and seated in front of a shock generator with an electrode that was attached to his wrist. The subject was instructed to give an electric shock to Mr. Wallace whenever Mr. Wallace gave an incorrect answer. The experimenter declared that although the shocks could be extremely painful, they would cause no permanent damage.

The shock generator had 30 switches, clearly marked sequentially from 15 to 450 volts. There were also labels on the switches ranging from "Slight Shock" to "Danger: Severe Shock" to two switches marked "XXX." The subject would read a series of word pairs to Mr. Wallace and then read the first word of each pair. Mr. Wallace, who had supposedly memorized the pairs, was instructed to select the correct association. He communicated his answers over an intercom. The subject (the teacher) was instructed to give a shock after every wrong answer. Furthermore, after every wrong answer the shock level was to be increased by 15 volts. Before beginning, each teacher received a sample 45-volt shock, in order to get an idea of what the learner would be going through. This was a real shock, the only real shock given in the experiment. Unknown to the subject, Mr. Wallace never received any electric shocks.

Mr. Wallace gave the wrong answer in a predetermined sequence. After each wrong answer, the subject was to increase the shock level by 15 volts and give Mr. Wallace a shock. After receiving a 150-volt shock, Mr. Wallace asked to be freed from the experiment. At 180 volts, he cried that he could no longer stand the pain. By 270 volts, his protests had become screams of agony. At 300 volts, Mr. Wallace pounded on the wall, mentioned his heart condition, and insisted that he be freed. After the 330-volt shock, Mr. Wallace fell silent. If the subject turned to the experimenter for guidance, as they typically did, the experimenter told them that no response was a wrong answer and that they should continue shocking.

If at any point, the subject showed a reluctance to continue, the experimenter would use a sequence of four prods, using as many as were needed to get the subject to obey. The first prod was "please continue"; the second prod was, "the experiment requires that you continue"; the third prod, "it's absolutely essential that you continue"; and the fourth, "you have no other choice, you must go on." The question that Milgram was interested in was how far people would proceed if they were asked to give increasingly powerful shocks to another person. Therefore, obedience to authority was measured by the maximum shock a subject would administer.

Each of the 40 subjects administered at least 300 volts. After 300 volts, the point at which the learner pounded on the wall, five subjects refused to continue with the next shock. However, 26 of the 40 subjects (65 percent) continued beyond "Danger: Severe Shock" to the last switch on the board marked "XXX." Every subject was willing to hurt someone at the experimenter's command. And almost two-thirds of the subjects were completely obedient to the experimenter. Keep in mind that the experimenter had no special authority to enforce his commands.

Milgram was convinced that the subjects really thought they were hurting someone. In postexperimental interviews, subjects generally said that they thought the shocks were extremely painful to the learner. Furthermore, many subjects showed signs of tension and stress. Like the high level of obedience itself, this was something Milgram had not anticipated. Subjects were observed to sweat, tremble, stutter, bite their lips, groan, and dig their fingernails into their flesh. Fourteen of the 40 subjects showed nervous laughter and smiling; three subjects had uncontrollable seizures. Milgram attributed the tension to a conflict between deeply ingrained tenets not to hurt others and the equally compelling tendency to obey those who are in authority. The results indicated that the drive to obey was stronger than the drive not to hurt someone against his will.

Milgram commented that measures obtained at one institution, rather than another, are irrelevant in terms of interpreting the findings in many areas of psychology. However, he reasoned, the fact that his obedience study took place at an esteemed university might have been an important factor. So Milgram conducted the same experiment in a rather run-down commercial building in Bridgeport, Connecticut. The laboratory was only marginally respectable in appearance, in contrast to the lab at Yale. The level of obedience was not significantly lower at Bridgeport than at Yale.

In a separate study, Milgram asked two confederates to defy the experimenter in the middle of the experiment. Ninety percent of the subjects followed their lead. This is not surprising in the light of Asch's conformity studies. In another variation, the subjects did not directly shock the learner. They would pull a switch and then a confederate would deliver the shock. In this situation, 37 out of 40 subjects participated until the very end.

Milgram related obedience in his experiment to obedience in Nazi, Germany. He said that his results raised the possibility that human nature, or more specifically, the kind of character produced in American democratic society, cannot be counted on to insulate its citizens from brutality and inhumane treatment under the direction of a malevolent authority. Milgram continues, "If in this study, an anonymous experimenter could successfully command adults to subdue a 47-year-old man and force on him painful electric shocks against his protests, one can only wonder what government with its vastly greater authority and prestige can command of its subjects."

KEY EXPERIMENTS ON CONFORMITY AND OBEDIENCE

Investigator	Strategy Used	Key Result
Sherif	Autokinetic effect	Individuals' estimates of movement conformed to group's
Asch	Comparing length of lines	Subjects yield to group pressure and choose incorrect line
Milgram	Experimenter prodded subject to give electric shock to other person	Subjects shocked person; majority continued shocking up to maximum voltage

Foot-in-the-Door Effect

Compliance is a change in behavior that occurs as a result of situational or interpersonal pressure. The **foot-in-the-door effect** demonstrates that compliance with a small request increases the likelihood of compliance with a larger request. For example, homeowners were first asked to sign a petition on safe driving. Several weeks later they were asked to place a large, unattractive billboard on their lawn that said "drive carefully." A control group of homeowners had not been asked to sign the petition, but were asked to put up a large billboard. Those who had first complied with the smaller request were much more likely to agree to the larger one.

Door-in-the-Face Effect

On the other hand, there is the **door-in-the-face effect**. This effect is one in which people who refuse a large initial request are more likely to agree to a later smaller request. College students were asked to serve as voluntary counselors at a juvenile detention center for a period of two years. Everyone refused this large request. When a second request was made to chaperone juveniles on a trip to the zoo, significantly more subjects agreed to this request than subjects in the control group, who were approached with the small request only.

The foot-in-the-door effect and the door-in-the-face effect seem contradictory, but they actually are not. The initial request in the door-in-the-face experiment is large and unreasonable, while the initial request in the foot-in-the-door experiment was quite reasonable, so the effects depend upon the nature of the original request.

SELF-PERCEPTION

Social psychologists are concerned with how our social lives influence our perspectives of ourselves Specifically, researchers have focused on the influence other peoples' views, our social roles, and our group memberships have on our perceptions of ourselves.

Clark and Clark Doll Preference Study

Clark and Clark (1947) studied ethnic self-concept among ethnically white and black children using the famous **doll preference** task. The experimenter showed each child a black doll and a white doll, and asked the child a series of questions about how the child felt about the dolls. The majority of white and black children preferred the white doll. This study was important because at the time, it highlighted the negative effects of racism and minority group status on the self-concept of black children. Additionally, it was used to argue against school segregation in the 1954 *Brown v. The Topeka Board of Education* Supreme Court case. However, subsequent research (since the 1960s) using improved methodologies (e.g., balancing the ethnicity of the experimenter), and perhaps partially due to changes in society, has shown that black children in fact hold positive views of their own ethnicity.

Dimensions of Personal Identity

Individuals have more than one dimension of personal identity—there are several factors that determine which identity will be enacted in particular situations. It is believed that our identities are organized according to a hierarchy of salience, or that which holds the most importance for us in each particular situation. For instance, male and female college students in same-sex groups were less likely to list gender in their self-descriptions than students in mixed-gender groups. Furthermore, researchers have found that the more salient the identity, the more we conform to the role expectations of the identities.

SOCIAL PERCEPTION

Primary/Recency Effects

Social perception is the name that social psychologists give to the ways in which we form impressions about the characteristics of individuals and of groups of people. The **primacy effect** refers to those occasions when first impressions are more important than subsequent impressions. Sometimes the most recent information we have about an individual is most important in forming our impressions; this is called the **recency effect**.

Attribution Theory

We form impressions of others, in part, through observation of their behavior. **Attribution theory** focuses on the tendency for individuals to infer the causes of other people's behavior. Fritz Heider (of balance theory fame) is one of the founding fathers of attribution theory. According to Heider, we are all naive amateur psychologists who attempt to discover causes and effects in events. Heider divided these causes into two main categories: dispositional and situational. This distinction is very important. Dispositional causes are those that relate to the features of the person whose behavior is being considered. These features include the beliefs, attitudes, and personality characteristics of the individual. Situational causes are external and are those that relate to features of the surroundings. Examples are threats, money, social norms, and peer pressure.

If you believed that the subjects in the Milgram experiment administered shocks primarily because they were evil, that's a dispositional attribution. If you believe that subjects delivered the shocks primarily in response to the power of the authority, that's a situational attribution. When you make a situational attribution you are, in effect, saying that it is the characteristics of the particular situation rather than the characteristics of the particular individual that are the primary cause of the behavior.

Researchers have identified several kinds of biases that occur in the attribution process. One of the most noted is this: when inferring the causes of others' behaviors, there is a general bias towards making dispositional attributions rather than situational attributions. This has been called the **fundamental attribution error**. The tendency to look for personality flaws in the Kitty Genovese witnesses and the Milgram subjects, rather than looking for situational influences that may have caused their behavior, can be considered an example of this error.

Halo Effect

The **halo effect** is another good example of the tendency for bias in evaluations of other people. It is the tendency to allow a general impression about a person ("I like Jill in general") to influence other, more specific evaluations about a person ("Jill is a good writer, Jill is trustworthy, Jill can do no wrong"). The halo effect explains why people are often inaccurate in evaluations of people that they either believe to be generally good, or those that they believe to be generally bad.

Belief in a Just World

M. J. Lerner studied the tendency of individuals to believe in a just world. In a just world, good things would happen to good people, and bad things would happen to bad people. Much of the recent research into belief in a just world (BJW) centers around developing measures that indicate the degree to which an individual believes in a just world. A strong belief in a just world increases the likelihood of "blaming the victim" since such a world view denies the possibility of innocent victims.

GROUPS

Social psychologists are also concerned with how being a member of a group affects individual behavior. Individual behavior is influenced by group norms, or expectations of behavior in given situations. The presence or involvement of others sometimes improves individual or group performance, and sometimes worsens it. Anonymity within groups also has been found to have an effect on behavior. Individuals are sometimes motivated to cooperate to attain group goals—other times, they are motivated to compete to attain individual goals.

Theodore Newcomb's Study

A famous experiment demonstrating the influence of group norms is the **Theodore Newcomb** study at a small woman's college, Bennington College (Bennington has since gone coed). Most of the women at Bennington came from wealthy, conservative families. Although more than two-thirds of the students' parents were Republican, the college itself had a very liberal atmosphere. Newcomb found that each year of a student's college career was marked by an increase in her liberalism. Put another way, over time, students increasingly accepted the norms of their community. One indicator was the 1936 United States presidential election between Roosevelt (a Democrat) and Langdon (a Republican). In the election, 66 percent of the parents voted for Langdon; and 62 percent of the freshmen also voted for Langdon, however, only 43 percent of the sophomores and 15 percent of the juniors and seniors voted for him.

Newcomb did a follow up 20 years later. Most of the women who had left the school as liberals remained liberals, and those who had left as conservatives remained conservatives. Women who had left as liberals generally married men of similar political beliefs. However, those liberals who ultimately married conservative men frequently returned to their old conservatism.

Edward Hall and Proxemics

Edward Hall suggests that there are cultural norms that govern how far away we stand from the people we're speaking to. In the United States, the proper distance to stand when you are talking to someone with whom you are intimate is somewhere around a foot, give or take a few inches. On the other hand, interactions between strangers in the United States usually take place several feet apart. If you doubt this, try stepping within a foot of a casual acquaintance to talk, and that person will probably back up or look otherwise uncomfortable. Incidentally, the study of how individuals space themselves in relation to others is called **proxemics**.

Zajonc's Theory

Zajonc argues that the presence of others increases arousal and consequently enhances the emission of dominant responses. During the early stages of learning, for example, dominant responses are likely to be wrong. If a person is learning a new dance step, the wrong movements are likely to be dominant. The presence of others, according to Zajonc, would enhance the wrong movements. For expert dancers, however, where the correct moves are likely to be dominant, the presence of others improves performance.

Social Loafing

Social loafing is a group phenomenon referring to the tendency for people to put forth less effort when part of a group effort than when acting individually. Take tug-of-war, for example. When six team members pull together we would expect that the total rope-pulling strength of the six-person team will equal the sum of the six individual rope-pulling strengths. It turns out that the team rope-pulling strength is half of the sum of the individual strengths. Other examples of this phenomenon include the amount of clapping done by spectators at sporting events and the productivity of a collective farm.

Anonymity

An interesting finding from social psychologist **Philip Zimbardo** is that people are more likely to commit antisocial acts when they feel anonymous within a social environment. When a person is anonymous, there is diminished restraint of unacceptable behavior. His study is called the **prison simulation**. He ran an ad in a university newspaper stating, "Wanted: Volunteers for an experiment on prison life, $15 per day, two weeks." Twenty-four applicants were selected. Half were randomly selected to be guards in the mock prison, and half were randomly assigned to be prisoners. Rather than tell them that they were selected to be prisoners, Zimbardo told them to go home to wait for his call. Instead of calling, Zimbardo sent the police department to arrest the mock prisoners; they were searched, handcuffed, taken to the police station where they were booked, and then driven blindfolded to the mock prison in the basement of a university. At the mock prison, they were stripped, deloused, and given loosely fitting smocks with identification numbers.

The student guards at the prison received no special training. They had been told to maintain law and order and that physical violence was prohibited. The guards wore khaki uniforms and silver reflector glasses. They had billy clubs, whistles, handcuffs, and keys to three small, barred cells and a storage closet to be used for solitary confinement.

On the second morning of the experiment, the prisoners rebelled by taking off their identification numbers and barricading their cell doors with beds. The guards responded by spraying them with carbon dioxide from a fire extinguisher, breaking into their cells, stripping the prisoners, and putting the ringleaders in solitary confinement. This was the only rebellion. The guards became more authoritarian and abusive in the time that followed. Before 36 hours had passed, one of the prisoners had to be released because of uncontrollable crying, fits of rage, and disorganized thinking. Three more prisoners had similar breakdowns; a fifth prisoner developed a psychosomatic rash. The experiment, which was intended to last for two weeks, had to be terminated at the end of six days. Remember, these were normal college students, randomly assigned to be prisoners or guards (there were no personality differences between the groups).

Zimbardo says that one of the major processes operating within the prison was **deindividuation**. Deindividuation refers to a loss of self-awareness and of personal identity. The subjects in the experiment lost their sense of who they were. Their sense of self was overwhelmed by the roles they were playing, and they began acting out those roles, forgetting that they were actually university students participating in an experiment.

Group Decision Making

Irving Janis has studied the ways that group decisions often go awry. Janis examined thousand of pages of historical documents about situations in which government officials had made what he considered to be serious blunders. These historical situations included the Bay of Pigs and the failure of America to be prepared for the attack on Pearl Harbor. According to Janis, judgment failed in these situations because the decision makers were in engaged in what he called **groupthink**. Groupthink refers to the tendency of decision-making groups to strive for consensus by not considering discordant information. An example of groupthink: The plan for the Bay of Pigs invasion stated that in the event of an unsuccessful initial landing, the invaders should retreat into the Escombre Mountains. However, no one in the planning group had looked at a detailed map. This would have shown them that the Escombre mountains and the initial landing area were separated by 80 miles of swamps and marshes.

Risky shift is another important factor social psychologists consider in group decision-making. Essentially, the risky shift refers to the finding that group decisions are riskier than the average of the individual choices (and this average riskiness of the individual choices can be considered to be an estimate of the group's original riskiness). One explanation for the risky shift is the **value hypothesis**. This hypothesis suggests that the risky shift occurs in situations in which riskiness is culturally valued. For example, riskiness in business ventures is culturally valued. In this situation, the less risky members of a group will compare themselves to the more risky members and the less risky will become riskier. However, it turns out that the risky shift might just be one specific example of a more general phenomenon.

In a 1968 experiment by **James Stoner**, dilemmas were presented to couples to examine the risky shift in controversial situations. For example, Stoner had a couple choose between allowing a pregnancy that would endanger the mother's life to continue and terminating that pregnancy. Stoner found a shift with group decisions toward caution instead of risk. Whatever the explanation for this seemingly contradictory finding, it is clear that the content of the item can determine the direction of the shift.

These seemingly contradictory findings have led researchers to speak about extremity shifts, noting that group decisions tend to be more extreme, but not necessarily more risky than the decisions of individuals. The leading current explanation for the extremity shift is **group polarization**. Group polarization refers to a tendency for group discussion to enhance the group's initial tendencies towards riskiness or caution. So, for instance, if a group originally has a tendency to be risky, further discussion will tend to make the group more risky. Likewise, if a group originally has a tendency to be cautious, further discussion will tend to make the group more cautious.

LEADERSHIP

Leadership and Communication

Leaders, even among a group of friends, seem to possess special qualities that separate them from followers. However, that's not the complete story. Research has found that leaders of groups engage in more communication than nonleaders. Furthermore, researchers found that by artificially increasing the amount a person speaks, that person's perceived leadership status also increases.

laissez faire - less efficient, organized,

Kurt Lewin's Study

In a famous study, **Kurt Lewin** conducted research to determine the effects of different leadership styles. Lewin manipulated the leadership styles used to supervise boys in an after-school program. Each group of boys experienced three different leadership styles: **autocratic, democratic,** and **laissez-faire.** Laissez-faire groups were less efficient, less organized, and less satisfying for the boys than the democratic groups. The autocratic groups were more hostile, more aggressive, and more dependent on their leader. Democratic groups were more satisfying for the boys and more cohesive than autocratic groups. The quantity of work in autocratic groups was greater than in the other groups, but work motivation and interest were stronger in the democratic groups.

COOPERATION AND COMPETITION

In **cooperation**, persons act together for their mutual benefit so that all of them can obtain a goal. In **competition**, a person acts for his or her individual benefit so that he or she can obtain a goal that has limited availability. Social psychologists are interested in understanding the ways in which people make decisions about engaging in cooperative and/or competitive behaviors.

Prisoner's Dilemma

The **prisoner's dilemma** has become a classic method of investigating people's choices to compete or cooperate. Here's a modified version of the dilemma. Consider the hypothetical case in which two men, prisoner A and prisoner B, have been taken into custody and separated. The district attorney is convinced that they're both guilty of a felony but he needs a confession from at least one prisoner in order to obtain a conviction. Each prisoner can either confess or not confess.

The results of each potential decision are diagrammed in Figure 9. If neither confesses, they will both be charged with a misdemeanor; if both confess, they will both be prosecuted for the felony and a moderate sentence will be recommended. If one confesses and the other doesn't, the confessor will have his or her charges dropped and the other prisoner will be prosecuted for the felony and a maximum sentence will be recommended. For either of the prisoners, the best possible outcome is to have the charges dropped. The second best outcome is being charged with a misdemeanor; the next best is to be charged with a felony but with a moderate sentence recommended; the worst outcome is to have the D.A. book the prisoner for a felony and recommend a maximum sentence.

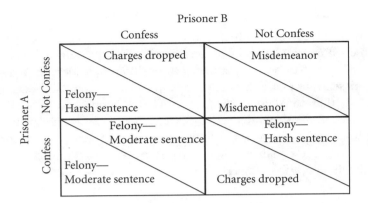

Figure 9: The Prisoner's Dilemma

A given person gains the most if he or she chooses to cooperate, and the other competes. Together, they lose the most if both compete. A given individual loses the most if he or she competes and the other cooperates. The logic of this dilemma can be used in analyzing many social interactions—including cooperation and competition in group panic situations and in pollution.

Why would one of the prisoners choose to compete rather than cooperate? Two reasons: one, the prisoner wants to get the best for him or herself; two, the prisoner doesn't trust the other prisoner and doesn't want to be left holding the bag (having a felony charge with a maximum sentence recommended). The D.A. is counting on at least one of the prisoners being self-interested or untrustworthy in order to get at least one confession and at least one conviction. However, the D.A. would prefer that neither of them cooperate with the other. In that case, both will confess and both will be charged with a felony.

Robber's Cave Experiment

Another study on cooperation and competition was conducted by **Muzafer Sherif**. Sherif and his colleagues created hostilities through competition and then reduced the hostilities through cooperation. This classic experiment took place at a boys' camp in Robber's Cave, Oklahoma. The subjects in this experiment were 22 twelve-year-old boys. Two groups of boys arrived separately at the camp and were taken to distant cabins. The camp was actually staffed by researchers and the groups did not know of each other's existence. During the first week, the boys within each group engaged in cooperative activities, that is, activities that required interdependent activity in order to obtain a goal. These included camping in the woods, improving a swimming place, and transporting canoes over rough land to water.

Sherif reports these developments: a status hierarchy, role differentiation for various tasks, norms for behavior, and self-adopted names for the groups. One called itself the Rattlers and the other the Eagles. The Rattlers, as the name indicates, developed norms of toughness such as not bothering to treat cuts. The Eagles however, developed norms such as not swearing and being polite. The first week created group allegiance within both groups.

After the first week, the groups were informed about each other's existence and a four-day competitive tournament was staged. The winners were to receive medals, a team trophy, and knives. The tournament was intended to create hostilities between the groups, which were effectively exhibited as the group members engaged in name calling, physical encounters, and raids on each other's cabins. When the Eagles were defeated during tug-of-war on the first day, they took down the Rattlers' flag and burned part of it. At the end of the tournament, both groups expressed a desire for no further contact.

The researchers' next step was to reduce the hostilities they had created. The first method was mere contact between group members. Seven contact situations were arranged, including going to the movies together and having meals together. These contacts failed to reduce hostility. Therefore, the researchers arranged activities in which the two groups had to cooperate to solve a problem. For example, there weren't enough camp funds to see a very popular film, *Treasure Island*. The boys discussed the problem and decided to pool their money. On another occasion, the two groups were on an outing and the truck broke down. The rope that had been used in the tug-of-war happened to be on the ground twenty feet from the truck. One of the boys suggested a tug-of-war against the truck. They started the truck by pulling it.

Sherif called the goals of obtaining the film and starting the truck **superordinate goals**. These goals are best obtained through intergroup cooperation. Sherif found that joint effort on these superordinate goals dramatically improved intergroup relations. The groups ultimately became quite friendly, mingled at the dining hall and had joint campfires. At the end of camp, the 22 boys chose to go home together on the same bus.

superordinate - intergroup cooperation.

IMPORTANT NAMES IN SOCIAL PSYCHOLOGY

Aronson, E., Linder, D.	Proposed **gain-loss principle** (an evaluation that changes will have more effect than an evaluation that remains constant)
Asch, S.	Studied **conformity** by asking subjects to compare the lengths of lines
Bem, D.	Developed **self-perception theory** as an alternative to cognitive dissonance theory
Clark, K., Clark, M.	Performed study on **doll preferences** in African American children; the results were used in the 1954 *Brown v. the Topeka Board of Education* Supreme Court case
Darley, J., Latané, B.	Proposed that there were two factors that could lead to non-helping: **social influence** and **diffusion of responsibility**
Eagly, A.	Suggested that **gender differences** in **conformity** were not due to gender, per se, but to differing social roles
Festinger, L.	Developed **cognitive dissonance theory**; also developed **social comparison theory**
Hall, E.	Studied norms for **interpersonal distance** in interpersonal interactions
Heider, F.	Developed **balance theory** to explain why attitudes change; also developed **attribution theory** and divided attributions into two categories: **dispositional** and **situational**
Hovland, C.	Studied **attitude change**
Janis, I.	Developed the concept of **groupthink** to explain how group decision making can sometimes go awry
Lerner, M.	Proposed concept of **belief in a just world**
Lewin, K.	Divided leadership styles into three categories: **autocratic**, **democratic**, and **laissez-faire**
McGuire, W.	Studied how **psychological inoculation** could help people resist persuasion

Milgram, S.	Studied **obedience** by asking subjects to administer electroshock; also proposed **stimulus-overload theory** explain differences between city and country dwellers
Newcomb, T.	Studied **political norms**
Petty, R., Cacioppo, J.	Developed **elaboration likelihood model of persuasion** (central and peripheral routes to persuasion)
Schachter, S.	Studied relationship between **anxiety** and the need for **affiliation**
Sherif, M.	Used **autokinetic effect** to study conformity; also performed **Robber's Cave experiment** and found that having superordinate goals increased intergroup cooperation
Zajonc, R.	Studied the **mere exposure effect**; also resolved problems with the **social facilitation effect** by suggesting that the presence of others enhances the emission of dominant responses and impairs the emission of nondominant responses
Zimbardo, P.	Performed **prison simulation** and used concept of deindividuation to explain results

SOCIAL PSYCHOLOGY PRACTICE SET

Time: 8 minutes

Directions: Each of the questions or incomplete statements below is followed by five suggested answers or completions. In each case, select the one that best answers the question or completes the statement.

1. Which of the following situations involving two people, P and O, and an object, X, will **NOT** be balanced according to Heider's balance theory?
   (A) P likes O, and they both like X
   (B) P likes O, and they both dislike X
   (C) P dislikes O, and they both dislike X
   (D) P dislikes O, P likes X, and O dislikes X
   (E) P dislikes O, P dislikes X, and O likes X

2. According to inoculation theory, a person's belief can be inoculated against a persuasive attack by
   (A) providing arguments to support the initial belief prior to the attack
   (B) providing arguments to support the initial belief subsequent to the attack
   (C) warning the individual that there will be an attack
   (D) anticipating the attacker's arguments and discrediting those arguments
   (E) refuting the persuasive attack subsequent to its presentation

3. The admonition that "you shouldn't take more love than you give" is most directly supported by
   (A) equity theory
   (B) the halo effect
   (C) the mere exposure effect
   (D) social comparison theory
   (E) the Romeo and Juliet effect

4. An experiment is staged so that on three occasions a subject overhears a confederate evaluate him. Which sequence of evaluations would lead the subject to be most attracted to the confederate, as predicted by Aronson's gain-loss principle?
   (A) Negative, negative, negative
   (B) Negative, negative, positive
   (C) Positive, negative, negative
   (D) Positive, positive, negative
   (E) Positive, positive, positive

5. A student is waiting for her first meeting with her faculty adviser. From inside the office, the student hears someone saying "Stop it . . . get your hands off me . . . "; and then hears the sound of furniture crashing.

   The student is a subject in a staged experiment, and he is waiting in one of four conditions: alone; with two passive confederates; with four passive confederates; or with two naïve subjects. If the results of this experiment follow the pattern of the Darley and Latané bystander intervention research, then which of the following sequences would correspond to decreasing frequency of helping behavior by students?

   (A) Four passive confederates, alone, two passive confederates, two naïve subjects

   (B) Four passive confederates, two passive confederates, two naïve subjects, alone

   (C) Two naïve subjects, two passive confederates, alone, four passive confederates

   (D) Alone, four passive confederates, two passive confederates, alone, two naïve subjects

   (E) Alone, two naïve subjects, two passive confederates, four passive confederates

6. Which of the following best illustrates an attempt to use the foot-in-the-door effect?

   (A) A salesperson tries to sell a radio to a customer for $75. The customer resists, and the salesperson lowers the price to $65.

   (B) A telephone solicitor calls a home and asks a person several questions about his reading habits. The solicitor then describes the benefits of subscribing to a newspaper he is selling.

   (C) An advertisement indicates that anyone who buys two CDs for $11.95 will be given a third CD "absolutely free."

   (D) A woman asks a friend for a loan of $1,000. The friend refuses. The woman then asks the friend for a loan of $250.

   (E) A salesperson tells a customer that if she does not buy a necklace at that moment, "somebody else probably will."

7. The performance of which of the following activities is LEAST likely to be facilitated by the presence of an audience?

   (A) Speed of winding a fishing reel
   (B) Memorizing a script
   (C) Running
   (D) Adding numbers
   (E) Taking a final examination

8. In an experiment that used threatened punishment to inhibit behavior, children were told not to play with very appealing toys after the experimenter left the room. Two levels of threat were involved: mild and severe. None of the children played with the toys. According to cognitive dissonance theory, how would you predict the children rated the attractiveness of the toys in the two different conditions after the experiment?

   (A) Equally unattractive
   (B) Toys in the severe-threat conditions were considerably less attractive than in the mild-threat condition
   (C) Toys in the mild-threat condition were considerably less attractive than in the severe-threat condition
   (D) Equally attractive
   (E) There was a slight significant difference toward the severe-threat condition toys being less attractive

9. The prisoner's dilemma is used to study

   (A) the autokinetic effect
   (B) recidivism in former convicts
   (C) affiliation and attraction
   (D) need complementarity
   (E) cooperation and competition

10. Which of the following theories is characterized by the assumption that individuals have a need to evaluate their own attitudes and abilities?

    (A) Social facilitation
    (B) Social comparison theory
    (C) Social influence
    (D) Social exchange theory
    (E) Equity theory

EXPLANATIONS FOR THE SOCIAL PSYCHOLOGY PRACTICE SET

1. C

If you remembered Heider's balance theory, this question was rather straight-forward. Recall that a triad will be balanced if P, the person whose balance is being considered, agrees with someone he likes or disagrees with someone he dislikes. A triad will be unbalanced when someone disagrees with someone he likes, or agrees with someone he dislikes. But don't just memorize these principles, think of the logic. If P likes O but they feel differently about object X, it's logical that there will be an inconsistency or imbalance. In both choices (A) and (B), P likes O and they agree about X so these situations are balanced. In choices (D) and (E), P disagrees with someone he dislikes so they are balanced. However, in choice (C), P dislikes O and they both dislike X; the fact that they both dislike X; means that they are in agreement. Because P agrees with someone he dislikes, this is an unbalanced situation. Therefore, answer choice (C) is correct.

2. D

McGuire's method of inoculation was to take a widely shared belief that had seldom been attacked and to subject it to a weak attack. He would argue against the belief and then refute the arguments. The individual would then be better protected against the natural attack. Choice (D), anticipating the actual arguments and discrediting these arguments, is correct. This does describe inoculation. The arguments that are going to be used in the actual attack are presented and refuted. Choices (A) and (B) refer to providing arguments to support the initial belief. However, McGuire used refuted counterarguments in inoculation, not supportive arguments. Choice (C), warning the individual that there would be an attack, is also incorrect. Although it is true that warning of an attack increases resistance, this does not describe inoculation. Finally, choice (E), refuting the persuasive attack subsequent to its presentation, is incorrect. In inoculation, arguments are refuted, but prior to the actual attack. Choice (E) would be analogous to receiving antibiotics after you've become sick. Although effective, this is not the same as being inoculated before you become sick. Therefore, choice (E) is incorrect.

3. A

One implication of this advice is that a relationship should have equality between what is given and what is taken. Therefore, answer choice (A)—equity theory—is correct. Equity theory suggests that each person compares his own ratio of cost to rewards to the other person's ratio and prefers it if the ratios are equal. This means that if a person is taking more than he is giving, the ratios will be unequal and the relationship will be unstable. The other answer choices have no direct bearing on the admonition. Choice (B), the halo effect, refers it to the tendency to use a general impression about another person to form judgments about specific qualities. If our overall impression is that someone is good, we may extend this to judgments that she is honest, humorous, kind, and intelligent. Choice (C), the mere exposure effect, refers to Zajonc's contention that mere repeated exposure to a stimulus enhances one's liking of it. Festinger's social comparison theory, choice (D), assumes that people have a need to evaluate their own opinions and abilities. Finally, choice (E), the Romeo and Juliet effect, refers to the observation that parental interference in a relationship often results in the opposite of its intended effect—it tends to increase, rather than decrease, romantic love.

4. B

If you understood the gain-loss principle, this choice was more compelling than the rest. The gain-loss principle states that an evaluation that changes will have more impact than an evaluation that remains constant. Therefore we will like someone more whose liking for us has increased, or shown a gain, than someone who has consistently liked us. Similarly, we will generally dislike a person more whose liking for us has decreased, or shown a loss, than someone who has consistently disliked us. The gain-loss principle leads to the prediction that a change from a negative to a positive evaluation, as in choice (B), will lead to greater liking than a uniformly positive evaluation, as in choice (E). A change from a positive to a negative evaluation, as in choices (C) and (D), or a uniformly negative evaluation as in choice (A), will lead to a greater or equal disliking. Choice (B) is the only situation in which there is an improvement in evaluations and, therefore, it is the correct answer choice.

5. **E**

In this experiment, we can assume that both social influence and diffusion of responsibility effects will operate—social influence because of the presence of other people in an ambiguous situation, and diffusion of responsibility because the number of people present varies. In Latané and Darley's research it was found that an individual alone was more likely to respond than an individual with other people. If there are other people, then an individual with a naïve subject is more likely to respond than an individual with a passive confederate. This has to do with the fact that a naïve subject is likely to reveal more concern than a person trained not to react. So with fellow naïve subjects, a person is less likely to define a situation as a nonemergency. Finally, an individual with two passive confederates is more likely to respond than an individual with four passive confederates. That's the diffusion of responsibility effect. So the final order, from most likely to least likely to help, is: alone, two naïve subjects, two passive confederates, four passive confederates, choice (E).

6. **B**

The foot-in-the-door effect refers to a tendency for compliance with a small request to increase the likelihood of compliance with a larger request. So you should have looked for an example that describes a small request followed by a larger one. In choice (B), a telephone solicitor asks several questions of a person. Asking a person to answer several questions is a small request. If he answers the questions, the solicitor has her foot in the door; she can then pose the larger request to buy the newspaper. Therefore, choice (B) is the best answer. In choice (A), a large request comes first and is followed by a slightly smaller request. Choices (C) and (E) are sales techniques but not the foot-in-the-door technique since there is not the sequence of a small request being followed by a larger one. Choice (D), which begins with a large request and ends with a request much smaller, is an application of the door-in-the-face effect. Therefore, the correct answer is choice (B).

7. **B**

Robert Zajonc summarized the evidence on social facilitation by saying that during training the presence of others impairs performance on that task. The presence of others only facilitates performance of the task after it has been mastered. Put another way, the acquisition of new responses is impaired by the presence of others while the performance of well-learned responses is facilitated. Choice (B), memorizing a script, is the most reasonable answer here. The other choices involve activities that we can assume are well-learned or at least better learned than a script that has not yet been memorized.

8. **C**

This experiment is a test of Leon Festinger's cognitive dissonance theory. We would explain the experiment in the following way: If you restrain yourself from a pleasant activity because of severe threat, then dissonance is reduced. That is, you feel there was a reason you restrained yourself. But, if you restrain yourself from a pleasant activity under only mild threat, you experience dissonance. So, in accordance with cognitive dissonance theory, the children in the mild-threat condition will convince themselves that the toys were not so attractive after all.

9. **E**

The prisoner's dilemma is used to study cooperation and competition. Answer choice (A) refers to Muzafer Sherif's study on conformity in groups. Answer choice (D), need complementarity, refers to the theory that suggests that you choose whom to enter into relationships with on the basis of whether you can mutually satisfy each others' needs. The other choices refer to other areas of study within social psychology.

10. **B**

Social comparison theory is characterized by the assumption that individuals have a need to evaluate their own attitudes and abilities. Let's take a look at the other answer choices. Answer choice (A), social facilitation, refers to the fact that the presence of others can enhance performance on well-learned tasks. Answer choice (C), social influence, is one of the situational factors Latané and Darley hypothesized to explain when people will help a bystander. Answer choice (D), social exchange theory, suggests that the more the rewards of entering a relationship with a person outweigh the costs, the more attracted you are likely to be to this person. Answer choice (E), equity theory, goes beyond social exchange theory and suggests that we weigh not only our cost-reward ratio, but also the cost-reward ratio of the other person.

CHAPTER FOUR

Developmental Psychology

OUTLINE

Historical Perspective

Research Methods

Nature/Nurture Controversy

Heredity
- Genetics
- Research Methods
- Genetic Disorders

Growth and Maturation
- Stages of Prenatal Development
- External Threats to Prenatal Development

Newborn Characteristics
- Reflexes

Cognitive Development
- Jean Piaget
- Lev Vygotsky

Language Development
- Components of Language
- Language Acquisition

Social and Emotional Development
- Sigmund Freud
- Erik Erikson

Temperament
- Thomas and Chess
- Research Methods

Early Social and Emotional Behavior
- Crying
- Social Smile
- Fear

Attachment
- Harry Harlow
- John Bowlby
- Mary Ainsworth
- Konrad Lorenz

Moral Development
- Lawrence Kolberg's Stages
- The Heinz Dilemma
- Carol Gilligan's Criticism

Newborn Characteristics
- Theoretical Perspectives
- Kohlberg's Stage Theory

Parenting
- Diane Baumrind
- Fatherhood

Developmental Psychology

The task of **developmental psychology** is to describe and explain changes in human behavior over time. In this chapter, we will review the history of the field of developmental psychology, research methodologies, genetics, major theoretical models, and research findings concerning social, emotional and cognitive development.

HISTORICAL PERSPECTIVE

In the Middle Ages, children were thought of as small, inferior adults who were expected to conform to adult standards for behavior at a very young age. In fact, medieval paintings depict children as miniature adults. It was during the Renaissance era that children were actually depicted in their own costumes and pictured at play. It is in the period that followed the Renaissance that we find the beginnings of modern thought concerning the nature of children.

In the 17th and 18th centuries, influential social philosophers helped broaden the public's views about children. One of these great thinkers was British philosopher **John Locke**, who, along with **Thomas Hobbes, George Berkeley, David Hume, James Mill**, and **John Stuart Mill**, formed the **British empiricist school of thought**. They believed that all knowledge is gained through experience. Locke asserted that a child's mind is considered a **tabula rasa**, or a blank slate, at birth. That is, children are born without predetermined tendencies and child development is completely reliant on experiences with the environment. It is the role of parents and society to mold the child to fit into society.

Nearly a century after Locke, **Jean-Jacques Rousseau** presented an opposing philosophical viewpoint. Rousseau believed that society was not only unnecessary, but also a detriment to optimal development. Rousseau conveyed his thoughts on child raising in a book called *Emile: Concerning Education*. Ostensibly the story of raising a young aristocrat, the book is in fact a comprehensive guide to pedagogy. *Emile* was so controversial in its day that the Archbishop of Paris denounced Rousseau, the book was banned, and Rousseau was forced to flee France to avoid arrest.

Beginning in the late 18th century, it became popular for physicians, loving relatives, and others to keep so-called baby biographies. These were diaries that, though often full of anecdotes and casual observations, contained detailed information concerning the sequence of physical and psychological development. One of the most informative and useful of these diaries was kept by **Charles Darwin**, who is most often linked to the concept of evolution. Evolutionary theory stressed the importance of studying the mind as it functioned to help the individual adapt to the environment, a central characteristic of the **functionalist system of thought**. Darwin's theory also caused researchers to become interested in the study of individual differences in abilities such as hearing, seeing, and problem solving.

It was the influence of Darwin's evolutionary thought that guided **G. Stanley Hall** in the work that earned Hall the title "the father of developmental psychology." Hall, who lived from 1846 to 1924, was one of the first psychologists to do empirical research on children. He compiled hundreds of questionnaires on the views and opinions of children and compared them by age. He was one of the founders of the American Psychological Association, and the founder of child and adolescent psychology.

John Watson (1878–1958), was an important early American psychologist whose theories were influential in the field of developmental psychology. Watson wrote an article published in *Psychological Review* called "Psychology as the Behaviorist Views It" that criticized the field of psychology as being too focused on mentalistic concepts. Watson believed in the importance of environmental influences in child development and he accepted Locke's view of the *tabula rasa*. Watson (1925) once wrote, "Give me a dozen healthy infants, well-formed, and my own special world to bring them up in and I'll guarantee to take any one at random and train him to become any type of specialist I might select—doctor, lawyer, artist, merchant-chief, and yes, even beggarman and thief—regardless of his talents, penchants, tendencies, abilities, and vocation and race of his ancestors." Watson's theory placed a great deal of responsibility on parents for raising competent children. Parents were charged with providing the right learning experiences, and to do so while avoiding overt, "sentimental" affection. Watson's view was extreme; he believed that emotions, as well as thought, were acquired through learning.

Watson also maintained that the only useful methods for the study of psychology were objective methods in the study of behavior. He believed that the field of psychology should never consider concepts such as consciousness, mental states, will, imagery, etc. As an early behaviorist (we discuss behaviorism in more detail in the personality and abnormal psychology and the learning and ethology chapters), Watson believed that the goal of psychology should be to predict behavioral responses given particular stimuli, and vice versa.

Arnold Gesell believed that development occurred as a maturational (or biological) process, regardless of practice or training. His developmental theories arose in contrast to those of his contemporary learning theorists and behaviorists in the 1920s and 1930s who focused on the importance of environmental factors, conditioning, learning, and practice. Gesell was a "nativist" in that he believed that much of development was biologically based and that the developmental blueprint existed from birth.

Another major perspective in the view of psychology is the **psychodynamic orientation**, a system of thought that arose out of a clinical, rather than academic or research setting. Originating in the work of **Sigmund Freud** (1856–1939), these theories stress the role of subconscious conflicts in the development of functioning and personality. Freud's ideas will also be covered in detail in this chapter.

In contrast to the beliefs of psychoanalytic and psychosocial theories, cognitive theories of development emphasize the thinking ability of people. In opposition to the behaviorists were the **cognitive structuralists,** an orientation most strongly influenced by the work of the late Swiss psychologist, **Jean Piaget** (1896–1980). Piaget saw children as more actively involved in their development—constructing knowledge of the world through their experiences with the environment. Piaget's theory will be covered in detail in this chapter.

RESEARCH METHODOLOGIES

There are three research methods frequently used in developmental psychology: **cross-sectional studies, longitudinal studies,** and **sequential cohort studies.** Cross-sectional studies compare groups of subjects at different ages. Longitudinal studies compare as specific group of people over an extended period of time. Sequential cohort studies combine cross-sectional and longitudinal research methods. In this combined approach, several groups of different ages are studied over several years.

RESEARCH METHODS IN DEVELOPMENTAL PSYCHOLOGY			
Type of study	**Groups studied at**		
	Time 1	Time 2	Time 3
Longitudinal study	Group 1	Group 1	Group 1
Cross-sectional study	Group 1, 2, 3	————	————
Sequential cohort	Group 1, 2, 3	Group 1, 2, 3	Group 1, 2, 3

Although the three types of studies just described are very useful, sometimes developmental psychologists want to take a more detailed look at the development of a particular child. This is called the clinical method or case study method. This method attempts to collate facts about a particular child and his or her environment in order to gain a better perspective.

NATURE/NURTURE CONTROVERSY

In developmental psychology, much of the discussion about determinants of behavior has centered on the extent to which hereditary factors versus environmental factors influence cognitive, social, and emotional behavior. This is the so-called **nature/nurture controversy.** On the **nature** side of this controversy is the position that human capabilities are innate (present at birth) and that individual differences are therefore largely an effect of the person's genetic makeup. On the other hand, the **nurture** side holds that human capabilities are determined by the environment and shaped by experience. In the past 30 years or so, the polarity between these two positions has largely disappeared. It is generally recognized that development is the result of a dynamic interaction between environmental and genetic forces.

HEREDITY

Genetics

To understand the mechanism of the influence of heredity on development, we must look at human genetic structure. There are usually questions of this sort on the GRE Psychology test, so read carefully.

The study of genetics was initiated by **Gregor Mendel**, an Austrian monk who lived in the 19th century. By carefully observing the inheritance of certain traits in pea plants, Mendel hypothesized the existence of the basic unit of heredity, the **gene**. He suggested that each specific trait was controlled by an alternative form of a gene, called an **allele**, and that each variation was represented by an allele that was either **dominant** or **recessive**. For any given gene there are two alleles.

In humans, both parents contribute a gene for each trait. If both parents contribute a dominant allele, or if one contributes a dominant allele and the other a recessive allele, the dominant allele will be expressed. If both parents contribute a recessive allele, the recessive allele will be expressed. Let's take eye color as an example (see Figure 1).

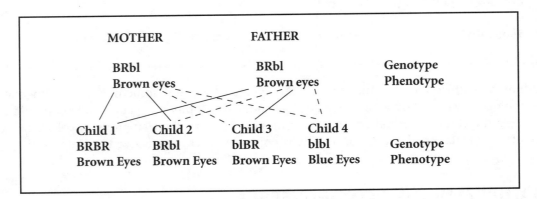

Figure 1. Dominant and Recessive Genes

Assume that the trait of brown eyes is dominant and the trait of blue eyes is recessive. Let's look at two parents who each have one blue eye allele and one brown eye allele. Consider the eye color of their children. Mendelian genetics states that parental genes are distributed randomly to all offspring. Given this random distribution, there are four equally likely possibilities of combining the alleles of the parents. First, a child could receive brown eye alleles from both parents (child 1). Second, a child could receive a brown eye allele from the mother and a blue eye allele from the father (child 2). Third, a child could receive a blue eye allele from the mother and a brown eye allele from the father (child 3). And finally, a child could receive blue eye alleles from both parents (child 4). In the first three cases, the child will have brown eyes. In the fourth, the child will have blue eyes even though both parents have brown eyes. Note that this does not mean that if our hypothetical parents have four children, three will necessarily have brown eyes and one will necessarily have blue eyes. It simply means that for any given child of these parents, there is a one in four chance of blue eyes and a three in four chance of brown eyes.

The total genetic complement (genetic makeup) of an individual is called the **genotype**. The total collection of expressed traits that is the individual's observable characteristics is called the **phenotype**. As we have seen, individuals with identical phenotypes can have different genotypes. For instance, in the diagram above, children 1 and 2 have the same phenotype (brown eyes), but have different genotypes. Identical genotypes can also produce different phenotypes, due to variations in the environment. For instance, genetically identical plants grown at altitudes 3,000 feet apart on the same mountain slope appear so dissimilar that if you saw them, you would not believe that they were even members of the same species.

Genes are located on **chromosomes**. It is on these chromosomes that we find the genetic information of the individual. The 23rd pair of chromosomes determines the sex of the child. If the 23rd pair of chromosomes is XX, the individual is female, but if it is XY, the individual is male. During reproduction, the mother's egg cell always contributes an X chromosome. The father, whose sperm cell contains either the X or the Y chromosome, can therefore contribute either an X or a Y.

The nucleus of each cell in the human body, except for sperm cells and egg cells, holds 23 pairs of chromosomes, 46 chromosomes in all. These cells in the human body are diploid. That is, the chromosomes they contain exist in pairs. The gametes (sperm and egg cells), however, are not diploid. These cells are haploid; they contain 23 single chromosomes. This arrangement is necessary for sexual reproduction because when the sperm and egg cells join during conception, the two haploid cells come together to make a full complement diploid of 23 chromosome pairs. In this way, each parent contributes a gene for each trait. Because the offspring of sexual reproduction receive genes from both parents, the genetic variability is far greater than in asexual reproduction.

Children can be said to have an average of 50 percent of their genes in common with each parent. This statistic is often used in psychological research to address the heritability of traits. In addition, siblings, including fraternal twins, also have 50 percent of their genes in common with each other. The number for identical twins is 100 percent.

We've talked about how genes can affect various physical characteristics such as gender and eye color, but genes are also thought to affect behavior. In fact, even very specific behaviors have a genetic basis. One of the clearest examples of this is **R. C. Tryon's** studies on the inheritance of maze-running ability in laboratory rats. Although this study was published in 1942, it still occasionally shows up on the GRE Psychology test.

Tyron tested a large group of laboratory rats on maze-running skill. The rats were given an equal number of trials to become familiar with the maze. On the basis of their performance, Tyron divided the rats into three groups: "**maze-bright**" rats, "**maze-dull**" rats, and intermediate rats.

Tyron utilized the technique of selective breeding in which rats with similar traits were mated. Tyron bred the maze-bright only with other maze-bright rats and bred maze-dull rats only with other maze-dull rats. The generation that resulted from this breeding was tested on the maze using the methods described above. Tyron again bred the maze-bright of this second generation with only other maze-brights and bred the maze-dull of this second generation only with other maze-dulls. Tyron used the same procedure over several generations, and found that the difference between the maze-bright and the maze-dull rats intensified from generation to generation. This provided evidence that learning ability had a genetic basis.

You might think that the maze-bright rats were better at running all sorts of mazes and were just generally more intelligent than the maze-dull rats, but further research showed that the performance of the two groups was different only on mazes of the type Tyron used. On mazes of other types, the maze-bright rats performed no better than the maze-dull rats.

Research Methods

Research that determines the degree of genetic influence on individual differences between people uses one of three methods: family studies, twin studies, and adoption studies. Since genetically related individuals are expected to be more similar phenotypically than genetically unrelated individuals, researchers often compare rates of similarity in a given characteristic among family members and rates of similarity among unrelated individuals. For example, family studies have determined that the risk of developing schizophrenia for children of schizophrenics is 13 times higher than in the general population. For siblings, the rate is 9 times higher. This has led psychologists to conclude that schizophrenia has a hereditary component. Family studies are limited, however, since families share both genetics and environments. Perhaps the pattern of increased rates of schizophrenia in families is a result of experiencing the same emotional climate in the home rather than genetically shared characteristics. Family studies cannot distinguish shared environment factors from genetic factors.

Twin studies, comparing **monozygotic (MZ)** and **dizygotic (DZ)** twins, are better able to distinguish the relative effects of shared environment and genetics. MZ twins are genetically identical, sharing 100 percent of their genes, whereas DZ twins share approximately 50 percent of their genes. The assumption is that both MZ and DZ twins share the same environment to the same degree and that differences between MZ and DZ twins are thought to reflect hereditary factors. For example, MZ twins tend to be more similar in regard to cognitive, social, and emotional characteristics than DZ twins, suggesting some genetic influence on these characteristics.

The underlying assumptions in twin studies have not gone unchallenged. Researchers have found that MZ twins are treated more similarly by people than DZ twins and that MZ twins tend to imitate each other more than DZ twins do. Therefore, the assumption that MZ and DZ twins share their environments to the same degree may not necessarily be valid.

To better measure genetic effects relative to environmental effects, researchers compared personality characteristics in twins who were raised together (in the same family) to twins raised apart (in different families). On personality measures, MZ twins raised in the same family are most similar. MZ twins reared apart are more similar on personality characteristics than DZ twins reared together. DZ twins reared apart are the least similar. Based upon this research, it seems that personality characteristics are somewhat heritable.

Finally, adoption studies also help us understand environmental influences and genetic influence on behavior. These studies compare the similarities between the biological parent and the adopted child to similarities between the adoptive parents and the adopted child. Researchers have found that adopted children's IQ is more similar to their biological parents' IQ than to their adoptive parents' IQ. This research suggests that IQ is heritable. Criminal behavior among boys shows a similar pattern of heritability.

Lewis Terman's study compared a group of children with high IQs (135 and above) with groups of children typical of the general population, to discover similarities and differences. The study was important in that it was the first to focus on "gifted" children, and that it was a large-scale longitudinal study that followed the development of the group over time, observing them every five years.

Genetic Disorders

Genetic effects on intelligence and behavior is evident in people afflicted with mental retardation. Mental retardation has several causes. **Down's syndrome** is a genetic anomaly in which the individual has an extra 21st chromosome. Individuals with Down's syndrome often have varying levels of mental retardation. One factor affecting the possibility of this genetic mutation is the age of the biological parents. Older parents (mothers and/or fathers) have an increased risk of having children with Down's syndrome.

Phenylketonuria (**PKU**), a genetic disorder, is a degenerative disease of the nervous system. PKU results when the enzyme needed to digest phenylalanine, an amino acid found in milk and other foods, is lacking. Today, infants are given tests for PKU and can avoid the severe effects of the disease with a strict diet. PKU was the first genetic disease that could be tested in large populations.

Sex chromosomes abnormalities can also occur. In males, possession of an extra X chromosome is known as **Klinefelter's syndrome**. These males have an XXY configuration. They're sterile and often have mental retardation. Females with only one X chromosome have **Turner's syndrome**. Turner's syndrome results in a failure to develop secondary sex characteristics. The individuals often have physical abnormalities such as short fingers and unusually shaped mouths.

GENETIC DISEASES	
Disease	**Description**
Down's Syndrome	A form of severe mental retardation that results from an extra 21st chromosome
PKU	A genetic defect in which the child lacks the enzyme needed to digest phenylalanine; can be controlled with a strict diet
Klinefelter's Syndrome	Found in males with an extra X chromosome
Turner's Syndrome	Found in females with only one X chromosome

GROWTH AND MATURATION

Stages of Prenatal Development

Prenatal developmental processes are also important to psychologists because of the importance a maturing nervous system and hormonal levels have on behavior. **Conception** takes place in the fallopian tubes where the ovum or egg cell is fertilized by the male sperm cell. These two types of cells are the human sex cells; they are called **gametes**. They combine to form a single cell called a **zygote** or **fertilized egg**. Shortly after fertilization, the zygote begins to divide in two.

The cells continue to develop and divide so that their numbers increase from two to four to eight to sixteen, and so on. During this period of cell division, the cellular mass travels down the fallopian tube into the uterus where it is implanted into the uterine wall. The **germinal period** lasts approximately two weeks from the time of conception. The next stage is called the **embryonic stage**, which lasts approximately eight weeks. During the embryonic stage the embryo increases in size by about two million percent or about 20,000 times.

During the **embryonic stage**, the embryo grows to about an inch long and begins to develop a human appearance. The limbs appear and the tail begins to recede. Fingers, toes, and external genitals appear. The male embryo begins to produce androgen in the testes. Nerve cells in the spine develop and the first behaviors, motion of the limbs, occur. The onset of the **fetal period**, which takes place during the third month, is marked by the beginning of measurable electrical activity in the brain. In the remaining months, the fetus continues to grow in size.

PRENATAL DEVELOPMENT: STAGES	
Stage	**Description**
Zygote	The sperm cell fertilizes the egg cell and forms a single cell—the zygote
Germinal period	The fertilized egg travels down the fallopian tube and is implanted into uterine wall
Embryonic period	The eight weeks following the germinal period; embryo increases in size by 2 million percent
Fetal period	Begins in the third month with measurable electrical activity in the fetus' brain

Thus far, we have considered prenatal development in a vacuum, without regard to the context in which it takes place. The first nine months of development are, of course, spent in the mother's uterus. Within this environment, temperature, chemical balance, orientation of the fetus with respect to gravity, and atmospheric pressure are all carefully controlled and remain relatively constant. The fetus is attached to the uterine wall and placenta by the umbilical cord. The placenta transmits nutrients to the fetus while returning waste-laden blood to the mother. Maternal blood supplies much of the proteins and amino acids needed for growth, although the embryo begins to produce them as well.

External Threats to Prenatal Development

A variety of external influences can have deleterious effects on the development of the fetus. Infants whose mothers contract rubella, or German measles, before the end of the second month run a high risk of cataracts, deafness, heart defects, and mental retardation. Other viral infections, measles, mumps, hepatitis, influenza, chicken pox, and herpes have been linked to various birth defects.

An unfortunate side effect of the revolution in pharmacology is that many drugs that help the mother can have damaging effects on the fetus she carries. The most noted of these drugs is thalidomide, a tranquilizer that was often prescribed in England during the 1950s. Mothers who took this drug while pregnant often gave birth to babies with missing and malformed limbs and defects of the heart, eyes, digestive tract, ears, and kidneys.

A variety of other influences on the maternal environment have been shown to adversely affect the fetus. Maternal malnutrition is considered to be a leading cause of abnormal development. Protein deficiency can retard growth, lead to mental retardation, and reduce immunities to disease. Maternal narcotic addiction produces chemically dependent infants who must undergo a traumatic withdrawal syndrome. Regular cigarette smoking can lead to slowed growth, increased fetal heart rate, and a greater chance of premature birth. Daily use of alcohol also leads to slowed growth and a slowed psychological development as well. Finally, prenatal exposure to X-rays has been strongly linked to retardation, defects of the skull, spinal cord and eyes, cleft palate, and limb deformities.

NEWBORN CHARACTERISTICS

Reflexes

After birth, although they may seem helpless, infants are actually equipped with well-developed somatic structures and a broad array of reflexes that help ensure survival. A reflex is a behavior that occurs automatically in response to a given stimulus. For example, the rooting reflex is the automatic turning of the head in the direction of a stimulus that touches the cheek—such as a nipple during feeding. Sucking and swallowing when an object is placed in the mouth are also examples of reflexes related to the feeding situation.

Other reflexes may have served an adaptive purpose in earlier stages of human evolution, but are currently used mainly in assessing infant neural development. By comparing the point in time at which each of these reflexes appear to the established norms, it is possible to tell whether neural development is taking place in the normal fashion. One such reflex is the Moro reflex: infants react to abrupt movements of their heads by flinging out their arms, extending their fingers and then bringing their arms back to their bodies and essentially hugging themselves. It has been speculated that this reflex may have developed during a time when our prehuman ancestors lived in trees and falling could be prevented by instinctive clutching. The Moro reflex usually disappears after four months and its presence at one year is a strong suggestion of developmental difficulties.

The Babinski reflex causes the toes to spread apart automatically when the sole of the foot is stimulated. The grasping reflex occurs when the infant closes his or her fingers around an object placed in his or her hand. Although reflexive behavior dominates the repertoire of the neonate, other behaviors occur as well. Newborn infants also kick, turn, and wave their arms. These uncoordinated, unconnected behaviors form the basis for later, more coordinated movements.

NEONATAL REFLEXES	
Reflex	**Description**
Rooting	Infants automatically turn their heads in the direction of stimuli applied to the cheek
Moro	Infants react to abrupt movements of their heads by flinging out their arms, extending their fingers, bringing their arms back to their body and then hugging themselves
Babinski	Infants' toes automatically spread apart when the soles of their feet are stimulated
Grasping	Infants automatically close their fingers around objects placed in their hands

COGNITIVE DEVELOPMENT

Jean Piaget

Jean Piaget is one of the most influential figures in developmental psychology, insisting that there are qualitative differences between adult and childhood thought. Piaget held that children pass through four stages of cognitive development, each stage being qualitatively different from the others. Piaget believed that cognitive growth is a continuous process that begins at birth and proceeds through these stages.

According to Piaget, during infancy children learn from interacting with the environment through reflexive behaviors. For example, based upon repeated experiences with the grasping reflex, infants learn that they can grasp things. Piaget refers to these organized patterns of behavior and/or thought as **schema** (the plural form is schemata). Infants develop behavioral schemata, characterized by action tendencies; older children develop operational schemata, characterized by more abstract representations of cognition.

An important principle in Piaget's theory is the principle of **adaptation**. According to Piaget, adaptation takes place through two complementary processes, **assimilation** and **accommodation**. Assimilation is the process of interpreting new information in terms of existing schemata. Accommodation occurs when new information doesn't really fit into existing schemata; it is the process of modifying existing schemata to adapt to this new information. (These terms are important to remember for the GRE Psychology Test, so be sure to keep them straight.)

Piaget's four stages of cognitive development are also very important to know for the GRE Psychology test: the **sensorimotor**, **preoperational**, **concrete operational**, and **formal operational** stages. During each stage, the child's mental processes are characterized by similar strategies. The stages are in an invariant sequence, each stage preparing the way for the one that follows it. Although we give the approximate ages for these stages, the most important thing to be aware of is the order in which a child progresses through these stages.

The **sensorimotor stage** is the first stage, lasting approximately from birth to age two. Three important concepts to remember related to this stage are: **primary and secondary circular reactions**, and **object permanence**. In primary circular reactions, the infant begins to coordinate separate aspects of movement. This is the advent of goal-oriented behavior. For instance, when the infant is hungry, he or she will suck indiscriminately, trying to gain satisfaction from putting something in his or her mouth. Because of the repetition of this behavior, it is referred to as circular. While primary circular reactions are restricted to motions concerned with the body, secondary circular reactions are directed towards manipulation of objects in the environment.

Object permanence occurs when the child realizes that objects continue to exist even though the child cannot perceive their existence. The saying "out of sight, out of mind" is literally true for infants who have not developed object permanence. Before object permanence develops, when you take a toy from an infant and hide it, the toy does not exist for the child anymore.

Object permanence marks the beginnings of representational thought. This means that the child has begun to make mental representations of external objects and events. Once the child begins this type of thought, the child has entered the **preoperational stage**. The preoperational stage lasts from about two years to seven years of age, and is characterized as the beginning of representational thought. During the preoperational stage, children have the capacity to understand the concept that objects continue to exist even though they cannot perceive their existence.

Another important feature of cognition during the preoperational stage is **centration**, or the tendency to be able to focus on only one aspect of a phenomenon. For example, children in the preoperational stage cannot take the perspective of other people and cannot understand that relationships are reciprocal. A girl in this stage might know that she has a sister, but will not be able to accurately tell you whether or not her sister has a sister. This is referred to as **egocentrism**.

In another example of centration, children in this stage are unable to understand the concept of **conservation**—the notion that physical properties of matter (such as volume and quantity) do not change simply because the appearance of the matter changes (providing, of course, that nothing is added or taken away). Piaget demonstrated this concept by showing preoperational children two identical beakers (A and B) filled to the same level with a colored liquid. He asked the children if each beaker contained the same amount of liquid—children in this stage are able to reply that yes, the amounts are identical. With the children watching,

Piaget then poured the contents of beaker B into beaker C (a taller, skinnier beaker). The water level of beaker C was several inches higher than beaker A. When asked which beaker contained the most water, preoperational children, focusing only on the detail of height, answer that beaker C contains more liquid. When beaker C is poured back into beaker B, the child will once again say that beaker A and beaker B are equal.

During the **concrete operational stage**, approximately ages seven to eleven, children can conserve and take the perspective of others into account, but are limited to working with concrete objects or information that is directly available. These children have difficulty with abstract thought.

Finally, with the approach of adolescence, the child enters the period of true **formal operations** and begins to "think like a scientist," that is, think logically about abstract ideas. The difference between this type of thought and concrete operations can be seen in Piaget's pendulum experiment. Children were given a pendulum in which they could vary the length of the string, the weight of the pendulum, the force of the push, and the height of the swing. They were asked to find out what determined the frequency of the swing. Children in the concrete operational stage manipulated the variables at random and even distorted the data to fit preconceived hypotheses. Adolescents, on the other hand, were able to hold all variables but one constant at a given time, proceed methodically, and discover, no matter what hypotheses they may have started with, that the length of the string alone affects the frequency.

Piaget had an interesting theory about the relationship between language and thought. You might think that improvements in children's linguistic abilities cause improvements in their thinking abilities; but that's not what Piaget suggested. Piaget believed that how we use language depends on which cognitive stage we are in. In other words, Piaget believed that it was the development of thought that directed the development of language.

PIAGET: STAGES OF COGNITIVE DEVELOPMENT

Stage	Description
Sensorimotor	Primary and secondary circular reactions; object permanence develops
Preoperational	Child has not mastered conservation
Concrete operational	Child masters conservation
Formal operational	Person has the ability to "think like a scientist"

Piaget's theories have been widely studied; however, his theories are not immune to criticism. A great deal of criticism has revolved around his use of the clinical method. Piaget preferred observation to statistical measures. Piaget's detractors say that such a method may be useful as a supplement, but that the true scientific study of a child demands empirical data that the clinical method cannot provide. Researchers have also failed to find evidence of formal operations in adolescents and in nontechnological cultures. Others argue that thinking like a scientist is not a true end point of a desirable or even particularly relevant developmental process.

Lev Vygotsky

Vygotsky's work has contributed to our understanding of cognitive development. For Vygotsky, the engine driving cognitive development is the child's internalization of various aspects of the culture—rules, symbols, language, and so on. As the child internalizes these various interpersonal processes, the child's cognitive activity develops accordingly. Vygotsky suggests that it's the internalization of various interpersonal and cultural rules and processes that drives cognitive development in children.

Vygotsky is known for his concept of the zone of proximal development, referring to those skills and abilities that have not yet fully developed but are in the process of development. The child needs guidance to demonstrate those skills and abilities. For example, a child may take a cognitive test and get a certain score. Now, the same child make take the same test with guidance from an adult, improving his or her score. The difference between the two scores indicates the zone of proximal development.

LANGUAGE DEVELOPMENT

Components of Language

It is generally accepted that there are four basic components of language: **phonology**, **semantics**, **syntax**, and **pragmatics**. Phonology refers to the actual sound stem of language. Children must learn to produce and recognize the sounds of language, separating them from environmental noises and speech sounds that do not denote differences in meaning. The ability to distinguish between differences in sound that do not denote differences in meaning and those differences in sound that do denote differences in meaning is called **categorical perception**. There are about 40 phonemes, or speech sounds in English.

Semantics involves the learning of word meanings. A child must learn that certain combinations of phonemes represent certain physical objects or events, and that certain words refer to entire categories, such as *women*, while others refer to specific members of categories, such as *mommy*.

Syntax refers to how words are put together to form sentences. The child must notice the effects of word order on meaning.

Finally, pragmatics consists of the actual efficient use of a language. Often the same sentence will have two or more very different meanings depending on how it is spoken. A child must learn to recognize these inflections and must learn to produce them as well.

An important precursor to language is **babbling**. Almost without exception, children —including deaf children—spontaneously begin to babble during their first year. In an important study, **Lenneberg, Rebelsky**, and **Nichols** (1965) showed that the age babbling begins is about the same for hearing children with hearing parents, hearing children with deaf parents, and deaf children. However, for hearing children, babbling continues and becomes more frequent, reaching its highest frequency between nine and 12 months. For deaf children, verbal babbling ceases soon after it begins. An interesting 1991 study by Petitto and Marentette, however, suggests that deaf children with parents using sign language appear to babble using their hands!

Language Acquisition

By around 18 months, the child may know dozens of words, but will usually utter them only one at a time. Because of this limitation, a word can mean more than one thing. For instance, depending on the child's intonation and/or accompanying gestures, the child could be using the word *apple* to label an apple, to ask for an apple, to ask whether a particular object is an apple, and so on. Between 18 and 20 months of age, a child will begin combining words.

Fundamentally, knowledge of a language is evidenced by the ability to produce novel, grammatically correct sentences while refraining from producing nongrammatically correct ones. It also implies the ability to distinguish between such sentences.

Around the age of two and a half to three, children begin producing longer sentences. As development continues, vocabulary increases rapidly. You might expect that grammatical errors would decrease in this time as well, but the opposite is true. As children begin to master complex general rules, we often see what is referred to as **errors of growth**, or overregulation. A child who once said, "I ran" will now say "I runned to the store." Many of these errors are universal and are not the result of environmental influence. For instance, almost all boys at this age use "hisself" instead of "himself," even though children probably never hear the word "hisself" used by an adult. It is thought that children are generalizing some internalized rule. This suggests that language acquisition is not the result of imitation and reinforcement, but the active application of a dynamic internalized set of linguistic rules.

For the most part, language is substantially mastered by the age of five. This would suggest that language acquisition is fairly simple. Yet many adults find learning a second language to be a difficult task. Indeed, the ease with which children learn their first language has led some psychologists to speculate that children must have some special innate capacity for language acquisition. The name most closely associated with this position is that of linguist Noam Chomsky.

Chomsky is known for his study of **transformational grammar**. He focused on syntactic transformations, or changes in word order that differ with meaning. Chomsky noted that children learn to make such transformations effortlessly at an early age. He therefore concluded that this ability must be innate. This innate capacity for language acquisition is sometimes called a **language acquisition device (LAD)**, and is thought to be triggered by exposure to language. The LAD enables infants to listen to and process sounds.

Nativists such as Chomsky believe in a critical period between age two and puberty for language acquisition. They believe that if a child was not exposed to language during this critical time, then being exposed to language later would be ineffective. It would have been unethical to design and conduct an experiment to test the theory. Unfortunately, a test case came to light with a victim of severe child abuse named **Genie**.

Genie was almost completely isolated from human contact from age two to thirteen, when she was discovered by authorities. Although she had been exposed to no language during this time, after training she was able to learn some aspects of syntax. Still, she was unable to master other aspects of syntax. What this may show us is that instead of a critical period in language development, there may be a sensitive period in language development. A sensitive period is the time when environmental input has maximal effect on the development of a particular ability. Most psychologists consider the sensitive period for language development to be before the onset of puberty.

SOCIAL AND EMOTIONAL DEVELOPMENT

Sigmund Freud

Sigmund Freud was a pioneer in charting personality and emotional growth. For Freud, human psychology and human sexuality are inextricably linked. In fact, Freud made the assertion that far from lying dormant until puberty, the **libido** (sex or life drive) is present at birth. Freud believed that libidinal energy and the drive to reduce libidinal tension were the underlying dynamic forces that accounted for human psychological process.

Freud hypothesized five distinct stages of psychosexual development. In each stage, children are faced with a conflict between societal demands and the desire to reduce the libidinal tension associated with different body parts. Each stage differs in the manner in which libidinal energy is manifested and the way in which the libidinal drive is met. Fixation occurs when a child is overindulged or overly frustrated during a stage of development. In response, the child then forms a personality pattern based on that particular stage, which persists into adulthood.

The first stage (0–1 year) is the **oral stage**. During this stage, gratification is obtained primarily through the putting of objects into the mouth by biting and sucking. Libidinal energy is centered on the mouth. An orally fixated adult would likely exhibit excessive dependency.

During the **anal stage** (one–three years), the libido is centered on the anus and gratification is gained through the elimination and retention of waste materials. Fixation during this stage would lead to either excessive orderliness or sloppiness in the adult.

From about ages three to six, the child passes through the phallic, or **Oedipal stage**. The central event of this stage is the resolution of the **Oedipal conflict** for male children, or the **Electra conflict**, the analogous conflict for female children. The male child envies his father's intimate relationship with his mother and fears castration at his father's hands. He wishes to eliminate his father and possess his mother, but the child feels guilty about his wishes. To successfully resolve the conflict, he deals with his guilt feelings by identifying with the father, establishing his sexual identity, and internalizing moral values. Second, the child to a large extent de-eroticizes, or sublimates his libidinal energy. This may be expressed through collecting objects or focusing on schoolwork. Freud did not elaborate much on the Electra complex, although he theorized a similar process for females. Since females cannot have castration fear (instead, they are thought to have "penis envy"), girls are expected to be less sex-typed, and be less morally developed.

Once the libido is sublimated, the child has entered the stage called **latency**, which lasts until puberty is reached.

For Freud, the final stage is the **genital stage**, beginning in puberty and lasting through adulthood. According to Freud, if prior development has proceeded correctly, at this point the person should enter into healthy heterosexual relationships. But if the sexual traumas of childhood have not been resolved, such behaviors as fetishism may result. Freud's theories are controversial and have been debated through the years, and are covered in more detail in the chapter on personality.

FREUD: STAGES OF PSYCHOSEXUAL DEVELOPMENT	
Stage	**Description**
Oral	Libidinal energy centered on the mouth; fixation can lead to excessive dependency
Anal	Toilet training occurs during this time; fixation can lead to excessive orderliness or messiness
Phallic	Oedipal conflict is resolved during this stage
Latency	Libido is largely sublimated during this stage
Genital	Begins at puberty; if previous stages have been successfully resolved, the person will enter into normal heterosexual relations

Erik Erickson

Erik Erikson's theory is a **psychosocial theory**. His theory holds that development is a sequence of central life crises. In each of these crises, there is a possible favorable outcome and a possible unfavorable outcome. Psychosocial theory emphasizes emotional development and interactions with the social environment. Erikson believed that development occurred through resolutions of conflicts between needs and social demands; these conflicts occur in stages.

According to Erikson, the first conflict, which takes place in the first year of life, is that of **trust versus mistrust**. If resolved successfully, the child will come to trust his or her environment as well as himself. If mistrust wins out, the child will often be suspicious of the world, possibly throughout his or her life.

The second stage is **autonomy versus shame and doubt** (1–3 years). The favorable outcome here is a feeling of will and an ability to exercise choice as well as self-restraint. A child will have a sense of competence and autonomy. The unfavorable outcome is a sense of doubt and lack of control—a feeling that what happens to one is the result of external influences rather than one's own volition.

The next psychological conflict confronted is **initiative versus guilt** (3–6 years). Favorable outcomes include purpose, the ability to initiate activities, and the ability to enjoy accomplishment. If guilt wins out, the child will be so overcome by the fear of punishment that the child may either unduly restrict him or herself, or may overcompensate by showing off.

If the crisis of **industry versus inferiority** (6–12 years) is resolved favorably, the child will feel competent, will be able to exercise his or her abilities and intelligence in the world, and to affect the world in the way that the child desires. Unfavorable resolution results in a sense of inadequacy, a sense of inability to act in a competent manner, and a low self-esteem.

During adolescence, the conflict between **identity versus role confusion** emerges. This stage encompasses what Erikson termed "physiological revolution." The favorable outcome is fidelity, the ability to see oneself as a unique and integrated person with sustained loyalties. Unfavorable outcomes are confusion of one's identity and a kind of amorphous personality that shifts from day to day.

The main crisis of young adulthood is **intimacy versus isolation**. Favorable outcomes are love, the ability to have intimate relationships with others, the ability to commit oneself to another person and to one's own goals. If this crisis is not favorably resolved, there will be an avoidance of commitment, a kind of alienation and distancing of oneself from others and one's ideals. Isolated individuals are either withdrawn, or only capable of superficial relationships with others.

Stage seven of Erikson's theory is the conflict of **generativity versus stagnation**, middle age. The successful resolution of this conflict results in an individual capable of being a productive, caring, contributing member of society. If this crisis is not overcome, one acquires a sense of stagnation and may become self-indulgent, bored, and self-centered with little care for others.

Finally, old age with approaching death brings about the crisis of **integrity versus despair**. One reflects on his or her life with either a sense of integrity or with a sense of despair. If favorably resolved, we will see wisdom, which Erickson defined as detached concern in life itself, assurance in the meaning of life, dignity, and an acceptance of the fact that one's life has been worthwhile; the individual is ready to face death. If not resolved favorably, there will be feelings of bitterness about one's life, a feeling that life has been worthless, and at the same time, fear over one's own impending death.

TEMPERAMENT

Temperament is considered by many psychologists to be the central aspect of an individual's personality. It refers to individual differences as well as an individual's pattern of responding to the environment. Temperament is thought to be somewhat heritable, to emerge early in life (during infancy), to be stable over time, and to be pervasive across situations. There is some disagreement in the field about how to best conceptualize and measure temperament. However, there are core concepts common to many temperament theories, such as activity level, negative emotionality, and sociability.

Thomas and Chess

Alexander Thomas and Stella Chess performed a longitudinal study to examine temperament. Based upon their study, they proposed three categories of infant emotional and behavioral style: "easy," "slow to warm up," and "difficult." At one extreme was the easy infant, who generally displayed a positive mood, regularity in bodily functions, and was easily adapted to new situations. At the other extreme was the difficult child who tended to have negative emotions, irregular bodily functions, and who tended to withdraw in new situations. In the middle of these two extremes was the slow to warm up child who initially withdrew, but was soon able to adapt to new situations.

Research Methods

Temperament is measured in three ways: parental reports of child behavior, observations in naturalistic settings (at home), and observations in laboratory settings. By relying on parental report through interviews or questionnaires the experimenter can be certain that the information is coming from someone very knowledgeable about the infant. Parents see their infants in a wide range of situations and know their infants best. However, this type of research also risks biased responses. Naturalistic observations allow for more objective measures, but are time-consuming. During laboratory observations, experimental methods can be used to measure specific behaviors during controlled conditions. The drawback is that these observations occur during an artificial situation, and may not be indicative of infant behavior during normal conditions.

EARLY SOCIAL AND EMOTIONAL BEHAVIOR

Although infants are not born with the ability to communicate through verbal language, they are equipped with capabilities of signaling to parents and other caregivers in the social environment.

Crying

Crying is one way that infants are equipped to communicate their needs. **Wolff** conducted research with newborn babies. Using spectograms, he identified three distinct patterns of crying: the basic cry, usually associated with hunger; the angry cry, associated with frustration; and the pain cry, following a painful stimulus. Interestingly, Wolff found that even nonparent adults react with heart-rate accelerations following infant pain cries. Eventually, infants learn that their caregivers respond to crying—as early as the second month. Wolff observed that infants will cry when a person they are looking at leaves the room, and cease when the person returns.

Social Smiling

One of the earliest social and communicative signals to appear in infants is the smile. At first, the smiling response is undifferentiated. Almost any stimulus is capable of producing what appears to be a smile. Then **social smiling**, or smiling associated with facelike patterns develops. At first, almost any face is sufficient to elicit a smile. At about five months, however, only familiar faces tend to elicit smiles.

Fear

The **fear response** also follows a certain developmental course from undifferentiated to increasingly specific. At first, fear is evoked through any sudden change in level of stimulation. Turning on a light in a dark room or darkening a bright room have the same effect. During the first year of life, an infant may experience separation anxiety and stranger anxiety. By the end of the first year, however, the fear response is reserved either for the sudden absence of a specific individual such as the mother or the presence of an object or person who in the past had been harmful to the child. Very often, the emotional response is context dependent. A novel stimulus may elicit a smile in a familiar context and may elicit fear if presented in an unfamiliar situation.

ATTACHMENT

Harry Harlow

Psychological studies of the early relationship between caregivers and their infants suggest that early bonding between parent and child is also important to emotional behavior. Probably the most well-known series of investigations on this subject have been those of **Harry Harlow**.

Harlow studied baby Rhesus monkeys separated from their mothers. In his most famous experiment, he took newborn monkeys from their mothers 6–12 hours after birth, and placed them in cages with so-called surrogate mothers. One type of surrogate mother was a wire cylinder with a feeding nipple attached, and the other type was a wood cylinder covered with terry cloth; the cloth-covered wood cylinder did not have a nipple and did not provide food. Perhaps surprisingly, the monkeys overwhelmingly preferred the cloth mother. From this, Harlow concluded that what he called "contact comfort" was more essential in bond formation than providing for physical needs.

Harlow also tried raising monkeys exclusively with either cloth or wire mothers and observed their subsequent social interactions. He found that the wire mother monkeys were less socially adept and took longer to socially integrate with other monkeys. He then raised some monkeys in total isolation and he found that these monkeys were severely dysfunctional. However, monkeys that were isolated for up to a year could be brought into monkey society by other monkeys. Indeed, Harlow discovered a phenomenon that he referred to as therapist monkeys—monkeys who took on the task of bringing these dysfunctional monkeys back into society. However, those monkeys which had been isolated for a year or more were beyond help. They were sexually inept, overly aggressive and would often be abused by other monkeys.

John Bowlby

A more naturalistic study on human children was done by **John Bowlby** during the last half of the 1940s. Bowlby studied children who were brought up in institutions such as foster homes and orphanages; in these institutions they were physically well-cared for but often lacked intimate bodily contact. Such children tended to be timid and asocial.

Bowlby identified several phases of the attachment process. In the first (pre-attachment) phase, which lasts several weeks, the infant reacts identically to every adult and smiling face. By about three months of age, the second phase of attachment is reached in which the infant discriminates between familiar and unfamiliar faces. Only at six months do we see the infant seeking out and responding specifically to the mother. From nine to 12 months, the bonding intensifies and the child begins expressing stranger anxiety—a fear of strangers. In the second year, the child reacts to the mother's absence with strong protest—he referred to this behavior as **separation anxiety**. In the third year, the child is able to separate from the mother without prolonged distress.

Mary Ainsworth

Mary Ainsworth demonstrated the universality of this sequence with a study of Ugandan infants. Ainsworth devised a laboratory experiment, the **"strange situation procedure,"** to study the quality of the parent (mother)-child attachment relationship. During the experiment, the attachment figure (the mother) brings the child into an unfamiliar room with many toys. A series of three-minute episodes follows. First the child is free to explore the room and play with the toys. Next, a stranger comes into the room remaining silent at first, and eventually talks to the mother and plays with the infant. Then the mother leaves the room and the stranger interacts with the infant. Next, the mother returns and the stranger departs. Then the infant is left alone in the room. Next, the stranger returns to the room and interacts with the infant. Finally, the mother returns and the stranger leaves the room.

Ainsworth observed and assessed infant behavior, focusing on the infant's reaction to separation and reunion behavior. Ainsworth classified behavior into three basic types: **insecure/avoidant attachment (Type A), secure attachment (Type B),** and **insecure/resistant attachment (Type C).** Insecure/avoidant infants are not distressed when left alone with the stranger, and avoid contact with the mother upon her return. Securely attached infants are mildly distressed during separations from the mother but greet her positively when she returns. Insecure/resistant infants are distressed during the separation and are inclined to resist physical contact with the mother upon her return.

Konrad Lorenz

A great deal of work on mother-infant bonding also comes from the field of ethology. Ethologists such as **Konrad Lorenz** have studied imprinting. Imprinting can be defined as the rapid formation of an attachment bond between an organism and an object in the environment. Ethologists have sought to determine which specific stimuli infants will attach to. Often the stimulus is a specific physical feature of the mother, or a specific movement. For instance, when Lorenz imitated the strut of a jackdaw, an infant jackdaw became attached to Lorenz. In other words, the bird became imprinted. The bird followed Lorenz about and preferred the company of humans to members of its own species. It even attempted to initiate mating rituals with humans. Lorenz's work led him to believe that all imprinting takes place during certain critical periods. Other ethologists reject this concept of a critical period however and prefer to speak of sensitive periods, as we discussed in the section about language development.

MORAL DEVELOPMENT

Lawrence Kolberg's Stages

Some of the most heated debates in developmental psychology have centered on the development of moral thought and action. A leading figure in this debate was **Lawrence**

Kohlberg. Kohlberg believed that there were three phases of moral thought with each phase consisting of two stages each, for a total of six stages. Each stage builds upon another and is associated with changes in cognitive structure.

The first phase is **preconventional morality**, during which right and wrong are defined by the hedonistic consequences of a given action (punishment or reward). The orientation during this stage is towards **punishment and obedience**. In stage two, there is an **orientation towards reciprocity**—an "I'll scratch your back, you scratch mine" orientation. Stage two has been called the **instrumental relativist stage**.

The second phase is the **conventional phase of morality** which is based on social rules. Once again, there are two stages in this phase. In the third stage, the emphasis is "**good girl, nice boy**" **orientation** in which one is looking for approval of others. The fourth stage sees morality defined by the rules of authority, and is therefore characterized by a "**law and order orientation**."

The third phase is called **post-conventional morality**, and once again, there are two stages in this phase. Stage five is what Kohlberg calls **social contract orientation**. Moral rules are seen as convention that is designed to ensure the greater good. Finally, stage six, according to Kohlberg, consists of acting according to a set of **universal ethical principles**.

The Heinz Dilemmma

Kohlberg has devised a test to determine the moral level of a given individual; this test consists of a series of hypothetical moral dilemmas. The subjects are asked what the character of a story should do and give a reason. Based on the reasoning they give, subjects can be placed in one of the six stages. One of these moral dilemmas is about a man named Heinz who lived in Europe. His wife was dying of a rare disease. There was a druggist in the town who invented a drug that could cure the disease. This drug cost him $200 to produce, yet he was selling it for $2,000. Heinz went to the druggist and asked him if he would lower the price. The druggist said "No. I invented it and I am going to make money from it." Heinz didn't have $2,000 and was desperate because his wife was going to die, so he broke into the druggist's office one night and stole the medication for his sick wife.

The question is, "Was Heinz right or wrong, and why?" A child in stage three might respond that Heinz was wrong because it is not nice to steal. Another child in stage three might respond that Heinz was right because it wouldn't be nice to let one's wife die. So the actual decision isn't as important as the thought processes that underlie it.

Carol Gilligan's Criticism of Kohlberg

Kohlberg's work has been strongly criticized. The postconventional phase has especially come under attack. **Carol Gilligan** asserts that males and females adopt different perspectives on moral issues and that these differences stem from the different ways in which boys and girls are raised. She points out that Kohlberg's research was done solely with males and therefore should not be used to evaluate the moral development of females. Gilligan's theory centers on the idea that women adopt an interpersonal orientation that is neither more or less mature than the rule-bound thinking of men. In other words, Gilligan argues that women's morality tends to be focused on caring and compassion, and that they are concerned with relationships and social responsibilities.

GENDER DEVELOPMENT

Theoretical Perspectives

Researchers have found gender differences in personality and social behavior, as well as in cognitive abilities (mathematical, spatial, and linguistic abilities). These findings have certainly enlivened the nature/nurture controversy mentioned earlier, as theorists from a broad range of perspectives have offered their explanations for gender differences.

Sociobiologists believe that gender role differences should be understood according to a evolutionary perspective—that men and women develop gender-stereotyped behaviors because of the historical survival function of these behaviors. Social learning theorists point to the social environment and emphasize that children model their behaviors after adults and other children of the same gender. Cognitive developmental theorists stress the importance of cognitions that children have concerning gender.

Kohlberg's Gender Stages

An example of a cognitive developmental theory was proposed by Kolberg, and is a three-stage theory of self-socialization. During the first stage, **gender labeling** (2–3 years of age), children achieve gender identity, that is, they realize that they are a member of a particular sex and accept the they are a boy or a girl and are able to label themselves as such. They are also able to label others in terms of their sex as well. The second stage, **gender stability** (3–4), marks the period when children can predict that they will still be a boy or a girl when they grow up, but this understanding is superficial and dependent upon a physical notion of gender. During the third stage, **gender consistency** (4–7 years), children understand the permanency of gender, regardless of what one wears or how one behaves.

Gender schematic processing theory, proposed by **Martin** and **Halverson**, builds on Kohlberg's theory. This theory holds that as soon as children are able to label themselves, they begin concentrating on those behaviors that seem to be associated with their gender, and paying less attention to those they believe are associated with the opposite gender.

PARENTING

Diane Baumrind

A great deal of research has been done on parental style and discipline, particularly by the psychologist **Diana Baumrind**. By measuring parental control, nurturance, clarity of communication, and maturity demands, she proposes three distinct parenting styles: **authoritarian**, **authoritative**, and **permissive**. Authoritarian parents tend to use punitive control methods and lack emotional warmth; authoritative parents have high demands for child compliance (but score low on punitive control methods), utilize positive reinforcement, and score high on emotional warmth; permissive parents score very low on control/demand measures.

Researchers have found that parenting style affects child behavior and is a major influence on a child's development. Children with authoritative parents are characterized as being more socially and academically competent. Children with authoritarian parents and permissive parents tend to have difficulties in school and in peer relations.

Fatherhood

Differences have been found in how fathers and mothers interact with children. The major difference you need to remember for the GRE Psychology test is that fathers tend to play more vigorously with their children than mothers do, while mothers tend to stress verbal over physical interactions. There are exceptions, but this is a pattern found in studies of behavior.

IMPORTANT NAMES IN DEVELOPMENTAL PSYCHOLOGY

Ainsworth, M.	Devised the "**strange situation**" to study attachment
Baumrind, D.	Studied the relationship between **parental style** and **aggression**
Bowlby, J.	Studied **attachment** in human children
Chomsky, N.	**Linguist** who suggested that **children have an innate capacity for language acquisition**
Erikson, E.	Outlined **eight stages of psychosocial development** covering the entire lifespan
Freud, S.	Outlined **five stages of psychosexual development**; stressed the importance of the **Oedipal conflict** in psychosexual development
Gesell, A.	Believed that development was due primarily to **maturation**
Gilligan, C.	Suggested that **males and females have different orientations toward morality**
Hall, G.	The **founder** of developmental psychology
Harlow, H.	Used **monkeys** and "surrogate mothers" to study the role of **contact comfort** in **bond formation**
Kohlberg, L.	Studied **moral development** using **moral dilemmas**
Locke, J.	British philosopher who suggested that infants had no predetermined tendencies, that they were blank slates (*tabula rasa*) to be written on by experience
Lorenz, K.	Studied **imprinting** in birds
Piaget, J.	Outlined **four stages of cognitive development**
Rousseau, J.	**French philosopher** who suggested that development could unfold without help from society
Terman, L.	Performed **longitudinal study** on **gifted children**
Tryon, R.	Studied the **genetic basis** of **maze-running** ability in rats
Vygotsky, L.	Studied **cognitive development**; stressed the importance of the zone of **proximal development**

DEVELOPMENTAL PSYCHOLOGY PRACTICE SET

Time: 8 minutes

Directions: Each of the questions or incomplete statements below is followed by five suggested answers or completions. In each case, select the one that best answers the question or completes the statement.

1. According to Piaget, the attainment of formal operations is characterized by
   - (A) understanding of object permanence
   - (B) preoperational thinking
   - (C) beginning of symbol usage
   - (D) ability to manipulate abstract concepts
   - (E) tertiary circular reactions

2. According to research in observational learning, which of the following statements is most accurate?
   - (A) A child will tend to display similar aggressive behavior after observing an adult hitting a doll
   - (B) It is not necessary to limit the amount of time school-age children spend watching television
   - (C) Children imitate only behavior displayed by their parents
   - (D) The development of social behavior in preschool children is derived primarily from innate tendencies
   - (E) Children are not likely to learn by merely observing the behavior of a social model

3. According to Freud, resolution of the Oedipal complex
   - (A) has no analogous process in girls
   - (B) depends on the antipathy of the child toward the father
   - (C) is a sign of emergent genital sexuality
   - (D) takes place only after the death of the mother
   - (E) is marked by a sublimation of libidinal energy

4. The tendency of infants to bring all novel objects to their mouths is an example of which of the following Piagetian processes?
   - (A) Assimilation
   - (B) Accommodation
   - (C) Sublimation
   - (D) Primary circular reaction
   - (E) Centration

5. Which of the following are true about Erikson's theory of development?
   - I. Erikson is a neo-Piagetian.
   - II. Erikson's approach is based the idea that people are products of their sexual instincts.
   - III. A significant factor of Erikson's theory is that it describes the entire lifespan.

   - (A) I only
   - (B) II only
   - (C) III only
   - (D) I and II only
   - (E) II and III only

6. Which of the following examples of child speech is LEAST likely to be considered an error of growth?

    (A) Mommy bringed me the ball
    (B) Jimmy hurt hisself
    (C) The two mans talked to me
    (D) No baby go store
    (E) I had the mostest fun on the slide

7. Who first showed that contact comfort was necessary for the formation of the mother-infant attachment bond?

    (A) Sigmund Freud
    (B) John Bowlby
    (C) Mary Ainsworth
    (D) Konrad Lorenz
    (E) Harry Harlow

8. A researcher is interested in studying the development of creativity in children. She develops an appropriate test and gives it to three groups of children: 3-year-olds, 4-year-olds, and 5-year-olds. Once a year for the next five years, she tests the creativity of her original subjects. This study is an example of a

    (A) cross-sectional study
    (B) sequential cohort study
    (C) longitudinal study
    (D) case study
    (E) none of the above

9. According to the Mendelian paradigm, which of the following statements is true?

    (A) If both parents have blue eyes, their offspring must have blue eyes
    (B) If both parents have brown eyes, their offspring must have brown eyes
    (C) If one parent has blue eyes and the other has brown eyes, their offspring cannot have blue eyes
    (D) If one parent has blue eyes and the other has brown eyes, their offspring will have gray eyes
    (E) Genes are located on the chromosomes in the nucleus of the cell

10. According to Erikson, which of the following is the central crisis of adolescence?

    (A) Identity versus confusion
    (B) Trust versus mistrust
    (C) Industry versus inferiority
    (D) Generativity versus stagnation
    (E) Intimacy versus isolation

EXPLANATIONS FOR THE DEVELOPMENTAL PSYCHOLOGY PRACTICE SET

1. D

Recall that Piaget's theory of cognitive development consists of four stages: sensorimotor, preoperational, concrete operations, and formal operations. It is in the stage of formal operations that the person acquires the ability to manipulate abstract concepts. Therefore, answer choice (D) is correct. Let's take a look at the other answer choices. Since formal operations is the final stage, you could have eliminated choices (A) and (E) because they are terms that describe a child's early development and occur during the sensorimotor stage. Object permanence is the child's realization that objects still exist even when they are out of sight; tertiary circular reactions are trial-and-error actions the child uses to investigate the environment. Therefore, choices (A) and (E) are incorrect. Choice (C), the beginning of symbol usage, appears long before the formal operations stage. Finally, answer choice (B) is incorrect because preoperational thinking, by definition, is different from formal operational thinking.

2. A

According to research on observational learning, a child will tend to display similar aggressive behavior after observing an adult hitting a doll. This was the result of Bandura's experiment with the Bobo Doll. In his experiment, Bandura found that children who had watched an adult model behave aggressively toward a Bobo doll performed similar acts themselves, even though the children hadn't been reinforced for committing such acts. Let's look at the other answer choices. Answer choice (B) talks about television watching, but does not say anything about the effects on learning or any other behavior, so it is incorrect. Answer choice (C) is incorrect because the adults the children imitated in Bandura's experiment were not their parents. Answer choice (D) refers to a biological basis for development, without any reference to observational learning, so it too is incorrect. Finally, answer choice (E) is just the opposite of what Bandura found in his experiment. Therefore, the correct answer is choice (A).

3. E

The resolution of the Oedipal complex is marked by a sublimation of libidinal energy. Recall that Freud's theory of psychosexual development includes five stages: oral, anal, phallic, latency, and genital. If you remembered that the genital stage is the last stage and that the Oedipal complex occurs in young boys during the phallic stage, you could have eliminated choice (C). Furthermore, if you remembered that resolution of the Electra complex, which occurs in girls, is an analogous process to the resolution of the Oedipal complex, you could have eliminated choice (A). Keep in mind that the question asks about the *resolution* of the Oedipal complex and you can take a closer look at choice (B) and eliminate that choice as well. Although it is true that the Oedipal complex consists of a male child's desire for his mother and antipathy for his father, the resolution of the complex depends on the child coming to terms with these feelings and sublimating his libido. Finally, answer choice (D) is also incorrect since the resolution of the Oedipal complex is not dependent on the death of the mother.

4. A

Answer choice (B), accommodation, might have been tempting because both assimilation and accommodation are key Piagetian concepts. Let's go over their definitions again. Assimilation is a process through which new information is incorporated into an existing schema. In this case, infants are using their "bring things to mouth" schema to bring the novel objects to their mouths. Accommodation is a process during which the infant's schema is changed to fit new information. Answer choice (C), sublimation, is a term used by Freud, not Piaget, and is therefore incorrect. Answer choice (D), primary circular reaction, is a pleasurable response that an infant discovers by chance and repeats over and over. These reactions are always centered on the infant's own body. Therefore, primary circular reactions would not involve the interaction between the infant and an object. Finally, answer choice (E), centration, is the tendency of preschool children to focus on only one aspect of a problem, even when two or more aspects may be relevant and is not related to the process that described in the question.

5. C

A significant factor of Erikson's theory is that it describes the entire lifespan. His eight stage theory covers the years from infancy to old age. Furthermore, whereas Freud's theory is psychosexual, Erikson's is psychosocial. Finally, although Erikson's theory differs from Freud's in several ways, Erikson is a neo-Freudian, not a neo-Piagetian. Because only Roman numeral option III is true, the correct answer is choice (C).

6. D

To answer this question you need to pick out just one answer that is NOT an error of growth. If you knew right off the bat what an error of growth is, then you could have answered the question directly. An error of growth is when a child overextends grammatical rules to words that adults would know don't follow the rules. For example, in choice (A), the child says *bringed* instead of *brought*. Looking through the answer choices, you may have been able to see a pattern in choices (A), (B), (C), and (E) of this kind of mistake, and therefore could have seen that choice (D) is the exception and thus the correct choice. In fact, choice (D) is an example of another speech pattern that occurs in children from about 18 to 24 months of age. Telegraphic speech is the term to describe early sentences that consist solely of content words and omit the less meaningful parts of speech such as articles, prepositions, pronouns, and auxiliary verbs.

7. E

Recall that Harlow separated newborn monkeys from their mothers. He then placed the newborn monkeys in a cage with two "surrogate mothers." One of the surrogate monkeys was a wire cylinder with a feeding nipple attached, the other was made of terry cloth, but with no feeding nipple. It turned out that the infant monkeys spent more time with the terry cloth monkey, especially if they were frightened by something. From this, Harlow concluded that "contact comfort" was an important factor in the formation of the attachment bond. Therefore, the correct answer is choice (E).

8. B

Recall that in a sequential cohort study subjects at different ages are studied repeatedly over several years. That's what is going on in the question stem, and therefore, answer choice (B) is correct. Answer choices (A) and (C) are often used in developmental psychology. In cross-sectional studies, members of different age groups are studied at the same time, and are then compared on the basis of their age. In longitudinal studies, the person conducting the study measures the same variable in one group of same-age subjects at a number of points in time. Answer choice (D), a case study, is also incorrect. Recall that, in a case study, the investigator seeks to record as completely as possible the actions of a very small number of individuals over a period of time. This is sometimes also called the clinical method.

9. A

The question is actually pretty simple if you remember that blue eyes are a recessive trait. If both parents have blue eyes that means they both have two recessive genes and can therefore only contribute these recessive genes to their children. Therefore, the offspring must have blue eyes. Answer (B) is incorrect. Both parents could have a recessive blue eye gene that was not expressed in them but that could be passed on to their children and expressed in their phenotypes. (C) is also incorrect. Again, the parent with the brown eyes could still have a recessive blue-eyed gene to contribute to the offspring genetic pool. (D) is incorrect because genes are not like paint. They can't be mixed. A gene is either expressed or it is not expressed. Finally, choice (E) is incorrect. Although genes are indeed located on chromosomes in the nucleus of the cell, this was not part of the Mendelian paradigm. Indeed, the laws of Mendelian genetics were formulated without knowledge of the actual physical transfer mechanism.

10. A

According to Erikson, adolescence is the period in which the child develops identity and the ability to sustain loyalty to self, others, and goals. Answer (B), trust versus mistrust is the first life crisis, the crisis of the first year. Answer (C) refers to the crisis that precedes adolescence and takes place from the sixth year through puberty. Answer (D), generativity versus stagnation, is the crisis of middle age and (E), intimacy versus isolation, is the crisis of early adulthood. Therefore, the correct answer is choice (A).

CHAPTER FIVE

Personality and Abnormal Psychology

OUTLINE

Historical Perspective

Theories of Personality and Abnormal Psychology

- Psychodynamic
  - Sigmund Freud
  - Carl Jung
  - Alfred Adler
  - Karen Horney
  - Ego Psychologists
  - Object Relations
- Behaviorism
  - John Dollard and Neal Miller
  - B. F. Skinner
  - Albert Bandura
  - Cognitive-Behavior Therapy
- Humanism
  - Kurt Lewin
  - Abraham Maslow
  - George Kelly
  - Carl Rogers
  - Victor Frankl

- Trait/Type Theorists
  - Type A/Type B
  - Raymond Cattell
  - Hans Eyseck
  - Gordon Allport
  - David McClelland
  - Herman Witkin
  - Julian Rotter
  - Machiavellianism
- Walter Mischel's Criticism

Understanding Mental Disorders

- *Diagnostic and Statistical Manual of Mental Disorders, Fourth Edition* (DSM-IV)
- Disorders First Diagnosed in Infancy
- Schizophrenia
- Mood Disorders
- Anxiety Disorders
- Somataform Disorders
- Dissociative Disorders
- Eating Disorders
- Personality Disorders

Diathesis-Stress Model

Primary Prevention

The Problem of Labeling

Personality and Abnormal Psychology

How do we define personality? To endeavor to do so is to get at the very root of psychology, namely, who a person really is, what makes a person tick, and why. Popular meanings of personality generally fall into one of two categories: the social skills and the salient impression one leaves on others. Closely linked to the study of personality is the study of abnormal behavior, or mental illness, a concern of philosophers since ancient times. When we speak of mental illness, we are speaking not only of the gross distortions in reality as is characterized by illnesses such as schizophrenia, but also the less severe difficulties that many people encounter dealing with everyday life.

This chapter will cover psychodynamic, behaviorist, type/trait, and phenomenological theories of personality and abnormal psychology, as well as some of the corresponding approaches of psychotherapy. Using the DSM-IV classification system, we will review some of the major categories of psychopathology: disorders first diagnosed in infancy, childhood, or adolescence; schizophrenic disorders; mood disorders; somataform disorders; dissociative disorders; eating disorders; and personality disorders. (Mental retardation is discussed in the chapter on developmental psychology, and deliriums and dementias are discussed in the physiological psychology chapter.)

HISTORICAL PERSPECTIVE

William Sheldon's early theory of personality defined physical/biological variables that he related to human behaviors. He characterized people by body type, relating body type (somatotypes) to personality type. He used the terms **endomorphy, mesomorphy,** and **ectomorphy** to characterize body types that were soft and spherical; hard, muscular, and rectangular; and thin, fragile and lightly muscled, respectively.

Early theories of abnormal behavior were similarly strange by today's standards: Abnormal behavior was seen as evidence of demonic possession or even witchcraft. However, beginning with the Renaissance, this view began to lose favor.

Some historians of psychology, most notably **E. G. Boring**, have suggested that the development of psychology is due not primarily to the efforts of great people, but to *Zeitgeist*, or the changing spirit of the times. Beginning with **Edward Titchener's method of introspection**, which formed the system of psychology called **structuralism**, a half dozen or so other major systems of psychology have developed over psychology's history, perhaps due to *Zeitgeist*: **functionalism, behaviorism, gestalt psychology, cognitive psychology, psychoanalysis,** and **humanism**.

Sigmund Freud's (1856–1939) theory of personality was the first comprehensive theory on personality and abnormal psychology. Most of Freud's predecessors emphasized consciousness and the power of reason in human behavior. Based upon his experience treating neurosis, Freud reversed this thinking and opened up a whole new perspective on personality. He pioneered the psychoanalytic system of thought in psychology. His theory will be covered in detail in this chapter.

Humanism developed as a system in the mid-20th century. It arose in opposition to both psychoanalysis and behaviorism. Humanistic psychology opposed the pessimism of the psychoanalytic perspective and the robotic concepts of behaviorism. Humanists believe in the notion of free will and the idea that people should be considered as wholes rather than in terms of stimuli and responses (behaviorism) or instincts (psychoanalysis). Important humanists include **Abraham Maslow** (1908–1970) and **Carl Rogers** (1902–1987). More information on these theorists is presented in this chapter.

Treatment options for people with mental illness have improved tremendously over time. Beginning in the 1500s, asylums were created to care for the mentally ill, where patients were treated like animals. Cells were dark dungeons with no provisions for heat in the winter. Hands and feet were chained and patients slept on straw rather than beds. They were kept shackled to the wall and were forced to sit in their own filth.

In 1792, **Philippe Pinel** was placed in charge of an asylum in Paris that was marked by the conditions just described. Pinel, however, believed that people with mental illness should be treated with consideration and kindness. He removed shackles from the patients, allowed them to go outside on hospital grounds, gave them beds to sleep on, and, in general, made sure the patients were treated humanely. As you might imagine, these changes had beneficial effects on the patients. These reforms spread to other asylums.

An important reformer in the United States was **Dorothea Dix**. From 1841 to 1881, she was a zealous advocate of treating the hospitalized mentally ill in a humane way. Her campaign was instrumental in improving the lives of the mentally ill in this country.

Advances were made in the later part of the 19th century in the biomedical understanding of physical and mental disorders. An important development was the discovery of the etiology (cause) of **general paresis**. General paresis was a disorder characterized by delusions of grandeur, mental deterioration, eventual paralysis, and death. It was eventually discovered that general paresis was due to brain deterioration caused by syphilis (which was untreatable until 1909), and that the mental disorder seen in the syndrome was caused by organic brain pathology. The idea that physiological factors could underlie mental disorders was an important advance in our understanding of abnormal psychology.

In 1938, **Cerletti** and **Bini** introduced the use of the electroshock for the artificial production of convulsive seizures in psychiatric patients. They believed that epileptic-like convulsions could cure schizophrenia (they were wrong). The convulsions were so violent that patients were in danger of fracturing vertebrae and other bones.

Between 1935 and 1955, tens of thousands of patients were subjected to **prefrontal lobotomies** to treat schizophrenia. In this surgical treatment, the frontal lobes of the brain were severed from the brain tissue. Unfortunately, this procedure also destroyed parts of the frontal lobe—the lobe of the brain responsible for most of the traits that make us distinctly human. Lobotomies didn't cure schizophrenia—it just made the patients easier to handle, since, in many cases, the patients became tranquil and showed an absence of feeling.

The introduction of antipsychotic drugs in the 1950s to treat schizophrenia changed the atmosphere in psychiatric hospitals. Surgeons stopped performing lobotomies and using electroshock therapy for schizophrenia as these antipsychotic drugs offered a major breakthrough in treatment modalities, with many formerly "hopeless" patients released from psychiatric hospitals completely.

Finally, in 1883, **Emil Kraepelin** published a textbook in which he noted that some symptoms of mental disorders occurred together regularly enough that the symptom patterns could be considered specific types of mental disorders. He then described these disorders and worked out a scheme of classifying these disorders integrating clinical data. Kraeplin's classification system was effective in summarizing what was known at the time. It was also a precursor to our current classification system, the DSM-IV.

THEORIES OF PERSONALITY AND ABNORMAL PSYCHOLOGY AND TREATMENT MODELS

We can categorize theories of personality into four areas: psychodynamic (psychoanalytic), behaviorist, phenomenological, and type and trait. There are great differences between these divisions in how personality is defined and how those theoretical perspectives explain abnormal personality; there are also differences within each division.

Psychodynamic

Sigmund Freud

The theories subsumed under **psychodynamic** or **psychoanalytic theory** postulate the existence of unconscious internal states that motivate the overt actions of individuals and determine personality. Sigmund Freud's model of personality was the structural dynamic model, and involved three major systems: the **id**, **ego**, and **superego**. The id is the reservoir of all psychic energy and consists of everything psychological that's present at birth. It functions according to the **pleasure principle** whose aim is to immediately discharge any energy build-up i.e., relieve tension. The **primary process** is the id's response to frustration operating under the dictum of "obtain satisfaction now, not later." For example, if a person gets hungry and food is unavailable, it is through the use of the primary process that a memory image of food might alleviate the frustration experienced. The mental image of the object is known as **wish-fulfillment**. However, since the person can't eat his mental image, another system forms.

Since the mental image cannot effectively reduce tension on a permanent basis, the ego and its mode of functioning, the **secondary process**, come into play. The ego operates according to the **reality principle**, taking into account objective reality as it guides or inhibits the activity of the id and the id's pleasure principle. The aim of the reality principle is to postpone the pleasure principle until the actual object that will satisfy the need has been discovered or produced. It must be emphasized that while the ego's functioning suspends the workings of the primary process, it does so only in service of the id to pragmatically meet the demands of objective reality. The mutual give and take of ego and secondary process with reality promotes the growth and elaboration of the psychological processes of perception, memory, problem solving, thinking, and reality testing. The ego can be understood to be the organization of the id; receiving its power from the id, it can never really be independent of the id.

The **superego** is similar to the id in that it too is not directly in touch with reality and strives for the ideal rather than the real. However, it represents the moral branch of personality, striving for perfection. There are two subsystems of the superego: the **conscience** and the **ego-ideal**. Whatever a child's caregivers say is improper and the child is punished for is incorporated into the child's conscience. Whatever they approve of and reward the child for tends to be incorporated into ego ideal. Ultimately, a system of right or wrong is substituted for the parental punishment—reward.

An **instinct** is an innate psychological representation (wish) of a bodily (biological) excitation (need). Instincts are the propelling aspects of Freud's dynamic theory of personality. Freud listed two general types of instincts: life and death instincts, sometimes called **Eros** and **Thanatos**, respectively. The life instincts serve the purpose of individual survival (hunger, thirst, and sex). The form of energy by which the life instincts perform their work is called **libido**. The death instincts also represent an unconscious wish for the ultimate absolute state of quiescence.

The ego's recourse to releasing excessive pressures due to anxiety are referred to as **defense mechanisms**. All defense mechanisms have two common characteristics: 1) they deny, falsify, or distort reality; and 2) they operate unconsciously. There are eight main defense mechanisms: **repression**, **suppression**, **projection**, **reaction formation**, **rationalization**, **regression**, **sublimation**, and **displacement**. **Repression** is the unconscious forgetting of anxiety-producing memories. **Suppression** is a more deliberate, conscious form of forgetting. **Projection** is when a person attributes his forbidden urges to others. For instance the thought, "I hate my uncle," may cause too much anxiety, so it gets turned into "My uncle hates me." In **reaction formation**, a repressed wish is warded off by its diametrical opposite. For example, a young boy who hates his brother and is punished for his hostile acts may turn his feelings into the exact opposite; he now showers his brother with affection. **Rationalization** refers to process of developing a socially acceptable explanation for inappropriate behavior or thoughts. **Regression** refers to a person reverting to an earlier stage of development in response to a traumatic event. **Sublimation** is transforming unacceptable urges into socially acceptable behaviors. In **displacement**, pent-up feelings (often hostility) are discharged on objects and people less dangerous than those objects or people causing the feelings. An example of displacement occurs when someone who is harassed by his boss at work goes home and provokes an argument with his wife.

Carl Jung

Later psychoanalytic theories have given more emphasis to interpersonal, sociological, and cultural influences, while maintaining their link with the psychoanalytic tradition. **Carl Jung** preferred to think of libido as psychic energy in general (not just psychic energy rooted in sexuality). Jung identified the ego as the conscious mind, and he divided the unconscious into two parts: the personal unconscious, similar to Freud's notion of the unconscious, and the **collective unconscious.** The collective unconscious is a powerful system that is shared among all humans and considered to be a residue of the experiences of our early ancestors. It includes images that are a record of common experiences, such as having a mother and a father. These images are the building blocks for the collective unconscious, referred to in Jung's theory as **archetypes.** An archetype is a thought or image that has an emotional element.

Major Jungian archetypes include: the **persona**, the **anima** and **animus**, the **shadow**, and the **self**. The **persona** is a mask that is adopted by a person in response to the demands of social convention. This archetype originates from social interactions in which the assumption of a social role has served a useful purpose to humankind throughout history. The **anima** (feminine) and the **animus** (masculine) help us to understand gender, the feminine behaviors in males, and the masculine behaviors in females. The **shadow** archetype consists of the animal instincts that humans inherited in their evolution from lower forms of life. The shadow archetype is responsible for the appearance in consciousness and behavior of unpleasant and socially reprehensible thoughts, feelings, and actions. The **self** is the person's striving for unity, and is the point of intersection between the collective unconscious and the conscious. Jung symbolized the self as a *mandala*, a Sanskrit word meaning *magic circle*. Jung saw the mandala as the mythic expression of the self, as the reconciler of opposites and as the promoter of harmony.

Jung also had a typology of personality. Jung distinguished two major orientations of personality: **extroversion** and **introversion.** Extroversion is an orientation toward the external, objective world. Introversion is an orientation toward the inner, subjective world. These two opposing orientations are both present in the personality, but ordinarily one of them is dominant. Jung also described four psychological functions: thinking, feeling, sensing, and intuiting. Typically, one of those four functions is more differentiated than the other three. Jung believed that these systems, attitudes, and functions all interact in dynamic ways to form personality.

Alfred Adler

Alfred Adler's theory turned the attention to immediate social imperatives of family and society (social variables) and their effects on unconscious factors. Adler was the originator of the concept of the inferiority complex—that is, the individual's sense of incompleteness, sense of imperfection, physical inferiorities, as well as social disabilities. According to Adler, it is striving toward superiority that drives the personality. This striving enhances the personality when it is socially oriented, that is, when the striving leads to endeavors that benefit all people; when the striving is selfish and not socially oriented, it becomes the root of personality disturbances.

The notions of the **creative self** and the **style of life** were also important to Adler's theory. The creative self is that force by which each individual shapes his or her uniqueness and makes his or her own personality. Style of life represents the manifestation of the creative self and describes a person's unique way of achieving superiority (as opposed to inferiority). The family environment is crucial in molding the person's style of life. (Adler coined the term "life style.")

Another important concept in Adler's theory of personality is **fictional finalism**. This is the notion that an individual is motivated more by his or her expectations of the future than by past experiences. According to Adler, human goals are based on a subjective or fictional estimate of life's values rather than objective data from the past.

Notice the difference between Freud, Jung, and Adler. Whereas Freud's major assumption is that behavior is motivated by inborn instincts and Jung's principal axiom is that a person's conduct is governed by inborn archetypes, Adler assumed that people are primarily motivated by striving for superiority.

Karen Horney

Karen Horney postulated that the neurotic personality is governed by one of ten needs. Each of these needs is directed toward making life and interactions bearable. Examples of these neurotic needs are the need for affection and approval, the need to exploit others, and the need for self-sufficiency and independence. While healthy people have the need for affection and the need for independence, Horney emphasizes that these neurotic needs resemble healthy ones except in four respects: one, they are disproportionate in intensity; two, they are indiscriminate in application; three, they partially disregard reality; and four, they have a tendency to provoke intense anxiety. For instance, someone with a neurotic need for self-sufficiency and independence would go to great extremes to avoid being obligated to someone else in any way. As the central focus of the person's life, it would be a neurotic need and not a healthy one.

Horney's primary concept is that of basic anxiety. This is based on the premise that a child's early perception of the self is important. A sense of helplessness as a child confuses the child, makes the child feel insecure, and produces basic anxiety in the child. To overcome basic anxiety and attain a degree of security, the child uses three strategies in his relationship with others: moving toward people to obtain the good will of people who provide security; moving against people, or fighting them to obtain the upper hand; and moving away, or withdrawing, from people. These three strategies are the general headings under which the ten neurotic needs fall. Healthy people use all three strategies, depending on the situation. However, the highly threatened child will use one of these strategies rigidly and exclusively, and this carries over into adult personality.

Ego Psychologists

A modification and extension of Freud's theory was initiated by his daughter, **Anna Freud**, and was the result of her work in psychotherapy with children. She suggested that psychoanalytic theory and psychotherapy could profit from more direct investigation of the conscious ego and its relation to the world, to the unconscious, and to the superego. She also augmented our understanding of the ego defense mechanisms. She is usually considered to be the founder of **ego psychology**.

Erik Erickson, another ego psychologist, provided a direct extension of psychoanalysis to the psychosocial realm. He expanded and reworked Freud's stages to cover the entire lifespan and in so doing showed how even negative events or conflicts could have positive effects on adult personality. He used this framework to describe the healthy person on his or her own terms and not merely as opposed to the unhealthy individual. A full discussion of Erikson's developmental stages is included in the developmental psychology chapter.

Object Relations

Object-relations theory also falls under the realm of psychodynamic theories of personality. In this context, "object" refers to the symbolic representation of a significant part of the young child's personality. Object-relations theorists look at the creation and development of these internalized objects in young children. Important object-relations theorists include **Melanie Klein**, **D. W. Winnicott**, **Margaret Mahler**, and **Otto Kernberg**.

Psychoanalytic Treatment

Psychoanalysis is probably the best known type of psychotherapy. This therapy was developed by Sigmund Freud and is an intensive, long-term treatment for uncovering repressed memories, motives, and conflicts stemming from problems in psychosexual development. Freud believed that by gaining insight into the repressed material, the energy being utilized to deal with the repressed conflict would be freed up and made available for further development.

Early in the development of psychoanalysis, Freud used **hypnosis** to free repressed thoughts from the patient's unconscious, but he later dropped that method in favor of alternative methods. Freud used **free association**, a technique whereby the client says whatever comes to his or her conscious mind regardless of how personal, painful, or seemingly irrelevant it may appear to be. Through free associations, the analyst and patient together reconstruct the nature of the client's original conflict. Freud also used **dream interpretation**. Freud believed that the defenses are relaxed and the mind is freer to express forbidden wishes and desires during dream states. Therefore, understanding patients' dreams leads to an understanding of their unconscious conflicts. **Resistance**, or an unwillingness or inability to relate to certain thoughts, motives, or experiences, is also a major part of analysis. Such things as forgetting dream material, missing a therapy session, blocking associations, and switching topics rapidly are indications of resistance and subject to analysis. And finally, **transference** involves attributing to the therapist attitudes and feelings that developed in the patient's relations with significant others in the past. It is through transference that the analyst can help recreate the patient's experiences so that the patient has an opportunity to uncover, acknowledge, and understand his or her relationships with others. The therapist too will experience a full array of emotions toward the patient at various points in the treatment. This is known as **countertransference** and must be understood by the therapist so that it does not impinge on the treatment in a counterproductive way. This is one of the reasons psychoanalysts-in-training undergo psychoanalysis themselves.

Classical psychoanalysis is very expensive and requires a larger commitment of time than most people can make. As a result, there have been many modifications in the treatment. The **neo-Freudian approaches** place much more emphasis on current interpersonal relationships and life situations than on childhood experience and psychosexual development.

Behaviorism

The basic assumption of behavior theory regarding personality development is that behavior is learned as people interact with their environment. Rather than focus on unconscious instincts, the **behaviorist theories of personality** tend to look first and foremost at behavior. **John Dollard** and **Neal Miller** blended some psychoanalytic concepts in a behavioral stimulus-response reinforcement learning theory approach. Dollard and Miller focused on conflicting motives or conflicting tendencies in the development of personality. **B. F. Skinner** considered personality to be a collection of behavior that happens to have been sufficiently reinforced to persist. That is to say, "personality" is the result of behavioral development of an organism. **Albert Bandura** also contends that learning principles are sufficient to account for personality development. The basis of his **social learning theory** is modeling observed behavior. Bandura stressed that learning occurs not only by having one's own behavior reinforced (as Skinner believes), but also by observing other people's behaviors being reinforced. This is called **vicarious reinforcement**, or more generally, vicarious learning.

Seligman's Learned Helplessness Theory of Depression

Martin Seligman conducted classic studies of "learned helplessness" in the 1960s. In these studies, he placed dogs in a cell with relatively high walls. He then administered a shock to the floor of the cell. Initially, the dogs would attempt to jump free of the cell and the shock. Over time, the dogs stopped jumping since they were unable to escape the cell. Later, Seligman replaced the high walls with relatively low walls. Nonetheless, when he administered a shock to the floor of the cell, the dogs did not jump, even though they could have easily escaped the cell if they had attempted to do so. Thus, the dogs had learned to be helpless.

Seligman and others extrapolated this to the realm of human depression and locus of control. Individuals who consistently face difficult situations from which they cannot escape learn to feel powerless to overcome their problems. Over time, this kind of environment can result in learned helplessness, an external locus of control (see the work of Julian Rotter later in this chapter), and depression.

Behavior Therapy

Behaviorists view maladjustment and abnormal behavior as learned through interactions between people and the environment. Individuals learn faulty coping patterns that are maintained by some kind of reinforcement. Although psychoanalysts consider the symptoms to be manifestations of some disorder, behaviorists consider the symptoms to *be* the disorder.

Behavior therapy has proven to be quite successful with certain problems, particularly phobias, impulse control problems, and personal care maintenance for people with mental retardation and hospitalized psychotic patients. We cover different types of behavior therapy in depth in the chapter on learning and ethology.

Cognitive-Behavior Therapy

Over the last few decades, cognitive-behavior therapy, blending cognitive and behavioral approaches, has developed. Essentially, cognitive-behavior therapy tries to change and restructure patient's distorted and/or irrational thoughts. **Beck's cognitive therapy for depression** and **Albert Ellis's rational-emotive therapy (RET)** are two examples. In Beck's therapy, the client might be asked to write down negative thoughts about himself or herself, figure out why they are unjustified, and come up with more realistic and less destructive cognitions. The basic assumption of Ellis's RET is that people develop irrational ways of thinking. Therefore, in Ellis's therapy, the therapist might challenge an irrational belief that the client has, helping him or her to recognize these beliefs and change them to more rational ones.

In contrast to behaviorists, psychoanalysts do not believe that symptom relief is adequate therapy. Because the underlying cause is still there, psychoanalysts suggest that new symptoms will develop to replace the old one. This is called **symptom substitution**. Naturally, behaviorists disagree with this viewpoint.

Humanism

Phenomenological theorists emphasize internal processes rather than overt behavior. Phenomenological psychologists are sometimes called humanistic because they focus on that which distinguishes us from animals. The concepts of phenomenology are similar to those of the existential theorists, since existential psychology employs phenomenological analysis. The Gestalt theory of personality, closely linked to both existential and humanistic theories, has a holistic view of the self.

Kurt Lewin

Kurt Lewin's field theory puts very little stock in constraints on personalities such as fixed traits, habits, or structures (e.g., id, ego, and superego). Lewin's theory was heavily influenced by Gestalt psychology. He saw personality as being dynamic and constantly changing. According to Lewin, a personality can be divided up dynamically into ever-changing regions that he called systems. Under optimal conditions, the regions within the personality are well articulated and function in an integrated fashion. When the person is under tension or an anxiety, however, articulation between various regions is generally diffused. Allport and Rogers's theories (to be discussed later) resemble Lewin's ideas of stressing more current behaviors and thought processes, as opposed to focusing on early developmental factors.

Abraham Maslow

Abraham Maslow, a humanistic theorist, is known for his hierarchy of human motives and for his views on self-actualization. Maslow proposed that needs were organized hierarchically ascending from basic needs to complex psychological needs. People strive for the higher-level needs only when their lower-level needs are met. Maslow's lowest levels of needs are the physiological and safety needs (food, shelter and so on). Next are belongingness and love needs, then esteem, cognitive, and aesthetic needs, and finally, the highest order of need: **self-actualization**, referring to the need to realize one's fullest potential. According to Maslow, most people don't reach self-actualization.

Maslow studied the lives of individuals whom he felt were self-actualizers (e.g., Beethoven, Einstein, George Washington Carver, and Eleanor Roosevelt). He identified several characteristics that these people had in common. These characteristics included a nonhostile sense of humor, originality, creativity, spontaneity, and a need for some privacy. According to Maslow, self-actualized people are more likely than non–self-actualized people to have what he called **peak experiences**: profound and deeply moving experiences in a person's life that have important and lasting effects on the individual.

George Kelly

George Kelly used himself as a model to theorize about human nature, and set aside the traditional concepts of motivation, drive, unconscious emotion, and reinforcement. Kelly hypothesized the notion of the individual as scientist, a person who devises and tests predictions about the behavior of significant people in his or her life. The individual constructs a scheme of anticipation of what others will do, based on his knowledge, perception, and relationships with these other people. The anxious person, rather than being the victim of inner conflicts and dammed-up energy (as in psychodynamic theory), is one who is having difficulty constructing and understanding the variables in his or her environment.

According to Kelly, psychotherapy is a process of insight whereby the individual acquires new constructs that will allow him or her to successfully predict troublesome events. Then, the individual will be able to direct these new constructs into already existing contructs.

Humanist-Existential Therapies

In general, humanist-existential therapies tend to emphasize the process of finding meaning in one's life by making one's own choices. Mental disorders tend to be viewed as stemming from problems of alienation, depersonalization, loneliness, and a lack of a meaningful existence. Humanistic therapy facilitates exploration into a client's thoughts and feelings. Existential approaches to therapy include empathy toward the client, as well as understanding, affirmation, and positive regard.

Carl Rogers

Carl Rogers identified himself with humanistic psychology, although his personality theory is basically phenomenological. He is most known for his psychotherapy technique known as **client-centered therapy**, **person-centered therapy**, or **nondirective therapy**. Rogers believed that people have the freedom to control their own behavior, and are neither slaves to the unconscious (as the psychoanalysts would suggest), nor subjects of faulty learning (as the behaviorists would suggest). The client is seen as being able to reflect upon his or her problems, make choices, take positive action, and help determine his or her own destiny.

One objective of Rogers's therapy is to help the client become willing and able to be himself or herself and to increase the congruence between what the person thinks he or she should be (the ideal self) and what he or she actually is. A climate of **unconditional positive regard** and understanding is provided to enhance this desired situation.

Victor Frankl

Victor Frankl, a survivor of Nazi concentration camps, is closely identified with the human search for meaning to existence. Mental illness and maladjustment, in Frankl's view, stems from a life of meaninglessness.

Trait/Type Theorists

Type theorists attempt to characterize people according to specific types of personality. **Trait theorists** attempt to ascertain the fundamental dimensions of personality. For our purposes, we will consider them together.

Type A/Type B

One well-known type theory divides personalities into two types: **Type A** and **Type B** personalities. Type A personality is characterized by behavior that tends to be competitive and compulsive. The Type B personality is generally laid-back and relaxed. Not surprisingly, type A personalities are more prone to heart disease than Type B personalities, and are most prevalent among middle- and upper-class men.

Raymond Cattell

Raymond Cattell, a trait theorist, used factor analysis (covered in the chapter on statistics, research methods, and testing) to measure personality in a more comprehensive way, attempting to account for the underlying factors that determine personality. Cattell identified sixteen basic traits, or relatively permanent reaction tendencies in individuals, that constitute the building blocks of personality.

Hans Eysenck

Hans J. Eysenck also used factor analysis to develop a theory of personality. He determined that the broad dimensions of personality were types, which were followed by more specific traits. Hans Eysenck's goal was to use scientific methodology to test Jung's division of **extroversion** and **introversion**. After extensive research, Eysenck distinguished two dimensions in which human personalities differed. One dimension was introversion-extroversion, and the second dimension was emotional stability–neuroticism. Still later, Eyseneck added another dimension that indicated **psychoticism**.

Gordon Allport

Gordon Allport, primarily a trait theorist, listed three basic types of traits or dispositions: **cardinal, central,** and **secondary**. Cardinal traits are traits around which a person organizes his or her life. For instance, Mother Teresa's cardinal trait may be self-sacrifice. Not everyone develops cardinal traits. Everyone though, has central and secondary traits. Central traits represent major characteristics of the personality that are easy to infer, such as honesty or fatalism. Secondary traits are more personal characteristics that are more limited in occurrence.

A major part of Allport's theory is the concept of **functional autonomy**. Functional autonomy means that a given activity or form of behavior may become an end or goal in itself, regardless of its original reason for existence. A hunter, for example, may have originally hunted in order to obtain food to eat. However, the hunter may continue to hunt even after there is enough food. Allport's theory suggests that the hunter may continue to hunt simply because of the enjoyment: that which began simply as a means to obtain a goal became the goal itself. The theory allows for many types of motives, as well as the uniqueness of motives in any individual.

Allport distinguished between an **idiographic** approach to personality and a **nomothetic** approach to personality (Allport borrowed these terms from the German philosopher Windelband). The idiographic approach to studying personality focuses on individual case studies, while the nomothetic approach focuses on groups of individuals and tries to find the commonalities between individuals. Allport insisted that personality theorists should use the idiographic approach and avoid the nomothetic approach. Allport later substituted the term *morphogenic* for idiographic and the term *dimensional* for nomothetic.

David McClelland

David McClelland identified a personality trait that is referred to as **the need for achievement** (nAch). People who are rated high in nAch tend to be concerned with achievement and have pride in their accomplishments. These individuals avoid high risks (to avoid risk of failing) and low risks (because easy tasks won't generate a sense of achievement). Additionally, they set realistic goals, and do not continue striving towards a goal if success is unlikely.

Herman Witkin

Herman Witkin endeavored to draw a relationship between an individual's personality and his or her perception of the world. Witkin classified people according to their degree of **field-dependence**. At one pole is the capacity to make specific responses to perceived specific stimuli (field-independence). At the other pole is a more diffuse response to a perceived mass of somewhat undifferentiated stimuli (field dependence). For example, people who are highly field-dependent will be more influenced by the opinions of others because they respond in a diffuse manner, not distinguishing separate ideas or even distinguishing their own ideas from those of others.

Julian Rotter

Another important area of personality research is **Julian Rotter's** work on **internal and external locus of control.** People with an internal locus of control tend to believe that they can control their own destiny. Those with an external locus of control tend to believe that outside events and chance control their destiny. Locus of control and self-esteem are related. People who attribute their success to ability (internal locus of control) tend to have higher self-esteem than people who attribute their success to luck or task ease (external locus of control). There is also a relationship between people's attributions of failure and self-esteem. People with high self-esteem tend to attribute their failures to bad luck or task difficulty (external locus of control) while people with low self-esteem tend to attribute their failures to lack of ability (internal locus of control).

Machiavellianism

"**Machiavellian**" is a personality trait that refers to someone who is manipulative and deceitful (from Niccolo Machiavelli's book, *The Prince*). People who score high on Machiavellianism tend to agree with statements such as "most people don't really know what's best for them," "the best way to handle people is to tell them what they want to hear," and "anyone who completely trusts anyone else is asking for trouble." Experiments have shown that people high in Machiavellianism are much more successful manipulators than those low in Machiavellianism.

Androgyny

Sandra Bem's theory on gender identity is related to personality theory. Sandra Bem's theory holds that because people can achieve high scores on measures of both masculinity and femininity on personality inventories, then masculinity and femininity must be two separate dimensions. **Androgyny** is defined as the state of being simultaneously very masculine and very feminine.

Mischel's Criticism

The notion of explaining behavior on the basis of personality types or traits has not gone unchallenged. Indeed, the concept of stable personality traits has been seriously challenged by **Walter Mischel**. Mischel believes that human behavior is largely determined by the characteristics of the situation rather than by those of the person.

UNDERSTANDING MENTAL DISORDERS

DSM-IV

Because there are so many ways in which psychopathology can manifest itself, it is useful to have a classification system for mental disorders. We will be using the system presented in the Fourth Edition of the *Diagnostic and Statistical Manual of Mental Disorders*, known as the **DSM-IV**, published by the American Psychiatric Association in 1994. The DSM-IV is the most widely accepted scheme (in the United States) for the classification of mental disorders. DSM-IV's classification scheme is not based on theories of etiology or treatments of different disorders. Rather, it is based on atheoretical descriptions of symptoms of the various disorders. For example, the DSM-IV doesn't list "neurosis" as a category of mental disorders, since neurosis is a theoretical term that is derived from psychoanalytic theory. (Questions about neurosis and the DSM have appeared on recent GRE Psychology tests.)

The DMS-IV has sixteen major diagnostic classes, some of which will be discussed. A hallmark of the DSM is its system of **multiaxial assessment**. In this system, clients are assessed on several different domains of information, all of which may help the clinician plan treatment. Five axes are included in the DSM-IV system. On **Axis I**, the clinician is to list the client's clinical disorders with exception of personality disorders and mental retardation. **Axis II** is for personality disorders and mental retardation. **Axis III** is used for recording any medical conditions that are potentially relevant to understanding or treating the client's mental disorder. **Axis IV** is used to indicate any psychosocial or environmental stresses that may influence progression, treatment, or outcome of the disorders from Axis I or Axis II. **Axis V** indicates the clinician's judgment of the client's overall functioning level. This judgment is assessed by using a **Global Assessment of Functioning (GAF)** scale that ranges from 0 to 100.

Disorders First Diagnosed in Infancy, Childhood, or Adolescence

Attention-deficit/hyperactivity disorder (ADD/HD) is characterized by developmentally atypical inattention and/or impulsivity-hyperactivity. Children with this disorder may have very short attention spans and have difficulty staying on task or with organizing tasks. These children are frequently unable to follow instructions or requests and are often unable to stick to activities for extended periods of time. Group situations are particularly difficult for these children. Hyperactivity manifests itself in motor activity such as excessive running or climbing, fidgeting, and restlessness. Impulsivity is manifested by an inability to delay gratification, impatience, and frequently interrupting others. Although the disorder typically occurs by age three, it is frequently not diagnosed until the child begins school. As many as three to five percent of school children may experience the symptoms of this disorder. The disorder is more prevalent in males than in females. Symptoms usually attenuate during adolescence.

The essential features of **autistic disorder** are lack of responsiveness to others (impairment in social skills), gross impairment in communication skills, and repetitive behaviors. Individuals with the disorder are often inflexibly routined and stereotyped. Children with autism may not cuddle or make eye contact, and may display little or no facial expression. Impairment in language skills, both receptive and expressive, is often present. Children with this disorder tend to be oversensitive to sensory stimuli such as sound, lights, color, odor, and/or touch. The disorder occurs in about two to five out of 10,000 individuals, and can be chronic. Only a small percentage of these individuals will be able to achieve an autonomous life with adequate social adjustments in adulthood.

Tourette's disorder, a tic disorder, is characterized by multiple motor tics (e.g., eye-blinking, skipping, deep knee bends) and one or more vocal tics (e.g., grunts, barks, sniffs, snorts, coughs, utterance of obscenities). Tics are sudden, recurrent, and stereotyped. The duration of the disorder is lifelong, but periods of remission may occur. Tourette's disorder occurs in approximately four to five individuals out of 10,000.

Schizophrenia and Other Psychotic Disorders

The term **schizophrenia** is a relatively recent term, coined in 1911 by Eugen Bleuler. Before Bleuler, schizophrenia was called *Dementia Praecox*, a term that has appeared on the GRE Psychology test. Schizophrenia literally means "split mind," since the disorder is characterized by gross distortions of reality and disturbances in the content and form of thought, perception, and affect. Unfortunately, this has led many lay people to confuse schizophrenia with multiple personality disorder (currently known as dissociative identity disorder). By "split mind," Bleuler did not mean that the mind is split into different personalities, but that the mind is split off from reality. Although no single feature need be present to diagnose schizophrenia, a person with schizophrenia may have any or all of the following symptoms: delusions, hallucinations, disorganized thought, inappropriate affect, and catatonic behavior.

Symptoms of schizophrenia are divided into positive and negative types. **Positive symptoms** *not good behaviors* are behaviors, thoughts, or affects added to normal behavior. Examples include delusions and hallucinations, disorganized speech, and disorganized or catatonic behavior. Positive symptoms are considered by some to be two distinct dimensions, the psychotic dimension (delusions and hallucinations) and the disorganized dimension (disorganized speech and behavior), perhaps with different underlying causes. **Negative symptoms** are those symptoms that involve the absence of normal or desired behavior. An example is flat affect, where the individual's emotional expression is blunted.

Delusions are false beliefs, discordant with reality, that are maintained in spite of strong evidence to the contrary. Common delusions include **delusions of reference, persecution,** and **grandeur**. Delusions of reference may involve the belief of an individual that others are talking about him or her. This individual may believe that common elements in the environment are directed at him or her. Delusions of persecution involve the belief that the person is being deliberately interfered with, discriminated against, plotted against, or threatened. Delusions of grandeur involve the belief by the patient that he or she is a remarkable person, such as an inventor, historical figure, or even the Queen of England. Other delusions involve the concept of thought broadcasting, which is the belief that one's thoughts are broadcast directly from one's head to the external world, and thought insertion, the belief that thoughts are inserted in one's head.

Hallucinations are perceptions that are not due to external stimuli but have a compelling sense of reality. Hallucinations can occur in all sensory modalities. The most common form of hallucination is auditory, involving voices that the individual perceives as coming from outside his or her head.

Disorganized thought is characterized by the loosening of associations. This may be exhibited as speech in which ideas shift from one subject to another on unrelated subjects in such a way that a listener would be unable to follow the train of thought. A patient's speech may be so disorganized that it will seem to have no structure—as though it were just words thrown together, incomprehensibly. This is sometimes called *word salad*. In fact, a person with schizophrenia may even invent new words. These new words are called *neologisms*.

A commom characteristic of schizophrenia is disturbance of affect, or the expression of emotion. Problems with affect may include **blunting**, in which there is a severe reduction in the intensity of affect expression; **flat affect**, in which there are virtually no signs of affective expression; or **inappropriate affect**, in which the affect is clearly discordant with the content of the individual's speech or ideation. For example, a patient with inappropriate affect may begin to laugh hysterically while describing a parent's death. Interestingly, it has become more difficult to assess the affective aspects of schizophrenia because the antipsychotic medications used in treatment frequently blunt and flatten affect as well.

Catatonic motor behavior refers to various extreme behaviors characteristic of some people with schizophrenia. The patient's spontaneous movement and activity may be greatly reduced or the patient may maintain a rigid posture, refusing to be moved. At the other extreme, catatonic behavior may include useless and bizarre movements not caused by any external stimuli.

Before schizophrenia is diagnosed, a patient often goes through a phase characterized by poor adjustment. This phase is called the **prodromal phase**. The prodromal phase is exemplified by clear evidence of deterioration, social withdrawal, role functioning impairment, peculiar behavior, inappropriate affect, and unusual experiences. This phase is followed by the **active phase** of symtomatic behavior.

If schizophrenia development is slow and insidious it is referred to as **process schizophrenia**, and prognosis for recovery is especially poor. If the onset of symptoms is intense and sudden, it is referred to as **reactive schizophrenia**, and the prognosis for recovery is better.

The DSM-IV divides schizophrenia into five subtypes: **catatonic, paranoid, disorganized, undifferentiated**, and **residual**. Since these are all subtypes of schizophrenia, people with these disorders tend to share the core symptoms; the patient's primary symptom(s) differentiate among the subtypes.

The primary symptom of the **catatonic** type of schizophrenia is a disturbance in motor behavior. Most notably, there is an alternation between extreme withdrawal of behavior (no movement, maintenance of a peculiar position for hours or days) and excitement or excessive movement. The **paranoid** type of schizophrenia is characterized by a preoccupation with one or more delusions or frequent auditory hallucinations. In this subtype there is a relative preservation of cognitive and affective functioning. The **disorganized** type of schizophrenia (formerly called *hebephrenic schizophrenia*) is characterized by flat or inappropriate affect and disorganized speech and behavior. The **undifferentiated** type of schizophrenia is diagnosed when the general criteria for the other categories are not met. The diagnosis of **residual** schizophrenia is used when there has been a previous schizophrenic episode, but positive psychotic symptoms are not currently displayed, although patients may still show disturbances and often negative symptoms.

Despite extensive research, the etiology of schizophrenia remains unclear. The leading biochemical explanation for schizophrenia is the **dopamine hypothesis**. Dopamine, a neurotransmitter, plays an important role in movement and posture in certain brain pathways. (A neurotransmitter is simply a chemical that helps individual neurons communicate with each other; see the chapter on physiological psychology.) The dopamine hypothesis suggests that the delusions, hallucinations and agitation associated with schizophrenia arise from an excess of dopamine activity at certain sites in the brain. A variant of this hypothesis is that the amount of dopamine is normal but that there is an oversensitivity to dopamine in the brain or that there are too many receptors that receive the dopamine. Evidence supporting the dopamine hypothesis comes from the effectiveness of antipsychotic drugs in treating schizophrenia.

The **double-bind hypothesis** of schizophrenia holds that as a child, the person with schizophrenia received contradictory and mutually incompatible messages from his or her primary caregiver (usually the mother). For instance, a mother may tell her child to be more affectionate, yet yell at or punish the child whenever the child approaches her. Torn between these contradictory messages, the child may begin to feel anxious, and these disorganized messages become internalized. From this point, the child begins to see his or her perceptions of reality as unreliable. Although this hypothesis is not widely supported, research has suggested that faulty family communication may play some role in explaining the origins of some forms of schizophrenia.

Mood Disorders

We all have times when we feel sad. Sometimes, we feel very sad, such as when we are grieving. During these periods, we might even say that we are "depressed." However, this is just part of normal human experience and not a mental disorder. In contrast, mood disorders are severe and persistent.

Major depressive disorder is characterized by at least one major depressive episode. In major depressive disorder, the essential feature is at least a two-week period during which there is a prominent and relatively persistent depressed mood, or loss of interest in all or almost all activities. Other symptoms include appetite disturbances, substantial weight changes, sleep disturbances, decreased energy, feelings of worthlessness or excessive guilt (sometimes delusional), difficulty concentrating or thinking, and thoughts of death or attempts at suicide. In order for major depressive disorder to be diagnosed, these symptoms must cause significant distress and/or impairment in functioning. As many as 15 percent of individuals with this disorder die by suicide.

The **bipolar disorders** (formerly known as manic-depression) are a major type of mood disorder characterized by both depression and mania. Manic episodes are often characterized by an abnormal and persistant elevated mood, accompanied by a decreased need for sleep. There is also flight of ideas and increased self-esteem. Judgment is usually impaired, sexual and other behavioral restraints are lowered, and the individual tends to be impatient with any attempts to restrain his or her behaviors. Manic episodes generally have a rapid onset and a briefer duration than depressive episodes. Bipolar I disorder has these manic episodes, whereas bipolar II disorder has **hypomania**. In contrast to mania, hypomania typically does not significantly impair functioning, nor are there psychotic features, although the individual may be more energetic and optimistic.

Dysthymic and **cyclothymic disorders** don't quite meet the criteria for major depressive and bipolar disorders, respectively, but essentially are characterized by similar, less severe symptoms.

Many etiologies have been proposed for mood disorders, ranging from genetics to sociocultural factors. The first explanation we will cover revolves around neurotransmitters. Recall from earlier in this chapter that neurotransmitters are chemicals that help individual neurons communicate with each other. Neurotransmitters that have been implicated in mood disorders include **norepinephrine** and **serotonin**. These two are often linked together into what is called the monoamine theory of depression, or sometimes the **catecholamine theory of depression**. These theories hold that too much norepinephrine and serotonin leads to mania, while too little leads to depression. Although more recent research has shown that it is not necessarily that simple, you should be aware of this theory for the GRE Psychology test.

Anxiety Disorders

There are more than ten disorders listed in the *anxiety disorders* portion of the DSM-IV. One type of anxiety disorder is a **phobia**. A phobia is simply an irrational fear of something that results in a compelling desire to avoid it. Most of the phobias that you are probably familiar with are what DSM-IV calls **specific phobias**. A specific phobia is one in which anxiety is produced by a specific object or situation. Claustrophobia is an irrational fear of closed places; acrophobia is an irrational fear of heights; cynophobia is an irrational fear of dogs; and so on. A more complicated kind of phobia is **agoraphobia,** or a fear of being in open places or in situations where escape might be difficult. Agoraphobics tend to be uncomfortable going outside their homes alone. **Social phobia** is characterized by anxiety that is due to social situations. These individuals have persistent fear when exposed to social/performance situations that may result in embarrassment.

Another type of anxiety disorder is **obsessive compulsive disorder (OCD)**. The disorder is characterized by repeated obsessions (persistent irrational thoughts) that produce tension and/or compulsions (irrational and repetitive impulses to perform certain acts) that cause significant impairment in a person's life. Loosely speaking, obsessions are thoughts and compulsions are behaviors. For instance, a person might obsess about dirt and compulsively wash his or her hands (to neutralize the anxiety produced by the obsession).

Somatoform Disorders

In general, **somatoform disorders** involve the presence of physical symptoms that suggest a medical condition but which are not fully explained by a medical condition. The afflicted person with somatoform disorder is not faking, but really believes that he or she has a medical condition. Examples include **conversion disorders** and **hypochondriasis**. A **conversion disorder** is characterized by unexplained symptoms affecting voluntary motor or sensory functions. Examples include paralysis when there is no neurological damage or even blindness when there is no evidence of damage to the visual system or brain. Incidentally, conversion disorder used to be referred to as *hysteria*. In **hypochondriasis**, the person is preoccupied with fears that he or she has a serious disease. These fears are based on a misinterpretation of one or more bodily signs or symptoms. These fears continue even after compete medical exams have proven that the person doesn't have the disease he or she claims to have.

Dissociative Disorders

In dissociative disorders, the person avoids stress by dissociating, or escaping from his or her identity. The person otherwise still has an intact sense of reality. Examples of dissociative disorders include **dissociative amnesia, dissociative fugue, dissociative identity disorder** (formerly multiple personality disorder), and **depersonalization disorder.**

Dissociative amnesia is characterized by an inability to recall past experience. The qualifier "dissociative" simply means that the amnesia is not due to a neurological disorder.

Dissociative fugue involves amnesia that accompanies a sudden, unexpected move away from one's home or location of usual daily activities. A person in a fugue state is confused about his or her identity and may even assume a new identity.

In **dissociative identity disorder** (formerly multiple personality disorder) there are two or more personalities that recurrently take control of a person's behavior. This disorder results when the components of identity fail to integrate. Two of the most famous cases that appear in the media are Sybil, who had 15 separate personalities, and Truddi Chase, who had 92 separate personalities. In most cases, the patients have suffered severe physical and/or sexual abuse as young children. After much therapy, the personalities can usually be integrated into one.

In **depersonalization disorder**, the person feels detached, like an outside observer of his or her mental processes and/or behavior. However, even during these times, the person still has an intact sense of reality.

Eating Disorders

Anorexia nervosa is characterized by a refusal to maintain a minimal normal body weight. The person with anorexia nervosa also has a distorted body image, and believes that he or she is overweight even when emaciated. In females, amenorrhea (the cessation of menstruation) is usually present. More than 90 percent of cases are female and 10 percent of hospitalized cases result in death due to starvation, suicide, or electrolyte imbalance.

Bulimia nervosa involves binge-eating accompanied by excessive attempts to compensate for it by purging, fasting, or excessive exercising. In bulimia nervosa, unlike anorexia nervosa, the individual tends to maintain a minimally normal body weight. At least 90 percent of the cases are female.

Personality Disorders

A personality disorder is a pattern of behavior that is inflexible and maladaptive, causing distress and/or impaired functioning in at least two of the following: cognition, emotions, interpersonal functioning, or impulse control. The DSM-IV lists ten personality disorders; we will cover four of the most common: **schizoid**, **narcissistic**, **borderline**, and **antisocial**. Passive-aggressive personality disorder has been deleted from the DSM-IV Classification of Personality Disorders. However, it is listed in the "Other Conditions That May Be a Focus of Clinical Attention" section of the DSM-IV.

Schizoid personality disorder is a pervasive pattern of detachment from social relationships and a restricted range of emotional expression. People with this disorder show little desire for social interactions; have few, if any, close friends; and have poor social skills. It should be noted that schizoid personality disorder is *not* the same as schizophrenia.

In **narcissistic personality disorder** there is a grandiose sense of self-importance or uniqueness, preoccupation with fantasies of success, an exhibitionistic need for constant admiration and attention, and characteristic disturbances in interpersonal relationships such as feelings of entitlement. As used in everyday language, narcissism refers to those who like themselves too much. However, people with narcissistic personality disorder have very fragile self-esteem and are constantly concerned with how others are viewing them. There may be marked feelings of rage, inferiority, shame, humiliation, or emptiness when these individuals are not viewed favorably by others.

People with **borderline personality disorder** show behavior that has features of both personality disorders and some of the more severe psychological disorders. In borderline personality disorder, there is pervasive instability in interpersonal behavior, mood, and self-image. Interpersonal relationships are often intense and unstable. There may be a profound identity disturbance manifested by uncertainty about self-image, sexual identity, long-term goals, or values. There is often intense fear of abandonment. Suicide attempts and self-mutilation (cutting or burning) are common.

Antisocial personality disorder has previously been referred to as psychopathic disorder and sociopathic disorder. The essential feature of the disorder is a pattern of disregard for, and violation of, the rights of others. This is evidenced by repeated illegal acts, deceitfulness, aggressiveness, and/or a lack of remorse for said actions. Serial killers who show no guilt for their actions, imposters, and many career criminals have this disorder.

DIATHESIS-STRESS MODEL

Psychologists are not interested in just describing the various types of mental disorders: they're also interested in why these disorders occur. The **diathesis-stress** model is a framework that can be used to examine the causes of mental disorders. A *diathesis* is a predisposition toward developing a specific mental disorder. It could be a genetic or anatomic abnormality, or a biochemical disorder that predisposes an individual to mental illness. Excessive stress operating on a person with a predisposition (diathesis) may lead to the development of the specific mental disorder. According to this model, an individual whose brain is oversensitive to dopamine and who also experiences excessive stress may be likely to develop schizophrenia. The diathesis-stress model reminds us that causal factors at the biological and psychological levels interact with each other.

PRIMARY PREVENTION

Efforts to seek out and eradicate conditions that foster mental illness and to establish the conditions that foster mental health are called **primary prevention**. Examples include increasing access to good prenatal and postnatal care, providing training in psychosocial skills to those who need it, promoting opportunities for education, and training parents in child-raising skills. Primary prevention is proactive, not reactive. It seeks to stop mental illness before it occurs rather than treating the illness after it occurs.

BEING LABELED "MENTALLY ILL"

David Rosenhan (1973) studied whether or not it was possible to be judged sane if you are in an "insane place" (a psychiatric hospital). Rosenhan and seven other "sane" people were admitted into different psychiatric hospitals by reporting auditory hallucinations. Each of these pseudopatients was diagnosed to have either paranoid schizophrenia or bipolar disorder and each was admitted. Once admitted, they acted normally in every way. Yet, because they had already been labeled as mentally ill, even normal activities were interpreted by the staff as evidence of mental illness. For instance, when they discussed their situation in a rational way with members of the staff, they were reported to be using the defense mechanism of intellectualization.

The pseudopatients remained in the hospitals an average of three weeks. Not one was identified as sane. In fact, when they were finally released (and they were only able to be released with the help of spouses and friends), the discharge diagnoses were either paranoid schizophrenia or bipolar disorder in remission. Rosenhan concluded that clinicians need to exercise greater care when judging normality and abnormality. Once someone is labeled mentally ill, the label never really goes away. Additionally, this study demonstrated that mental illness could be feigned, as well as misdiagnosed.

Thomas Szasz, an outspoken critic of labeling people mentally ill, argues that most of the disorders treated by clinicians are not really illnesses. Rather, they are traits or behaviors that differ from the cultural norm. Szasz argues that labeling people as mentally ill is a way to force them to change and conform to societal norms rather than allowing them to attack the societal causes of their problems. The phrase to associate with Szasz is the name of his most famous book, *The Myth of Mental Illness*.

SYSTEMS OF PSYCHOLOGY: A BRIEF OVERVIEW

System	Key People	Important Concepts/Goals/Methods
Structuralism	Titchener	Breaks consciousness into elements by using introspection
Functionalism	James, Dewey	Stream of consciousness; studies how mind functions to help people adapt to environment; attacked structuralism
Behaviorism	Watson, Skinner	Psychology as objective study of behavior; attacked mentalism and the use of introspection; attacked structuralism and functionalism
Gestalt	Wertheimer, Köhler, Koffka	Whole is something other than the sum of its parts; attacked structuralism and behaviorism
Cognitive	Chomsky	Behaviorism is not an adequate explanation for human behavior; humans think, believe, are creative
Psychoanalysis	Freud, Jung, Adler	Behavior is a result of unconscious conflicts, repression, defense mechanisms
Humanism	Maslow, Rogers	Looks at people as wholes; humans have free will; psychologists should study mentally healthy people, not just mentally ill/maladjusted ones

IMPORTANT NAMES IN PERSONALITY

Adler, A.	**Psychodynamic theorist** best known for the concept of **inferiority complex**
Allport, G.	**Trait theorist** known for the concept of **functional autonomy**; also distinguished between **idiographic** and **nomothetic** approaches to personality
Bandura, A.	**Behaviorist theorist** known for his **social learning theory**; did modeling experiment using punching bag ("Bobo" doll)
Bem, S.	Suggested that masculinity and femininity were two separate dimensions; also linked with concept of **androgyny**
Cattell, R.	**Trait theorist** who used **factor analysis** to study personality
Dollard, J. and Miller, N.	Behaviorist theorists who attempted to study **psychoanalytic concepts within a behaviorist framework**; also known for their work on **approach-avoidance conflicts**
Erikson, E.	**Ego psychologist** whose **psychosocial stages of development** encompass entire lifespan
Eysenck, H.	**Trait theorist** who proposed two main dimensions on which human personalities differ: **introversion-extroversion** and **emotional stability-neuroticism**
Freud, A.	Founder of **ego psychology**
Freud, S.	Originator of the **psychodynamic** approach to **personality**
Horney, K.	**Psychodynamic theorist** who suggested there were three ways to relate to others: **moving toward, moving against,** and **moving away from**
Jung, C.	**Psychodynamic theorist** who broke with Freud over the concept of libido; suggested that the unconscious could be divided into the **personal unconscious** and the **collective unconscious**, with archetypes being in the collective unconscious
Kelly, G.	Based personality theory on the notion of "**individual as scientist**"
Kernberg, O.	**Object-relations theorist**
Klein, M.	**Object-relations theorist**
Lewin, K.	**Phenomenological personality theorist** who developed **field theory**

Mahler, M.	**Object-relations theorist**
Maslow, A.	**Phenomenological personality theorist** known for developing a **hierarchy of needs** and for the concept of **self-actualization**
McClelland, D.	Studied **need for achievement** (**nAch**)
Mischel, W.	**Critic of trait theories** of personality
Rogers, C.	**Phenomenological personality theorist**
Rotter, J.	Studied **locus of control**
Sheldon, W.	Attempted to relate **somatotype** (body type) to personality type
Skinner, B. F.	**Behaviorist**
Winnicott, D. W.	**Object-relations theorist**
Witkin, H.	Studied **field-dependence** and **field-independence** using the rod and frame test

PERSONALITY PRACTICE SET

Time: 8 minutes

Directions: Each of the questions or incomplete statements below is followed by five suggested answers or completions. In each case, select the one that best answers the question or completes the statement.

1. A person gets a good grade on a midterm exam and believes that the good grade was due to an easy test. This statement is most relevant to which of the following theorists?
   (A) Abraham Maslow
   (B) Julian Rotter
   (C) Sandra Bem
   (D) Gordon Allport
   (E) Raymond Cattell

2. The sociological school of psychoanalysis, as represented by such theorists as Adler and Horney, is different from Freud in its
   (A) increased emphasis on environmental influences on personality
   (B) designation of the unconscious as a secondary force in personality development
   (C) emphasis on cognitive/rational elements of personality
   (D) decreased emphasis on the individuality of behavior
   (E) institution of the ego with the same instinctual origin as the id

3. Horney originally put forward a list of ten needs which are acquired as a consequence of trying to find solutions for the problem of disturbed relationships. Later, she classified these "neurotic" needs under
   (A) two headings: for and against
   (B) three headings: toward, against, and away
   (C) four headings: toward, against, away, and ambivalent
   (D) three headings: for, against, and ambivalent.
   (E) four headings: for, against, withdrawn, and disturbed

4. Which of the following statements is NOT characteristic of the ego, according to Freud?
   (A) The ego acts as a bridge between libidinal forces and realistic demands.
   (B) The ego mediates between the id and the superego.
   (C) The ego is governed by the reality principle.
   (D) The ego aims to discharge energy.
   (E) The ego is in the service of the id.

5. Jung's chief criticism of Freudian theory was mostly directed against Freud's
   (A) overemphasis on the defense mechanisms
   (B) determinism
   (C) teleological tendencies
   (D) strong emphasis on ego functioning
   (E) insistence that sexual motives were the basis of neurosis

6. Adler's individual psychology is associated with all of the following concepts EXCEPT
   (A) superiority strivings
   (B) inferiority
   (C) introversion/extroversion
   (D) fictional finalism
   (E) uniqueness of the individual

7. We know of people in German concentration camps during World War II who continued to help others even though their own survival was in doubt. This causes the most problems for which of the following theorists?

(A) Jung
(B) Skinner
(C) Adler
(D) Witkin
(E) Maslow

8. Which of the following behavioral theorists is (are) most closely associated with psychoanalytic theory?

(A) Albert Bandura
(B) Raymond Cattell
(C) Gordon Allport
(D) John Dollard and Neal Miller
(E) Carl Jung

9. The description "He's tall and muscular" would be most relevant to which of the following theorists?

(A) Gordon Allport
(B) Alfred Adler
(C) Julian Rotter
(D) Albert Bandura
(E) William Sheldon

10. An investigator used a test to measure masculinity and femininity in a large sample of college students, consisting of equal numbers of males and females. The test showed that 30 percent of the sample was androgynous. This finding is most relevant to which of the following propositions?

(A) Genotypic sex exerts the greatest influence on gender identity.
(B) Gender roles become less differentiated after puberty, as hormone levels reach equilibrium.
(C) Adults who model both "masculine instrumentality" and "feminine expressiveness" are the ones most likely to raise androgynous offspring.
(D) Rather than being at two ends of a spectrum, masculinity and femininity are two separate traits that can coexist within an individual.
(E) Men are not more likely than women to be androgynous.

EXPLANATIONS FOR THE PERSONALITY PRACTICE SET

1. B

The statement in the question stem is most relevant to the theory of Julian Rotter. Recall that Rotter's contribution was the distinction between internal and external locus of control. A person with an internal locus of control would believe that she controls her own destiny whereas a person with an external locus of control would be very fatalistic about his destiny. In the question stem, the student is providing evidence that he has an external locus of control—by stating that the test was easy, rather than attributing her good grade to intelligence or studying (internal locus of control). Answer choice (A), Abraham Maslow, was the personality theorist you should associate with the terms hierarchy of needs and self-actualization. Answer choice (C), Sandra Bem, is the theorist associated with the concept of androgyny. Answer choice (D), Gordon Allport, was a trait theorist who talked about three kinds of traits: cardinal, central, and secondary. Finally, answer choice (E), Raymond Cattell, was another trait theorist, and he is most noted for using factor analysis in his personality theorizing.

2. A

This is correct because environmental refers not only to the physical environment, but also to the social environment. By definition, environmental refers to all those stimuli that impinge on the individual that are outside the individual. Answer choice (B) is incorrect because the unconscious remains a primary force in personality development for these theorists as it was for Freud. Looking at (C), although the sociological school did talk about cognitive, rational elements of personality, this area was not particularly emphasized. Choice (D) is incorrect because these theorists did continue to focus on individuality. Finally, choice (E) is incorrect because the designation of the ego as instinctual with the id did not arise with Adler or Horney but with the later ego psychologists.

3. B

Toward, against and away. Moving toward people is exemplified by the need for love. Moving away from people is exemplified by the need for independence. Finally, moving against is exemplified by the need for power. Each of these headings represents a basic orientation towards others and oneself. Horney finds in these different orientations the basis for inner conflict. Note that these three attitudes are not in themselves indicative of disturbance. It's only when one of these is strictly and irrationally adhered to that we see disturbance.

4. D

It is NOT true that the ego aims to discharge energy. Answer choice (D) is true of the id, not the ego. The ego aims to postpone discharge of energy until reality conditions are suitable for gratification. Let's look at the other answer choices. Answer choice (A) gives a general description of the ego's mediating role. Answer choice (B) refers to another role of the ego. Since both the id and the superego are oblivious to reality conditions, they sometimes make demands that are conflicting. It is the ego's role to mediate these conflicts. Choice (C) is also true of the ego. While the id works under the pleasure principle, the ego works under the reality principle. The ego is ultimately in the service of the id. Thus (E) a true statement.

5. E

Jung's criticism was directed against Freud's insistence that sexual motives were the basis of neurosis. Jung took a much broader view than Freud of the motivating forces behind behavior. For Jung, behavior was motivated by a continuous life urge which had for its aim wholeness and the completion of creative development. This is a broader concept than Freud's libido. Therefore, the correct answer is choice (E). Choices (A) and (D) are incorrect. These were not points of concern for Jung regarding Freudian theory. Choice (B) is incorrect because both Freud and Jung shared the concept of determinism, the belief that behavior could be traced back to specific motives, even if they disagreed as to what these motives were. Finally, choice (C) is incorrect because it was Jung, not Freud, who insisted on the importance of teleology; that is, Jung believed that there was a definite purpose to man's development and to his behavior.

6. C

The classifications of introversion and extroversion were originated by Jung. The other four concepts belong to Adler. Superiority strivings, choice (A), are a motivating force for behavior according to Adler.

Choice (B), inferiority, gives rise to either sickness or compensatory behavior. Answer choice (D), fictional finalism, refers to the notion that an individual is motivated more by his or her expectations of the future than by past experiences. Finally, answer choice (E), the uniqueness of the individual, is strongly acknowledged by Adler and it gives rise to his concepts of the creative self and the style of life. Therefore, the correct answer —the answer choice not associated with Adler—is choice (C), introversion/extroversion.

7. E

The information presented in the question stem causes the most problems for Maslow's theory. Recall that Maslow proposed that needs were organized hierarchically. Thus, people would strive for the higher-level needs only when their lower-level needs were met. Maslow's lowest levels of needs are the physiological and safety needs: food, shelter, and so on. Following this are the belongingness and love needs. Esteem needs, are higher on the hierarchy, with the highest order need being self-actualization. Certainly, with imperative concerns for their own safety and well-being, the prisoners at the concentration camps shouldn't have cared at all for their fellow prisoners, because this caring is reflective of a higher level of need; according to Maslow's theory, prisoners shouldn't have helped other prisoners. Yet, help they did. This poses a problem for Maslow's theory, and therefore, the correct answer choice is (E).

8. D

John Dollard and Neal Miller were behavioral theorists who were also associated with psychoanalytic theory. In fact, their theory can be considered an attempt to merge the best features of behavioral theory with the best features of psychoanalytic theory into a unified whole. Therefore, the correct answer is choice (D). Let's look at the other answer choices. Albert Bandura, answer choice (A), is a behavioral theorist who is known for social learning theory. Raymond Cattell, answer choice (B), is a trait theorist who used the statistical technique of factor analysis in his theorizing. Gordon Allport, choice (C), was also a trait theorist. He talked about cardinal, central, and secondary traits. Finally, choice (E), Carl Jung, was a psychoanalytic theorist. You might have been tempted by this answer choice if you didn't read the question carefully. Note the phrase "behavioral theorists" in the question stem! Jung was not a behavioral theorist.

9. E

William Sheldon's system of constitutional psychology would be most concerned with the description given. Recall that Sheldon related body type (what he called *somatotype*) to various personality characteristics. Although largely discredited, Sheldon still occasionally appears on the GRE Psychology test. It should be emphasized that the description in the question stem would not be irrelevant to other theorists. For example, Bandura might conceivably talk of the quality of the interaction between person and social environment as being affected by body shape. But Sheldon remains the best choice, and so the correct answer is choice (E).

10. D

Androgynous people are those people who are both very masculine and very feminine. According to Sandra Bem, the existence of androgyny suggests that masculinity and femininity are not two ends of the same scale (otherwise, being high in one would necessarily lead to being low in the other), but are two separate scales. Therefore, a finding that 30 percent of the investigator's sample was androgynous would indicate that masculinity and femininity are two separate traits. Therefore, the correct answer is choice (D). Let's take a look at the other answer choices. Choice (B) can be eliminated because this study alone cannot answer questions about the development of gender identity. We can also rule out choices (A) and (E). It is possible that the information in the question-stem could be relevant to these issues, if the results were broken down by gender, but we're not given that information. That leaves choices (C) and (D). Choice (C) talks about the effects of parent gender typing on androgyny. This was not a dimension that was measured in the study.

IMPORTANT NAMES IN ABNORMAL PSYCHOLOGY

Beck, A.	Cognitive behavior therapist known for his therapy for **depression**
Bleuler, E.	Coined the term *schizophrenia*
Dix, D.	19th century American advocate of **asylum reform**
Ellis, A.	Cognitive behavior therapist known for his **rational-emotive therapy (RET)**
Freud, S.	Developed **psychoanalysis**
Kraepelin, E.	Developed system in 19th century for **classifying mental disorders**; DSM-IV can be considered to be a descendant of this system
Pinel, P.	**Reformed French asylums** in late 18th century
Rogers, C.	Developed **client-centered therapy**, a therapy that was based upon the concept of **unconditional positive regard**
Rosenhan, D.	Investigated the **effect of being labeled mentally ill** by having pseudopatients admitted into mental hospitals
Seligman, M.	Formulated **learned helplessness** theory of **depression**
Szasz, T.	Suggested that most of the mental disorders treated by clinicians are not really mental disorders; wrote *The Myth of Mental Illness*

ABNORMAL PSYCHOLOGY PRACTICE SET

Time: 8 minutes

Directions: Each of the questions or incomplete statements below is followed by five suggested answers or completions. In each case, select the one that best answers the question or completes the statement.

1. All of the following are listed as disorders in *DSM-IV* except for
    (A) obsessive-compulsive disorder
    (B) neurotic disorder
    (C) anorexia nervosa
    (D) hypochondriasis
    (E) Tourette's disorder

2. Which of the following is NOT a technique used in Freudian therapy?
    (A) Analysis of resistance
    (B) Free association
    (C) Dream interpretation
    (D) Hypnotic suggestion
    (E) Analysis of transference

3. The goal of primary prevention is to
    (A) reduce the possibility of mental disorder occurring
    (B) reduce the impact or duration of a problem
    (C) reduce the long-term consequences of disorders
    (D) improve the conditions at mental hospitals
    (E) none of the above

4. Which of the following people was instrumental in improving the conditions in mental hospitals?
    (A) Rosenhan
    (B) Szasz
    (C) Pinel
    (D) Freud
    (E) Von Meduna

5. The learned helplessness model put forth by Seligman is a model of which of the following?
    (A) Schizophrenia
    (B) Autism
    (C) Depression
    (D) Obsessive-compulsive disorder
    (E) Mania

6. *The Myth of Mental Illness* was written by
    (A) David Rosenhan
    (B) Dorothea Dix
    (C) Albert Ellis
    (D) The American Psychiatric Association
    (E) Thomas Szasz

7. Which of the following are <u>NOT</u> symptoms of dissociative fugue?

    I.   A sudden, unexpected travel away from home
    II. Identity confusion
    III. Hallucinations

    (A) I only
    (B) II only
    (C) III only
    (D) I and II only
    (E) II and III only

8. Unconditional positive regard is associated with

    (A) Wolpe's systematic desensitization therapy
    (B) Ellis's rational-emotive therapy
    (C) Beck's cognitive therapy
    (D) Rogers's client-centered therapy
    (E) Freud's psychoanalysis

9. Delusions, flat affect, and catatonic behavior are all symptoms of

    (A) schizophrenia
    (B) bipolar disorder
    (C) multiple personality disorder
    (D) schizoid personality disorder
    (E) somatoform disorder

10. A predisposition toward developing a specific mental disorder is a(n)

    (A) transference
    (B) attributional style
    (C) paresis
    (D) etiology
    (E) diathesis

EXPLANATIONS FOR THE ABNORMAL PSYCHOLOGY PRACTICE SET

1. B

"Neurotic disorder" is not listed in the DSM-IV. DSM-IV attempts to be atheoretical, and since neurosis is a term that is actually based on psychoanalysis, DSM-IV does not use it. The other four answer choices are all disorders listed in DSM-IV. Answer choice (A), obsessive-compulsive disorder, is characterized by persistent thoughts that the individual recognizes are irrational (obsessions) and/or irrational and repetitive impulses to perform certain acts (compulsions). Answer choice (C), anorexia nervosa, is a serious eating disorder characterized by a refusal to maintain a minimal normal body weight. In answer choice (D), hypochondriasis, the person is preoccupied with fears that he has a serious disease. Finally, Tourette's disorder, answer choice (E), is characterized by multiple motor tics and one or more vocal tics.

2. D

Hypnotic suggestion is not used in Freudian therapy. This was a tricky question because Freud *did* originally use hypnosis, but quickly stopped doing so when he realized that it was ineffective for his purposes. Let's look at the other answer choices. Resistance refers to the patient's unwillingness or inability to mention certain thoughts, motives, or experiences to the therapist. By analyzing the patient's resistance, the therapist can help break though the resistance and uncover the repressed material. Answer choice (B), free association, is a fundamental technique of psychoanalysis (the name for Freud's therapy). The patient is to say whatever comes to mind no matter how personal, painful, or irrelevant it may seem to be. Answer choice (C), dream interpretation, is also used in psychoanalysis. The analyst tries to discover the latent content of the patient's dreams in order to better understand that patient's unconscious conflicts. Finally, transference occurs when the patient applies attitudes and feelings towards significant others to the therapist. Analyzing the transference is a major part of psychoanalysis as it allows the analyst to recreate the patient's experience at an earlier point in time.

3. A

The goal of primary prevention is to stop mental illness before it occurs by changing the conditions that foster mental illness. In order to do this, primary prevention efforts tend to focus on increasing mental health by improving environmental and societal conditions. Answer choice (B) actually refers to secondary prevention. An excellent example of secondary prevention is crisis intervention, such as counseling to victims of a crime or disaster. Answer choice (C) refers to tertiary prevention, which is aimed at restoring someone to mental health after a breakdown has occurred. Trying to improve conditions at mental hospitals, answer choice (D), would be an example of tertiary prevention.

4. C

Philippe Pinel was instrumental in improving the conditions in mental hospitals. In 1792, Pinel was placed in charge of a Parisian asylum that essentially treated its patients as if they were beasts. Pinel reformed the asylum and began treating the patients with kindness and humanity. These reforms soon spread to other asylums. Answer choices (A) and (B) might have tempted you. Both David Rosenhan and Thomas Szasz have looked at the effects of being labeled mentally ill. Rosenhan and several colleagues feigned mental illness in order to get admitted to a mental hospital. Once admitted, they acted sanely, yet discovered that their actions were still interpreted by the staff members as being evidence of insanity. Thomas Szasz argued that most of the disorders treated by clinicians were not really illnesses, but rather labels applied to those who differed from the cultural norm. Although both Rosenhan and Szasz have changed the way we view those with mental illness, the best answer is choice (C), Philippe Pinel. Answer choice (D), Sigmund Freud, was the founder of psychoanalysis and answer choice (E), Von Meduna, was the person who speculated that epileptic-like convulsions might cure schizophrenia, thus setting the stage for the development of electroconvulsive therapy.

5. C

Learned helplessness is a model of depression. As originally proposed, learned helplessness describes the situation in which an individual gives up because he sees no connection between his behavior and desired reinforcement. The more recent version of this theory suggests that whether the noncontingency between response and reinforcement leads to depression depends on the attribution made by the person as the cause of the noncontingency.

6. E

In this book, Thomas Szasz suggests that much of what is labeled mental illness is simply behavior that differs from the cultural norm. Furthermore, Szasz argues that labeling people "mentally ill" is nothing more than an attempt to force them to conform to the societal norm. David Rosenhan, choice (A), was the psychologist who conducted and participated in the study where nonmentally ill people were admitted to mental hospitals by feigning mental illness. Even after these pseudopatients stopped feigning mental illness, the label of "mentally ill" stuck to them. Dorothea Dix, answer choice (B), was a 19th century American who was a zealous advocate of treating the hospitalized mentally ill in a humane way. Albert Ellis, choice (C), developed rational-emotive therapy (RET). RET tries to change patients' irrational beliefs by forcibly challenging them. Finally, the American Psychiatric Association, answer choice (D) is the author and publisher of *DSM-IV*, a manual used for classifying mental disorders.

7. C

Hallucinations are not a symptom of dissociative fugue. Dissociative fugue involves amnesia plus a sudden, unexpected flight away from one's home or location of usual daily activities. A person in a fugue state will be confused about his identity, and may even assume a new identity. Roman numeral options I and II are both symptoms of dissociative fugue, leaving only Roman numeral option III as not a symptom of dissociative fugue. Therefore, the correct answer is choice (C).

8. D

Unconditional positive regard is associated with Rogers's client-centered therapy. The primary goal of Rogerian therapy is to help the person to be himself and to increase the congruence between the client's ideal self and his actual self. To aid in this, the therapist must care about the client, even when the client reveals thoughts and feelings that the therapist is uncomfortable with. Therefore, the therapist's caring must be unconditional. Let's go through the other answer choices. We didn't discuss answer choice (A), Wolpe's systematic desensitization therapy, in this chapter—we do so in the chapter on learning and ethology. Wolpe's therapy is as behaviorist therapy that is used primarily to treat phobias; the word *desensitization*, a behaviorist term, should have steered you away from this choice. Choices (B) and (C)—Ellis' rational-emotive therapy and Beck's

cognitive therapy—are both cognitive therapies designed to help the client change irrational and distorted beliefs about himself and his situation. Finally, answer choice (E), Freud's psychoanalysis, is used to help uncover material that the patient has kept out of conscious awareness.

9. A

Delusions, flat affect, and catatonic behavior are all symptoms of schizophrenia. Delusions are false beliefs, discordant with reality, that are maintained in spite of strong evidence to the contrary. Common delusions include delusions of persecution and delusions of grandeur. Flat affect refers to the case where the patient shows almost no signs of emotional expression (and recall that affect is simply a fancy term for emotion). Finally, catatonic behavior refers to movement disorders that can range from extreme rigidity to useless and bizarre movements not caused by any external stimuli. Therefore, the correct answer is choice (A). Let's look at the other answer choices. Bipolar disorder is the name for the disorder that used to be called manic-depressive disorder. It is characterized by extreme mood swings between mania and depression. In multiple personality disorder, the patient has two or more personalities that recurrently take control of her behavior. Remember that schizophrenia and multiple personality disorder are two completely different illnesses. In schizoid personality disorder, there is a pervasive pattern of detachment from social relationships and a restricted range of emotional expression. Delusions and catatonic behavior are not symptoms of this disorder. Schizoid personality disorder is not the same as schizophrenia, nor is it a less severe form of schizophrenia. Finally, somatoform disorder is a general term for those disorders that involve the presence of physical symptoms which, although they suggest a medical condition, are not fully explained by medical data.

10. E

A predisposition toward developing a specific mental disorder is a *diathesis*. The diathesis-stress model argues that mental illness results from the interaction between a predisposition to develop a particular disorder (the diathesis) and excessive stress. So, for instance, the diathesis for schizophrenia might be an oversensitivity to dopamine in the brain (although this is still being researched). You might have been tempted to choose choice (B). As we saw in our discussion of learned helplessness and depression, it may be the case that making certain types of causal attributions may predispose one to develop depression, but there's still a debate on that issue, and, at any rate, we were looking for something more general. Regarding choice (D), it is true that etiology refers to the study of the causes of disorders, but there are many different types of causes: predisposing causes, precipitating causes (the condition that actually triggers the disorder), primary causes (conditions without which the disorder cannot occur), and so forth. Therefore, the best is answer choice (E): a predisposition toward developing a specific mental disorder is a diathesis.

CHAPTER SIX

Physiological Psychology

OUTLINE

Historical Perspective

Central and Peripheral Nervous Systems

- Nerve Cells
- Human Nervous System

Anatomy of the Brain

- Anatomical Subdivisions of the Brain
- Cerebral Hemispheres

Neurons and Glial Cells

- Neurons
- Glial Cells

Neural Transmission

- Electrical Properties of Nerve Cells
- Action Potentials and Electrical Conduction
- Chemical Transmission
- Postsynaptic Potentials

Neurotransmitters

- Acetylcholine
- Monoamine Neurotransmitters
- GABA
- Peptides

Psychopharmacology

- Sedative-Hypnotics
- Behavioral Stimulants
- Antipsychotic Drugs
- Narcotics

The Endocrine System

- Communication Systems
- Glands and Hormones
- Sexual Development
- Female Reproductive Cycle

Neuropsychology

- Research Methods
- Clinical Disorders

Sleep and Sleep Disorders

- Reticular Formation
- Circadian Rhythms
- Brain Waves and Sleep Stages
- Sleep Disorders

Perception of Emotion and Physiology

- James-Lange Theory
- Cannon-Bard Theory
- Schachter-Singer Theory

Physiological Psychology

The physiology of behavior has received increasing attention in recent decades. In fact, it has become one of the hottest areas of contemporary research in psychology. This chapter will review everything from history of physiological psychology to the neuroanatomy of the brain. We will discuss the physiology of emotion and memory, sleep and arousal, motor control, and motor reflexes. We will cover research methods used to study the physiology of behavior, and identify important researchers you should know for the GRE Psychology test. We will also discuss selected disorders of the nervous system and explore the role of psychopharmacology in treating them. The key associations we highlight throughout the review are important to learn because these may help you make the crucial link between a test question and the right answer choice.

HISTORICAL PERSPECTIVE

Researchers in the 19th century began to think about behavior from a physiological perspective. Many of these early thinkers formed the foundation of current knowledge about neuroanatomy, linking the functions of the specific areas of brain with thought and behavior.

Franz Gall (1758–1828) had one of the earliest theories that behavior, intellect, and even personality might be linked to brain anatomy. He developed the doctrine of phrenology. The basic idea was that if a particular trait were well developed, then the part of the brain responsible for that trait would expand. This expansion, according to Gall, would push the area of the skull that covered that part of the brain outward and therefore cause a bulge on the head. Although phrenology was quickly shown to be false, it did generate serious research on brain functions, and was the impetus for the work of **Pierre Flourens** in the early 19th century.

Flourens's was the first person to study the functions of the major sections of the brain. He did this by **extirpation** (also known as **ablation**). In extirpation, various parts of the brain are surgically removed, and the behavioral consequences are observed. (Flourens did most of his work on pigeons.) Flourens's work led to his assertion that the brain had specific parts for specific functions, and that the removal of one part weakens the whole brain.

William James (1842–1910) believed that it was important to study how the mind functioned in adapting to the environment. His view was among the first theories that formed **functionalism**, a system of thought in psychology that was concerned with studying how mental processes help individuals adapt to their environments. His important theory on the link between physiology and emotional experience is covered in this chapter.

John Dewey, who lived from 1859–1952, is another important name in functionalism, since his 1896 article is seen as its inception. This article criticized the concept of the reflex arc, covered in detail in this chapter, which breaks the process of reacting to stimulus into discrete parts. Dewey believed that psychology should focus on the study of the organism as a whole as it functioned to adapt to the environment.

Around 1860, **Paul Broca** added to the knowledge of physiology by examining the behavioral deficits of people with brain damage. He was the first person to demonstrate that specific *functional impairments* could be linked with specific brain lesions. Broca found that a man who'd been unable to talk was actually unable to do so because of a lesion in a specific area on the left side of the brain. This area of the brain is referred to as **Broca's area**, and will be covered in detail in this chapter.

Another early example of the relation between brain lesions and functional behavior is the famous case of **Phineas Gage**. In 1848, Gage was injured when an explosive charge sent an iron rod through the front of his skull. Gage survived the injury with relatively minor physical impairments. However, there were notable differences in his personality. Before the injury, he was a persistent and energetic employee—afterwards he was totally unpredictable, profane, and intolerant. His friends simply concluded that he was "no longer Gage." These changes make sense now that we know more about the functions of the prefrontal cortex. The functions of the prefrontal cortex will be covered in detail in this chapter.

Early theorists also proposed that some sort of nervous system underlies behavior. **Johannes Müller** identified the law of specific nerve energies. This law states that each sensory nerve is excited by only one kind of energy (e.g., light or air vibrations). Furthermore, the brain interprets any stimulation of that nerve as being that kind of energy. Sensation depends more on the part of the brain that the nerves stimulate than on the particular stimulus that activates them.

Hermann von Helmholtz was the first to measure the speed of a nerve impulse. By actually measuring the speed of impulse in terms of reaction, Helmholtz is often credited with the transition of psychology into the field of the natural sciences. The nervous system will also be covered in detail in this chapter. Around the turn of the century, **Sir Charles Sherrington** first inferred the existence of synapses. Many of his conclusions have held over time—except for one. He thought that synaptic transmission was an electrical process, but we now know that it is primarily a chemical process.

CENTRAL AND PERIPHERAL NERVOUS SYSTEMS

Nerve Cells

Generally speaking, there are three kinds of nerve cells in the nervous system: sensory neurons, motor neurons, and interneurons. **Sensory neurons** (also known as **afferent neurons**) transmit sensory information from receptors to the spinal cord and brain. **Motor neurons** (also known as **efferent neurons**) transmit motor information from the brain and spinal cord to the muscles. **Interneurons** are found between other neurons and are the most numerous of the three types of neurons. Interneurons are located predominantly in the brain and spinal cord and are linked to reflexive behavior. This type of behavior is controlled by neural circuits called **reflex arcs**. Behavior that is crucial to survival is controlled by **reflexes**.

When receptors in the foot detect pain, for instance, when you step on a nail, the pain signal is transmitted by sensory neurons up to the spinal cord. At that point, the sensory neurons connect with interneurons, which then relay pain impulses up to the brain. Because interneurons in the spinal cord are closer to your foot, it would be faster if they could tell your foot to move instead of waiting for the brain to do it instead. In fact, this is exactly what happens in the reflex arc. Sensory neurons first send out impulses signaling the presence of pain. As soon as the impulses arrive at the spinal cord, interneurons immediately transmit that information to the motor neurons. Without wasting any time, the motor neurons tell your foot to step away from the nail. Bear in mind that the original sensory information still makes its way up to the brain. But by the time it arrives there, the muscles have already responded to the pain, thanks to the reflex arc.

As mentioned earlier, functionalists such as John Dewey criticized the breaking down of reflex processes into separate stimuli and responses. Functionalists preferred to study the process as a whole. To break down the reflex arc into different motor and sensory phases, was, for Dewey, a useless artificial separation.

Human Nervous System

Let's turn now to the overall structure of the human nervous system, which is diagrammed in Figure 1. The nervous system can be broadly divided into two primary components: the **central** and **peripheral nervous systems.** The central nervous system, or **CNS**, is composed of the brain and spinal cord. The peripheral nervous system, in contrast, is made up of nerve tissue and fibers outside the brain and spinal cord, i.e., the PNS connects the CNS to the rest of the body. The peripheral nervous system is subdivided into **somatic** and **autonomic nervous systems.**

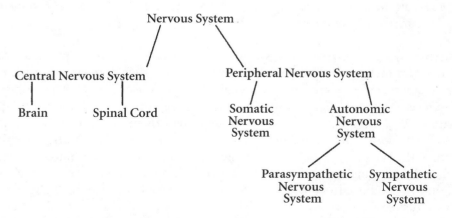

Figure 1. Major Subdivisions of the Nervous System

The somatic nervous system consists of sensory and motor neurons distributed throughout the skin and muscles. Sensory neurons transmit information through **afferent fibers**. Motor impulses, in contrast, travel along **efferent fibers.** Since it's easy to confuse these two, try to remember them like this: sensory impulses travel along <u>a</u>fferent fibers, which <u>a</u>scend up to the brain; motor impulses travel along <u>e</u>fferent fibers, which <u>e</u>xit the brain and spinal cord on their way down to the muscles. GRE Psychology tests tend not to ask much about the somatic nervous system.

The autonomic nervous system appears often on the GRE Psychology test, so it's worth knowing in some detail. Pioneering work in regard to the autonomic nervous system, or **ANS**, was done by **Walter Cannon**.

The ANS generally regulates heartbeat, respiration, digestion, and glandular secretions. In other words, the ANS manages the involuntary muscles associated with many internal organs and glands. The ANS also helps regulate body temperature by activating sweating or shivering, depending on whether we are too hot or too cold. The main thing to understand about these functions is that they are automatic, or independent of conscious control. Note the similarity between the words *autonomic* and *automatic*. This association makes it easy to remember that the autonomic nervous system manages automatic functions such as heartbeat, respiration, digestion, and temperature control.

The ANS has two subdivisions: the **sympathetic nervous system** and the **parasympathetic nervous system**. These two branches often act in opposition to one another, meaning that they are antagonistic. An illustration of this is that the sympathetic nervous system acts to accelerate heartbeat and inhibit digestion. Activation of the parasympathetic nervous system, in contrast, decelerates heartbeat and increases digestion.

The main role of the parasympathetic nervous system is to conserve energy. It is associated with resting and sleeping states, and acts to reduce heart and respiration rates. The parasympathetic nervous system is also responsible for managing digestion. The parasympathetic nervous system thus promotes **"resting and digesting"**—a phrase that captures what you need to know for the test. **Acetylcholine** is the neurotransmitter responsible for parasympathetic responses in the body.

In contrast, the sympathetic nervous system is activated whenever you face stressful situations. This can include everything from a mild stressor, such as keeping up with your schoolwork, to emergencies that mean the difference between life and death. The sympathetic nervous system is closely associated with fear and rage reactions, also known as "fight or flight" reactions. Because the sympathetic nervous system often appears on the test, it's a good idea to know some specific physiological responses associated with **"fight or flight"** reactions. When the sympathetic nervous system is activated, the body mobilizes for fighting for one's life or for running for one's life. Therefore, there are increases in heart rate, blood-sugar level, and respiration. In contrast to the parasympathetic activation, "fight or flight" reactions act to decrease digestive processes. The sympathetic nervous system also causes the pupils in the eyes to dilate (open wilder) in order to increase the amount of visual information reaching the retina. Also, the neurotransmitter adrenaline is released into the bloodstream during fear and rage reactions. An "adrenaline rush" gives you more energy than usual in order to contend with emergencies; it helps you run faster or fight harder at times when you need everything you've got. Overall, most of the physiological responses associated with the sympathetic nervous system act in ways to maximize energy for quick responses to threatening situations.

THE ANATOMY OF THE BRAIN

Throughout this section we'll be referring to Figure 2, which identifies various anatomical structures inside the human brain. As we discuss different parts of the brain, it's important to remember the functions of these brain structures. Different parts of the brain perform remarkably different functions. For instance, one part of the brain processes sensory perception while an entirely different part of the brain manages the internal organs. For complex functions such as waving hello to a friend, several brain regions work together. For the GRE Psychology test, you need to know some of the basics about how the brain integrates input from different regions.

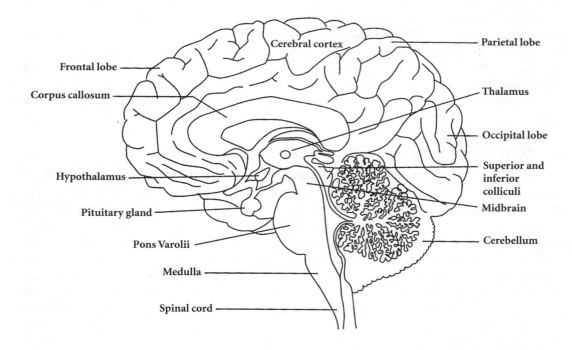

Figure 2. Anatomical Structures Inside the Human Brain

The human brain can be divided into three basic subdivisions: the **hindbrain**, the **midbrain**, and the **forebrain**. Located where the brain meets the spinal cord, the **hindbrain's** primary functions include balance, motor coordination, breathing, digestion, and general arousal processes such as sleeping and waking. In short, the hindbrain manages vital functioning necessary for survival. Just above the hindbrain is the **midbrain**, which manages sensorimotor reflexes that also promote survival. The midbrain receives sensory and motor information. Above the midbrain is the **forebrain**, which is associated with complex perceptual, cognitive, and behavioral processes. Among its other functions, the forebrain is associated with emotion and memory; it is the forebrain that has the greatest influence on human behavior.

The forebrain's functions are not absolutely necessary for survival, but are associated instead with the intellectual and emotional capacities most characteristic of humans. Also, notice that brain structures associated with basic survival are located at the base of the brain, and that brain structures linked with more complex functions are located higher up.

The meaningful connection between brain location and functional complexity is no accident. In evolutionary terms, the hindbrain and midbrain were the first brain structures to develop. Together they form what's called the **brainstem**, which is sometimes referred to as the most primitive region of the brain. The next brain region to evolve was the **limbic system**, a group of neural structures primarily associated with emotion and memory. Aggression, fear, pleasure, and pain are all behaviors involved with the limbic system. The most recent evolutionary development of the human brain was the **cerebral cortex**, which is the outer covering of the cerebral hemispheres. In humans the cerebral cortex is associated with everything from language processing to problem solving, and from impulse control to long-term planning. The term for evolutionary development in humans is **phelogeny** (there's a good chance it will appear on the test).

Anatomical Subdivisions of the Brain

The hindbrain contains the **medulla oblongata**, a lower brain structure that is responsible for regulating vital functions such as breathing, heartbeat, and blood pressure. The **pons** lies above the medulla and contains sensory and motor tracts between the cortex and the medulla. At the top of the hindbrain, mushrooming out of the pons, is the **cerebellum**, a structure that helps maintain posture and balance and coordinates body movements. Damage to the cerebellum causes clumsiness, slurred speech, and loss of balance (alcohol impairs the functioning of the cerebellum, and similarly affects sleep and balance). The **reticular formation** extends from the hindbrain into the midbrain and is composed of an intricate network of nerve fibers. It primarily regulates arousal and alertness (sleeping and waking). Anesthetics cause unconsciousness by depressing activity of the reticular formation. Remember that the reticular formation is associated with *a*rousal, *a*lertness, and *a*ttention. If you remember these "A's," you'll be ready for this on the exam.

The midbrain is associated with involuntary reflex responses triggered by visual or auditory stimuli. There are several prominent nuclei in the midbrain, two of which are collectively called **colliculi**. The **superior colliculus** receives visual sensory input, and the **inferior colliculus** receives sensory information from the auditory system. The inferior colliculus has a role in reflexive reactions to sudden noises. You can keep them straight be remembering that the *s*uperior colliculi are associated with *s*eeing.

The forebrain is above the midbrain and is divided into two cerebral hemispheres (to be discussed in detail later). The **thalamus** is a structure within the forebrain that serves as an important relay station for incoming sensory information, including all senses except for smell. After receiving incoming sensory impulses, the thalamus sorts them, and then transmits them to the appropriate areas of the cerebral cortex. The thalamus is a sensory "way-station."

ANATOMICAL SUBDIVISIONS OF THE BRAIN

Major Division and Principal Structures	Functions
Forebrain	Complex perceptual, cognitive, and
Cerebral cortex	behavioral processes
Basal ganglia	Movement
Limbic system	Emotion and memory
Thalamus	Sensory relay station
Hypothalamus	Hunger and thirst; emotion
Midbrain	
Inferior and superior colliculi	Sensorimotor reflexes
Hindbrain	
Cerebellum	Refined motor movements
Medulla oblongata	Vital functioning (breathing, digestion)
Reticular formation	Arousal and alertness

The **hypothalamus**, subdivided into the **lateral hypothalamus**, **ventromedial hypothalamus**, and **anterior hypothalamus,** serves homeostatic functions, and is a key player in emotional experience during high arousal states, aggressive behavior, and sexual behavior. The hypothalamus also helps control some endocrine (hormone) functions, as well as the autonomic nervous system.

The hypothalamus serves many homeostatic functions, which are self-regulatory processes that maintain a stable equilibrium within the body. Receptors in the hypothalamus regulate metabolism, temperature, and water balance. When any of these functions are out of balance, the hypothalamus detects the problem and signals the body to correct the imbalance. For the test, remember that maintenance of water balance in the body—**osmoregulation**—is performed by **osmoreceptors** in the hypothalamus. **Walter Cannon** developed the conceptualization of homeostasis. The hypothalamus is also important in **drive** behaviors—hunger, thirst, and sexual behavior.

The **lateral hypothalamus** (LH) is referred to as the hunger center because it has special receptors thought to detect when your body needs more food or fluids. In other words, the lateral hypothalamus tells you when to begin eating and drinking. When this part of the hypothalamus is destroyed in lab rats, they refuse to eat and drink and would starve to death if not force-fed through tubes. This disorder is called **aphagia**. Remember that the root word *phagos* means eating. The same root word appears in *esophagus*, the tube leading from the mouth to the stomach. To remember the association between the lateral hypothalamus and aphagia, think of *l*acking *h*unger, or LH, which are also the initials for *l*ateral *h*ypothalamus. Additionally, the LH plays a role in rage and fighting behaviors.

The **ventromedial hypothalamus (VMH)** is identified as the "satiety center," and tells you when you've had enough to eat. Brain lesions to this area usually lead to obesity. A name for this disorder is **hyperphagia**, or excessive eating. To remember the connection between the ventromedial hypothalamus and hyperphagia, remember hyperphagia refers to being *v*ery *h*ungry (the initials, VH, can also stand for *v*entromedial *h*ypothalamus).

The hypothalamus is also a key player in emotional experience during high arousal states. The hypothalamus's job is to manage the **"fight or flight" responses** associated with the sympathetic nervous system. In the early 1920s, researchers first discovered the hypothalamus's role in rage and fighting through classic experiments conducted with cats. When researchers removed the cat's cerebral cortex but left the hypothalamus in place, the cat displayed a pattern of pseudo-aggressive behavior that was called "sham rage"—lashing of the tail, arching of the back, clawing and biting—except that rage was spontaneous or triggered by the mildest touch. These animals displayed random rage that was not necessarily directed at the provocation (as it is in normal rage responses). The researchers concluded that the cortex typically inhibits this type of response.

When the researchers removed the cat's cortex and hypothalamus together, the outcome was very different. The cat no longer showed any signs of sham rage, and much rougher stimulation was required before the cats showed defensive behavior. So, without the cerebral cortex, animals have little or no control over defensive and aggressive behavior. Furthermore, without the hypothalamus, animals seem to lack the ability to defend themselves against threats to their survival. Without both the cortex and the hypothalamus, the cats lacked the ability to coordinate and organize emotional responses.

Electrical stimulation of the **anterior hypothalamus** causes an increase in aggressive sexual behavior. When the anterior hypothalamus is stimulated, lab animals are willing to mount just about anything (including inanimate objects). In many species, damage to the anterior hypothalamus leads to permanent inhibition of sexual activity. A useful mnemonic is that damage to the *a*nterior hypothalamus results in *a*sexual behavior. The hypothalamus also plays a role in arousal. An easy way to remember the hypothalamus's function is to think of "the four F's": feeding, fighting, fleeing, and sexual functioning.

THE HYPOTHALAMUS	
Major Subdivisions	**Primary Functions**
Lateral Hypothalamus	Hunger center—lesions lead to aphagia (i.e., *Lacking Hunger*)
Ventromedial Hypothalamus	Satiety center—lesions lead to hyperphagia (i.e., *Very Hungry*)
Anterior Hypothalamus	Sexual activity—lesions lead to inhibition of sexual activity (i.e., *Asexuality*)

In the middle of the brain are a group of structures known as the **basal ganglia** (not shown in Figure 2). The basal ganglia coordinates muscle movement as it receives information from the cortex and relays this information (via the extrapyramidal motor system) to the brain and the spinal cord. The **extrapyramidal motor system** gathers information about body position (from areas such as the basal ganglia) and carries this information to the brain and spinal cord. Basically, it helps to make our movements smooth and our posture steady. One chronic disease associated with the basal ganglia is **Parkinson's disease**, characterized by jerky movements and uncontrolled resting tremors. The basal ganglia may also play a role in **schizophrenia**.

The **ventricles** are fluid-filled cavities in the middle of the brain that link up with the spinal canal that runs down the middle of the spinal cord. The ventricles and the spinal canal are filled with the same **cerebrospinal fluid**. Researchers have linked abnormally enlarged ventricles with a pattern of symptoms often seen in **schizophrenia**—social withdrawal, flat affect, and catatonic states.

The **limbic system** comprises a group of interconnected structures looping around the central portion of the brain, and is primarily associated with emotion and memory. Its primary components include the **septum**, **amygdala**, and **hippocampus**, although this system does also include portions of the hypothalamus and cortex. Phylogenetically, the limbic system was the second major area of the brain to evolve; it lies in the oldest part of the cerebral hemispheres.

The **septum** (or **septal area**) is one of the primary pleasure centers in the brain. Mild stimulation of the septal area is reported to be intensely pleasurable and sexually arousing. For the GRE Psychology test, it's worth noting that **James Olds** and **Peter Milner** discovered this phenomenon back in the 1950s. They demonstrated that when rats could stimulate their septal regions at will, the rats found it so pleasurable that they preferred it to eating, even after going 24 hours without food. It is worth noting that reward sites are not confined solely to the septum. The septum also acts to inhibit aggression. If the septal area is damaged, aggressive behavior goes unchecked and results in vicious behavior called **septal rage**.

The **amygdala** is a structure that plays an important role in defensive and aggressive behaviors; it has a dual effect on behavior. Researchers base this observation on studies of animals and humans with brain lesions. When the amygdala is damaged, aggression and fear reactions are markedly reduced. Lesions to the amygdala result in docility and hypersexual states. **Heinrick Klüver** and **Paul Bucy** performed studies that linked the amygdala with defensive and aggressive behavior in monkeys. These researchers identified changes in animals that resulted from bilateral removal of the amygdala as **Klüver-Bucy syndrome**.

The **hippocampus** plays a vital role in learning and memory processes. Researchers originally discovered the connection between memory and the hippocampus the hard way. Parts of the temporal lobes—including the amygdala and hippocampus—were removed in a famous patient now known to the world as H.M. This surgery was performed in order to control epileptic seizures. After surgery, H.M.'s intelligence was largely intact, but he suffered a drastic and irreversible loss of memory for anything new. This kind of memory loss is called **anterograde amnesia** and is characterized by not being able to establish new long-term memories, whereas memory for distant events is usually intact. The opposite kind of memory loss, **retrograde amnesia**, refers to memory loss of events that transpired before brain injury. It has become painfully clear that the hippocampus should not be removed to control epileptic seizures. **Brenda Milner** described H.M.'s memory problems in detail.

THE LIMBIC SYSTEM	
Brain Structure	**Primary Functions**
Septum	A pleasure center identified by Olds and Milner; inhibits aggression; lesions produce "sham rage"
Amygdala	Defensive and aggressive behavior; studied by Klüver & Bucy; lesions produce docility and hypersexual states
Hippocampus	Memory; lesions produce anterograde amnesia

The outer surface of the brain is called the **cerebral cortex**. In Latin, cortex means *bark*. The cortex is sometimes called the **neocortex**, with the prefix *neo* meaning new. The term neocortex is a good reminder that the cortex is the most recent brain region to evolve. Rather than having a smooth surface, the cortex has numerous bumps and folds called **convolutions**. The convoluted structure of the brain provides increased cellular mass. If you were to look at the cortex from above, you'd see that it has two halves, or **cerebral hemispheres**. The surface of the cortex is divided into four lobes—the **frontal lobe**, **parietal lobe**, **occipital lobe**, and **temporal lobe**. These lobes are identified in Figure 3, which shows a side view of the left cerebral hemisphere. It may help for you to remember the names of the lobes by remembering F-POT (frontal, parietal, occipital, temporal).

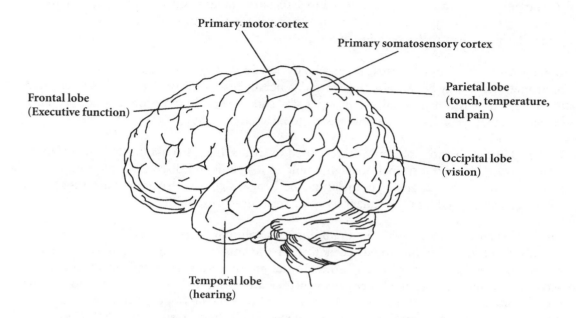

Figure 3. The Left Cerebral Hemisphere (from the side)

The **frontal lobe** is comprised of two basic regions—the **prefrontal lobes** and the **motor cortex**. Overall, the prefrontal cortex serves an executive function in which it supervises and directs the operations of other brain regions. This lobe supervises processes associated with perception, memory, emotion, impulse control, and long-term planning. The **prefrontal cortex** thus governs and integrates numerous cognitive and behavioral processes.

It may be helpful to illustrate how the prefrontal cortex manages these various cognitive and emotional processes. In memory, for instance, the role of the prefrontal cortex is not to store any memory traces, but rather to remind you that you have something to remember. To regulate attention and alertness, the prefrontal cortex communicates with the reticular formation in your brainstem, telling you either to wake up or relax, depending on the situation.

Because it integrates information from different cortical regions, the prefrontal cortex is a good example of an **association area**—an area that combines input from diverse brain regions. For example, multiple inputs may be necessary to solve a complex puzzle, to plan ahead for the future, or to reach a difficult decision. Association areas are generally contrasted with **projection areas**, which receive incoming sensory information or send out motor-impulse commands. Examples of projection areas include the **visual cortex**, which receives visual input from the retina, and the **motor cortex**, which sends out motor commands to the muscles.

In humans the amount of cortex devoted to association areas is substantially larger than the amount devoted to projection areas. In other mammals, however, projection areas are generally larger than the association areas.

Damage to the prefrontal cortex impairs its overall supervisory functions. A person with a prefrontal lesion may be more impulsive and generally less in control of his or her behavior, or depressed. It is not unusual, for instance, for someone with a prefrontal lesion to make vulgar and inappropriate sexual remarks, or to be apathetic.

In the 1950s, **prefrontal lobotomies** were used to treat **schizophrenia**. In these lobotomies, surgeons would insert a scalpel through a hole in the skull and disconnect the frontal lobe from the limbic system and hypothalamus, both of which are associated with mood and emotion. This procedure is no longer used for treating schizophrenia.

The **motor cortex**, identified in Figure 3, initiates voluntary motor movements by sending neural impulses down the spinal cord toward the muscles. As such, it is considered a projection area in the brain. The neurons in the motor cortex are arranged systematically according to the parts of the body to which they are connected. Starting at the top of the motor cortex, motor neurons are connected to the toes of the opposite foot. As you move down the motor cortex you find an orderly sequence of cells corresponding to the foot, then the leg, the torso, the hand, the face, etc. Because certain sets of muscles require more motor control than others, they take up more space in the motor cortex than you would expect from their relative size in the body.

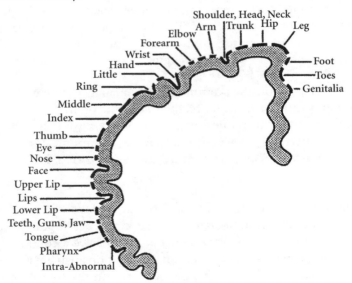

Figure 4. The Somatosensory Cortex

A third part of the frontal lobe worth mentioning is **Broca's area**, which is vitally important for speech production. Broca's area is usually found in only one hemisphere, the so-called "dominant" hemisphere, which for most people is the left hemisphere.

The **parietal lobe** is located to the rear of the frontal lobe. The **somatosensory cortex** is located in the parietal lobe and is involved in somatosensory information processing. This projection area is the destination for all incoming sensory signals for touch, pressure, temperature, and pain. Despite certain differences, the somatosensory cortex and motor cortex are very closely related. In fact, they are so interrelated they sometimes are described as a single unit: the **sensorimotor cortex**.

The central region of the parietal lobe is associated with spatial processing and manipulation. This region makes it possible for you to orient yourself in three-dimensional space, to do spatial manipulation of block designs, and to apply spatial-orientation skills such as those required for map reading.

The **occipital lobes**, at the very rear of the brain, contain the visual cortex, which is sometimes called the **striate cortex**. *Striate* means furrowed or striped, which is how the visual cortex appears when examined under a microscope. Researchers understand the visual cortex better than many other brain regions. Important advances are credited in particular to **David Hubel** and **Torsten Wiesel**. Their work on the physiology of visual perception is outlined in detail in the chapter on sensation and perception. Areas in the occipital lobe have also been implicated in learning and motor control.

The **temporal lobes** are associated with a number of functions. The **auditory cortex** and **Wernike's area** are located in the temporal lobe. Wernicke's area is associated with language reception and comprehension. It is this area of the brain that enables us to understand spoken language. The temporal lobe also serves in memory processing, emotional control, and language. Studies have shown that electrical stimulation of the temporal lobe can evoke memories for past events. This makes sense, because it turns out the hippocampus (the brain structure most associated with memory) is located inside the temporal lobe. It is important to note that the lobes, although having seemingly independent funtions, are not independent. Often a sensory modality may be represented in more than one area.

Cerebral Hemispheres

In most cases, but not all, one side of the brain communicates with the opposite side of the body. In such cases, we say a cerebral hemisphere communicates **contralaterally**. For example, the motor neurons on the left side of your brain activate movements on the right side of your body. In other cases (for instance smell), cerebral hemispheres communicate with the same side of the body. In such cases, the hemispheres communicate **ipsilaterally**.

We distinguish between **dominant** and **nondominant hemispheres**. Because the brain mostly communicates contralaterally with the body, the dominant hemisphere is generally located opposite to the hand used for writing. Given that most people write with their right hands, it makes sense that the left hemisphere is dominant for most people. It's estimated that the left hemisphere is dominant in about 97 percent of all people.

The dominant hemisphere (usually the left) is primarily analytic in function, making it well-suited for managing details. For instance, language, logic, and math skills all are all located in the dominant hemisphere. Language production (**Broca's area**) and language comprehension (**Wernicke's area**) entail speaking and understanding all the specific words and meanings that make up language, clearly a very detail-oriented task.

Many behaviors involve control of both hemispheres, whereas language is typically controlled by only one hemisphere, usually the left, and as mentioned earlier, Broca's area and Wernicke's area are both located in the dominant hemisphere. Broca's area has been determined as the articulation center of the brain—controlling the muscles necessary for speech production. Wernicke's area is the comprehension center for both spoken and written language, receiving input from the auditory cortex and visual cortex, respectively. As such, it makes sense that Broca's and Wernicke's areas are associated with the dominant hemisphere.

In contrast, the nondominant hemisphere serves a less prominent role in language. It is more sensitive to the emotional tone of spoken language, and permits us to recognize whether people are happy, depressed, or anxious just by the sound of their voice. The dominant hemisphere thus screens incoming language to analyze its content, and the nondominant hemisphere interprets it according to its emotional tone. Thus the minor (nondominant) hemisphere plays a supportive role.

The nondominant hemisphere (usually the right hemisphere) is also associated with intuition and creativity, and music and spatial processing. Neither creativity, intuition, nor music processing are particularly logical in nature, so it makes sense that they operate primarily out of the nondominant (minor) hemisphere. To remember spatial processing, think of a *spa*cious concert hall where you listen to music—*spa*cious, *sp*atial processing. The nondominant hemisphere simultaneously processes the pieces of a stimulus and assembles them into a holistic image.

Roger Sperry and **Michael Gazzaniga** studied the effects of severing the **corpus callosum**, a large collection of fibers connecting the left and right hemispheres (see Figure 2). Sperry and Gazzaniga studied epileptic patients whose corpus callosum was severed in a last-ditch effort to limit their convulsive seizures. Sperry was able to determine that the corpus callosum allows a sharing of information between the two hemispheres in a coordinated fashion. In a "split brain" patient, in whom the corpus callosum has been severed, each hemisphere has its own function and specialization that is no longer accessible to the other. Associate *sp*lit brain with *Sp*erry and Gazzaniga.

REMEMBER THE DIFFERENCES BETWEEN LEFT AND RIGHT CEREBRAL HEMISPHERES		
Function	**Left Hemisphere "Dominant"**	**Right Hemisphere "Nondominant"**
Visual system	Letters, words	Faces
Auditory system	Language-related sounds	Music
Language	Speech, reading, writing, arithmetic	Emotions
Movement	Complex voluntary movement	
Spatial processes		Geometry
		Sense of direction

* Remember, the left hemisphere is "dominant" in <u>right-handed people</u>. This is because most nerve tracts cross over from one side of the brain to the other side of the body. For <u>left-handed people</u> "dominant" functions (language, complex movement, etc.) are generally associated with the right side of the brain.

NEURONS AND GLIAL CELLS

Neurons

All neurons have four basic parts: **the cell body** (also known as the **soma**), the **dendrites**, the **axon**, and the **terminal buttons**. Each region is identified in Figure 5. The cell body contains the nucleus of the cell, making it the neuron's energy center. Dendrites branch out from the cell body to receive incoming information from other neurons via postsynaptic receptors. External stimulation of the dendrites can lead a neuron to "fire," or generate an electrical impulse. The end of the axon branches out into numerous terminal buttons, each containing tiny vesicles, or sacs, filled with **neurotransmitters**. These transmitters are chemical substances that the vesicles release whenever the neuron "fires," allowing neurotransmitters to flow into the tiny space separating terminal buttons of one neuron from the dendrites of adjacent neurons (the synapse). Hence, the neuron is able to transform chemical energy to electrical energy and vice versa.

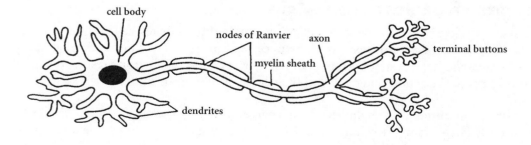

Figure 5. The Major Structures of the Neuron

All information passing between neurons via neurotransmitters must make it across a tiny gap called the synapse. Depending on which neurotransmitters are released into the synapse, these chemicals may stimulate a neural impulse in an adjacent neuron. The entire cycle then repeats itself in the second neuron.

Glial Cells

It's useful to think of neurons as information carriers. We'll make an analogy to the function of the U.S. Marines, whose primary job is to get information through to the other side of the synapse. For the Marines to do their job, however, they need logistical support: proper food and housing, medical care, etc. In the neural system, these supporting and caretaking functions are performed by specialized nonneural cells known as **glial cells**. The most important function of glial cells is to insulate **axons** by enclosing individual axons in a protective **myelin sheath** (by the way, not all axons are myelinated). One purpose of this myelin sheath is to insulate nerve fibers from one another. Myelination also plays an important role in the conduction velocity or speed of of an impulse. The myelin sheath is divided into myelinate and unmyelinated areas along the axon, which allows an impulse to transmit down the axon in a saltatory manner. This saltatory conduction is faster than normal conduction along an unmyelinated axon.

Dendrites differ from **axons** in two crucial respects. The first difference is that most axons are myelinated and dendrites are not myelinated. Also the branching pattern of dendrites (see Figure 5) can change significantly throughout the lifetime, whereas axons typically remain a certain way throught aging. Even when damaged, dendrites can still regenerate new branches and thereby replace neural connections that might otherwise be lost. Axons cannot regenerate in this manner, and therefore, the branching of an axon is kept fairly constant. The second crucial difference between axons and dendrites is in their functions: dendrites are typically receptors of information, whereas axons are generally the communciation avenue of a nerve cell.

NEURAL TRANSMISSION

Electrical Properties of Nerve Cells

Neural conduction *within* the neuron, including among the dendrites, cell body, and axon is an *electrical process*. Neural transmission *between* neurons is a *chemical process* that always occurs at the synapse. In a step-by-step manner, we will review the neuron's resting potential, various stages of the action potential, and the release of neurotransmitters.

The **resting potential** is a slight electrical charge (a negative charge) stored inside the neuron's cell membrane—a charge just waiting to be transformed into a nerve impulse. Because this energy potential is present when the neuron is at rest, it is called a resting potential.

The **cell membrane** plays an important role in the resting potential and this potential is sometimes called the **membrane potential**. The cell membrane is a thin layer of fatty molecules that separates the inside of the neuron from the outside. This membrane is **semipermeable**; it's a partial barrier that allows some substances to pass through but blocks the passage of others.

To understand the process of neurotransmission, we are most interested in small, electrically charged particles called **ions**. Smaller ions can pass through the cell membrane, but larger ions are blocked. It's a little like a kitchen sifter: smaller bits of flour pass through, but larger lumps of flour stay inside the sifter. Similarly, large electrically charged ions are too big to pass through the cell membrane, so they remain trapped where they are. These ions can have either a positive or negative electrical charge. Many large ions trapped inside the cell membrane have a negative charge. When charged particles are separated, this is the resting state of the neuron. The charge outside the neuron is more positive (more positively charged ions) than the inside of the neuron. This results in a net negative charge inside the neuron. The neuron is this resting stage is said to be **polarized.**

To illustrate the dynamics of the resting potential, we will discuss two positively charged ions, potassium and sodium ions, and a special mechanism called the **sodium-potassium pump**. Generally speaking, potassium ions are located inside the cell and sodium ions are outside the cell. The sodium ions move from outside the cell membrane to the inside and the potassium ions move from the inside of the cell to the outside of the cell. If nothing controlled the inward flow of sodium ions, these positively charged ions would balance out the negative charge built up on the inside of the cell membrane. Without getting into the laws of electricity, let's just say that the inward flow of sodium ions would eventually cancel out the resting potential, meaning that there would be no stored-up energy available to create a nerve impulse. To maintain the resting potential (slight negative charge inside the cell membrane), the cell membrane has to actively "pump" the positively charged sodium ions back outside, as well as keep the potassium ions inside the cell. This is done by the sodium-potassium pump.

Action Potentials and Electrical Conduction

The complete firing of the neuron is a four-stage event that includes the **resting potential**, **depolarization**, the **action potential spike**, and **hyperpolarization**. The whole cycle happens very quickly, usually taking no more than a tiny fraction of a second.

Whenever a cell membrane is at its resting potential, we say that it is **polarized**. When we measure its intensity, the polarization associated with the resting potential is about −70 millivolts. **Depolarization**, the second stage in the action potential, occurs when a stimulus has been significant enough to cause the membraine's potential to increase to the threshold potential, typically about −50mV. The depolarization is the actual "firing of the neuron."

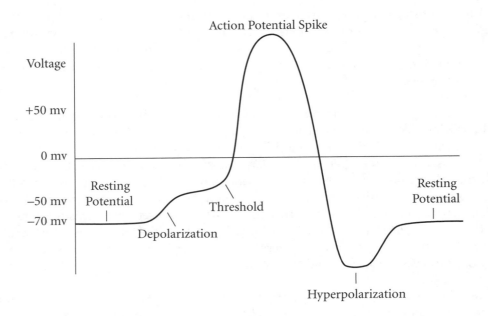

Figure 6. The Action Potential

Upon reaching this threshold, the membrane produces a rapid electrical pulse, identified in Figure 6 as the **action potential spike**. The pulse occurs when the cell membrane's charge suddenly becomes positive (depolarization) for a tiny fraction of a second. How does this sudden reversal of the membrane's charge occur? After reaching its threshold, the membrane suddenly allows passage of sodium ions into the cell. Whereas before there was a partial barrier limiting the number of sodium ions entering the membrane, now there is nothing to stop these positively charged ions from rushing into the cell. This rush of positive charges into the cell changes the cell membrane from negative to a positive charge. During the third step of the action potential, the cell membrane is **repolarized**. The cell membrane then quickly switches back to a negative charge by letting positively charged potassium ions rush back outside the cell membrane. After these positively charged ions leave the cell, more negatively charged ions are once again left inside, and the cell membrane's original negative charge is restored. The cell is then said to be repolarized.

The restoration of membrane's negative charge happens so quickly that the membrane briefly overshoots its original negative charge from the resting potential. This last stage, is known as **hyperpolarization** and is depicted in Figure 6. During this stage, the membrane becomes hyperpolarized (more polarized), which is to say, farther away from a neutral charge of 0 millivolts than during the resting potential. During this last stage of the neuron's firing cycle, the cell membrane becomes resistant once again to the inflow of positively charged sodium ions, and its internal voltage gradually returns to the original resting potential, completing the cycle.

ELECTRICAL CONDUCTION WITHIN NEURONS		
Location	**Type of Conduction**	**Description**
Dendrite	<u>**Graded potentials**</u>	• Intensity proportional to external stimulation
	Excitatory Postsynaptic Potentials (EPSPs)	• Increase likelihood of action potential
	Inhibitory Postsynaptic Potentials (IPSPs)	• Decrease likelihood of action potential
Axon	<u>**Action potential**</u>	• All-or-Nothing Law—once action potentials are triggered, they all reach the same voltage
	1. Resting potential	• Maintained by sodium-potassium pump
	2. Depolarization	• Moves voltage to threshold triggering action potential spike
	3. Action potential spike	• Absolute refractory period begins
	4. Hyperpolarization	• Relative refractory period begins
	<u>**Conduction properties**</u>	• Action potentials maintain same voltage during travel
	Myelination	• The thicker the insulation, the faster the conduction
	Saltatory conduction	• Action potential skips along Nodes of Ranvier
Terminal buttons	<u>**Chemical transmission begins**</u>	• Action potential releases neurotransmitters into synapse

Once an action potential is triggered, the neuron can't fire again until the action potential completes part of its firing cycle. During this interval, the neuron is said to be in its **refractory** period. The neuron's refractory period is divided into two stages. The period corresponding to the depolarization (the inrush of sodium ions) is called the **absolute refractory period**; this is the achievement of the action potential. During the absolute refractory period, the neuron is completely unresponsive to additional stimulation. Once the neuron has achieved its action potential spike, it begins the **relative refractory period**, which corresponds to repolarization (when potassium ions rush out). Often, the cell is repolarized too much, that is to say it is **hyperpolarized**. During hyperpolarization, a stronger stimulation is required to reach threshold potential than when the cell is at normal resting potential.

The action potential is governed by the **all-or-nothing law**—when depolarization reaches the critical threshold, −50 millivolts, the neuron is going to fire, each time, every time. Once the action potential begins, its voltage always peaks at the same intensity, usually about +35mV, regardless of the intensity of the stimulation that triggered it.

The action potential originates at the **axon hillock**, a small elevation on a neuron where the axon meets the cell body. It is at the axon hillock where the **graded potential** in the cell body is converted into the all-or-nothing potential of the axon. The action potential is then transmitted as an electrical impulse along the axon toward its ultimate destination, the terminal buttons.

The basic function of **myelin** is to insulate the axon and to speed up conduction. The efficient conduction along a myelinated axon is called **saltatory conduction**. The myelin sheath along an axon is not continuous; it has gaps called **nodes of Ranvier** where the axon is uncovered (unmyelinated). The depolarization actually occurs at the nodes, the conduction jumping from node to node. When the action potential reaches one node, it triggers a new action potential at the node next to it. The main idea is that the action potential skips from node to node, which is faster than having a single impulse traveling sequentially down the axon. Also, by regenerating the action potential at each node, the neural impulse moves down the axon without losing any of its intensity.

Chemical Transmission

At the end of the axon are the **terminal buttons**. When an action potential reaches the terminal buttons, it triggers the release of chemical substances known as **neurotransmitters** into the synapse.

The terminal button is positioned close to, but not actually touching, the dendrite of an adjacent neuron. The space in between the terminal button and the dendrite is the **synapse**, sometimes called the **synaptic cleft**. The membrane of the terminal button that faces the synapse is known as the **presynaptic membrane**. Inside this membrane are tiny sacks called **vesicles** that store neurotransmitters. On the other side of the synapse, within the dendrite, is the **postsynaptic membrane** of an adjacent neuron that has **receptors** on it. When an action potential releases the neurotransmitters, these chemical substances flood into the synapse. Within the synapse, three things can happen to the neurotransmitters: (a) they can attach themselves to receptor sites on the postsynaptic membrane; (b) they can remain in the synapse, where they are destroyed and washed away by other biochemical substances; or (c) they can be drawn back into the vesicles of the terminal buttons via a process called **reuptake**.

Specific kinds of neurotransmitters can bind to receptor sites on the postsynaptic membrane only if those receptor sites are specially constructed to receive them. The main idea is that neurotransmitters fit into receptor sites just like keys fit into locks. If you don't have the right neurotransmitter key, it won't fit into the receptor-site lock. If the transmitter does fit and attach itself to the receptor site in a process called **binding**, then communication between nerve cells occurs. After the neurotransmitter binds to the postsynaptic receptors, the neurotransmitters are eliminated from the synapse through either reuptake or by being destroyed.

Synaptic transmission receives considerable attention in scientific research because the synapse is where certain drugs act to change behavior. This applies to pharmaceutical drugs as well as recreational drugs sold on the street. Specific neurotransmitters are linked to different moods or behavior.

Postsynaptic Potentials

Once the neurotransmitter binds to the receptor site on the dendrite, it generates a tiny electrical charge called a postsynaptic potential, or PSP. Depending on the transmitter and the receptor site, one of two things can happen. It can make the neuron more likely to fire or less likely to fire. When the postsynaptic potential makes it more likely that a neuron will fire, it is known as an **Excitatory PostSynaptic Potential**, or **EPSP**. When the postsynaptic potential makes it less likely to fire, it is called an **Inhibitory PostSynaptic Potential**, or **IPSP**.

Postsynaptic potentials in the dendrites are **graded potentials**, which means their voltage can vary in intensity. Postsynaptic potentials are thus not subject to the all-or-nothing law that characterizes the action potentials in axons. In graded potentials the voltage depends directly on how much the receptor sites are stimulated by neurotransmitters. With graded potentials, if relatively few transmitters bind to the receptor sites, the resulting postsynaptic potential will be weak. If more transmitters bind to the receptor sites, the postsynaptic potential will be stronger. Another characteristic of graded potentials is that as they spread out from the original site of stimulation, their voltage gradually weakens as they travel along the dendrites. In contrast, action potentials retain their strength as they travel along the axon.

Researchers have come to understand the link between neurotransmitters and behavior by studying animals with very simple neural networks. **Eric Kandel** studied simple neural networks in *aplysia*, which are sea snails with large, easily identifiable nerve cells. Kandel studied neural activity associated with reflexes that govern the movement of the *aplysia's* gills. When lightly touched, *aplysia* normally withdraw their gills automatically. As the sea snails gradually learned that this stimulation was harmless, they stopped withdrawing their gills: this is called **habituation**. Kandel found that after *aplysia* learned to ignore stimulation of their gills, the neurons governing the gill-withdrawal reflex released smaller amounts of neurotransmitters than before. In other words, Kandel demonstrated that changes in synaptic transmission underlie changes in behavior. This finding is important because it identifies specific changes in the neuron that explain a simple learned behavior.

NEUROTRANSMITTERS

Acetylcholine

Acetylcholine is a neurotransmitter found in both the central and peripheral nervous systems. In the parasympathetic nervous system, acetylcholine is used to transmit nerve impulses to the muscles. In the central nervous system, acetylcholine has been linked to **Alzheimer's disease**, an illness resulting in progressive and incurable memory loss. Alzheimer's disease is specifically associated with a loss of acetylcholine in neurons that connect with the hippocampus, which you may recall is an important memory structure in the brain.

Monoamine Neurotransmitters

Epinephrine, norepinephrine, and **dopamine** are three closely related neurotransmitters known as **catecholamines**. Due to similarities in their molecular composition, these three transmitters are also loosely classified as **monoanimes**, or **biogenic amines**. The most important thing to know about the catecholamines is that they all play important roles in the experience of emotions.

Norepinephrine, also known as **noradrenaline**, is involved in controlling alertness and wakefulness. For the GRE Psychology test, it is also important to know that norepinephrine is implicated in mood disorders such as **depression** and **mania**. One theory holds that too much norepinephrine results in mania, which is characterized by intense euphoria and impaired judgment. When there is too little norepinephrine, the result is depression. Another neurotransmitter, **serotonin**, has also been linked to depression and will be discussed in greater depth later.

Dopamine is a neurotransmitter that plays an important role in movement and posture. High concentrations of dopamine are normally found in the **basal ganglia** (brain structures that help make our movements smooth and our posture steady).

Imbalances in dopamine transmission have been found to play a role in schizophrenia. An important theory about the origin of this mental illness is called the **dopamine hypothesis of schizophrenia**. The dopamine hypothesis argues that delusions, hallucinations, and agitation associated with schizophrenia arise from either too much dopamine or from an oversensitivity to dopamine in the brain. Evidence for this theory comes from different sources. Drugs like amphetamines enhance the action of dopamine at the synapse. If taken over a long period of time, amphetamines produce excessive dopamine activity that can result in amphetamine psychosis, a disorder closely resembling paranoid schizophrenia. Second, antipsychotic medications, such as a class of drugs called the **phenothiazines**, are thought to reduce the sensitivity of dopamine receptors. The less sensitive the receptors are to dopamine, the less likely the person is to experience schizophrenic symptoms. Although the dopamine hypothesis of schizophrenia is an important theory, it is not conclusive; researchers continue to explore the origins of this disease.

If you recall the connection between the basal ganglia and **Parkinson's disease**, you may be wondering whether dopamine plays a role in this disease as well. Indeed, Parkinson's disease is thought to result from a loss of dopamine-sensitive neurons in the basal ganglia (specifically, in the substantia nigra, a part of the basal ganglia). Disruptions of dopamine transmission lead to resting tremors and jerky motor movements. Consequently, when antipsychotic medication is given to people with schizophrenia over a long period of time, there is an interference with dopamine transmission. Ultimately, these patients begin to show side effects resembling the motor disturbances seen in Parkinson's disease. This side effect of antipsychotic medication is called **tardive dyskinesia**.

Motor disturbances in Parkinson's disease can be treated with a drug called **L-dopa,** a synthetic substance that increases dopamine levels in the brain. Before discovery of L-dopa, researchers tried giving Parkinson's patients oral doses of dopamine, but this technique did not work. When ingested orally, the dopamine was blocked from entering the brain by something known as the blood-brain barrier. Unlike dopamine, L-dopa can make it past the blood-brain barrier in order to increase production of dopamine in the brain. Unfortunately, L-dopa can have unwanted side effects—when L-dopa leads to an oversupply of dopamine in the brain, it can produce psychotic symptoms in Parkinson's patients.

Along with the catecholamines, **serotonin** is loosely classified as a monoamine or biogenic-amine transmitter. Serotonin is generally thought to play roles in regulating mood, eating, sleeping, and arousal. Like norepinephrine, serotonin is thought to play a role in depression and mania. An oversupply of serotonin is thought to produce manic states; an undersupply is thought to produce depression. It is precisely this concept that led to the production of a class of antidepressants known as **selective serotonin reuptake inhibitors**, such as Prozac.

It is worth emphasizing the similarities between theories linking oversupplies of norepinephrine or serotonin to mania, and undersupplies with depression. Indeed, these two theories are sometimes lumped together and described as the **monoamine theory of depression**.

GABA

The neurotransmitter, **GABA** (gamma-amino butyric acid) produces inhibitory postsynaptic potentials and is thought to play an important role in stabilizing neural activity in the brain. GABA exerts its effects by causing hyperpolarization in the postsynaptic membrane.

Peptides

Studies suggest that **peptides**, which are two or more amino acids joined together, are also involved in neurotransmission. The synaptic action of **neuromodulators** (also called **neuropeptides**) involves a more complicated chain of events in the postsynaptic cell than that of regular neurotransmitters. Neuromodulators are therefore relatively slow and have longer effects on the postsynaptic cell than neurotransmitters. The endorphins, which are natural pain killers produced in the brain, are the most important peptides to know about. The **endorphins** and **enkephalins** are very similar in structure to morphine and other opiates.

NEUROTRANSMITTERS AND ASSOCIATED BEHAVIORS AND DISORDERS

Neurotransmitter	Behavior	Disorders
Acetylcholine	Voluntary muscle control	Alzheimer's Disease
Epinephrine (adrenaline)	"Fight or flight" responses	
Norepinephrine (noradrenaline)	Wakefulness and alertness	Depression and Mania
Dopamine	Smooth movements and steady posture	Schizophrenia Parkinson's Disease
Serotonin	Mood, sleep, eating, dreaming	Depression and Mania
GABA	Brain "stabilizer"	Anxiety Disorders
Endorphin (a peptide)	Natural pain killer	

PSYCHOPHARMACOLOGY

Psychopharmacology, a subdiscipline of physiological psychology, is the science of how drugs affect behavior. Psychoactive drugs, which include both psychiatric and illegal drugs, produce their main effects by modifying neurotransmission. Psychopharmacology is also concerned with the development of medications to treat mental illness.

Sedative–Hypnotics

In general, **sedative-hypnotic drugs**—also known as **depressants**—act to slow down the functioning of the central nervous system. At low doses, these drugs reduce anxiety; at medium doses, they produce sedation; and at high doses, they induce anesthesia or coma. Sedative-hypnotic drugs are **synergistic**, or additive in effect. In other words, when two different drugs are taken together, their combined effect is greater than either drug alone. Alcohol and barbiturates make a particularly dangerous combination that can easily result in a coma.

The sedative-hypnotics include the **benzodiazepines** and **barbiturates**. Generally speaking, these drugs facilitate and enhance the action of GABA, which stabilizes brain activity. Barbiturates are relatively potent tranquilizers often used as sedatives. The benzodiazepines are tranquilizers often used to reduce anxiety. Valium is classified as a benzodiazepine.

Another common sedative-hypnotic is **alcohol**. Alcohol abuse can result in memory disturbances, such as blackouts. Chronic alcoholics sometime suffer from **Korsakoff's syndrome**, which produces even more serious disturbances in memory. One of the major symptoms is anterograde amnesia (memory loss for anything new). Korsakoff's doesn't arise directly from drinking too much alcohol. It is traced to a vitamin deficiency in thiamin, also known as Vitamin B$_1$. This vitamin deficiency arises from malnutrition that often occurs in chronic alcoholics.

Behavioral Stimulants

Behavioral stimulants are a class of drugs that increase behavioral activity by increasing motor activity or by counteracting fatigue. **Amphetamines** speed up the central nervous system in ways that mimic the action of sympathetic nervous system. These drugs are thought to stimulate receptors for dopamine, norepinephrine, and serotonin.

Antidepressants, which are classified as behavioral stimulants, are used to treat symptoms of clinical depression. Antidepressants often elevate mood, increase overall activity level and appetite, and improve sleep patterns. The main antidepressants to know about for the GRE Psychology test are the **tricyclics** and the **MAO inhibitors**.

Tricyclic antidepressants are thought to reduce depression by facilitating the transmission of norepinephrine or serotonin at the synapse. They are called tricyclic because of their chemical structure. The tricyclics block the reuptake of monoamines. MAO inhibitors do just what their name implies: they inhibit the action of an enzyme called MAO, which normally breaks down and deactivates norepinephrine and serotonin in the synapse. By suppressing the action of this enzyme, MAO inhibitors increase the supply of norepinephrine and serotonin.

Prozac inhibits the reuptake of serotonin, and increases the supply of serotonin in the synapse. Prozac is one of a new class of antidepressants called **Selective Serotonin Reuptake Inhibitors (SSRIs)**.

Methylphenidate, which is better known by its brand-name Ritalin®, is an amphetamine used to treat hyperactive children who suffer from **attention deficit disorder**. This behavioral stimulant increases alertness and decreases motor activity in hyperactive children.

Antipsychotic Drugs

Thorazine, chlorpromazine, phenothiazine, and **haloperidol (Haldol)** are antipsychotic drugs, and are effective in treating the delusional thinking, hallucinations, and agitation commonly associated with **schizophrenia**. Most are thought to block receptor sites for dopamine, making it difficult for this transmitter to bind to the postsynaptic membrane. They are therefore thought to reduce sensitivity to dopamine, reducing delusions, hallucinations, and agitation.

Lithium carbonate is prescribed to treat **bipolar disorder**, a mood disorder formerly known as manic-depression. Bipolar disorder is characterized by marked mood swings alternating between manic highs and depressive lows. Lithium is an effective mood stabilizer and eliminates 70–90 percent of symptoms associated with bipolar disorder. Lithium prevents mood swings and is extremely effective in controling acute manic symptoms.

Narcotics

Opium, **heroin**, and **morphine** are narcotics, and are among the most effective pain-relieving drugs available. Many narcotics bind directly to opiate receptors in the brain, which normally respond to the body's own naturally produced pain killers: endorphins. Artificial pain killers such as heroin and morphine alleviate pain by mimicking the effects of naturally occurring pain killers.

Psychedelics are a mixed class of drugs that alter sensory perception and cognitive processes. The GRE Psychology test is unlikely to probe your knowledge of these illegal drugs (cannibis, mescaline, psilocybin).

MAJOR PSYCHOACTIVE DRUGS		
Drug	**Affects**	**Medical Uses**
Sedative-Hypnotics:		
Benzodiazepines *(Valium)*	GABA	Minor tranquilizer (reduces anxiety)
Barbiturates	GABA	Sedatives
Behavioral-Stimulants:		
Amphetamines	Norepinephrine, dopamine	Narcolepsy
Tricyclics and MAO inhibitors	Norepinephrine, serotonin	Depression
Methylphenidate *(Ritalin)*	Dopamine	Attention Deficit Disorder
Antipsychotic Drugs:		
Chlorpromazine *(Thorazine)*	Dopamine	Schizrenia
Haloperidol *(Haldol)*	Dopamine	Schizophrenia
Lithium	Unknown	Bipolar disorder
Narcotics (Opiates):		
Heroin and morphine	Opiate receptors	Pain killers

THE ENDOCRINE SYSTEM

Communication Systems

We've already discussed the relatively fast communication network—the nervous system —which uses chemical messages called neurotransmitters. The **endocrine system** is the other internal communication network in the body, and it uses chemical messengers called **hormones**. The endocrine system is somewhat slower than the nervous system, because hormones travel to their target destinations through the bloodstream.

The endocrine system is involved in slow and continuous bodily process—for example, thyroid hormones regulate general body growth. The endocrine system does respond quickly when we face life-threatening situations. One endocrine gland produces the hormone adrenaline (also known as epinephrine) that increases energy available for "fight or flight" reactions (recall that adrenaline also sometimes acts as a neurotransmitter). Epinephrine is, therefore, a chemical that can act as both a neurotransmitter and a hormone. The endocrine system also regulates sexual arousal and other functions associated with sexual reproduction.

Glands and Hormones

The endocrine system shares many of the characteristics with the hypothalamus. Remember the four "F's": feeding, fighting, fleeing, and sexual functioning? The hypothalamus works directly with the pituitary gland, the so-called "master gland" of the endocrine system. The **pituitary gland**, located at the base of the brain is divided into two parts: the **anterior** and **posterior**. It is the anterior pituitary that is the master since it releases hormones that regulate activities of endocrine glands. However, the hypothalamus controls the anterior pituitary. The pituitary secretes various hormones into the bloodstream that travel to other endocrine glands located elsewhere in the body to activate them. Once activated by the pituitary, a given endocrine gland manufactures and secretes its own characteristic hormone into the bloodstream. This chemical messenger then signals a specific internal organ like the heart or liver to change its functioning.

Sexual Development

Hormones that are regulated by the hypothalamus and anterior pituitary also play a role in initiating, maintaining and halting development of primary and secondary sex characteristics. Primary sex characteristics are present at birth: sex organs, or gonads (ovaries or testes), and external genitalia. In contrast, secondary sex characteristics do not appear until puberty—for females, enlarged breasts and widened hips, for males facial hair and deeper voices.

There are two kinds of sex chromosomes: X chromosomes and Y chromosomes. At conception, the embryo always inherits an X chromosome from the mother but may receive either an X or a Y chromosome from the father. When a fetus inherits two X chromosomes, it is genetically female; when it inherits an X and a Y chromosome, it is genetically male. The genetic sex of a child is determined upon fertilization, however, the development of physical characteristics of the fetus occurs later.

THE PHYSIOLOGY OF MOTIVATION AND BEHAVIOR

Structure	Primary Functions
Cortical structures:	
Prefrontal lobe	• Executive management of emotional arousal and impulse-control
Auditory Cortex	• Emotional tone of language is processed in the "nondominant" hemisphere (in right-handed people, the right side of the brain)
Subcortical structures:	
Limbic system	• The septum is a pleasure center in the brain; the amygdala is associated with defensive and aggressive behavior
Hypothalamus	• "Four F's": feeding, fighting, fleeing, and sexual functioning
Reticular Formation	• A hindbrain structure associated with high and low arousal states
Autonomic Nervous System:	
Sympathetic Nervous System	• Activated in "fight or flight" situations; facilitates rapid expenditure of energy
Endocrine System:	
Epinephrine (adrenaline)	• A hormone associated with "fight or flight" responses; effects include increased sugar output of liver; increased heart rate
Neurotransmitters:	
Catecholamines	• Dopamine is associated with schizophrenia; norepinephrine (noradrenaline) is associated with depression and mania
Serotonin	• Associated with depression and mania
GABA	• Associated with anxiety disorders

Male development, for example, requires the presence of hormones called **androgens** during critical stages of fetal development. Androgens refer to male hormones, and the most important androgen to remember is **testosterone**. Just after conception, the Y chromosome initiates production of androgens. Normal development of the testes and penis then proceeds. If the fetus does not produce or cannot use androgens, development will follow the female pattern, regardless of chromosomal genetic sex. This rare phenomenon is called **androgen-insensitivity syndrome**. Anatomic development of a female fetus does not need female hormones, but merely the absence of androgens.

MAIN ENDOCRINE GLANDS AND THEIR FUNCTIONS	
Gland	**Function of released hormones**
Hypothalamus	Controls release of <u>pituitary hormones</u>
Pituitary	Often called "the master gland"; triggers hormone secretion in many other endocrine glands
Thyroid	Affects metabolism rate; growth and development
Adrenal medulla	Produces <u>adrenaline</u> (epinephrine), which increases sugar output of liver; also increases heart rate; "fight or flight" response
Ovaries	<u>Estrogen</u> stimulates female sex characteristics; <u>progesterone</u> prepares uterus for implantation of embryo
Testes	<u>Testosterone</u> produces male sex characteristics; relevant to sexual arousal

During puberty, the pituitary gland produces and releases **gonadoptropic hormones**, which are also called **gonadotropins**. These chemical messengers activate a dramatic increase in the production of hormones by the testes or ovaries. In males, gonadotropic hormones stimulate the testes to produce sperm. They also stimulate a surge in testosterone levels which leads to facial hair and deepening of the voice, that is, development and maintenance of secondary sexual characteristics. In females, gonadotropic hormones stimulate the ovaries to secrete estrogen which accelerates development of female genitalia and has a role in the menstrual cycle.

Female Reproductive Cycle

Hormones also play a role in the female reproductive cycle: the menstrual cycle in humans and primates, the estrus cycle in other mammals. First, the pituitary gland secretes a hormone called **follicle stimulating hormone (FSH)**, which does exactly what its name implies. It stimulates the growth of an ovarian follicle, which is a small protective sphere surrounding the egg or ovum. **Luteinizing hormone (LH)** is associated with ovulation, which is the release of the egg from one of the ovaries. At various stages during this cycle the ovaries manufacture and secrete two hormones: **estrogen** and **progesterone**. Increasing levels of estrogen are associated with the maturation and release of the egg or ovum from the ovary. The function of progesterone is to prepare the uterus for implantation of the fertilized egg. One way to remember this is to say that *progesterone* promotes *pregnancy*. It makes sense when you think of its root words: *pro* and *gestation*. If an ovum is fertilized by a sperm cell, the ovum begins to divide, and will soon attach itself to the uterine wall. If the ovum is not fertilized, estrogen and progesterone levels decrease, at which point menstruation begins.

CLASSIFICATION OF HUMAN SEX HORMONES	
Principal Hormone (Gland where Produced)	**Examples of Effects**
Testosterone (testes)	Maturation of male genitalia; production of sperm, growth of facial and pubic hair
Estrogen (ovaries)	Maturation of female genitalia; growth of breasts; growth of uterine lining
Progesterone (ovaries)	Maintenance of uterine lining
Gonadotropins (pituitary)	
• **Follicle-stimulating hormone**	Development of ovarian follicle
• **Luteinizing hormone**	Ovulation

NEUROPSYCHOLOGY

Neuropsychology is the term used to refer to the study of functions and behaviors associated with specific regions of the brain. It is most often applied in research settings, where researchers attempt to associate very specific areas in the brain to behavior, and clinical settings where patients are treated for brain lesions. Neuropsychology has its own experimental methodology and technology.

Research Methods

Studying human patients with brain lesions is one way that researchers have studied the functions of the brain. One problem in studying human brain lesions is that they are rarely isolated to specific brain structures. When several brain structures are damaged, it becomes difficult for researchers to attribute a specific functional impairment to any one brain region. The impairment could just as easily be attributed to any other region that suffered damage.

One method utilized for studying the relationship of brain and behaviors is to study brain lesions in lab animals. The advantage of this approach is that precisely defined brain lesions can be created in animals. **Ablation** (or **extirpation**) refers to any surgically induced brain lesion. Researchers might also produce lesions by inserting tiny electrodes inside the brain and then selectively applying intense heat, cold, or electricity to specific brain regions. The device used to locate brain areas when electrodes are implanted to make lesions or stimulate nerve cell activity is called a **stereotaxic instrument**. Although these techniques may seem cruel, they have greatly increased our understanding of comparable neural structures in humans.

Another method involves electrically stimulating and recording brain activity. This approach was first used by **Wilder Penfield**. Before operating on the brain, Penfield stimulated the patient's cortex with an electrode, which is a thin wire carrying a small electrical charge. This kind of stimulation leads individual neurons to fire, thereby activating the behavioral or perceptual processes associated with those neurons. For instance, if the electrode stimulates neurons in the motor cortex, it leads to specific muscle movements. If the electrode stimulates the visual cortex, the patient "sees" flashes of light that are not really there. By using electrical stimulation, Penfield mapped out different areas on the brain's surface. Neurosurgeons rely on the assistance of the patient (who is awake and alert) to make cortical maps. Because there are no pain receptors in the brain, only local anesthesia is required for this kind of neurosurgery.

Electrodes have also been used in lab animals to study deeper regions of the brain. Depending on where electrodes were implanted, researchers have found that brief bursts of electrical current can elicit sleep, sexual arousal, rage, or terror. Once the electrode is turned off, these behaviors cease.

Another use of electrodes is to record electrical activity of the brain. In some studies individual neurons are recorded by inserting ultrasensitive microelectrodes into single brain cells, whose electrical activity is recorded. One example of single-cell recording is the work of **David Hubel** and **Torsten Wiesel**. Their pioneering work on individual brain cells in the visual cortex of cats is covered in the chapter on sensation and perception. Recording is similar to stimulation in that they both involve electrodes, but stimulation is for studying new activity, whereas, recording monitors an ongoing activity.

Electrodes can also enable researchers to record electrical activity generated by large numbers of neurons. One technique involves placing several electrodes on the surface of the head. Broad patterns of electrical activity can thus be detected and recorded by using an **electroencephalograph**. This machine produces an **electroencephalogram**, **EEG** for short. Because this procedure is noninvasive (i.e., it does not cause any brain damage), it is commonly used with human subjects. In fact, sleep research relies heavily on EEGs.

Another noninvasive procedure is **regional cerebral blood flow** (**rCBF**), which detects broad patterns of neural activity based on increased blood flow to different parts of the brain. When a specific cognitive function, such as listening to music, activates specific areas of the brain, the blood flow to that region increases. In this example, blood flow to the right auditory cortex increases because that is where music is processed in most people's brains. A special device that can detect radioactivity in the bloodstream (after a person inhales a harmless radioactive gas) records increased regional cerebral blood flow. This research method uses noninvasive computerized scanning devices to generate pictures of the brain. **CAT scans**, **PET scans**, and **MRIs** are all computerized scanners.

MAJOR RESEARCH METHODS IN PHYSIOLOGICAL PSYCHOLOGY

Techniques	Description
Lesions and ablations	Localized brain damage (lesions) or brain surgery (ablations) used to study functions of specific brain areas
Stereotaxic instrument	Used to locate brain areas when implanting electrodes in order to make lesions, or to stimulate and/or record nerve cell activity
Electrical stimulation and recording of neurons	Used to study activity of individual nerve cells
Noninvasive imaging and recording techniques	Methods used with living human subjects
• **Electroencephalograph (EEG)** • **Regional Cerebral Blood Flow (rCBF)** • **Positron Emission Tomography (PET Scans)**	Different devices used to indicate activity in various parts of the human brain at a given time
• **Computer Axial Tomography (CAT Scans)**	Devices used to reveal structures of the brain in a living person

Clinical Disorders

Depending on the location of a lesion and amount of neural damage, brain lesions will affect perceptual or behavioral functions in more or less specific ways. The most important name to associate with the study of neuropsychological disorders is the Russian neurologist, **A. R. Luria.** He wrote about many of the disorders covered in this section.

Let's begin with aphasias, or language disorders, which are associated with Broca's and Wernicke's areas. Broca's aphasia refers to impairments in producing spoken language. Not surprisingly, Broca's aphasia is associated with lesions to Broca's area (language production); Wernicke's aphasia is associated with damage to Wernicke's area (understanding spoken language). It's worth noting the root words for *aphasia*: in Greek, *a* means "not," and *phasia* means "speech."

Damage or surgical removal of the hippocampus, a brain structure in the limbic system, is associated with **anterograde amnesia**, or disturbance in memory for events after brain injury occurs. An especially severe case was Brenda Milner's patient, H.M., mentioned earlier in this chapter.

Agnosia affects perceptual recognition. The Greek roots for *agnosia* mean "not knowing." In visual agnosia, there is an impairment in visual recognition. That is, although the person can see an object, let's say a comb, he or she is not able to know or recognize what it is. Note that visual perception and recognition are separate processes that occur in separate areas of the visual cortex. Visual perception is registered in the projection area of the visual cortex, whereas recognition is processed in nearby association areas. Therefore, damage to the cortical area results in visual agnosia, which impairs a person's ability recognize visual objects without interfering with his or her ability to see.

Apraxia is an impairment in the organization of motor action. The Greek root words for *apraxia* mean "inability to act." Apraxia is characterized by an inability to execute a simple motor response to a verbal command. In one form of the disorder, simple actions such as striking a match to light a cigarette become utterly fragmented and disorganized. A patient with apraxia may strike a match against the box and keep striking it again and again even after the match is lit; or he may light the match but then put it in his mouth. Notice that this behavior is not indicative of motor paralysis. The patient can perform each part of lighting the cigarette by itself. Instead, the patient has problems executing the step-by-step sequence entailed in everyday acts.

In apraxia, the projection areas in the motor cortex, which send motor impulses down to the muscles, remain more or less intact. Instead, the problem seems to arise from damage to the nearby association areas, which organize simple motor movements into predictable voluntary acts.

Dementias are neurological disorders characterized by a loss in intellectual functioning. Alzheimer's disease is one example of dementia, primarily associated with progressive memory loss. Patients with Huntington's chorea and Parkinson's disease also present symptoms of dementia. Cognitive deficits occur at a much slower rate, and deficits are less severe than in Alzheimer's disease. The motor symptoms in Huntington's chorea (loss of motor control) and Parkinson's disease (resting tremors, muscle rigidity) are quite severe, however.

NEUROPSYCHOLOGICAL DISORDERS

Disorder	Description	Major Subtypes
Aphasia	Impairment of language functions	• *Broca's aphasia* disturbs ability to <u>produce</u> language • *Wernicke's aphasia* disturbs ability to <u>understand</u> language
Amnesia	Impairment of memory functions	• *Anterograde amnesia* disturbs memory for events <u>after</u> brain injury occurs • *Retrograde amnesia* disturbs memory for events <u>before</u> brain injury occurs
Agnosia	Impairment in perceptual recognition of objects	• *Visual agnosia* disturbs visual recognition • *Tactile agnosia* disturbs tactile (touch) recognition
Apraxia	Impairment of skilled motor movements	

SLEEP AND SLEEP DISORDERS

Reticular Formation

The **reticular formation**, a neural structure located in the brain stem, keeps our cortex awake and alert. If the reticular formation is disconnected from the cortex (for example, because the connecting fibers are damaged in an accident), the result will be that the person sleeps for most of the day.

Circadian Rhythms

Our daily cycle of waking and sleeping is regulated by internally generated rhythms, or **circadian rhythms**. In humans and other animals, the circadian rhythm approximates a 24-hour cycle that is somewhat affected by external cues such as night and day. These external cues seem to effect only minor changes in the internal rhythm. In experiments where there is no alternation between light and dark, humans and other animals appear to keep roughly the same 24-hour waking and sleeping cycle. However, with no alternation between light and dark, this cycle may be slightly longer or shorter than 24 hours.

Brain Waves and Sleep Stages

One way we study sleep is by recording brain wave activity occurring during the course of a night's sleep. This is done with an **electroencephalograph**, or **EEG**, which records a gross average of the electrical activity in different parts of the brain. There are four characteristic EEG patterns that correspond to different stages of waking ad sleeping—**beta, alpha, theta,** and **delta waves**. There is a fifth wave that corresponds to **REM** sleep, which is the time during the night when we have most of our dreams. These sleep stages form a complete cycle lasting about 90 minutes.

Beta and alpha waves characterize brain wave activity when we are awake. Beta waves have a high frequency and occur when the person is alert or attending to some mental task that requires concentration (rearrange the letters in *beta* and remember that *beta* waves *beat* all the others). Beta waves occur when neurons are randomly firing. Alpha waves occur when we are awake but relaxing with our eyes closed, and are somewhat slower than beta waves. Alpha waves are also more synchronized than beta waves.

As soon as you doze off, you enter **Sleep Stage 1**, which is detected on the EEG by the appearance of sleep spindles—short bursts of alpha waves. At this point, EEG activity is characterized by slower frequencies and the waveform becomes irregular and jagged. Also, the size or voltage of the waves begins to increase. As you fall deeper asleep, you enter **Sleep Stage 2**. The EEG shows theta waves and becomes progressively slower and "K complexes" occur. As you fall more deeply asleep you enter **Sleep Stage 3**. EEG activity grows progressively slower until only a few sleep waves per second are seen. These low-frequency, high voltage sleep waves are called delta waves. Remember this by associating the *d*elta waves with being *d*eeply asleep. **Sleep Stage 4** is the deepest sleep state of the full sleep cycle. The delta waveform reaches its slowest rate and the sleep spindles are at their steepest. During this stage, it becomes especially difficult to rouse someone from the sleep.

Remember the sequential order of these brain waves—beta, alpha, theta, delta—by combining their first letters to form "BAT-D," and remember that a bat sleeps during the day. Get it? BAT for beta, alpha and theta waves, and D for delta waves.

We spend proportionally more time in **Rapid Eye Movement** (**REM**) sleep than during any other time in the life span. REM is also called desynchronized sleep and "paradoxical sleep." REM sleep is paradoxical because its EEG brain waves look a lot like beta brain waves (although they are desynchronized), but our muscle tone remains relaxed. Even though our limb muscles are relaxed during REM sleep, our eyes are constantly moving.

Sleep Disorders

What about sleepwalking, sleep talking, and night terrors (experiences of intense anxiety that lead people to awaken screaming in terror)? It turns out that these sleep phenomena typically occur during non-REM sleep.

During periods of extreme sleep deprivation, people begin to experience extreme distress: they sometimes even have hallucinations that resemble symptoms of psychotic disorders. When people are only deprived of their REM sleep, but allowed to sleep during all other sleep stages, they tend to become irritable during waking states. They also report having trouble concentrating. After people who have been deprived of REM sleep are allowed to sleep without being disturbed, they compensate for the loss of REM sleep by spending more time than usual in REM sleep. This phenomenon is called **REM rebound**.

SLEEP WAVES AND EEGs		
Sleep Stages	**Brain Waves**	**Description**
Awake	Beta waves	Person is awake and alert; fast EEG activity
	Alpha waves	Person is awake, but relaxed and with eyes closed; slower EEG activity
Stage 1	Theta waves	Person is lightly sleeping; EEG activity shows "sleep spindles" and K complexes appear
Stage 2	Theta waves	
Stage 3	Delta waves	Person is more deeply asleep; progressively slower EEG activity and steeper "sleep spindles"
Stage 4	Delta waves	Person is in deepest sleep; slowest EEG activity and steepest "sleep spindles," relaxed muscle tone; decreased respiration and heart rates
REM sleep (Rapid Eye Movement)		"Paradoxical" sleep; fast but irregular EEG activity, similar to alpha waves; relaxed muscle tone; associated with dreaming

Insomnia is a disturbance affecting the ability to fall asleep and/or stay asleep. **Narcolepsy,** in contrast, is a condition characterized by lack of voluntary control over the onset of sleep. The narcoleptic has sudden, brief periods of sleep. Another sleep disorder is **sleep apnea,** which is an inability to breathe during sleep, sometimes for more than a minute. People with this disorder awaken often during the night in order to breathe.

PERCEPTION OF EMOTION AND PHYSIOLOGY

There are three prominent theories of how we experience emotion, all named for the theorists who first presented them.

James-Lange Theory

William James and Carl Lange proposed the **James-Lange theory of emotions** during the late 19th century, arguing that we become aware of our emotion after we notice our physiological reactions to some external event. James wrote that "we feel sorry because we cry, angry because we strike, afraid because we tremble." This theory emphasized the role of the peripheral nervous system.

Cannon-Bard Theory

Walter Cannon and Philip Bard, objecting to the James-Lang theory, argued the **Cannon-Bard theory**, that awareness of emotions reflects our physiological arousal and our cognitive experience of emotion. This theory postulates that bodily changes and emotional feelings occur simultaneously. Unlike the James-Lange theory, this more recent theory gives the brain a more central role in our subjective experience of emotion. Cannon discovered that any activation of the sympathetic nervous system (part of the peripheral nervous system) essentially produced the same physiological response: increased heart rate, perspiration, trembling, etc. Cannon and Bard argued that subjective experience of emotion must affect specific neural circuits in the brain, and that different circuits probably correspond to different emotions. For instance, one brain circuit might correspond to sadness and another to euphoria. Regardless of which neural circuits are activated (central nervous system), Cannon and Bard argued that emotional responses also include simultaneous physiological arousal of the sympathetic nervous system.

Schacter-Singer Theory

Stanley Schacter and **J. E. Singer** proposed another theory known as the **two-factor theory of emotion.** According to this theory, the subjective experience of emotion is based on the interaction between changes in physiological arousal and cognitive interpretation of that arousal. In absence of any clear emotion-provoking stimulus, interpretation of physiological arousal depends on what is happening in the environment around us. In other words, in some situations a person will label physiological arousal as anger, and in other situations the same arousal will be interpreted as euphoria. Thus, it is the individual's appraisal of the situation that determines the interpretation.

In a famous experiment, Schacter and Singer injected subjects with adrenaline, which increases physiological arousal. Half of the subjects was told that the drug increases arousal; the other half was told that they were injected with a vitamin. Each subject was then asked to wait in a room with another "subject"—actually, this subject was a confederate. The confederate acted silly and joyful and played with paper airplanes. Those subjects who were not told of the effects of the adrenaline injection reported feeling euphoria, while those subjects who were told to expect arousal (due to the drug) did not feel euphoria. Basically, once the physiological arousal was induced by the adrenaline, the subjects would label their emotions based upon the information that they had available. This information includes both past experiences and current environmental cues.

MAJOR THEORIES OF EMOTION

Theory	Key Associations
James-Lange Theory	Argued that we recognize emotions based on how our body reacts: "We feel sorry because we cry, angry because we strike, afraid because we tremble."
Cannon-Bard Theory	Argued that emotions reflect physiological arousal of the autonomic nervous system *and* specific neural circuits in the brain
Schachter-Singer Theory	Argued that unspecified physiological arousal will be labeled as different emotions depending on mental response to environmental stimulation

IMPORTANT NAMES IN PHYSIOLOGICAL PSYCHOLOGY

Broca, P.	French anatomist who identified the part of the brain primarily associated with *producing* spoken language: i.e., **Broca's area**.
Cannon, W.	Physiologist who studied the autonomic nervous system, including "**fight or flight**" reactions; investigated homeostasis; and with Bard, proposed the **Cannon-Bard theory of emotions**
Kandel, E.	Demonstrated that **simple learning behavior** in sea snails (Aplysia) is associated with **changes in neurotransmission**
James, W. and Lange, C.	Proposed the **James-Lange theory** of emotions
Klüver, H. and Bucy, P.	Studied **loss of normal fear and rage reactions** in monkeys resulting from **damage to temporal lobes**; also studied the **amygdala's role in emotions**
Luria, A.	Russian neurologist who studied how **brain damage** leads to **impairment in sensory, motor, and language functions**
Milner, B.	Studied severe **anterograde amnesia** in **H.M.**, a patient whose hippocampus and temporal lobes were removed surgically to control epilepsy
Olds, J., and Milner, P.	Demonstrated existence of **pleasure center** in the brain using "self-stimulation" studies in rats
Penfield, W.	Canadian neurosurgeon who used electrodes and **electrical stimulation** techniques to "**map**" out different parts of the **brain** during surgery
Schachter, S. and Singer, J.	Proposed the **Schachter-Singer theory of emotions**
Sherrington, C.	English physiologist who first inferred the existence of **synapse**
Sperry, R., and Gazzaniga, M.	Investigated **functional differences** between **left and right cerebral hemispheres** using "split-brain" studies
Wernicke, C.	German neurologist who identified the part of the brain primarily associated with *understanding* spoken language—i.e., **Wernicke's area**

PHYSIOLOGICAL PSYCHOLOGY PRACTICE SET

Time: 8 minutes

Directions: Each of the questions or incomplete statements below is followed by five suggested answers or completions. In each case, select the one that best answers the question or completes the statement.

1. Which of the following is associated primarily with the nondominant cerebral hemisphere?
    (A) Broca's area
    (B) Recognition of faces
    (C) Mathematics
    (D) Writing
    (E) Logic

2. Which of the following describes the correct sequence of electrical activity as it passes through a single nerve cell?
    (A) Axon, dendrite, soma, vesicle
    (B) Soma, cell body, dendrite, vesicle
    (C) Soma, vesicle, dendrite, axon
    (D) Dendrite, soma, axon, vesicle
    (E) Dendrite, cell body, vesicle, axon

3. Disturbances in nerve tracts for certain neurotransmitters have been linked with various psychiatric disorders and degenerative diseases. Which of the following pairings is NOT correct?
    (A) Dopamine and schizophrenia
    (B) Norepinephrine and depression
    (C) Serotonin and mania
    (D) Acetylcholine and Alzheimer's disease
    (E) GABA and Parkinson's disease

4. The hormone DES (diethylstilbestrol) was given to women during the 1950s and 1960s to prevent miscarriages. Physicians later learned that DES stimulated testosterone production, which in some cases led to unwanted side effects. If taken during the first trimester of pregnancy, DES resulted in which of the following?
    (A) Masculine-looking genitalia in female fetuses
    (B) Feminine-looking genitalia in male fetuses
    (C) Hemophilia in male fetuses
    (D) Phenylketonuria (PKU) in female fetuses
    (E) Down's syndrome in male fetuses

5. After suffering a stroke that damaged his left occipital lobe, Bill's ability to speak and understand language remained intact. Nevertheless, he was unable to identify simple visual stimuli, such as letters from the alphabet. He was able to accurately copy these visual stimuli on a piece of paper. Bill's symptoms suggest which of the following disorders?
    (A) apraxia
    (B) aphagia
    (C) aphasia
    (D) agnosia
    (E) amnesia

6. Neurons generally cannot fire at rates exceeding 1,000 impulses per second. This maximum firing rate can be largely attributed to

    (A) excitatory postsynaptic potentials
    (B) spatial summation
    (C) temporal summation
    (D) absolute refractory periods
    (E) relative refractory periods

7. Which of the following best characterizes the difference between the sympathetic and parasympathetic nervous systems?

    (A) Voluntary movements versus involuntary movements
    (B) Energy expenditure versus energy conservation
    (C) Peripheral nervous system versus somatic nervous system
    (D) Sensory neurons versus afferent nerve fibers
    (E) All-or-nothing versus graded potentials

8. Which of the following is associated with the hypothalamus?

    (A) Refined body movements
    (B) Lateral geniculate nucleus
    (C) Spatial perception
    (D) Long-term planning
    (E) Homeostatic regulation

9. John goes out on a date with Lisa. He orders a bowl of soup, which, unknown to him, is spoiled. After eating the soup, he feels slightly light-headed. John attributes his light-headedness to being in love with Lisa. This can be best explained by which of the following theories?

    (A) James-Lange
    (B) Cannon-Bard
    (C) Schachter-Singer
    (D) Hubel-Wiesel
    (E) Wever-Bray

10. REM sleep is characterized by which of the following?

    (A) Sleep walking
    (B) Delta waves
    (C) Night terrors
    (D) Dreams
    (E) Sleep spindles

EXPLANATIONS FOR THE PHYSIOLOGICAL PSYCHOLOGY PRACTICE SET

1. B

The only clue you have to work with in question 1 is the term "nondominant hemisphere," which in most people is the right cerebral hemisphere. You may recall that the nondominant hemisphere is associated with emotion, creativity, spatial orientation, and music, none of which appear as answer choices. Choices (A) and (D) have to do with language. You may recall that language is governed by the dominant hemisphere, so we can eliminate these choices. This narrows our selection to three contenders. If you recall the memory aid for the functions associated with the dominant hemisphere, you know that the dominant hemisphere is, in most people, the left hemisphere and that it handles language, logic, and that most logical of sciences, mathematics. This leaves us with only one answer remaining, and that is choice (B), recognition of faces. This answer actually makes sense if you recall that the nondominant hemisphere is associated with recognizing the overall form of something. To recognize a person's face is a function of recognizing its general form. Accordingly, this cognitive function is typically processed in the nondominant hemisphere.

2. D

Question 2 requires a basic grasp of the structure of individual nerve cells. The correct answer is (D). This answer indicates that electrical activity begins in the dendrites, which receive incoming information from other neurons. The electrical activity then flows from the dendrites into the soma or cell body of the neuron. If there is enough electrical activity the neuron will "fire," i.e., generate an electrical impulse which then travels down the axon toward the terminal buttons, where the synaptic vesicles are located. Once stimulated by the nerve impulse, the vesicles release chemical neurotransmitters into the synapse. These transmitters may stimulate electrical activity in the dendrites of adjacent neurons, thus starting the whole process over again.

3. E

The only incorrect pairing is choice (E), GABA and Parkinson's disease. The key to answering this question was to remember the strong associations between dopamine, schizophrenia, and Parkinson's disease.

Choice (A), dopamine and schizophrenia, is fully consistent with these associations. Remember, schizophrenia is often associated with an oversensitivity to dopamine, and Parkinson's disease with a loss of dopamine cells in the substantia nigra of the basal ganglia. Choice (E), however, incorrectly links Parkinson's disease with GABA rather than dopamine. You may recall that GABA is an amino acid that stabilizes neural activity in the brain.

Let's look at the remaining answer choices. Answer choices (B) and (C) form a cluster. Both norepinephrine and serotonin are monoamine neurotransmitters, and both are thought to play a role in affective disorders such as mania and depression. On the test don't be surprised if you see norepinephrine paired with mania or depression. Similarly, serotonin may be paired with mania or depression as well. Choice (D), acetylcholine and Alzheimer's disease, correctly identifies the neurotransmitter associated with Alzheimer's disease. Therefore, the only incorrect pairing is answer choice (E): GABA and Parkinson's disease.

4. A

By stripping away excess verbiage, we can rephrase question 4 as follows: "What is the effect of artificially high testosterone levels in fetal development?" Then, by looking at the answer choices, we can see that the answer must involve differential effects in male and female fetuses. To answer this question, it may help to review how primary sex characteristics, i.e., external genitalia and internal reproductive organs, are determined during fetal development. Chromosomal sex is determined at conception: XX chromosomes normally leads to female development and XY chromosomes to male development. Genetic messengers on the Y chromosome normally initiate testosterone production in males, which leads to fetal development of testes and male genitalia. In absence of testosterone, female genitalia develop in female and male fetuses alike, thus ignoring chromosomal sex. This information helps us select between choices (A) and (B), which form an opposing pair. We know that the absence of testosterone, not excess levels, leads to female genitalia in males and females alike. It thus follows that artificially high testosterone levels are not likely to lead to choice (B), feminine-looking genitalia in male

168 KAPLAN

fetuses. We also know that high testosterone levels during fetal development of girls normally don't occur, because females lack the Y chromosome that initiates its production. If DES artificially increases testosterone levels, it makes sense that it would lead to masculine-looking genitalia in females and, therefore, the correct answer is choice (A). If you've already read the chapter on developmental psychology, you may have recognized that choices (D) and (E) both refer to genetic disorders. PKU and Down's syndrome are both associated with mental retardation. Choice (C), hemophilia is associated with a defective gene responsible for blood-clotting.

5. D

Question 5 requires a basic grasp of neuropsychological disorders. Choice (A), apraxia, refers to a disturbance in the ability to organize and sequence motor movements. Based on Bill's ability to copy the letters he sees, his motor control seems unaffected by his stroke. Choice (B), aphagia, refers to a disturbance in eating that may result from damage to the lateral hypothalamus. Bill's impairment cannot result from choice (C), aphasia, because his stroke does not affect his language ability. This leaves us with choices (D) and (E), agnosia and amnesia. We know that Bill's ability to see remains intact because without his vision he would be unable to copy anything. Nevertheless, he is unable to identify letters in the alphabet, indicating his stroke affects his ability to recognize simple visual stimuli. This leads us to the correct answer choice (D), agnosia, which refers to a disorder in perceptual recognition. Although choice (E), amnesia, may have tempted you, this answer is incorrect. The memory disturbances associated with amnesia typically do not affect basic school skills we learned as children, which includes recognition of letters from the alphabet.

6. D

You may have found question 6 somewhat difficult. The correct answer is (D), absolute refractory periods. During the absolute refractory period, external stimulation, no matter how intense, will not trigger a new action potential. Immediately after the absolute refractory period is the relative refractory period, when the neuron is hyperpolarized. If external stimulation is strong enough to offset this hyperpolarization, a new action potential can be triggered during the relative refractory period. Now let's imagine a situation where there is constant external stimulation that is sufficiently intense to trigger an action potential the exact moment the neuron enters the relative refractory period. That means the instant the absolute refractory period ends, a new action potential begins. Because each new impulse is associated with its own absolute refractory period, the duration of the absolute refractory period effectively determines the number of neural impulses that can occur per second. For example, if the absolute refractory period lasts one millisecond, then no more than a thousand neural impulses can occur in a second. If there were no absolute refractory period, the neuron would be able to fire continuously. Let's look at the other answer choices. Answer choice (A), excitatory postsynaptic potentials, are tiny electrical charges that make the postsynaptic neuron more likely to fire. We didn't discuss answer choices (B) and (C), spatial and temporal summation, in the chapter. They refer to the ways that postsynaptic potentials can join together to make the postsynaptic neuron either more likely to fire (if excitatory postsynaptic potentials are being summed) or less likely to fire (if inhibitory postsynaptic potentials are being summed). But, that's not what the question stem is about, so the correct answer is choice (D).

7. B

Question 7 is really asking about the autonomic nervous system, which is divided into sympathetic and parasympathetic branches. If you were able to recall that high arousal states, especially "fight or flight" reactions, are associated with the sympathetic branch, and that vegetative states, such as resting or sleeping, are associated with the parasympathetic branch, then answering this question would have been relatively easy. Answer choice (B), energy expenditure versus energy conservation, succinctly describes the opposition between the two branches of the autonomic nervous system. Answer choice (A), voluntary versus involuntary movements, isn't correct. Both branches of the autonomic nervous system are associated with involuntary movements, such as heartbeat, digestion, glandular secretions, etc. Answer choice (C), peripheral versus somatic nervous systems, isn't correct because the somatic nervous system is a part of the peripheral nervous system. (And by the way, don't forget that the autonomic nervous system is also a part of the peripheral nervous system.) Answer choice (D) isn't correct because sensory neurons are afferent nerve fibers, and thus can't be in opposition with one another. Finally, answer choice (E), all-or-nothing versus graded potentials, is incorrect. This answer choice describes a difference between the presynaptic axon and the postsynaptic dendrite. The action potential, as it travels along the axon, is governed by the all-or-nothing law. It either fires or it doesn't and, if it fires, it fires at the same voltage every time. On the other hand, in the dendrite, the postsynaptic potential varies in voltage. Hence, it is called a graded potential.

8. E

Here's a question about the hypothalamus for which the four F's by themselves won't help you find the answer. The correct response to question 8 is (E), homeostatic regulation. Remember, homeostasis is an ongoing process of self-regulation that maintains a balanced internal environment. The hypothalamus plays a key role in maintaining this equilibrium by regulating body temperature, water balance, and metabolism. We can eliminate choice (A), refined body movements, because this is associated with the cerebellum. We briefly mentioned that choice (B), the lateral geniculate nucleus, is a subdivision of the thalamus. More detailed discussion of the lateral geniculate nucleus is found in the sensation and perception chapter. Choice (C), spatial perception, is associated with the parietal lobe of the cerebral cortex. Finally, choice (D), long-term planning, is a function of the prefrontal cortex in the frontal lobe.

9. C

According to the Schachter-Singer theory of emotion, when physiological arousal occurs without any obvious cause, a person will search the environment for something to explain the arousal and thus give it emotional meaning. So, in this example, John is feeling the effects of the spoiled soup, but doesn't realize that the effects are due to the soup. Therefore, he searches his environment for something to explain the arousal. Since he's out on a date, he assumes his feelings are related to the woman he is out with, and thus attributes his light-headedness to love. Choices (A) and (B) are also theories of emotion. According to the James-Lange theory, we become aware of our emotions only after we notice our physiological reactions to some external event. Therefore, according to this theory, we feel afraid of the bear because we have run from it. This is the opposite of the "common-sense" approach which would suggest that we run away from the bear because we are afraid. The Cannon-Bard theory suggests that the subjective experience of emotion must also involve specific neural circuits in the brain. Answer choices (C)

and (D), Hubel and Wiesel and Wever-Bray, respectively, are discussed in detail in the sensation and perception chapter. We briefly mentioned Hubel and Wiesel in this chapter when discussing the visual cortex Wever and Bray formulated a theory of pitch perception known as the volley principle.

If you didn't know the answer, you could have narrowed down the possible answer choices by clustering. Answer choices (A), (B) and (C) could have been clustered together because they are all theories of emotion. Because the information in the question stem appears to have something to do with emotion, you could have therefore eliminated answer choices (D) and (E) and guessed from the remaining three answer choices.

10. D

REM sleep is characterized by dreams. Dreams occur during REM sleep—something you should probably memorize by test day. Let's take a look at the other answer choices. Both delta waves and sleep spindles, choices (B) and (E), are names for characteristic patterns of brain activity that occur during various stages of sleep. Delta waves occur during sleep stages 3 and 4, while sleep spindles occur during stages 2, 3, and 4. Neither of these patterns of brain activity occurs during REM sleep. In fact, during REM sleep, the pattern of brain activity resembles alpha waves, a brain wave pattern that occurs when we are awake. Choices (A) and (C) are also incorrect, as both sleep walking and night terrors occur during non-REM sleep. You should be aware that nightmares, which *do* occur during REM sleep, are different from night terrors, which *don't* occur during REM sleep. Night terrors are experiences of intense anxiety that lead the person to awaken screaming in terror, yet with no memory of a dream. During these episodes, attempts to comfort the person are relatively unsuccessful and, upon awakening in the morning, the person has amnesia for the event. Night terrors are much more common in children than adults.

CHAPTER SEVEN

Sensation and Perception

OUTLINE

Historical Perspective

Psychophysics

- Absolute Thresholds
- Difference Thresholds
- Frechner's Law and Steven's Law
- Signal Detection Theory

Sensory Information Processing

- Reception
- Transduction
- Projection Areas

Vision

- The Structure of the Eye
- Visual pathways in the Brain
- Brightness Perception
- Color Perception
- Depth Perception
- Form Perception
- Motion Perception

Visual Constancies

Visual Illusions

Visual Perception and Experience

Auditory System

- Dimensions of Sound
- Structure of the Ear
- Auditory Pathways in the Brain
- Pitch Perception
  - Helmhotz's Place-Resonance Theory
  - Frequency Theory
  - Békésy's Traveling Wave

Other Senses

- Taste
  - Receptors for Taste
  - Pathways in the Brain
  - Primary Tastes
- Smell
  - Interaction Between Taste and Smell
  - Receptors
  - Olfactory Pathways in the Brain
  - Pheromones
- Touch
  - Receptors for Touch
  - Somatosensory Cortex
  - Two-Point Thresholds
  - Physiological Zero
  - Gateway Theory of Pain
- Vestibular Sense
- Kinesthetic Sense
- Proprioception

Perception and Attention

- Selective Attention
- Yerkes-Dodson Law

HISTORICAL PERSPECTIVE

In 1834, **Ernst Weber** published a book called *De Tactu*, which was an investigation of muscle sense. His book introduced the notion of **just noticeable difference (jnd)** in sensation, an important concept to the field of psychophysics. In the mid-18th century, Gustav Fechner, another psychophysics researcher, discovered the relationship between physical stimuli and psychological responses to stimuli. Fechner formulated what he called **Weber's Law**, which was the mathematical expression of Weber's discovery about just noticeable differences. Both of their ideas will be covered in detail in this chapter.

Sir Francis Galton was one of the first researchers interested in individual differences. For six years, Galton maintained an anthropometric lab in which he measured the sensory abilities of *nearly 10,000 people*. His work not only contributed to what we know about how people differ in their sensory abilities, but it also influenced researchers focusing on other aspects of behavior.

Gestalt psychology was founded by **Max Wertheimer** (1880–1943), beginning with a visual illusion referred to as the **phi phenomenon**, discussed in detail in this chapter. Briefly, Wertheimer's studies led him to conclude that the experience of this visual illusion has a wholeness about it that is different from the sum of its parts. He, like other Gestalt psychologists, believed that an analysis of experience into parts is not a valid way of studying our conscious experience.

PSYCHOPHYSICS

Psychophysics is concerned with measuring the relationship between physical stimuli and psychological responses to the stimuli. One of the most important concepts in sensory perception to understand is the concept of threshold. There are two main types of thresholds—the **absolute threshold** and the **difference threshold**.

ABSOLUTE THRESHOLDS

The **absolute threshold** is the minimum of stimulus energy that is needed to activate a sensory system. It is the amount of stimulus that an individual can perceive. It turns out that human sensory systems are amazingly sensitive. To get an idea of how sensitive they are, here are some absolute thresholds (you do not need to know these for the GRE Psychology test; just be aware that these are approximate, and they vary from person to person). The absolute threshold for taste is a teaspoon of sugar dissolved in two gallons of water. Furthermore, on a clear dark night with no other lights shining, the eye can detect the light of one candle burning 30 miles away! So, when we are talking about an absolute threshold, we're talking about how bright or how loud a stimulus must be before it is perceived.

Another word for threshold is **limen.** For instance, *subliminal* **perception** refers to perception of stimuli below a threshold—in this case, below the threshold of conscious awareness. Therefore, subliminal perception refers to perception that occurs without conscious awareness. Contrary to what you may have heard, there is little practical value to using subliminal perception to sell products.

Difference Thresholds

In a **difference threshold**, we're concerned with how different two stimuli (in magnitude) must be before they are perceived to be different. This amount is called the difference threshold. If, for example, experimenters wanted to find the difference threshold for a 100 ounce weight (6 $\frac{1}{4}$ pounds), they would compare a **standard stimulus** (100 ounce weight) to a **comparison stimulus**, which is different from the value of the standard stimulus. The subject's task is to adjust the comparison stimulus's weight until it matches that of the standard stimulus. In this case, the subject would do so by adding and/or subtracting weight from the comparison stimulus. At some point, the subject will think that the comparison stimulus is equal to the standard stimulus, even though it isn't. After repeated trials, the differences between the weight of the standard stimulus and the comparison stimuli are averaged—this value is the difference threshold. For example, let's say that we find that the difference threshold for a 100 ounce weight is 2 ounces. Therefore, on average, a 101 ounce weight will usually feel equally heavy as a 100 ounce weight, while, on average, a 98 or 102 ounce weight will feel just lighter or heavier.

Related to the difference threshold is the **just noticeable difference**, abbreviated **jnd**. Both difference thresholds and jnds measure the same things, but in different units. In the example above, 2 ounces is the point where a difference in weight is noticeable—the just noticeable difference. So 2 ounces would equal 1 jnd; 4 ounces would equal 2 jnds, and so forth. The jnd is the amount of change necessary to predict the difference between two stimuli.

The important part of determining difference thresholds is not the difference between the standard and average comparison stimuli, but their *ratio*. For example, let's assume that in an experiment, it is determined that the difference threshold for a standard stimulus of 10 candles is 1 candle. That is, 11 candles look just noticeably brighter than ten candles. If you were in a room lit by 10,000 candles as the standard stimulus, the difference threshold would be about 1,000 candles. Notice that in each case the difference threshold is $\frac{1}{10}$ of the standard stimulus.

This relationship has been formalized in **Weber's law**, which states that the change in stimulus intensity needed to produce a jnd divided by the stimulus intensity of the standard stimulus is a constant. Mathematically, you will see this expressed as ? I/I = K. ? I means delta I (ΔI), or change in intensity. You may sometimes see it expressed as ? S/S = K. The constant, K, is sometimes called **Weber's fraction** or **Weber's constant**. Note that the smaller the K, the better the sensitivity. So, when we have 10 candles we can make out that 11 candles appear brighter, the constant is equal to $\frac{11-1}{10}$. This equals $\frac{1}{10}$ or .1. When we start out with 1,000 candles, the constant is the same: $\frac{100}{1,000}$, or .1.

You might be wondering how Weber's law fits the observed data. In all sense modalities that have been scaled, Weber's law fits the data except at very low and very high intensities.

THRESHOLDS	
Concept	**Explanation**
Absolute threshold	The amount of stimulus energy needed for a person to say that she perceives it
Difference threshold	The amount of stimulus energy that needs to be added to or subtracted from a stimulus for a person to say that she notices a difference
JND	One jnd needs to be added to or subtracted from a stimulus for a person to say that she notices the difference
Weber's law	What's important in producing a jnd is not the absolute difference between the two stimuli, but the ratio of them

Fechner's Law and Steven's Law

Fechner's law expresses the relationship between the intensity of the sensation and the intensity of the stimulus. Fortunately, it's not likely that you'll need to know the actual equation, but you should be comfortable with its purpose: to relate the intensity of the stimulus to the intensity of the sensation. Fechner derived his law from Weber's law and determined the sensation increases more slowly as intensity increases.

Around the middle of the 20th century, S. S. Stevens performed some experiments that suggested that Fechner's law might be incorrect. He found that his results were best fit by another equation, which has come to be known as **Stevens's power law**. It also relates the intensity of the stimulus to the intensity of the sensation.

Signal Detection Theory

When we measure thresholds in experiments, we are really measuring what the person says she perceived that she sensed rather than what she actually sensed. **Signal detection theory** suggests that other, nonsensory factors influence what the subject says she senses. These nonsensory factors include experiences, motives, and expectations. For instance, a cautious person may want to be absolutely certain that he or she heard a tone before responding, "Yes, I heard a tone." On the other hand, someone else might need to have only an inkling that he or she heard a tone before responding, "Yes, I heard a tone." These are excellent examples of **response bias**, which refers to the tendency of subjects to respond in a particular way due to nonsensory factors. Unlike the earlier psychophysics, signal detection theory gives us a way to measure both how well the subject can sense the stimulus (sensitivity) *and* response bias.

In the basic signal detection experiment, there are two experimenter-controlled situations possible on a particular trial: either a stimulus is presented or it isn't presented. Now, even if a stimulus isn't presented, your sensory systems are still excited by background noise, such as the random firings going on in the nervous system. Therefore, trials in which the stimulus isn't presented are called noise trials; these are also called catch trials. In signal detection lingo, the stimulus is called a signal. Each trial is either a signal trial or a noise trial. On each trial, the subject is asked to indicate whether or not a signal was present. In Figure 1, there are four possible outcomes for each trial. Hits (when a signal is presented and the subject perceives the stimulus), Misses (when a signal is presented and the subject does not perceive the stimulus), False Alarms (when no signal is presented and the subject perceives a stimulus), and Correct Negatives (when no signal is presented and the subject does not perceive a stimulus). **Receiver Operating Characteristic (ROC)** curves are employed by many researchers to graphically summarize a subject's responses by measuring the operating (sensitivity) characteristics of a subject receiving signals. **John A. Swets** refined the use of ROC carves; his name may come up on a signal detection question on the exam.

Subject's Response

"Yes"   "No"

	"Yes"	"No"
Signal Present	Hit	Miss
Signal Absent	False Alarm	Correct Rejection (Correct Negative)

Figure 1. Signal Detection Theory

SIGNAL DETECTION THEORY: KEY CONCEPTS

Concept	Description
Response bias	Measures how risky the subject is in sensory decision-making; based upon nonsensory factors
Sensitivity	Measures how well the subject can sense the stimulus
ROC curve	Used to graphically summarize a subject's responses in a signal detection experiment

SENSORY INFORMATION PROCESSING

While you should have some familiarity with smell, taste, and touch, you need to have a good understanding of vision and audition because most of the questions about sensation and perception on the GRE Psychology test concern these two senses. Let's look at what sensory systems have in common (there have been questions about this on previous editions of the GRE Psychology test).

The first step in all sensory information processing is **reception**. Each sensory system has receptors to react to physical external energy. The second step is **transduction**. Transduction is the translation of physical energy into neural impulses or action potentials. Once transduction occurs, the electrochemical energy is sent to various **projection areas** in the brain along various **neural pathways** and can be processed by the nervous system.

COMMONALITIES OF SENSORY SYSTEMS	
Item	**Description**
Receptors	Respond to physical stimuli
Transduction	Translates physical energy to neural impulses
Projection areas	Brain areas that further analyze sensory input

VISION

The Structure of the Eye

There are several parts of the eye that you need to be familiar with: the **cornea, pupil, iris, lens,** and especially the **retina**. The **cornea**, the clear, domelike window in the front of your eye, gathers and focuses the incoming light. The **pupil**, the hole in the iris, contracts in bright light, and expands in dim light to let more light in. The **iris**, the colored part of the eye, has involuntary muscles and autonomic nerve fibers. It controls the size of the pupil and therefore, the amount of light entering the eye. The **lens**, which lies right behind the iris, helps control the curvature of the light coming in and can focus near or distant objects on the retina.

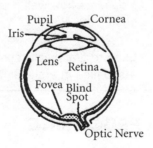

Figure 2. The Eye

The **retina** is in the back of the eye and is like a screen filled with neural elements and blood vessels. It is the image-detecting part of the eye. The **duplexity** or **duplicity theory of vision** states that the retina contains two kinds of photoreceptors. The organization of the retinal cells makes light pass through intermediate sensory neurons before reaching, and stimulating the photoreceptors. This is illustrated in Figure 3. There is a blind spot where the optic nerve leaves the eye, and there are no photoreceptors here.

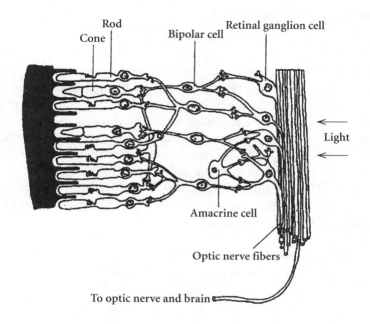

Figure 3. The Organization of Cells in the Retina

Questions about **rods** and **cones** are always on the GRE Psychology test, so you should be able to compare the two. **Cones** are basically used for **color vision** (remember: *cones* and *color* both begin with *c*) and for perceiving fine **detail**. Cones are most effective in bright light, and allow us to see chromatic and achromatic colors. In reduced illumination, the **rods** function best and allow perception only of achromatic colors. Rods have low sensitivity to detail and are not involved in color vision.

There are many more rods than cones in the human eye. However, the middle section of the retina, called the **fovea**, contains only cones. As you move further away from the fovea, the number of rods increases while the number of cones decreases. Therefore, visual acuity is best in the fovea and the fovea is most sensitive in normal day light vision. At the periphery of the retina, there are only rods.

The connection between the receptors (the rods and cones) and the optic nerve is not direct. There are several layers of neurons in between: **horizontal, amacrine, bipolar cells,** and **ganglion cells.** Rods and cones connect with bipolar neurons, which connect with ganglion cells. The ganglion cells group together to form the optic nerve. Because there are many, many more receptors than ganglion cells, each ganglion cell has to represent the combined activity of many rods and cones. This results in a loss of detail as information from the photoecepters is combined. The greater the number of receptors that converge through the bipolar neurons onto one ganglion cell, the more difficult it becomes to make out the fine detail. On average, the number of cones converging onto individual ganglion cells is smaller than the number of rods converging onto individual ganglion cells. Therefore, cones have a greater sensitivity to fine detail than rods do.

Visual Pathways in the Brain

As you can see in Figure 4, the image of the stimulus on the right side of each eye's visual field forms the left half of each eye's retina and the image of the stimulus on the left side of each eye's visual field forms on the right half of each eye's retina. As we trace the optic nerves back into the brain, the first significant event occurs at the **optic chiasm**. Here the fibers from the nasal half of the retina (closer to the nose) cross paths. The nasal fibers from the left eye go to the right side of the brain and the **nasal fibers** from the right eye go the left side of the brain. However, the fibers from the temporal halves of the retina (away from the nose, closer to the temples) do not cross paths. The **temporal fibers** from the left eye go to the left side of the brain and the temporal fibers from the right eye go to the right side of the brain. As you can see from Figure 4, all the information from the left visual field of both eyes is processed in the right cerebral hemisphere and all the information from the right visual field of both eyes is processed in the left hemisphere.

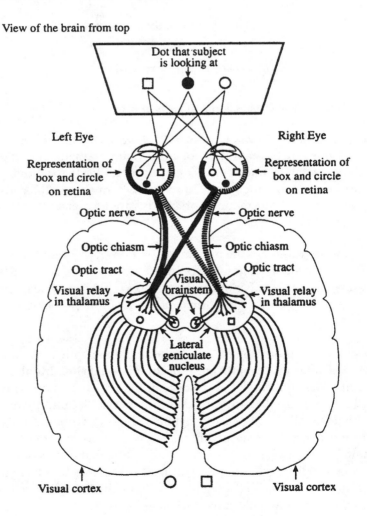

Figure 4. Visual Pathways in the Brain

From the optic chiasm, the information goes to several different places in the brain: the **lateral geniculate nucleus** of the **thalamu**s, the **visual cortex** in the **occipital lobe**, and the **superior colliculus**—you need to have these memorized by the test day. Remember that the word *occipital* has two *c*'s in the middle, so you use the *occipital lobe* to *see*. Also, if you remember that the visual system is more important, even superior, for the GRE Psychology test, you can recognize that the *superior colliculus*, and not the inferior colliculus, is involved in vision.

Hubel and **Wiesel's** work on the visual cortex earned a Nobel Prize in 1981. Hubel and Wiesel found a neural basis for **feature detection theory**, which suggests that certain cells in the cortex are maximally sensitive to certain features of stimuli. They distinguished three different types of cells: **simple**, **complex**, and **hypercomplex**. The responses of simple cells give information about the orientation and boundaries of an object. The responses of complex cells give more advanced information about orientation, such as movement. The responses of hypercomplex cells give information about more abstract concepts such as object shape. The idea that single cells give information about such specific features was considered an amazing breakthrough.

Hubel and Wiesel measured cell responses using the latest research methodologies available to sensory psychologists at the time: single-cell recording. This method involves placing a microelectrode in the cortex so sensitive that it could record responses of a single cell. A microelectrode is so small that its tip cannot be seen with an ordinary microscope! This technique is sometimes called *recording from single nerve fibers*.

FEATURE DETECTION CELLS IN THE CORTEX	
Type of Cell	**Responds to Information About**
Simple	Orientation
Complex	Movement
Hypercomplex	Shape

Perception

related to illumination, but it is not the same thing as illumination. is a physical, objective measurement that is simply the amount of light falling **Brightness** is the *subjective* impression of the intensity of a light stimulus.

There are several factors involved in how we perceive brightness. The first one is **adaptation**. When you adapt to a darker environment, such as a dark movie theater, you experience **dark adaptation**. When you first walk into the theater, you have problems seeing, but as your eyes became accustomed to the dark, you are soon able to see better—you have adapted. Part of the reason for dark adaptation is that light reaching the photoreceptors before you entered the theater bleached the photopigment in the rods. The rods have only one photopigment, a photochemical called **rhodopsin**, and you should know this photopigment for the test. Rhodopsin is made up of a vitamin A derivative, called **retinal**, and a protein, called **opsin**. When a molecule of rhodopsin absorbs a photon of light, the pigment begins to decompose, or split, into retinene and opsin. This is called bleaching. After bleaching, it takes time for the pigments to regenerate. As you sit in the darkness, waiting for the movie to begin, the rhodopsin begins to regenerate, and you begin to see better. Since vitamin A is crucial for the resynthesis of rhodopsin, people who have serious vitamin A deficiencies have problems seeing in the dark.

When you walk out of the dark movie theater into a bright sunny day, the visual process that takes place is called (not surprisingly) light adaptation. Less is known about the physiological basis for this.

Another important factor in brightness perception is **simultaneous brightness contrast**. Basically, a target area of a particular luminance appears brighter when surrounded by a darker stimulus than when surrounded by a lighter stimulus. An explanation of this phenomenon is **lateral inhibition**. Essentially, lateral inhibition works just like it sounds: adjacent retinal cells inhibit one another. In other words, if a cell is excited, neighboring cells will be inhibited. Because the surrounding cells are inhibited, they do not fire as often, and the corresponding area appears not as bright. Lateral inhibition is an important part of our visual perception because it sharpens and highlights the borders between dark and light areas.

BRIGHTNESS PERCEPTION: KEY CONCEPTS	
Concept	**Explanation**
Illumination	An *objective* measurement of the amount of light falling on a surface
Brightness	The *subjective* impression of the intensity of a stimulus
Dark adaptation	Caused by the regeneration of rhodopsin, the photopigment in the rods
Lateral inhibition	Adjacent retinal cells inhibit one another; sharpens and highlights borders between light and dark areas

Color Perception

Color perception is related to the wavelength of the light entering the eye. The human eye can see wavelengths from about 400 to about 800 nanometers. The idea that color and light are related was probably made clear to you in an elementary school science or art class, when you took a prism and shone light through it. Recall that the prism broke the light into different colors of the spectrum: red, orange, yellow, green, blue, indigo, and violet.

In order to understand color perception, you need to understand the difference between **additive** and **subtractive color mixture**. **Subtractive color mixture** occurs when we mix pigments. You are probably familiar with this kind of mixing from your kindergarten experiences with finger paints. It's likely that the color combinations you know are subtractive mixtures (like blue and yellow make green). The mixture of pigments is subtractive.

Additive color mixing has to do with lights, and since what our eyes see are lights, an understanding of additive color mixture is important to understanding how we see color. The primary colors here are blue, green, and red, not the yellow, blue and red of subtractive color mixture. Sometimes this leads to surprising results. In additive color mixing, if you were to mix red and green lights, you would get yellow. (No, that was not a mistake—adding red and green lights gives you yellow.)

If a stimulus does not emit its own light, then we perceive it by processing the light reflected off of it. An apple appears red because the wavelengths that appear red to us are reflected by the apple while all the other wavelengths are absorbed.

There are two basic theories of color vision. The first is called the **Young-Helmhotz** theory, or the **trichromatic theory**. This theory suggests that the retina contains three different types of color receptors (cones), which are differentially sensitive to different colors. One is maximally sensitive to red, one is maximally sensitive to blue, and one is maximally sensitive to green, and all colors are produced by combined stimulation of these receptors. Light enters the eye, hits the retina, and the three types of receptors are stimulated to varying degrees. It is the ratio of activity in the receptors that determines color. Young demonstrated that you could mix the three primary lights and produce all of the other colors of the spectrum.

The second theory of color vision derives from **Ewald Hering's** criticism of the trichromatic theory. Essentially, Hering held that yellow must be one of the primary colors and that yellow was a basic color along with red, blue, and green. Hering further suggested that his four primaries (red, blue, green, and yellow) were arranged in opposing pairs, so that one opponent process would signal the presence of red or green, and another would signal the presence of blue or yellow. For instance, the color red would excite a red-green cell, while green would inhibit a red-green cell. An implication of this is that since a cell's response cannot both increase and decrease simultaneously, you could never have a reddish-green. And if you think about it, it's very hard to imagine what a reddish-green would look like. In addition to his red-green and blue-yellow, Hering also included one more opposing pair to code the brightness, namely black-white. Not surprisingly, this theory is called the **opponent-process theory of color vision**.

Neither Hering nor Helmholtz had the sophisticated physiological methods available today. Modern research, able to observe individual cells, suggests that Helmholtz was right: There are indeed three types of cones in the retina, each one maximally sensitive to a different primary color. Modern research has also shown that Hering's opponent-process theory applies to other cells in the visual system, such as the cells in the lateral geniculate nucleus in the brain.

THEORIES OF COLOR VISION	
Theory	**Basic Idea**
Young-Helmholtz (trichromatic)	Three types of color receptors: red, blue, green
Hering (opponent process)	Three opposing pairs: red-green, blue-yellow, black-white

There is one other concept related to color that you should be familiar with: **afterimages**. It was the concept of afterimages that led Hering to his theory. An afterimage is a visual sensation that appears after prolonged or intense exposure to a stimulus. Of most interest here are those afterimages that involve color. For instance, if you stare at a red square for several minutes and then transfer your gaze to a white piece of paper, you will see a green square, not a red square. Afterimages have been used to support Hering's theory of color vision, since the color of the afterimage will be the "opposite" of the original color.

Depth Perception

Considering that the image on our retina is only two-dimensional, the fact that we see three dimensions is really quite amazing. A good portion of the explanation was provided by George Berkeley in 1709 when he listed various cues for depth. The two-dimensional image on the retina has certain characteristics that signal the three-dimensionality of the actual object. **Interposition**, which is also called **overlap**, refers to the cue for **depth perception** when one object (A) covers, or overlaps with another object (B). We see object (A) as being in front. **Relative size** is another cue for depth perception. As an object gets farther away, its image on the retina gets smaller. You can tell how far away something is from you relative to another object by comparing the size of the images on the retina with what you know about their actual sizes. **Linear perspective** refers to the convergence of parallel lines in the distance. In other words, lines which are actually parallel appear to converge on the horizon. Since you know that the lines don't actually converge, you can use this cue in forming your impression of depth.

Three important depth cues are not included in Berkeley's work. The first one, which comes from the work of **J. J. Gibson**, are **texture gradients**. Texture gradients refer to the variations in perceived surface texture as a function of the distance from the observer. The more distant parts of a scene appear to have smaller, more densely packed elements. Furthermore, sudden changes in texture generally signal either a change in distance or a change in direction (for example, a corner). There are several examples of texture gradients in Figure 5.

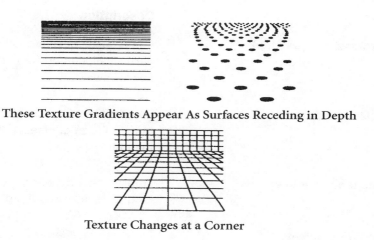

These Texture Gradients Appear As Surfaces Receding in Depth

Texture Changes at a Corner

Figure 5. Texture Gradients

Another depth cue is **motion parallax**. Next time you are in a car or train, look out the window and fix your gaze on an object about halfway between you and the horizon. You'll notice that objects closer to you than your fixation point appear to move in the same direction you do. The perceived speed at which these objects appear to move also varies depending on how close the object is to your fixation point. The variation in apparent speed and motion is called motion parallax. When an object rather than the perceiver moves, the motion of that object gives us cues about the relative depth of parts of the object. This is a special kind of motion parallax called the **kinetic depth effect**.

The final cue to depth perception is called **binocular disparity**, or sometimes **stereopsis**. This cue depends on the fact that the distance between the eyes provides us with two slightly disparate views of the world. The degree of disparity between the retinal images of the eyes due to the slight differences in the horizontal position of each eye in the skull is called **binocular parallax**. When the brain combines these two views, we get a perception of depth, or stereopsis. By the way, as much as ten percent of the population cannot take advantage of stereopsis in depth perception. However, thanks to the other depth cues presented above, they can still perceive depth. Stereopsis is the only depth cue that requires two eyes and is therefore called a **binocular depth cue**. The other depth cues, which require the use of only one eye, are called **monocular depth cues**.

The tool used in stereopsis research is called a stereoscope. Stereoscopes go back to the 19th century and give the impression of depth to a flat picture by presenting to each eye a separate and slightly different picture, corresponding to the retinal image that would have occurred in each eye had the three-dimensional scene been viewed normally.

CUES FOR DEPTH PERCEPTION

Cue	Description
Interposition (Overlap)	If one object covers another, the partially hidden object is seen as farther away
Relative size	Comparison of retinal size of object to actual size of objects gives cue to depth
Linear perspective	Parallel lines appear to converge as they recede into the distance
Texture gradients	As scene recedes from viewer, the surface texture of the object appears to change
Motion parallax	When observer moves, objects in a stationary environment appear to move relative to distance from observer
Binocular disparity (Stereopsis)	Each eye sees a slightly different scene; when the brain combines the scenes, we get perception of depth

Perception of Form

The perception of form is really about how we abstract perceptual objects such as the book in front of you out of the array of blobs and contours appearing on our retina. Perceptual objects exist only in our mind, and not in the retinal image. The most important concepts to consider in form perception are **figure** and **ground**. The figure is the integrated visual experience that stands out at the center of attention. The ground is simply the background against which the figure appears. For instance, if you are looking at a ball that is resting on a field of grass, the ball is the figure and the ground consists of many elongated shapes (the blades of grass). Sometimes, figure and ground can change, as in the famous "face-vase" which is presented in Figure 6.

Figure 6. Figure and Ground

If you look at the picture long enough, what you see will begin to oscillate: first you will see the vase, then two faces in profile, and then a vase again. When you see the vase, the white part of the picture is the figure and the black part of the picture is the ground. When you see the two faces, the opposite is true.

How is it that we manage to separate the figure from the ground, given that the retinal image is just a collection of blobs and contours? Gestalt psychologists and others have contributed a great deal to our understanding of these issues. There are five laws that explain form perception: **proximity**, **similarity**, **good continuation**, **closure**, and **prägnanz**. Figure 7 shows examples of the first four laws.

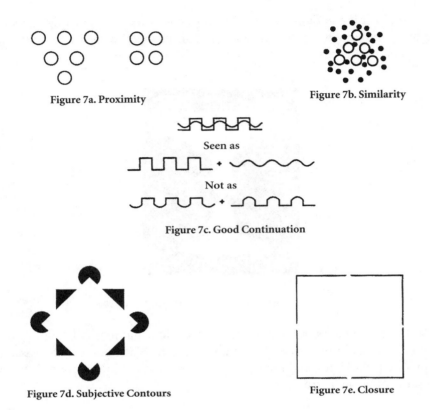

Figure 7a. Proximity

Figure 7b. Similarity

Seen as

Not as

Figure 7c. Good Continuation

Figure 7d. Subjective Contours

Figure 7e. Closure

The **law of proximity**, depicted in 7a, says that elements close to one another tend to be perceived as a unit. In this figure, we don't see ten dots, we see a triangle and a square. The **law of similarity** says that objects that are similar tend to be grouped together. In Figure 7b, we see the big hollow dots as a triangle against a background. The **law of good continuation**, Figure 7c, says that elements that appear to follow in the same direction (such as a straight line or a simple curve) tend to be grouped together. That is, there is a tendency to perceive continuous patterns in stimuli rather than abrupt changes. Some researchers have argued that the phenomena of subjective contours may arise from this law. **Subjective contours** have to do with perceiving contours, and therefore, shapes, that are not present in the physical stimulus. Once again, as with much of Gestalt psychology, the phenomena of subjective contours is better displayed than described. In Figure 7d, subjective contours lead to the perception of a white diamond on a black square with its corners lying on the four circles. The law of closure says that when a space is enclosed by a contour it tends to be perceived as a figure. Closure also refers to the fact that certain figures tend to be perceived as more complete (or closed) than they really are. In Figure 7e, we don't see four right angles, we see a square, even though all four sides aren't present. All these laws operate to create the most stable, consistent, and simple figures possible within a given retinal array. Taken altogether, this process is called the **law of prägnanz**. Prägnanz encompasses the other laws and says that perceptual organization will always be as regular, simple, and symmetric as possible.

GESTALT LAWS OF ORGANIZATION	
Law	**Description**
Proximity	Elements close to one another tend to be perceived as a unit
Similarity	Elements that are similar to one another tend to be grouped together
Good continuation	Elements that appear to follow in the same direction tend to be grouped together
Closure	The tendency to see incomplete figures as being complete
Prägnanz	Perceptual organization will always be as "good" (i.e., regular, simple, symmetrical, etc.) as possible

Gestalt psychologists have also considered how figure-ground configurations are represented in the brain. **Wolfgang Kohler** addresses this issue via the **theory of isomorphism.** The theory of isomorphism suggests that there is a one-to-one correspondence between the object in the perceptual field and the pattern of stimulation in the brain. Isomorphism hasn't fared well empirically, but the concept has appeared on the GRE Psychology test.

Modern theories of object recognition assume at least two major types of psychological processing: **bottom-up processing** (data-driven processing) and **top-down processing** (conceptually driven processing). **Bottom-up processing** refers to object perception that responds directly to the components of incoming stimulus on the basis of fixed rules. It then sums up the components to arrive at the whole pattern (such as in feature detection). **Top-down processing** refers to object perception that is guided by conceptual processes such as memories and expectations that allow the brain to recognize the whole object and then recognize the components. If we did only bottom-up processing, we would not be very efficient at recognizing objects; on the other hand, if we did only top-down processing, we would see only what we expected to see. The distinction between top-down and bottom-up processing is relevant for all senses, not just vision.

TYPES OF PROCESSING	
Type	**Description**
Bottom-Up Processing (Data-driven processing)	Responds directly to components of incoming stimulus on the basis of fixed rules and then sums up components to arrive at the whole pattern
Top-down processing (Conceptually driven processing)	Guided by conceptual processes such as memories and expectations that allow the brain to recognize whole objects and *then* the components

Motion Perception

There are five different ways to make a light look like it's moving: **real motion**, **apparent motion** (**stroboscopic movement**, or the **phi phenomenon**), **induced motion**, **autokinetic effect**, and **motion aftereffect** (**waterfall illusion**). **Real motion** involves actually moving the light. **Apparent motion** is an illusion that occurs when two dots flashed in different locations on a screen seconds apart are perceived as one moving dot. **Induced motion** is the illusion of movement occurring when everything around the spot of light is moved. The **autokinetic effect** is an illusion that occurs when a spot of light appears to move erratically in a dark room, simply because there is no frame of reference. Finally, the **motion aftereffect** occurs when you first view a moving pattern, such as stripes moving off to the right (or a waterfall), and then you view a spot of light: the spot of light will appear to move in the opposite direction.

ILLUSIONS OF MOTION	
Illusion	**Description**
Apparent motion (Phi)	When two or more stationary lights flicker in succession they tend to be perceived as a single moving light
Induced motion	A stationary point of light appears to move when the background moves
Autokinetic effect	A stationary point of light when viewed in an otherwise totally dark room appears to move; probably caused by involuntary eye movements
Motion aftereffect	If a moving object is viewed for an extended period of time, it will appear to move in an opposite direction when the motion stops

VISUAL CONSTANCIES

Before discussing visual constancies, it is important to distinguish between proximal stimuli and distal stimuli. The distal stimulus is the actual object or event out there in the world and the proximal stimulus is the information our sensory receptors receive about the object. In the case of vision, the proximal stimulus is the image on the retina. The task of perception is to appropriately perceive the distal stimulus.

If all we had was the proximal stimulus to perceive the world, the world would appear very chaotic. An approaching friend would appear to grow larger as she came nearer to you (remembering that the closer the object, the larger the retinal image). There are four major constancies in visual perception: **size constancy**, **shape constancy**, **lightness constancy**, and **color constancy**. These are all phenomena that help us make sense of our environment, by allowing us to make sense of retinal images.

In order to explain **size constancy**, we should first consider visual angles. The visual angle determines the size of the image on the retina. The two things that determine the visual angle (and thus the retinal size of the object) are the size of the object and the distance between the object and the eye. If the distance remains constant, the bigger the object, the bigger the visual angle, and thus, the bigger the retinal size. If the object size remains constant, the closer the object, the larger the visual angle, and thus the larger the retinal size. You can see a diagram of this in Figure 8.

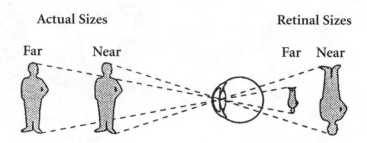

Figure 8. Distance and Retinal Size

So, if an object is first four feet away, and then eight feet away, the retinal size of the object is halved. However, our perception of the size of that object is not halved. In fact, our perception of the object's size probably stays about the same. It has been shown that the maintenance of size constancy depends on perceived distance. As it becomes harder to determine the distance of an object from the observer, size constancy diminishes.

Emmert's law describes the relationship between size constancy and apparent distance. It is not as important to remember the name of the law as it is to remember what the law, later generalized into the size-distance invariance principle, says. Simply stated, it says that size constancy depends on apparent distance. The farther away the object appears to be, the more the scaling device in the brain will compensate for its retinal size by enlarging our perception of the object.

Erroneous depth information confuses our notion of size in certain situations. Figure 9 is an illustration of one such example, the **Ames room**. In this example, the back left corner of the room is almost twice as far away as the back right corner, and there are distortions in the floor-to-ceiling height. However, if you view the room through the peephole provided, the trapezoidal shape of both the back wall and the windows at the rear of the room make the room look like a normal rectangular room, with a back wall apparently perpendicular to the line of sight. Thus, someone standing by the larger left rear window appears equally far away as someone standing at the closer right rear window even though the visual angles subtended by the two people are quite different. The person on the left appears much smaller than the equally sized person on the right because you have been fooled into believing that the difference in visual angles is not due to a difference in distance. Incidentally, the Ames room demonstration remains compelling even when you know what you're looking at.

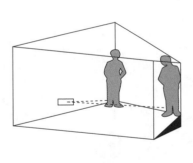

Actual construction

Perceived appearance

Figure 9. The Ames Room

Another illusion that involves inappropriate size constancy scaling is the **moon illusion**. The moon on the horizon appears to be larger than when the moon is at its zenith, despite the fact that both moons are the same size (in actuality and on the retina). One explanation is that the moon is seen larger on the horizon because of distance cues like buildings.

Another constancy is **shape constancy**: we see, for instance, a rectangular door as rectangular, even though, in the course of opening and closing the door, its retinal shape can be anything from a trapezoid to a rectangle to a rather thin line. Shape constancy scaling seems to have something to do with how we judge the relative depth of the different parts of the stimulus based on its retinal image.

Lightness constancy refers to the fact that, despite changes in the amount of light falling on an object (illumination), the apparent lightness of the object remains unchanged. So, for instance, even when the sun goes behind the clouds, the sail on a boat still appears white, rather than gray. This occurs because levels of illumination are the same for both the object and the background.

Color constancy refers to the fact that the perceived color of an object does not change when we change the wavelength of the light we see. So, for instance, when you put on amber sunglasses, you can still identify the colors of most of the objects you see.

VISUAL CONSTANCIES	
Constancy	**Explanation**
Size constancy	Tendency for the perceived size of an object to remain constant despite variations in the size of its retinal image
Shape constancy	Tendency for the perceived shape of an object to remain constant despite variations in the shape of its retinal image
Lightness constancy	Tendency for the perceived lightness of an object to remain constant despite changes in illumination
Color constancy	Tendency for the perceived color of an object to remain constant despite changes in the spectrum of light falling on it

VISUAL ILLUSIONS

An illusion is an erroneous percept. There are a few simple visual illusions that may appear on the GRE Psychology test. The most common illusions are the **Müller-Lyer**, **Hering**, **Ponzo**, **Wundt**, and the **Poggendorff illusions**. These are displayed in Figure 10.

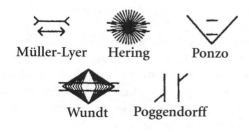

Figure 10. Visual Illusions

The two horizontal lines in the Müller-Lyer illusion are the same size, as are the two horizontal lines in the Ponzo illusion. In the Hering and Wundt illusions, the two horizontal lines are straight and parallel. Finally, in the Poggendorff illusion, the diagonal line on the bottom is a continuation of the diagonal line on the top.

Another type of illusion is a **reversible figure**. A reversible figure is a stimulus pattern in which two alternative, equally compelling, perceptual organizations spontaneously oscillate. A good example of a reversible figure is the Necker cube, pictured in Figure 11.

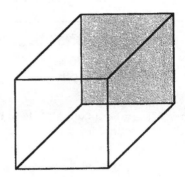

Figure 11. Reversible Figure

VISUAL PERCEPTION AND EXPERIENCE

Past experience has a large effect on perception. Over time, we develop perceptual sets that make perception, or (top-down processing), easier. Are babies, with limited experiences, therefore confronted by what William James called "a blooming, buzzing confusion"?

There are two major research methods for studying visual perception in infants: **preferential looking** and **habituation**. Fantz designed the **preferential looking** method. In this method, two different stimuli are presented side by side. The amount of time spent looking at each one is recorded. If there is a difference in the time spent looking at each stimuli, then it can be inferred that the infant can discriminate between the two stimuli, and the one the infant looks at the longest is the stimuli preferred. Fantz found that even very young infants prefer to look at relatively complex and socially relevant stimuli, such as a mother's face. They preferred to look at patterns rather that uniform surfaces.

The **habituation** method rests on the finding that when a new stimulus is presented to an infant, the infant will orient towards it. In this method, one stimulus is initially presented to the infant. Once the infant stops attending to this stimulus, the experimenter will introduce a new stimulus. If the infant cannot tell the difference between the old and new stimuli, the infant will remain disinterested. However, if the infant orients to the new stimulus, it is inferred that the infant can tell the difference between the old and the new stimuli.

Over the first two months of life, the visual areas of the cerebral cortex develop rapidly. At birth, infants are unable to discern fine details but are able to follow an object or light with their eyes when it is placed in the center of their visual field. Furthermore, newborns can perceive color, simple figures, sharp contrast, and can even see in dim light. As development continues, the baby's ability to see fine detail constantly improves.

Much work has also been done on infant depth perception. The primary tool in these experiments is the "**visual cliff**," developed in the early 1960s by Eleanor Gibson and Richard Walk. This clever setup assesses whether or not an infant is able to perceive depth. The visual cliff is a table set up to create the illusion that the left half of the table is much lower than the right half, so that it looks like there is a cliff in the middle of it. It's all very safe because the entire table is covered by a level piece of clear glass. The infant is placed on one side of the visual cliff while the child's mother stands on the other side of the visual cliff. Even at six months of age, infants will not attempt to cross that cliff. Therefore, researchers can infer that even very young infants can perceive depth.

It is difficult to separate out the contributions of nature and nurture to perceptual development in human infants without rearing them in visually impoverished environments. Since such procedures are unethical, researchers have relied on animal studies. Most find that experience plays an important role in the development of the visual system, and that there are sensitive periods during which the experience is maximally effective. However, it should be noted that the results of these animal studies do not necessarily generalize to humans.

METHODS USED TO STUDY INFANT VISUAL PERCEPTION

Method	Explanation
Preferential looking	Two different stimuli are presented side by side; if infant looks longer at one of them, it is inferred that the infant can perceive the difference between the stimuli
Habituation	A stimulus is presented to infant, infant eventually stops attending to it; a different stimulus is presented, if the infant attends to it, it is inferred that the infant can perceive the difference between the old and new stimuli
Visual cliff	An apparatus designed by Gibson and Walk to assess infant depth perception
Animal experiments	Sometimes used to assess contributions of nature and nurture to the development of vision

AUDITORY SYSTEM

Dimensions of Sound

Sound is basically just a wave of mechanical pressure and a sound wave can be described by specifying certain values. These values are the objective dimensions of sound. The only two you really need to be familiar with are **frequency** and **intensity**. **Frequency** is the number of cycles per second and is measured in units of **Hertz (Hz)**. One Hz is one cycle per second. Frequency is inversely related to wavelength. That is, the shorter the wave length, the higher the frequency. Human sensitivity ranges from about 20 Hz to about 20,000 Hz, with maximum sensitivity at about 1,000–3,000 Hz, depending on age and hearing ability.

Intensity, the amplitude or height of the air-pressure wave, is measured in **bels** (named after Alexander Graham Bell). However, since a bel is a rather large unit relative to normal hearing levels, we generally talk in terms of tenths of a bel, or **decibels**. The more decibels, the noisier the sound is. Sounds above 140 decibels tend to be painful to the human ear. Intensity is related to loudness.

There are at least eight subjective dimensions of sound. The three you should be familiar with are **loudness**, **pitch**, and **timbre**. Early researchers incorrectly thought that there were one-to-one correspondences between loudness and intensity and between pitch and frequency. Loudness can not be measured in decibels, and pitch cannot be measured in Hertz. For our purposes, **loudness** can be considered to be the subjective experience of the magnitude or intensity of the sound. **Pitch** can be considered to be the subjective experience or perception of the frequency of the sound. In other words, pitch is what distinguishes between a low tone and a high tone. We will be discussing some theories of pitch perception later on in this chapter. **Timbre** refers to the quality of a particular sound. So, for instance, even when played at the same pitch and the same loudness, a note on the piano sounds different from a note on the clarinet. Timbre is related to the complexity of the sound wave or the mixture of the frequencies.

DIMENSIONS OF SOUND	
Dimension	**Description**
Objective dimensions	
Frequency	The number of cycles per second; measured in Hertzes
Intensity	The amplitude of the sound wave; measured in decibels
Subjective dimensions	
Pitch	The subjective experience of the frequency of the sound
Loudness	The subjective experience of the intensity of the sound
Timbre	Refers to the quality of the sound

Structure of the Ear

There are three main parts to the ear: the **outer ear**, the **middle ear**, and the **inner ear**. A sound wave first reaches the fleshy part of the ear visible from the outside. This is called the **pinna**. The main function of the pinna is to channel sound waves into the auditory canal, also in the outer ear. The auditory canal channels the sound to the **eardrum**, also called the **tympanic membrane**. The membrane vibrates in phase with the incoming sound waves, moving back and forth at a high rate for high-frequency sounds, and more slowly for low-frequency sounds. Incidentally, a soft whisper displaces the tympanic membrane about four billionths of an inch, about the width of a single hydrogen molecule.

The middle ear has three tiny bones, called **ossicles**, which are the smallest bones in your body. These ossicles, common called the **hammer**, **anvil**, and **stirrup** (scientifically called the **malleus**, **incus**, and **stapes**) transmit the vibrations of the tympanum to the inner ear.

The edge of the stirrup rests on the **oval window**, which is the entrance to the inner ear. The inner ear contains the **cochlea**, which is filled with a saltwater-like fluid called **cochlear fluid**. There are a couple of membranes that run the length of the cochlea; the most important is the **basilar membrane**. The **Organ of Corti** rests on the basilar membrane along its entire length. The Organ of Corti is composed of thousands of hair cells. These hair cells are the receptors for hearing, analogous to the rods and cones in the eye. When these hair cells bend, the bending is transduced into electrical charges in some way not fully understood. These signals are then transmitted out of the cochlea along the nerve fiber, which then connects to other nerve fibers in the **auditory nerve**.

Hair cells bend when sound waves upon tympanic membrane cause the bones in the middle ear to vibrate. The movement of the last of the ossicles, the stirrup or stapes, causes the oval window to vibrate. This causes the cochlear fluid to vibrate at the same frequency. This vibration causes movement down in the basilar membrane, a traveling wave that in turn causes the hair cells to bump into the relatively immovable tectorial membrane above them. The movement of the basilar membrane due to vibration in the cochlear fluid causes the hair cells to bend.

The auditory pathways in the brain are a bit more complex than the visual pathways. The basic circuit is that the auditory nerve projects to the superior olive, the inferior colliculus, and the medial geniculate nucleus in the thalamus, and finally to the temporal cortex.

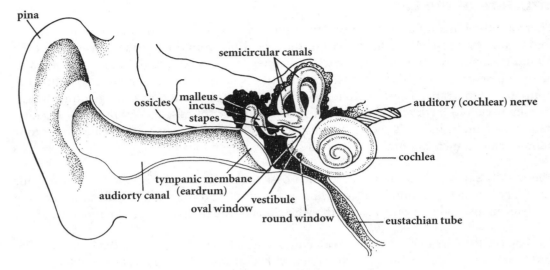

Figure 12. The Human Ear

Pitch Perception

Helmholtz's Place-Resonance Theory

The neural basis of pitch perception has something to do with the basilar membrane. It is the movement of the basilar membrane that determines our perception of pitch. According to **place theory**, proposed by **Helmholtz** and **Young**, each different pitch causes a different place on the basilar membrane to vibrate. These different places of disturbance would, in turn, cause different hair cells to bend.

Frequency Theory

An alternative theory, **frequency theory**, suggests that the basilar membrane vibrates as a whole, and that the rate of vibration equals the frequency of the stimulus. Further, this vibration rate is then directly translated into the appropriate number of neural impulses per second. If a tone of 500 Hz causes the basilar membrane to vibrate 500 times per second, the vibrations would cause nerve fibers in the auditory nerve to fire at 500 impulses per second, so the pitch is determined by the frequency of impulses traveling up the nerve. This theory, however cannot be applied to tones above 1,000 Hz. Wever and Bray modified the frequency theory by proposing the volley principle, which states that high rates of neural firing can be maintained if nerve fibers work together.

Békésy's Traveling Wave

In the early 1960s, **Von Békésy** found that the movement of the basilar membrane is maximal at a different place along the basilar membrane for each different frequency (although the whole basilar membrane vibrates for any given stimulus). High frequencies maximally vibrate the membrane near the part of the cochlea close to the oval window; low frequencies maximally vibrate near the apex, or tip of the cochlea. This is sometimes called Békésy's traveling wave theory. However, Von Békésy also found that low frequency tones, less than 400 Hz, maximally displaced a very broad part of the basilar membrane.

To sum up all the research, the frequency theory is operative for tones up to about 500 Hz, place theory is operative for tones higher than about 4,000 Hz, and both mechanisms are operative between 500 and 4,000 Hz.

OTHER SENSES

Taste and Smell

Taste, like smell, is a chemical sense. They both require receptors to have actual contact with the molecules that make up the stimulus. The receptors for taste are groups of cells called **taste buds** found in little bumps on the tongue called **papillae**. The **smell receptors** are in the upper nasal passage of the nose called the **olfactory epithelium**. Taste information travels to the **taste center** in the **thalamus**, while **smell** information travels to the **olfactory bulb** in the brain.

Touch

The sense of touch is actually quite complex and is generally described by four broad categories: pressure, pain, warmth, and cold. There are at least five different types of receptors that receive tactile information. They are the Pacinian corpuscles (deep pressure) Meissner corpuscles (touch) Merkle discs, Ruffini endings (warmth), and free nerve endings. Transduction occurs in the receptors, and information travels to the **somatosensory cortex** in the parietal lobe of the brain.

There are three concepts related to touch perception that are important to know for the GRE Psychology test: **two-point thresholds**, **physiological zero**, and **gate theory of pain**. **Two-point theory** refers to the minimum distance necessary between two points of stimulation on the skin such that the points will be felt as two distinct stimuli. The size of the two-point threshold depends on the density of nerves in particular areas of the skin. Temperature is judged relative to **physiological** zero, or the temperature of the skin. When we talk about feeling cold, it is likely that a stimulus has caused the skin temperature to drop below physiological zero. The **gate theory of pain** is associated with its authors Ronald Melzach and Patrick Wall, and proposes that there is a special "gating" mechanism that can turn pain signals on or off, thus affecting whether we perceive pain or not. The gating mechanism is located in the spinal cord, and is able to block sensory input from large, thick sensory fibers, before the brain is able to receive the pain signals.

TOUCH: KEY CONCEPTS	
Concept	**Explanation**
Two-point threshold	The minimum distance necessary between two points of stimulation on the skin such that the points will be felt as two distinct stimuli
Physiological zero	A neutral temperature perceived to be neither hot nor cold
Gate theory of pain	The theory that there is a gating mechanism in the spinal chord that turns pain signals on and off

Proprioception and the Vestibular and Kinesthetic Senses

Proprioception is the general term for our sense of bodily position and includes aspects of both the vestibular and kinesthetic senses. The **vestibular sense** has to do with our sense of balance and of our bodily position relative to gravity. The receptors for balance, the semicircular canals, are in the inner ear, above and behind the cochlea. They are depicted in the drawing of the ear (Figure 12). The **kinesthetic sense** has to do with the awareness of body movement and position, specifically, with muscle, tendon, and joint position since the receptors are at or near them.

BRAIN STRUCTURES IMPORTANT IN SENSATION AND PERCEPTION	
Structure:	**Sensory system:**
Lateral geniculate nucleus in the thalamus	Vision
Superior colliculus	Vision
Visual cortex in occipital lobe	Vision
Inferior colliculus	Audition
Medial geniculate nucleus in the thalamus	Audition
Auditory cortex in temporal lobe	Audition
Somatosensory cortex	Touch

ATTENTION AND PERCEPTION

Selective Attention

Donald Broadbent proposed that selective attention acts as a **filter** between sensory stimuli and our processing systems. If a stimulus is attended to, it will be passed through the filter and analyzed further. If it is not, it will be lost. According to Broadbent, selection attention is an all-or-nothing process if we attend to something, we don't attend to everything else. More recent evidence indicates that this is not the case.

The cocktail party phenomenon is one example of how you can attend to something you are interested in, while not totally ignoring background noise. You could be having a conversation with one person, when all of a sudden, your ears perk up because someone half a room away mentions your name. Despite the fact that you were attending to the conversation and not attending to the background noise, you heard your name mentioned. So it seems that selective attention is not an all-or-none filter, but more of a loudness control that dampens, but does not completely block out, ancillary stimuli.

In order to study selective attention in the lab, psychologists have used a technique called **dichotic listening**. In this technique, the two ears are simultaneously presented with two different messages. Generally, listeners are asked to shadow, that is, to repeat one of the messages as it is presented. Using this method, it has been demonstrated that observers can indeed attend to one message and dampen out the other one.

Yerkes-Dodson Law

Maintaining attention seems to depend, at least partially, on maintaining a certain amount of arousal. Common sense would probably lead you to think that the more aroused we are, the more attentive and competent we will be. However, studies relating arousal level to performance suggest that our common sense may be wrong. The Yerkes-Dodson law states that performance is worst at extremely low or extremely high levels of arousal, and optimal at some intermediate level. Figure 13 is a graphical representation of the Yerkes-Dodson law.

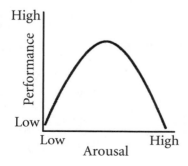

Figure 13. The Yerkes-Dodson Law

IMPORTANT NAMES IN SENSATION AND PERCEPTION

Békésy, G.	Empirical studies led to **traveling wave theory of pitch** perception which, at least partially, supported Helmholtz's place-resonance theory
Berkeley, G.	Developed a list of **depth cues** that help us to perceive depth
Broadbent, D.	Proposed **filter theory of attention**
Fechner, G.	Developed **Fechner's law**, which expresses the relationship between the intensity of the stimulus and the intensity of the sensation
Gibson, E. and Walk, R.	Developed the **visual cliff** apparatus, which is used to study the development of depth perception.
Gibson, J.	Studied **depth cues** (especially **texture gradients**) that help us to perceive depth
Helmholtz, H.	Developed **Young-Helmholtz trichromatic theory of color vision**; developed **place-resonance theory of pitch** perception
Hering, E.	Developed **opponent process theory of color vision**
Hubel, D. and Wiesel, T.	Studied **feature detection** in visual cortex and discovered **simple**, **complex**, and **hypercomplex cells**
Köhler, W.	Developed theory of **isomorphism**
Melzack, R. and Wall, P.	Proposed **gate theory of pain**
Stevens, S. S.	Developed **Stevens's law** as an alternative to Fechner's law
Swets, John A.	Refined **ROC** curves in **signal detection** theory
Wever, E. and Bray, C.	Proposed **volley theory of pitch** perception in response to a criticism of the frequency theory of pitch perception
Yerkes, R. and Dodson, J.	Developed **Yerkes-Dodson Law** which states that performance is best at intermediate levels of arousal

SENSATION AND PERCEPTION PRACTICE SET

Time: 8 minutes

<u>Directions:</u> Each of the questions or incomplete statements below is followed by five suggested answers or completions. In each case, select the one that best answers the question or completes the statement.

1. The tendency to perceive continuous patterns in stimuli is called
   - (A) good continuation
   - (B) closure
   - (C) proximity
   - (D) similarity
   - (E) linear perspective

2. Which of the following determine perceived size?
   - I. Retinal size
   - II. Perceived distance
   - III. Pupil size

   - (A) I only
   - (B) II only
   - (C) III only
   - (D) I and II only
   - (E) II and III only

3. The experiments of Hubel and Wiesel suggest a physiological basis for
   - (A) stereopsis
   - (B) visual feature detection
   - (C) depth perception
   - (D) color perception
   - (E) sound localization

4. A researcher has a subject place her hand in beaker one, which contains 105° F water. The subject reports that the water feels lukewarm. The researcher then has the subject place her hand into beaker two, which contains 140° F water. Following this, the subject again places her hand into beaker one and reports that the 105° water now feels cold. This finding is best explained by changes in
   - (A) physiological zero
   - (B) the temperature of the water in beaker one
   - (C) the room temperature
   - (D) the subject's response bias
   - (E) the subject's two-point threshold

5. Staring at a red stimulus for a while leads to a green afterimage. This supports
   - (A) Békésy's theory
   - (B) Hering's opponent-process theory
   - (C) Helmholtz's trichromatic theory
   - (D) Wever's volley principle
   - (E) the duplexity theory

6. The dispute between the place theory and the frequency theory has to do with the action of the
    (A) basilar membrane
    (B) ossicles
    (C) inferior colliculus
    (D) somatosensory cortex
    (E) fovea

7. An individual taking caffeine pills to stay awake during an all-night study session finds that he is incapable of writing his term paper effectively. Unable to sleep, he immaculately cleans his apartment. Such performance is best predicted by the
    (A) opponent-process theory
    (B) cocktail party phenomenon
    (C) filter theory
    (D) Yerkes-Dodson law
    (E) signal detection theory

8. Semicircular canals are involved in which sense?
    (A) auditory
    (B) kinesthetic
    (C) olfactory
    (D) vestibular
    (E) visual

9. In an experiment on vision, stimuli of different magnitudes are presented to a subject who is then asked to respond "yes" if he sees the stimulus and "no" if he does not. Using this procedure, the experimenter is likely to find that a subject with a high sensitivity will
    (A) say "yes" more times than "no"
    (B) have more hits than false alarms
    (C) have a high absolute threshold
    (D) have a low difference threshold
    (E) also have a high response bias

10. Which of the following statements regarding the perception of fine detail is (are) true?
    I.   Visual acuity is gained at the expense of color vision
    II. Your cones must be functional
    III. Light must hit the periphery of the retina

    (A) I only
    (B) II only
    (C) I and II only
    (D) I and III only
    (E) II and III only

EXPLANATIONS FOR THE SENSATION AND PERCEPTION PRACTICE SET

1. A

The tendency to perceive continuous patterns in stimuli is called good continuation. Answer choice (B), closure, has to do with filling in gaps in the stimuli and answer choice (C), proximity, has to do with judging that stimuli belong together because they are physically near each other. Answer choice (D), similarity, has to do with judging stimuli that belong together because they are similar. Choices (A), (B), (C), and (D) can be clustered together because they are all Gestalt laws of perceptual organization. Answer choice (E), linear perspective, is an outlier because it is a depth cue and not a Gestalt law. In a question of this format, an outlier is not likely to be correct. And if you were not sure which one of the Gestalt laws was being referred to, you could have made a good guess from the names alone based on your general vocabulary knowledge.

2. D

Retinal size and perceived distance determine perceived size. The retinal size of the image is a term used interchangeably with "visual angle" and is determined by the actual size of the object and its distance from the eye. We also mentioned in our discussion of size constancy that perceived distance has a lot to do with perceived size. However, pupil size has to do with how much light is let into the eye, not with perceived size. Therefore, since only Roman numeral statements I and II determine perceived size, the correct answer choice is (D). If you were unsure of which answer choice to choose, you could have used the Roman numeral strategy of considering answer choices that do include Roman numeral statements that you are sure should be included in the correct choice and eliminating answer choices that include the statements that you are sure should not be included. So, if you were able to rule out Roman numeral statement III, you could have ruled out choices (C) and (E), which would have left you with only three choices to guess from.

3. B

Make a strong association between Hubel and Wiesel and feature detection. Hubel and Wiesel discovered certain cells in the visual cortex that were involved in detecting various features of stimuli. While the only way to be sure that choice (B) is correct is to know the

association, you still could have narrowed down your choices by eliminating answer choice (E) with a fair amount of confidence since it is an outlier: It is the only answer choice that concerns audition. The first four answer choices all have to do with vision.

4. A

Physiological zero is essentially a neutral temperature that is perceived to be neither hot nor cold. We judge temperature relative to physiological zero, and what physiological zero is at any moment is affected by the context. Thus, whether a temperature of 80° Fahrenheit feels warm or cool depends on whether we have just left an air-conditioned room or a sauna. Likewise, whether the 105° F water feels warm or cold depends on what the subject's physiological zero is. The first time the subject dipped her hand in the 105° water, the hand's physiological zero was below 105°. Therefore, the water felt lukewarm. The second time the subject dipped her hand in the 105° water, the hand's physiological zero was at a very warm 140° F, so the water felt cold. Thus, what changed was the physiological zero. The temperature of the water in beaker one didn't change—it remained at 105°—and the room temperature didn't change.

Response bias, choice D, may have tempted you, but only if you didn't know the signal detection theory definition of the term. Response bias is based on nonsensory factors; even if some bias is introduced, there is also a major change in physiological zero. The two-point threshold (E) refers to the minimum distance necessary between two points of stimulation on the skin such that the points will be felt as two distinct stimuli.

5. B

Recall that Hering posits four primary colors: red, green, yellow, and blue and that these four colors are grouped into two opposing pairs: red-green and blue-yellow. A physiological basis for this theory has been suggested since certain cells have been found that are excited by blue light and inhibited by yellow light (and similar red-green cells have been found). If you've ever experienced afterimages, you'll notice that the color of the afterimage of a red stimulus is always green; the afterimage of a green stimulus is always red. The same relationship holds for blue and yellow. Notice how

Hering's theory allows us to predict the color of the afterimage. Thus, afterimages would appear to provide some support for Hering's opponent-process theory. Choices (B), (C), and (E) cluster in that they are all theories of vision while choices (A) and (D) are theories of pitch perception. Of the contenders—the (B), (C) and (E) cluster—choices (B) and (C) are more likely since they are, theories of color vision. Helmholtz's trichromatic theory really doesn't give us any basis on which to predict what color a particular afterimage would be. Helmholtz's theory suggests that there are three types of cones that are maximally sensitive to different wavelengths (which correspond to the primary colors of blue, green, and red). The duplexity theory of vision essentially states that vision is based on two types of cells—rods and cones—that differ in structure and function. It is too general a theory to be the correct answer here.

6. A

Recall that both the place theory and the frequency theory have to do with pitch perception. The place theory suggests that the neural coding of pitch perception depends on where the basilar membrane is maximally displaced, since different frequencies cause different areas of the basilar membrane to be maximally displaced. On the other hand, the frequency theory suggests that the important thing is the frequency of the vibration of the basilar membrane: that the basilar membrane vibrates in resonance with the frequency of the incoming sound. So the dispute clearly has to do with what happens at the basilar membrane. You may have correctly slected choice (A) by remembering the strong association between pitch perception and the basilar membrane. None of the other answer choices are associated with pitch perception. Answer choice (B), the ossicles, are the three small bones in the middle ear that send the auditory stimulus to the inner ear via the oval window. Answer choice (C), the inferior colliculus, is an area of the brain where auditory information is analyzed. The other two answer choices have nothing to do with audition. Answer choice (D), the somatosensory cortex is an area of the brain that has to do with touch, and the fovea, answer choice (E), is a part of the eye.

7. D

The first thing that you have to do is to figure out what's going on in the question stem. Keep in mind that we're looking for a theory or phenomenon that will best explain the *performance* of the student on the school and housekeeping tasks. This alone should be enough to eliminate (A) which is a theory about color vision. You may have also been able to eliminate choices (B) and (C) because they have to do with selective attention. Okay, so what's going in the question stem? Well, caffeine is a stimulant, so our student is pretty aroused. This alone may have clued you into the Yerkes-Dodson law if you recalled that it has to do with the relationship between arousal and performance. And, if you hadn't done it already, you should have ruled out choice (E), signal detection theory. Signal detection theory comes from psychophysics and it has to do with discerning a signal from unimportant background noise. Breaking down the name suggests that this choice has to do with perceiving signals, which is not going on here. So, by this point you could have arrived at the correct choice by process of elimination. Our moderately aroused student is unable to perform difficult tasks (writing a research paper) optimally, yet is fully capable of performing simple housekeeping tasks. And this points to the Yerkes-Dodson law. Remember that the basic Yerkes-Dodson law says that the optimal level of arousal for good performance is a moderate one. However, what we mean by moderate depends on how difficult the task is. The optimal level of arousal for easy tasks is higher than that for more difficult tasks.

8. D

Semicircular canals are involved in the vestibular sense. The vestibular sense has to do with our sense of balance and provides information regarding the rotation and position of the head. The semicircular canals contain the receptors for this sense. You may have confused this with choice (B), the kinesthetic sense, which concerns our awareness of skeletal movement and position. If you thought the correct choice was (A), the auditory system, you may have been misled by the fact that the semicircular canals are located within the inner ear.

9. B

Someone with a relatively high sensitivity would tend to have more hits than false alarms. That is, they would respond "yes" to the presentation of a signal more than they would say "yes" when no signal is presented. Sensitivity basically has to do with how often a subject responds correctly. A high sensitivity means that the subject is correct more often than he is incorrect. And this is what choice (B) indicates. Choice (A) is not correct because the percentage of "yes" and "no" responses has more to do with the subject's response bias, or decision criterion, than with his sensitivity. Also, saying "yes" more than "no" does not mean that the subject is correct more often than not, which is our concern here. Now let's look at the other choices. (C) and (D) both have to do with thresholds. If you recognized that this is a signal detection experiment, you may have quickly eliminated these choices. However, if you were uncertain of whether this was a signal detection vignette, you still could have ruled out these choices with a little more thought. Someone with a relatively high sensitivity would be very sensitive to the stimuli and would therefore be able to detect relatively low stimulus intensities. Consequently, we would expect this individual to have a *low* absolute threshold, and this means that she would be able to detect stimuli of low intensities. Therefore, answer choice (C) is incorrect. Furthermore, just by looking at the question stem, we can rule out choice (D). Based on the procedure listed in the question stem, the experimenter won't be able to find out anything about difference thresholds. Notice that the subject is only being asked to respond "yes, I saw the signal" or "no, I did not see the signal." If the experimenter wanted to determine a difference threshold, she'd have to ask if two stimuli were different from each other. Clearly, that's not what is going on in the question stem and, therefore, answer choice (D) is incorrect. Finally, choice (E) has to do with response bias. Response bias refers to the subject's tendency to say "Yes, I saw the stimulus" or "No, I did not see the stimulus." According to signal detection theory, sensitivity and response bias are independent. Someone with high sensitivity could have a high response bias or a low response bias.

10. **B**

Only Roman numeral statement II is true. Your recollection of the duplexity theory of vision, which refers to the different functions and characteristics of rods and cones, would serve you well here. Cones are needed for high visual acuity as well as color vision. With this in mind, you can eliminate Roman numeral statement I. Therefore, because you know that Roman numeral statement I cannot be included in the correct answer choice, you can eliminate answer choices (A), (C), and (D) as they all include Roman numeral statement I. Regarding Roman numeral statement III, recall that the cones are most concentrated, and therefore visual acuity is greatest, in the fovea, which is located near the center of the retina. As you move out towards the periphery, there are less and less cones and more and more rods. So, light that hits the periphery of the retina will stimulate rods, not cones. Therefore, Roman numeral statement III is incorrect: to discriminate fine detail, light should hit and stimulate the cones in the fovea.

CHAPTER EIGHT

Learning and Ethology

OUTLINE

Classical Conditioning

- Pavlov's Experiment
- Important Terms
- Explanations for Classical Conditioning

Operant Conditioning

- Thorndike's Law of Effect
- B. F. Skinner
- Types of Operant Conditioning
- Reinforcement Versus Punishment
- Discriminative Stimulus
- Schedules of Reinforcement
- Shaping

Behavior Therapies

- Classical Conditioning
- Operant Conditioning

Challenges to Conditioning

- Problem Solving
- Cognitive Maps
- Instinctual Drift

Ethologists

- Lorenz
- Fixed-Action Patterns
- Sign Stimuli and Releasers

Evolutionary Theory

- Darwin
- Fitness and Altruism
- Sociobiology

Learning and Ethology

The psychological study of learning and research concerning the way in which animals and people learn has been very productive over the past 50 years or so. In this chapter, we will review the history of the field, provide detailed explanations of classical conditioning and operant conditioning, discuss behavioral therapies, cover challenges to learning theories, and briefly discuss ethology and evolutionary theory as it relates to learning.

HISTORICAL PERSPECTIVE

Edward Thorndike (1874–1949) is one of the early psychologists who studied learning. He is considered to be a part of the **functionalist** system of thought, focusing on how the mind functioned in adapting to the environment. He is also considered to be an early behaviorist, since as a result of his study of the objective behavior of animals, he developed the **law of effect**, which formed the basis for operant conditioning. The law of effect is discussed in detail in this chapter.

One of the original experiments on learning that founded the behaviorist system of thought was a **classical conditioning** experiment that would be considered highly unethical today. In 1920, **John Watson**, one of the early founders of behaviorism, conducted an experiment with an 11-month-old child, Little Albert. At the beginning of this experiment, Albert was not afraid of white laboratory rats—in fact, he reached for them. Watson would present Albert with a white rat, and then make a startlingly loud noise behind Albert's head. Eventually Albert learned to associate the white rat with the loud noise. Albert began to show a fear response to the white rat, a rabbit, and even a mink coat. **Ivan Pavlov**, another name associated with classical conditioning, will be covered in detail in this chapter.

After Watson, **behaviorism** became the dominant system of psychology in the United States, and remained so until about 1960. **Clark Hull's theory of motivation**, or **drive-reduction theory**, suggested that the goal of behavior is to reduce biological drives: that is, reinforcement occurs whenever a biological drive is reduced. Other behaviorists such as **Edwin Guthrie** and **B. F. Skinner** will be covered in this chapter.

The 1930s, largely due to the work of **Konrad Lorenz**, marked the beginning of **ethology** as a recognized discipline. Lorenz rejected the idea that animal behavior could be understood in the laboratory. Instead, he believed that an understanding of animal behavior could be gained only out in the field. By observing the animal in its natural environment, he was able to describe the animal's behavior in great detail, and by studying the context in which a particular behavior took place, he could begin to analyze the function that the behavior served. Ethologists study animals in their natural environment, rather than in the laboratory.

CLASSICAL CONDITIONING

Classical conditioning, or **respondent conditioning**, is a result of learning connections between different events. For instance, we learn that thunder follows lightning, the smell of food is followed by dinner, and darkened lights in a theater mean that the movie is about to begin.

Ivan Pavlov is usually credited with the founding of the basic principles of classical conditioning. He noticed that through experience, stimuli that previously had no relation to a specific reflex could come to trigger that reflex. Pavlov made this discovery while he was studying the reflex of salivation of dogs in response to food. A **reflex** is simply an unlearned response that is elicited by a specific **stimulus**. For example, when food powder is placed into dogs' mouths, they reflexively salivate. The dogs don't learn this; it is reflexive. However, a specific type of stimulus is required in order for the salivation to occur. Dogs don't just naturally salivate when a bell is rung, for example, since the bell is a **neutral stimuli** in this example.

However, something interesting happened when Pavlov regularly presented a neutral stimulus—the ringing of a bell—*before* putting the food in the dogs' mouths. Initially, the dogs did not react much when they heard the bell ring. However, after this procedure was repeated several times, the dogs began to salivate when they heard the bell ring. In fact, the dogs would salivate even if Pavlov just rang the bell, and did not deliver any food. This is an example of classical conditioning.

Through repeated trials, the originally insignificant stimulus, the bell ring, became significant for the dogs. They came to realize that once they heard the bell ring, the food would soon be placed in their mouths. Technically, we can say that the bell ring became **paired**, or **associated**, with placing the meat powder in the dogs' mouths. Once this association was made, the dogs began to salivate when they heard the bell ring. In other words, the dogs had become conditioned to salivate in response to the bell ring.

The food was the **unconditioned stimulus** (UCS), which when placed in the mouth resulted in the **unconditioned response** (UCR) of salivation. These are called unconditioned because the animals' salivation is the natural response to the stimulus and didn't need to learned (conditioned). After conditioning, the new stimulus (the bell in this example) that elicits the response is called the **conditioned stimulus** (CS); the animals' response to the conditioned stimulus (salivation) is called the **conditioned response** (CR). They are both called conditioned because the animal had to learn to salivate to the bell.

CLASSICAL CONDITIONING: KEY PHRASES

Phrase	Explanation
Unconditioned stimulus	A stimulus that can reflexively elicit a response
Unconditioned response	A response reflexively elicited by an unconditional stimulus
Conditioned stimulus	A stimulus that, after conditioning, is able to elicit a nonreflexive response
Conditioned response	A response that, after conditioning, is elicited by a conditioned stimulus

A crucial factor in success of classical conditioning is the timing of the CS and UCS. Notice that in Pavlov's experiment, the CS was presented before the UCS; the bell ring was presented before the food powder. This is called forward conditioning. For classical conditioning to work, the CS has to be presented before the UCS. **Acquisition** is the term used to describe the period during which an organism is learning the association of the stimuli.

Once classical conditioning occurs, it can be unlearned through a process called **extinction**. In extinction, we repeatedly present the CS without the UCS. So, for instance, we would ring the bell, but not give the dog any food powder. If we do this repeatedly, the dog will eventually stop salivating in response to the bell ring. The conditioned behavior is not **reinforced**, and becomes extinct.

After extinction occurs, will the CS (the bell ring) never again elicit the CR of salivation? The answer is no. After a period of rest, presenting the bell ring without the UCS will actually elicit a weak CR of salivation. This is called **spontaneous recovery**. Of course, further extinction training will once again cause the animal to stop salivating to the bell ring.

Generalization is the tendency for stimuli similar to the CS to elicit the CR. In our example, the dog might begin to salivate to bells of a different pitch and/or timbre, or maybe even to chimes. We see evidence of stimulus generalization in phobias. For instance, if a child is bitten by a large dog, he is liable to fear not only large dogs, but also small dogs.

CLASSICAL CONDITIONING: SOME KEY CONCEPTS

Concept	Explanation
Forward conditioning	Presenting the UCS following the CS
Backward conditioning	Presenting the CS following the UCS; generally unsuccessful
Extinction	Repeatedly presenting the CS without the UCS
Spontaneous recovery	After extinction and a period of rest, presenting the CS without the UCS will again elicit a weak CR
Generalization	After conditioning, the tendency for stimuli similar to the original CS to elicit the CR

Classical conditioning appears to have limited usefulness for humans. After all, we can pair stimuli only when one of the stimuli (the UCS) elicits a reflex, and people have relatively few reflexes. Fortunately, two other classical conditioning phenomena expand the usefulness and applicability of classical conditioning tremendously.

In **second-order conditioning**, a neutral stimulus is paired with a CS rather than an UCS. There are two stages involved in second-order conditioning. Stage 1 is regular classic conditioning, for example, conditioning a dog to salivate to a bell ring. In stage 2, we present a new UCS stimulus—a flash of light, for example—just before presenting the CS (the bell ring), but without presenting the food powder. After several of these trials, the dog will salivate to the light flash alone. We could even do third-order conditioning by presenting the tick of a metronome followed by the light flash. Eventually the dog will begin to salivate to the ticking of the metronome.

In **sensory preconditioning**, two neutral stimuli are paired together and then one of the neutral stimuli is paired with an UCS. Once again, there are two stages involved here. In stage 1, we pair two neutral stimuli, say a flash of light and a bell ring. Remember that both of these are neutral stimuli. After several trials, we move on to stage 2, where we pair the bell with the UCS of food powder. After the animal salivates to the bell alone, we then test for the effect of sensory preconditioning by flashing the light without either ringing the bell or presenting the food. It turns out that even thought the light flash and the food were never directly paired, the light flash elicits salivation.

SECOND ORDER CONDITIONING VERSUS SENSORY PRECONDITIONING

Type	Stimuli presented during stage 1*		Stimuli presented during stage 2*		Stimuli presented during testing stage*
Second-order	CS,	UCS	Neutral,	CS	Neutral
	bell ring,	*food*	*light flash,*	*bell ring*	*light flash*
Sensory preconditioning	Neutral$_1$,	Neutral$_2$	Neutral$_2$ (becomes CS), UCS		Neutral$_1$
	light flash,	*bell ring*	*bell ring,*		*food light flash*

* Stimuli are listed in order of presentation; hence in the first stage of second-order conditioning, the CS is presented before the UCS. Stimuli in italics are the stimuli used in our example above.

Until the late 1960s, psychologists believed that classical conditioning occurred because the CS and the UCS were presented in succession. They believed that temporal contiguity of the CS and UCS were essential to the conditioning. However, in the late 1960s, **Robert Rescorla** performed some brilliant experiments that suggested classical conditioning was a matter of learning signals for the UCS. To the extent that the CS is a good signal and that it has informational value, or is a good predictor of the UCS, the CS and UCS will become associated and classical conditioning will occur. His approach is sometimes called a **contingency explanation of classical conditioning**.

Other researchers suggested that Rescorla's explanation didn't go far enough. Not only must the CS and UCS be contingent, the CS must also provide nonredundant information about the occurrence of the UCS in order for conditioning to occur. The relevant experimental procedure here is called **blocking**.

The original blocking experiment had two stages. In the first stage, rats heard a hissing noise and were then given an electrical shock. The hissing noise is the CS and the shock is the UCS. After repeated trials, the rats began to show fear of the hissing noise alone. In stage 2, the hissing noise and a light were presented at the same time, followed by the UCS. This procedure was repeated several times. Now there are two CSs: the hissing noise and the light. If classical conditioning were based on contingency alone, then we would expect the rat to show a fear response to the light. In fact, the light is as good a predictor of the UCS as the hissing noise is, and we know that rats showed a fear response to the hissing noise. Therefore, we would expect the light to become associated with the shock and would expect the rat to show a fear response to the light. However, when the light was presented alone, the rat did not show a fear response to it, thus providing evidence that the rats did not learn the association between the light and the shock. What's going on here? Well, the rat learned in stage 1 of the experiment that the hissing noise was a good predictor of the shock. In stage 2, the light provided no additional information useful for predicting when shock will occur, so the rats just ignored the light. Therefore, for classical conditioning to occur, it's not enough for the CS and the UCS to be contingent; the CS must also provide useful, that is, nonredundant, information about the occurrence of the UCS.

CLASSICAL CONDITIONING: EXPLANATIONS THAT HAVE BEEN PROPOSED FOR WHY IT WORKS	
Concept	**Explanation**
Contiguity	CS and UCS are contiguous (near) in time
Contingency	CS is a good signal for UCS
Blocking	CS is a good signal for UCS *and* provides nonredundant information about the occurrence of the UCS

OPERANT CONDITIONING

Operant conditioning, sometimes called **instrumental conditioning** or reward learning, is based on learning the relationship between one's actions and their consequences. Much of what you'll be reading about in this section is probably already familiar to you since you use operant conditioning principles in your daily life. Operant behavior is controlled by consequences.

One of the pioneers of operant conditioning was **E. L. Thorndike**. Around the 20th century, Thorndike proposed the **law of effect**: if a response is followed by an annoying consequence, the animal will be less likely to emit the same response in the future.

B. F. Skinner agreed with Thorndike's contention that environmental consequences affect the probability of response, but he rejected Thorndike's stress on mentalistic terms such as "satisfying" and "annoying." Skinner further developed the study of operant conditioning, distinguishing four important concepts: **positive reinforcement**, **negative reinforcement**, **punishment**, and **extinction**.

In **positive reinforcement**, the probability that the desired response will be performed is increased by giving the organism something it wants (reward) whenever it makes the desired response. Essentially, positive reinforcement refers to the case where you reward someone in order to increase the frequency of a particular behavior. For example, if you give your dog a biscuit (reward) every time he comes to your call, your dog will learn to respond in order to get a treat. Therefore, your dog will come to your call more often.

In **negative reinforcement**, the probability that the desired response be performed is increased by taking away or preventing something undesirable whenever the desired response is made. Negative reinforcers can be "turned off" once the desired response has been achieved. There are two types of negative reinforcement: **escape** and **avoidance**. In **escape**, the behavior removes something undesirable. For example, the loud annoying buzzer that tells you that your car seat belt is not fastened can be taken away by fastening your seat belt. In **avoidance**, the organism gets a warning that an aversive stimulus will soon occur, and the appropriate response completely avoids the aversive stimulus. For example, heeding the warning inherent in a stop sign: If you stop first before entering the intersection, you are likely to avoid a crash. In avoidance, your behavior stops an aversive stimulus from ever happening.

In reinforcement, whether positive or negative, behavior is being affected: it is more likely that you will, in the future, perform the same behavior under similar circumstances. In **punishment**, however, the probability that a response will be made is decreased by giving the organism something undesirable whenever the response is made. For example, sending a child to his or her room (something undesirable) because he or she wrote on the walls, decreases the probability that she will write on the walls in the future. When the stimulus is applied, it is punishment; when removed, it is negative reinforcement.

You might think that Skinner would define a reinforcer as something that is good, and a punisher as something that is bad. But that's not what he did. The goal of punishment is to decrease the probability of a particular behavior, while the goal of negative reinforcement is to increase the probability of a particular behavior. According to Skinner, we don't know whether something is a reinforcer or a punisher until we look at the effect it has on the behavior. For example, if a child is reprimanded for clowning around in class, is the child's behavior being reinforced or punished? The correct response is "it depends on whether or not the child's clowning around increased in frequency or decreased in frequency." If the child clowns around more after the reprimand, then the reprimand is actually a reinforcer. Maybe the child actually likes the attention he or she gets from the reprimand.

OPERANT CONDITIONING: BASIC TYPES

Type	Characteristic	Effect on Probability of Response
Positive reinforcement	Behavior is rewarded	Increases probability
Negative reinforcement		
Escape	Behavior removes something undesirable	Increases probability
Avoidance	Behavior avoids something undesirable	Increases probability
Punishment	Behavior causes something undesirable	Decreases probability
Extinction	Behavior that used to bring reward no longer does so	Decreases probability

Another important concept to understand related to operant conditioning is the **discriminative stimulus**, which is a stimulus condition that indicates that the organism's behavior will have consequences. We'll illustrate with a classic operant conditioning task: a pigeon pecking at a key to get a food pellet. The food pellet functions as a positive reinforcement, increasing the pigeon's pecking behavior. Above the key, we then place a light that illuminates periodically. When the light is on, the pigeon will get a food pellet whenever it pecks the key. However, regardless of how much the pigeon pecks the key when the light is off, it will not get a food pellet. So, the pigeon's actions can be reinforced only when the light is on. The discriminative stimulus, abbreviated as SD, is the illuminated light. This stimulus becomes a situation for operant response.

Generalization, a concept from classical conditioning, also applies to operant conditioning. Let's say that we train an animal to peck for food when a green light is on (the green light is the SD). After the training occurs, the animal will peck not only when the green light is on, but also when similar colored lights are on. In fact, the closer the color of the light is to green, the more likely the animal will peck. Generalization is an extremely important principle of learning.

Researchers have found interesting effects when partially reinforcing behavior. For example, if we train rat A that each time it presses a lever, it will receive food, and we trained rat B that every other time it presses a lever, it will receive food, they would both press the lever fairly often. If we began extinction training, however, where neither rat receives food after a lever press, in which rat do you think extinction will take the longest? Rat B. It turns out that it takes longer to extinguish the lever press for the rat who acquired the response while receiving only occasional reinforcement. This is called the **partial reinforcement effect**.

Gambling is another example of this effect. Once you sit down and begin gambling, it's hard to stop, even though your behavior is reinforced by only an occasional win.

There are four basic types of partial reinforcement, called **schedules of reinforcement: fixed-ratio (FR)**, **variable-ratio (VR)**, **fixed-interval (FI)**, and **variable interval (VI)**. In **FR**, the organism receives reinforcement only after a fixed number of responses, for instance, after every five lever presses, an animal receives a food pellet. In **VR**, the animal receives reinforcement after a varying number of responses. For example, on a VR 5 schedule, the animal will receive, on average, a food pellet for every five lever presses. On any particular trial, the food pellet could come on the second lever press, or the fifth lever press, or the 17th lever press. In a **FI** schedule, the animal will be reinforced on the first response after a fixed period of time has elapsed since the last reinforcement. For example, an animal on a FI 45 second schedule will receive the food pellet for the first lever press after 45 seconds have elapsed since the last reinforcement. On a **VI** schedule, the animal will be reinforced for the first response made after a variable amount of time has elapsed since the last reinforcer. However, in VI, there is an average time interval period. Using this terminology, what could we call the situation where the animal is being reinforced for every response? It's called FR 1 schedule, also called a **continuous reinforcement schedule (CRF)**.

In order to make the different schedules of reinforcement easier to remember, let's look at some human examples for each of these schedules. An example of a fixed ratio (FR) schedule in the work-place would be one in which a worker receives money for, say, every 1,000 envelopes stuffed. A classic example of a variable ratio (VR) schedule is a slot machine: dropping a coin in a slot machine will be reinforced, by winning, every so often. An example of variable interval (VI) schedule is a parent responding to a crying child. From the child's perspective, the response of interest is the crying and the reinforcement is the parent responding to the child. This is a variable interval schedule because most parents, after responding to a cry, will not go back to the child if she cries immediately after the reinforcement. Rather, the parent will usually wait a little while. So, a certain time interval has to pass before the child will be reinforced for crying. Exactly what that time interval is will vary depending on the situation.

The schedule most resistant to extinction is the variable ratio (VR) schedule. A good way to remember this is to look at the abbreviation for the name of this schedule. The variable ratio schedule is abbreviated VR, which can also stand for *very resistant*. By the way, the variable ratio schedule also produces the most rapid response rate of the four basic schedules. VR can also stand for *very rapid* response rate.

SCHEDULES OF REINFORCEMENT

Schedule	Definition	Example
Fixed-ratio	Behavior will be reinforced after a fixed number of responses	Piece work
Variable-ratio	Behavior will be reinforced after a varying number of responses	Slot machines
Fixed-interval	Behavior will be reinforced for the first response after a fixed period of time has elapsed since the last reinforcement	Going to office to pick up bimonthly paycheck
Variable-interval	Behavior will be reinforced for the first response after a varying period has elapsed since the last reinforcement	Parent responding to crying child (from child's perspective)

Shaping is another operant conditioning phenomenon. Let's say you want to train your dog to fetch your slippers. In order to do this, you'd have to wait until your dog actually fetched your slippers the first time so you could reinforce the behavior, so that your dog would fetch your slippers again, and so forth. The question is, though, would your dog ever fetch your slippers the first time? You'd probably be waiting forever because fetching slippers is not something dogs naturally do. In shaping, you reinforce successive approximations to the desired behavior. So, for instance, you might begin by reinforcing your dog every time she looks at your slippers. After she's doing that consistently, you would stop reinforcing her for just looking at your slippers, and reinforce her only when she walks toward your slippers. Once she's doing this consistently, you reinforce her only for picking up the slippers, and so on. This is an oversimplified example. Shaping would actually take longer than this, and would require much smaller steps. Shaping is sometimes called **differential reinforcement**. This is a technique whereby you reinforce the desired response while extinguishing others.

BEHAVIOR THERAPIES

Although conditioning is relevant in our daily lives, it is especially relevant for, and important in, the treatment of various psychopathologies. There are many psychotherapies based on conditioning models: they are called **behavior therapies** and/or **behavior modification**. We can divide behavior therapies into two groups: those based on classical conditioning and those based on operant conditioning.

Therapies based on classical conditioning are used primarily with phobias, but can also be used with obsessive-compulsive disorders. A phobia is an irrational fear. One explanation for phobia is that they develop through classical conditioning: a learned association between an aversive US and a CS, the CS being what the person became afraid of. Therefore, one of the simplest ways to get rid of a phobia is through extinction. By repeatedly presenting the feared object, the CS, without the associated US that originally elicited the fear, the fear response to the CS will decrease and will eventually be eliminated. However, this is easier said than done. For example, let's consider someone with a cat phobia. By definition, this fear is irrational. If the person is exposed to cats several times, the person would learn that there is nothing to fear. The fear response will undergo extinction. The therapist just needs to find a way to expose the client to the source of fear.

One way of exposing clients to their irrational fears is called **flooding**. In flooding, the client experiences the CS (in this case, cats) without the US that originally elicited fear. The therapist might, for example, force the client to hold a cat. After having experienced the cat-holding as harmless, the person learns that cats need not be avoided.

Implosion, another behavior therapy, works on the same principle as flooding, but here the client only imagines the fearful situation. In fact, in implosion, the client is asked to imagine the anxiety-producing situation. So, by intensely concentrating on the fearful stimulus in a way that nothing fearful can happen, the person is able to confront the phobia.

A criticism of both flooding and implosion is that they force the client to experience a great deal of anxiety at the beginning of the therapy. In order to reduce the initial anxiety, a psychologist by the name of Joseph Wolpe developed the technique of **systematic desensitization**. This process uses a hierarchy of anxiety-producing situations coupled with the use of relaxation techniques. The individual, while in a deeply relaxed state, is asked to imagine the least anxiety producing situation in the hierarchy. The principle is that an individual cannot experience these contradictory emotions (relaxation and anxiety) simultaneously. The individual then proceeds up the hierarchy until the relaxation responses are reinforced to the anxiety-invoking stimulus. This is called **counter-conditioning**.

Another therapy based on classical conditioning is called **conditioned aversion**. Aversion therapy is used when the client is attracted to a behavior that the client and/or therapist find undesirable. This therapy has been used to help, among others, people with alcohol problems, people with addictions to cigarettes, and people with various fetishes. In conditional aversion, the stimulus that attracts the client becomes paired with an aversive unconditioned stimulus associated with a punishment. The negative feelings will be associated to the undesirable behavior and the client will therefore no longer be attracted to the behavior.

THERAPIES BASED ON CLASSICAL CONDITIONING	
Therapy	**Explanation**
Flooding	Forcing the client to directly experience the feared object (the CS)
Implosion	Forcing the client to imagine the feared object (the CS)
Systematic desensitization	Forcing the client to imagine the feared object (the CS) while trying to ensure that the client stays relaxed by using deep relaxation and an anxiety hierarchy
Conditioned aversion	Pairing a desired CS with an aversive UCS

Therapies based on operant conditioning attempt to alter the consequences of the client's behavior. The goal of these therapies is to change the client's behavior by changing the reinforcement contingency that is associated with the behavior. The therapist utilizes different kinds of operant conditioning: positive reinforcement, negative reinforcement, punishment, and extinction to modify client behavior. This approach is generally called **contingency management**. Specific examples include: **behavioral contracts**, **time-out procedures**, **token economies**, and the **Premack principle**.

A **behavioral contract** is a negotiated agreement between two parties that explicitly states the behavioral change that is desired and indicates consequences of certain acts. Behavioral contracts are most often used where the goal of the therapy is to improve various interpersonal situations. In these cases, behavioral contracts generally state that one person will perform the behaviors desired by the second person in return for the second person performing the behaviors desired by the first person.

The idea behind the **time-out** is that the undesirable behavior occurs in situations that reinforce the behavior. Therefore, if you can remove the client from the reinforcing situation before he receives reinforcement for his behavior, the behavior will not be reinforced and will, therefore, eventually cease.

Token economies are given for desirable behaviors and are taken away for various undesirable behaviors. These tokens can later be exchanged by the client for a wide array of rewards and privileges. Token economies have been especially useful in mental hospitals where desirable behaviors might include aiding in self-care, making one's own bed, interacting well with other patients or staff, and so on.

The **Premack principle** simply states that a more preferred activity can be used to reinforce a less preferred activity. This principle is often applied by parents requiring children to do homework before they can play. If parents want the child to study more often they tell the child that he or she can play after studying for an hour each day after school. The parent would be using the more preferred activity, playing, to reinforce the less preferred activity, studying.

THERAPIES BASED ON OPERANT CONDITIONING

Therapy	Explanation
Contingency management	A general name for therapies that attempt to change the client's behavior by altering the consequences of the behavior
Behavioral contract	A written agreement that explicitly states the consequences of certain acts; useful in resolving interpersonal conflicts
Time-out	Removing the client from the potentially reinforcing situation before he can receive reinforcement for the undesirable behavior
Premack principle	Using a more preferred activity to reinforce a less preferred activity

CHALLENGES TO THE BEHAVIORISTS

Theorists challenging behaviorism have raised a very important question: Can all learning be explained by a simple conditioning model? Perhaps animals are more flexible and intelligent than the behaviorists think. To illustrate this point of disagreement, let's compare the research on **problem solving**.

E. L. Thorndike conducted a series of experiments to prove that problem solving is best explained by the **law of effect**. Thorndike would place a hungry cat in what he called a **puzzle box**. Essentially, a puzzle box is a cage that the animal can open by some simple action, such as pressing a lever or pulling a loop. He also placed a dish of food just outside of the box. As you might expect, the first time a cat is in a puzzle box, it will try almost anything to get out: meowing, biting the bars, striking out in all directions. Eventually, by chance, it happens to press the correct lever that opens the door. Once the cat gets out of the puzzle box once, it escapes the puzzle box at a quicker rate on each subsequent trial. Does the cat have a cognitive understanding or insight about how to get out of the puzzle box? Thorndike's answer was a clear *no*. According to Thorndike, this is merely trial-and-error learning. The correct response is reinforced by the food and the other responses are not. Thorndike argued that all problem solving was of the trial-and-error type.

Wolfgang Köhler (cofounder of the school of Gestalt Psychology) disagreed with Thorndike. Although Köhler conceded that the animals in Thorndike's experiment learned through trial and error, he suggested that those animals were forced into trial-and-error learning because of the situation. He argued that given the opportunity, some animals could learn by **insight**. Insight is the perception of the inner relationships between factors that are essential to solving a problem.

To prove his point, Köhler looked at problem solving in chimpanzees. He placed the chimps in enclosed play areas and placed food in their sight, but out of reach (suspended high above them). Typically, chimps would begin their efforts by trying to get the food directly, that is, by reaching for it. After that approach failed, they would typically stop and survey the situation. After a period of time, and often suddenly, they would try a different approach based on a novel way of using items in the cage. So, for instance, they would use sticks, or would climb up upon boxes to reach the food. To Köhler, this suggested that chimps used insight to solve the problem of the unreachable food. This presents a challenge to the models of conditioning we talked about before because it is difficult to explain insight on the basis of conditioning.

Köhler is not alone in suggesting alternatives to the simple conditioning model. **Edward Tolman** conducted experiments with rats in mazes to show that behavior isn't always simply a matter of stimulus-response reinforcement learning. The phrase to associate with Tolman is **cognitive map**. As the name implies, a cognitive map is a mental representation of a physical space. Tolman was able to show that rats were able to form cognitive maps of various mazes. If a familiar path through the maze was blocked, the rats were able to utilize their cognitive map to adopt an alternative route through the maze.

To challenge behaviorist theories, researchers also point to evidence that different species have different inborn predispositions to learn different things in different ways. These predispositions are called **biological constraints**, and they affect both classical conditioning and operant conditioning.

The **Garcia effect** (discovered by **John Garcia**) was illustrated in a classical conditioning experiment with thirsty rats. The rats in group A are allowed to lick a tube that releases water sweetened with saccharin. The rats in group B are allowed to lick another tube that releases unsweetened water while simultaneously flashing a light and making a clicking noise. For convenience, we'll call this water *bright-noisy water*. For half of group A and half of group B, the conditioned stimulus (the water) is paired with a pain-inducing shock, and for the other half of each group, the conditioned stimulus is paired with a nausea-inducing drug. The four groups of rats are diagrammed in Figure 1. In group 1, the pairing is between the unconditioned stimulus (UCS) of shock and the conditioned stimulus (CS) of sweet water. In group 2, the pairing is between the UCS of the nauseating drug and the CS of sweet water. In group 3, the pairing is between the UCS of shock and the CS of bright-noisy water. Finally, in group 4, the pairing is between the UCS of the nauseating drug and the CS of bright-noisy water.

		USC	
		Shock	Nauseating drug
CS	Sweet water	Group 1	Group 2
	Bright-noisy water	Group 3	Group 4

Figure 1. Garcia's Experiment

You would think that classical conditioning would occur in all four groups and that all the groups would show an aversion to the CS, regardless of whether the particular CS was sweet water or bright-noisy water. This is certainly what classical conditioning would predict. It turns out that conditioning was successful only for groups 2 and 3. Even though standard classical conditioning procedures were used, the rats in groups 1 and 4 did not show any conditioning. Those rats who received the UCS of nausea-inducing drug showed a conditioned aversion to the sweet water but NOT to the bright-noisy water. Conversely, the rats who had received the UCS of shock showed a conditioned aversion to the bright-noisy water but NOT to the sweet water.

Why does this occur? What we are seeing here is **preparedness**. The rats seem to have an inborn tendency to associate certain stimuli with certain consequences. Rats are biologically wired to associate illness with something they ingested and to pair sights and sound with externally induced pain. Hence, conditioning did not occur in groups 1 and 4.

We see this kind of thing in humans as well. People tend to associate illness with something they've eaten. This can be a serious problem with cancer patients receiving chemotherapy. Certainly, they understand that the treatment is making them ill and not the food they eat, but the biological wiring causes some aversions to food anyway. Researchers are trying to avoid this problem by giving the patients some novel food, for instance, a new and strange flavor of ice cream, to eat right before the treatment. It's helpful if the patients develop an aversion to a food they will never come across outside of the chemotherapy situation instead of developing an aversion to a nutritive food.

These studies of taste-aversion learning have also posed additional problems for classical conditioning. First, learned taste aversion can occur after only one trial. One pairing of the CS and UCS is all it takes. This is unlike most of classical conditioning where many trials are required for the conditioning to fully develop. Second, subsequent experiments on taste-aversion learning have shown that such learning can take place even if the UCS occurs up to 24 hours after the CS. Usually, the optimal time period between the CS and UCS is several seconds after the CS. But typically, if you become ill up to 24 hours after eating a new food, you will probably be averse to eating any more of that food.

Biological constraints are also vitally important in operant conditioning. One such constraint is **instinctual drift**. We've suggested to you that operant conditioning can be used to teach animals to do some pretty amazing things. This is certainly true, and in fact, you've probably seen some examples on TV. You might have seen the pigeons who play table tennis or the dog who can plunk out simple tunes on a toy piano. **Keller** and **Marion Breland**, like most other behavioral psychologists in the 1950s, believed that operant conditioning could be used to train animals to do pretty much anything. However, they soon discovered otherwise.

The Brelands used shaping in an attempt to train a raccoon to pick up coins and deposit them into a piggy bank. First they reinforced the raccoon for picking up a coin, then they reinforced the raccoon for picking up the one coin and depositing it into the bank. However, this proved to be somewhat difficult. Upon picking up the coin, the raccoon didn't want to put it in the piggy bank. The raccoon would rub the coin against the container, clutch it, and let it drop into the piggy bank only after a fair amount of hesitation. Then next step, reinforcing the raccoon for picking up two coins at the same time and putting them both into the piggy bank, was not at all successful. The raccoon would pick up the two coins, rub them together, dip them partly into the bank, and then take them out again. The raccoon never did learn to drop the two coins into the bank. What's going on here? Instinctual drift. The raccoon was reverting to a species-specific behavior pattern. When raccoons catch crayfish, they instinctively rub the crayfish and dip them into water to remove the shell. That's essentially what the raccoon was doing with the coins.

Albert Bandura demonstrated by this classic "Bobo doll" experiment that behavior could be learned by observation, or what he termed **vicarious reinforcement**. See the social psychology chapter for a discussion of this experiment.

CHALLENGES TO BEHAVIORISM: BASIC CONCEPTS	
Concept	**Description**
Problem-solving	
Thorndike (behaviorist)	Problem solving due to trial-and-error learning
Köhler	Problem solving is insightful
Cognitive maps (Tolman)	Animals have mental maps of physical spaces
Observational learning (Bandura)	Observing others' behavior can affect your own behavior
Preparedness (Garcia)	Animals are prepared to learn connections between certain stimuli
Instinctual drift (the Brelands)	Instinctual ways of behaving are able to override behaviors learned through operant conditioning

Ethology

Ethology is the study of animal behavior under natural conditions, and is radically different from behaviorism. The evidence pointing to the effects of biological constraints on learning was of no surprise to ethologists. Ethologists tended to concern themselves with behaviors that are characteristic of a particular species: **species-specific**, or **species-typical behaviors.** Since species-specific behaviors tend to have an instinctual basis, the early ethologists tended to look at instinctual behavior. This contrasted with the behaviorists who concerned themselves with learned behavior. Ethologists also employ different research methods than other psychologists. Recall that the behaviorists tend to bring the animals into the lab and study only simple behaviors such as salivation, key-pecking, and lever-pressing. In contrast, ethologists observe animal behavior in the animal's natural habitat and tend to look at more complex behavior.

As mentioned earlier in this chapter, Konrad Lorenz's research established the field of ethology. Some of his work, specifically, his research on imprinting, was discussed in the chapter on developmental psychology. Other ethologists, like **Niko Tinbergen**, introduced experimental methods into the field, enabling the construction of controlled conditions outside of a laboratory.

If you observed the behavior of animals in their natural habitat, you would observe that certain action patterns are relatively stereotyped and appear to be species-typical. These actions are called **fixed-action patterns** (**FAP**). Because they are considered innate, it is perhaps easy to confuse an FAP with a Pavlovian unconditioned response, which is also considered to be innate. The difference is that an FAP tends to be more complex than a Pavlovian unconditioned response. So, for instance, an unconditioned response might be something like salivation or an eyeblink whereas an FAP might be something like rolling an egg back to a nest, or a species-typical courtship ritual.

FAP's are triggered by **sign stimuli** or **releasers**. In general, a specific FAP will be elicited by only one sign stimulus or releaser. Although sign stimuli and releasers are often used interchangeably, there is a difference between the two. Sign stimuli are features of a stimulus that are sufficient to bring about a particular FAP. Releasers, on the other hand, are sign stimuli that function as signals from one animal to another. A release is a particular environmental stimulus that sets off a specific behavior.

For an example of a sign stimulus, let's look at one of the most famous experiments in ethology: Tinbergen's experiment on aggression in male sticklebacks. The stickleback is a fish whose males establish territories during the spring breeding season. If a male swims into the territory of another male, he's likely to be attacked. Tinbergen and his associates found that the red belly of the invading stickleback was the most important element in triggering the aggressive behavior, since even a crude model with the belly painted red was apt to be attacked. Therefore, a red belly is a sign stimulus, and in fact, also a releaser, which triggers aggression in male sticklebacks during the spring.

One of the interesting things about this experiment was that Tinbergen was able to design a model that elicited the aggressive response more often than an actual male stickleback. A stimulus that is more effective at triggering the FAP than the actual stimulus found in nature is called a **supernormal stimulus**.

The fixed-action pattern follows automatically once the organism perceives the sign stimulus. In fact, even if the stimulus is removed in the middle of the behavioral sequence the animal will continue to perform the actions as if the stimulus was still present. Because of this, ethologists have suggested that there must be some mechanism in the animal's nervous system that serves to connect the stimulus with the right response. They call this mechanism an **innate releasing mechanism** (**IRM**).

ETHOLOGY: BASIC CONCEPTS	
Concept	**Explanation**
Fixed-action patterns (FAP)	A stereotyped behavior sequence that does not have to be learned by the animal
Sign stimuli	Features of a stimulus sufficient to bring about a particular FAP
Releaser	A sign stimulus that triggers social behaviors between animals
Supernormal stimulus	A model more effective at triggering an FAP than the actual sign stimulus found in nature
Innate releasing mechanism (IRM)	A mechanism in the animal's nervous system that connects sign stimuli with the correct FAPs

Reproductive isolating mechanisms are behaviors that prevent animals of one species from attempting to mate with animals of a closely related species. They work by providing an animal with a way of identifying others of its own species. An example is the species-specific call given by black-headed gull males, enabling black-headed gull females to find them. Isolating mechanisms are found only in locations where closely related species share a common environment.

In other research, **Karl von Frisch** and others have found that honey bees are able to communicate the direction and the distance of a food source to their fellow hive members by means of special movement patterns, often called dances. The mechanism is a complex one and an infinite source of interest to ethologists.

The picture of ethology presented so far is a bit outdated, and in that sense, perhaps a bit misleading. Modern ethologists tend to deemphasize the instinctual bases of behavior and focus more on the question of *why* the animal behaves as it does and not in some other manner. To answer the question, ethologists attempt to discover the evolutionary significance of various behaviors.

Charles Darwin believed that **natural selection** is the key to evolution. His theory is based on the premise that not every member of a species is equally successful at surviving and reproducing. Furthermore, there is variation between individual members of the same species, and at least some of this variation has a genetic basis. To the extent that a genetic variation increases the chances of reproduction, it will tend to be passed down to the next generation.

DARWIN'S THEORY OF NATURAL SELECTION: STEP-BY-STEP

Step 1: There are genetic differences between members of a species.

Step 2: If a specific genetic variation increases the chances of reproduction, it will tend to be passed down to the next generation.

If a specific genetic variation decreases the chances of reproduction, it will tend to not be passed down to the next generation.

Step 3: Over time, more and more members of the species will tend to have the genetic variation that increases their chance of reproduction and less and less of the species will tend to have the genetic variation that decreases their chance of reproduction.

What does all this have to do with behavior? To talk about this, we need to introduce the concept of **reproductive fitness**, or the number of offspring that live to be old enough to reproduce. It is suggested that animals will act to increase their reproductive fitness. If the animal's behavior decreases its reproductive fitness, it's called **altruism**. Altruism is difficult to explain with classical Darwinian theory. Since the altruist is putting itself in danger, and if doing so does not help its offspring (or potential offspring), the behavior will actually decrease its reproductive fitness. However, animals are known to put themselves at risk for fellow species-members.

The **theory of kin selection** suggests that animals act to increase their **inclusive fitness**, rather than their reproductive fitness. Inclusive fitness takes into account not only the number of offspring who survive to reproductive age, but also the number of your other relatives who survive to reproductive age.

FITNESS AND ALTRUISM		
Type of Fitness	**Characteristic**	**Relationship to Altruism***
Reproductive fitness	Takes into account the number of offspring that live to be old enough to reproduce	Altruism is problematic
Inclusive fitness	Takes into account the number of offspring that live to be old enough to reproduce and the number of other relatives who live to reproductive age	Altruism is not problematic

* In this context, altruism can be defined as an action that increases the reproductive fitness of other members of the species while decreasing your own.

Modern ethology is generally considered to be a branch of biology, zoology, or **sociobiology**, which studies how various social behaviors increase fitness. The scientist most associated with sociobiology is **E. O. Wilson**. Wilson is adamant in his belief that behavior is due to a complex and dynamic interplay between genetics and the environment. The goal of ethology is to test hypotheses about the effect of social behavior on fitness.

IMPORTANT NAMES IN LEARNING AND ETHOLOGY

Bandura, A.	Studied **observational learning**
Breland, K. and Breland, M.	Discovered and studied **instinctual drift**
Darwin, C.	Proposed a **theory of evolution** with **natural selection** as its centerpiece
Garcia, J.	Studied **taste-aversion learning** and proposed that some species are biologically prepared to learn connections between certain stimuli
Köhler, W.	Studied insight in **problem solving**
Lorenz, K.	Ethologist who studied **unlearned**, **instinctual behaviors** in the natural environment
Pavlov, I.	Discovered the basic principles of **classical conditioning**
Premack, D.	Suggested the **Premack principle**: that a more-preferred activity could be used to reinforce a less-preferred activity
Rescorla, R.	Performed experiments which showed that **contiguity could not fully explain classical conditioning**; proposed **contingency theory of classical conditioning**
Skinner, B. F.	Developed principles of **operant conditioning**
Thorndike, E.	Proposed the **law of effect**; used **puzzle boxes** to study problem solving in cats
Tinbergen, N.	Ethologist who introduced **experimental methods** into **field situations**
von Frisch, K.	Ethologist who studied **communication in honey bees**
Watson, J.	Performed experiment on **Little Albert** that suggested that the **acquisition of phobias** was **due to classical conditioning**
Wilson, E. O.	Developed **sociobiology**
Wolpe, J.	Developed method of **systematic desensitization** to eliminate phobias

LEARNING AND ETHOLOGY PRACTICE SET

Time: 8 minutes

<u>Directions:</u> Each of the questions or incomplete statements below is followed by five suggested answers or completions. In each case, select the one that best answers the question or completes the statement.

1. Which of the following types of operant conditioning increase(s) the probability of a particular response?

    I.   Positive reinforcement
    II. Negative reinforcement
    III. Punishment

    (A) I only
    (B) II only
    (C) III only
    (D) I and II only
    (E) II and III only

2. E. O. Wilson is a major proponent of

    (A) operant conditioning
    (B) classical conditioning
    (C) sociobiology
    (D) altruism
    (E) instinctual drift

3. You turn on the can opener to open the dog food and your dog begins to salivate. The sound of the can opener is a(n)

    (A) unconditioned stimulus
    (B) conditioned response
    (C) unconditioned response
    (D) conditioned stimulus
    (E) neutral response

4. If a CS becomes associated with a UCS, and then later, a neutral stimulus is paired with the CS but not the UCS, will the neutral stimulus elicit a conditioned response?

    (A) Yes, because of sensory preconditioning
    (B) Yes, because of second-order conditioning
    (C) No, because the neutral stimulus is never associated with the UCS
    (D) Yes, but only if the neutral stimulus is similar to the CS
    (E) No, because only the UCS can elicit the CR

5. If it works as planned, which of the following is the best example of escape?

    (A) A client misses a session, so the therapist charges an extra fee
    (B) A teacher gives detention to all late students
    (C) A parent rescinds a curfew because a child gets good grades
    (D) A doctor gives a lollipop to all children who do not cry when they get a shot
    (E) A child is warned that if he doesn't clean his room, he will be punished. The child cleans his room.

6. If a teacher wanted to get an extremely shy student to participate in class events using shaping she might

    (A) reprimand the child each time he does not participate
    (B) utilize a time-out procedure
    (C) write a note to the child's parents
    (D) initially reinforce the student each time he looked up from his desk
    (E) only reinforce the child for speaking up

7. Which of the following is NOT based on operant conditioning?

    (A) contingency management
    (B) behavioral contracting
    (C) implosion
    (D) token economies
    (E) Premack principle

8. Köhler's experiment on chimpanzee problem solving demonstrated that

    (A) insight can be explained by trial-and-error learning
    (B) not all learning is trial-and-error
    (C) trial-and-error learning never occurs
    (D) chimpanzees used cognitive maps to find the bananas
    (E) chimpanzees do not learn by trail and error

9. Which of the following best states John Garcia's major contribution to classical conditioning?

    (A) Classical conditioning is based on contingency
    (B) Classical conditioning is due to instinctual drift
    (C) Classical conditioning is actually a type of operant conditioning
    (D) Classical conditioning is affected by the animals' biological make-up
    (E) Classical conditioning is based on contiguity alone

10. Which of the following was instrumental in the founding of ethology?

    (A) E. L. Thorndike
    (B) John Watson
    (C) B. F. Skinner
    (D) Konrad Lorenz
    (E) Ivan Pavlov

EXPLANATIONS FOR THE LEARNING AND ETHOLOGY PRACTICE SET

1. D

Only positive reinforcement and negative reinforcement increase the probability of a particular response. The key to correctly answering this question was to remember that negative reinforcement is *not* the same as punishment and that in negative reinforcement the response removes something, or the threat of something, that is undesirable to the behaver. Roman numeral options I and II both increase the probability of a particular response, and answer choice (D) is the correct one. If you did not know the correct answer, you could have used Roman numeral strategy to help you eliminate answer choices. In other words, consider those answer choices which *do* include options you are sure should be included in the correct choice and eliminate those answer choices that include options you are sure should *not* be included to narrow down your choices.

2. C

E. O. Wilson is a major proponent of sociobiology. Sociobiology is a branch of science that investigates the effect various social behaviors have on fitness. Choices (A) and (B) are both incorrect. The major proponent of operant conditioning was B. F. Skinner and the major proponent of classical conditioning was Ivan Pavlov. Choice (E) is also incorrect. Instinctual drift refers to the fact that certain instinctive behaviors can override learned behaviors when the two are in conflict. The main psychologists here have been Marion and Keller Breland. Answer choice (D) might have tempted some of you. Although sociobiology does try to explain altruism, Wilson is primarily known as a sociobiologist exploring a range of social behaviors and their effect on fitness.

3. D

The sound of the can opener is a conditioned stimulus. Recall that a conditioned stimulus is a previously neutral stimulus that became associated with an unconditioned stimulus, and so began to elicit the conditioned response. In this case, the unconditioned stimulus is the food and the conditioned response is the salivation. The first time the dog heard the can opener, it did not salivate. However, eventually, the dog learned to salivate to the can opener. Choices (A) and (C) are both incorrect. The sound of the can opener is neither the unconditioned stimulus nor the unconditioned

response. Recall that the unconditioned stimulus elicits the unconditioned response. The animal does not need to learn this connection: it occurs automatically. In this case, the unconditioned stimulus is the food and the unconditioned response is the salivation in response to the food. The animal does not need to learn to salivate to the food: it does so automatically. Therefore, these are both unconditioned. (B) is wrong; the conditioned response is the salivation at the sound of the can opener. Answer choice (E) might have tempted some of you. Although there is no such thing as a neutral response, there is such a thing as a neutral stimulus. Recall that a neutral stimulus is a stimulus that has not previously been associated with the unconditioned stimulus. The sound of the can opener was a neutral stimulus prior to the conditioning.

4. B

The neutral stimulus will elicit a conditioned response because of second-order conditioning. Recall that second-order conditioning consists of two stages. The first stage consists of classical conditioning where a CS becomes associated with a UCS. In the second stage, the CS becomes paired with a neutral stimulus. We know that second-order conditioning occurred because when we now present the neutral stimulus alone, it elicits the CR. Because this procedure is precisely what is being described in the question stem, the correct answer choice is (B). Answer choice (A) is incorrect. Although it is true that the neutral stimulus will elicit the CR, this is due to second-order conditioning and not to sensory preconditioning. Recall that the major difference between second-order conditioning and sensory preconditioning is the order of the two stages. In the first stage of sensory preconditioning, two neutral stimuli become associated and in the second stage, classical conditioning takes place between a UCS and one of the neutral stimuli, which then becomes a CS. This is not what is being described in the question stem. Answer choice (C) is also incorrect. As we've discussed, the neutral stimulus will elicit the CR. Answer choice (D) may have tempted some of you. It is true that a neutral stimulus that is similar to the CS will tend to elicit the conditioned response. This is called stimulus generalization. However, the question stem provides a description of second-order conditioning and in second-order conditioning, the neutral stimulus does not have to be similar to the CS in order to elicit the conditioned response. Finally, answer choice (E) is also incorrect. Remember that an unconditioned stimulus elicits an unconditioned response and that a conditioned stimulus elicits a conditioned response. An unconditioned stimulus cannot elicit a conditioned response.

5. C

Recall that in escape, something undesirable is removed by the behavior. The undesirable thing here is the curfew, and, if the child gets good grades, it will be removed. Therefore, the correct answer choice is (C). Let's contrast this with answer choice (E). Answer choice (E) is an example of avoidance. Choice (E) might have tempted you because both escape and avoidance are types of negative reinforcement. In avoidance, however, the organism is given a warning that an aversive stimulus is imminent. If the organism heeds the warning by making the appropriate response, the aversive stimulus will be completely avoided. Answer choice (A) is punishment. The fee that the therapist charges will reduce the probability that the client will miss another session. Answer choice (B) is also punishment. Finally, answer choice (D) is positive reinforcement. Giving the child a lollipop for not crying increases the probability that in the future, under the same circumstances, the child will not cry.

6. D

Shaping involves differentially reinforcing successive approximations to the desired behavior. The desired behavior in this case is participation in class events. We can't just reinforce the child when he speaks up, because the child, being extremely shy, is not likely to do so. If we want to shape, we begin by reinforcing something that the child does do and which is somehow related to the desired behavior. So the teacher might reinforce him, perhaps with a smile or a piece of candy, whenever he looked up from his desk. After the child regularly looked up from his desk, the teacher would cease to reinforce that behavior and would reinforce only the behavior of, say, nodding. After the child was nodding, the teacher would stop reinforcing that behavior and reinforce another behavior, until the child was being reinforced only for participating in class events. Answer choice (A) is an example of punishment. Answer choice (B), time-out, involves removing someone from the reinforcing environment as soon as she begins to perform an undesired behavior. Answer choice (C) is

incorrect. Although it might be appropriate to write such a note, such note writing is not a part of the shaping. Finally, answer choice (E) is incorrect. As mentioned above, the child is unlikely to speak up at all. If the child never makes that response, it could never be reinforced, nor would this be shaping.

7. C

Implosion is based on classical conditioning, not operant conditioning. In implosion, the patient imagines what it is that he fears. The theory behind implosion is that the phobia was formed when the CS, a neutral stimulus, became associated with an aversive UCS. This caused the CS to come to elicit anxiety and, thus, the client became phobic toward the CS. In implosion, the goal is to present (in imagination) the CS, the phobic object, without its associated UCS. Thus extinction of the anxiety should occur. Therefore, choice (C) is correct. Answer choices (A), (B), (D), and (E) are all based on operant conditioning. Contingency management is a general term that describes therapies based on operant conditioning. A behavioral contract is a written agreement that explicitly states the consequences—the rewards and the punishments—for various behaviors. Token economies are based on rewarding and punishing behaviors by awarding or taking away tokens. These tokens can then be exchanged for something desirable. The Premack principle holds that being allowed to perform certain behaviors can reinforce other less preferred activities. Therefore, the only item listed not based on operant conditioning is answer choice (C).

8. B

Not all learning is trial-and-error. Recall that Köhler did his experiment on problem solving in response to Thorndike's assertion that all learning was trial-and-error. Köhler was trying to demonstrate that at least some animals in some situations can solve problems not by trial-and-error, but by insight. To demonstrate this, Köhler placed chimpanzees in large enclosures and suspended bananas out of their direct reach. The chimpanzees were able to reach the bananas only when they used an object in their environment in a novel way. Typically, the chimps would begin by trying to reach the food directly. Upon failing, they would typically stop, survey the situation, and then suddenly realize that they could reach the bananas by using something in their environment as a tool. To Köhler, this suggested that the chimps were using insight to solve the problem. Furthermore, because of the suddenness of the solution, Köhler believed that insight could not be explained by trial-and-error learning. Therefore, answer choice (A) is incorrect. Answer choice (C) is also incorrect. Köhler did not believe that trial-and-error learning never occurred, just that learning didn't have to be trial-and-error. In fact, Köhler agreed with Thorndike that Thorndike's cats did use trial-and-error. By the same token though, Köhler believed that Thorndike's cats had to use trial-and-error because the experimental setup did not allow them to do otherwise. Choice (D) is also incorrect. The person who did the studies on cognitive maps was Tolman. A cognitive map is a cognitive representation of a physical space essentially, a map of what occurs where. Finally, answer choice (E) is incorrect. Chimpanzees, according to Köhler, learn both by trail-an-error and insight.

9. D

Classical conditioning is affected by the animals' biological make-up. Specifically, Garcia's experiment was on learned taste aversion. He found that rats were able to associate food with illness and light with shock but were not able to associate light with illness or food with shock. This suggested to him that animals had certain instinctual predispositions to associate certain stimuli and to not associate certain other stimuli. This was especially important because it showed that not every CS could be paired with a specific UCS and that what could or couldn't be paired was due to the animals' biological make-up. Therefore, the correct answer is (D). Answer choice (A) is incorrect. Recall that contingency refers to the CS being a good predictor of the UCS. Although it is true that classical conditioning is based, at least in part, on contingency, this was Rescorla's major contribution and not Garcia's. Answer choice (B) is also incorrect. Instinctual drift refers to the fact that nature has provided species of animals with certain built-in, instinctual, ways of behaving which are able to override behaviors learned through operant conditioning. Instinctual drift was a contribution of the Brelands who did their work on operant conditioning and not classical conditioning. Choice (C) is incorrect. Although there is evidence that operant and classical conditioning may interact with each other, it is not correct to say that classical conditioning is a type of operant conditioning. Finally, answer choice (E) is incorrect. Contiguity refers to the nearness in time of the CS and the UCS. It used to be thought that this was the basis for classical

conditioning, but we know now that it is not. In fact, Garcia's experiment on learned food aversions helped to disprove this. Garcia's rats were able to make the association between the food and the sickness even though, in some cases, the onset of the sickness did not occur until 24 hours after they had eaten the food. Since the food and the sickness occurred 24 hours apart, they are certainly not contiguous, and therefore, answer choice (E) is incorrect.

10. D

Konrad Lorenz was instrumental in the founding of ethology. Choice (A), E. L. Thorndike, is the psychologist who formulated the law of effect, which states that if a response is followed by a satisfier, the stimulus-response bond will be strengthened, and if a response is followed by an annoyer, the stimulus-response bond will be weakened. John Watson, choice (B), is the behaviorist who performed the unethical "Little Albert" classical conditioning experiments. Choice (C), B. F. Skinner, is the person you should associate with operant conditioning. Finally, answer choice (E), Ivan Pavlov, is the person associated with classical conditioning.

CHAPTER NINE

Cognitive Psychology

OUTLINE

Historical Perspective

Research Methods in Cognitive Psychology

Memory

- Ebinghaus's Experiments
- Encoding, Storage, and Retrieval
  - Retrieval Methods
  - Memorization
- Stage Theory of Memory
  - Sensory Memory
  - Short-Term Memory
  - Long-Term Memory
- Procedural Memory
- Declarative Memory
- Semantic Memory
  - Spreading Activation Model
  - Semantic Feature Comparison Model
- Levels-of-Processing Theory
- Paivio's Dual Code Hypothesis
- Forgetting
- Facilitating Memory

- Reconstructive Memory
- Eyewitness Memory
- Zeigarnik Effect

Thinking

- Problem Solving
- Creativity
- Decision Making
  - Heuristics

Language

- Theories of Language Development
  - Chomsky's Work
- The Relationship Between Language and Thought
  - Whorfian Hypothesis
- Gender and Language Development

Intelligence

- Charles Spearman and the *g* Factor
- Louis Thurston
- Robert Sternberg's Triarchic Theory
- Howard Gardner's Theory of Multiple Intelligences
- Raymond Catell's Theory

Information Processing

Metapsychology

> ## Cognitive Psychology
>
> Cognitive psychology is a broad and diverse field dealing with topics as varied as memory, language, creativity, problem solving, decision making, and intelligence. Some material on language is in the developmental psychology chapter; attention, a topic that is vital to our understanding of cognition, is covered in the sensation and perception chapter. In this chapter, we will discuss the history of cognitive psychology, memory, information processing, thinking, language, and intelligence.

HISTORICAL PERSPECTIVE

The history of modern memory research can be said to begin in 1885 with **Hermann Ebbinghaus**. His unusual experiments are among the most well-known in the field of psychology. Briefly, he used meaningless strings of letters to study the capacity of our memory system. We will cover the nature of his experiments in detail in this chapter.

Edward Titchener (1867–1927) belonged to the system of thought referred to as or specific **structuralism**. The goal of structuralism was to break consciousness down into its elements, or specific mental structures. To accomplish this, Titchener used the method of introspection: he asked subjects to report on their current conscious experiences. Not only did he study the higher mental processes, but he did so in a laboratory setting. Titchener's work spawned three other systems of thought in reaction to structuralism: **functionalism**, **behaviorism**, and **Gestalt psychology**. It is also noteworthy to mention that Titchener was a Wundt-trained psychologist and that Wundt also relied on the method of introspection.

Noam Chomsky, a linguist, paved the way for modern cognitive psychology with an eloquent critique of B. F. Skinner's 1957 book *Verbal Behavior*. Chomsky opposed the behaviorist's position that speech is best explained by operant conditioning, that language is acquired by reinforcement. Chomsky argued that since children say things that they could not have heard adults say (e.g., errors in growth; see the developmental psychology chapter), and that since even adults use language in novel and creative ways, speech could not possibly be due to reinforcement. Chomsky believed that language study is the most viable route to understanding the mind. He is credited with inspiring much research on cognition. His ideas will be covered in detail in this chapter.

RESEARCH METHODS

Three general research methods are used in the study of human cognition. The measurement of the time elapsed between a stimulus presentation and the subject's response to it, or **reaction time**, has often provided insight into the organization of cognitive processes. This method is sometimes called mental chronometry. Measurements focused on **eye movements** have also been used to study reading and language comprehension. This method is especially useful because the eye movements are an "on-line" measure: that is, they can be measured as the subject is actually performing tasks. Finally, **brain imaging** has started to become more and more important as researchers have tried to associate various cognitive processes to various parts of the brain.

RESEARCH METHODS IN COGNITIVE PSYCHOLOGY	
Method	**Description**
Reaction time	Elapsed time between stimulus presentation and the subject's response to it
Eye movements	An "on-line" measure of information processing
Brain imaging	Used to associate various cognitive processes with various parts of the brain

MEMORY

Ebbinghaus's Experiments

Hermann Ebbinghaus's famous experiment used nonsense syllables—for example, QAS and CEG—to study memory using himself as subject. He would memorize the items in the list, one at a time and in the order they appeared on the list. After one list, he distracted himself by trying to learn many other such lists. Ebbinghaus measured how much of the original list he remembered by using what he called the **method of savings**. In the method of savings, after memorizing the initial list, he compared the number of times he had to read the list in order to rememorize it. If he rememorized the list faster than he originally memorized it, he concluded that he had remembered something from the first time. To quantify the amount of savings, Ebbinghaus subtracted the number of trials it took to rememorize the list from the number of trials it originally took to memorize the list. He then divided this quantity by the original number of trials and multiplied everything by 100 to come up with a percent.

Let's say it takes you 20 trials to memorize a list. On the next day, you rememorize the list, but this time it takes you only eight trials. You would subtract 8 from 20 and divide the result by 20, and multiply by 100. Your savings in this case would be 60 percent.

By using this method over various time intervals, Ebbinghaus came up with his **forgetting curve**, which is depicted in Figure 1. The horizontal axis indicates the number of days between the time the list was originally learned and the time the list was relearned. The vertical axis indicates the percent savings. Notice that the percent savings originally decreases rapidly, but then reaches a plateau after which decrease in percentage savings is minimal. In other words, without practice, we forget rapidly, then at a certain point (in this case, five days), forgetting occurs at a much lesser rate. With practice, however, this forgetting curve would look different.

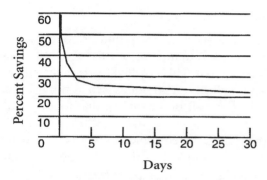

Figure 1. Ebbinghaus's Forgetting Curve

Ebbinghaus's study was so influential that for the next several decades, when psychologists studied memory for verbal material, they tended to use nonsense syllables. For the most part, although there were exceptions, the study of memory for meaningful material didn't really begin until the 1950s.

Mental Processes Involved in Memory

Modern theories of memory suggest that there are three mental processes or stages of memory: **encoding**, **storage**, and **retrieval**. Encoding involves putting new information into memory, storage involves retaining the information over time, and retrieval is recovery of the stored material at a later time. The tip-of-the-tongue phenomenon, where you feel like you're on the verge of remembering something, but continue to be unsuccessful doing so, is a problem with retrieval.

MENTAL PROCESSES INVOLVED IN MEMORY	
Process	**Definition**
Encoding	Putting information into memory
Storage	Retaining information in memory
Retrieval	Recovering the information in memory

The two most common methods of retrieval are **recall** and **recognition**. **Recall** involves independently reproducing the information that you have been previously exposed to. Short answer and fill in the blank questions tend to test recall. On the other hand, **recognition** involves realizing that a certain stimulus event is one you have seen or heard before. Multiple-choice questions tend to test recognition.

According to the **generation-recognition model**, a recall task taps the same basic process of accessing information in memory as does a recognition task. However, a recall task requires an additional processing step. You have to generate information rather than simply recognize information presented.

Researchers have found that under certain conditions, our memory system varies in effectiveness. For example, when asked to memorize a list of words, those words presented at the end of the list are remembered best. This is called the **recency effect**. The items presented first are also remembered fairly well, although not as well as things presented last. This effect is called the **primacy effect.** It's the stuff in the middle that we forget most often.

Another interesting effect that occurs when subjects are asked to memorize and then recall words is called **clustering**. For an example, let's think about what might happen if you were given the list of words below and asked to memorize them:

Bird
Dog
Pear
Purple
Red
Banana
Cat
Mango
Green

As you try to memorize the list, you would probably break it down into three clusters: animals, fruits and colors. When asked to recall them, you would probably recall the words in those clusters, listing the words in groups that go together.

MEASURING RETRIEVAL: KEY CONCEPTS	
Concept	**Definition**
Recall	Reproducing information you have previously been exposed to
Recognition	Realizing that a certain stimulus event is one you've seen or heard before
Generation-recognition	An attempt to explain why you can usually recognize more than you can recall; model suggests that recall involves the same mental process involved in recognition plus another process not required for recognition
Order effects	
Recency effect	Words presented at the end of a list are remembered best
Primacy effect	Words presented at the beginning of a list are remembered second-best
Clustering	When asked to recall a list of words, people tend to recall words belonging to the same category

Stage Theory of Memory

The **stage theory of memory** has been a very influential theory in cognitive psychology, and will likely appear on the GRE Psychology test. This theory holds that there are several different memory systems and that each system has a different function. Furthermore, the theory suggests that memories enter the various systems in a specific order. These three memory systems are called **sensory memory**, **short-term memory**, and **long-term memory** (incidentally, many psychologists today prefer to use the phrase *working memory* instead of short-term memory).

Sensory Memory

Sensory memory contains fleeting impressions of sensory stimuli. **Visual memory** is sometimes called **iconic memory**, and auditory memory is sometimes called **echoic memory**. Information does not last long in this memory; at most, for a few seconds.

To find out how much information could be retained in sensory memory, early researchers used a method called the **whole-report procedure**. In this method, subjects looked for a fraction of a second at a visual display of nine items such as the one shown in Figure 2. They were then asked to recall as many of the items as they could. On average, subjects could remember only about four of the nine items. Researchers interpreted this as evidence that the capacity of sensory memory was only four items. However, a young researcher by the name of **George Sperling** suspected that this might not be an accurate indication of the capacity of sensory memory.

$$
\begin{array}{ccc}
B & X & O \\
R & T & P \\
W & Q & L
\end{array}
$$

Figure 2. A sample 3 by 3 Array Used to Study Sensory Memory

Sperling devised a method called the **partial-report procedure**. Like the earlier researchers, he used a 3 x 3 matrix of letters. Like earlier researchers, he flashed the array for a fraction of a second. However, unlike earlier researchers, he asked the subjects to report only one row of the array. Immediately after the presentation of the array of letters, a high, medium, or low tone was presented, indicating to the subjects which row to recall. Notice that the subjects didn't know beforehand what row they had to recall. Therefore, the subjects couldn't focus on just one row. It turned out that, regardless of which row Sperling asked for, the subjects' recall was nearly perfect, thus suggesting that the capacity of sensory memory was about 9 items. Other experiments with larger arrays confirmed the 9-item limit. So, in the whole report method, as the subjects were reporting what they saw, their sensory memory of the array was decaying. By the time the subjects reported about four of the stimuli, the memory had already decayed. Sterling's procedure, however, avoided this problem.

Short-Term Memory

In real life, we are bombarded with sensations at any given moment. What happens to all of this input? Well, most of the information just leaves your sensory memory within a few seconds. However, information that you attend to goes from your sensory memory into your **short-term memory**. Short-term memory can be thought of as the link between our rapidly changing sensory memory and the more lasting long-term memory.

How long information remains in short-term memory depends on what is done with it. If nothing is done with the information, it will remain in short-term memory for only about 20 seconds. However, if the information is rehearsed, it can stay in short-term memory for a relatively long time, as long as you keep rehearsing the information (as when you repeat a phone number you want to remember). This is called **maintenance rehearsal**.

There is a limit to the amount of information that can be kept in short-term memory. George Miller found that seven (plus or minus two) pieces, or chunks, of information can be stored in short-term memory. Chunks are meaningful units of information. To get a sense for how chunking information into seven or fewer units of information can be an effective method for using your short-term memory, imagine trying to remember the following list of numbers: 1 9 7 6 1 8 1 4 1 6 4 3 1 4 7 5 1 2 0 3. You could probably remember about seven of these numbers. If, however, you chunk the numbers, you could probably remember all of them: 1976, 1814, 1643, 1475 and 1203. Breaking the numbers down into five years will make it much easier to remember all of the numbers.

Long-Term Memory

The phenomenon of chunking is an important interaction in behavior and long-term memory. **Long-term memory** can be considered to be the permanent storehouse of your experiences, knowledge, and skills. Items in long-term memory can be brief or can last a lifetime. One of the ways we get information into long-term memory is by using **elaborative rehearsal**, which involves organizing the material and associating it with information you already have in long-term memory.

TYPES OF REHEARSAL		
Type	**Definition**	**Use**
Maintenance	Repeating the information	Keeping the information in short-term memory
Elaborative	Organizing the information and associating it with information already in long-term memory	Getting the information into long-term memory

There are two types of long-term memory: **procedural memory** and **declarative memory**. **Procedural memory** has to do with remembering how things are done. It includes things like how to tie your shoelaces, how to swim, how to ride a bike, etc. **Declarative memory** is where explicit information is stored. Sometimes it is called fact memory. There are two types of declarative memory: **semantic memory** and **episodic memory**. **Semantic memory** has to do with remembering general knowledge, especially the meanings of words and concepts. **Episodic memory** refers to memories for particular events, or episodes, that you have personally experienced.

LONG-TERM MEMORY	
Type	**Concerned With**
Procedural memory	Remembering how to do things
Declarative memory	Remembering explicit information
Semantic memory	Remembering general knowledge
Episodic memory	Remembering particular events you have personally experienced

Encoding

In general, encoding for verbal material in short-term memory differs from that of long-term memory. Encoding for verbal material in short-term memory tends to be phonological or acoustic, rather than visual. For example, when asked to recall letters from short-term memory, confusions tend to occur with letters that sound alike, e.g., D and T, rather than with letters that look alike, e.g., D and O. On the other hand, items in long-term memory are more likely to be encoded on the basis of their meaning. This assertion is supported by studies of **semantic priming**. In the usual semantic priming task, the subject has to decide whether a stimulus is a word or a nonword. In one classic experiment, subjects were presented with pairs of words, some of which were semantically related (e.g., NURSE-DOCTOR) and some of which were not (e.g., NURSE-BUTTER). The subjects' task was to press a yes button if both words were real words and to press a no button if both words were not real words. The response time was quicker if the two words were semantically related.

ENCODING: SHORT-TERM MEMORY VERSUS LONG TERM MEMORY	
Memory System	**Encoding of Verbal Material Likely to Be Based On**
Short-term memory	Phonology
Long-term memory	Meaning

Semantic Memory

The question of how semantic memory is organized has aroused much interest. Researchers have used the **semantic verification task** to investigate this area. Recall that semantic memory, which is part of long-term memory, has to do with remembering general knowledge, especially the meanings of words and concepts. In the semantic verification task, subjects are asked to indicate whether or not a simple statement presented is true or false. The experimenter measures the time it takes the subject to respond, or the **response latency**. The idea is that the pattern of response latencies will provide information on how semantic knowledge is stored in memory.

In 1975, **Collins** and **Loftus** proposed the **spreading activation model**. A portion of their model is represented in Figure 3. The key to understanding this model is to remember that the shorter the distance between two words, the closer the words are related in the semantic memory. So, for instance, according to Figure 3, ambulance and fire engine are more closely related than ambulance and street. Using the semantic verification task, subjects will respond to questions about ambulances and fire engines quicker than questions about ambulances and streets.

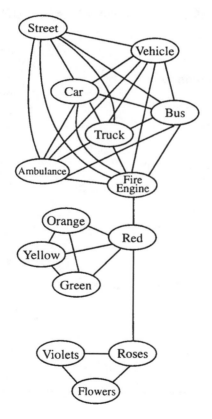

Figure 3. The Spreading Activation Model

The **semantic feature-comparison model** was proposed by **Smith**, **Shoben**, and **Rips** in the early 1970s. This model suggests that concepts are represented by sets of features, some of which are required for that concept, and some of which are typical of that concept. So, for instance, the concept of "college" is represented by the features *has faculty* (required), *offers degrees* (required), *has fraternities* (typical), and so on. Let's see what this model predicts in a semantic verification task. Example sentence 1: A robin is a bird. The first step is to compare the characteristics of robins with the characteristics of birds. Remember, these lists of features are stored in your semantic memory, so this whole process is fairly quick and automatic. If there is much overlap between the lists of characteristics, as there is in this case, you respond TRUE fairly quickly. If there is no, or very little overlap, you respond FALSE fairly quickly. On the other hand, if there is some overlap, it will take you longer to reach a decision. For example, you would respond fairly quickly to the following: "a robin is a bird"; and "a horse is a fish." When faced with a sentence like, "a turkey is a bird," it may take a little longer, since there is some overlap between the feature lists for *turkey* and *bird*, but not a lot since a turkey is a relatively atypical bird.

SEMANTIC MEMORY: KEY CONCEPTS

Concept	Description
Semantic verification task	Method used to investigate the organization of semantic memory
Spreading activation model	Semantic memory organized into map of interconnected concepts; the key is the distance between the concepts
Semantic feature-comparison model	Semantic memory contains feature lists of concepts; the key is the amount of overlap in the feature lists of the concepts

---

Levels-of-Processing Theory

Although the stage theory of memory has been widely accepted, it has also been challenged. The most influential competing theory has been the **levels-of-processing theory**, sometimes called the **depth-of-processing theory**. This theory was proposed by **Craik** and **Lockart**, and suggests that what determines how long you will remember material is not what memory system it gets into (they suggest that there is only one memory system), but the way in which you process the material. They postulated that an item entering into memory is analyzed in stages.

According to Craik and Lockart's theory, there are three ways, or levels, in which information can be processed. First is **physical** (visual), by focusing on the appearance, size, and shape of the information. Second is **acoustical**, by focusing on the sound combinations words have. The third is **semantic**, by focusing on the meaning of the word. These three ways demand different amounts of mental effort. The first way demands very little effort, the third way (the deepest level) demands more effort. The deeper the processing, and the greater the effort, the better your memory will be of the material. The later stages (deeper levels) of processing also includes connecting the information with other information in memory.

Paivio's Dual-Code Hypothesis

Another theory of memory is **Paivio's dual-code hypothesis**. According to this theory, information can be stored (or encoded) in two ways: visually and verbally. Abstract information tends to be encoded verbally, whereas concrete information tends to be encoded visually (i.e., as an image) and verbally. So, for instance, the word *virtue* would be encoded verbally while the word *elephant* would be encoded both visually and verbally.

So far, what we've said about memory might make it seem as if memory is like a giant tape recorder: picking up the incoming stimuli, recording them, and spitting them out again. However, memory is actually much more complex than this. It's more like a food processor. What comes out doesn't necessarily look like what went in. Psychologists actually think of memory as the result of a dynamic interplay between what we experience and what we already know.

An important concept here is **schema** (the plural form is **schemata**). Schemata are conceptual frameworks we use to organize our knowledge. We interpret our experiences, and therefore remember them in terms of our existing schemata. As you might imagine, trying to make our experiences fit into our existing schemata can lead to distortions in our memories. Furthermore, if we have a tough time matching up our experiences with a schema, we will have difficulty remembering it.

Forgetting

An early explanation for why we forget was the **decay theory**, which holds that if the information in long-term memory is not used or rehearsed, it will, eventually be forgotten. One of the problems with this theory is that it assumes that what you've learned in the time that has elapsed between memory and attempted retrieval makes no difference. However, we now know that it does.

Much modern research on long-term memory has focused on forgetting. One such theory, **inhibition theory,** suggests that forgetting is due to the activities that have taken place between original learning and the later attempted recall. There are two basic types of inhibition: **retroactive** and **proactive**. In **proactive inhibition**, what you learned earlier interferes with what you learn later. For instance, if you learn French as a second language, and then Spanish as a third language, you may find that as you are learning Spanish, you occasionally speak in French. **Retroactive inhibition** occurs when you forget what you learned earlier as you learn something new. For instance, if you learn List A, then learn List B, but find that you can't recall list A anymore, you've encountered retroactive inhibition.

Facilitating Memory

Sometimes it may seem like we've forgotten something when what's actually going on is **encoding specificity**. Encoding specificity is the assumption that recall will be best if the context at recall approximates the context during the original encoding. So, for instance, if you know that you're going to be taking a test in a classroom, you should try to study, if not in that particular classroom, at least in a room that has some of the features of that particular classroom. A special case of encoding specificity is **state-dependent learning**. State-dependent learning suggests that recall will be better if your psychological or physical state at the time of recall is the same as your state when you memorized the material. For example, if you were upset when you memorized the material, you will probably have better recall of it if you are upset at the time of recall.

Mnemonic devices are techniques that we use to improve the likelihood that we will remember something. **Chunking**, as we discussed earlier in this chapter, is one method. **The method of loci** is a system of associating information with some sequence of places with which you are familiar. For instance, let's say that you have to remember a list of ten words; you mentally place each one of these words alongside something you see on the pathway between your dorm room and your classroom. Once you can remember where you've placed everything, you're set. People can remember things for months if they associate what they have to learn with a sequence of places well known to them.

Reconstructive Memory

Sir Frederick Bartlett studied memory in a classic study that used the "War of the Ghosts," a Native American folk tale. In the study, Bartlett found that subjects reconstructed the story in line with their own expectations and schema for a ghost story.

The important thing to remember in relation to Bartlett is that prior knowledge and expectations influence recall.

Eyewitness Memory

Elizabeth Loftus has studied eyewitness memories and the tendency for eyewitnesses to be influenced or confused by misleading information. She has found that much of eyewitness memory (and testimony) can be erroneous for myriad reasons. Her work has been influential in both legal and psychological fields. More recently, she has studied the accuracy of repressed memories that return later in life.

Zeigarnik Effect

The **Zeigarnik effect** refers to the tendency to remember incomplete tasks better than completed tasks. For example, it's easier to remember the chores you haven't completed than the chores you have completed.

THINKING

Problem Solving

Psychologists have also been interested in understanding how the problem-solving process takes place. In particular, much research has focused on impediments to effective problem solving. Let's look at the **Luchins water-jar problem** as an example. In this task, subjects are presented with three empty jars, a list of the capacities of each jar, and they are asked to obtain a particular amount of water in one of the jars. Here's a typical problem:

	Jar A	Jar B	Jar C	Desired Amount
Problem A	29	3	7	20
Problem 1	21	127	3	100
Problem 2	14	163	20	109
Problem 3	18	43	10	5
Problem 4	9	42	6	21
Problem 5	20	59	4	31
Problem 6	23	49	3	20

Let's look at problem A as a sample problem. For this problem, if you pour water from Jar A into Jar B until B is filled, this will leave you with 26 quarts of water in Jar A. You should then empty Jar B and once again pour water from Jar A into Jar B, empty Jar B, and pour from Jar A to Jar B one more time. Once you have filled up Jar B three times, you will have 20 quarts of water left in Jar A.

Based upon the problem above, you've probably discovered a pattern that will help you solve the other problems. In problem 1, you would fill Jar B with water, pour water from Jar B into Jar A until it was filled, and then pour water from Jar B into Jar C, empty Jar C, and pour the water from B into C again. This would leave you with 100 quarts of water in Jar B. Try solving the other problems.

How did you solve problem 6? It could be solved using the pattern of responses above, or it could be solved a much simpler way. Simply by filling Jar A and pouring water from Jar A into Jar C, you would have 20 quarts of water left in Jar A. If you had done problem 6 first, you would have no doubt noticed this. However, since you did problem 6 last, after getting used to the more complicated method, you probably didn't even consider the simple method. This is because you have developed a **mental set**, or a tendency to keep repeating solutions that worked in other situations. So, past experience affects the strategies we use to solve problems. Inappropriate sets can be impediments to effective problem solving.

Another impediment to effective problem solving is **functional fixedness**. As an example, let's look at the following scenario: You walk into a room and see a box of matches, some tacks, and a candle. Your task is to mount the candle on the wall so that it can be used without the wax dropping on the floor. Before reading on, try to solve the problem.

If you're like most people, you had problems with the task. You might have thought of tacking the candle to the wall, but that doesn't work since the wax would still drop to the floor. The solution is to realize that the box the matches are in can serve not just as a container for the matches, but as a holder for the candle. The solution, therefore, is to tack the box to the wall and put the candle in the box. This way, the candle wax will go into the box and not on the floor. Why was it difficult to find this solution? Because people tend to get used to certain things having certain functions. We think of a box as *container* and we have problems thinking of a box as *candle holder*. Functional fixedness can be defined as the inability to use a familiar object in an unfamiliar way.

Creativity

Closely related to problem solving is **creativity**. Cognitive psychologists think of creativity as a cognitive ability that results in new ways of viewing problems or situations. Unfortunately, we still don't have much empirical evidence about the creative process, but it's an interesting subject to consider. Have you ever noticed that creative solutions often occur to you when you're thinking of something else, or suddenly, in what can be described as a "eureka" experience?

The most famous attempt to measure creativity is **Guilford's** test of **divergent thinking**. Divergent thinking is thinking that involves producing as many creative answers to a question as possible. For instance, if you are asked, "What can you use a brick for," you might answer, "to make a building," or "to build a wall." But these are not very creative answers as they are tied to the usual use of a brick as a building aid. More creative people might answer that they could use a brick as a candleholder, or they could paint "Happy Birthday" on it and give it to their best friend as a birthday gift. In divergent thinking, an individual's thoughts diverge along multiple paths of possibilities.

Decision Making

Heuristics

We make decisions every day, some insignificant (what should I wear today) and others very important (what graduate school should I choose). Two psychologists, **Daniel Kahneman** and **Amos Tversky** have investigated how our decision-making process can sometimes go awry.

Kahneman and Tversky found that humans use **heuristics**, basically short-cuts or rules of thumb, to make decisions. The **availability heuristic** is used when we try to decide how likely something is. When we use this heuristic, we make our decisions based upon how easily similar instances can be imagined. In other words, in using the availability heuristic, we use the information most readily available in memory to make our decisions. Often, the use of this heuristic leads us to a correct decision, but not always. As an example, answer the following question: "Are there more words in the English language that start with the letter 'K' or that have 'K' as their third letter?"

What did you decide? If you are like most people, you probably answered that there are more words that begin with the letter "K" than have "K" as their third letter. In fact, this is wrong. There are actually at least twice as many words in English that have "K" as the third letter than that begin with "K." Most people approach this question by trying to think of words that begin with "K" and words that have "K" as their third letter. Because we're so used to categorizing words by their first letter, it is easier to think of words beginning with "K." Using this availability heuristic, most people come to the erroneous conclusion.

The **representativeness heuristic** involves categorizing things on the basis of whether they fit the prototypical, stereotypical, or representative image of the category. As with the availability heuristic, the use of this heuristic often leads to correct decisions, but can sometimes lead us astray. Using prototypical or stereotypical factors rather than actual numerical information about which category is more numerous is called **base-rate fallacy**.

While heuristics can lead us astray, they are essential to speedy and effective decision-making. Heuristics are often used by experts in a given field. In order to win at chess, you've got to be able to think ahead several moves before you decide which move you're going to make. On any particular turn, you may have 15 or 20 possible moves (and the list of all the possible moves you can make is called the problem space). If you tried to think about all of the possible consequences of all of these possible moves, it would take you a really long time to make a decision. There are heuristics, however, that you can use to quickly eliminate from consideration some of the possible moves. For example, you need to protect the king, you want to control the center squares, you don't want to needlessly put any of your pieces in danger. Now, if effective decision-making in chess requires the use of heuristics, then certainly, decision-making in real-life, where there are usually many more options available, requires the use of heuristics even more so.

THINKING: KEY CONCEPTS	
Concept	**Explanation**
Problem solving	
Mental sets	Tendency to keep repeating solutions that worked in other situations
Functional fixedness	The inability to use a familiar object in an unfamiliar way
Creativity	
Divergent thinking	Attempting to produce as many creative answers to a question as possible
Decision-making	
Heuristics	Short-cuts and rules of thumb we can use in making decisions
Availability heuristic	Making decisions about frequencies based upon how easy it is to imagine the items involved
Representativeness heuristic	Categorizing things on the basis of whether they fit the prototypical image of the category
Base-rate fallacy	Ignoring the numerical information about the items being referred to when categorizing them

LANGUAGE

Language is another important study of cognitive psychology. Let's begin by talking about the different components of language (and we previously discussed some of these in the developmental psychology chapter). **Phonemes** are the smallest sound units of language. For example, the word *field* consists of four phonemes: the *f* sound, the *e* sound, the *l* sound, and the *d* sound. **Morphemes** are the smallest units of meaning in a language. For instance, the word *walked* consists of two morphemes, *walk*, indicating action, and *ed*, indicating that the action took place in the past. The word *troubleshooter* consists of three morphemes: *trouble, shoot, er*. **Semantics** deals with the meaning of words and sentences, and **syntax** deals with the grammatical arrangement of words in sentences.

Theories of Language Development

The major theoretical perspectives in language development include **learning theory** and early **cognitive developmental theory** (Jean Piaget). Briefly, learning theorists believe that language is acquired through classical conditioning, operant conditioning, and/or modeling. B. F. Skinner is a proponent of this perspective. Cognitive developmental theorists believe that language has to do with the child's capacity for symbolic thought, which develops toward the end of the sensorimotor period. This perspective holds that language continues to develop according to the child's cognitive level. For example, the acquisition of comparison terms like *more than* or *less than* occurs about the same time that cognition develops from preoperational to concrete operational thought.

Chomsky's Work

Noam Chomsky critiqued the behaviorist perspective on language, and proposed a **nativist theory** of language acquisition. Because children across the world produce speech so early in their development (12–18 months) and become fluent by about five years old, Chomsky believed that there must be some sort of innate, biologically based mechanism for language acquisition. Chomsky proposed a **language acquisition device (LAD)**, which is built-in advanced knowledge of rule structures in language.

We'll address two important aspects of Chomsky's theory of grammar, the distinction between **deep** and **surface grammatical structure**, and the concept of **transformational rules**. The **surface structure** of a sentence is the actual word order of the words in a sentence. The **deep**, or **abstract structure** is an underlying form that specifies the meaning of the sentence. For instance, the following sentences all have different surface structures but similar deep structures: 1) The boy picked up the book; 2) The boy picked the book up; and 3) The book was picked up by the boy. Furthermore, sometimes sentences with the same surface structure have different meanings. For instance, "They are eating apples" can mean that *some people are eating apples*, or that *those apples are for eating*.

Transformational rules tell us how we can change one structure into another. For instance, the sentences "The house is green" and "Is the house green?" are related by a transformational rule including the set of rules that tell us how to change a statement to a question.

The Relationship Between Language and Thought

Benjamin Whorf proposed the **Whorfian hypothesis**, also called the **linguistic relativity hypothesis**, which suggests that our perception of reality, the way that we think about the world, is determined by the content of language. Basically, language affects the way we think and not the other way around. For instance, the Eskimo language has a wide variety of names for different types of snow, whereas the English language has only one. Therefore, according to the Whorfian hypothesis, Eskimos are better at discriminating between different types of snow than English speakers are. As you might imagine, this is a somewhat controversial notion, and there is evidence both for it and against it.

LANGUAGE: KEY CONCEPTS	
Concept	**Definition**
Components of language	
Phonemes	The smallest sound units
Morphemes	The smallest units of meanings
Syntax	The grammatical arrangement of words and sentences
Semantics	The meanings of words and sentences
Noam Chomsky	
Surface structure	The actual order of words in a sentence
Deep structure	An underlying form that specifies the meaning of the sentence
Transformational rules	Tell us how we can change from one sentence form to another (e.g., from a sentence in the active voice to a sentence in the passive voice)
Whorfian hypothesis	The hypothesis that language determines how reality is perceived

Gender Differences in Language Development

While gender studies remain controversial, **Eleanor Macoby** and **Carol Jacklin** found evidence of better verbal abilities in girls in their studies.

INTELLIGENCE

There has been much debate concerning the definition of intelligence. **Charles Spearman** suggested that individual differences in intelligence are largely due to variations in the amount of a general, unitary factor, which he called *g*. **Louis Thurstone** identified seven abilities which he called **primary mental abilities** (e.g., verbal comprehension, number ability, perceptual speed, general reasoning) and used factor analysis with factors more specific than *g* but more general than *s*. **Robert Sternberg's triarchic theory** suggests that there are three aspects to intelligence: componential (e.g., performance on tests), experiential (creativity) and contextual (street smarts/business sense). **Howard Gardner's theory** is called the **theory of multiple intelligences**, with seven defined: linguistic ability, logical-mathematical ability, spatial ability, musical ability, bodily-kinesthetic ability, interpersonal ability, and intrapersonal ability. Gardner argues that Western culture values the first two abilities over the others. After all, these are the two abilities tested by traditional IQ tests.

Some theorists have tried to study what happens to intelligence as we develop. **Raymond Cattell** divided mental abilities into two major types: **fluid intelligence** and **crystallized intelligence**. Fluid intelligence is described as the ability to quickly grasp relationships in novel situations and make correct deductions from them. Solving analogies requires fluid intelligence. In contrast, crystallized intelligence is an ability to understand relationships or solve problems that depend on knowledge acquired as a result of schooling or other life experiences. Cattell suggested that crystallized intelligence increases throughout the lifespan, since it is dependent on education and experience, but that fluid intelligence gradually increases throughout childhood and adolescence (paralleling an increase in neurological maturation), levels off in young adulthood, and begins a steady decrease with advanced age (decline with neurological degeneration).

INTELLIGENCE AND THE LIFESPAN: CATTELL'S THEORY	
Type of Intelligence	**Course Throughout Lifespan**
Fluid intelligence	Increases throughout childhood and adolescence, levels off in young adulthood, and begins a steady decline with advanced age
Crystallized intelligence	Increases throughout the lifespan

Arthur Jensen is a prominent educational psychologist who studied intelligence. He claimed that intelligence as measured by IQ tests was almost entirely genetic in nature and that you could not teach someone to score higher on IQ tests. He also focused on differences in IQ scores across racial lines, and provoked a great deal of controversy with this line of inquiry.

INFORMATION PROCESSING

Accounts of human information processing used to assume that the brain processed information serially: that it performs one stage of processing at a time. In the mid 1980s, **McClelland** and **Rumelhart** published a two-volume book about parallel distributed processes (PDP), proposing that information processing is distributed across the brain and is done in a parallel fashion.

METAPSYCHOLOGY

"Meta" refers to the ability to reflect upon something. **Metacognition** and **metamemory** refer to a person's ability to think about and monitor cognition and memory, respectively. For instance, as you are reviewing major psychological concepts for the GRE Psychology test, you are probably thinking about whether or not it will be difficult to remember everything, whether mnemonic devices would help, etc.

IMPORTANT NAMES IN COGNITIVE PSYCHOLOGY

Bartlett, F.	Investigated the role of **schemata** in memory; concluded that **memory** is largely a **reconstructive process**
Cattell, R.	Divided intelligence into **fluid intelligence** and **crystallized intelligence** and looked at how they change throughout the lifespan
Chomsky, N.	Distinguished between the **surface structure** and **deep structure** of a sentence; studied **transformational rules** that could be used to transform one sentence into another
Collins, A. and Loftus, E.	Devised the **spreading activation model of semantic memory**
Craik, F. and Lockhart, R.	Developed the **levels-of-processing theory of memory** as an alternative to the stage theory of memory
Ebbinghaus, H.	Studied **memory** using **nonsense syllables** and the **method of savings**
Gardner, H.	Proposed a **theory of multiple intelligences** that divides intelligence into seven different types, all of which are equally important; traditional IQ tests measure only two of the seven types
Guilford, J.	Devised **divergent thinking** test to measure **creativity**
Kahneman, D. and Tversky, A.	Investigated the use of **heuristics** in **decision-making**; studied the **availability heuristic** and the **representativeness heuristic**
Loftus, E.	Studied **eyewitness memory** and concluded that our memories can be altered by presenting new information or by asking misleading questions
Luchins, A.	Used the **water-jar problem** to study the effect of **mental sets** on **problem-solving**
Macoby, E. and Jacklin, C.	Found support for **gender differences** in verbal ability

McClelland, J. and Rumelhart, D.	Suggested that the **brain processes information** using **parallel distributed processing (PDP)**
Miller, G.	Found that the **capacity of short-term memory** is seven (plus or minus two) items
Paivio, A.	Proposed **dual-code hypothesis**
Smith, E., Shoben, E., and Rips, L.	Devised the **semantic feature-comparison model** of **semantic memory**
Spearman, C.	Suggested that individual **differences in intelligence** were largely due to differences in amount of a **general factor** called g
Sperling, G.	Studied the **capacity** of **sensory memory** using the **partial-report method**
Sternberg, R.	Proposed **triarchic theory** that divides **intelligence** into three types: **componential**, **experiential**, and **contextual**
Thurstone, L.	Used **factor analysis** to study primary **mental abilities**—factors more specific than g, but more general than s
Whorf, B.	Hypothesized that **language determines how reality is perceived**

COGNITIVE PSYCHOLOGY PRACTICE SET

Time: 8 minutes

Directions: Each of the questions or incomplete statements below is followed by five suggested answers or completions. In each case, select the one that best answers the question or completes the statement.

1. A student learned a monologue from Shakespeare's *Twelfth Night* and then, a month later, learned a monologue from *King Lear*. Every time he tried to recite the monologue from *Lear* he began reciting the *Twelfth Night* monologue. This is known as

    (A) the Method of Loci
    (B) the method of savings
    (C) proactive inhibition
    (D) encoding specificity
    (E) retroactive inhibition

2. Which of the following theorists invented the concept of the method of savings?

    (A) Ebbinghaus
    (B) Bartlett
    (C) Chomsky
    (D) Craik
    (E) Loftus

3. If someone had ten objects to remember and she chose to do so by putting one on each street corner between her house and school, what method would she be using?

    (A) chunking
    (B) Method of Loci
    (C) encoding specificity
    (D) Zeigarnik effect
    (E) retroactive organization

4. For Noam Chomsky, the semantic interpretation of a sentence comes from

    (A) surface structure
    (B) inhibition theory
    (C) deep structure
    (D) divergent thinking
    (E) transformational rules

5. Which of the following best illustrates the difference between semantic and episodic memory?

    (A) Remembering how to tie your shoes versus remembering where you bought your last pair of shoes
    (B) Remembering the meaning of *phenomenon* versus remembering how *phenomenon* is spelled
    (C) Knowing the meaning of words versus remembering where you went to school
    (D) Remembering your trip to France versus remembering your trip to high school
    (E) Remembering where you live versus remembering how to dial a phone

6. Upon being asked to list various uses for a blanket, Lillian responds "a parachute, a basketball net, and fake icing for a small sculpture of a cake." Lillian is using

    (A) parallel distributed processing
    (B) metacognition
    (C) crystallized intelligence
    (D) divergent thinking
    (E) transformational rules

7. Three groups of subjects were presented with a list of 30 words, presented one at a time by the experimenter. Subjects in Group 1 were told to indicate whether the word had less than or more than five letters. Subjects in Group 2 were told to indicate whether the word referred to an agent or an action. Finally, subjects in Group 3 were told to indicate whether the word had one syllable or two syllables. After the list is presented, the subjects are asked to write down as many words as they can remember. According to the levels-of-processing theory, which of the following answer choices describes the order of number of words subjects in each group recalled, from most to least?

    (A) 1, 3, 2
    (B) 1, 2, 3
    (C) 2, 3, 1
    (D) 3, 1, 2
    (E) 3, 2, 1

8. Who hypothesized a general or *g* factor to intelligence?

    (A) Robert Sternberg
    (B) Charles Spearman
    (C) Louis Thurstone
    (D) Howard Gardner
    (E) David Wechsler

9. According to the stage theory of memory, information can go through memory in which order?

    (A) Sensory memory, long-term memory, short-term memory
    (B) Iconic memory, short-term memory, long-term memory
    (C) Echoic memory, iconic memory, long-term memory
    (D) Short-term memory, long-term memory, sensory memory
    (E) Long-term memory, sensory memory, short-term memory

10. You hear an excerpt of music and your companion asks you who wrote it. You've never heard it before, but reply that it's likely that Bach wrote it. Your judgment can be best explained on the basis of

    (A) proactive inhibition
    (B) divergent thinking
    (C) representativeness
    (D) the method of loci
    (E) procedural memory

EXPLANATIONS FOR THE COGNITIVE PSYCHOLOGY PRACTICE SET

1. C

Proactive inhibition is when something learned in the past makes it more difficult to remember something being learned in the present. Retroactive inhibition, choice (E), means that later material makes the recalling of earlier material difficult. Let's look at the other answer choices. The method of loci, answer choice (A), involves associating what you have to remember with a sequence of places you are familiar with. Answer choice (B), the method of savings, refers to Ebbinghaus's method of measuring memory. Finally, encoding specificity, choice (D), states that recall will be best if the context of the recall approximates the context of the original encoding.

2. A

The method of savings was invented by Ebbinghaus, answer choice (A). Bartlett, choice (B), worked on schemata and reconstructed memories. Chomsky, answer choice (C), is the person behind the theory of grammar that distinguished between the surface and deep structures of a sentence. Choice (D), Craik, was one of the theorists who proposed the levels-of-processing theory of memory. Finally, choice (E), Loftus, was the psychologist who did the ground-breaking work on memory and eyewitness testimony.

3. B

Recall that the method of loci involves associating what you need to remember with some sequence of places with which you are familiar. Answer choice (A), chunking, is incorrect. A chunk is a meaningful unit of information. Recall that in the chapter, we chunked individual numbers into years, and this allowed us to remember all of the numbers. Answer choice (C), encoding specificity, is the assumption that recall will be best if the context at recall approximates that context during the original encoding. Answer choice (D), the Zeigarnik effect, refers to Zeigarnik's finding that, if the person is interested in the outcome of the task, she would have better recall of incomplete tasks than completed tasks. Finally, answer choice (E), although it may have tempted you, was just a made-up answer choice. Therefore, the correct answer is choice (B).

4. C

The semantic interpretation of a sentence comes from its deep structure. Recall that semantics deals with the meaning of sentences. Recall also that Chomsky proposed a distinction between the surface structure of a sentence and the deep structure of a sentence. The surface structure is the actual order of the words in the sentence. In contrast, the deep structure specifies the meaning of the sentence. Let's look at some of the other answer choices. Choice (B), inhibition theory, is a theory of forgetting. Choice (D), divergent thinking, is thinking that involves producing as many creative answers to a question as possible. Guilford used the divergent thinking task to assess creativity. Finally, choice (E), transformational rules, refers to how we can change from one sentence structure to another, for instance, from an active sentence to a passive sentence.

5. C

Let's review some definitions. Long-term memory can be divided into two types: procedural memory and declarative memory. Procedural memory has to do with remembering how things get done whereas declarative memory is where explicit information is stored. There are two types of declarative memory: semantic memory and episodic memory. Semantic memory has to do with remembering general knowledge whereas episodic memory has to do with remembering particular events you have personally experienced. Semantic memory is sort of like an encyclopedia while episodic memory is sort of like an autobiography. If you remembered these definitions, this was an easy question. The correct answer is (C): knowing the meaning of words has to do with semantic memory and remembering where you went to school has to do with episodic memory. Let's look at the other answer choices. In choice (A), remembering how to tie your shoes has to do with procedural memory whereas remembering where you bought your last pair of shoes has to do with episodic memory. Both items in answer choice (B) would be stored in semantic memory. Since both parts of answer choice (D) involve memories of events that you personally experienced, they would both be stored in episodic memory. Finally, in answer choice (E), remembering where you live has to do with episodic memory and remembering how to dial a phone has to do with procedural memory.

6. D

Recall that divergent thinking was the task used by Guilford to assess creativity. It involves coming up with as many creative answers to a question as possible, and certainly, Lillian is being very creative. Let's look at the other answer choices. Answer choice (A), parallel distributed processing (PDP), is incorrect. PDP assumes that information is processed in the brain, not in series, but in parallel and that such information processing is widely distributed across the brain. This is a relatively new theory that was proposed in the mid-1980s by McClelland and Rumelhart. Although it might very well be true that divergent thinking takes place in the brain in parallel distributed form, answer choice (A) is not the best answer choice. Answer choice (B), metacognition, refers to the ability to think about and monitor one's own cognitive acts. Answer choice (C), crystallized intelligence, refers to the ability to understand relationships or solve problems that depend on knowledge acquired as a result of schooling or other life experiences. Finally, answer choice (E), transformational rules, refers to Chomsky's theory of language. Recall that transformational rules are rules that tell us how we can change from one sentence structure to another.

7. C

Question 7 deals with Craik and Lockhart's levels-of-processing theory of memory. This theory, an alternative to the stage theory of memory, suggests that what determines how long you will remember material is the way in which you process the material. They suggest three different ways information can be processed: physical, acoustical, and semantic. Physical processing involves focusing on the physical characteristics of the letters. Subjects in Group 1 processed the information in this way. Acoustical processing involves focusing on the way the information sounds. Subjects in Group 3 processed the information in this way. Finally, semantic processing involves focusing on the meaning of the information. By being asked whether the words referred to an action or an agent (an agent is the person or thing performing the action), subjects in Group 2 had to use semantic processing to process the information. The levels-of-processing theory suggests that these three different ways of processing information require different amounts of mental energy, with physical processing requiring the least energy and semantic processing requiring the most. This theory also suggests that the deeper the processing, and thus, the greater the energy

required, the better your memory of the material. Hence, Group 2 ought to remember the material the best, followed by Group 3, and finally Group 1. Therefore, the correct answer is choice (C).

8. B

According to Charles Spearman, individual differences in intelligence were largely attributable to differences in the g factor. Choice (A), Robert Sternberg, was the psychologist who proposed the triarchic theory of intelligence. Answer choice (C), Louis Thurstone, may have been tempting since he, like Spearman, used factor analysis to study intelligence. However, Thurstone identified seven primary mental abilities whose scope was somewhere in-between that of g and s. Answer choice (D), Howard Gardner, proposed a theory of multiple intelligences in which he divided intelligence into seven equally important types. Finally, as we'll find out in the chapter on tests and measurements, David Wechsler devised several tests of intelligence, including the WAIS, the WISC, and the WPPSI.

9. B

The stage theory of memory suggests that information begins in the sensory memory. If you attend to this information, it moves on to the short-term memory. Finally, information may enter the long-term memory. Based just on this information, it would appear that all five answer choices are incorrect. However, in order to answer this question correctly, you needed to remember that visual sensory memory is called iconic memory and that auditory sensory memory is called echoic memory. If the information is visual, the information can go from the iconic memory to the short-term memory to the long-term memory. Therefore, the correct answer to this question is choice (B).

10. C

This was a tough question. Let's look at it in more detail. You hear a piece of music you've never heard before and your companion asks you who wrote it. How are you going to figure it out? More than likely, you'll think about whether the music has features that are typical of the various composers you're familiar with. You realize that this piece has features typical of a Bach composition, therefore, you tell your companion that it's likely that Bach wrote it. In other words, you're basing your conclusion on representativeness. Recall that the representativeness heuristic involves categorizing things on the basis of whether they fit the prototypical image of the category. Let's look at the other answer choices. Choice (A), proactive inhibition is exemplified by the phrase "You can't teach an old dog new tricks" and refers to the phenomenon in which what you learned earlier interferes with what you try to learn later. Choice (B), divergent thinking, refers to the process of coming up with as many creative answers to a question as you are able to. Choice (D), the method of loci, is a mnemonic device used to help remember a list of items. To use this method, you associate what you have to memorize with some sequence of places with which you are familiar. Finally, answer choice (E), procedural memory, has to do with remembering how to do things.

CHAPTER TEN

Research Design, Statistics, Tests, and Measurements

OUTLINE

Historical Perspective

Research Design

- Hypothesis
- Variables
- Types of Research
- Populations and Samples
- Confounding Variables

Problems in Research Design

- Experimenter Bias
- Demand Characteristics
- External Validity

Descriptive Statistics

- Frequency Distributions
- Measures of Central Tendency
- Measures of Variability
- Distributions, Percentiles, and z-scores
- Correlation Coefficients

Inferential Statistics

- Significance Testing
- Errors in Significance Testing
- Types of Significance Tests
- Meta-Analysis

Tests and Measurements

- Score Interpretation
- Reliability
- Validity
- Scales of Measurement
- Types of Ability Tests
- Personality Tests
- Interest Tests

Research Design, Statistics, Tests, and Measurements

Psychology is a science using scientific methods of research design and statistics. Included here is basic information on the scientific method as applied to the field of psychology, with definitions, types of research design used in psychological research, various methods of subject selection, and potential problems in research design.

Statistics are also essential for designing and evaluating psychological tests. Therefore, this chapter is organized so that information on statistics is presented before tests and measurements. We cover descriptive and very basic inferential statistics, as well as the ways in which tests and measurements are designed and interpreted. Although you do not need to memorize long formulas or prepare for complex computations, there are some important basics for you to know about how to analyze data once you've collected it.

HISTORICAL PERSPECTIVE

Perhaps the most significant historical moment in psychology research was the first psychology laboratory founded by **William Wundt** in 1879. Wundt brought together earlier work in philosophy, physiology, and psychophysics to create psychology as a science. What was Wundt's psychology like? Over the past 25 years, our understanding of his ideas has changed rather dramatically. We used to think of his psychology as being rather sterile and narrow, and just not very interesting. We'd think of a rather unscientific introspection and of a striving to reduce consciousness to its elements. Actually, Wundt believed that experimental psychology has a very limited use: that methodology could not be used to study the higher mental processes such as memory, thinking, and language. To study the higher mental processes, Wundt proposed a sort of cultural psychology.

A contemporary of Wundt's, **Hermann Ebbinghaus** showed that higher mental processes could be studied using experimental methodology. As you may recall from the cognitive psychology chapter, Ebbinghaus studied memory using nonsense syllables. He showed that at least one of the higher mental processes could be studied empirically using good experimental methodology.

Another contemporary of Wundt's, **Oswald Kulpe**, also disagreed with Wundt fundamentally. Wundt believed that whenever you thought of something, an image of that thing formed in your mind, that is, there could be no thought without a mental image. Kulpe, on the other hand, strongly believed that there could be imageless thought; he performed experiments to prove his hypothesis.

James McKeen Cattell, who studied under Wundt, introduced mental testing to the United States. Much later, in 1905, **Binet** collaborated with **Simon** to publish the first intelligence test, known as the **Binet-Simon test**. The purpose of the test was to assess the intelligence of French school children to ascertain which children were too mentally retarded to benefit from ordinary schooling. Binet also introduced the concept of mental age, or the age level that a person functions at intellectually, regardless of their actual chronological age. Later, **William Stern** developed an equation to compare mental age to chronological age, which came to be known as the intelligence quotient, or **IQ**. In 1916, Lewis Terman revised the Binet-Simon test for use in the United States. This became known as the **Stanford-Binet Intelligence** test.

RESEARCH DESIGN

The Hypothesis and Research Variables

The first step in research design involves identifying a problem to study and formulating a **hypothesis**, or a tentative and testable explanation of the relationship between two or more **variables**. A variable is a characteristic or property that varies in amount or kind, and can be measured (e.g., height, weight, mental abilities, physical abilities, personality characteristics, and so on). So, if a researcher is interested in the effect of one variable, breakfast, on another variable, academic performance, the hypothesis might be something like: "If you have a good breakfast, you will perform better academically than if you do not have a good breakfast."

As you read that sample hypothesis, some questions may have popped up in your mind. What does the researcher mean by a *good breakfast*? What does the researcher mean by *perform better academically*? In other words, what are the **operational definitions**: how does the researcher plan to define the variables in the experiment so that the variables are measurable? An operational definition of a good breakfast might be a breakfast high in protein. An operational definition of academic performance might be the number of correct responses on a spelling test.

HYPOTHESIS: KEY CONCEPTS	
Concept	**Definition**
Hypothesis	A tentative and testable explanation of the relationship between two or more variables
Variable	A factor that varies in amount or kind and can be measured
Operational Definitions	State how the researcher will measure the variables

Now that we have operationally defined the variables in our research, we can refine our hypothesis. Our new hypothesis might be something like "Those who have a high-protein breakfast will do better on a spelling test than those who have a low-protein breakfast." We now also have a more specific definition of hypothesis: a tentative and testable explanation of the relationship between one or more independent variables, and one or more **dependent variables**. The **independent variable (IV)** is the variable whose effect is being studied the variable that the experimenter manipulates. In this example, we are studying the effect of protein content in breakfast food on spelling test performance, so protein content is the IV. The **dependent variable (DV)** is the response that is expected to vary with differences in the independent variable. In this example, we are interested in how performance on the spelling exam, the DV, varies with different levels of protein. The dependent variable is said to depend on the action.

INDEPENDENT AND DEPENDENT VARIABLES		
Type	**Definition**	**Example**
Independent Variable	The variable whose effect is being studied	Breakfast type
Dependent Variable	The variable expected to change due to variations in the independent variable	Spelling test performance

There is distinction between the *number* of IVs and the *number of levels* in the IV. The levels of the IV are simply the values the IV has in a study. In our example, we have one IV, breakfast protein content, but we may have multiple levels of protein content. If we give one group of subjects a low-protein breakfast and another a high-protein breakfast, there would be two levels of the IV. If we give one group of subjects a no-protein breakfast, one group a low-protein breakfast, and a third group a high-protein breakfast, there would be three levels of the IV.

Research Types

There are three basic types of research: true experiments, quasi-experiments, and correlational studies. We will illustrate the differences between these three using our example.

To test the hypothesis in our example, one strategy the researcher could use would be to go into an elementary school class, give a spelling test, and ask each member of the class exactly what she or he had for breakfast. From their reports, the researcher could figure out the protein levels of the breakfasts. In this example, the researcher is *not* manipulating the IV. Because the researcher does not manipulate the IV in this example, this study is a **correlational** study.

Alternatively, the researcher could have taken the same class of children, and instead of allowing the students to eat breakfast at home, the researcher could have fed them breakfast in the classroom. For example, the researcher could **randomly assign** the students in the classroom into groups: half of the class might receive a breakfast containing three grams of protein, and the other half a breakfast that contains ten grams of protein. The students could then be given a spelling test. In this example, the researcher controls, or manipulates, the levels in the IV. Since the researcher uses random assignment *and* manipulates the IV, this is a **true experiment**. Finally, researchers using a **quasi-experimental design** do not use random assignment and lack sufficient control over the variables and, therefore, definitive statements on causal factors cannot be made.

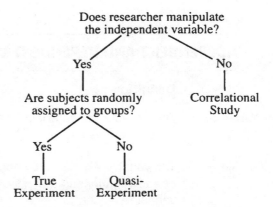

Figure 1. Types of Research

In the three types of research just mentioned, the researcher is interested in looking at the relationship between at least two variables. The next type of research we will discuss does not have this restriction. In this kind of study, the researcher does not intervene at all in what is being studied. Rather, the researcher is observing what naturally occurs. Not surprisingly, this is called **naturalistic observation**, sometimes also called **field study**.

TYPES OF RESEARCH	
Type	**Characteristic(s)**
Naturalistic observation	Researcher does not intervene, measures behavior as it naturally occurs
Correlational	IV not manipulated
Quasi-experiment	IV manipulated, subjects not randomly assigned to groups
True experiment	IV manipulated, subjects randomly assigned to groups

Populations and Samples

In theory, researchers have to make a lot of decisions about the ideal subject to be studied in research. In reality, they usually use whomever is most convenient to study (very often this means students of introductory psychology classes). Needless to say, this is not the best method for selecting subjects. Before selecting subjects, researchers have to determine what population the researcher wants to generalize the results to. Does the researcher hope to draw conclusions about all people? All elementary school children? All second graders? All second graders in New York City schools?

If a researcher is interested in studying a small enough group, for example, all second grade students in a particular classroom, the researcher can run every member of the population through the experiment. However, if the population is larger, say all second graders in the United States, it would be too expensive, if even possible, to run every member of the population of second graders through the experiment. The only alternative is to run the experiment on a subset of the population, or a **sample**.

How do researchers select samples from the population that they are interested in studying? The researcher needs to select a sample that is representative of the population of interest. One technique for selecting such a sample is **random selection**, meaning that each member of the population has an equal chance of being selected for the sample. Another technique is called **stratified random sampling**. This is a technique of assuring that each subgroup of the population is randomly sampled in proportion to its size.

POPULATIONS AND SAMPLES	
Concept	**Explanation**
Population	The group the researcher wishes to generalize her results to
Representative sample	Sample is a miniature version of the population
Random sample	Every population member has an equal chance to be selected for the sample
Stratified random sample	Relevant subgroups of the population are randomly sampled in proportion to size

Researchers also have to decide which subjects will receive the different levels of the IV. There are three options here: a **between-subjects design**, a **matched-subjects design**, and a **within-subjects design**.

Between-Subjects Design

In a **between-subjects design**, each subject is exposed to only one level of each independent variable. The subjects are assigned randomly to groups and subjects in a given group do not receive the same level of independent variable as members of another group. For example, some subjects are assigned to the high-protein group, and some are assigned to the low-protein group. We could therefore reasonably assume that the groups are equal in terms of any subject variables that might affect our DV, such as intelligence or motivation. However, statistical theory tells us that even with random assignment, it is possible that the groups might differ on these variables merely due to chance.

Matched-Subjects Design

Let's assume that there is a strong relationship between spelling test performance and intelligence. The experimenter may want to make sure that both groups have, on the average, roughly, the same level of intelligence. The experimenter could match subjects on the basis of the variable that he or she wants to control, in this case, intelligence. This design is called, not surprisingly, a **matched-subjects design**. For example, assume there are twelve subjects in the experiment, six subjects per group. Subjects in one group would be given high protein breakfasts and subjects in the other group would be given low-protein breakfasts. Let's assume that their IQ scores are as listed below:

Subject Number	IQ	Subject Number	IQ
1	110	7	98
2	103	8	110
3	100	9	120
4	104	10	118
5	97	11	95
6	100	12	95

To match the subjects, we would take the two top IQs, subjects 9 and 10, and randomly assign each one into the two groups (high protein and low protein groups). The next two highest IQs, subjects 1 and 8, would also be randomly assigned to the two groups, and so on. The result of these pairings is as follows:

Matched Pair #	Low-Protein Group Subject # (IQ)	High-Protein Group Subject # (IQ)
1	9 (120)	10 (118)
2	8 (110)	1 (110)
3	2 (103)	4 (104)
4	6 (100)	3 (100)
5	5 (97)	7 (98)
6	11 (95)	12 (95)

The pairing ensures that both groups are approximately equal on the matching variable, in this case, intelligence.

Within-Subjects Design

It is also possible to match subjects on every variable at the same time. How? We can pair each subject with himself or herself by using the same subjects in both groups. This is called a **within-subjects design**, or a **repeated-measures design**. The subject's own performance is the basis of comparison. In our example, we could give all subjects a low-protein breakfast on day one, and then give them all a spelling test. We could then give all subjects a high-protein breakfast on day two, and then give them all a spelling test. The crucial thing here is that each subject is exposed to more than one condition, allowing the researcher to separate the effects of individual differences in intelligence from the effects of the IV, the level of protein in the breakfast.

A problem with the within-subjects design in our particular example is that people may just do better on the second test because they are more familiar with the test format. If all subjects have the high-protein breakfast on the second day, the improvement in performance may be due to increased familiarity with the exam than due to their breakfast. Or they may do worse on the second test because of boredom. To eliminate this problem the experimenter can use **counterbalancing** to counteract these order effects. This can be done by assigning half of the subjects to experience the low-protein breakfast first, and the other half to experience the high protein breakfast first. All subjects will still experience both levels, just in different orders.

EXPERIMENTAL DESIGNS			
Type	Experimental Condition 1	Experimental Condition 2	One-to-One Pairing?
Between	Group 1	Group 2	No
Matched	Group 1	Group 2	Yes
Within	Group 1	Group 1	Not applicable— there is only one group

Confounding Variables

The major goal of research is to figure out if there is a causal relationship between the independent and dependent variable, that is, to find out if changes in the IV cause changes in the DV. In order to reasonably infer that a causal relationship exists, researchers need to be able to discount any other variables that could differentially effect the DV. These variables are called **confounding variables**. These are unintended independent variables.

Despite attempts to create a well-designed experiment, experiments can contain confounding variables. Let's say we run our experiment on breakfast type and spelling test performance. We obtain the subjects, using appropriate sampling methodology. We bring the subjects into our lab and randomly assign the subjects to one of two groups. The subjects in the first group are given a high-protein breakfast: three scrambled eggs, four strips of bacon, buttered toast, and a glass of orange juice. The subjects in the second group are given a low-protein breakfast, say, a bowl of Sugar-Free Veggie O's. We then give all the subjects a spelling test, and subjects in the high-protein group do better on the spelling test than subjects in the low-protein group. Now, since we have manipulated the IV and randomly assigned subjects to groups, we have run a true experiment. But can we infer a causal relationship between amount of breakfast protein and spelling test performance?

In order to answer that question, we need to be able to discount any other possible causes of the differences in spelling test performance between the two groups. Let's start thinking of some possible causes. What about calorie differences between the two groups? This could conceivably cause a difference in spelling test scores. Here, calorie count would be a possible confounding variable.

We could design a study using a **control group design** by treating both groups equally in all respects except that the cereal for one group (the control group) contains no protein whereas the cereal for the other group (**the experimental group**) has ten grams of protein injected into it. The control group is the group that does not receive the treatment; the experimental group is the group that receives the treatment. If we run this experiment and find a significant difference between the two groups, we know that the difference cannot be due to differences in calories, because we've held the number of calories constant. We can be more confident that it is the difference in protein content that is causing the difference in spelling test performance.

Nonequivalent Group Design

In a **nonequivalent group design**, the control group is not necessarily similar to the experimental group since the researcher doesn't use random assignment. This is common in educational research because you can't randomly assign subjects to different classes. For example, if a researcher wants to see if a new method for teaching reading is better than the usual method, the researcher might assign the new method to one class and the usual method to another class, and measure each subject's increase in reading skill from the beginning to the end of the study.

POTENTIAL PROBLEMS IN RESEARCH DESIGN

Experimenter bias, or the fact that due to his or her expectations, the experimenter might inadvertently treat groups of subjects differently, may influence the results of the experiment. Alternatively, the experimenter might also let his or her expectations affect how the results of the experiment are interpreted. One way to control for experimenter bias is a technique called **double-blinding**. In a double-blind experiment, neither the researcher who interacts with the subjects nor the subjects themselves know which groups received the IV or which level of the IV. If the subjects do not know whether they are in the treatment or control group, but the researchers know, it is called a **single-blind experiment**.

Demand characteristics refer to any cues that suggest to subjects what the researcher expects from them. These are overall effects of the situation on a subject's behavior. The assumption is that if subjects have an idea what the researcher expects, they will perform as expected. To give an example, suppose a researcher is studying problem-solving skills. The experimenter might get a baseline measurement of skill level, and then give one group training on problem-solving skills, and allow other group to watch TV. Subjects receiving the training might realize that the experimenter expects them to do better on the second test, and may try to do well on the second test as a result.

A special kind of demand characteristic is the **placebo effect**. For example, let's say that we're testing a drug to see if it will reduce anxiety. When people are given a drug, they usually expect that the drug will be effective. If you give subjects a sugar pill, and tell them that it will reduce anxiety, the subjects' anxiety will usually decrease.

Finally, the **Hawthorne effect** refers to the tendency of people to behave differently if they know that they are being observed. To control for the Hawthorne effect, researchers use a control group design, and observe *both* the control group and the experimental group.

External validity has to do with how generalizable the results of an experiment are. If the results of a laboratory experiment on helping behavior using college sophomores as research subjects cannot be generalized to people in general, and to behavior outside of the laboratory, then the study lacks external validity.

POTENTIAL PROBLEMS IN RESEARCH DESIGN

Problem	Explanation	Possible Remedy
Experimenter bias	Experimenter's expectations or attitudes that can affect results	Double-blinding
Demand characteristics	Cues in research situation that suggest to the subject what is expected	Deception?
Placebo effect	A type of demand characteristic where a placebo has a beneficial effect on the subjects	Control groups
Hawthorne effect	The effect that being observed has on behavior	Control groups

DESCRIPTIVE STATISTICS

There are two basic types of **statistics: descriptive statistics** and **inferential statistics**. Descriptive statistics is concerned with organizing, describing, quantifying, and summarizing a collection of actual observations. In inferential statistics, researchers generalize beyond actual observations. That is, inferential statistics is concerned with making an inference from the sample involved in the research to the population of interest and to provide an estimate of popular characteristics.

A very simple data set is presented below:

Weight (in pounds)

0

1

1

1

2

3

3

7

9

Frequency Distributions

We can use graphs and charts to summarize the data collected. Figure 2 is an example of a **frequency distribution** using the sample data set. Not surprisingly, it is a graphic representation of how often each value occurs. There is one instance of 0 pounds, 3 instances of 1 pound, and so on.

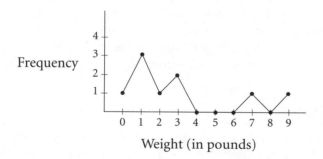

Figure 2. Frequency Distribution

Measures of Central Tendency

Measures of central tendency are also used in descriptive statistics. Measures of central tendency include the **mode**, the **median**, and the **mean**. These three measures all provide estimates of the average score.

The **mode** is the value of the most frequent observation in a set of scores. In our example, the mode is 1 pound. If there are two values that are tied for being the most frequently occurring observation, the data has two modes, or is **bimodal**. A distribution can also have three modes, or four modes, etc. This makes mode different from the other two measures of central tendency, as there can be only one mean and one median. If all the values in a distribution occur with equal frequency, that distribution has no mode.

The **median** is the middle value when observations are ordered from least to most or from most to least. The median is not the halfway point between the numerical value of the highest score and the numerical value of the lowest score. The median is the number that divides the distribution in half. In other words, once the data is ranked in numerical order, the median should be the number in the middle of the ranking. In our example, the median is 2, because there are four numbers below it (0, 1, 1, and 1) and four numbers above it (3, 3, 7, and 9). If you have an even number of data points, you must add the two middle-most numbers and divide by two. It might help to remember what a median is if you consider the median on the highway: the median divides the lanes in half. Likewise, the median of a data set divides the data set into two equal halves.

The **mean** is the numerical halfway point between the highest score and the lowest score, the arithmetic average. To calculate a mean, add all of the scores in your set of data and divide this sum by the number of scores. Adding the scores in our simple set of data gives us a total of 27. Since we have 9 scores, we divide our sum, 27, by 9 which gives us 3. Therefore, the mean of our distribution is 3.

How will extreme scores effect these measures of central tendency? Extreme scores, or **outliers**, affect the mean, median, and mode differently. Let's change the 9 in our data set to an extremely high score, 72. What happens to the median and the mode? They stay the same. The mean, however, becomes 10. The mean is therefore the measure of central tendency most sensitive to extreme scores. If you have extreme scores in your data set and are interested in a representative score for any individual, it usually makes more sense to use the median instead of the mean as your measure of central tendency.

Measures of Variability

The **range**, **standard deviation**, and **variance** are also important descriptive statistics: they are measures of **variability**, or **dispersion**, of scores. If the scores in the distribution are all the same, then there is no variability. If the scores are very spread out, then the variability is high. The **range** is simply the smallest number in the distribution subtracted from the largest number. In our example, 9 minus 0 equals a range of 9. The **standard deviation** provides a measure of the typical distance of scores from the mean. The **variance** is simply the square of the standard deviation and is a description of how much each score varies from the mean. If the standard deviation is 5, the variance would be 25. If the variance is 36, the standard deviation would be 6. Both the standard deviation and the variance must be either 0 or a positive number, since there can be no negative values to these measures of "distance."

MEASURES OF DISPERSION	
Measure	**Description**
Range	Highest score minus lowest score
Standard deviation	"Average" scatter away from the mean (also the square root of the variance)
Variance	The square of the standard deviation

Distributions, Percentiles, and *z*-Scores

Knowing the standard deviation of a distribution can actually be quite useful, especially if the distribution of scores forms a normal distribution. The normal distribution forms a symmetrical bell-shaped curve, as depicted in Figure 3. Similar to the frequency distribution, the horizontal axis gives us the values (standard deviations) and the vertical axis gives us the frequency of the values.

If scores form a normal distribution, and you know how many standard deviations away from the mean your score is, you can also determine what **percentile** your score is at. The percentile tells us the percentage of scores that fall at or below that particular score. If your score on the GRE Psychology test is at the 90th percentile, then 90 percent of test takers obtained scores at or below your score. Note, this does not mean that you got 90 percent correct. It just means that relative to the other people taking the test, you scored as well or better than 90 percent of the test takers. Because of the special properties of the normal distribution, we know what the percentages are at 1, 2, and 3 standard deviations (3 standard deviations is the extent of what you will need to know for the GRE Psychology test) above and below the mean. The percentages, which you should memorize, are depicted in Figure 3. Sixty-eight percent of scores will fall within 1 standard deviation; 96 percent will fall within 2 standard deviations; and 4 percent will fall beyond 2 standard deviations.

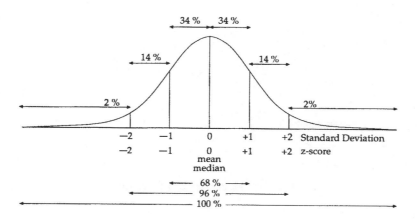

Figure 3. Percentages and the Normal Distribution

A **z-score** is another way of calculating how many standard deviations above or below the mean your score is. To determine z-scores, you subtract the mean of the distribution from your score, and divide the difference by the standard deviation. Negative z-scores fall below the mean, and positive z-scores fall above the mean. For example, if the mean of a set of scores was 20, the standard deviation was 15, and your score was 50, your z-score would be (50-20)/15, or 2. In other words, your score falls 2 standard deviations above the mean.

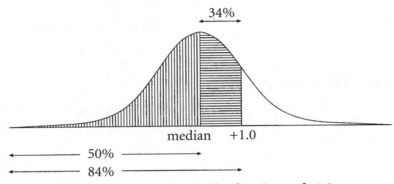

Figure 4. Finding the Percentile of a z-Score of +1.0

To find percentiles for normal distributions, we need to figure out what percentage of scores occurs below the score in question. Drawing a picture of the normal distribution sometimes helps. Figure 4 illustrates how to find the percentile of a z-score of +1. The scores that occur below z-scores of +1 can be divided into two groups: those scores that occur between the mean and a z-score of +1 (34 percent), denoted by horizontal lines in Figure 3, and those that occur below the mean (50 percent), denoted by the vertical lines in Figure 4. The total percentage of scores below a z-score of +1 is 50 percent + 34 percent = 84 percent. Thus, in a normal distribution, 84 percent of scores will fall below a score with a z-score of +1.

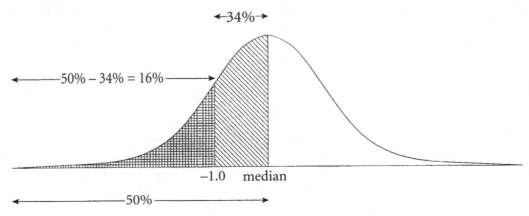

Figure 5. Finding the Percentile of a z-Score of −1.0

If you need to find the percentile occurring below a *z*-score of –1, you would need to figure out what percentage of scores is denoted by the area with crossed vertical and horizontal lines in Figure 5. We don't know directly the percentage of scores that occur below a *z*-score of –1.0, but we can figure it out. Since we know that 50 percent of the scores fall below a *z*-score of 0, and we know that 34 percent of scores fall between *z*-scores of 0 and –1, then by subtracting 50 percent–34 percent, we can figure out the percentage of scores denoted by the area with crossed vertical and horizontal lines: 16 percent.

There is a method for approximating *z*-scores, but it still requires that you memorize Figure 3. To figure out the percentile represented by your *z*-score, just add up all the percentages to the left of it. If you're given a *z*-score of +2.0, add $2 + 14 + 34 + 34 + 14 = 98$. So a *z*-score of +2.0 will be at about the 98th percentile.

From time to time, a question pops up on the GRE Psychology test about what would happen if you converted every score in a distribution to a *z*-score. Without going through the reasoning behind it, just know that if you have a distribution of *z*-scores and calculate the mean and standard distribution, the mean of the distribution of *z*-scores will always be zero and the standard deviation will always be 1. This is true regardless of whether the distribution is normal or not and regardless of what the mean and the standard deviation of the original distribution were.

PERCENTILES AND *z*-SCORES: SOME KEY CONCEPTS	
Concept	**Explanation**
Percentile	Indicates the percentage of scores that fall at or below a given score (e.g., if your score is at the 90th percentile, 90 percent of the scores fall at or below your score)
z-Score	Indicates the number of standard deviations your score is away from the mean
Normal distribution	About 68 percent of the scores within 1 standard deviation of the mean; about 96 percent of the scores fall within 2 standard deviations of the mean

Scores can also be converted into **T-scores**. The T-score distribution has a mean of 50 and a standard deviation of 10. So, for instance, a T-score of 60 is one standard deviation above the mean. Because of their nice round numbers, T-scores are often used in test score interpretation.

Because the normal distribution is symmetrical and has its greatest frequency in the middle, the mean, median and mode of a normal distribution are identical. In skewed distributions, as in Figure 6, where the distributions of scores are not identical, the mean, median, and mode will not be identical.

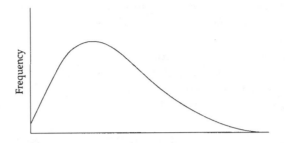

Figure 6. A Skewed Distribution

Correlation Coefficients

Correlation coefficients are another type of descriptive statistic that measure to what extent, if any, two variables are related. Two variables are related if knowing the value of one variable helps you predict the value of the other variable. Correlations help us understand the relationship and degree of association between two variables.

The correlation coefficient allows us to mathematically specify how well we can predict the value of the second variable given the corresponding value of the first variable. Correlation coefficients range from −1.00 to +1.00. So, if a question on the GRE Psychology test asks you to interpret a correlation coefficient of +1.3, the correct answer would be something like "a mathematical error has been made."

If two variables have a **positive correlation**, it means that a change in value of one of the variables tends to be associated with a change in the same direction of the value of the other variable. As the value of one variable increases, the value of the second tends to increase as well in a linear fashion. On the other hand, if two variables have a **negative correlation**, a change in value of one of the variables tends to be associated with a change in the opposite direction of the other variable. So, as the value of one variable increases, the value of the second variable tends to decrease. *When we say that two variables are correlated, we do not necessarily mean that the two variables have a cause and effect relationship.* Ice cream sales and drownings are positively correlated, but we can't inter a causal relationship between the two. The fact that both increase in summer may be a significant factor. However, the correlation suggests a relationship.

The numerical value of the correlation tells us how strong the relationship is. The closer a correlation coefficient is to +1 or −1, the more sure we can be of our prediction. If you have a perfect correlation, either +1 or −1, then given a value of one variable, you can predict, with absolute certainty, the value of the second variable. Note that a negative correlation does not indicate a lack of relationship. As the correlation coefficient moves closer to zero, the less sure you become about your prediction. Finally, if two variables have a correlation of zero, knowing the value of the first variable does not at all help you predict the value of the second variable.

The graphical representation of correlational data is called a **scatterplot**. Let's take a look of an example about the relationship between high school grade point average and college grade point average. The data are as follows:

Person	High School GPA	College GPA
1	4.0	3.7
2	2.5	3.0
3	3.7	3.9
4	1.8	2.1
5	3.2	3.4
6	2.3	2.7
7	2.8	2.4
8	3.9	4.0
9	3.0	3.3
10	2.9	2.7

The scatterplot of this data is given in Figure 7. As you can see, high school GPA is represented on the horizontal axis, and college GPA is represented on the vertical axis.

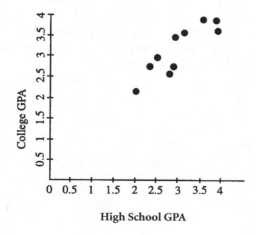

Figure 7. A Scatterplot

Once we have a scatterplot, we can draw what we call the **best-fitting straight line** through the dots. Figures 8, 9, and 10 are illustrations of scatterplots with best fitting straight lines. The most important information to get from the scatterplot is the direction, or the slope, or the line. Figure 8 illustrates a positive correlation: as the score on Test 1 increases, so does the score on Test 2. Figure 9 illustrates a negative correlation: as the score on Test 1 increases, the score on Test 2 decreases. Figure 10 illustrates a correlation of zero. Notice that knowing a person's score on Test 1 does not allow you to predict the person's score on Test 2.

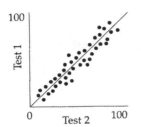 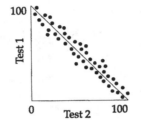 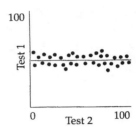

Figure 8. A Positive Correlation   **Figure 9. A Negative Correlation**   **Figure 10. No Correlation**

Correlation is also the cornerstone of a technique known as **factor analysis.** Factor analysis attempts to account for the interrelationships found among various variables by seeing how groups of variables "hang together." The process of actually performing a factor analysis is quite complex; however, you may be asked to do an "armchair" factor analysis on the GRE Psychology test.

Below is a correlation matrix, which is a table that shows the correlations between various pairs of variables. For instance, the correlation between variable A and variable B is +.85; the correlation between variable A and variable C is +.79, and so forth. The correlation between a variable and itself is +1.00. Now, to the extent that two variables measure the same thing, the correlation between those two variables will be high. We want to look through the correlation matrix to see which variables are highly correlated with each other. A cluster of variables highly correlated with each other is assumed to be measuring the same thing. This thing is called a **factor** (hence the name *factor analysis*).

	A	B	C	D	E	F
A	1.00	.85	.79	.05	.02	.04
B		1.00	.95	.01	.03	.01
C			1.00	.03	.07	.06
D				1.00	.93	.89
E					1.00	.97
F						1.00

In our correlation matrix, variables A, B, and C have a lot in common with each other, since they are highly correlated with one another. Furthermore, variables A, B, and C have nothing in common with variables D, E, and F. On the other hand, D, E, and F are highly correlated with one another. Therefore, our armchair factor analysis has detected two separate factors: one measured by variables A, B and C, and the other measured by variables D, E, and F.

INFERENTIAL STATISTICS

Inferential statistics allow us to use a relatively small batch of actual observations to make conclusions about the entire population of interest. We make these kinds of conclusions in real life, when, for instance, we conclude that an entire batch of soup doesn't have enough pepper based on a taste of just one small spoonful. As the name suggests, inferential statistics is concerned with making inferences, or generalizations, from samples to populations. Inferential statistics gives us powerful tools for making conclusions about populations based only upon data obtained from samples, while taking into account the possibility for error.

Significance Testing

A **significance test** is one tool researchers use to draw conclusions about populations based upon research conducted on samples. With a significance test, the researcher is trying to show that one hypothesis (the **research hypothesis**, or the **alternative hypothesis**) is supported by the data by showing that other possible hypotheses (represented by the **null hypothesis**) are inconsistent with the data collected. Experimental hypotheses are confirmed by disconfirming the null hypothesis—by showing that it is not supported by the data. The null hypothesis is that the population mean is the same as the sample mean.

Let's assume that we're interested in the effect of gender on problem-solving skills. Our subjects are 25 men and 25 women, and the task measuring problem-solving skills is a list of 15 logic problems. The DV is the number of problems solved; our IV is gender; our research hypothesis is that gender has an effect on problem-solving skills; and our null hypothesis is that there is no difference between the mean problem-solving score for the population of men and the mean problem-solving score for the population of women.

In significance testing, we test our null hypothesis against the data we obtained from our sample. If the two groups in our experiment differ on the dependent variable measured, the difference could reflect a real difference, or a difference due to chance, or random error. If the mean score of the women is 8 and the mean score of the men is 10, we have a different of 2 points between the two means. Significance tests can help determine if a 2 point difference is a real difference, or due to chance.

A significance test can tell us the probability that our observed difference is due to chance, that is, the probability that we could have obtained such a difference if our null hypothesis, that there is no difference between the two groups, was indeed true. If it is unlikely that the 5-point difference was due to chance, then we can reject the null hypothesis and accept the alternative, or the research hypothesis. We could conclude that a breakfast high in protein is associated with higher spelling test scores, as compared to a breakfast low in protein.

If the significance tells us that the probability our observed difference is due to chance is high, we can accept our null hypothesis and reject the alternative, or research hypothesis. So, for instance, if we found that there was a 97 percent probability that the observed difference between the two groups was due only to chance, we would conclude that the difference observed does not reflect a true difference between the male and female populations.

On the other hand, a low probability means that it is *un*likely that the observed difference is due only to chance. Therefore, we would strongly suspect that our independent variable was at least partially responsible for our observed difference. In this case, we could reject the null hypothesis and accept our research, or alternative hypothesis.

If we reject the null hypothesis, the observed difference is **statistically significant**. Who decides what probability represents statistically significance? The researcher decides before collecting data by establishing a **criterion of significance**. By convention, psychologists usually use 5 percent as their criterion of significance. That is, most psychologists are willing to reject the null hypothesis only if they are very sure that observed differences are not due solely to chance. If they obtain a significance level equal to or less than 5 percent, the results are statistically significant, and they reject the null hypothesis. If they do their study and obtain a significance level greater than 5 percent, their results are not statistically significant and they must accept the null hypothesis. The criterion of significance is sometimes also called the **alpha level**.

SIGNIFICANCE TESTING PROCESS	
Step 1	Formulate alternative and null hypotheses based on your research hypothesis.
Step 2	Decide on a criterion of significance (usually 5 percent).
Step 3	Collect data.
Step 4	Perform significance test on your data in order to obtain the significance level.
Step 5	Compare the obtained significance level to the criterion of significance. If the significance level is less than the criterion of significance, the results are statistically significant. Otherwise the results are statistically insignificant.
Step 6	If the results are statistically significant, reject the null hypothesis. If the results are statistically insignificant, accept the null hypothesis.

Errors in Significance Testing

In the process of testing the statistical significance of research results, there are possibilities of error. There are two types of errors a researcher could make: Type I or Type II errors. Figure 11 refers to errors in significance testing.

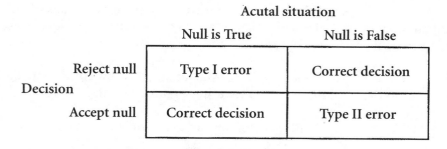

Figure 11. Errors in Significance Testing

Researchers could mistakenly reject the null hypothesis, committing a Type I error, represented in the upper left-hand corner of Figure 11. In this case, there is really no difference between the population values mentioned in the null hypothesis and a statistically significant result was obtained just by chance. In other words, a true null hypothesis was rejected. The likelihood of making a Type I error is the same as the criterion of significance the researcher chooses. For instance, if the researcher chooses a criterion of 5 percent, then, there is a 5 percent chance of making a Type I error. With this criterion, if the null hypothesis is rejected, there are 5 chances out of 100 that the decision is wrong.

The second error a researcher can make is to accept the null hypothesis, when it is, in fact, false. This is called a Type II error, represented in the lower right-hand corner of Figure 10. In this case, a statistically insignificant result was obtained and the null hypothesis was accepted, even though the null hypothesis was, in fact, false. What is the probability of making a Type II error? Well, it's rather complex and the details are beyond the scope of the GRE Psychology test. You probably just need to remember that the probability of making a Type II error is called **Beta**, after the Greek letter.

To conclude, the purpose of significance testing is to make an inference about a population on the basis of sample data. Statistical significance does not tell us anything about whether or not the research is poorly designed, or whether or not the results are trivial or meaningless. Sample size is related to significance levels: the larger the size of the sample, the smaller the difference between the groups has to be in order to be significant. Therefore, if you use really large sample sizes and you get a statistically significant result, the difference between the groups on the DV measure might be so small as to make the results trivial.

Types of Significance Tests

There are three kinds of significance tests that have appeared on the GRE Psychology test: the **t-test**, **ANOVA** and **chi-square test**. You won't need to know how to calculate them, but you will need to know how to use them. Briefly, t-tests are used to compare the means of two groups. For more than two groups, analyses of variance (ANOVAs) are used. A chi-square test tests the equality of two frequencies or proportions.

ANOVAs estimate how much group means differ from each other by comparing the between-group variance to the within-group variance using a ratio, called the F ratio:

$$\text{F ratio} = \frac{\text{Between-group variance estimate}}{\text{Within-group variance estimate}}$$

Using our breakfast example, let's say we establish groups receiving high-protein, medium-protein, and low-protein diets. If the protein level doesn't make a difference on spelling test scores, we would expect an F ratio of near 1. That is, the mean scores on spelling test are about the same for each group, (and should therefore be the about the same as the difference between individuals within each group) regardless of the level of protein in the breakfast.

Let's look at another example. Let's say that the variance within the groups is low: children receiving low protein breakfasts all score relatively low; children receiving medium protein breakfasts all score in the medium range; and children receiving high protein breakfasts all score relatively high. Let's also say that the variance among the means of the groups is comparatively high, that is, the mean score of the low-protein group is relatively low, as compared to the medium-protein group; and the medium protein group scores relatively low, as compared to the high-protein group. In this case, we would expect the value of F to be larger, and more likely to be significantly significant.

ANOVAs can also be used to determine if there is any interaction between two or more IVs. Let's return to our breakfast example and add gender as a second IV. Below are the hypothetical results from our experiment:

		Gender	
		Female	Male
Breakfast	High protein	70	60
type	Low protein	65	75

You will notice that females do better on spelling tests, on average, if given a high protein breakfast. On the other hand, if you look at the male results, you'll see that the males actually did better when given a low-protein breakfast. Given this data, if someone asked you whether it was good to have a high-protein breakfast before taking a spelling test, you'd have to answer, "It depends on whether you're a female or a male." That's because there is an interaction between the two independent variables. An interaction occurs whenever the effects of one independent variable are not consistent for all levels of the second independent variable. ANOVAs can assess interactions and this technique helps ascertain if the IV influenced the DV.

Chi-square tests are significance tests that work with **categorical**, rather than numerical data. If you think back on the statistics we've talked about so far, you'll recall that the dependent variable has usually been some kind of score, for example, the number of correct answers on a spelling test. When the data collected are not numbers, but names or categories, such as male or female, and you are making inferences about data of this type, you could use a chi-square test. Categorized measurement is also called **nominal** since it involves classifying or naming.

When summarizing categorical data, we wind up with frequencies or proportions. So, if 150 individuals are asked whether they are Democrats or Republicans, data might be given in numbers, i.e., 80 people Democrats and 70 are Republicans (frequencies), or 53 percent are Democrats and 47 percent were Republicans (proportions).

TYPES OF SIGNIFICANCE TESTS	
Type	**Use/Explanation**
T-test	Use when you have two groups
ANOVA	Use when you have more than two groups
Factorial design	Each level of a given independent variable occurs with each level of the other independent variables
Interaction	When the effects of one independent variable are not consistent for all levels of the other independent variables
Chi-square test	Use when individual observations are names or categories

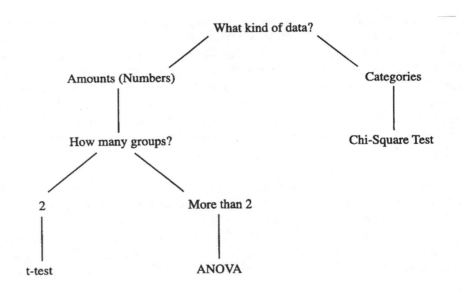

Figure 12. Significance Tests

Meta-Analysis

Meta-analysis is a statistical procedure that can be used to make conclusions on the basis of data from different studies. If researcher A publishes a study on therapeutic outcomes and researcher B publishes a similar study using different methods, we can use meta-analysis to combine the results of these studies and come up with a more general conclusion.

TESTS AND MEASUREMENTS

Score Interpretation

Based upon the information we've covered so far in this chapter, you know that statistics help to analyze data after we've collected it. However, statistics can also come in handy when we design and evaluate the psychological tests that we use to collect data. Let's review some standardized tests and measurements that measure attitudes, motivation, personality traits, or abilities.

Norm-Referenced Testing

First, let's look at two ways that test results can be interpreted: **norm-referenced** and **domain-referenced**. **Norm-referenced** testing involves assessing an individual's performance in terms of how that individual performs in comparison to others. For example, "Erika did better in spelling than 99 percent of second graders tested." In other words, we compare the test taker's performance to that test's norms. Test norms are derived from standardized samples; the samples should be large and representative of the population to whom the particular test will be administered.

One problem with norm-referenced testing is that the population to whom the tests will be administered can, and often does, change. If the population of interest changes, then the original standardization sample would no longer be representative of the population.

Domain-Referenced Testing

Domain-referenced testing, sometimes called **criterion-referenced testing**, is concerned with the question of what the test taker knows about a specified content domain. Performance on such a test is described in terms of what the test taker knows or can do. An example of domain-referenced testing is the written test you must take for your driver's license. What's important is not how you score in relation to your peers, but whether you have mastery of the rules of the road.

Reliability

Reliability is the consistency with which a test measures whatever it is that the test measures. High reliability means that the test measures are dependable, reproducible, and consistent. We would expect that an individual would score about the same when retested on the same test or a comparable form of the test. In practice, no test is perfectly reliable.

So, what makes a good test? One way to determine whether a test is good is to think about how close a person's score is to his or her true score. The standard error of measurement (SEM) is an index of how much, on average, we expect a person's observed score to vary from the score the person is capable of receiving based on actual ability. The best SEM would be zero, but since no test is perfect, this is not possible. The smaller the test's SEM, the better. The SEM provides information in regard to a test's reliability.

There are three basic methods used to establish the reliability of a test. In the **test-retest method**, the same test is administered to the same group of people twice. This method estimates the inter-individual stability of test scores over time. In the **alternate-form method**, the examinees are given two different forms of a test that are taken at two different times. The final method is called **split-half reliability**, where test takers only take one test, but that one test is divided into equal halves. Scores on one half are correlated with the scores on the other half. In all of these methods, a correlation coefficient is then calculated using the pairs of scores. A high positive correlation ($\geq +.80$) indicates a high level of reliability.

METHODS OF ASSESSING RELIABILITY		
Type of Reliability	**Correlation between:** First Score	Second Score
Test-retest	Test 1	Test 1 (given to same person second time)
Alternate-form	Test 1	Test 2 (given to same person as Test 1)
Split-half	Score on one-half of Test 1	Score on one-half of Test 1

Validity

Validity is concerned with the extent to which a test actually measures what it is purports to measure. All types of validity assessment examine the relationship between performance on the test in question and other independent and objective sources of information about the knowledge or behaviors or interest. The evidence used to determine validity depends on the nature of the test itself, and more specifically, what the test is used for.

Content validity refers to its coverage of the particular skill or knowledge area that it is supposed to measure. If a test is supposed to measure knowledge of 20th century American History, the test items should include questions about 20th century American History.

Face validity refers to whether or not the test items appear to measure what they are supposed to measure. If you are interested in measuring knowledge of 20th century American History, but you give subjects a test on 20th century European History, the test will lack face validity.

Criterion validity has to do with how well the test can predict an individual's performance on an established test of the same skill or knowledge area. **Cross validation** involves testing the criterion validity of a test on a second sample, after you demonstrated validity using an initial sample.

Construct validity refers to how well performance on the test fits into the theoretical framework related to what it is you want the test to measure. If, for example, social adeptness is related to intelligence, then in order for your test of social adeptness to have construct validity, people who score high on your test of social adeptness should also score high on tests of intelligence. This is called **convergent validity**. In order to show that a test has construct validity, researchers also have to show that performance on the test is not correlated with other variables theory predicts that test performance should not be related to. This is called **discriminant validity**.

AN EXAMPLE OF TEST VALIDITY

What We Want to Know	Type of Validity We're Concerned With
Does the test measure various facets of American history?	Content
Does the test look like it measures knowledge of American history?	Face
Does test performance indicate number of previous American history courses taken?	Criterion Concurrent
Does test performance predict future success as history major?	Predictive
Is test performance related to, e.g., interest in history?	Construct Convergent
Is test performance not related to, e.g., test-taking experience?	Discriminate

A test with zero reliability will have zero validity; however, a test can have perfect reliability and very little validity. In other words, reliability is a precondition for validity, but the opposite is not necessarily true. Let's say that you wanted to measure creativity by asking children to swim as far as they could. Such a test would have high reliability, that is, if repeated, they would probably swim about the same distance each time. However, your test would not be a valid measure of creativity.

Scales of Measurement

There are four basic types of measurement scales: **nominal**, **ordinal**, **interval**, and **ratio**. A **nominal** scale of measurement (also called a **categorical** scale) labels observations so that observations can be categorized, for instance, Democratic-Republican, girl-boy, blue eyes-brown eyes. In an ordinal scale, observations are ranked in terms of size or magnitude, for example, highest score on spelling test, second highest score on spelling test, and so on. An **interval scale**, uses actual numbers (not ranks), such as the number correct on a spelling test. In **ratio scaling**, unlike interval scales, there is a true zero point that indicates the total absence of the quantity being measured. For example, a temperature of 0° does not mean that there is no temperature, and therefore could not be considered a ratio scale.

Multiplication and division are meaningful only on measurements made using ratio scales, whereas subtraction and addition are meaningful on ratio and interval scales. It makes sense, for example to say that a temperature of 30° F is 60° less than a temperature of 90° F; it makes no sense to say that 90° F is three times as hot as 30° F.

SCALES OF MEASUREMENT			
Scale Type	**Characteristic(s)**	**Example**	**Arithmetic Operations**
Nominal/categorical	Names	Political affiliation	None
Ordinal	Ranks	Order of finish in horse race	None
Interval	Equal intervals	Temperature (in °F)	Addition/ Subtraction
Ratio	Equal intervals + true zero point	Income	All (Add/ Subtract/ Multiply/Divide)

Ability Tests

There are two types of **ability tests: aptitude tests** and **achievement tests. Aptitude tests** are used to predict what one can accomplish through training. In other words, they are used to predict future performance; aptitude tests include intelligence tests. **Achievement tests,** on the other hand, attempt to assess what one knows or can do now; they can test adequacy of learning content and skill.

IQ is a well-known measure of intelligence aptitude using an equation comparing mental age to chronological age. IQ is mental age divided by chronological age, multiplied by 100. An IQ of 100 indicates that a person's mental age is equal to his or her chronological age. One of the problems with the **ratio IQ**, though, is that after a certain age, chronological age increases while mental age does not. Therefore, even if your mental age remains constant, your IQ will decrease with age. In order to get around this problem, the 1960 revision of the Stanford-Binet used **deviation quotients.** Essentially, a deviation IQ score tells us how far away a person's score is from the average score for the particular age group the subject is a member of. Therefore, the deviation IQ represents the individual's standing among his or her same-aged cohort.

THE INTELLIGENCE QUOTIENT	
Type of IQ	**Definition**
Ratio IQ	$\dfrac{\text{Mental Age}}{\text{Chronological Age}} \times 100$
Deviation IQ	Indicates how well a person performed on an IQ test relative to her/his same-age peers

A major group of intelligence tests is the **Wechsler tests.** Unlike the Stanford-Binet, which is organized by age levels, the Wechsler tests have all items of a given type grouped into subtests. These items are arranged in order of increasing difficulty within each subtest. The Wechsler tests have two broad subscales: a verbal scale which is based on information, vocabulary, and similar skills; and a performance scale, which is derived from tests of manipulative skill, eye-hand coordination, and speed.

Wechsler developed three major IQ tests: the **Wechsler Preschool and Primary Scale of Intelligence (WPPSI),** the **Wechsler Intelligence Scale for Children (WISC),** and the **Wechsler Adult Intelligence Scale (WAIS).** All have been revised, and are now called the **WPPSI-R,** the **WISC-R** and the **WAIS-R,** and they are used with preschoolers, school-aged children (5–16 years old) and adults (16 years and older), respectively. The **WAIS-III** is the current version utilized for adult intelligence testing.

Personality Tests

Personality Inventories

Personality tests are also frequently used in psychological research. A **personality inventory** is a self-rating device usually consisting of somewhere between 100 and 500 statements. The subject is asked to determine if the given statements apply to him or her. Although these structured tools are quite reliable, the veracity of responses is not guaranteed. For example, if an item should appear that says, "I occasionally steal," most people would tend to answer "no" regardless of whether or not they occasionally steal. The perceived social acceptability of a response is just one factor that can effect the accuracy of tests that involve self-reporting.

One of the major personality inventories is the **Minnesota Multiphasic Personality Inventory**, or **MMPI**. The MMPI consists of 550 statements to which subjects respond "true," "false," or "cannot say." The MMPI yields scores on ten clinical scales, measuring things such as depression, schizophrenia, and masculinity/femininity. It has scales that can indicate whether the person is careless, faking answers, misrepresenting him or herself, or distorting responses, whether it is being done intentionally or unintentionally. High scores on these scales can lead to the rejection of the test record. The purpose of the MMPI is to aid in the assessment of various clinical disorders.

To develop the MMPI, Hathaway and McKinley used the **empirical criterion-keying approach**. They tested thousands of questions and retained those that differentiated between patient and nonpatient populations, even if the item didn't seem to have anything to do with abnormality. The authors examined the responses of patient groups with different diagnoses. Each criterion group's responses formed the basis of a particular clinical scale, so that if a new patient answered questions in the same way that, say, the depressive criterion group did, that patient would receive a high depression score.

A revision of the MMPI, the MMPI-2 (1989) added content scales. These scales were formed using items derived from theoretical concerns rather than from an empirical criterion-keying approach. So for instance, to form the low self-esteem content scale, the test authors selected items that ought to be related to low self-esteem. Hence, the original clinical scales have been supplemented with content scales that were developed using a more theoretical approach.

The **California Psychological Inventory** (**CPI**), is another personality inventory that is based on the MMPI. It was developed to be used with normal populations from age 13 and up. It is especially oriented to high school and college students. This particular test consists of 20 scales, including 3 validity scales, used to assess test-taking attitudes. Through a series of 462 true-false items, the CPI measures such personality traits as dominance, sociability, self-control, and femininity. Like the MMPI, all scores are expressed as standard scores with a mean and standard deviation derived from standardization samples.

Projective Tests

Projective tests are different from personality inventories in two basic ways: First, the stimuli in a projective test are relatively ambiguous; second, the test taker is not limited to a small number of possible responses. A test taker is given the stimuli and asked to interpret what he or she sees. This means that the scoring of a projective test is subjective, whereas the scoring of personality inventories is objective.

One of the most famous projective tests is called the **Rorschach inkblot** test, created by Hermann Rorschach. The test is made up of 10 cards that are reproductions of ink blots. The cards are presented to the subject in a specific order with very specific instructions to describe what it is that the blots remind the subject of. The clinician then interprets the results based upon what the person saw and the spontaneous remarks that the person may have made.

Another projective test is the **Thematic Apperception Test** (TAT). The **TAT** was devised by Morgan and Murray and consists of twenty simple pictures depicting scenes that have ambiguous meanings. For example, one picture might be a boy staring sadly at a violin. The test-taker is told to tell a story about what is happening, to give the events leading up to what is happening in the picture, and to provide an ending. It is important to remember that like the Rorschach, there is no standardized scoring method for the TAT. Scoring is qualitative and the clinician has to rely on his or her clinical skills.

A projective test devised especially for children is the **Blacky pictures**. This test consists of 12 cartoonlike pictures that feature a little dog named Blacky. Developed according to psychoanalytic theory, each picture depicts Blacky in a situation designed to correspond to a particular stage of psychosexual development. The test taker is asked to tell stories about the pictures he or she is shown.

The **Rotter Incomplete Sentences Blank** is an example of a sentence completion test, another projective technique researchers and clinicians use. The test taker is provided with 40 sentence stems and is asked to complete them. The theory is that the test taker will fill in the blanks with whatever is on his or her mind.

There is an interesting effect, the "**Barnum effect**," which refers to the tendency of people to accept and approve of the interpretation of their personality that you give them. It is relatively simple to generate a "report" from stereotyped statements; these reports are readily accepted as accurate. The Barnum effect is a form of pseudovalidation.

PERSONALITY TESTS	
Type of Test and Examples	**Definition**

Personality inventory
 	
    MMPI
    CPI
	Self-rating device consisting of statements that can be answered by the person taking the test; the test taker is given a limited number of ways to respond to the statements (e.g., *yes, no, uncertain*)

Projective tests
 	
    Rorschach inkblot test
    TAT
    Rotter incomplete sentences
	Relatively ambiguous stimuli are presented to the test-taker; the test taker is asked to interpret the stimuli

Interest Testing

Interest testing is usually used to assess an individual's interest in different lines of work. The best known test of this kind is the **Strong-Campbell Interest Inventory**. This inventory is organized like a personality inventory, and in fact, like the MMPI, was developed using an empirical criterion-keying approach. Test-takers are given lists of interests and asked to indicate whether they like or dislike the interest listed. In other sections of the test, the test-taker is asked to indicate his or her preference for one of the two paired items. The interpretation of the results is based, at least partly, on Holland's model of occupational themes. Holland divided interests into six types: realistic, investigative, artistic, social, enterprising, and conventional. That's why it is sometimes called the **RIASEC** system.

IMPORTANT FORMULAS IN STATISTICS

Mean
$$\frac{\text{Sum of observations}}{\text{Number of observations}}$$

Median The number that divides the data in half

Mode The number with the highest frequency

Range Highest score—lowest score

Standard deviation The square root of the variance

Variance The square of the standard deviation (or, to put it another way, the standard deviation times the standard deviation)

z-score
$$\frac{\text{Your score minus the mean}}{\text{Standard deviation}}$$

RESEARCH DESIGN AND STATISTICS PRACTICE SET

Time: 8 minutes

Directions: Each of the questions or incomplete statements below is followed by five suggested answers or completions. In each case, select the one that best answers the question or completes the statement.

1. A researcher is interested in the effect exercise has on the spatial frequency perception of people with Uhthoff's symptom. She takes 30 people with Uhthoff's symptom and divides them into two groups. One group is told to exercise for 15 minutes and the other group is told to rest for 15 minutes. When the 15 minutes are up, each subject is presented with two pictures of the same object, one blurry and one clear, and asked whether the two pictures are metamers or not. Which of the following is the most appropriate test?

   (A) Sandler's A statistic
   (B) T-test
   (C) ANOVA
   (D) Chi-square test
   (E) Hierarchical analysis

2. Which of the following is the defining characteristic of random sampling?

   (A) The sample is a stratified sample.
   (B) The sample is a miniature version of the population.
   (C) The researcher haphazardly selects subjects for her sample.
   (D) The sample is representative of the population.
   (E) Each member of the population has an equal chance of being selected for the sample.

3. Which of the following can help control for experimenter bias?

   (A) Double-blinding
   (B) Randomly assigning subjects to groups
   (C) Using control groups
   (D) Demand characteristics
   (E) ANOVA

4. What is the mean of the following distribution? 1, 1, 7, 8, 8

   (A) 1
   (B) 2
   (C) 5
   (D) 7
   (E) 8

5. All else being equal, which correlation coefficient is strongest?

   (A) −0.70
   (B) 0.00
   (C) +0.20
   (D) +0.65
   (E) +1.05

6. If a distribution has a lot of variability, which of the following is true?

   (A) The variance will be relatively small.
   (B) The mean will be relatively high.
   (C) The standard deviation will be relatively small.
   (D) The distribution will be skewed.
   (E) The standard deviation will be relatively high.

7. A researcher is interested in studying the effect of noise on the problem-solving abilities of elementary school students. She uses two classes of fourth grade students and tests them on a 10-problem test. When one class takes the test, she turns on a radio, keeping it off for the other class. This is an example of a

   (A) true experiment
   (B) quasi-experiment
   (C) correlational study
   (D) naturalistic observation
   (E) longitudinal study

8. The psychology department chair at the local University is interested in finding out which of two experimental psychology textbooks is better received by students. Two sections of the experimental psychology class are being offered next semester. The section that meets during the day uses text A and the section that meets at night uses text B. At the end of the semester, students in both sections will be asked to rate the text they used. Which of the following is most likely to confound this study?

   (A) The number of psychology courses students had prior to enrolling in the experimental psychology class
   (B) The university the study is taking place at
   (C) The text used in each section
   (D) The time of day each section meets
   (E) None of the above

9. A positively skewed distribution has a mean of 75.3 and a standard deviation of 20.15. If all the scores in the distribution are transformed into z-scores, what will the mean and standard deviation of the new distribution be?

   (A) 0 and 1, respectively
   (B) 0 and 20.15, respectively
   (C) 75.3 and 1, respectively
   (D) 75.3 and 20.15, respectively
   (E) Because the distribution is skewed, the new mean and standard deviation cannot be determined from the information given

10. A Type II error occurs

    (A) whenever a true null hypothesis is accepted
    (B) whenever a false null hypothesis is rejected
    (C) whenever a false null hypothesis is accepted
    (D) whenever a true null hypothesis is rejected
    (E) whenever a statistically <u>in</u>significant result is obtained

EXPLANATIONS FOR THE RESEARCH DESIGN AND STATISTICS PRACTICE SET

1. D

This was a tricky question. It required you to cut through the verbiage to get to the meat of the question. The question to ask is "What kind of data do we have?" Well, what is being measured is whether two pictures are perceived as metamers. Now, you don't need to know what metamers are to figure out that this is not an amount, it's a category. Two pictures are either metamers or they are not, just like someone is either a boy or a girl. Because we're not dealing with amounts, neither a t-test nor an ANOVA is appropriate here. Therefore, answer choices (B) and (C) are incorrect. Since we're only dealing with categories, the researcher should do a chi-square test. Therefore, the correct answer choice is (D). Choices (A) and (E) aren't likely to be correct answers because you have probably never seen or heard of them before. If you can't even recall seeing a statistics answer choice before, chances are it's too obscure to be the correct answer on the GRE psychology test. You could then have guessed from the remaining three answer choices, and remember, when you can narrow down the answer choices, it's in your best interest to guess.

2. E

For a sample to be random, each member of the population must have an equal chance of being selected for the sample. Random sampling does not insure that the sample will be representative of the population, so answer choice (D) is incorrect. And, by the way, that's why some researchers use stratified random sampling. If you remember, our definition of a representative sample is that the sample is a miniature version of the population. Therefore, answer choice (B) is incorrect. Answer choice (C) is also incorrect. Selecting a truly random sample requires much planning, much thinking, and much difficult work. If you haphazardly select subjects for your sample, you will probably *not* wind up with a truly random sample. Finally, answer choice (A) is also incorrect as no mention is made of any variables to be stratified on. If you didn't know the answer, but remembered what a representative sample was, you could have ruled out choices (B) and (D) as being synonymous and guessed from the remaining three answer choices.

3. A

Double-blinding can control for experimenter bias. If the persons dealing with the subjects and gathering the data do not know which level of the independent variable the subjects received, they will not have any expectations regarding the differential performance of the groups, and thus experimenter bias will be controlled. Choices (B) and (C) are incorrect. Although they are procedures that can help control for other confounding variables, they do not help control for experimenter bias. Choice (D) has to do with cues in the research situation that suggest to the subject what is expected of them. Choice (E) is a statistical procedure that doesn't control for experimenter bias.

4. C

The mean is 5. Remember, to obtain the mean, you first add up the values of all the observations in the distribution, so $1 + 1 + 7 + 8 + 8$ equals 25. You then divide this total by the number of observations, in this case, 5. So, 25 divided by 5 equals 5. Answer choice (D) is incorrect; 7 is the median, not the mean. Remember that the median is the number that divides the scores in half. Answer choices (A) and (E) are incorrect, because 1 and 8 are the modes, not the mean. Remember that the mode is the value that has the highest frequency. In this case there are two values that have the highest frequency, so there are two modes.

5. A

In a question of this sort, you want to disregard the sign of the correlation coefficient and see which number is biggest. Since .70 is bigger than .65, a correlation coefficient of −.70 is stronger than one of +.65. Therefore, choice (A) is correct. Choice (E) might have tempted some of you, because it is the highest number. However, it is impossible to have a correlation coefficient above +1.00 or below −1.00.

6. E

If a distribution has a lot of variability, the standard deviation will be relatively high. The standard deviation provides an index of the average scatter away from the mean. The greater the variability, the greater the scatter. Answer choices (A) and (C) are incorrect. Since the variance is the square of the standard deviation, if the variance is relatively small, the standard deviation will be relatively small, thus suggesting that there will be relatively low variability. Answer choice (D) is also incorrect. Whether or not a distribution is skewed does not depend on the amount of variability. Finally, answer choice (B) is incorrect. The mean can be relatively high and you can still have little variability.

7. B

This is a tricky question, but you can answer it using a process of elimination. Recall that when presented with a question such as this one, the first question to ask yourself is "Does the researcher manipulate the independent variable?" The independent variable here is the noise level (the dependent variable is the score on the problem-solving test). The researcher does indeed manipulate the noise level. She does so by turning the radio on and off. Therefore, the correct answer is not choice (C), a correlational study, because, in a correlational study, the researcher does not manipulate the independent variable. The next question that needs to be asked is whether the subjects are randomly assigned to the groups. Because the researcher is using preset groups, namely, the two classes, she can't randomly assign her subjects to the two conditions. Therefore, the correct answer is (B): a quasi-experiment. Answer choice (A), a true experiment, is incorrect because in a true experiment, the researcher both manipulates the independent variable and randomly assigns subjects to groups. Answer choice (D) is also incorrect. This study cannot be an example of naturalistic observation because the researcher intervenes, both in manipulating the independent variable and in testing the students. Finally, answer choice (E) is incorrect. This study is not a longitudinal study: the researcher is not interested in comparing different age groups over time. So, since this researcher manipulates the independent variable but does not randomly assign the subjects to the two conditions, the correct answer is (B).

8. D

There might be a difference between the students who would take a night class and those who would take a day class. For instance, night classes might attract relatively older students, who might rate textbooks differently than day students, perhaps because of differences in motivation, life experiences, etc. So, time of day might confound this study. Answer choice (C), the text used in

each section, cannot be a confounding variable because it is the independent variable. Answer choice (B), the university the study took place at, cannot be a confounding variable because it is held constant. Answer choice (A), however, cannot be dismissed so easily. It is true that there will be variation in the number of psychology courses students have had and it is conceivable that this variable could affect the rating of a psychology textbook, but it is not likely that this variable will be systematically related to the independent variable. That is, it is not likely that most of the students with lots of psychology courses will take the night class and that most of the students with few psychology courses will take the day class, or vice versa. In other words, it is likely that the effect of this variable will randomize out and will not differentially effect the ratings of the two groups.

9. A

Whenever you transform all the scores in a distribution into z-scores, the z-scores will always have a mean of 0 and a standard deviation of 1. It does not matter what the old mean and standard deviation were: a distribution of z-scores always has a mean and standard deviation of 0 and 1, respectively, and it doesn't matter that the distribution was skewed. Therefore, the correct answer choice is (A). You might have been tempted by some of the distracter items in the question stem. Don't be thrown by them. Just figure out what you need to know and go from there.

10. C

Type II error occurs whenever a false null hypothesis is accepted. Answer choices (A) and (B) are not errors and answer choice (D) is a Type I error, since you are falsely rejecting a true null hypothesis. Answer choice (E), however, can't be dismissed so easily. When a statistically insignificant result is obtained, the researcher accepts the null hypothesis. While it it is true that Type II errors can only occur when the researcher accepts the null hypothesis, this does *not* mean that a Type II error is made whenever the researcher accepts the null hypothesis; rather it means that accepting the null hypothesis *sometimes* leads to a Type II error. Therefore, choice (E) is incorrect and the only correct answer choice is (C).

IMPORTANT NAMES IN TESTS AND MEASUREMENTS

Binet, A. and Simon, T.	Developed the **Binet-Simon intelligence test**; introduced the concept of **mental age**
Holland, J.	Developed the **RIASEC model** of occupational themes
Jensen, A.	Suggested that there were **genetically based racial differences in IQ**; this suggestion has been much criticized
Morgan, C. and Murray, H.	Developed the **Thematic Apperception Test** (**TAT**), a projective test designed to measure personality
Rorschach, H.	Developed the **Rorschach inkblot** test, a projective test designed to measure personality
Rotter, J.	Developed a **sentence completion test**; a projective test designed to measure personality
Stern, W.	Developed the concept of the **ratio IQ**
Strong, E. and Campbell, D.	Developed the **Strong-Campbell Interest Inventory**; used to assess interest in different lines of work (actually, they didn't work together: Campbell revised an earlier test of Strong's)
Terman, L.	Revised the Binet-Simon intelligence test; revision became known as the **Stanford-Binet IQ Test**
Wechsler, D.	Developed several intelligence tests for use with different ages (the **WPPSI**, **WISC**, and **WAIS**); these tests yield three deviation IQs: a verbal IQ, a performance IQ, and a full-scale IQ

TESTS AND MEASUREMENTS PRACTICE SET

Time: 8 minutes

Directions: Each of the questions or incomplete statements below is followed by five suggested answers or completions. In each case, select the one that best answers the question or completes the statement.

1. A projective technique is
   (A) a method by which people's personalities can be assessed via their responses to ambiguous stimuli
   (B) a defense mechanism
   (C) an objective test in which the subject responds "True," "False," or "Cannot say"
   (D) a subtest on the WAIS
   (E) any test that measures personality

2. The developer of a clinical psychology aptitude test reports that the correlation between scores on it and scores on a test of interpersonal skills is +.45. This correlation provides some evidence that the clinical psychology aptitude test has
   (A) face validity
   (B) content validity
   (C) a ratio scale
   (D) construct validity
   (E) alternate-form reliability

3. A test mainly concerned with predicting future performance is
   (A) an aptitude test
   (B) an achievement test
   (C) a chi-squares test
   (D) a T test
   (E) an IQ test

4. If a person's observed score is 105, and the standard error of measurement is 15, what is that person's true score?
   (A) 15
   (B) 90
   (C) 105
   (D) 120
   (E) It cannot be determined from the information given.

5. What type of validity hinges largely on actions and decisions made before any test items are actually administered?
   (A) Criterion
   (B) Construct
   (C) Content
   (D) Predictive
   (E) Convergent

6. A 4-year old, Mary, has an IQ score of 200. An 8-year old, Jimmy, has an IQ score of 100. A 10-year old, Johnny, has an IQ of 90. Assuming that these are not deviation IQs, which child has the highest mental age?
   (A) Mary
   (B) Jimmy
   (C) Johnny
   (D) Neither; all children have the same mental age.
   (E) Mental age cannot be determined from the information given.

7. Which of the following statements about reliability is true?
    I. Reliability is important only in aptitude tests
    II. Reliability refers to the consistency with which the test measures whatever it measures
    III. Reliability refers to how well the test measures what you want it to measure

    (A) I only
    (B) II only
    (C) III only
    (D) I and II only
    (E) II and III only

8. When a person says "Molly is smarter than John," she is employing which measurement scale?

    (A) Nominal
    (B) Ordinal
    (C) Interval
    (D) Ratio
    (E) Categorical

9. The MMPI can best be classified as a(n)

    (A) computer-adaptive test
    (B) projective test
    (C) personality inventory
    (D) intelligence test
    (E) achievement test

10. One of the dangers of individual intelligence testing is that the examinees may get bored if the questions are too easy or become frustrated if the items are too difficult. To get around this problem, some intelligence tests are arranged so that the more difficult questions are presented only to the examinees who have gotten the easier questions correct. This is an example of

    (A) cross-validation
    (B) construct validity
    (C) adaptive testing
    (D) norm-referenced interpretation
    (E) projective testing

EXPLANATIONS FOR THE TESTS AND MEASUREMENTS PRACTICE SET

1. A

Examples of projective tests include the Rorschach test and the TAT. Answer choice (B), a defense mechanism, is incorrect. This might have tempted you because projection is a defense mechanism, but that's not what's being asked about in the question stem (defense mechanisms were discussed in the chapter on personality and abnormal personality). Answer choice (C) describes personality inventories, such as the MMPI. Personality inventories are not projective tests. Answer choice (D), the WAIS, is an intelligence test. Finally, as implied above, answer choice (E) is incorrect. Projective tests are only one type of personality test.

2. D

In this context, a construct refers to a theoretical framework related to what you want the test to measure. It seems apparent that any theoretical framework for clinical psychology aptitude would include something about interpersonal skills. Therefore, a moderately high correlation between a test of it and a test of clinical psychology aptitude suggests that the clinical psychology test has some construct validity. Answer choice (A), face validity, has to do with whether the questions on the test appear to be measuring clinical psychology aptitude. The only way to "measure" face validity is by informally examining the test, and by concluding that the questions on the test appear to have to do with clinical psychology aptitude. That is not what is happening in the question stem, so answer choice (A) is incorrect. Answer choice (B), content validity, is also incorrect. Content validity has to do with how well the test questions sample the different aspects of clinical psychology aptitude. To assess that, you would want to have, say, a list of important indicators of clinical psychology aptitude and see how many of these indicators are tested in the test. Content validity is assessed by critically examining the test items and comparing the breadth of material covered with what should be covered. Choice (C), a ratio scale, is also incorrect. Recall that you have a ratio scale when there are both equal intervals between the points on your scale and a true zero point. Finally, answer choice (E), alternate-form reliability, is also incorrect. Alternate-form reliability is a method of assessing reliability where the test taker takes two different forms of a test at two different times, one form at each time. It

is true that, in the question stem, subjects are taking two different tests, but the two tests are not different forms of the same test.

If you did not know the test answer, you could have reduced the number of contending answer choices to three by clustering. You could have clustered answer choices (A), (B), and (D), because they all have to do with validity. Answer choices (C) and (E), which don't cluster, could then be eliminated as outliers. In a question of this format, it is likely that the correct answer choice will reside in a cluster.

3. A

An aptitude test is concerned with predicting future performance. Answer choice (B) is incorrect because achievement tests are primarily concerned with assessing present skills and abilities. An example of an achievement test is the typical final exam given at the end of a class in order to assess how much the students have learned. Answer choices (C) and (D) are statistical tests used in research. Finally, answer choice (E), an IQ test, may have tempted you, but IQ tests don't always have a direct relationship to future performance.

4. E

The person's true score, which is the theoretical score equal to what the examinee truly deserves, cannot be determined from the information given. A person's true score is a theoretical number; it can only be estimated.

5. C

Content validity is determined before test items are administered. Remember, a test has content validity if it includes items that adequately sample the major components of the skill or trait being measured. Content validity is considered when assembling a test, before it's administered. Answer choice (A), criterion validity, is incorrect. Criterion validity has to do with how well the test can predict an individual's future performance in designated activities. Therefore, you can't assess criterion validity until after you have administered the test. Answer choice (D), predictive validity, is a type of criterion validity where the performance you are trying to predict with the test occurs a relatively long time after the test administration. Answer choice (B), construct validity, in general has to do with two things: whether performance on the test is correlated with other variables your theory predicts test performance should be related to and whether performance on the test is not correlated with other variables your theory predicts test performance should not be related to. You can't assess construct validity until after you have administered the test. Answer choice (E), convergent validity, is also incorrect. Convergent validity is a type of construct validity concerned specifically with whether or not test performance is correlated with other variables your theory predicts it should be related to. Thus, only content validity hinges largely on actions and decisions made before any test items are actually administered.

6. C

In some ways, question 6 was a tricky question. You knew that the IQ scores listed in the question stem were not deviation IQs. The only other option, therefore, is that the scores were ratio IQ scores. Once you realized this, you had to remember the formula for ratio IQ scores: IQ equals mental age divided by chronological age, multiplied by 100. To find the mental age, you had to multiply the chronological age by the IQ score, and then divide that product by 100. Let's see how this works. Mary's chronological age is 4 and her IQ is 200. Multiplying them together gives us 800. Dividing 800 by 100 gives us her mental age, which is 8. By using this procedure, you would have found out that Jimmy's mental age is also 8, while Johnny's mental age is 9. Therefore, Johnny has the highest mental age of the three children.

7. B

Reliability refers to the consistency with which the test measures whatever it is that the test measures. However, reliability does not refer to how well the test measures what you want it to measure. That characteristic of a test is called validity—and it is very important that you know the difference between reliability and validity by test day. Furthermore, it is not true that reliability is only important in aptitude tests. Reliability is important in all tests, because, regardless of the type of test we're talking about, if it doesn't measure whatever it measures consistently, it's pretty much useless. Therefore, since Roman numeral options I and III are false and option II is true, the correct answer choice is (B).

8. B

All the person in the example is saying is that if you were to rank Molly and John on intelligence, Molly would have a higher rank than John. Because ordinal scales are based on ranks, the correct answer is (B), an ordinal scale. The person in the example is not saying *how much* smarter Molly is than John so she is employing neither an interval nor a ratio scale. Therefore, choices (C) and (D) are not correct. Further, because she is ranking people, she cannot be employing a nominal scale, another name for a categorical scale. If she were using a nominal or categorical scale, all she could say would be something like "Her name is Molly and his name is John" or "Molly is a psychology major and John is a sociology major." Therefore, choices (A) and (E) are not correct. In fact, since nominal and categorical scales are the same thing, and since there can not be more than one correct answer choice, you could have eliminated both these choices at the outset.

9. C

Recall that the MMPI is a personality test that consists of 550 statements to which the test takers respond "true," "false," or "cannot say." Answer choice (A) is incorrect because, unlike a computer-adaptive test, every person who takes the MMPI is asked the same questions. Answer choice (B), a projective test, is incorrect because a projective test is a way of assessing personality by showing the test taker some kind of ambiguous stimulus and having them respond to it. The statements on the MMPI are not ambiguous, at least not in the way that a Rorschach ink blot is. Answer choice (D), an intelligence test, is incorrect because an intelligence test measures abilities or aptitudes for intellectual performance whereas the MMPI assesses personality. Finally, answer choice (E), an achievement test, is incorrect because an achievement test measures what one can do now as a result of some prior training.

10. C

Recall that adaptive testing involves adapting the difficulty level of a test to the abilities of the examinees. That is what is being talked about in the question stem. The examinees with the higher ability level are being presented with more difficult questions. So, this is an example of adaptive testing. Answer choice (A), cross-validation, is incorrect. Cross-validation refers to testing the criterion validity of a test on a second sample of examinees. Answer choice (B), construct validity, is discussed in explanation 2. Choice (D), norm-referenced interpretation, is also incorrect. The question stem does not mention how the test results will be interpreted, and nearly any test could be interpreted by either a norm-referenced interpretation or a domain-referenced interpretation. Finally, answer choice (E), projective testing, is also incorrect. A projective test is a type of personality test, and since the question stem specifically refers to intelligence tests, (E) is incorrect.

Section Three:
Practice Tests and Explanations

PRACTICE TEST I ANSWER SHEET

1 (A) (B) (C) (D) (E)   27 (A) (B) (C) (D) (E)   53 (A) (B) (C) (D) (E)   79 (A) (B) (C) (D) (E)

2 (A) (B) (C) (D) (E)   28 (A) (B) (C) (D) (E)   54 (A) (B) (C) (D) (E)   80 (A) (B) (C) (D) (E)

3 (A) (B) (C) (D) (E)   29 (A) (B) (C) (D) (E)   55 (A) (B) (C) (D) (E)   81 (A) (B) (C) (D) (E)

4 (A) (B) (C) (D) (E)   30 (A) (B) (C) (D) (E)   56 (A) (B) (C) (D) (E)   82 (A) (B) (C) (D) (E)

5 (A) (B) (C) (D) (E)   31 (A) (B) (C) (D) (E)   57 (A) (B) (C) (D) (E)   83 (A) (B) (C) (D) (E)

6 (A) (B) (C) (D) (E)   32 (A) (B) (C) (D) (E)   58 (A) (B) (C) (D) (E)   84 (A) (B) (C) (D) (E)

7 (A) (B) (C) (D) (E)   33 (A) (B) (C) (D) (E)   59 (A) (B) (C) (D) (E)   85 (A) (B) (C) (D) (E)

8 (A) (B) (C) (D) (E)   34 (A) (B) (C) (D) (E)   60 (A) (B) (C) (D) (E)   86 (A) (B) (C) (D) (E)

9 (A) (B) (C) (D) (E)   35 (A) (B) (C) (D) (E)   61 (A) (B) (C) (D) (E)   87 (A) (B) (C) (D) (E)

10 (A) (B) (C) (D) (E)   36 (A) (B) (C) (D) (E)   62 (A) (B) (C) (D) (E)   88 (A) (B) (C) (D) (E)

11 (A) (B) (C) (D) (E)   37 (A) (B) (C) (D) (E)   63 (A) (B) (C) (D) (E)   89 (A) (B) (C) (D) (E)

12 (A) (B) (C) (D) (E)   38 (A) (B) (C) (D) (E)   64 (A) (B) (C) (D) (E)   90 (A) (B) (C) (D) (E)

13 (A) (B) (C) (D) (E)   39 (A) (B) (C) (D) (E)   65 (A) (B) (C) (D) (E)   91 (A) (B) (C) (D) (E)

14 (A) (B) (C) (D) (E)   40 (A) (B) (C) (D) (E)   66 (A) (B) (C) (D) (E)   92 (A) (B) (C) (D) (E)

15 (A) (B) (C) (D) (E)   41 (A) (B) (C) (D) (E)   67 (A) (B) (C) (D) (E)   93 (A) (B) (C) (D) (E)

16 (A) (B) (C) (D) (E)   42 (A) (B) (C) (D) (E)   68 (A) (B) (C) (D) (E)   94 (A) (B) (C) (D) (E)

17 (A) (B) (C) (D) (E)   43 (A) (B) (C) (D) (E)   69 (A) (B) (C) (D) (E)   95 (A) (B) (C) (D) (E)

18 (A) (B) (C) (D) (E)   44 (A) (B) (C) (D) (E)   70 (A) (B) (C) (D) (E)   96 (A) (B) (C) (D) (E)

19 (A) (B) (C) (D) (E)   45 (A) (B) (C) (D) (E)   71 (A) (B) (C) (D) (E)   97 (A) (B) (C) (D) (E)

20 (A) (B) (C) (D) (E)   46 (A) (B) (C) (D) (E)   72 (A) (B) (C) (D) (E)   98 (A) (B) (C) (D) (E)

21 (A) (B) (C) (D) (E)   47 (A) (B) (C) (D) (E)   73 (A) (B) (C) (D) (E)   99 (A) (B) (C) (D) (E)

22 (A) (B) (C) (D) (E)   48 (A) (B) (C) (D) (E)   74 (A) (B) (C) (D) (E)   100 (A) (B) (C) (D) (E)

23 (A) (B) (C) (D) (E)   49 (A) (B) (C) (D) (E)   75 (A) (B) (C) (D) (E)   101 (A) (B) (C) (D) (E)

24 (A) (B) (C) (D) (E)   50 (A) (B) (C) (D) (E)   76 (A) (B) (C) (D) (E)   102 (A) (B) (C) (D) (E)

25 (A) (B) (C) (D) (E)   51 (A) (B) (C) (D) (E)   77 (A) (B) (C) (D) (E)   103 (A) (B) (C) (D) (E)

26 (A) (B) (C) (D) (E)   52 (A) (B) (C) (D) (E)   78 (A) (B) (C) (D) (E)   104 (A) (B) (C) (D) (E)

105 Ⓐ Ⓑ Ⓒ Ⓓ Ⓔ   135 Ⓐ Ⓑ Ⓒ Ⓓ Ⓔ   165 Ⓐ Ⓑ Ⓒ Ⓓ Ⓔ   195 Ⓐ Ⓑ Ⓒ Ⓓ Ⓔ
106 Ⓐ Ⓑ Ⓒ Ⓓ Ⓔ   136 Ⓐ Ⓑ Ⓒ Ⓓ Ⓔ   166 Ⓐ Ⓑ Ⓒ Ⓓ Ⓔ   196 Ⓐ Ⓑ Ⓒ Ⓓ Ⓔ
107 Ⓐ Ⓑ Ⓒ Ⓓ Ⓔ   137 Ⓐ Ⓑ Ⓒ Ⓓ Ⓔ   167 Ⓐ Ⓑ Ⓒ Ⓓ Ⓔ   197 Ⓐ Ⓑ Ⓒ Ⓓ Ⓔ
108 Ⓐ Ⓑ Ⓒ Ⓓ Ⓔ   138 Ⓐ Ⓑ Ⓒ Ⓓ Ⓔ   168 Ⓐ Ⓑ Ⓒ Ⓓ Ⓔ   198 Ⓐ Ⓑ Ⓒ Ⓓ Ⓔ
109 Ⓐ Ⓑ Ⓒ Ⓓ Ⓔ   139 Ⓐ Ⓑ Ⓒ Ⓓ Ⓔ   169 Ⓐ Ⓑ Ⓒ Ⓓ Ⓔ   199 Ⓐ Ⓑ Ⓒ Ⓓ Ⓔ
110 Ⓐ Ⓑ Ⓒ Ⓓ Ⓔ   140 Ⓐ Ⓑ Ⓒ Ⓓ Ⓔ   170 Ⓐ Ⓑ Ⓒ Ⓓ Ⓔ   200 Ⓐ Ⓑ Ⓒ Ⓓ Ⓔ
111 Ⓐ Ⓑ Ⓒ Ⓓ Ⓔ   141 Ⓐ Ⓑ Ⓒ Ⓓ Ⓔ   171 Ⓐ Ⓑ Ⓒ Ⓓ Ⓔ   201 Ⓐ Ⓑ Ⓒ Ⓓ Ⓔ
112 Ⓐ Ⓑ Ⓒ Ⓓ Ⓔ   142 Ⓐ Ⓑ Ⓒ Ⓓ Ⓔ   172 Ⓐ Ⓑ Ⓒ Ⓓ Ⓔ   202 Ⓐ Ⓑ Ⓒ Ⓓ Ⓔ
113 Ⓐ Ⓑ Ⓒ Ⓓ Ⓔ   143 Ⓐ Ⓑ Ⓒ Ⓓ Ⓔ   173 Ⓐ Ⓑ Ⓒ Ⓓ Ⓔ   203 Ⓐ Ⓑ Ⓒ Ⓓ Ⓔ
114 Ⓐ Ⓑ Ⓒ Ⓓ Ⓔ   144 Ⓐ Ⓑ Ⓒ Ⓓ Ⓔ   174 Ⓐ Ⓑ Ⓒ Ⓓ Ⓔ   204 Ⓐ Ⓑ Ⓒ Ⓓ Ⓔ
115 Ⓐ Ⓑ Ⓒ Ⓓ Ⓔ   145 Ⓐ Ⓑ Ⓒ Ⓓ Ⓔ   175 Ⓐ Ⓑ Ⓒ Ⓓ Ⓔ   205 Ⓐ Ⓑ Ⓒ Ⓓ Ⓔ
116 Ⓐ Ⓑ Ⓒ Ⓓ Ⓔ   146 Ⓐ Ⓑ Ⓒ Ⓓ Ⓔ   176 Ⓐ Ⓑ Ⓒ Ⓓ Ⓔ   206 Ⓐ Ⓑ Ⓒ Ⓓ Ⓔ
117 Ⓐ Ⓑ Ⓒ Ⓓ Ⓔ   147 Ⓐ Ⓑ Ⓒ Ⓓ Ⓔ   177 Ⓐ Ⓑ Ⓒ Ⓓ Ⓔ   207 Ⓐ Ⓑ Ⓒ Ⓓ Ⓔ
118 Ⓐ Ⓑ Ⓒ Ⓓ Ⓔ   148 Ⓐ Ⓑ Ⓒ Ⓓ Ⓔ   178 Ⓐ Ⓑ Ⓒ Ⓓ Ⓔ   208 Ⓐ Ⓑ Ⓒ Ⓓ Ⓔ
119 Ⓐ Ⓑ Ⓒ Ⓓ Ⓔ   149 Ⓐ Ⓑ Ⓒ Ⓓ Ⓔ   179 Ⓐ Ⓑ Ⓒ Ⓓ Ⓔ   209 Ⓐ Ⓑ Ⓒ Ⓓ Ⓔ
120 Ⓐ Ⓑ Ⓒ Ⓓ Ⓔ   150 Ⓐ Ⓑ Ⓒ Ⓓ Ⓔ   180 Ⓐ Ⓑ Ⓒ Ⓓ Ⓔ   210 Ⓐ Ⓑ Ⓒ Ⓓ Ⓔ
121 Ⓐ Ⓑ Ⓒ Ⓓ Ⓔ   151 Ⓐ Ⓑ Ⓒ Ⓓ Ⓔ   181 Ⓐ Ⓑ Ⓒ Ⓓ Ⓔ   211 Ⓐ Ⓑ Ⓒ Ⓓ Ⓔ
122 Ⓐ Ⓑ Ⓒ Ⓓ Ⓔ   152 Ⓐ Ⓑ Ⓒ Ⓓ Ⓔ   182 Ⓐ Ⓑ Ⓒ Ⓓ Ⓔ   212 Ⓐ Ⓑ Ⓒ Ⓓ Ⓔ
123 Ⓐ Ⓑ Ⓒ Ⓓ Ⓔ   153 Ⓐ Ⓑ Ⓒ Ⓓ Ⓔ   183 Ⓐ Ⓑ Ⓒ Ⓓ Ⓔ   213 Ⓐ Ⓑ Ⓒ Ⓓ Ⓔ
124 Ⓐ Ⓑ Ⓒ Ⓓ Ⓔ   154 Ⓐ Ⓑ Ⓒ Ⓓ Ⓔ   184 Ⓐ Ⓑ Ⓒ Ⓓ Ⓔ   214 Ⓐ Ⓑ Ⓒ Ⓓ Ⓔ
125 Ⓐ Ⓑ Ⓒ Ⓓ Ⓔ   155 Ⓐ Ⓑ Ⓒ Ⓓ Ⓔ   185 Ⓐ Ⓑ Ⓒ Ⓓ Ⓔ   215 Ⓐ Ⓑ Ⓒ Ⓓ Ⓔ
126 Ⓐ Ⓑ Ⓒ Ⓓ Ⓔ   156 Ⓐ Ⓑ Ⓒ Ⓓ Ⓔ   186 Ⓐ Ⓑ Ⓒ Ⓓ Ⓔ
127 Ⓐ Ⓑ Ⓒ Ⓓ Ⓔ   157 Ⓐ Ⓑ Ⓒ Ⓓ Ⓔ   187 Ⓐ Ⓑ Ⓒ Ⓓ Ⓔ
128 Ⓐ Ⓑ Ⓒ Ⓓ Ⓔ   158 Ⓐ Ⓑ Ⓒ Ⓓ Ⓔ   188 Ⓐ Ⓑ Ⓒ Ⓓ Ⓔ
129 Ⓐ Ⓑ Ⓒ Ⓓ Ⓔ   159 Ⓐ Ⓑ Ⓒ Ⓓ Ⓔ   189 Ⓐ Ⓑ Ⓒ Ⓓ Ⓔ
130 Ⓐ Ⓑ Ⓒ Ⓓ Ⓔ   160 Ⓐ Ⓑ Ⓒ Ⓓ Ⓔ   190 Ⓐ Ⓑ Ⓒ Ⓓ Ⓔ
131 Ⓐ Ⓑ Ⓒ Ⓓ Ⓔ   161 Ⓐ Ⓑ Ⓒ Ⓓ Ⓔ   191 Ⓐ Ⓑ Ⓒ Ⓓ Ⓔ
132 Ⓐ Ⓑ Ⓒ Ⓓ Ⓔ   162 Ⓐ Ⓑ Ⓒ Ⓓ Ⓔ   192 Ⓐ Ⓑ Ⓒ Ⓓ Ⓔ
133 Ⓐ Ⓑ Ⓒ Ⓓ Ⓔ   163 Ⓐ Ⓑ Ⓒ Ⓓ Ⓔ   193 Ⓐ Ⓑ Ⓒ Ⓓ Ⓔ
134 Ⓐ Ⓑ Ⓒ Ⓓ Ⓔ   164 Ⓐ Ⓑ Ⓒ Ⓓ Ⓔ   194 Ⓐ Ⓑ Ⓒ Ⓓ Ⓔ

Practice Test I

Time: 170 Minutes
Questions: 215

Directions: Each of the questions or incomplete statements below is followed by five suggested answers or completions. In each case, select the one that best answers the questions or completes the statement.

1. Which of the following is not an important determinant when considering the effects of modeling on learning?

    (A) the role of reinforcement
    (B) retention of the material modeled
    (C) the sex of the model
    (D) the functional value of the model's behavior
    (E) the nature of the material being modeled

2. The period in which a female of the species is sexually receptive is known as

    (A) courting
    (B) estrus
    (C) gestation
    (D) copulation
    (E) menstruation

3. Which of the following is NOT a morpheme?

    (A) the "s" in "dogs"
    (B) the "dog" in "dogs"
    (C) the "ed" in "learned"
    (D) the "ou" in "soup"
    (E) the "bio" in "biology"

4. Which of the following is most closely associated with the field of sociobiology?

    (A) B F. Skinner
    (B) E. L. Thorndike
    (C) E. O. Wilson
    (D) Ivan Pavlov
    (E) John B. Watson

5. The sound of a sizzling frying pan causes Rudolpho to salivate uncontrollably. The sound of the sizzling frying pan is a(n)

    (A) unconditioned stimulus
    (B) conditioned stimulus
    (C) unconditioned response
    (D) conditioned response
    (E) neutral stimulus

6. Ernst Weber introduced the notion of

    (A) physiological zero
    (B) response bias
    (C) just noticeable difference
    (D) motion parallax
    (E) subliminal processing

7. Dichotic listening tasks are used to study

    (A) selective attention
    (B) spontaneous recovery
    (C) good continuation
    (D) echoic memory
    (E) habituation

8. Which of the following is based on the principles of classical conditioning?

    (A) token economies
    (B) differential reinforcement
    (C) systematic desensitization
    (D) contingency management
    (E) unconditional positive regard

9. Which of the following can be inferred from most twin studies?

    (A) Differences between dizygotic twins are most likely the product of environmental factors.
    (B) Differences between monozygotic twins are most likely the product of environmental factors.
    (C) Differences between monozygotic and dizygotic twins are most likely the product of environmental factors.
    (D) Differences between dizygotic twins are most likely the product of genetic factors.
    (E) Differences between monozygotic twins are most likely the product of genetic factors.

10. Which of the following is commonly referred to as the father of developmental psychology?

    (A) G. Stanley Hall
    (B) Sigmund Freud
    (C) Erik Erikson
    (D) William James
    (E) John Locke

11. If two individuals have the same phenotype, that means that they

    (A) have the same genes for a particular trait
    (B) have the same expressed traits for a particular trait
    (C) possess the same number of chromosomes
    (D) are both hybrids
    (E) are genetically identical

12. Each of the following is true about *z*-scores EXCEPT

    (A) the mean of a distribution of *z*-scores is 0
    (B) the standard deviation of a distribution of *z*-scores is 1
    (C) about 68 percent of scores fall between a *z*-score of −1 and a *z*-score of +1
    (D) about 96 percent of scores fall between a *z*-score of −2 and a *z*-score of +2
    (E) there is no correlation between *z*-scores and T-scores

13. All of the following increase the probability of a particular response occurring EXCEPT

    (A) positive reinforcement
    (B) negative reinforcement
    (C) shaping
    (D) punishment
    (E) differential reinforcement

GO ON TO THE NEXT PAGE

14. Axis II of the DSM IV is used for

(A) clinical disorders and other conditions
(B) personality disorders and mental retardation
(C) general medical conditions
(D) psychosocial and environmental problems
(E) Global Assessment of Functioning

15. A social psychologist finds that subjects who drink coffee before viewing a videotape of a comedian find her to be funnier than subjects who did not drink coffee. These results best support

(A) the James-Lange theory
(B) innoculation theory
(C) the cognitive-physiological theory of emotion
(D) social comparison theory
(E) social facilitation

16. The door-in-the-face effect describes a process in which

(A) a person who complies with a small request is more likely to comply with a larger request
(B) a person who complies with a small request is less likely to comply with a larger request
(C) a person who complies with a small request and then refuses a larger request is judged less favorably than he was prior to complying with the smaller request
(D) a person who complies with an initial large request is less likely to comply with a second large request
(E) a person who refuses a large request is more likely to comply with a smaller request

17. A child's parents only allow her to play video games after she has completed all of her homework for that night. This reward system is consistent with

(A) the Premack principle
(B) the Garcia effect
(C) observational learning
(D) systematic desensitization
(E) a token economy

GO ON TO THE NEXT PAGE

18. "Give me a group of infants, and if I could control the world in which they are raised, I could predict which will become doctors and which will become sculptors." This statement is most likely based on

    (A) the utilization of the methods of classical conditioning
    (B) the Freudian explanation of human behavior
    (C) an early behaviorist conception of the nature of human development
    (D) a functionalistic emphasis on the adaptive nature of behavior
    (E) a firm opposition to determinism

19. If a patient is diagnosed as having a demyelinizing disease in which myelin degenerates from around the bodies of axons, which of the following is likely to occur?

    (A) faster nerve conduction times
    (B) slower nerve conduction times
    (C) retrograde degeneration and eventual cell death
    (D) cortical brain lesions
    (E) rerouting of nerve impulses

20. A two-year-old who wants her bottle simply says "bottle." This is an example of

    (A) a schema
    (B) a holophrase
    (C) a neologism
    (D) an oversimplification
    (E) a heuristic

21. Conrad found that subjects had a fairly high error rate when asked to recall groups of six letters, even when the letters were always drawn from a ten-letter pool that remained in view throughout the study. The error rate was found to be related to

    (A) the sounds of the letters involved
    (B) the order of the letters involved
    (C) whether the letters were upper case or lower case
    (D) whether the letters were all vowels or consonants
    (E) the number of previous presentations

22. The main difference between the Minnesota Multiphasic Personality Inventory (MMPI) and the California Personality Inventory (CPI) is that

    (A) the CPI is more applicable to "normal" groups
    (B) the MMPI is more applicable to "normal" groups
    (C) the CPI is a projective test
    (D) the MMPI is a projective test
    (E) the CPI is based on the DSM IV

23. Jung's archetypes include all of the following EXCEPT

    (A) persona
    (B) shadow
    (C) anima
    (D) animus
    (E) superego

GO ON TO THE NEXT PAGE

24. The "blind spot" refers to

    (A) the area of the retina that contains only rods and no cones
    (B) the area of the retina that contains only cones and no rods
    (C) the area where the optic nerve connects with the retina
    (D) the place in the optic chiasm where the optic nerves cross
    (E) the area on the cornea where an astigmatism occurs

25. Two pins are placed so close to each other on a subject's finger that they are perceived as a single point. This is because the pins have not reached the

    (A) absolute threshold
    (B) just noticeable difference
    (C) two-point threshold
    (D) action potential
    (E) gate theory of pain

26. The central difference between Freud's pleasure principle and his reality principle is that

    (A) the reality principle is more salient early in life
    (B) the pleasure principle can only be understood through hypnosis
    (C) the pleasure principle is associated with the ego whereas the reality principle is associated with the superego
    (D) the reality principle responds to demands from the environment by delaying gratification
    (E) the reality principle only emerges in individuals who are self-actualized

27. According to Carl Rogers, the goal of therapy is to achieve

    (A) self-actualization
    (B) internal locus of control
    (C) congruence
    (D) self-satisfaction
    (E) peak experiences

28. The word "bugs" consists of

    (A) one morpheme and three phonemes
    (B) one morpheme and four phonemes
    (C) two morphemes and three phonemes
    (D) two morphemes and four phonemes
    (E) three morphemes and three phonemes

Questions 29 and 30 refer to the following paragraph:

Most people who are labeled "mentally ill" are not really "sick" in the medical sense but exhibit behavior which deviates from ethical, legal, or social norms. This behavior would best be viewed as "problems in living" and not the result of organic malfunctioning. Applying the label "mentally ill" creates problems for the person which increases his inability to cope with the stresses in his life. Treatment, then, should be directed toward better coping mechanisms for everyday life.

29. This paragraph would most likely have been written by

    (A) Sigmund Freud
    (B) Melanie Klein
    (C) Thomas Szasz
    (D) Harry Stack Sullivan
    (E) Adolph Meyer

GO ON TO THE NEXT PAGE

30. Which of the following treatment approaches would be the most dissatisfactory following this model?

    (A) somatic-based treatment
    (B) psychoanalysis
    (C) client-centered therapy
    (D) behavior modification
    (E) cognitive therapy

31. Which of the following is the least accepted of Freud's ideas in current psychoanalytic theory?

    (A) the concept of reaction formation
    (B) the theory of infantile sexuality
    (C) the belief that humans have a death instinct
    (D) the concept of repression
    (E) the importance of unconscious conflict expression in dreams

32. According to Julian Rotter, someone who credits her success to luck and fate is exhibiting a personality characteristic known as

    (A) belief in a just world
    (B) extroversion
    (C) internal locus of control
    (D) external locus of control
    (E) learned helplessness

33. C. G. Jung is associated with each of the following EXCEPT

    (A) the collective unconscious
    (B) extroversion/introversion
    (C) archetypes
    (D) peak experiences
    (E) anima/animus

34. Albert Bandura claimed that individuals can learn new behaviors by observing other people's behaviors being reinforced. He referred to this phenomenon as

    (A) social loafing
    (B) vicarious reinforcement
    (C) symptom substitution
    (D) functional autonomy
    (E) field dependency

35. Which of the following terms refers to an approach to personality that focuses on individual case studies as opposed to groups?

    (A) individuated
    (B) nomothetic
    (C) idiographic
    (D) cardinal
    (E) field-independent

36. Lewin and his colleagues in their 1939 study of leadership styles found that

    (A) laissez-faire groups had the greatest productivity
    (B) the productivity of the democratic groups was greater than that of autocratic groups
    (C) autocratic leaders were better liked than democratic leaders
    (D) autocratic leaders created more hostility than democratic leaders
    (E) the personality traits of a leader had a greater effect than his leadership style

GO ON TO THE NEXT PAGE

37. Which of the following figures is most closely associated with the concept of the inferiority complex?

    (A) Victor Frankl
    (B) Erik Erikson
    (C) Alfred Adler
    (D) Kurt Lewin
    (E) Konrad Lorenz

38. Which of the following is NOT categorized as a personality disorder according to the DSM IV?

    (A) narcissistic
    (B) antisocial
    (C) impulsive
    (D) borderline
    (E) schizotypal

39. A pollster wishes to know if there is any significant association between political affiliations and favorite sports teams. Which statistic should be employed to decide this question?

    (A) correlation coefficient
    (B) chi square
    (C) independent-subjects *t*
    (D) within-subjects *t*
    (E) analysis of variance

40. Sandra Bem is most closely associated with which of the following terms?

    (A) androgyny
    (B) achievement
    (C) persuasion
    (D) aggression
    (E) empathy

41. Which of the following personality disorders is associated with a pervasive pattern of detachment from social relationships and a restricted range of emotional expression?

    (A) schizoid
    (B) narcissistic
    (C) histrionic
    (D) borderline
    (E) antisocial

42. Sandy got the highest score in her class on her final exam. She attributes her success to lucky guesses and a lot of easy questions. She is demonstrating

    (A) an internal locus of control
    (B) an external locus of control
    (C) a need for acceptance
    (D) a need for achievement
    (E) field independence

43. According to William Sheldon's system of somatotypes, which of the following body types would correspond to an inhibited, intellectual personality?

    (A) somatomorph
    (B) mesomorph
    (C) endomorph
    (D) ectomorph
    (E) heliomorph

GO ON TO THE NEXT PAGE

44. Which of the following refers to the tendency of individuals to agree with and accept personality interpretations that are provided?

   (A) the Zodiac effect
   (B) the Barnum effect
   (C) the Hawthorne effect
   (D) the placebo effect
   (E) the halo effect

45. Macoby and Jacklin found support for which of the following gender differences?

   (A) better mathematical skills in girls
   (B) better mathematical skills in boys
   (C) better spatial ability in girls
   (D) better verbal ability in girls
   (E) better verbal ability in boys

46. In social psychology, the autokinetic effect was used by Sherif in his study of

   (A) conformity
   (B) aggression
   (C) leadership
   (D) person perception
   (E) altruism

47. Which of the following is NOT an example of primary prevention of mental illness?

   (A) Drug Abuse Resistance Education (DARE)
   (B) prenatal health care
   (C) Narcotics Anonymous (N.A.)
   (D) genetic screening
   (E) a child development program that targets "at-risk" children

48. Two hundred undergraduates were asked to choose their favorite vegetable from a list of 20 vegetables. What kind of data would be gathered in this study?

   (A) ordinal
   (B) ratio
   (C) interval
   (D) nominal
   (E) subliminal

49. "Blaming the victim" is a process most closely associated with

   (A) diffusion of responsibility
   (B) deindividuation
   (C) belief in a just world
   (D) scapegoating
   (E) prejudice

50. If a distribution has relatively low variability, which of the following is true?

   (A) the variance will be relatively large
   (B) the mean will be relatively low
   (C) the standard deviation will be relatively large
   (D) the distribution will be skewed
   (E) the standard deviation will be relatively low

51. When extremely excited, Marsha has a harder time throwing darts than when she is mildly excited. This behavior is consistent with which of the following?

   (A) the Zeigarnik effect
   (B) the Hawthorne effect
   (C) Weber's law
   (D) the Yerkes-Dodson law
   (E) the fundamental attribution error

GO ON TO THE NEXT PAGE

52. The appearance of afterimages of different colors than the original stimulus is used as support for

    (A) opponent process theory
    (B) tri-color theory
    (C) place theory
    (D) frequency theory
    (E) gate theory

53. A rat which is lesioned in the cerebellum would probably exhibit

    (A) obstinate progression
    (B) loss of muscle tonus causing paralysis
    (C) seizure activity with motor symptoms
    (D) defective regulation of involuntary functions
    (E) clumsy, exaggerated voluntary motor behavior

54. The groupthink process is NOT characterized by

    (A) inhumane solutions
    (B) critical thinking
    (C) restricted discussion
    (D) group cohesiveness
    (E) excessive riskiness

55. The field theory was developed by

    (A) Solomon Asch
    (B) Leon Festinger
    (C) Fritz Heider
    (D) Carl Hovland
    (E) Kurt Lewin

56. A two-sided communication is best defined as a communication

    (A) which is not supported by at least one member of the group
    (B) from both a high and low credibility source
    (C) in which a person argues a position contrary to his own beliefs
    (D) which includes arguments both for and against a position
    (E) which includes both the image and sound of the communicator

57. The systematic study of how humans position themselves in relation to others is called

    (A) haptics
    (B) chronemics
    (C) proxemics
    (D) spatial relations
    (E) orthography

58. Stanley Milgram's classic experiment in social psychology is most closely associated with

    (A) persuasion
    (B) conformity
    (C) leadership
    (D) altruism
    (E) attraction

59. The statement "she stole from the store because she is a thief" is an example of which of the following?

    (A) the fundamental attribution error
    (B) the just world bias
    (C) the base-rate fallacy
    (D) cognitive dissonance
    (E) equity theory

GO ON TO THE NEXT PAGE

60. Which of the following is NOT used by cognitive psychologists to measure cognitive processes?

    (A) eye movements
    (B) gaze durations
    (C) latency
    (D) semantic recognition
    (E) free association

61. According to a subject's mental set, a baseball bat is used to hit a baseball. However, in a problem solving task, the subject uses the baseball bat to prop open a door. This is an example of

    (A) functional fixedness
    (B) divergent thinking
    (C) metacognition
    (D) deductive reasoning
    (E) inductive reasoning

62. Festinger : cognitive dissonance ::

    (A) Chomsky : transformational grammar
    (B) Bandura : radical behaviorism
    (C) Neisser : tri-color theory
    (D) Whorf : cognitive depression theory
    (E) Skinner : social learning theory

63. Which of the following is a central tenet of the Gestalt school?

    (A) Psychology is the study of adaptive acts.
    (B) The elements of mind are images, thoughts, and affective states.
    (C) A perception must be studied in its whole or molar form.
    (D) The concept of mind and other mentalistic terms are meaningless.
    (E) The human mind is subject to powerful unconscious forces which can control behavior.

64. The work of Paul Broca led him to conclude that:

    (A) the inability to speak is always psychogenically induced
    (B) the brain area responsible for speech is usually localized to the right frontal lobe
    (C) hearing can be explained by his theory of resonance
    (D) aphasia can have an organic basis
    (E) extirpation is particularly useful for the study of human subjects

GO ON TO THE NEXT PAGE

65. Fechner

    (A) disputed the existence of laws which described the relation of matter to consciousness
    (B) quantified Weber's statement of the relationship between stimulus and sensation
    (C) challenged Helmholtz's conception of limen
    (D) published a text called *Elements of Physiological Psychology*
    (E) discarded the method of limits in favor of the clinical method

66. Watson said that the goal of behaviorism is to predict the response if the stimulus is known and to predict the stimulus if the response is known. Which of the following is NOT used by Watson to study behavior?

    (A) simple observation
    (B) conditioned reflex studies
    (C) instrumental control studies
    (D) the method of hits
    (E) verbal reports on visceral reactions

67. Franz Joseph Gall is most closely associated with which of the following?

    (A) ectomorphism
    (B) phrenology
    (C) *tabula rasa*
    (D) eugenics
    (E) stream of consciousness

68. An example of ordinal data would be

    (A) lining up a gym class from shortest to tallest
    (B) measuring the exact weights of the students in a gym class
    (C) measuring the pulse of students before and after strenuous physical activity
    (D) placing students into different groups based on the first letter of their last names
    (E) measuring the time of day when students perform best on a given task

69. Walter Mischel's main criticism of personality tests was that they

    (A) fail to measure the most interesting aspects of personality
    (B) focus on personality traits which are less important than situational factors
    (C) focus too heavily on positive personality traits
    (D) focus too heavily on negative personality traits
    (E) rely too heavily on introspection

70. A high school teacher walks around the room more and speaks more clearly when being observed by her principal. This is an example of

    (A) the placebo effect
    (B) the Hawthorne effect
    (C) the availability heuristic
    (D) a double-blind experiment
    (E) cohort effects

71. A Type I error occurs

    (A) whenever a true null hypothesis is accepted
    (B) whenever a false null hypothesis is rejected
    (C) whenever a false null hypothesis is accepted
    (D) whenever a true null hypothesis is rejected
    (E) whenever a statistically insignificant result is obtained

72. The first official laboratory for psychology was founded in Leipzig in 1879 by

    (A) Rene Descartes
    (B) Jean Piaget
    (C) Edward Titchener
    (D) Wilhelm Wundt
    (E) Sigmund Freud

73. According to the DSM IV, each of the following is a category of mental disorders except

    (A) substance-related disorders
    (B) personality disorders
    (C) mood disorders
    (D) memory disorders
    (E) sleep disorders

74. The American Psychology Association (APA) was founded by

    (A) William James
    (B) Stanley Hall
    (C) John Dewey
    (D) Francis Galton
    (E) Wilhelm Wundt

75. Which of the following statements is NOT true of imprinting?

    (A) It takes place only between members of the same species.
    (B) Prenatal perception appears to play a role in some imprinting.
    (C) It has been theorized to be a factor causing aggression in humans.
    (D) More than two siblings may imprint to a mother at the same time.
    (E) In some species, it is thought to take place within a certain time after birth.

76. Which stimulus does NOT trigger the start of a behavior?

    (A) consummatory stimulus
    (B) sign stimulus
    (C) supernormal stimulus
    (D) motivating stimulus
    (E) releaser

77. A psychiatrist would include his client's Global Assessment of Functioning (GAF) in which of the following?

    (A) the MMPI
    (B) the DSM IV
    (C) the Myers-Briggs
    (D) the Stanford-Binet
    (E) the CPI

GO ON TO THE NEXT PAGE

78. An example of a projective personality test would be the

    (A) Minnesota Multiphasic Personality Inventory (MMPI)
    (B) California Personality Inventory (CPI)
    (C) Goodenough Draw-a-Man Test
    (D) Rorschach Inkblot Test
    (E) Stanford-Binet Intelligence Scale

79. If the mean IQ of Americans is 100 with a standard deviation of 16, what percentage of Americans would you expect to score at or below a 132 on an IQ test?

    (A) 34 percent
    (B) 48 percent
    (C) 68 percent
    (D) 84 percent
    (E) 98 percent

80. Which of the following is NOT categorized as a dissociative disorder according to the DSM IV?

    (A) amnesia
    (B) obsessive-compulsive disorder
    (C) fugue
    (D) identity disorders
    (E) depersonalization

81. On a hypothetical test, it has been established that any student taking the test will always score at a point that exactly reflects that student's actual ability. Which of the following would be true of this test?

    (A) The test would have a standard deviation of 0.
    (B) The test would have a variance of 0.
    (C) The test would have a standard error of measurement of 0.
    (D) The test would no face validity.
    (E) The test would have an alpha level of less than 0.05.

82. "Pattern recognition is said to occur when the animal pushes the target button corresponding to the symbol *W* on 75 percent of the trials presenting the symbol." This excerpt from a research paper methodology section is meant to adhere to the principle of

    (A) empirical verification
    (B) controlled observation
    (C) operational definition
    (D) statistical generalization
    (E) hypothesis testing

83. "I see a bear, my heart starts racing, I start trembling, and I begin to run. From these bodily responses, I understand that I am afraid." This understanding of emotion is consistent with

    (A) the James-Lange theory
    (B) the Cannon-Bard theory
    (C) the opponent-process theory
    (D) the encoding-specificity principle
    (E) the availability heuristic

84. Having never seen a sparrow before, Jawarhi identifies the sparrow as a bird because it has wings, and birds have wings. This is an example of

    (A) a schema
    (B) a script
    (C) an algorithm
    (D) metacognition
    (E) functional fixedness

85. Jenny has been to Memphis on three different weekends, and every time she has been there, it has rained. Based on this information, Jenny determines that it's always raining in Memphis. This is an example of

    (A) divergent thinking
    (B) the availability heuristic
    (C) perseveration
    (D) spreading activation
    (E) mental sets

86. Gibson and Walk used a "visual cliff" experiment to study

    (A) figure-ground discrimination
    (B) depth perception
    (C) feature detection
    (D) signal detection theory
    (E) motion perception

87. A stationary point of light when viewed in an otherwise totally dark room appears to move. This is an example of

    (A) apparent motion
    (B) induced motion
    (C) the autokinetic effect
    (D) good continuation
    (E) binocular disparity

88. parameter : statistic ::
    population mean :

    (A) standard deviation
    (B) sample mean
    (C) normal distribution
    (D) observation
    (E) theoretical advantage

89. Which of the following measures is most sensitive to outlying observations?

    (A) mean
    (B) median
    (C) mode
    (D) variance
    (E) standard deviation

90. In a clinical trial, a cigarette smoker is given a mildly painful shock each time she sees a pack of cigarettes. This trial is an example of

    (A) learned helplessness
    (B) cognitive dissonance
    (C) conditioned aversion
    (D) differential reinforcement
    (E) spontaneous recovery

GO ON TO THE NEXT PAGE

91. The reinforcement schedule that is most difficult to extinguish is

    (A) fixed-ratio schedule
    (B) variable-ratio schedule
    (C) fixed-interval schedule
    (D) variable-interval schedule
    (E) continuous schedule

92. A normal distribution of 200 scores has a mean of 30 and a standard deviation of 4. Joe received a score of 38. Each of the following is true of his score EXCEPT

    (A) his percentile rank is approximately the 98th percentile
    (B) his score is equivalent to a z-score of +2
    (C) his score is two standard deviations from the mean
    (D) approximately 48 percent of the total scores lie between his score and the mean
    (E) approximately 68 percent of students scored lower than he did

93. The Ajax Scale of Creativity has a +0.15 correlation with four other standardized creativity scales. Also, a correlation of +1.00 exists between the scores of any student who takes the Ajax Scale of Creativity twice. This indicates that the Ajax has

    (A) high content validity but low reliability
    (B) moderate external validity and moderate reliability
    (C) low face validity but high reliability
    (D) low criterion validity but high reliability
    (E) low internal validity but high external validity

94. Faith learned to speak French at dinner parties where she normally had a few glasses of wine. Now, she finds that she is better able to speak French after a drink or two. This is an example of

    (A) state-dependent learning
    (B) the Law of Effect
    (C) the Method of Loci
    (D) tip-of-the-tongue phenomenon
    (E) transformational grammar

95. If a dog's owner wanted to teach the dog to catch a frisbee using shaping she might

    (A) scold the dog each time it did not chase the frisbee
    (B) place the dog in "time-out" if it did not catch the frisbee
    (C) only give the dog a reinforcer when it successfully caught the frisbee
    (D) initially reinforce the dog each time it picked up or sniffed the frisbee
    (E) pair the sight of the frisbee with an unconditioned stimulus

96. Tinbergen discovered that a male stickleback reacts more aggressively to a model of a fish than to an actual fish. The model that produces a more aggressive response is an example of

    (A) a paranormal stimulus
    (B) a supernormal stimulus
    (C) the primacy effect
    (D) a positive reinforcer
    (E) a negative reinforcer

97. Chemicals that act as messengers between animals are referred to as

   (A) hormones
   (B) pheromones
   (C) amacrines
   (D) polymorphisms
   (E) anachrones

98. The Method of Loci is an example of

   (A) the primacy effect
   (B) the recency effect
   (C) a mnemonic
   (D) a heuristic
   (E) an algorithm

99. According to current psychological thinking, children's earliest sentences are considered telegraphic in the sense that

   (A) one utterance follows predictably from the next
   (B) many words and word endings are missing
   (C) meaning is often communicated in codelike personal idiom
   (D) they are often so garbled that they are readily understood only by the parents, who act as "telegraphic operators" by interpreting them
   (E) we can infer knowledge of complex syntactic structures from such simple utterances

Questions 100 and 101 refer to the following sentence:

The dog and the cat lived in a house with Mary.

100. Which of the following is true of the sentence above?

   (A) "Mary lived in a house with the dog and the cat" shares the same surface structure.
   (B) "Mary lived in a house with the dog and the cat" shares the same deep structure.
   (C) The word "lived" is made up of one morpheme.
   (D) The sentence is structured according to phonological rules.
   (E) The deep structure and surface structure of this sentence are identical.

101. Chomsky would agree with which of the following statements about the sentence above?

   (A) It has its own unique surface structure.
   (B) It is made up of four morphemes.
   (C) It is made up of four phonemes.
   (D) It requires a transformational grammar to be syntactically correct.
   (E) It is an example of a language acquisition device (LAD).

GO ON TO THE NEXT PAGE

102. A fixed-action pattern differs from a conditioned response in that

    (A) fixed-action patterns are triggered by a conditioned stimulus
    (B) fixed-action patterns are triggered by releasing stimuli
    (C) fixed-action patterns are always aggressive
    (D) fixed-action patterns are easier to extinguish
    (E) fixed-action patterns are a form of imprinting

103. A dog that had been conditioned to scratch behind its ears by rubbing against a rough surface suddenly returns to scratching behind its ears with its paw. This is an example of

    (A) spontaneous recovery
    (B) instinctual drift
    (C) homeostasis
    (D) first-order conditioning
    (E) second-order conditioning

104. The primary deficit in anterograde amnesia is

    (A) impaired long-term learning
    (B) faster forgetting than normal subjects
    (C) a frequently reversible storage deficit
    (D) difficulty remembering past events
    (E) not a chunking deficit

105. Which of the following visual display tasks requires the longest amount of time for processing and recall?

    (A) recalling a probe stimulus which was part of a previous 10 number display
    (B) reporting whether a probe stimulus was part of a previous 10 number display
    (C) correctly locating a probe stimulus which occurred early in a string of 10 numbers
    (D) correctly locating a probe stimulus which occurred late in a string of 10 numbers
    (E) recalling a probe stimulus which was part of a previous display of 10 faces

106. Which of the following examples would be consistent with Benjamin Whorf's hypothesis on language?

    (A) a young child refers to a horse as a *doggie* prior to learning the word *horse*
    (B) an adolescent raised in a culture with no word for *snow* refers to it instead as *cold white rain*
    (C) a young child uses the word *sheeps* to refer to more than one *sheep*
    (D) an adolescent raised in a culture with no word for the color *green* can still recognize *green* as distinct from *blue*
    (E) girls have been found to be faster and more accurate with language learning than boys are

GO ON TO THE NEXT PAGE

107. The fact that we remember only the main details in a story and retell it with various "fillers" is supportive of which theory?

    (A) reconstructive
    (B) reappearance
    (C) regressive
    (D) free recall
    (E) wholist

108. Which of the following is NOT one of the four basic components of language?

    (A) phonology
    (B) morphology
    (C) syntax
    (D) semantics
    (E) pragmatics

109. All other things being equal, which of the following correlation coefficients is the strongest?

    (A) -0.88
    (B) 0.00
    (C) $+0.15$
    (D) $+0.75$
    (E) $+1.05$

110. Which of the following is NOT one of Gestalt psychology's five laws of form perception?

    (A) closure
    (B) similarity
    (C) relative size
    (D) proximity
    (E) good continuation

111. Which of the following is used to study visual perception in infants?

    (A) autokinetic effect
    (B) dichotic listening
    (C) semantic recognition
    (D) preferential looking
    (E) visual agnosia

112. The main difference between the theory of color vision put forth by Young-Helmholz and that put forth by Hering is that Hering's theory

    (A) emphasizes the importance of the three types of color receptors: red, blue, and green
    (B) emphasizes the importance of three opposing pairs of color receptors: red-green, blue-yellow, and black-white
    (C) is based more on top-down processing than Young-Helmholz
    (D) is based more on bottom-up processing than Young-Helmholz
    (E) incorporates the activity of rods in color perception

113. Which of the following would probably acquire language the fastest?

    (A) a girl exposed to only one language
    (B) a boy exposed to only one language
    (C) a girl exposed to two languages
    (D) a boy exposed to two languages
    (E) all children would acquire language at roughly the same rate

GO ON TO THE NEXT PAGE

114. Which type of memory is being tested when you take a multiple-choice test?

    (A) Method of Loci
    (B) Recognition
    (C) Savings method
    (D) Free recall
    (E) Eidetic

115. Which of the following is the best way to present a tone in order to enhance memory of quickly vanishing letters on a tachistoscopic display?

    (A) just as the letters are vanishing from the screen
    (B) one second after the letters have vanished from the screen
    (C) five seconds after the letters have vanished from the screen
    (D) with an inhibiting stimulus to create metacontrast
    (E) along with an array of flashing lights

116. Jeff made a list of classic movies he wanted to see in no particular order. When asked to reconstruct the list, he successfully listed all the detective movies, then all the comedies, and then all the Westerns. This is an example of

    (A) chunking
    (B) recency
    (C) clustering
    (D) primacy
    (E) assimilation

117. Which of the following is an example of the brief storage of events at the sensory level?

    (A) eidetic memory
    (B) iconic memory
    (C) transitory memory
    (D) spontaneous memory
    (E) elaborative memory

Questions 118 and 119 refer to the following paragraph.

The relationship between fatigue and clerical errors is under investigation. A group of 15 clerks volunteers to proofread a list of 500 words for spelling errors. The first list is presented to the clerks at 10 A.M. The same group is then asked to proof a comparable, but not identical list at 6 P.M., after the clerks have been working all day.

118. This type of design is known as

    (A) 2 × 3 factorial design
    (B) independent-subjects design
    (C) nested design
    (D) matched-pair design
    (E) within-subjects design

119. The independent variable of interest in this experiment is the

    (A) type of word list
    (B) hour of the working day
    (C) number of errors per list
    (D) individual differences in clerical ability
    (E) number of words per list

GO ON TO THE NEXT PAGE

120. A graphical representation of correlational data is called a

   (A) bell curve
   (B) chi square
   (C) scatterplot
   (D) bimodal distribution
   (E) skewed distribution

121. According to Helmholtz and Young, the neural basis for pitch perception is

   (A) the frequency at which the ossicles vibrate
   (B) the frequency at which the tympanic membrane vibrates as a whole
   (C) the frequency at which the basilar membrane vibrates as a whole
   (D) the location on the ossicles that vibrates
   (E) the location on the basilar membrane that vibrates

122. Harry Harlow's experiments with wire and cloth surrogate mothers demonstrated the importance of

   (A) insight learning
   (B) contact comfort
   (C) kin selection
   (D) instinctual drift
   (E) releasing stimuli

123. Both bats and marine mammals use which of the following to perceive their environments?

   (A) infrasound
   (B) echolocation
   (C) stereotaxis
   (D) delta waves
   (E) neural desynchrony

124. Kandel's studies of the sea slug *aplysia* were used to support the hypothesis that

   (A) even simple animals like sea slugs respond to contact comfort
   (B) even simple animals like sea slugs are capable of insight learning
   (C) basic changes in neural pathways are heritable
   (D) basic changes in neural pathways occur with changes in learning and memory
   (E) chemical cues, as well as visual and auditory cues, are used in proprioception

125. Which statement best summarizes current views on feature detectors in the auditory and visual systems?

   (A) Feature detectors have been clearly demonstrated in both modalities.
   (B) Feature detectors are clearly evident in the visual system, and hypothesized to exist in the auditory system.
   (C) Feature detectors are hypothesized to exist only in the visual system.
   (D) Both systems were once thought to rely on feature detectors, but currently a signal detection theory prevails.
   (E) Feature detectors are important only for relatively simple stimuli.

GO ON TO THE NEXT PAGE

126. Afferent pathways are involved in which of the following sensory systems?

    (A) visual, tactile, kinesthetic, and auditory only
    (B) visual, tactile, olfactory, and kinesthetic only
    (C) kinesthetic only
    (D) kinesthetic and auditory only
    (E) all sensory systems

127. Damage to the ventromedial region of the hypothalamus would most likely result in which of the following?

    (A) hyperphagia
    (B) hypophagia
    (C) agnosia
    (D) apraxia
    (E) aphasia

128. In most right-handed people, the left hemisphere is dominant for all of the following EXCEPT

    (A) speech production
    (B) perception of meaningful sounds
    (C) perception of nonsense syllables
    (D) application of syntactic rules
    (E) perception of melody

129. Two-point discrimination is assessed in the study of

    (A) visual acuity
    (B) auditory thresholds
    (C) cutaneous sensitivity
    (D) binocular depth perception
    (E) the somatosensory strip

130. The "fight or flight" response to a perceived threat is associated with increased activity of

    (A) the sympathetic nervous system
    (B) the parasympathetic nervous system
    (C) the cerebral cortex
    (D) the corpus collosum
    (E) the basal ganglia

131. The action potential "jumps" along an axon. The gaps in a myelinated axon that the action potential "jumps" to are called the

    (A) Islets of Langerhorn
    (B) Broca's area
    (C) Nodes of Ranvier
    (D) terminal buttons
    (E) Wernicke's area

132. Albert Ellis's rational-emotive therapy (RET) is an example of

    (A) psychoanalytic therapy
    (B) humanistic therapy
    (C) existential therapy
    (D) cognitive-behavioral therapy
    (E) nondirective therapy

GO ON TO THE NEXT PAGE

133. A therapist feels she can no longer treat a hypochondriacal patient because the secondary gain is too great to overcome. This means that

 (A) the symptom is reducing the tension or conflict
 (B) the advantages derived from the illness outweigh the discomfort created by the illness
 (C) the ongoing mentation is directly related to the id and characteristic of unconscious mental activity
 (D) the ongoing mentation is primarily related to the functions of the ego and preconscious thought
 (E) the patient is expressing unconscious impulses in actions

134. The belief that the analyst must serve as an object onto which hostile impulses are projected is most consistent with the work of

 (A) Sigmund Freud
 (B) Melanie Klein
 (C) Anna Freud
 (D) Margaret Mahler
 (E) D. W. Winnicott

135. If a neuron will not fire regardless of the amount of stimulation, it is most likely

 (A) at its resting potential
 (B) in its absolute refractory period
 (C) in its relative refractory period
 (D) an afferent neuron
 (E) an efferent neuron

136. Schizophrenia was formerly known as

 (A) Huntington's disease
 (B) *dementia praecox*
 (C) Pick's disease
 (D) Tay-Sachs disease
 (E) cretinism

137. If an individual is facing the psychosocial crisis of identity versus role confusion, according to Erik Erikson's model, that individual is most likely

 (A) a preadolescent
 (B) an adolescent
 (C) a young adult
 (D) a middle-aged adult
 (E) an elderly adult

138. Lawrence Kohlberg developed a theory of moral development using which of the following hypothetical situations?

 (A) the prisoner's dilemma
 (B) the Heinz dilemma
 (C) Gulden's paradox
 (D) the tragedy of the Commons
 (E) the Damocles dilemma

GO ON TO THE NEXT PAGE

139. Which of the following statements best characterizes the relationship between genotype and phenotype?

    (A) Phenotype determines genotype.
    (B) Genotype determines phenotype.
    (C) The genotype and phenotype work in a complementary fashion during the child's development.
    (D) The genotype is the organism's finite potential which interacts with the environment to form the phenotype.
    (E) The genotype reflects pure hereditary influences while the phenotype reflects those of the environment.

140. Which of the following glands is frequently referred to as the "master gland" since it regulates the activity of many other glands?

    (A) thyroid
    (B) adrenal
    (C) pituitary
    (D) sweat
    (E) pineal

141. When people are deprived of REM sleep, they compensate by spending more time in REM sleep at a later time. This is commonly known as

    (A) the all-or-nothing-law
    (B) the phi phenomenon
    (C) the rebound effect
    (D) equilibration
    (E) lateral inhibition

142. According to Piaget, understanding of "conservation" is a characteristic of which of the following stages?

    (A) preoperational
    (B) formal operational
    (C) concrete operational
    (D) postoperational
    (E) sensorimotor

143. Lithium salts have been found to be an effective treatment for

    (A) Tourette's syndrome
    (B) Down's syndrome
    (C) schizophrenia
    (D) bipolar disorder
    (E) multiple personality disorder

144. A seventeen-year-old subject with a family history of schizophrenia exhibited no symptoms of schizophrenia prior to the death of his mother. Soon after his mother's death, psychotic symptoms begin to appear and he is diagnosed with schizophrenia. This scenario is most consistent with which of the following?

    (A) dopamine hypothesis
    (B) diathesis-stress model
    (C) Weber's Law
    (D) Steven's Law
    (E) Yerkes-Dodson Law

145. Chomsky theorized that humans possess an innate ability to acquire language. He referred to this as

    (A) a transformational grammar
    (B) a language acquisition device
    (C) a fixed-action pattern
    (D) a deep structure
    (E) a surface structure

GO ON TO THE NEXT PAGE

146. Which of the following statements can be made about a one-year-old infant who responds to a sudden repositioning of his head by flinging out his arms and stretching out his fingers?

    (A) The child is displaying appropriate behavior for his age.
    (B) The child appears fearful and may be developing an infantile phobia.
    (C) Further reflexive testing must be conducted to determine if the child is developmentally delayed.
    (D) The child may be developmen-tally delayed, but about ten percent of all children display this behavior until age two.
    (E) The child is severely developmentally delayed and may never outgrow this primitive response.

147. Which of the following theorists is credited with first inferring the existence of synapses?

    (A) Johannes Muller
    (B) Franz Gall
    (C) William James
    (D) Hermann von Helmholtz
    (E) Charles Sherrington

148. The uncovering and discharge of repressed emotion is called

    (A) transference
    (B) abreaction
    (C) libido
    (D) projection
    (E) congruence

149. If a neonate is touched on the cheek, she will turn her head in that direction. Which of the following statements concerning this behavior is true?

    (A) It is known as the turning reflex.
    (B) It is an example of a nonadaptive reflex.
    (C) If an object other than a nipple repeatedly touches the cheek, the behavior is soon extinguished.
    (D) Failure of this reflex to disappear within a week of birth may be a sign of developmental difficulty.
    (E) In its adaptive function, this reflex is closely linked with two other reflexes.

150. Joseph Wolpe developed a behavior therapy that uses classical conditioning to relieve anxieties and phobias. This form of behavior therapy is known as

    (A) systematic desensitization
    (B) person-centered therapy
    (C) assertiveness training
    (D) self-actualization
    (E) token economy

151. Abraham Maslow is well known for his concept of

    (A) object-relations theory
    (B) cognitive-behavioral theory
    (C) hierarchy of needs
    (D) learned helplessness
    (E) authoritarianism

GO ON TO THE NEXT PAGE

152. The psychopharmaceuticals known as SSRIs

    (A) increase the release of serotonin into the synapses
    (B) increase postsynaptic sensitivity to serotonin
    (C) limit the reuptake of serotonin in the synapses
    (D) are synthetic chemicals that mimic the effects of serotonin
    (E) are a highly effective class of antipsychotics

153. Electroconvulsive shock therapy (ECT) has been found to be an effective intervention for

    (A) eating disorders
    (B) anxiety disorders
    (C) schizophrenia
    (D) severe depression
    (E) dissociative fugues

154. In order to perceive fine details of an object in full daylight, one should

    (A) look off to one side of the object
    (B) close one eye
    (C) look so that the retinal image falls on the fovea
    (D) first fully dark-adapt the eyes
    (E) look slightly above the object

155. The study of communication in honeybees is most closely associated with

    (A) Karl Von Frisch
    (B) Konrad Lorenz
    (C) Niko Tinbergen
    (D) E. O. Wilson
    (E) G. Stanley Hall

156. The breeding of "maze bright" and "maze dull" rats is associated with which of the following?

    (A) Harry Harlow
    (B) Karl Von Frisch
    (C) Eric Kandel
    (D) Edward Thorndike
    (E) R. C. Tyron

157. It has been demonstrated that a tone of a single frequency causes a wide area of the basilar membrane to vibrate. Whose theory of pitch perception was disconfirmed by this finding?

    (A) Helmholtz
    (B) Von Békésy
    (C) Rutherford
    (D) Wever
    (E) Hertz

158. The phenomenon of dark adaptation is primarily a function of the regeneration of

    (A) rhodopsin
    (B) retinal
    (C) opsin
    (D) lamellae
    (E) chromatic pigments

159. Kohler's experiments with chimpanzees demonstrate that chimps are capable of which type of learning?

    (A) one-trial learning
    (B) insight learning
    (C) trial-and-error learning
    (D) state-dependent learning
    (E) imitative learning

160. Birds have been known to use each of the following to navigate EXCEPT

    (A) atmospheric pressure
    (B) infrasound
    (C) magnetic sense
    (D) star compass
    (E) echolocation

161. Which sensory modality is most integrated with the limbic system?

    (A) visual
    (B) auditory
    (C) tactile
    (D) olfactory
    (E) kinesthetic

162. All of the following terms are associated with client-centered therapy EXCEPT

    (A) empathy
    (B) unconditional positive regard
    (C) positive, trusting environment
    (D) nondirective
    (E) will to power

163. Victor Frankl's existential approach to therapy centers around

    (A) meaningfulness
    (B) unconditional positive regard
    (C) operant conditioning
    (D) classical conditioning
    (E) drive reduction

164. Which of the following symptoms is most likely in a patient with Tourette's syndrome?

    (A) delusions and hallucinations
    (B) eating disturbances
    (C) refusal to go to sleep at night
    (D) the irresistible urge to utter obscenities
    (E) memory impairment at both short-term and long-term levels

165. A patient is given a diagnosis of social phobia after an intake evaluation. The most likely presenting complaint was fear of

    (A) being alone in public places
    (B) closed spaces
    (C) high places
    (D) going crazy
    (E) being embarrassed or scrutinized by others

166. A man was picked up by the police 100 miles from his home, reporting to be someone other than who his identification named. A mental-status examination showed him to be quite confused. The most likely diagnosis would be

    (A) catatonic schizophrenia
    (B) paranoid schizophrenia
    (C) multiple personality disorder
    (D) psychogenic amnesia
    (E) psychogenic fugue

GO ON TO THE NEXT PAGE

167. Which of the following will NOT be balanced according to Heider's balance theory?

    (A) Jim dislikes Myra, Myra likes Thai food, and Jim dislikes Thai food
    (B) Jim dislikes Myra, Myra dislikes Thai food, and Jim dislikes Thai food
    (C) Jim likes Myra, Myra dislikes Thai food, and Jim dislikes Thai food
    (D) Jim likes Myra, Myra likes Thai food, and Jim likes Thai food
    (E) Jim dislikes Myra, Myra dislikes Thai food, and Jim likes Thai food

168. Which of the following is a negative symptom of schizophrenia?

    (A) perceptual hallucinations
    (B) delusions
    (C) flat affect
    (D) disorganized speech
    (E) disorganized behavior

169. The expression *familiarity breeds contempt* directly contradicts which of the following?

    (A) equity theory
    (B) the halo effect
    (C) the mere exposure effect
    (D) social comparison theory
    (E) the Romeo and Juliet effect

170. Which of the following studied group decision-making and groupthink?

    (A) Solomon Asch
    (B) Daryl Bem
    (C) Irving Janis
    (D) Muzafer Sherif
    (E) William McGuire

171. Which of the following developmental psychologists was noted for covering psychosocial development across an entire lifespan?

    (A) Sigmund Freud
    (B) Jean Piaget
    (C) Erik Erikson
    (D) Harry Harlow
    (E) Carol Gilligan

172. Damage to the hippocampus would most likely result in

    (A) difficulty understanding language
    (B) difficulty producing language
    (C) difficulty controlling emotional reactions, such as fear and anger
    (D) difficulty encoding new information into long-term memory
    (E) difficulty processing sensory information

173. A woman asks her friend for a loan of $100 dollars. After her friend refuses, she asks for a loan of $10 and her friend agrees. This is an example of

  (A)   the door-in-the-face phenomenon
  (B)   the foot-in-the-door phenomenon
  (C)   social facilitation
  (D)   balance theory
  (E)   cognitive dissonance

174. The Kitty Genovese case is associated with which of the following?

  (A)   groupthink
  (B)   the bystander effect
  (C)   the halo effect
  (D)   the just world bias
  (E)   the Barnum effect

175. Which of the following tools provides the best analogy for DNA?

  (A)   A mathematician's compass, which is used for drawing identical forms of various sizes
  (B)   A painter's brush, which is used to put various elements of a composition together on a canvas
  (C)   A cobbler's last, which serves a the model for many styles of shoe, all the same size
  (D)   A photographer's camera, which records exactly what occurs
  (E)   A draftsman's template, which identically copies a given number of shapes or symbols

176. Prior to viewing a debate, subjects are exposed to information that anticipates and discredits one of the debater's arguments. After the debate, subjects were more likely to disagree with this debater's view than a control group which received no information related to his arguments. This scenario is consistent with

  (A)   equity theory
  (B)   inoculation theory
  (C)   the mere exposure effect
  (D)   social comparison theory
  (E)   social exchange theory

177. Each of the following brain regions is paired with a corresponding function EXCEPT

  (A)   frontal lobe : problem solving and reasoning
  (B)   occipital lobe : visual processing
  (C)   parietal lobe : somatosensory processing
  (D)   temporal lobe : memory
  (E)   cerebellum : coordination and balance

178. Carol Gilligan's criticism of Kohlberg's theories of moral development centers around

  (A)   gender differences in orientations towards morality
  (B)   a lack of emphasis on socialization
  (C)   an absence of cross-cultural support
  (D)   the way in which morality is operationalized
  (E)   problems with his emphasis on psychosocial stages

GO ON TO THE NEXT PAGE

179. Despite working fewer hours than her coworkers, Melanie receives a promotion and a raise. Instead of feeling happy, Melanie feels guilty. This is best explained by

    (A) social-exchange theory
    (B) gain-loss theory
    (C) equity theory
    (D) foot-in-the-door phenomenon
    (E) door-in-the-face phenomenon

180. Which of the following is associated with an extra 21st chromosome?

    (A) Turner's syndrome
    (B) Kleinfelter's syndrome
    (C) Down's syndrome
    (D) Tourette's syndrome
    (E) Pickwickian syndrome

181. Which of the following is NOT a technique used in Freudian therapy?

    (A) free association
    (B) free recall
    (C) dream interpretation
    (D) analysis of transference
    (E) analysis of resistance

182. Which of the following treatment modalities would be most useful in enhancing the skills of patients with severe mental retardation?

    (A) token economy
    (B) psychoanalysis
    (C) cognitive therapy
    (D) systematic desensitization
    (E) client-centered therapy

183. An experimenter wants to study cooperation and competition in adolescents. Which of the following would be most useful to this study?

    (A) the Heinz dilemma
    (B) the prisoner's dilemma
    (C) the autokinetic effect
    (D) the phi phenomenon
    (E) the strange-situation procedure

184. A subject takes longer naming the color of the ink used when the word *green* is written in red than when the word *button* is written in red. This is an example of

    (A) the Stroop effect
    (B) automatic processing
    (C) metacognition
    (D) the opponent-process theory
    (E) the prisoner's dilemma

185. Fertilization of human eggs normally takes place in the

    (A) uterus
    (B) ovaries
    (C) fallopian tubes
    (D) cervix
    (E) urethra

186. According to Piaget, the ability to "think like a scientist" is characteristic of which of the following developmental stages?

    (A) preoperational
    (B) sensorimotor
    (C) concrete operational
    (D) formal operational
    (E) postconventional

187. The main advantage of a heuristic over an algorithm is that a heuristic

    (A) considers every possible solution to a problem
    (B) involves metacognition
    (C) is faster than an algorithm
    (D) is an example of divergent thinking
    (E) avoids functional fixedness

188. When asked to recall the months of the year, young children often recall January and February and November and December better than the months in between. This is an example of

    (A) retroactive interference
    (B) proactive interference
    (C) elaboration
    (D) primary and secondary inhibition
    (E) primacy and recency effects

189. Which of the following is an example of a recognition task?

    (A) fill-in-the-blank questions
    (B) essay questions
    (C) multiple-choice questions
    (D) paraphrasing exercises
    (E) true-false questions

190. According to Freud, the Oedipal conflict is normally resolved during which of the following stages?

    (A) oral
    (B) genital
    (C) latency
    (D) anal
    (E) phallic

191. Suzie is learning to bowl. She finds that when she bowls in a group, she performs better than when she bowls alone. This is consistent with

    (A) social comparison theory
    (B) social facilitation
    (C) social influence
    (D) equity theory
    (E) social exchange theory

192. According to Piaget, the sensorimotor stage is characterized by

    (A) primary and secondary circular reactions
    (B) concrete operations
    (C) formal operations
    (D) conservation
    (E) centration

193. Vygotsky is best known for his concept of

    (A) zone of proximal development
    (B) transformational grammar
    (C) psychosocial crises
    (D) strange situation
    (E) object permanence

GO ON TO THE NEXT PAGE

194. Convergent and divergent thinking were first defined by

    (A) Herbert Simon
    (B) J. P. Guilford
    (C) Martin Seligman
    (D) Joseph Wolpe
    (E) Raymond Cattell

195. Reaction times decrease on a semantic recognition task when the word *ice* appears prior to the word *snow*. This is an example of

    (A) semantic priming
    (B) selective attention
    (C) insight learning
    (D) mediation
    (E) bottom-up processing

196. Louie refuses to go to costume parties because he knows how people behave at such parties. He has likely developed which of the following about parties?

    (A) a prototype
    (B) a heuristic
    (C) a script
    (D) a divergence
    (E) a convergence

197. Stability and introversion are two major dimensions of personality hypothesized by

    (A) Abraham Maslow
    (B) Hans Eysenck
    (C) Erik Erikson
    (D) Sigmund Freud
    (E) George Kelley

198. Which of the following statements is consistent with Walter Mischel's perspective on personality?

    (A) Personality traits are best studied using factor analysis.
    (B) Only cardinal traits are worthy of study.
    (C) The majority of traits studied are based on studies of mentally ill populations.
    (D) A nomothetic approach to personality is preferable to an ideographic approach.
    (E) Trait theory is based on flawed assumptions about the consistency of human behavior across situations.

199. Which of the following terms is associated with Henry Murray and the Thematic Apperception Test?

    (A) hierarchy of needs
    (B) belief in a just world
    (C) locus of control
    (D) authoritarianism
    (E) need to achieve

GO ON TO THE NEXT PAGE

200. According to Mendelian genetics, which of the following statements is true?

(A)   If both parents have brown eyes, their offspring must have brown eyes.

(B)   If one parent has blue eyes and one has brown eyes, their offspring must have brown eyes.

(C)   If both parents have brown eyes, their offspring could have blue eyes.

(D)   If both parents have blue eyes, their offspring could have brown eyes.

(E)   If both parents are heterozygous, their offspring must be heterozygous.

201. The term *reaction formation* is most likely to be encountered in descriptions of

(A)   client-centered therapy
(B)   group therapy
(C)   behavior modification
(D)   psychoanalysis
(E)   psychodrama

202. In a psychoanalytic case study, Alex criticizes his brother Joe's tendency to steal things when in fact Alex, not Joe, has been caught shoplifting on several occasions. According to psychoana-lytic theory, Alex is most likely displaying which of the following defense mechanisms?

(A)   projection
(B)   countertransference
(C)   repression
(D)   compensation
(E)   rationalization

203. According to Baumrind, which parenting style is associated with the most socially and academically competent children?

(A)   permissive
(B)   authoritative
(C)   authoritarian
(D)   democratic
(E)   assertive

204. Which of the following defense mechanisms relates to the analyst's feelings towards the patient?

(A)   sublimation
(B)   projection
(C)   transference
(D)   countertransference
(E)   identification

205. Which of the following represents the correct progression of Piaget's four stages of cognitive development?

(A)   preoperational, concrete operational, formal operational, sensorimotor

(B)   preoperational, sensorimotor, concrete operational, formal operational

(C)   sensorimotor, preoperational, concrete operational, formal operational

(D)   sensorimotor, preoperational, formal operational, concrete operational

(E)   preoperational, formal operational, concrete operational, sensorimotor

GO ON TO THE NEXT PAGE

206. The child's game of "peek-a-boo" centers around which of the following developmental concepts?

    (A) schema
    (B) conservation
    (C) concrete operations
    (D) formal operations
    (E) object permanence

207. The process of interpreting new information in terms of an existing schema is termed

    (A) assimilation
    (B) accommodation
    (C) centration
    (D) conservation
    (E) ideation

208. Which of the following terms is NOT associated with Mary Ainsworth's studies of Ugandan infants?

    (A) strange situation
    (B) insecure/avoidant attachment
    (C) insecure/aversive attachment
    (D) insecure/resistant attachment
    (E) secure attachment

209. "I used to think I wasn't a Trojans fan. Then I went to three Trojans games last season. Now I think I am a Trojans fan." This statement is most consistent with which of the following?

    (A) social comparison theory
    (B) cognitive dissonance
    (C) belief in a just world
    (D) foot-in-the-door phenomenon
    (E) balance theory

210. Janine is attractive and assertive. She arrives at work on time each day, and never complains. When her cowork-ers are asked to assess Janine's intel-ligence, they consistently rate her much higher than she scores on an intelligence test. This is an example of

    (A) the mere exposure effect
    (B) the Hawthorne effect
    (C) the halo effect
    (D) the placebo effect
    (E) the fundamental attribution error

211. According to the Zimbardo study, wearing uniforms has been found to promote

    (A) depression
    (B) social loafing
    (C) authoritarianism
    (D) deindividuation
    (E) reactance

212. A group discussing how best to handle insubordinate employees moves from an initial position where the employees would receive a verbal reprimand to the conclusion that insubordinate employees will be summarily dismissed. This is an example of

    (A) group polarization
    (B) social comparison
    (C) social exchange
    (D) reactance
    (E) social facilitation

213. Sasha has been playing solitaire on her computer for months. She believes that she has become a good player, and seeks out other solitaire players to determine exactly how good she is. This behavior is consistent with

    (A) the James-Lange theory
    (B) innoculation theory
    (C) social loafing
    (D) social comparison theory
    (E) social facilitation

214. A person with low self-esteem would most likely attribute his success to

    (A) stable causes
    (B) unstable causes
    (C) internal causes
    (D) external causes
    (E) direct causes

215. The Robber's Cave experiment focused was used to study

    (A) the prisoner's dilemma
    (B) groupthink
    (C) social facilitation
    (D) group and intergroup interactions
    (E) political norms

STOP! END OF TEST.

PRACTICE TEST I ANSWER KEY

1.	C	29.	C	57.	C	85.	B
2.	B	30.	A	58.	B	86.	B
3.	D	31.	C	59.	A	87.	C
4.	C	32.	D	60.	E	88.	B
5.	B	33.	D	61.	B	89.	A
6.	C	34.	B	62.	A	90.	C
7.	A	35.	C	63.	C	91.	B
8.	C	36.	D	64.	D	92.	E
9.	B	37.	C	65.	B	93.	D
10.	A	38.	C	66.	D	94.	A
11.	B	39.	B	67.	B	95.	D
12.	E	40.	A	68.	A	96.	B
13.	D	41.	A	69.	B	97.	B
14.	B	42.	B	70.	B	98.	C
15.	C	43.	D	71.	D	99.	B
16.	E	44.	B	72.	D	100.	B
17.	A	45.	D	73.	D	101.	A
18.	C	46.	A	74.	B	102.	B
19.	B	47.	C	75.	A	103.	B
20.	B	48.	D	76.	D	104.	A
21.	A	49.	C	77.	B	105.	A
22.	A	50.	E	78.	D	106.	B
23.	E	51.	D	79.	E	107.	A
24.	C	52.	A	80.	B	108.	B
25.	C	53.	E	81.	C	109.	A
26.	D	54.	B	82.	C	110.	C
27.	C	55.	E	83.	A	111.	D
28.	D	56.	D	84.	A	112.	B

113. A	143. D	173. A	203. B
114. B	144. B	174. B	204. D
115. B	145. B	175. E	205. C
116. C	146. C	176. B	206. E
117. B	147. E	177. D	207. A
118. E	148. B	178. A	208. C
119. B	149. E	179. C	209. B
120. C	150. A	180. C	210. C
121. E	151. C	181. B	211. D
122. B	152. C	182. A	212. A
123. B	153. D	183. B	213. D
124. D	154. C	184. A	214. D
125. A	155. A	185. C	215. D
126. E	156. E	186. D	
127. A	157. A	187. C	
128. E	158. A	188. E	
129. C	159. B	189. C	
130. A	160. E	190. E	
131. C	161. D	191. B	
132. D	162. E	192. A	
133. B	163. A	193. A	
134. E	164. D	194. B	
135. B	165. E	195. A	
136. B	166. E	196. C	
137. B	167. B	197. B	
138. B	168. C	198. E	
139. D	169. C	199. E	
140. C	170. C	200. C	
141. C	171. C	201. D	
142. C	172. D	202. A	

EXPLANATIONS TO PRACTICE TEST I

1. C

Each of the wrong answer choices in this question is an important determinant when considering the effects of modeling on learning. Reinforcement, choice, retention, functional value of the model's behavior, and the nature of the material being modeled, all can and do influence the effects of modeling on learning. Only the sex of the model, (C) is irrelevant. Be very careful when selecting choices that emphasize sex differences on the GRE Psychology test. Except in a few key instances, choices that focus on sex differences frequently are distracters.

2. B

Estrus is the term used by comparative psychologists to refer to the period of time in which the female of the species is sexually receptive. Courting refers to behaviors intended to result in coupling. Gestation is the period of time in which an unborn offspring is within its mother. Copulation refers specifically to sexual intercourse, and menstruation refers to the process whereby the old uterine lining is discharged from the female of a species.

3. D

A morpheme refers to the smallest unit of meaning in a word. Only (D), *ou*, does not represent a single unit of meaning. The *ou* in *soup* is a single phoneme, or sound, but does not represent anything meaningful. Note that the *s* in a word like *dogs*, and the *ed* in *learned* both represent morphemes since they change the meaning of the word. The *s* in *dogs* makes the word plural, and the *ed* in *learned* changes the word to its past tense.

4. C

E. O. Wilson is widely considered to be among the foremost sociobiologists. Sociobiology is the controversial field that attempts to link human behavior to its evolutionary roots. B. F. Skinner and John Watson are associated with behaviorism. Ivan Pavlov is associated with classical conditioning, and E. L. Thorndike is connected to learning theory.

5. B

This question focuses on classical conditioning. The sound of the sizzling frying pan is not an unconditioned stimulus since if it was never paired with the unconditioned stimulus (food), it would not cause the unconditioned response (salivation). Therefore, the sound of the sizzling frying pan is a conditioned stimulus that elicits the conditioned response of salivation.

6. C

Ernst Weber introduced the concept of a "just noticeable difference." A just noticeable difference is the smallest difference between two stimuli that allows them to be perceived as distinct stimuli. Physiological zero is the temperature that is perceived as neither hot nor cold. Motion parallax is one way in which depth perception is perceived.

7. A

Dichotic listening tasks were first used extensively by Broadbent to study selective attention. Dichotic listening tasks require a subject to listen to and shadow what they hear in one ear and ignore distracting information that enters the other ear.

8. C

Only systematic desensitization is associated with classical conditioning. Token economies, differential reinforcement or shaping, and contingency management are more correctly associated with operant conditioning. Unconditional positive regard is a central concept in the client-centered approach to therapy propounded by Carl Rogers.

9. B

Dizygotic (or fraternal) twins develop from two fertilized eggs. Monozygotic (or identical) twins develop from a single fertilized egg. As a result, monozygotic twins are identical genetically, and any differences that develop between the twins must be the result of environmental factors. Keep in mind that dizygotic twins should be no more similar genetically than any other pairs of siblings.

10. A

G. Stanley Hall is generally considered the father of developmental psychology. Freud is generally considered the father of psychoanalysis. Erik Erikson is an important developmental psychologist whose work appeared well after Hall. William James is an important figure in the history of psychology in the United States, and an early proponent of the functionalist school. He also coined the term *stream of consciousness*. John Locke is an empiricist philosopher who coined the term tabula rasa to refer to the blank slate that is the human mind prior to experience.

11. B

It is important to understand the differences between genotype and phenotype for the GRE Psychology test. Phenotype refers to the expressed traits for a given trait, so (B) is correct. Genotype refers to the genetic foundation that causes the traits to be expressed. Remember that two individuals can have the same phenotype but different genotypes.

12. E

Remember that on "all of the following EXCEPT" questions, you must find the one answer choice that does not apply. In this case, (E) is correct, since z-scores and T-scores are closely related. z-scores are expressed in terms of number of standard deviations above or below the mean. The mean score for a distribution is scored at 0, and one standard deviation up or down would be scored at +1 or −1. T-scores work the same way, except that the mean score is scored at 50, and every 10 points up or down represents a standard deviation. Also note that the information provided in choices (C) and (D) gives you good information about the percentages of scores that fall below or between one or two standard deviations.

13. D

Only punishment, (D), does not increase the probability of a particular response occurring. Punishment decreases the probability of a particular response occurring. Negative reinforcement, choice (B), refers to the reinforcement that occurs when an aversive agent is removed (e.g., a baby who stops crying when fed is unknowingly using negative reinforcement on her parents).

14. B

Axis II of the DSM-IV is used for personality disorders and mental retardation so (B) is correct. Each of the incorrect choices refers to another axis of the DSM-IV. Axis I is used for general medical conditions; Axis III is used for clinical disorders and other conditions; Axis IV is used for psychosocial and environmental problems;

and Axis V is used for the Global Assessment of Functioning.

15. C

Drinking coffee is likely to increase the physiological arousal of a subject. According to the James-Lange theory, choice (A), these physiological states would cause a specific type of emotion, regardless of the situation or the subject's cognitions. Since subjects were watching a comedy, the cognitive-physiological theory of emotion, choice (C), would easily explain why they labeled the increased arousal as heightened amusement. Remember to associate Schacter and Singer with the cognitive-physiological theory of emotion. Inoculation theory, choice (B), is a distracter since it is associated with persuasion, and social comparison and social facilitation both refer to unrelated theories from social psychology.

16. E

Like it sounds, the "door-in-the-face" phenomenon refers to the increased likelihood of complying with a small request after refusing to comply with a small request. It should not be confused with the "foot-in-the-door" phenomenon in which the likelihood of complying with a large request is increased after complying with a small request, choice (A).

17. A

The Premack principle states that a less favorable behavior or activity can be reinforced by a more favorable behavior or activity. In this case, playing video games reinforces doing homework.

18. C

This quote is similar to one widely attributed to John B. Watson, an early behaviorist. It is consistent with behaviorist emphasis on the influence of environmental factors on behavior. (A) is wrong because it focuses too narrowly on classical conditioning. (B) is wrong because a Freudian approach would want to consider unconscious drives and unresolved childhood conflicts. (D) is wrong because a functionalist approach would not focus so heavily on controlling the environment to dictate behavioral outcomes. (E) is wrong since determinism is implied rather than opposed in the quotation.

19. B

Myelinization allows for faster nerve conduction time as the action potential "jumps" from node to node along the axon. Demyelinization, consequently, would result in slower nerve conduction times, choice (B).

20. B

The *term holophrase* refers to the tendency of infants in the early stages of language acquisition to use a single word to express themselves. A schema, choice (A), is a way of organizing information, a term used by Piaget. A neologism, choice (C), is a newly coined term. A heuristic, choice (E), is a rule of thumb used as a short cut to reach a solution.

21. A

Conrad found that letters that sounded similar were most likely to be confused with one another. This lent support to the idea that the rehearsal that takes place in short-term memory has an acoustic component.

22. A

The key distinction between the MMPI and the CPI has appeared frequently on the GRE Psychology test. The two personality inventories are quite similar and differ primarily on the basis of the representativeness of the samples used to establish their norms. The MMPI was normed using a more clinical population than the CPI. Therefore, choice (A) is correct since the CPI was normed using a more "normal" sample that would be more applicable to a "normal" population.

23. E

Jung's archetypes include the anima, the animus, the persona, and the shadow. The superego is more closely linked to Freudian theory and is not included among Jung's archetypes.

24. C

The "blind spot" refers to the area where the optic nerve connects to the retina. There are no rods or cones in this area, so no visual perception occurs at this location.

25. C

In touch perception, the two-point threshold refers to the amount of distance between two pins necessary for each to be perceived as a distinct sensation. The absolute threshold and action potential both refer to nerve conduction. Just noticeable difference, or JND, is a measure of the amount of change necessary to predict the difference between two stimuli of differing force.

26. D

Freud's reality principle centers on delaying gratification, so choice (D) works here. The reality principle emerges after the pleasure principle. The pleasure principle is the initial narcissistic orientation that does not respond to demands from the environment. Choice (A) is wrong since the reality principle is less salient than the pleasure principle early in life. Choice (B) is simply incorrect: hypnosis is irrelevant to this question. Choice (C) is off the mark since the pleasure principle is more aptly paired with the id and the reality principle is better paired with the ego. Choice (E) is wrong since self-actualization is not a necessary requirement for the reality principle.

27. C

Although all the answer choices deal with aspects of humanistic psychology, only choice (C) uses a term that is specifically connected to Rogers. Rogers claimed that the goal of psychotherapy was congruence between who one is and one's ego ideal. Self-actualization, choice (A), and peak experiences, choice (E), are terms to associate with Abraham Maslow rather than Carl Rogers. Internal locus of control, choice (B), comes from the work of Julian Rotter.

28. D

When dealing with a word like *bugs* on the GRE Psychology Test, you may be asked to determine the number of phonemes or morphemes in the word. Phonemes refer to the smallest units of sound or phonetic speech. *Bugs* consists of four phonemes: *b, u, g,* and *s*. Morphemes refer to the smallest units of meaning. *Bugs* consists of two morphemes: *bug* and *s*. Note that the *s* here is a morpheme since it changes the meaning of the word to represent more than one bug.

29. C

Associate the name Thomas Szasz with his book entitled *The Myth of Mental Illness*. This quote is quite consistent with the main thesis of this book, which is that mental illness is social construction, and that the term is applied to people who are not sick in a medical sense, but instead deviate from certain societal norms.

30. A

Somatic-based therapy, choice (A), would not be consistent with the view put forth in the excerpt here. Somatic-based therapy would involve treatments that would be effective with physical or biochemical disorders. Since the passage here is more consistent with the view that mental illness is not physical or biochemical in nature, choice (A) would be inconsistent with the author's view, and would therefore be the correct answer.

31. C

Freud's concept of a death wish or *thanatos* is the least accepted among the choices presented here. Each of the other four answer choices has received considerable support among contemporary psychoanalysts.

32. D

Julian Rotter is connected to the idea of an internal or external locus of control. Someone who credits herself for her success or failure is demonstrating an internal locus of control. Someone who credits external factors like luck or fate is demonstrating an external locus of control. So choice (D) is correct here.

33. D

Jung is associated with the collective unconscious, extroversion/introversion, archetypes, and the anima/animus. So choices (A), (B), (C), and (E) are out. Maslow rather than Jung is linked to the term *peak experiences*, choice (D).

34. B

Bandura is associated with social learning theory and the Bobo doll experiment. In much of his research, Bandura found that behaviors that are witnessed could be reinforced. He termed this kind of reinforcement *vicarious reinforcement* so choice (B) works here.

35. C

Gordon Allport used the terms nomothetic and idiographic to classify two types of approaches to personality theory. A nomothetic approach focuses on group and societal norms. An idiographic approach focuses on individual case studies. So (C) is your best bet here.

36. D

Lewin's classic study of leadership styles defined three types of leadership styles: autocratic, democratic, and laissez-faire. Autocratic leaders tended to create more hostility than democratic leaders, so (D) is on target here.

37. C

Alfred Adler's work included seminal research into the need for superiority and the development of the inferiority complex.

38. C

The DSM IV includes numerous classifications of mental disorders, including personality disorders. Narcissistic, antisocial, borderline, and schizotypal personality disorders are among the disorders listed in DSM IV. Only choice (C), impulsive personality disorder, does not appear in DSM IV.

39. B

Any time you are placing groups or individuals into different nominal categories or groups, you need to use the chi-square to analyze your data. So choice (B) is the correct answer here. A correlational coefficient, choice (A), is used when determining if two scores are correlated (either positively or negatively). A t-test, choices (C) and (D), is used to determine if there are significant differences between two groups and the data is numerical in nature. An analysis of variance (ANOVA), choice (E), is used to determine if there are significant differences among more than two groups or variables.

40. A

Sandra Bem studied gender roles, and should be associated with tests of androgyny. Subjects who score high on both masculinity and femininity scales of her personality inventory are classified as androgynous.

41. A

A pervasive pattern of detachment from social relationships and a restricted range of emotional expression characterize the schizoid personality disorder.

42. B

Locus of control centers around how one attributes the cause of events in one's life. If we attribute our success to our ability and effort, that demonstrates an internal locus of control. If, like Sandy in our example here, we attribute our success to luck and environmental factors (like the easiness of the test) we are demonstrating an external locus of control, choice (B).

43. D

Although William Sheldon's theories regarding body types have fallen out of favor in mainstream psychology these days, they sometimes appear on the GRE Psychology test. The three body types he describes are ectomorph, endomorph, and mesomorph. The ectomorph, choice (D), is associated with an inhibited, intellectual personality.

44. B

The Barnum effect, choice (B), is the term used for the tendency of individuals to agree with and accept personality interpretations that are provided. The Hawthorne effect, choice (C), refers to the effect of observation on performance.

45. D

Psychological studies of gender differences have been a subject of much controversy in recent years. Among the more well-established and frequently tested studies are those of Macoby and Jacklin. They found that girls tend to exhibit better verbal ability than boys, choice (D).

46. A

Sherif used the apparent motion associated with the autokinetic effect to study conformity, choice (A). The autokinetic effect is the visual illusion whereby a stationary light appears to move in a dark room. Subjects in Sherif's study reported movement that was consistent with the estimates that were offered before their estimate.

47. C

Primary prevention takes place prior to the development of a mental illness or disorder. Only choice (C), Narcotics Anonymous, occurs after the onset of a mental disorder. Each of the other answer choices is a preventative measure designed to avoid the emergence of mental disorders.

48. D

Nominal data refers to data that is grouped according to names of categories. Ratio and interval data, choices (B) and (C), refer to data that is more numerically based. Ordinal data, choice (A), involves sorting objects according to their rank or order.

49. C

Research into "belief in a just world," choice (C), centers around how individuals make judgments based on an underlying (and oftentimes erroneous) assumption that good things happen to good people and bad things happen to bad people. As a result, subjects who demonstrate a high level of belief in a just world are likely to assume that a victim did something bad to result in their negative circumstances.

50. E

Variability is measured by the variance or standard deviation of a distribution. A distribution with high variability would have a large variance and large standard deviation. A distribution with low variability would have a smaller variance and standard deviation, choice (E).

51. D

The Yerkes-Dodson law centers around performance and arousal. The main thing to remember regarding the Yerkes-Dodson law is that individuals tend to perform best with a moderate level of arousal. Too much and too little arousal results in poorer performance. In this example, Marsha performs better when mildly excited than when extremely excited. This is right in line with Yerkes-Dodson.

52. A

Edward Hering's opponent process theory for color vision posits that color is perceived through the action of three opponent processes, one for red-green, one for blue-yellow, and one for black-white. Afterimages (also known as the McCollough effect) that appear after staring at a color for a long period of time provide support for the opponent process theory.

53. E

The cerebellum is responsible for smoothing movements and balance. Damage or removal of the cerebellum would therefore result in clumsy, exaggerated voluntary motor behavior.

54. B

Irving Janis's studies of group behavior determined that groupthink could result in irrational decision-making when an insular group makes decisions without questioning assumptions or thinking critically. Inhumane solutions, restricted discussion, group cohesiveness, and excessive riskiness are all qualities of groupthink. Of the choices presented, only critical thinking is not indicative of groupthink.

55. E

Field theory was first put forth by Kurt Lewin. He also discussed the difference between field-dependence and field-independence among individuals. Field-dependent individuals are more influenced by environmental factors and the perceptions of others.

56. D

Two-sided communication is communication that includes arguments both for and against a position.

57. C

Proxemics is the study of how humans position themselves in space in relation to others. The name you should associate with proxemics is Edward Hall.

58. B

Milgram's classic study involved subjects believing they were administering shocks to a subject. In reality, no shocks were administered. The main object of the study was to observe obedience and conformity. Although an experimenter was instructing the real subjects to perform seemingly inhumane tasks, these subjects did not question or resist administering apparently painful shocks to another human being.

59. A

The fundamental attribution error is the tendency to attribute the behavior of others to dispositional factors while attributing one's own behavior to situational factors. In this case, stating that "she stole from the store because she is a thief" is attributing the behavior of another to dispositional factors (i.e., she is a thief).

60. E

Among the answer choices provided, only free association is not a measure used by cognitive psychologists to measure cognitive processes. Eye movements, gaze durations, latency (or response times), and semantic recognition are all measures used by cognitive psychologists.

61. B

Divergent thinking runs contrary to functional fixedness, choice (A). Functional fixedness involves seeing each object in terms of a single fixed function. If an individual is able to think of new or unforeseen uses for an object or an item when solving a problem, then that individual is demonstrating divergent thinking. In the example provided here, it requires divergent thinking to use a baseball bat in a new and unexpected way.

62. A

Festinger coined the term *cognitive dissonance* and performed studies to establish that it does in fact exist. Similarly, Chomsky coined the term *transformational grammar* and performed studies to establish that it does in fact exist. Each of the other answer choices involves an incorrect pairing of researcher and theory.

63. C

The Gestalt school of psychological thought focuses on perception and the perception of wholes. Choice (D) is true of the behaviorist school. Choice (E) applies to psychoanalytic thought.

64. D

Broca discovered that an area in the left frontal lobe was associated with speech production. He found that patients with aphasia tended to have damage to this area, which is now termed Broca's area. His findings demonstrated that aphasia could have an organic basis. Choice (A) is wrong since aphasia may be induced in a number of ways. Choice (B) states incorrectly that speech centers are located in the right, not left, frontal lobe. Choice (C) is way off base. It deals with hearing perception, not language production. Choice (E) introduces the term *extirpation* which has appeared on recent GRE Psychology tests (as has its synonym, *ablation*). Extirpation, or ablation, is the intentional lesioning or removal of regions of the brain. For obvious reasons, it is not commonly used in the study of human subjects.

65. B

Fechner is best known for his quantification of Weber's statement of the relationship between stimulus and sensation.

66. D

Watson and the behaviorists use all of the methods described in the answer choices except for the method of hits. The method of hits is a technique used in signal detection research.

67. B

You should associate Franz Joseph Gall with phrenology. Phrenology attempts to associate lumps on the head with personality traits. Not surprisingly, phrenology has fallen out of favor in psychology. Ectomorphism, choice (A), is associated with William Sheldon and his also largely discredited theory of a somatic basis to personality. *Tabula rasa*, choice (C), is linked to John Locke. Eugenics, choice (D), is frequently associated with E. O. Wilson and sociobiology. Stream of consciousness, choice (E), is a term coined by William James.

68. A

Ordinal data involves ordering or ranking items. Out of the examples given, only lining students up in gym class from shortest to tallest deals with this kind of data. Weighing students or recording their pulse rates are examples of ratio variables. Placing students into groups according to their last names is an example of nominal data.

69. B

Mischel criticized personality tests for their narrow focus on permanent, dispositional traits. Mischel felt that situational factors were more important determinants of behavior.

70. B

The Hawthorne effect refers to the influence of being observed on behavior. In this example, the teacher performs differently (and better) when being observed by her principal.

71. D

Type I and Type II errors appear frequently on the GRE Psychology test. A Type I error occurs when a true null hypothesis is rejected. In other words, a Type I error occurs when a study claims that significant results exist when in fact they do not. A Type II error occurs when a false null hypothesis is accepted. That means that significant results are not noticed.

72. D

Wilhelm Wundt established the first psychology laboratory in Leipzig in 1879. Wundt is frequently referred to as the founder of psychology. His studies used introspection to analyze the nature of consciousness.

73. D

Substance-related disorders, personality disorders, mood disorders, and sleep disorders are all listed as categories of mental disorders in DSM IV. Of the choices listed, only memory disorders do not have their own category in DSM IV.

74. B

Stanley Hall founded the American Psychological Association (APA) in 1892.

75. A

Imprinting is an important concept in ethology. Associate Konrad Lorenz with the term imprinting. As Lorenz demonstrated with young birds, animals may imprint on animals from different species, and even on objects. Each of the remaining choices provides accurate information about imprinting.

76. D

Four of the five answer choices refer to triggers to behavior from ethology and comparative psychology. Only the phrase *motivating stimulus* is not a term for a behavior trigger.

77. B

The Global Assessment of Functioning (GAF) scale is part of the DSM IV. It is an overall score between 0 and 60 that is recorded on Axis V of the DSM IV.

78. D

A projective personality test is a test in which the subject supposedly projects his or her thoughts onto an ambiguous stimulus. The Rorschach Inkblot Test is a classic example of a projective personality test. The MMPI and the CPI are normed personality inventories. The Goodenough Draw-A-Man Test is a cross-cultural test of a child's ability to draw a man. The Stanford-Binet Intelligence Scale is an intelligence test.

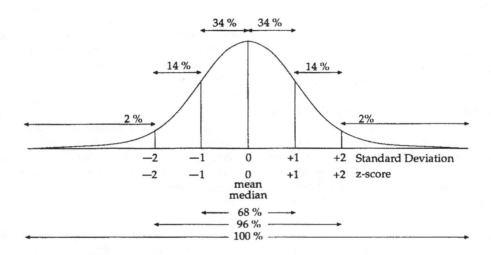

79. E

You need to memorize the percentages of students who fall within one, two, and three standard deviations from the mean. Sixty-eight percent of scores in a distribution fall within one standard deviation from the mean. That means that 34 percent of scores in a normal distribution fall between the mean and one standard deviation up, and 34 percent of scores fall between the mean and one standard deviation down. Twenty-eight percent of scores fall between one and two standard deviations from the mean. That means that 96 percent of scores fall between the mean and two standard deviations up or down. Four percent of scores fall beyond two standard deviations from the mean. That means two percent of students score above two standard deviations up, and two percent score below two standard deviations down. In terms of this question, a score of 132 is two standard deviations of 16 above the mean of 100. So 98 percent of scores would be at or below 132 on the test described in this question.

80. B

Among the answer choices listed here, only obsessive-compulsive disorder is not classified as a dissociative disorder. Obsessive-compulsive disorder is classified as an anxiety disorder.

81. C

The standard error of measurement (SEM) represents the likelihood that a test-taker will receive the same score on multiple applications of the same measure. In the example here, since any student will receive the same exact score no matter how many times they take the test, the standard error of measurement (SEM) for the hypothetical test would be 0. Standard deviation and variance are measures of variability. Face validity centers around whether a scale measures what it intends to measure. Alpha levels refer to the chance that differences between parametric statistics are due to chance.

82. C

The sentence in quotes here provides a clear and measurable way of determining when "pattern recognition is said to occur." This is an example of an operational definition.

83. A

The James-Lange theory states that emotional attributions are based on physiological sensations. Cannon-Bard theory attempted to refute James-Lange theory, stating that physiological sensations and cognitions act in parallel during emotional processing.

84. A

Piaget refers to schema as organized patterns of behavior or thought. These schemas are then adjusted through adaptation as new information appears. In the example given, Jawarhi has a schema for birds that assumes that birds have wings. When Jawarhi sees something new that has wings, he attempts to incorporate that new instance into his existing schema. A script, choice (B), refers to a behavioral protocol expected in certain situations. An algorithm, choice (C), is a mathematical technique for arriving at a solution to a problem. Metacognition, choice (D), is thinking about thinking. Functional fixedness, choice (E), is the tendency in problem solving to view objects and tools as having a single fixed function.

85. B

The availability heuristic refers to the tendency to make decisions based on available data. In the example described here, Jenny decides that Memphis is rainy based on the three instances when she was in Memphis. She is relying on the information she has available, but fails to consider the weather in Memphis all the times she has not been there. Divergent thinking, choice (A), refers to thinking outside of functionally fixed bases. Perseveration, choice (C), refers to the tendency to stay focused on certain thoughts for prolonged periods of time. It is a symptom associated with schizophrenia. Spreading activation, choice (D), refers to the tendency of semantic processing to spread from a single word or node to related words or nodes. A mental set, choice (E), refers to a given set of potential solutions to a problem held by a given person.

86. B

Gibson and Walk used a "visual cliff" with infants to study the development of depth perception. Even at six months of age, infants will not attempt to crawl across a visual cliff of clear glass.

87. C

The perceived motion of a stationary light in an otherwise totally dark room is an example of the autokinetic effect. This effect is important both in studies of perception and in Sherif's studies of conformity.

88. B

In parametric statistics, a parameter relates to the mean of the population itself. The statistic refers to the mean of the sample itself. Differences between the sample mean and the population mean allow researchers to make inferences about statistically significant differences between samples.

89. A

Frequently, the GRE Psychology test will ask for the measure of central tendency that is most sensitive to outlying observations. Always remember that the average or arithmetic mean is most sensitive to outlying observations, and is least indicative of central tendency when dealing with a skewed distribution. Hence, when discussing income, for instance, the median income is used as a better indicator of central tendency than the mean income.

90. C

Conditioned aversion is a behavioral therapy most often used to eliminate addictive behaviors like cigarette smoking. This technique pairs an aversive unconditioned stimulus with the behavior that needs to be extinguished. Learned helplessness, choice (A), refers to Seligman's classic studies involving dogs, shocks, and depression. Seligman found that subjects placed in negative situations that they could not avoid developed depressive symptoms. Cognitive dissonance, choice (B), refers to Festinger's work involving changing dissonant cognitions to coincide better with one's behaviors. Differential reinforcement, choice (D), refers to shaping, or using operant conditioning in small increments to get a subject to behave in a desired fashion. Spontaneous recovery, choice (E), refers to learning studies that demonstrate that after extinction and a period of rest, presenting the CS without the UCS will again elicit a weak CR.

91. **B**

This question, along with many variations like it, appears frequently on the GRE Psychology test. Remember that the *variable ratio* (VR) reinforcement schedule is *very resistant* (VR) to extinction. It is also the reinforcement schedule connected to addictive gambling behavior.

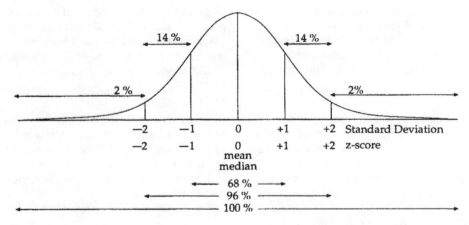

92. **E**

This question states that "each of the following answer choices is true EXCEPT." That means that four answer choices will contain accurate information, and only one will be off target. A score of 38 on a test with a mean of 30 and a standard deviation of 4 would be two standard deviations above the mean. Remember that 34 percent of scores fall between the mean and one standard deviation up and 34 percent of scores fall between the mean and one standard deviation down. So 68 percent of scores fall within one standard deviation from the mean. Joe received a score that was two standard deviations above the mean. Remember that 14 percent of scores fall between one and two standard deviations above the mean. So only two percent score at or above two standard deviations above the mean. That means that 98 percent score lower than Joe, and not 68 percent as described in choice (E). Note that questions like this one can be mined for a great deal of information. Should another statistic question appear that tests percentile to standard deviation conversions, be sure to refer back to questions like this one.

93. **D**

The ability of a measure to produce the same results across multiple administrations is referred to as its reliability. In this case, the Ajax Scale of Creativity has +1.00 correlation for any student who takes it more than once. This indicates that the measure has a high degree of reliability. Criterion validity refers to how well a test can predict an individual's performance on an established test of the same skill or knowledge area. Since this test has only a +0.15 correlation to other tests of creativity, it would be seen as having low criterion validity. So (D) is the only choice that works.

94. **A**

State-dependent learning refers to the phenomenon whereby it is easier to perform a task when in the same state one was in when one first learned the task. In the example described here, Faith performs better when in the same state she was in when she first learned to speak French.

95. **D**

Shaping or differential reinforcement refers to operant conditioning that takes place over very small increments. In the example described in this question, rather than only reinforcing the desired behavior (catching a frisbee), the dog's owner would use shaping to gradually move the dog's behavior towards the desired outcome. This might begin by initially reinforcing the dog each time it picked up or sniffed the frisbee, choice (D).

96. B

A supernormal stimulus is a sign stimulus that provokes a more extreme reaction than the natural stimulus. In this case, the model provokes a more aggressive response than an actual fish. Thus, the model is a supernormal stimulus.

97. B

Chemicals that act as messengers between animals are referred to as *pheromones*. Pheromones frequently act via olfactory (smell) receptors. They differ from hormones, choice (A), in that pheromones communicate with other animals whereas hormones communicate within a single organism.

98. C

The Method of Loci is a classic mnemonic or memory tool that involves associating terms with locations one is already familiar with.

99. B

Children's earliest sentences are considered telegraphic in that they frequently omit many words or word endings. Among the terms to associate with children's earliest phrases is the *holophrase*, in which a complete thought is expressed through a single word or phrase.

100. B

Chomsky did a great deal of work centering on the surface structure and deep structure of language. The surface structure refers to the actual appearance and word order of the sentence. The deep structure refers to the semantic meaning of the sentence. Through the use of transformational grammars, multiple surface structures can refer to a single deep structure. In this example, choice (B) has the same deep structure as "the dog and the cat lived in the same house as Mary." Note that this sentence has a different surface structure, but the same deep structure as the sentence provided in the example.

101. A

Each sentence has its own unique surface structure. No two sentences can have the same surface structure. If

they did, they would be the same sentence. This sentence is made up of more than four morphemes (units of meaning) and more than four phonemes (units of sound), so (B) and (C) are out. The sentence is currently grammatically correct, so (D) is out. A Language Acquisition Device (LAD), choice (E), is the term used by Chomsky to refer to the innate propensity in humans for language acquisition.

102. B

A fixed-action pattern refers to a series of complex behaviors that are triggered by a single releasing stimulus. Generally speaking, fixed-action patterns correspond to instinctual or innate behaviors.

103. B

Instinctual drift refers to the tendency for natural or instinctual behaviors to spontaneously reappear during conditioning trials. In this example, the dog's instinctive behavior of scratching its ears with its paw returns despite the conditioning.

104. A

Anterograde amnesia refers to the inability to retrieve information that one was exposed to after a trauma. It should be differentiated from retrograde amnesia, choice (D), which refers to a loss of access to information from before a trauma. Since anterograde amnesia is associated with the inability to encode and retrieve new information, it impairs long-term learning, choice (A).

105. A

Different tasks require more or less processing and recall time. Of the choices presented here, choices (B), (C), and (D) all refer to tasks that either require reporting that a probe stimulus was present in an earlier trial, or correctly locating the probe in a string of numbers. Each of these tasks requires less depth of processing than the free recall which is asked for in (A) and (E). (A) would take longer than (E) since we recall and process faces more quickly than numbers.

106. B

Whorf's hypothesis is that language can influence perception. Choice (B) is the most in line with this sort of thinking. In a culture with no word for snow, snow is perceived instead as *cold white rain*.

107. A

Much as it sounds, a "reconstructive" theory refers to a theory of memory in which much of what is recalled is reconstructed. This is consistent with the example in which only the main details in a story are recalled with "fillers" that flesh out the story.

108. B

The four basic components of language are phonology (sound), syntax (structure), semantics (meaning), and pragmatics (practical usage). Only choice (B), morphology, is a distracter that is not one of the basic components of language.

109. A

Correlation coefficients reflect the level to which to variables change in direct relation to each other. A correlation coefficient of −1.00 represents a perfect negative correlation, a correlation coefficient of 0.00 represents no correlation, and a correlation coefficient of +1.00 represents a perfect positive correlation. In the examples given, −0.88 represents the strongest correlation. Keep in mind that a negative correlation can be stronger than a positive one, and that a correlation coefficient must fall between −1.00 and 1.00. Choice (E) represents a correlation coefficient that cannot be obtained.

110. C

Of the five answer choices presented here, only relative size, choice (C), is not one of Gestalt psychology's five laws of form perception. Closure, similarity, proximity, good continuation, and *pragnänz* are the five Gestalt laws of form perception.

111. D

Preferential looking is one technique used to study visual perception in infants. This technique tracks the infant's gaze and notes which stimuli the infant prefers to look at.

112. B

Hering is associated with the opponent process theory of color perception. According to this theory, color is perceived through the action of three opposing pairs of color receptors: red-green, blue-yellow, and black-white. Note that choice (A) is more consistent with Young-Helmhotz tri-color theory of color perception than with Hering and opponent process theory.

113. A

One of the few gender differences that have been supported by recent studies involves girls and language acquisition. Girls have been found to acquire language more quickly than boys. Similarly, studies have demonstrated that children exposed to a single language tend to acquire it more rapidly than children exposed to more than one language. Consequently, a girl exposed to only one language would acquire it faster than any of the other options that appear here.

114. B

Recognition refers to the ability to recognize the correct answer when you see it. This can be differentiated from recall or free recall, choice (D), which would describe fill-in-the-blank question types.

115. B

A tone that occurs one second after a letter vanishes from a tachistoscopic display would enhance memory of the letters since they would still be in sensory memory at that time.

116. C

Clustering is the term used to describe the technique used in this question. It refers to the enhanced recall associated with grouping terms into semantically linked clusters.

117. B

Iconic and echoic memory refer to the brief storage of events at the sensory level prior to encoding to a deeper level (e.g., short-term or long-term memory). Eidetic memory, choice (A), refers to exceptional or "photographic" memory.

118. E

Since the same subjects are used for both trials, this design would be described as within-subjects design or repeated measures design. Such a design is most often contrasted with between-subjects design that presents different trials to different groups.

119. B

The independent variable is the variable that is manipulated and/or studied by the experimenter. The influence of the independent variable is measured via the dependent variable. In the example here, hour of the working day at which the test is administered is the independent variable and the dependent variable is the number of errors per list.

120. C

A scatterplot is the term used for a graphical representation of correlational data. The slope of the scatterplot corresponds to the correlation coefficient. A bell curve is the term used to describe the shape of the normal distribution. Chi-square is the statistical test used to evaluate nominal data.

121. E

Helmholtz and Young should be associated with the place theory of pitch perception. This theory is contrasted with the frequency theory of pitch perception. Place theory holds that the location on the basilar membrane that vibrates determines the perceived pitch. Frequency theory holds that the frequency at which the basilar membrane vibrates as a whole determines perceived pitch.

122. B

Harlow's studies of monkeys found that young monkeys preferred the contact comfort provided by a surrogate cloth mother despite the fact that they could only get sustenance from a surrogate wire mother. These studies have been used to emphasize the importance of contact comfort.

123. B

Both bats and marine mammals (like whales and dolphins) have been found to use echolocation to perceive their environments.

124. D

Kandel studied learning in simple organisms like the aplysia since their nervous systems were quite simple and easily observed. He found that as the *aplysia* learned new behavioral responses, their neural pathways underwent related changes.

125. A

Feature detectors have been demonstrated in both visual and auditory modalities. Choice (E) is incorrect since very complex feature detectors have been found in the visual modality.

126. E

All four sensory systems that appear in this question involve the action of afferent pathways. Afferent pathways ascend to the brain, and consequently are closely connected to any sensory system. Efferent pathways exit the brain and are more involved in motor skills and functioning.

127. A

The ventromedial hypothalamus is central to appetite regulation. Damage to this region of the brain will result in hyperphagia (or overeating). A good mnemonic for this region is that damage to the ventromedial hypothalamus makes one very hungry. Hypophagia is the term for not eating enough. Agnosia is the inability to perceive or recognize stimuli. Apraxia refers to the inability to manipulate objects or perform simple motor tasks. Aphasia refers to the inability to produce or comprehend speech.

128. E

Associate the left brain in right-handed people with language comprehension and production. Consequently, speech production, perception of meaningful sounds, of nonsense syllables, and application of syntactic rules would all reside in the left-brain of right-handed individuals. Musical ability, spatial ability, and some mathematical and artistic abilities have been linked to the right brain of right-handed people.

129. C

Two-point discrimination refers to the ability to perceive two tactile points as distinct from each other. It is associated with cutaneous sensitivity and touch perception.

130. A

The "fight or flight" response refers to the increase in pulse and blood pressure that is associated with the presence of a perceived threat. These changes are linked to increased activity of the sympathetic nervous system. The parasympathetic nervous system is the complementary system of the autonomic nervous system associated with feeding and resting. The corpus callosum is the bridge of nervous tissue that connects the two hemispheres of the brain and allows them to communicate with one another.

131. C

The action potential "jumps" along the myelinated axon from gap to gap. These gaps are referred to as the nodes of Ranvier. Broca's area is the region in the left brain of right-handed subjects associated with language production. Wernicke's area is the region in the right brain of right-handed subjects associated with language comprehension. Terminal buttons are located at the end of the axon. Terminal buttons release neurotransmitters into the synapse when activated by the action potential.

132. D

Albert Ellis's rational-emotive therapy (RET) is an example of cognitive-behavioral therapy.

133. B

Secondary gains refer to perceived advantages that are afforded a patient due to an illness. It is a phrase frequently associated with hypochondria. In this example, the therapist is stating that the advantages gained by the illness outweigh the discomfort created by the illness.

134. E

A therapeutic approach that centers around the analyst or patient as an object is most aptly termed object-relations therapy. One of the foremost proponents of the object-relations school was D. W. Winnicott.

135. B

If a neuron will not fire regardless of the amount of stimulation, that neuron must have recently fired and has now entered into the absolute refractory period.

136. B

Schizophrenia was formerly known as *dementia praecox*.

137. B

Erik Erikson's model of psychosocial development centers on the resolution of a series of crises over the course of one's life. The crisis of identity versus role confusion is normally resolved during adolescence.

138. B

Kohlberg used the Heinz dilemma in the development of his theory of moral development. The prisoner's dilemma is an important hypothetical situation used by social psychologists to study cooperation and competition.

139. D

An organism's genotype refers to its genetic blueprint. The phenotype refers to how the genotype is expressed through interactions between the genes and the environment. Note that choice (B) is incorrect since genotype alone does not determine phenotype. The environment plays a factor as well. Choice (E) is incorrect since it undervalues the importance of genotype on phenotypic expression.

140. C

The pituitary gland is frequently referred to as the master gland since it regulates the activity of several other glands.

141. C

The phenomenon whereby an individual deprived of REM sleep compensates by spending more time in REM sleep when possible is referred to as the rebound effect.

142. C

Connect conservation with Piaget and the beaker experiment. In this classic experiment, Piaget poured the contents of one beaker into another. Since the two beakers had different diameters, the water rose to a higher level in the narrower beaker. Subjects in the preoperational stage were unable to realize that both beakers contained the same amount of water. Subjects in the concrete operational stage were able to understand that although they appeared to contain different amounts of water, both beakers contained the same amount of water.

143. D

The use of lithium salts has been found to be an effective somatic treatment for bipolar disorder.

144. B

The diathesis-stress model of mental illness states that the onset of a mental illness involves the interaction of two key factors. First, the subject must have a diathesis or genetic predisposition for the disorder. Then a stressor of some kind must be in place to cause the diathesis to manifest itself as a full-blown mental disorder. In the example provided with this question, the diathesis is demonstrated by the family history of schizophrenia, and the stressor is the death of the subject's mother. The dopamine hypothesis states that schizophrenia results from overactivity of or oversensitivity to the neurotransmitter dopamine.

145. B

Chomsky referred to humans' innate ability to acquire language as a language acquisition device or LAD. Chomsky also coined the term *transformational grammar* to describe the different ways in which unique surface structures or sentences can be formed from a single deep structure or semantic meaning.

146. C

A one-year-old who responds to a sudden repositioning of his head by flinging out his arms and stretching his fingers is demonstrating the Moro reflex. This response is inappropriate for a one-year-old, so choice (C) is correct.

147. E

Charles Sherrington is credited with being the first to infer the existence of synapses or gaps between neurons.

148. B

Freud used the term *abreaction* to describe the uncovering and discharge of a repressed emotion. Abreaction is viewed as an essential aspect of the therapeutic process by psychoanalysts. The release of energy associated with abreaction is also termed *catharsis*.

149. E

The head-turning reflex described in this question is associated with neonates. It has adaptive functions, similar to the sucking reflex, that allow newborns to nurse. It is similar to the Palmar reflex which is also adaptive in that it allows neonates to grasp something placed in their hands.

150. A

Associate Joseph Wolpe with systematic desensitization. Systematic desensitization is a treatment for phobias that involves guided visualization and presenting the threatening stimulus under relaxed conditions.

151. C

Abraham Maslow is well known for his concept of a hierarchy of needs. This hierarchy of needs was frequently represented as a pyramid in which basic needs like food and shelter are presented at the base, and more abstract and higher order needs are presented higher up. Maslow should also be associated with peak experiences and self-actualization.

152. C

SSRI is an acronym for selective serotonin reuptake inhibitors. These drugs limit the reuptake of serotonin in the synapses and have proved to be effective in the treatment of depression.

153. D

While electroconvulsive shock therapy (ECT) is a controversial treatment due to its extreme mental and physical demands, it is still used as a treatment for severe cases of depression.

154. C

The fovea is the area of the retina with the highest concentration of cones. In order to perceive fine details in full daylight, one should look so that the retinal image falls on the fovea. Keep in mind that in low light or darkness, the activity of the rods is more important than that of the cones. Hence, looking to the side can aid with detail perception in the dark.

155. A

Karl Von Frisch is the ethologist to associate with the study of communication in honeybees. Associate Konrad Lorenz with birds, imprinting, and the field of ethology as a whole. Tinbergen is linked with the study of fish and sticklebacks in particular. E. O. Wilson should be associated with the field of sociobiology. G. Stanley Hall, the "father of psychology," is an outlier, and easy to eliminate.

156. E

Associate the breeding of maze-bright and maze dull rats with R. C. Tryon. Associate Harlow with contact comfort and wire and cloth mother studies with monkeys. Von Frisch studied communication among honeybees. Kandel studied *aplysia* and neural learning. Associate Thorndike with learning theory and Law of Effect.

157. A

Helmholtz is associated with the place theory of pitch perception. This theory holds that pitch perception is linked to the region of the basilar membrane that vibrates. This theory would be disconfirmed by finding that a single tone causes the basilar membrane to vibrate as a whole.

158. A

Rhodopsin is the pigment to associate with dark adaptation and visual perception. It is also the pigment to associate with the functioning of the rods.

159. B

Kohler's studies with chimpanzees demonstrated that chimps were capable of insight learning. In one classic study using a chimp named Sultan, Kohler found that a chimp could use tools and demonstrate insight to solve a puzzle and achieve a goal.

160. E

Birds have been found to use atmospheric pressure, infrasound, magnetic sense, and a star compass to assist with navigation. They have not been known to use echolocation.

161. D

The olfactory (smell) modality is most integrated with the limbic system. Numerous links have been made between olfaction and memory. The olfactory bulbs are one of the oldest regions of the brain and are located near the limbic system, which is also an older region of the brain.

162. E

Client-centered therapy is associated with empathy, unconditional positive regard, positive, trusting environment, and a nondirective approach. Only the will to power, choice (E), is not associated with the client-centered approach put forth by Carl Rogers.

163. A

Victor Frankl's existential approach to psychotherapy centers on the concept of meaningfulness. Unconditional positive regard is associated with Carl Rogers's client-centered approach. Operant conditioning is associated with B. F. Skinner and behaviorism. Classical conditioning is associated with Ivan Pavlov. Drive reduction is associated with psychoanalytic theory.

164. D

One of the most common symptoms linked to Tourette's syndrome is the irresistible urge to utter obscenities.

165. E

Social phobia is characterized by a persistent fear of being embarrassed or scrutinized by others.

166. E

A psychogenic fugue is characterized by a loss of identity accompanied by wandering long distances from one's normal routine.

167. B

Since Jim dislikes Myra and dislikes Thai food, imbalance occurs because Myra, also disliking Thai food, is on Jim's side on the issue of this cuisine. All the other answer choices show balance in the Heider triangle.

168. C

Negative symptoms of schizophrenia involve the absence of normal cognitive or emotional expression or behavior. Positive symptoms of schizophrenia involve the presence of abnormal cognitive or emotional expression or behavior. Perceptual hallucinations, delusions, disorganized speech, and disorganized behavior all are positive symptoms of schizophrenia. Only flat affect is a negative symptom among the answer choices presented here.

169. C

The mere exposure effect demonstrates that individuals are more attracted to people and things they are exposed to more often. This would run contrary to the expression "familiarity breeds contempt."

170. C

Associate Irving Janis with group decision-making and groupthink. Solomon Asch studied conformity. Daryl Bem is associated with self-perception theory. Muzafer Sherif is associated with conformity studies. William McGuire studied persuasion.

171. C

Erik Erikson is frequently noted for his development of a theory of psychosocial development that covers an entire lifespan. His theory involved a series of crises that are addressed at different stages in one's life.

172. D

The hippocampus is the region of the brain that has been linked to encoding and retaining information in long-term memory. Damage to the hippocampus is linked to memory impairment.

173. A

The door-in-the-face phenomenon is associated with persuasion studies. This phenomenon states that people are more likely to comply with a small request after refusing a large request. The example here of refusing a loan of $100 then agreeing to a loan of $10 fits nicely into this model.

174. B

The Kitty Genovese case involved a woman who was attacked in the courtyard of an apartment in Kew Gardens, Queens. Although numerous tenants heard her cries, no one responded to assist her. This famous case is associated with the bystander effect and the diffusion of responsibility.

175. E

DNA is really a series of proteins that serve as a template for the other proteins that will attach to it. In that sense it is most similar to a draftsman's template that identically copies a given number of shapes or symbols.

176. B

Inoculation theory is related to persuasion. It centers on the idea that a subject can be inoculated to a particular side to an issue by being exposed to information that anticipates or discredits that position.

177. D

The frontal lobe is associated with problem solving and reasoning, so (A) is out. The occipital lobe is associated with visual processing, so (B) can be eliminated. The parietal lobe is associated with somatosensory processing, so (C) is out. The cerebellum is associated with coordination and balance so (E) is out. Only

choice (D) incorrectly pairs the temporal lobe with memory. Memory is more closely linked to the limbic regions of the brain and the hippocampus.

178. A

Carol Gilligan is an important feminist psychologist who questioned many of Kohlberg's assumptions about moral development along gender lines.

179. C

Equity theory states that we expect to be rewarded for our good behavior, and punished for our poor or negligent behavior. When that equity does not exist, our emotions respond accordingly. In this case, Melanie feels guilty about receiving a promotion and a raise she does not deserve. This is consistent with equity theory.

180. C

Down's syndrome is linked to an extra 21st chromosome. It is also linked to mental retardation. Turner's syndrome and Klinefelter's syndrome are associated with chromosomal irregularities involving the sex chromosomes. In Klinefelter's syndrome, a male has an extra X chromosome. In Turner's syndrome, a female has only one X chromosome. Tourette's syndrome is associated with muscle tics and the uncontrollable urge to utter obscenities.

181. B

Free association, dream interpretation, analysis of transference, and analysis of resistance are all techniques used in Freudian therapy. Only free recall is not a technique used in Freudian therapy.

182. A

Token economies have been found to be extremely effective forms of behavior modification for severely mentally retarded patients.

183. B

The Prisoner's dilemma is a classic hypothetical situation in which two parties can either cooperate cohort, or cheat on their cohort. If both cooperate with their cohort, they face a medium sentence. If one cooperates and one cheats, the cooperating subject receives an extreme sentence, while the cheating subject gets off with no sentence. If both subjects cheat, both receive an extreme sentence. This dilemma has been used in social psychology and in game theory to study when subjects cheat, when subjects cooperate, and when it is in their best interest to do one or the other.

184. A

The Stroop effect refers to the delay in response time described in this question. When asked to say the color of ink that a word is written in, subjects take longer to say a color word that does not coincide with the color of ink. Studies of the Stroop effect have shed light on semantic processing and perception.

185. C

Fertilization of human eggs normally takes place in the fallopian tubes. The ovaries are the female sex organs where eggs are produced and released. The uterus is the place where the developing embryo resides.

186. D

According to Piaget, the ability to "think like a scientist" is an indicator that one has reached the formal operational stage of development. Piaget associated this stage of development with his pendulum experiment.

187. C

An algorithm is a complex and mathematically exhaustive way of arriving at the solution to a problem. A heuristic is a short cut or rule of thumb that may not always get you to the correct solution, but will get you to your solution more quickly than an algorithm. An algorithm is helpful in that it will always find the solution to a problem, but frequently it will take longer than desired to get there.

188. E

Primacy and recency effects are phenomena discussed in memory research. These effects state that it is easier to remember items at the beginning (primacy) and end (recency) of a list. In this example, the early and late months are remembered better, which is consistent with primacy and recency effects.

189. C

Multiple-choice questions, like the ones on this test, are a type of recognition task. As the name implies, recognitions only require you to recognize the correct information rather than generate or recall that information yourself.

190. E

According to Freud, the Oedipal conflict is normally resolved during the phallic stage. The Oedipal conflict centers on a boy's sexual attraction to his mother. Its female counterpart is known as the Electra complex.

191. B

According to social facilitation theory, when learning a relatively easy task like bowling, the presence of others enhances one's performance. Associate the name Zajonc with social facilitation theory.

192. A

Piaget noted that primary and secondary circular reactions were a characteristic of the sensorimotor stage. Primary and secondary circular reactions are repeated simple behaviors that are intended to manipulate the environment. The tendency of infants to repeatedly put things in their mouths is an example of these kinds of behaviors.

193. A

Vygotsky is a developmental psychologist known for his development of the concept of a zone of proximal development. The zone of proximal development centers on the notion that the infant or child develops in relation to its social environment, chiefly its mother. The child will perform differently and better when in close proximity to its mother.

194. B

Convergent and divergent thinking were first defined by J. P. Guilford. Convergent thinking is necessary when there is a single solution to a problem. Divergent thinking is helpful when there are multiple creative outcomes or solutions to a problem.

195. A

The shorter reaction times described in this question would be consistent with the notion of semantic priming. Semantic priming is associated with spreading activation and the idea that semantic nodes are primed by the activation of nearby nodes when exposed to related words.

196. C

A script refers to a procedural schema or expected way in which a process or event will occur. In this example, Louis has a preconceived idea of "how people behave at parties." These preconceptions would comprise his "party" script.

197. B

Hans Eysenck was a theorist who developed a dimensional approach to personality centering on variation along certain major traits. Eysenck posited that stability-instability and introversion-extroversion were two important dimensions upon which to observe personality.

198. E

Mischel was an ardent critic of trait theories of personality. Mischel criticized trait theories because they placed far too much emphasis on fixed, dispositional traits that did not vary across situations. Mischel adopted a more situational understanding of personality where the environment played an important role.

199. E

Henry Murray and the Thematic Apperception Test should be associated with the need to achieve. This test was a projective test involving ambiguous story cards. According to Murray, subjects' apperceptions of the story would indicate which needs were most important to them.

200. C

According to Mendelian genetics, there are dominant and recessive genes. Brown eyes are a dominant trait, and blue eyes are a recessive trait. What that means is that if an individual has blue eyes, she has two recessive blue eye genes. If an individual has brown eyes, however, she may have two dominant brown eye genes or she may have one dominant brown eye gene and one recessive blue eye gene. Since the brown eye gene is dominant, it will be expressed, and the individual will have brown eyes. Notice that if two individuals each possess a gene for blue eyes and a gene for brown eyes, their offspring may have blue eyes if they receive the gene for blue eyes from each parent. Thus, if both parents have brown eyes, their offspring could have blue eyes.

201. D

The term *reaction formation* comes from psychoanalysis. It refers to a defense mechanism in which a patient responds with the opposite reaction from what he genuinely feels.

202. A

Projection involves shifting unacceptable feelings or actions to another person. In this example, Alex is projecting his distaste for his own actions onto his brother. Countertransference refers to the analyst's transfer of unconscious feelings or wishes onto a patient. Repression refers to not allowing threatening material into consciousness. Compensation involves excelling in one area to make up for shortcomings elsewhere. Rationalization refers to justifying or rationalizing behavior or feelings that cause guilt.

203. B

According to Baumrind, the most effective parenting style is authoritative. She contrasted this style with permissive and authoritarian parenting styles, and found that authoritative parenting produced the most socially and academically competent children.

204. D

Countertransference refers to the tendency of the analyst to project his or her feelings onto the patient. According to psychoanalysis, this is inevitable and unavoidable. It is important, however, that the analyst is conscious of this defense mechanism when treating a patient. It is also a reason why psychoanalysts are required to undergo analysis themselves.

205. C

The correct progression through Piaget's four stages of cognitive development is sensorimotor stage, preoperational stage, concrete operational stage, and formal operational stage.

206. E

The child's game of "peek-a-boo" centers around the idea that when a child does not see you, he thinks you are not there. This is why it is such a surprise each time you reveal yourself. This corresponds to the development of object permanence. Object permanence is the awareness that objects (and people) do not cease to exist when we no longer see them. Understanding object permanence is an important milestone in a child's cognitive development.

207. A

The process of interpreting new information in terms of an existing schema is termed assimilation. By contrast, accommodation refers to adjustments made to an existing schema to incorporate new instances and information.

208. C

Ainsworth's studies of Ugandan children involved placing children in a "strange situation" where their mother left them briefly. She then observed how they responded. She found that several different types of attachment were evident. These included insecure/avoidant attachment, insecure/resistant attachment, and secure attachment. She did not discuss an insecure/aversive attachment.

209. B

Cognitive dissonance is the theory put forth by Festinger that centers on the desire to relieve dissonance between behaviors and cognitions. In this example, the statement demonstrates how a cognition changed based on behavior that was inconsistent with a previous cognition. If I think I'm not a Trojans fan, but I attend several Trojans games, my behavior is inconsistent with my cognitions, and I enter into a state of dissonance. In order to resolve that dissonance, I change my cognitions to match my behavior. In this example, I come to think that I am a Trojans fan, and the dissonance dissipates.

210. C

The halo effect refers to the tendency to attribute additional positive qualities to individuals who already possess positive qualities. In this example, Janine has several positive qualities, so her coworkers attribute to her the additional positive quality of intelligence even though she scores poorly on intelligence tests.

211. D

The Zimbardo study involved creating a prisonlike scenario with one group of subjects becoming the prisoners, and another group of subjects becoming the guards. Zimbardo found that the use of roles, uniforms, and a rigid social structure resulted in subjects losing their sense of themselves and their ability to question what they were doing. The term *deindividuation* is associated with this phenomenon and this study.

212. A

Studies of group decision-making and groupthink have found that groups tend to move towards riskier and more extreme decisions than individual decision-makers. This tendency of groups to move towards extremes or "poles" when making decisions is called group polarization.

213. D

Festinger's social comparison theory centers around the idea that we need others to understand our own ability, and that we will actively seek others out to compare their performance with our own.

214. D

Attribution of success to external causes is common for individuals with low self-esteem. Such individuals, along with depressed individuals, have also been found to attribute failures to internal causes.

215. D

The Robber's Cave experiment is a classic study of group and intergroup interactions. In this study, two groups of boys were formed at a camp. The development of group norms and interactions between groups were studied in depth.

PRACTICE TEST II ANSWER SHEET

1 (A) (B) (C) (D) (E)   27 (A) (B) (C) (D) (E)   53 (A) (B) (C) (D) (E)   79 (A) (B) (C) (D) (E)

2 (A) (B) (C) (D) (E)   28 (A) (B) (C) (D) (E)   54 (A) (B) (C) (D) (E)   80 (A) (B) (C) (D) (E)

3 (A) (B) (C) (D) (E)   29 (A) (B) (C) (D) (E)   55 (A) (B) (C) (D) (E)   81 (A) (B) (C) (D) (E)

4 (A) (B) (C) (D) (E)   30 (A) (B) (C) (D) (E)   56 (A) (B) (C) (D) (E)   82 (A) (B) (C) (D) (E)

5 (A) (B) (C) (D) (E)   31 (A) (B) (C) (D) (E)   57 (A) (B) (C) (D) (E)   83 (A) (B) (C) (D) (E)

6 (A) (B) (C) (D) (E)   32 (A) (B) (C) (D) (E)   58 (A) (B) (C) (D) (E)   84 (A) (B) (C) (D) (E)

7 (A) (B) (C) (D) (E)   33 (A) (B) (C) (D) (E)   59 (A) (B) (C) (D) (E)   85 (A) (B) (C) (D) (E)

8 (A) (B) (C) (D) (E)   34 (A) (B) (C) (D) (E)   60 (A) (B) (C) (D) (E)   86 (A) (B) (C) (D) (E)

9 (A) (B) (C) (D) (E)   35 (A) (B) (C) (D) (E)   61 (A) (B) (C) (D) (E)   87 (A) (B) (C) (D) (E)

10 (A) (B) (C) (D) (E)   36 (A) (B) (C) (D) (E)   62 (A) (B) (C) (D) (E)   88 (A) (B) (C) (D) (E)

11 (A) (B) (C) (D) (E)   37 (A) (B) (C) (D) (E)   63 (A) (B) (C) (D) (E)   89 (A) (B) (C) (D) (E)

12 (A) (B) (C) (D) (E)   38 (A) (B) (C) (D) (E)   64 (A) (B) (C) (D) (E)   90 (A) (B) (C) (D) (E)

13 (A) (B) (C) (D) (E)   39 (A) (B) (C) (D) (E)   65 (A) (B) (C) (D) (E)   91 (A) (B) (C) (D) (E)

14 (A) (B) (C) (D) (E)   40 (A) (B) (C) (D) (E)   66 (A) (B) (C) (D) (E)   92 (A) (B) (C) (D) (E)

15 (A) (B) (C) (D) (E)   41 (A) (B) (C) (D) (E)   67 (A) (B) (C) (D) (E)   93 (A) (B) (C) (D) (E)

16 (A) (B) (C) (D) (E)   42 (A) (B) (C) (D) (E)   68 (A) (B) (C) (D) (E)   94 (A) (B) (C) (D) (E)

17 (A) (B) (C) (D) (E)   43 (A) (B) (C) (D) (E)   69 (A) (B) (C) (D) (E)   95 (A) (B) (C) (D) (E)

18 (A) (B) (C) (D) (E)   44 (A) (B) (C) (D) (E)   70 (A) (B) (C) (D) (E)   96 (A) (B) (C) (D) (E)

19 (A) (B) (C) (D) (E)   45 (A) (B) (C) (D) (E)   71 (A) (B) (C) (D) (E)   97 (A) (B) (C) (D) (E)

20 (A) (B) (C) (D) (E)   46 (A) (B) (C) (D) (E)   72 (A) (B) (C) (D) (E)   98 (A) (B) (C) (D) (E)

21 (A) (B) (C) (D) (E)   47 (A) (B) (C) (D) (E)   73 (A) (B) (C) (D) (E)   99 (A) (B) (C) (D) (E)

22 (A) (B) (C) (D) (E)   48 (A) (B) (C) (D) (E)   74 (A) (B) (C) (D) (E)   100 (A) (B) (C) (D) (E)

23 (A) (B) (C) (D) (E)   49 (A) (B) (C) (D) (E)   75 (A) (B) (C) (D) (E)   101 (A) (B) (C) (D) (E)

24 (A) (B) (C) (D) (E)   50 (A) (B) (C) (D) (E)   76 (A) (B) (C) (D) (E)   102 (A) (B) (C) (D) (E)

25 (A) (B) (C) (D) (E)   51 (A) (B) (C) (D) (E)   77 (A) (B) (C) (D) (E)   103 (A) (B) (C) (D) (E)

26 (A) (B) (C) (D) (E)   52 (A) (B) (C) (D) (E)   78 (A) (B) (C) (D) (E)   104 (A) (B) (C) (D) (E)

105	Ⓐ Ⓑ Ⓒ Ⓓ Ⓔ	135	Ⓐ Ⓑ Ⓒ Ⓓ Ⓔ	165	Ⓐ Ⓑ Ⓒ Ⓓ Ⓔ	195	Ⓐ Ⓑ Ⓒ Ⓓ Ⓔ
106	Ⓐ Ⓑ Ⓒ Ⓓ Ⓔ	136	Ⓐ Ⓑ Ⓒ Ⓓ Ⓔ	166	Ⓐ Ⓑ Ⓒ Ⓓ Ⓔ	196	Ⓐ Ⓑ Ⓒ Ⓓ Ⓔ
107	Ⓐ Ⓑ Ⓒ Ⓓ Ⓔ	137	Ⓐ Ⓑ Ⓒ Ⓓ Ⓔ	167	Ⓐ Ⓑ Ⓒ Ⓓ Ⓔ	197	Ⓐ Ⓑ Ⓒ Ⓓ Ⓔ
108	Ⓐ Ⓑ Ⓒ Ⓓ Ⓔ	138	Ⓐ Ⓑ Ⓒ Ⓓ Ⓔ	168	Ⓐ Ⓑ Ⓒ Ⓓ Ⓔ	198	Ⓐ Ⓑ Ⓒ Ⓓ Ⓔ
109	Ⓐ Ⓑ Ⓒ Ⓓ Ⓔ	139	Ⓐ Ⓑ Ⓒ Ⓓ Ⓔ	169	Ⓐ Ⓑ Ⓒ Ⓓ Ⓔ	199	Ⓐ Ⓑ Ⓒ Ⓓ Ⓔ
110	Ⓐ Ⓑ Ⓒ Ⓓ Ⓔ	140	Ⓐ Ⓑ Ⓒ Ⓓ Ⓔ	170	Ⓐ Ⓑ Ⓒ Ⓓ Ⓔ	200	Ⓐ Ⓑ Ⓒ Ⓓ Ⓔ
111	Ⓐ Ⓑ Ⓒ Ⓓ Ⓔ	141	Ⓐ Ⓑ Ⓒ Ⓓ Ⓔ	171	Ⓐ Ⓑ Ⓒ Ⓓ Ⓔ	201	Ⓐ Ⓑ Ⓒ Ⓓ Ⓔ
112	Ⓐ Ⓑ Ⓒ Ⓓ Ⓔ	142	Ⓐ Ⓑ Ⓒ Ⓓ Ⓔ	172	Ⓐ Ⓑ Ⓒ Ⓓ Ⓔ	202	Ⓐ Ⓑ Ⓒ Ⓓ Ⓔ
113	Ⓐ Ⓑ Ⓒ Ⓓ Ⓔ	143	Ⓐ Ⓑ Ⓒ Ⓓ Ⓔ	173	Ⓐ Ⓑ Ⓒ Ⓓ Ⓔ	203	Ⓐ Ⓑ Ⓒ Ⓓ Ⓔ
114	Ⓐ Ⓑ Ⓒ Ⓓ Ⓔ	144	Ⓐ Ⓑ Ⓒ Ⓓ Ⓔ	174	Ⓐ Ⓑ Ⓒ Ⓓ Ⓔ	204	Ⓐ Ⓑ Ⓒ Ⓓ Ⓔ
115	Ⓐ Ⓑ Ⓒ Ⓓ Ⓔ	145	Ⓐ Ⓑ Ⓒ Ⓓ Ⓔ	175	Ⓐ Ⓑ Ⓒ Ⓓ Ⓔ	205	Ⓐ Ⓑ Ⓒ Ⓓ Ⓔ
116	Ⓐ Ⓑ Ⓒ Ⓓ Ⓔ	146	Ⓐ Ⓑ Ⓒ Ⓓ Ⓔ	176	Ⓐ Ⓑ Ⓒ Ⓓ Ⓔ	206	Ⓐ Ⓑ Ⓒ Ⓓ Ⓔ
117	Ⓐ Ⓑ Ⓒ Ⓓ Ⓔ	147	Ⓐ Ⓑ Ⓒ Ⓓ Ⓔ	177	Ⓐ Ⓑ Ⓒ Ⓓ Ⓔ	207	Ⓐ Ⓑ Ⓒ Ⓓ Ⓔ
118	Ⓐ Ⓑ Ⓒ Ⓓ Ⓔ	148	Ⓐ Ⓑ Ⓒ Ⓓ Ⓔ	178	Ⓐ Ⓑ Ⓒ Ⓓ Ⓔ	208	Ⓐ Ⓑ Ⓒ Ⓓ Ⓔ
119	Ⓐ Ⓑ Ⓒ Ⓓ Ⓔ	149	Ⓐ Ⓑ Ⓒ Ⓓ Ⓔ	179	Ⓐ Ⓑ Ⓒ Ⓓ Ⓔ	209	Ⓐ Ⓑ Ⓒ Ⓓ Ⓔ
120	Ⓐ Ⓑ Ⓒ Ⓓ Ⓔ	150	Ⓐ Ⓑ Ⓒ Ⓓ Ⓔ	180	Ⓐ Ⓑ Ⓒ Ⓓ Ⓔ	210	Ⓐ Ⓑ Ⓒ Ⓓ Ⓔ
121	Ⓐ Ⓑ Ⓒ Ⓓ Ⓔ	151	Ⓐ Ⓑ Ⓒ Ⓓ Ⓔ	181	Ⓐ Ⓑ Ⓒ Ⓓ Ⓔ	211	Ⓐ Ⓑ Ⓒ Ⓓ Ⓔ
122	Ⓐ Ⓑ Ⓒ Ⓓ Ⓔ	152	Ⓐ Ⓑ Ⓒ Ⓓ Ⓔ	182	Ⓐ Ⓑ Ⓒ Ⓓ Ⓔ	212	Ⓐ Ⓑ Ⓒ Ⓓ Ⓔ
123	Ⓐ Ⓑ Ⓒ Ⓓ Ⓔ	153	Ⓐ Ⓑ Ⓒ Ⓓ Ⓔ	183	Ⓐ Ⓑ Ⓒ Ⓓ Ⓔ	213	Ⓐ Ⓑ Ⓒ Ⓓ Ⓔ
124	Ⓐ Ⓑ Ⓒ Ⓓ Ⓔ	154	Ⓐ Ⓑ Ⓒ Ⓓ Ⓔ	184	Ⓐ Ⓑ Ⓒ Ⓓ Ⓔ	214	Ⓐ Ⓑ Ⓒ Ⓓ Ⓔ
125	Ⓐ Ⓑ Ⓒ Ⓓ Ⓔ	155	Ⓐ Ⓑ Ⓒ Ⓓ Ⓔ	185	Ⓐ Ⓑ Ⓒ Ⓓ Ⓔ	215	Ⓐ Ⓑ Ⓒ Ⓓ Ⓔ
126	Ⓐ Ⓑ Ⓒ Ⓓ Ⓔ	156	Ⓐ Ⓑ Ⓒ Ⓓ Ⓔ	186	Ⓐ Ⓑ Ⓒ Ⓓ Ⓔ	216	Ⓐ Ⓑ Ⓒ Ⓓ Ⓔ
127	Ⓐ Ⓑ Ⓒ Ⓓ Ⓔ	157	Ⓐ Ⓑ Ⓒ Ⓓ Ⓔ	187	Ⓐ Ⓑ Ⓒ Ⓓ Ⓔ	217	Ⓐ Ⓑ Ⓒ Ⓓ Ⓔ
128	Ⓐ Ⓑ Ⓒ Ⓓ Ⓔ	158	Ⓐ Ⓑ Ⓒ Ⓓ Ⓔ	188	Ⓐ Ⓑ Ⓒ Ⓓ Ⓔ	218	Ⓐ Ⓑ Ⓒ Ⓓ Ⓔ
129	Ⓐ Ⓑ Ⓒ Ⓓ Ⓔ	159	Ⓐ Ⓑ Ⓒ Ⓓ Ⓔ	189	Ⓐ Ⓑ Ⓒ Ⓓ Ⓔ	219	Ⓐ Ⓑ Ⓒ Ⓓ Ⓔ
130	Ⓐ Ⓑ Ⓒ Ⓓ Ⓔ	160	Ⓐ Ⓑ Ⓒ Ⓓ Ⓔ	190	Ⓐ Ⓑ Ⓒ Ⓓ Ⓔ	220	Ⓐ Ⓑ Ⓒ Ⓓ Ⓔ
131	Ⓐ Ⓑ Ⓒ Ⓓ Ⓔ	161	Ⓐ Ⓑ Ⓒ Ⓓ Ⓔ	191	Ⓐ Ⓑ Ⓒ Ⓓ Ⓔ		
132	Ⓐ Ⓑ Ⓒ Ⓓ Ⓔ	162	Ⓐ Ⓑ Ⓒ Ⓓ Ⓔ	192	Ⓐ Ⓑ Ⓒ Ⓓ Ⓔ		
133	Ⓐ Ⓑ Ⓒ Ⓓ Ⓔ	163	Ⓐ Ⓑ Ⓒ Ⓓ Ⓔ	193	Ⓐ Ⓑ Ⓒ Ⓓ Ⓔ		
134	Ⓐ Ⓑ Ⓒ Ⓓ Ⓔ	164	Ⓐ Ⓑ Ⓒ Ⓓ Ⓔ	194	Ⓐ Ⓑ Ⓒ Ⓓ Ⓔ		

Practice Test II

Time: 170 Minutes
Questions: 220

<u>Directions:</u> Each of the questions or incomplete statements below is followed by five suggested answers or completions. In each case, select the one that best answers the questions or completes the statement.

1. Susan, who is moderately critical of the present government, gets involved in heated political discussions with her college classmates. On her next visit home, her parents notice how much more critical of the government she has become. Which of the following is the LEAST likely explanation for her attitude change?

   (A) group polarization
   (B) the mere exposure effect
   (C) social facilitation
   (D) the risky shift phenomenon
   (E) conformity

2. The tendency to attribute one's own feelings and thoughts to an external object is known as

   (A) personification
   (B) displacement
   (C) cathexis
   (D) projection
   (E) sublimation

3. The administration of unavoidable shock prior to avoidance learning results in what phenomenon when avoidance training begins?

   (A) The animal jumps over the barrier if the shock is strong enough.
   (B) The animal jumps over the barrier and avoids the shock every time.
   (C) Trial-and-error learning
   (D) Insightful learning
   (E) The animal makes no effort to escape the shock.

4. The Whorfian hypothesis states that

   (A) language largely determines the way in which we perceive the world
   (B) the way we perceive the world affects our language development
   (C) the way we observe the world contradicts our way of speaking
   (D) previous experience causes us to fixate on incorrect solutions to problems
   (E) we fixate in an effort not to be distracted from correct solutions

5. Every time an alarm clock rings, the subject is hit in the eye with a puff of air from a blow dryer. This causes the subject to blink. After a while, the subject blinks her eyes as soon as the alarm clock rings. The eye blink that is caused by the blow dryer is called

   (A) the conditioned stimulus
   (B) the unconditioned response
   (C) the unconditioned stimulus
   (D) the conditioned response
   (E) habituation

6. Systematic desensitization is a form of therapy most closely associated with the work of

   (A) Joseph Wolpe
   (B) Carl Rogers
   (C) Albert Ellis
   (D) Richard Lazarus
   (E) Jacob Moreno

7. A poll shows that people tend to believe that tornadoes kill more people than asthma, even though, at least in the United States, asthma actually causes about 20 times more deaths than tornadoes. Which of the following could best explain the poll results?

   (A) the Hawthorne effect
   (B) the availability heuristic
   (C) divergent thinking
   (D) the representativeness heuristic
   (E) social loafing

8. If a person's score on the WAIS is one standard deviation below the mean, his IQ score would be at about what percentile?

   (A) 2
   (B) 10
   (C) 16
   (D) 34
   (E) 84

9. Impaired language comprehension following a stroke would most probably be diagnosed as

   (A) dyslexia
   (B) aphagia
   (C) Wernicke's aphasia
   (D) Broca's aphasia
   (E) retrograde amnesia

10. Which of the following stages postulated by Erikson corresponds most closely to Freud's oral stage of development?

    (A) trust versus mistrust
    (B) initiative versus guilt
    (C) integrity versus despair
    (D) incorporation versus dependence
    (E) autonomy versus shame and doubt

11. Door-to-door salespeople who are paid on commission and maintain high levels of perseverance despite infrequent sales display an effect of

    (A) a fixed-ratio schedule
    (B) a fixed-interval schedule
    (C) a variable-interval schedule
    (D) a variable-ratio schedule
    (E) successive approximations

GO ON TO THE NEXT PAGE

12. What three styles of parenting did Baumrind identify?

   (A) autocratic, democratic, laissez-faire
   (B) authoritarian, authoritative, permissive
   (C) preconventional, conventional, postconventional
   (D) moving against, moving toward, moving away from
   (E) prototaxic, parataxic, syntaxic

13. Investigations into the influence of group pressure on perceptual judgments reveal that

   (A) Many people obey orders even though they object strongly to what they are doing.
   (B) The less ambiguous the stimulus, the more likely it is that the subject will conform to group pressure.
   (C) The more ambiguous the stimulus, the more likely it is that the subject will conform to group pressure.
   (D) A pressure group is more effective in getting a subject to conform if group opinion is not unanimous.
   (E) Group pressure cannot influence something as personal as perceptual judgments.

14. Which of the following statements characterizes the cognitive-structuralist orientation in developmental psychology?

   (A) The child is a "blank slate."
   (B) Sexual drives play an important role in early development.
   (C) There are no qualitative differences between the psychological processes of children and adults.
   (D) The child is a passive receptor of stimuli.
   (E) The child actively constructs her own knowledge.

15. Which of the following yields a balanced structure, according to Heider's balance theory?

   (A) Jack likes Jill and both like football
   (B) Jack dislikes Jill and both like football
   (C) Jack dislikes Jill and both dislike football
   (D) Jack likes Jill but only Jill likes football
   (E) Jack likes Jill, Jack likes football, and Jill likes baseball

16. In order to solve a particular problem, subjects must use a hammer and a nail as units of measurement. This experiment is most directly concerned with

   (A) demand characteristics
   (B) crystallized intelligence
   (C) functional fixedness
   (D) semantic priming
   (E) response generalization

17. Which of the following concepts is most closely associated with Allport?

    (A) striving for superiority
    (B) moving away from others
    (C) object displacement
    (D) functional autonomy
    (E) phenomenal field

18. Many pedestrians observe a motorist sideswipe a parked car, but none reports the incident. This behavior is an example of

    (A) social proximity
    (B) pluralistic ignorance
    (C) diffusion of responsibility
    (D) altruism
    (E) imitation

19. "Paradoxical sleep" is so called because

    (A) its EEG pattern is much slower than would be expected in sleep
    (B) it is so easy to wake someone in paradoxical sleep
    (C) its EEG pattern resembles that of the waking state more than that of slow-wave sleep
    (D) it is apparently unnecessary; organisms deprived of paradoxical sleep do not compensate for the loss when allowed to resume sleeping
    (E) investigators are unsure as to what transpires during this sleep stage

20. In reciting the alphabet for a school play, Julie says the first ten letters in perfect order but then slips up and recites the remaining letters in incorrect order. This is an example of

    (A) physical processing
    (B) selective attention
    (C) the recency effect
    (D) Emmert's law
    (E) the primacy effect

21. The most important assumption made by Piaget about intelligence is that

    (A) the organism passively takes in information
    (B) crystallized intelligence increases throughout the life span
    (C) social interaction and transmission are at the core of learning
    (D) assimilation and accommodation are necessary for the development of intelligence
    (E) thought arises from actions

22. The afterimage of an object on a wall appears larger as the viewer moves further away from it because

    (A) the size of the retinal image remains constant
    (B) motion parallax tends to make objects appear larger
    (C) the perceived size of the image changes inversely with perceived distance
    (D) the size of the retinal image is increasing
    (E) Emmert's law has no effect on afterimages

GO ON TO THE NEXT PAGE

23. The MMPI was originally constructed by including items that discriminated between patient groups and "normals." Therefore, it relied on the concept of

    (A) predictive validity
    (B) concurrent validity
    (C) construct validity
    (D) content validity
    (E) alternate-form reliability

24. Which principles are contrasted in the following figure?

    ] [ ] [ ] [ ] [ ]

    (A) similarity versus closure
    (B) continuity versus common fate
    (C) proximity versus similarity
    (D) *prägnanz* versus closure
    (E) proximity versus closure

25. One hundred students are given a mathematics test and no more than 20 of their scores are the same. The ten top-scoring students are called Group A. Which of the following descriptive statistics will have a higher value if generated from the distribution of Group A scores than from the entire distribution of the hundred scores?

    (A) median
    (B) mode
    (C) range
    (D) the correlation between math test scores and spelling test scores for the students
    (E) standard deviation

26. Which of the following is due to the regeneration of rhodopsin?

    (A) lateral inhibition
    (B) light adaptation
    (C) stereopsis
    (D) dark adaptation
    (E) simultaneous brightness contrast

27. The law of effect was first formulated by

    (A) John Garcia
    (B) B. F. Skinner
    (C) Edward Thorndike
    (D) Edward Tolman
    (E) E. O. Wilson

28. Bowlby's major contribution to theories of child development grew out of studies of

    (A) fraternal and identical twins
    (B) children separated from their parents
    (C) recessive gene inheritance
    (D) imitation and modeling as causes of aggression
    (E) IQ scores and heredity

29. In the auditory system, transduction takes place at the

    (A) inferior colliculus
    (B) pinna
    (C) olfactory epithelium
    (D) Pacinian corpuscles
    (E) Organ of Corti

GO ON TO THE NEXT PAGE

30. A person sees an accident, runs away, and feels afraid. This sequence is explicitly predicted by which of the following theories?

    (A) Sheldon's theory
    (B) Cannon-Bard theory
    (C) Schachter-Singer theory
    (D) James-Lange theory
    (E) signal detection theory

31. In Freudian theory, primary process thought

    (A) refers to the attempt to satisfy needs irrationally, with no consideration of reality
    (B) refers to the desires expressed by the elementary school child
    (C) describes the same phenomenon as Piaget's concept of egocentric speech
    (D) is dependent upon the successful development of the ego
    (E) develops primarily as a response to superego demands

32. Calculating standard deviations could most directly assess whether

    (A) Drug A is more effective than Drug B
    (B) students who spend more at the college bookstore achieve better grades
    (C) the difference in height between women who took vitamins as children and women who didn't is due to chance
    (D) the price of corn was subject to greater daily fluctuations during July than the price of wheat
    (E) the median income of families living in New York is less than that of families living in Boston

33. Which of the following is a physical property of sound?

    (A) loudness
    (B) frequency
    (C) pitch
    (D) timbre
    (E) hue

34. Associating a list of items you need to remember with a sequence of specific places is called

    (A) encoding specificity
    (B) chunking
    (C) cognitive mapping
    (D) the Method of Loci
    (E) the hypothetico-deductive method

35. The split-half procedure is a method of

    (A) sampling groups
    (B) studying dominant and nondominant brain functions
    (C) measuring reliability
    (D) rejecting the null hypothesis
    (E) assessing validity

36. A study following the lives of gifted children may be classified as a

    (A) longitudinal study
    (B) true experiment
    (C) cross-sectional study
    (D) quasi-experiment
    (E) control group study

GO ON TO THE NEXT PAGE

37. Which of the following theories challenged Helmholtz's theory of color vision?

    (A) frequency theory
    (B) oppponent-process theory
    (C) isomorphism
    (D) trichromatic theory
    (E) place-resonance theory

38. A young child who does not smile at people and who is indifferent to cuddling presents behavior typical of

    (A) enuresis
    (B) separation anxiety disorder
    (C) autistic disorder
    (D) attention-deficit/hyperactivity disorder
    (E) pica

39. McClelland and Rumelhart developed the idea of

    (A) functional fixedness
    (B) the dual-code hypothesis
    (C) reconstructive memory
    (D) parallel distributed processing
    (E) the encoding specificity principle

40. The primary feature of catatonic schizophrenia is

    (A) motor abnormalities
    (B) auditory hallucinations
    (C) inappropriate affect
    (D) paranoia
    (E) delusional thinking

41. The essential assumption of the theory of cognitive dissonance is that

    (A) when attitudes and behavior are incongruent, a state of tension exists
    (B) attitudes are permanent and unchanging
    (C) a change in attitude is not always immediately obvious
    (D) people organize behavior to make it meaningful
    (E) behavior can be modified

42. When a child acquires the ability to represent the world internally through the use of symbols, she enters which of Piaget's stages of cognitive development?

    (A) sensorimotor
    (B) secondary circular reactions
    (C) concrete operational
    (D) preoperational
    (E) formal operational

43. Albert Ellis is most closely associated with which of the following types of psychotherapy?

    (A) Gestalt therapy
    (B) primal therapy
    (C) psychodrama
    (D) client-centered therapy
    (E) rational-emotive therapy

44. The nondominant hemisphere is more adept at

    (A) verbal tasks
    (B) arithmetic
    (C) logical propositions
    (D) remembering the gist of a story, rather than the words themselves
    (E) spatial organization

45. One object partially blocks your view of a second object and, therefore, the first object is seen as being closer to you than the second object. This is an example of

(A) relative size
(B) good continuation
(C) interposition
(D) the Poggendorff illusion
(E) overregularization

46. Bandura's studies of aggression suggest that

(A) frustration is a necessary antecedent condition of aggressive modeling
(B) observation of aggressive responses increases the likelihood of aggressive behavior in children
(C) adult models are more influential than peer models in stimulating aggression in children
(D) girls have a stronger innate tendency toward aggression than boys
(E) direct expression of hostile feelings is most common in children with high frustration tolerance

47. Which type of drug is indicated for the treatment of depression?

(A) tricyclics
(B) Thorazine
(C) Haldol
(D) chlorpromazine
(E) Ritalin

48. A morpheme may best be defined as

(A) an orderly arrangement of words in a syntactical sequence
(B) a single word used to convey an complex idea
(C) the meaning of a word in any given context
(D) the smallest unit of language that conveys a meaning
(E) a class of closely related speech sounds regarded by speakers of a language as a single sound

49. Olds and Milner discovered that

(A) rats raised in a "rich" environment develop more dendritic spines
(B) rats electrically stimulate themselves if electrodes are placed in the septal region of their brains
(C) individual behavioral traits, such as a rat's maze running ability, are inheritable
(D) sickness caused by X-radiation can be used to condition rats' preferences for food pellet taste
(E) lesions to a rat's hypothalamus disrupt its eating behavior

50. The babbling behavior of six month old infants

(A) is similar for nearly all children, including deaf infants
(B) develops more slowly in children born to mute parents
(C) is absent if the child is deaf
(D) is more frequent and consistent in girls than in boys
(E) is characterized by the absence of aspirate "h" sounds

GO ON TO THE NEXT PAGE

51. The Ames room experiment demonstrates

    (A) the principle of closure
    (B) the influence of gender on size constancy
    (C) the importance of binocular cues for depth perception
    (D) the effect of retinal disparity on simultaneous brightness contrast
    (E) the influence of apparent distance on the perception of size

52. Galton's major contribution to psychology was his

    (A) work towards making the institutional treatment of the mentally ill more humane
    (B) explanation of the phi phenomenon
    (C) creation of standardized measures of intelligence
    (D) theory of infantile sexuality
    (E) focus on individual differences

53. According to Piaget, a child who is confident that the quantity of milk in a glass does not change when it is poured into a glass of a different shape is probably

    (A) in the closing period of the sensorimotor stage of development
    (B) between three and five years old
    (C) able to conserve volume
    (D) in the preoperational stage of cognitive development
    (E) engaging exclusively in egocentric patterns of play

54. The technique used to extinguish fear by forcing the patient to remain in the anxiety-arousing situation is called

    (A) inhibition
    (B) flooding
    (C) desensitization
    (D) implosion
    (E) time-out

55. The client-centered therapy of Carl Rogers differs from Freudian therapy most substantially in that the Rogerian therapist

    (A) refers to the patient as a "client"
    (B) places strong emphasis on the concept of transference
    (C) does not attempt to be as observant as a psychoanalyst
    (D) is more directive
    (E) does not emphasize tracing the development of her client's personality from its earliest beginnings

56. The dual-code hypothesis suggests that

    (A) words processed semantically are remembered better than words processed acoustically
    (B) abstract information is encoded visually and verbally
    (C) words which are low in imagery tend to be recalled better than words which are high in imagery
    (D) concrete information tends to be recalled better than abstract information
    (E) feature lists for a category contain both required and typical features of instances in that category

57. The tip-of-the-tongue phenomenon is due to a difficulty in

   (A) encoding
   (B) storage
   (C) retrieval
   (D) working memory
   (E) semantic verification

58. When a child reacts to a novel experience by changing his behavior in response to environmental demands, the resulting modification of his mental structures is referred to by Piaget as the process of

   (A) accommodation
   (B) assimilation
   (C) adaptation
   (D) organization
   (E) acquisition

59. Which of the following pairs is correct?

   (A) Festinger—attribution theory
   (B) Milgram—cognitive dissonance theory
   (C) Bandura—social learning theory
   (D) Garcia—instinctual drift
   (E) Pearson—depth perception

60. In his studies of memory, Ebbinghaus used the method of savings to determine the

   (A) amount of material retained from a prior learning task
   (B) number of trials taken to relearn old material
   (C) amount of time taken to unlearn old material and learn something new
   (D) efficacy of using nonsense syllables to study memory
   (E) usefulness of Zipf's law

61. The brain structure that plays a critical role in "motivated" behaviors such as eating and sexual activity is the

   (A) thalamus
   (B) cerebral cortex
   (C) amygdala
   (D) corpus callosum
   (E) hypothalamus

62. Removal of the hippocampus is most likely to lead to

   (A) sham rage
   (B) narcolepsy
   (C) anterograde amnesia
   (D) retrograde amnesia
   (E) lethargy

63. The best scale of aggression which a social scientist may employ to claim that "Joe is twice as aggressive as Jim," would be a(n)

   (A) nominal scale
   (B) ordinal scale
   (C) interval scale
   (D) ratio scale
   (E) logarithmic scale

64. Attribution theory

   (A) explains why cultural truisms are susceptible to persuasive arguments against them
   (B) is concerned with the cognitive bases upon which actions are performed
   (C) is rarely accurate
   (D) is responsible for breakthroughs in attitude measurement
   (E) is concerned with the ways in which people organize behavior and make it meaningful

GO ON TO THE NEXT PAGE

65. A person who is impatient, compulsive, and competitive is likely to be diagnosed as having a(n)

    (A) obsessive-compulsive personality disorder
    (B) Type A personality
    (C) Type B personality
    (D) Machiavellian personality
    (E) external locus of control

66. An experimenter who has been carefully trained in the techniques of self-observation uses himself as his subject. He attempts to analyze his own immediate experience into its elements. This study would most likely occur in the laboratory of

    (A) John Watson
    (B) George Sperling
    (C) Max Wertheimer
    (D) Hermann von Helmholtz
    (E) Edward Titchener

67. Which of the following studied the effect of misleading questions on eyewitness testimony?

    (A) Frederic Bartlett
    (B) Elizabeth Loftus
    (C) Mary Calkins
    (D) Charles Spearman
    (E) Howard Gardner

68. Syntax is concerned with

    (A) how consonants are combined to make phonemes
    (B) how phonemes are combined to make morphemes
    (C) how morphemes are combined to make words
    (D) how words are combined to make sentences
    (E) how sentences are combined to make paragraphs

69. A patient walks with a jerky, uncoordinated motion. A good preliminary diagnosis would be damage to the

    (A) hypothalamus
    (B) thalamus
    (C) amygdala
    (D) reticular activating system
    (E) cerebellum

70. Which of the following drugs would most likely be used to treat an acute schizophrenic episode?

    (A) diphenylhydantoin
    (B) MAO inhibitor
    (C) L-Dopa
    (D) chlorpromazine
    (E) diazepam

71. Milgram's experiments on obedience demonstrated that

    (A) most subjects refused to give extremely painful electric shocks to an innocent victim
    (B) most subjects did obey the command to give extremely painful electric shocks to an innocent victim
    (C) only subjects scoring high on a measure of authoritarian personality agreed to shock an innocent victim
    (D) the subject's moral values were more important than the tendency to obey an authority figure's command
    (E) male subjects were found to give significantly more painful shocks to an innocent victim than female subjects

72. The Young-Helmholtz theory postulates the existence of three types of cones in the retina. Later research has confirmed the presence of such receptor cells in the retina. This sequence BEST illustrates

    (A) Kuhn's theory of the development of science
    (B) the empirical method
    (C) the clinical method
    (D) natural monism
    (E) the hypothetico-deductive method

73. Berko and Chomsky would be likely to agree that

    (A) use of holophrases represents the first step in language acquisition
    (B) language is taught by waiting for certain verbalizations to occur and then rewarding them
    (C) cognitive development is driven by the internalization of interpersonal processes
    (D) certain innate structures account for acquisition of language and grammar
    (E) language is learned through repeated imitations of the specific utterances of others

74. The wife of Mr. L, an extremely hard-working man with a stressful occupation, reports to the police that he has been missing for two days. Investigation reveals that Mr. L. is now living in a different state under a new name and cannot recall his former identity. Mr. L. is most likely suffering from

    (A) dissociative fugue
    (B) multiple personality disorder
    (C) obsessive-compulsive disorder
    (D) dysthymic disorder
    (E) agoraphobia

75. Harlow's work with monkeys and surrogate mothers suggests that

    (A) bottle-fed infants are usually less attached to their mothers than breast-fed infants
    (B) infants are less likely to explore their environments when they can experience maternal comforting instead
    (C) attachment may not be directly related to the provision of food
    (D) infant monkeys generally refuse all milk but that of their mother
    (E) infants will cling to any object that provides food

76. Resolution of an avoidance–avoidance conflict is most like

    (A) putting all one's eggs in one basket
    (B) choosing between a pay raise and a different job
    (C) choosing between a pay raise and a longer vacation
    (D) choosing between the carrot and the stick
    (E) choosing the lesser of two evils

GO ON TO THE NEXT PAGE

77. Confabulation is often a symptom of

    (A) obsessive neurosis
    (B) Korsakoff's syndrome
    (C) schizophrenia
    (D) bipolar disorder
    (E) dissociative fugue

78. All of the following made important contributions to psychophysics EXCEPT for

    (A) Hermann von Helmholtz
    (B) Gustav Fechner
    (C) S. S. Stevens
    (D) Ernst Weber
    (E) John Swets

79. Which person is correctly linked with his area of interest?

    (A) Jung—collective unconscious
    (B) Allport—nomothetic approach to personality
    (C) Breuer—fictional finalism
    (D) Dollard and Miller—field theory
    (E) Witkin—need for achievement

80. Which of the following concepts is least directly related to psychotherapeutic technique?

    (A) systematic desensitization
    (B) retroactive inhibition
    (C) flooding
    (D) implosion
    (E) transference

81. Iconic memory refers to

    (A) visual working memory
    (B) auditory working memory
    (C) visual short-term memory
    (D) visual sensory memory
    (E) auditory sensory memory

82. The custom that a majority vote is sufficient for a measure to become law is most closely analogous to

    (A) the process which determines the resting potential of a membrane
    (B) the process which determines the postsynaptic potential
    (C) the all-or-nothing law governing the action potential
    (D) the regulation of synaptic activity
    (E) the operation of an analog computer

83. Comparison of students' GRE scores with their later graduate school grade point averages (GPAs) would probably be used to analyze the GRE's

    (A) content validity
    (B) concurrent validity
    (C) predictive validity
    (D) test-retest reliability
    (E) split-half reliability

84. Which of the following psychologists were influential in the development of the intelligence test?

    (A) Henry Murray
    (B) Alfred Adler
    (C) Erik Erikson
    (D) Kurt Lewin
    (E) Alfred Binet and David Wechsler

85. Phobias are usually treated most successfully through the technique of

    (A) systematic desensitization
    (B) electroconvulsive therapy
    (C) psychoanalysis
    (D) transactional analysis
    (E) client-centered psychotherapy

86. Which of the following is used to measure the time it takes to perform various mental processes?

    (A) habituation
    (B) bottom-up processing
    (C) magnetic resonance imaging
    (D) mental chronometry
    (E) shadowing

87. Under dim light, a researcher repeatedly displays several objects to a subject, so that each time the image falls on a different area of the subject's retina. What is the expected result?

    (A) Object discrimination will be worst in the fovea.
    (B) Object discrimination will be best in the fovea.
    (C) Color discrimination will be best in the fovea.
    (D) Color discrimination will be best at the periphery of the retina.
    (E) Visual sensitivity will be the same across the retina.

88. Which of the following is the best example of an idiographic approach to personality?

    (A) A psychologist uses factor analysis to analyze the results of a personality test.
    (B) A psychologist analyzes case studies to determine each person's unique personality structure.
    (C) A psychologist analyzes case studies to determine what traits people vary on.
    (D) A psychologist studies normal subjects, not abnormal ones.
    (E) A psychologist correlates personality traits with body shape.

89. Subjects are presented with one of the following learning experiences:

Condition I: Learn A $\rightarrow$ Learn B $\rightarrow$ Recall A
Condition II: Learn A $\rightarrow$ Learn B $\rightarrow$ Recall B

    If a subject in Condition I cannot recall A, it is probably due to

    (A) proactive inhibition
    (B) interference learning
    (C) retroactive inhibition
    (D) the isolation effect
    (E) the Einstellung effect

90. The importance of vicarious learning was most clearly demonstrated by

    (A) Carl Jung
    (B) E. O. Wilson
    (C) Raymond Cattell
    (D) Albert Bandura
    (E) Keller Breland

GO ON TO THE NEXT PAGE

91. If the olfactory sense were eliminated, a blindfolded person tasting a peeled apple and a peeled raw potato would most likely

    (A) experience the same tastes as usual
    (B) be unable to distinguish between the taste of the apple and the taste of the potato
    (C) taste the apple as sweeter than usual
    (D) taste the potato as more bitter than usual
    (E) taste the potato as sweeter than usual

92. Aggressive behavior appears to be inhibited by the

    (A) amygdala
    (B) hypothalamus
    (C) medulla oblongata
    (D) septum
    (E) adrenal medulla

93. A school psychologist wishes to test a second-grade student for possible mental retardation. The most appropriate test to use would probably be the

    (A) Stanford-Binet Intelligence Test
    (B) MMPI
    (C) WAIS
    (D) Thematic Apperception Test
    (E) IRT

94. The unconscious process most closely associated with the phenomenon of transference is

    (A) displacement
    (B) sublimation
    (C) reaction-formation
    (D) primary process thinking
    (E) fixation

95. Assume that if a person has a particular genetic disease, there's a 50 percent chance that his sibling will also have the disease. If an afflicted person has a fraternal twin, what is the chance that the fraternal twin has the disease?

    (A) 100 percent
    (B) 75 percent
    (C) 50 percent
    (D) 25 percent
    (E) 0 percent

96. In their experiments concerning cognitive influences on emotions, Schachter and Singer found that

    (A) "informed" subjects, in the presence of the angry confederate, became angry
    (B) "uninformed" subjects became either angry or euphoric, depending on the confederate's behavior
    (C) "informed" and "uninformed" subjects were equally affected by the actions of the confederate
    (D) "informed" subjects became angry, but not euphoric, in imitation of the confederate
    (E) "uninformed" subjects became euphoric, but not angry, in imitation of the confederate

GO ON TO THE NEXT PAGE

97. According to the theories of Thomas Szasz,

    (A) mental deficiency is predominately an organic syndrome
    (B) IQ is determined mainly by genetic factors
    (C) neurotic behavior stems from disordered early parent/child relationships
    (D) schizophrenia usually results from chemical abnormalities
    (E) mental illness is largely a social and legal problem

98. An experimenter accepts the null hypothesis when it is false. Which of the following is true?

    (A) She has made a Type I error.
    (B) She has made a Type II error.
    (C) Her results were statistically significant.
    (D) The criterion of significance was too large.
    (E) The experiment does not have predictive validity.

99. If the difference threshold for a standard stimulus of 20 grams is 2 grams, then, according to Weber's law, the difference threshold for a standard stimulus of 50 grams is

    (A) 2 grams
    (B) 3 grams
    (C) 4 grams
    (D) 5 grams
    (E) 10 grams

100. Lithium is most often used to treat

    (A) bipolar disorder
    (B) undifferentiated schizophrenia
    (C) somatoform disorder
    (D) dissociative fugue
    (E) dysthymic disorder

101. The method of studying development using groups of people that vary in age and are measured at the same time is called

    (A) longitudinal study
    (B) field study
    (C) matched-subjects design
    (D) quasi-experiment
    (E) cross-sectional study

102. Which of the following findings is most likely to weaken a sociobiological explanation for the evolution of dominance hierarchies?

    (A) Lower-ranking males live longer.
    (B) Higher-ranking males have greater access to food sources.
    (C) Higher-ranking males are more likely to mate with higher-ranking females.
    (D) The brothers of high-ranking males reproduce more than the brothers of low-ranking males.
    (E) There is an inverse relationship between rank and inclusive fitness.

GO ON TO THE NEXT PAGE

103. Reproductive isolating mechanisms are most likely to evolve in a situation where

    (A) robins and gulls live in close proximity to each other
    (B) two troops of baboons share a territory
    (C) two different species of ducks live in close proximity to each other
    (D) females are only sexually receptive at certain times
    (E) males and females are sexually dimorphic

104. In contrast to bulimia, anorexia is characterized by

    (A) binge-eating
    (B) a fear of gaining weight
    (C) a refusal to maintain a minimal normal body weight
    (D) repeated purging
    (E) misuse of laxatives

105. One would expect an action potential to travel most quickly in

    (A) a long, thick myelinated fiber
    (B) a long, thin myelinated fiber
    (C) a short, thick unmyelinated fiber
    (D) a short, thin, myelinated fiber
    (E) a long, thick unmyelinated fiber

106. George Sperling discovered that sensory memory could contain about how many pieces of information?

    (A) 1
    (B) 4
    (C) 7
    (D) 9
    (E) 30

107. In an experiment, the control group should be treated in the same way as the experimental group except for

    (A) receiving different levels of the independent variable
    (B) receiving different levels of the dependent variable
    (C) completing pretest measures
    (D) completing post-test measures
    (E) receiving different levels of the confounding variable

108. Which of these illnesses is related to abnormality in the dopaminergic system?

    (A) schizophrenia only
    (B) Parkinson's disease only
    (C) Alzheimer's disease only
    (D) Parkinson's disease and schizophrenia
    (E) Parkinson's disease and Alzheimer's disease

109. The dominant hemisphere of the brain

    (A) usually controls the nondominant hand
    (B) is especially adept at spatial tasks
    (C) is the more "intuitive" hemisphere
    (D) works independently of the nondominant hemisphere
    (E) controls the expression and comprehension of language

110. The statistical method used to elicit information concerning the component parts of intelligence is known as

    (A) factor analysis
    (B) construct validity
    (C) Spearman's *g* factoring
    (D) hypothesis testing
    (E) task analysis

111. A child with a mental age of 10.7 and a chronological age of 9.5 would have a ratio IQ of about

    (A) 132
    (B) 125
    (C) 113
    (D) 103
    (E) 89

112. Which of the following is a natural pain killer?

    (A) GABA
    (B) dopamine
    (C) serotonin
    (D) endorphins
    (E) Prozac

113. Which neurotransmitter is inhibitory?

    (A) epinephrine
    (B) dopamine
    (C) serotonin
    (D) acetylcholine
    (E) GABA

114. In a particular species of gulls, the sight of an egg which has rolled from the nest stimulates the gull to attempt to roll the egg back. As an experiment, an ethologist moves an actual egg from the gull's nest to the ground and, next to it, places a similar-looking, but slightly smaller egg. If the gull pushes the smaller egg back to the nest instead of its own egg, which description would best fit the smaller egg?

    (A) sign stimulus
    (B) innate releasing mechanism
    (C) super-normal stimulus
    (D) fixed-action pattern
    (E) reproductive isolating mechanism

115. Piaget's approach to investigating the thought processes underlying a given verbal response is best described as

    (A) the method of varied comparisons
    (B) introspective analysis
    (C) a longitudinal study
    (D) projective testing
    (E) the clinical method

116. "Mama stayed near Baby Duck
    Since first she saw the light;
    Now Baby follows Mama's trail
    All morning, noon, and night."

    The baby duck's behavior is an example of

    (A) separation anxiety
    (B) the need for contact comfort
    (C) autism
    (D) stranger anxiety
    (E) imprinting

GO ON TO THE NEXT PAGE

117. A key feature of the DSM-IV is its

    (A) focus on the etiology of mental disorders
    (B) multiaxial system of assessment
    (C) focus on theoretical issues
    (D) behaviorist outlook
    (E) dimensional approach to classification

118. The approaches of Horney and Adler shared an emphasis on

    (A) the importance of biological instincts
    (B) the role of repressed sexual drives
    (C) the significance of social relationships in psychological development
    (D) the nature of approach-avoidance convicts
    (E) the coordination between actual and perceived self images

119. Group A reads a report in support of the view that food additives do not pose a health hazard. The report is attributed to the president of a company that produces artificial flavorings and colorings. Group B reads the same report, but it is attributed to a noted consumer magazine. Agreement with the position advocated by the report was measured before, immediately after, and four weeks after reading. The sleeper effect would be illustrated by which of the following tables of results? (The higher the number, the greater the agreement.)

	Before	Imm. After	4 weeks After
(A) A:	5.6	5.8	6.3
B:	5.5	7.4	6.8
(B) A:	5.6	5.8	5.8
B:	5.5	7.4	7.9
(C) A:	5.6	5.8	5.2
B:	5.5	7.4	7.9
(D) A:	5.6	5.8	5.2
B:	5.5	7.4	6.8
(E) A:	5.6	5.8	6.3
B:	5.5	7.4	7.9

120. The most severe forms of mental retardation tend to be associated with

    (A) low socioeconomic status
    (B) physiological damage to the brain
    (C) cultural-familial retardation
    (D) malnutrition
    (E) a deprivation of environmental stimulation during infancy

GO ON TO THE NEXT PAGE

121. Experimental use of the visual cliff is based on the assumption that

    (A) infants will always follow the sound of their mothers' voices
    (B) infants can perceive the presence of the glass which stops them from falling over the cliff
    (C) infants cannot tell when they may be venturing into dangerous positions
    (D) infants are willing to risk a fall in order to approach their mothers
    (E) the infants' unwillingness to venture onto the "deep" side of the apparatus shows that they are capable of perceiving the apparent drop

122. A man is shown two photographs of himself: one is a mirror image and the other is a true image. He prefers the mirror image. When the man is shown mirror and true image photographs of a friend, he prefers the true image of his friend. This best illustrates

    (A) the primacy effect
    (B) social comparison theory
    (C) self-perception theory
    (D) the fundamental attribution error
    (E) the mere exposure effect

123. In the DSM-IV, multiple personality disorder is categorized as a(n)

    (A) schizophrenic disorder
    (B) dissociative disorder
    (C) anxiety disorder
    (D) somatoform disorder
    (E) personality disorder

124. A first-grade child is given a test of cognitive abilities and scores at the first-grade level. The same child then retakes the test with help and guidance from a teacher and scores at the third-grade level. This finding most directly supports

    (A) Jean Piaget's theory of conservation
    (B) Leon Festinger's theory of cognitive dissonance
    (C) Albert Bandura's theory of observational learning
    (D) Lev Vygotsky's theory of the zone of proximal development
    (E) Alfred Binet's theory of mental age

125. An athlete who has never run a mile in less than four minutes during solitary training runs a mile race in a time of 3:56 before a large crowd at a track meet. This most clearly exemplifies the theory of

    (A) social influence
    (B) imitation
    (C) social facilitation
    (D) proximity
    (E) overcompensation

126. Studying to avoid a bad grade is an example of

    (A) positive reinforcement
    (B) negative reinforcement
    (C) punishment
    (D) escape
    (E) extinction

GO ON TO THE NEXT PAGE

127. An electric shock administered to the paw of a cat will elicit foot withdrawal. Before the shocks are administered, a green light is flashed. Eventually, the green light elicits foot withdrawal. The green light would be labeled

    (A) the unconditioned response
    (B) the conditioned response
    (C) the unconditioned stimulus
    (D) the conditioned stimulus
    (E) the dependent variable

128. Zajonc's research has shown that in the presence of others

    (A) performance of dominant responses deteriorates, while performance of nondominant responses improves
    (B) performance of dominant responses improves, while performance of nondominant responses deteriorates
    (C) performance of all types of responses improves
    (D) performance of all types of responses deteriorates
    (E) performance of correct responses improves

129. When a person learns by observing the consequences of someone else's behavior, he is experiencing the phenomenon of

    (A) conforming behavior
    (B) learning to learn
    (C) obedience to authority
    (D) accidental learning
    (E) vicarious learning

130. Early diagnosis offers hope of avoiding the effects of

    (A) narcissistic personality disorder
    (B) schizophrenia
    (C) senile dementia
    (D) Down's syndrome
    (E) PKU

131. Feature detection is an example of

    (A) top-down processing
    (B) an ROC curve
    (C) bottom-up processing
    (D) transduction
    (E) field dependence

132. A lesion of the ventromedial hypothalamus will most likely produce

    (A) hyperphagia
    (B) aphasia
    (C) aphagia
    (D) adipsia
    (E) increased ACTH levels

133. Consistency theories are based on the assumption that

    (A) individuals desire a coherent system of thoughts and beliefs
    (B) attitudes are ultimately nonmeasurable, since they are purely internal psychological events
    (C) the difficulties people have making decisions are psychologically significant
    (D) people's attitudes are largely determined by their parents and peer groups
    (E) people have a need to find causes for the behavior of others

GO ON TO THE NEXT PAGE

134. Which of the following statements about the limbic system is true?

   (A) It is rarely found in mammals.
   (B) Lesions of portions of it may result in unpredictable, vicious behavior.
   (C) It was the first part of the brain to evolve.
   (D) It is part of the reticular activating system.
   (E) Lesions of portions of it may inhibit sensorimotor processing.

135. Regions and boundaries are central to the personality theory of

   (A) George Kelly
   (B) Karen Horney
   (C) John Dollard
   (D) Kurt Lewin
   (E) David McClelland

136. The theory that early attachment behaviors may be traced to innate psychological tendencies centers on the process of

   (A) affiliation
   (B) social facilitation
   (C) peer group pressure
   (D) imprinting
   (E) genetic determinism

137. Which of the following is most likely to produce cognitive dissonance?

   (A) "I'll go to this movie or none at all."
   (B) "I enjoy working here, although I don't know exactly why."
   (C) "I spend time with her, but I don't really like her."
   (D) "I can't stand him, and he doesn't like me either."
   (E) "I've stopped overeating because my clothes were getting too tight."

138. An average 10-month old infant will most likely

   (A) exhibit stranger anxiety
   (B) display the Moro reflex
   (C) have mastered conservation
   (D) be entering the zone of proximal development
   (E) be in the middle of Freud's anal stage of psychosexual development

139. The XO chromosome combination in females is primarily associated with

   (A) PKU
   (B) Klinefelter's syndrome
   (C) Down's syndrome
   (D) aggressive antisocial behavior
   (E) Turner's syndrome

GO ON TO THE NEXT PAGE

140. Which of the following statements about neurosis is true?

    (A) It is not a category of mental disorder in the DSM-IV.
    (B) It was used by Freud to indicate disorders where reality testing was impaired.
    (C) The term was originally coined by Emil Kraepelin.
    (D) General paresis is a type of neurosis.
    (E) ECT was originally used by Von Meduna to treat neurosis.

141. A telemarketer calls customers and asks them a few questions about their long-distance service. She then asks them to change their long-distance carrier. The telemarketer is attempting to take advantage of the

    (A) inoculation theory
    (B) foot-in-the-door effect
    (C) door-in-the-face effect
    (D) elaboration likelihood model
    (E) sleeper effect

142. John goes to a party, gets drunk, and is introduced to a coworker. At work the next day, John sees the coworker, but does not remember her name. That night, however, John goes to a party, drinks, sees the coworker, and remembers her name. Which of the following can best explain this sequence of events?

    (A) retroactive inhibition
    (B) spreading activation
    (C) metamemory
    (D) fluid intelligence
    (E) state-dependent learning

143. Which of the following suggested that differences in intelligence could be largely attributed to differences in a single factor?

    (A) J. P. Guilford
    (B) Charles Spearman
    (C) Alfred Binet
    (D) David Wechsler
    (E) L. L. Thurstone

144. Which of the following theorists attempted to relate personality to perception?

    (A) William Sheldon
    (B) Herman Witkin
    (C) Abraham Maslow
    (D) Neal Miller
    (E) Richard Lazarus

145. After a boating accident at summer camp, Jimmy came home and refused to ride the Staten Island ferry with his mother. This was probably due to

    (A) backward conditioning
    (B) stimulus discrimination
    (C) flooding
    (D) stimulus generalization
    (E) shaping

146. In which of the following are the Freudian stages in the correct order?

    (A) oral, latency, phallic
    (B) oral, anal, latency
    (C) genital, oral, anal
    (D) anal, phallic, Oedipal
    (E) Oedipal, phallic, latency

GO ON TO THE NEXT PAGE

147. If a psychologist wanted to test someone to see whether previous experience affected his ability to solve problems, she might use the

    (A) Rorschach test
    (B) Wechsler Adult Intelligence Scale
    (C) factor analysis
    (D) Luchins water-jar problem
    (E) process of brainstorming

148. A researcher is interested in the effect that meeting the university president has on students' perceptions of the university. To obtain subjects for her research, the researcher stands at the entrance of the performing arts building and selects every fifth student who enters the building. This method is an example of

    (A) random sampling
    (B) stratified random sampling
    (C) representative sampling
    (D) selecting a population
    (E) none of the above

149. What can a researcher conclude if the correlation between variable A and variable B equals −1.00?

    (A) Variables A and B are causally related.
    (B) Variables A and B are not at all related.
    (C) Knowing the value of one of the variables allows you to predict with absolute certainty the corresponding value of the other variable.
    (D) Variable A is causally related to variable B but variable B is not necessarily causally related to variable A.
    (E) Knowing the value of one of the variables does not help you to predict the value of the other variable.

150. Petty and Cacioppo developed

    (A) the elaboration likelihood model of persuasion
    (B) cognitive dissonance theory
    (C) the mere exposure effect
    (D) the concept of groupthink
    (E) the concept of belief in a just world

151. The length of the prodromal phase of schizophrenia is most directly relevant to the

    (A) process-reactive distinction
    (B) amount of family support
    (C) learned helplessness theory
    (D) utility of psychoanalysis in treating schizophrenia
    (E) development of fugue states

GO ON TO THE NEXT PAGE

152. An amusement park which presents performances by animals takes account of instinctual drift in its training procedures. Which of the following is most relevant to the training?

    (A) Because of learned food aversions, potential reinforcers should be selected carefully.
    (B) Because biological predispositions for learning particular behaviors may exist, animals can be more easily trained on some tasks than on others.
    (C) Animals can only behave instinctively.
    (D) Because animals are best prepared to learn during sensitive and critical periods, instinctual drift will not be a problem if training is conducted during these periods.
    (E) Animals can learn to perform any response.

153. Which of the following theorists most stressed the importance of maturation in development?

    (A) Jean Piaget
    (B) John Locke
    (C) Arnold Gesell
    (D) Lev Vygotsky
    (E) Lawrence Kohlberg

154. A child enjoys working in the garden. Her parents are trying to decide whether they should start paying her for her work. Which of the following most strongly suggests that they ought not to pay their child?

    (A) source credibility
    (B) the overjustification effect
    (C) belief perseverance
    (D) locus of control theory
    (E) the double-bind hypothesis

155. Dorothea Dix is most noted as

    (A) an important precursor to psychoanalysis
    (B) an early follower of Jean Charcot
    (C) the founder of the first psychological clinic in the United States
    (D) the founder of structuralism
    (E) an important 19th century crusader for the improvement of mental hospitals

156. If a fetus inherits an X chromosome from its mother and a Y chromosome from its father, but does not produce androgens, it will

    (A) have a feminine genotype and a masculine phenotype
    (B) have a masculine genotype and a masculine phenotype
    (C) have a masculine genotype and a feminine phenotype
    (D) have a feminine genotype and a feminine phenotype
    (E) be hermaphroditic

157. The sentence "He placed the flask under the table," if not recalled perfectly two days later, is most likely to be recalled as which of the following?

    (A) She placed the flask under the table.
    (B) He put the bottle under the table.
    (C) He placed the flask on the table.
    (D) He laced the cask under the table.
    (E) He tabled the motion and asked to adjourn.

158. Ablation of the lateral geniculate nucleus would most likely affect which sensory system?

    (A) audition
    (B) olfaction
    (C) kinesthesis
    (D) vision
    (E) gustation

159. Early computer simulations of chess-playing tended to use brute processing force—the computer would evaluate every possible move and then choose the best one. Modern simulations, though, tend to program rules of thumb into the computer in order to reduce the reliance on brute force in deciding the next move. These rules are called

    (A) chunks
    (B) heuristics
    (C) operational matrices
    (D) transformations
    (E) perceptual sets

160. If reliability is 0.00, which of the following is true?

    (A) The standard error of measurement is relatively high.
    (B) The standard error of measurement is relatively low.
    (C) The test is too long.
    (D) Validity is high.
    (E) A mathematical error has been made.

161. According to Wolfgang Köhler, when one of his chimps fastened two sticks together to reach a bunch of bananas, it was showing evidence of

    (A) trial-and-error learning
    (B) a fixed-action pattern
    (C) classical conditioning
    (D) instinctual drift
    (E) insight

162. In a double-blind experiment

    (A) neither the subjects nor the researchers interacting with them know which groups received which level of the independent variable.
    (B) nobody knows which groups received which level of the independent variable.
    (C) the subjects do not know which groups received which level of the independent variable, but the researchers interacting with them do know.
    (D) neither the subjects nor the researchers interacting with them know which groups received which level of the dependent variable.
    (E) the Hawthorne effect is not a problem.

GO ON TO THE NEXT PAGE

163. A program to increase self-esteem in elementary school children could be considered to be an example of

   (A) primary prevention
   (B) secondary prevention
   (C) tertiary prevention
   (D) retroactive prevention
   (E) response prevention

164. John sees Andrea yelling at the TV during a football game and thinks to himself that Andrea is aggressive. A week later, John yells at the TV during a football game and thinks to himself that he is doing so because it is an important game for his team. This is an example of

   (A) the halo effect
   (B) the recency effect
   (C) the fundamental attribution error
   (D) dispositional attributions
   (E) situational attributions

165. Which of the following concepts is most associated with Abraham Maslow?

   (A) archetype
   (B) peak shift
   (C) hierarchy of needs
   (D) anxiety hierarchy
   (E) need for achievement

166. Which of the following statements about the Babinski reflex is true?

   (A) It normally persists until adolescence.
   (B) It is another name for the grasping reflex.
   (C) It consists of turning the head towards a source of noise.
   (D) It is a reaction to a sudden head movement.
   (E) It consists of extending the toes when the sole of the foot is stimulated.

167. The volley principle can be considered an improvement on

   (A) Helmholtz's place-resonance theory
   (B) frequency theory
   (C) the traveling wave
   (D) opponent-process theory
   (E) the duplexity theory

168. Which of the following would be most likely to argue that researchers should investigate the effects various social behaviors have on fitness?

   (A) John Garcia
   (B) Keller Breland
   (C) Francis Galton
   (D) E. O. Wilson
   (E) John Bowlby

169. The ability to quickly grasp relationships in novel situations and make correct deductions from them requires

   (A) crystallized intelligence
   (B) fluid intelligence
   (C) parallel processing
   (D) episodic memory
   (E) transformational rules

170. A researcher wishes to run an experiment, but is concerned that variations in the subjects' intelligence quotients (IQs) might confound the results. All of the following are possible solutions to this problem EXCEPT for

    (A) using a matched-subjects design
    (B) holding IQ level relatively constant
    (C) running a double-blind experiment
    (D) randomly assigning subjects to groups
    (E) adding IQ as another independent variable

171. Which leadership style tends to produce the most satisfied members?

    (A) autocratic
    (B) authoritative
    (C) authoritarian
    (D) laissez-faire
    (E) democratic

172. Which of the following describes a major difference between Kohlberg's and Gilligan's theories of moral development?

    (A) One theory emphasizes rewards and punishment; the other emphasizes classical conditioning.
    (B) One theory emphasizes an interpersonal orientation in moral decisions; the other emphasizes individual ethical principles.
    (C) One focuses on psychosocial factors; the other focuses on psychosexual factors.
    (D) One is based on psychoanalysis; the other is based on behaviorism
    (E) One uses a stage model; the other does not.

173. Follicle-stimulating hormone is secreted by the

    (A) ovaries
    (B) testes
    (C) pituitary gland
    (D) hypothalamus
    (E) sensorimotor cortex

GO ON TO THE NEXT PAGE

174. An investigator wishes to construct a test to assess potential for entrepreneurial success. He comes up with 1,000 potential test items, and gives these items to 750 owners of successful small businesses and 750 people whose small businesses failed. He then constructs the test using those items which tended to be answered differently by the successful owners and the nonsuccessful owners. This test development procedure is called

    (A) the split-half method
    (B) item response theory
    (C) the empirical criterion-keying approach
    (D) meta-analysis
    (E) counterbalancing

175. Subjects are asked to read two stories: one from their culture and one from an unfamiliar culture. In a surprise recall test, subjects are then asked to retrieve the story from memory. Bartlett's reconstructive theory would predict that

    (A) subjects' recall will be better when the story is not from their culture
    (B) subjects' recall will be better when the story is from their culture
    (C) subjects will only be able to remember 7 ± 2 sentences in the stories
    (D) recall will be equally accurate for all stories
    (E) subjects will process stories from their culture in a parallel fashion and will process stories from the other culture serially

176. Autoshaping is important because

    (A) it suggests that operant conditioning and classical conditioning work in similar ways
    (B) it explains conditioned suppression
    (C) it is an example of avoidance
    (D) if pigeons can be taught to peck on keys, pigeons can be taught to do anything
    (E) it shows that behaviors thought to be solely due to operant conditioning may have a classical conditioning component

177. An adult knows that *bit* and *pit* refer to two different things, but that *bit* said by a female and *bit* said by a male refer to the same thing. This is evidence of

    (A) assimilation
    (B) an innate language acquisition device
    (C) formal operational thinking
    (D) categorical perception
    (E) proximal development

178. If the gene for blue eyes is recessive and if a child has blue eyes, which of the following must be true?

    (A) Both parents have blue eyes.
    (B) The child's sibling has brown eyes.
    (C) Each parent has at least one blue-eye gene.
    (D) At least one parent must have blue eyes.
    (E) Each parent has one blue-eye and one brown-eye gene.

179. A researcher wants to study the effect of response bias and sensitivity on the perception of changes in frequency. She would most likely use

    (A) Weber's law
    (B) Fechner's law
    (C) Stevens's law
    (D) signal detection theory
    (E) ANOVA

180. Which method is used to assess cooperation and competition?

    (A) stimulus overload
    (B) blocking
    (C) spreading activation
    (D) the prisoner's dilemma
    (E) Robber's Cave experiment

181. Which of the following is the best example of reactance?

    (A) A high school student enrolls in the choir, then changes her mind.
    (B) A toddler is told that she can only go out to play after she cleans her room.
    (C) A student refuses to do homework because the members of her in-group refuse to do homework.
    (D) A boyfriend and girlfriend continue to go out with each other even though they don't love each other anymore.
    (E) A mother tells her child not to start smoking, so the child goes in back of the garage and smokes.

182. Jenny refuses to study for an exam, saying that fate will decide her grade. Which of the following provide plausible explanations for her behavior?

    (A) self-monitoring
    (B) the placebo effect
    (C) the Hawthorne effect
    (D) the halo effect
    (E) locus of control

183. When a father tells a child that she can go out and play after she does her homework, he is using

    (A) the Premack principle
    (B) instinctual drift
    (C) sensory preconditioning
    (D) autoshaping
    (E) insight

184. A subject in an experiment wears a set of earphones that allow different messages to be given to each ear. The subject is asked to repeat one of the messages aloud as she hears it. This technique is called

    (A) auditory processing
    (B) the traveling wave
    (C) spreading activation
    (D) shadowing
    (E) parallel distributed processing

GO ON TO THE NEXT PAGE

185. The depth-of-processing theory predicts that you will most likely remember that the word *milk* occurred in a list of words if you focus on

    (A) how the words in the list are pronounced
    (B) how many syllables the words in the list have
    (C) how the words in the list look on the printed page
    (D) what the items in the list are used for
    (E) what words rhyme with the words in the list

186. Which of the following is used to implant electrodes in specific brain areas?

    (A) PET scan
    (B) stereotaxic instrument
    (C) reticular formation
    (D) EEG
    (E) oscilloscope

187. Which of the following concepts is most relevant to signal detection theory?

    (A) absolute threshold
    (B) just noticeable difference
    (C) ROC curve
    (D) iconic memory
    (E) echoic memory

188. The hypothesis that mood disorder is caused by an interaction between a genetic disturbance and separation from loved ones would be most relevant to which of the following?

    (A) psychoanalysis
    (B) behaviorism
    (C) monoaminergic theory
    (D) diathesis-stress
    (E) humanism

189. A researcher is interested in the relationship between political affiliation and eye color. Therefore, she asks people whether they are Democrats, Republicans, or Independents and what their eye color is—blue, brown, green, or other. The appropriate statistical test would be a(n)

    (A) t-test
    (B) ANOVA
    (C) goodness of fit test
    (D) chi-square test
    (E) ANCOVA

GO ON TO THE NEXT PAGE

190. Genie suffered from a terrible form of child abuse and was completely isolated from human contact from age 2 to age 13. She was then discovered and began to receive language training. Although she learned some language, certain aspects of language still eluded her. The fact that Genie was able to learn some language argues most strongly AGAINST

    (A) a critical period for language
    (B) a sensitive period for language
    (C) the importance of attachment for later adjustment
    (D) the importance of contact comfort
    (E) a zone of proximal development for language

191. Karl von Frisch is most noted for his research into

    (A) communication in honey bees
    (B) taste aversion in rats
    (C) the misbehavior of raccoons
    (D) egg-rolling in gulls
    (E) aggression in male sticklebacks

192. Electroconvulsive therapy is used mostly for treating

    (A) schizophrenia that has not responded to the antipsychotic drugs
    (B) depression where there is a high risk of suicide
    (C) obsessive-compulsive disorder
    (D) fetishism
    (E) antisocial personality disorder

193. If a researcher asks a subject to memorize a list of words and then asks her to fill out a questionnaire about how she memorized the list, the researcher is probably studying

    (A) recognition memory
    (B) semantic priming
    (C) metamemory
    (D) retroactive inhibition
    (E) spreading activation

194. A subject listens to a tape recording of an ambiguous sound and is asked to describe what he heard. This is most analogous to which of the following tests?

    (A) Thematic Apperception Test
    (B) CPI
    (C) MMPI
    (D) Blacky pictures
    (E) Rorschach inkblot test

195. Latent learning depends most strongly on which of the following distinctions?

    (A) respondent versus classical conditioning
    (B) negative reinforcement versus punishment
    (C) contiguity versus contingency
    (D) continuous reinforcement versus partial reinforcement
    (E) learning versus performance

196. A cross-sectional design could be considered to be an example of a

    (A) longitudinal design
    (B) matched-subjects design
    (C) between-subjects design
    (D) within-subjects design
    (E) true experiment

GO ON TO THE NEXT PAGE

197. People will tend to stay in a relationship if their rewards outweigh their costs. This is predicted by

    (A) social-exchange theory
    (B) equity theory
    (C) need complementarity
    (D) gain-loss principle
    (E) social comparison theory

198. Bipolar disorder is

    (A) a severe form of depression
    (B) characterized by episodes of depression and mania
    (C) a form of schizophrenia where the person cycles between schizophrenia and normality
    (D) best treated by Valium
    (E) a more recent term for cyclothymic disorder

199. Which of the following would be most likely to criticize trait theory?

    (A) Raymond Cattell
    (B) William Sheldon
    (C) Starke Hathaway
    (D) James McKeen Cattell
    (E) Walter Mischel

200. All of the following are used to study perceptual development EXCEPT

    (A) the visual cliff
    (B) habituation
    (C) preferential looking
    (D) animal experiments
    (E) the rod and frame apparatus

201. Beliefs can be made resistant to attack by presenting refuted counter-arguments. This is the basic premise of

    (A) the door-in-the-face effect
    (B) the risky shift
    (C) inoculation theory
    (D) the elaboration likelihood model of persuasion
    (E) belief perseverance

202. A researcher wants to test the hypothesis that the number of bystanders affects the probability of helping behavior. She sets up three conditions:one with no bystanders, one with two bystanders, and one with four bystanders. Which of the following is true?

    (A) There is one independent variable having three levels.
    (B) There are three independent variables having one level each.
    (C) There is one independent variable and three dependent variables.
    (D) There is one independent variable having four levels.
    (E) There are three independent variables and one dependent variable.

203. A sixth grade student needs to learn the colors of the rainbow in the correct order for a test. Why would learning "Roy G. Biv" be helpful?

    (A) It can be more easily visualized.
    (B) It is less susceptible to retroactive inhibition.
    (C) It uses fewer pieces of information.
    (D) It invokes the Zeigarnik effect.
    (E) It is an example of telegraphic speech.

204. A person who is high in both masculinity and femininity is said to be

    (A) transsexual
    (B) mesomorphic
    (C) amorphous
    (D) androgynous
    (E) bisexual

205. Which archetype represents the feminine side of men?

    (A) persona
    (B) anima
    (C) animus
    (D) shadow
    (E) self

206. The fundamental rule of psychoanalysis is that the patient is to say whatever comes into her mind, no matter how embarrassing or trivial it might appear to be. This best describes

    (A) transference
    (B) countertransference
    (C) free association
    (D) projection
    (E) latent content

207. After constructing the final exam for a developmental psychology class, the instructor analyzes the test to make sure that it adequately samples the material covered in the course. The instructor is assessing the test's

    (A) concurrent validity
    (B) discriminant validity
    (C) split-half reliability
    (D) alternate-form reliability
    (E) content validity

208. George Miller found that short-term memory could contain about how many chunks of information?

    (A) 1
    (B) 4
    (C) 7
    (D) 10
    (E) 13

209. Damage to the left visual cortex will

    (A) impair vision in only the right eye
    (B) impair vision in only the left eye
    (C) leave a person with no vision
    (D) impair vision for images of objects falling on the left half of each eye's retina
    (E) impair vision for images of objects falling on the right half of each eye's retina

210. The theory of kin selection was proposed to explain

    (A) altruism
    (B) instinctual drift
    (C) preparedness
    (D) contiguity
    (E) imprinting

211. Which of the following is a principal function of the parietal lobe?

    (A) visual processing
    (B) auditory processing
    (C) long-term planning
    (D) receptive language
    (E) spatial processing

GO ON TO THE NEXT PAGE

212. What does a sign stimulus trigger?

    (A) an FAP
    (B) a releaser
    (C) a supernormal stimulus
    (D) a conditioned response
    (E) an unconditioned response

213. A researcher finds that the same individuals are rated as less attractive when they are identified as criminals than when they are not so identified. This best illustrates

    (A) reactance
    (B) the halo effect
    (C) the mere exposure effect
    (D) belief perseverance
    (E) the fundamental attribution error

214. The autokinetic effect occurs when a subject views

    (A) a spot of light in a dark room
    (B) a spot of light superimposed on a vertical line
    (C) two or more lights flashing consecutively
    (D) a highly saturated hue for a prolonged period
    (E) objects, using only monocular vision

215. A researcher presents pictures to subjects for them to memorize. A week later, the researcher shows those pictures, interspersed with several new pictures, to the subjects. The subjects' task is to indicate which pictures they have seen before. The researcher is most likely studying

    (A) recall memory
    (B) recognition memory
    (C) semantic memory
    (D) semantic verification
    (E) echoic memory

216. The presence of a large number of people tends to increase the likelihood of wild, impulsive behavior. Which of the following is LEAST likely to be a plausible explanation for this phenomenon?

    (A) deindividuation
    (B) anonymity
    (C) diffusion of responsibility
    (D) functional autonomy
    (E) group polarization

217. Which of the following best describes Kelly's basic approach to personality?

    (A) Behavior is determined by unconscious forces.
    (B) Behavior is determined by the family structure.
    (C) People have a need to control the environment.
    (D) People have a hierarchy of needs.
    (E) Behavior is determined by a person's trait structure.

218. You've tried all morning to use the phone, but have not been able to because you can't get a dial tone. You finally stop trying. Later, in the afternoon, you decide to try to use the phone again. Your afternoon behavior is an example of

    (A) extinction
    (B) shaping
    (C) a fixed-action pattern
    (D) spontaneous recovery
    (E) stimulus generalization

219. Which of the following theorists is matched with the correct concept?

    (A) Maslow—self-actualization
    (B) Cattell—mesomorphy
    (C) Eysenck—approach-avoidance conflict
    (D) Titchener—functionalism
    (E) Adler—archetypes

220. In a normal distribution, approximately what percentage of cases will fall within two standard deviations of the mean?

    (A) 34%
    (B) 48%
    (C) 68%
    (D) 96%
    (E) 100%

STOP! END OF TEST.

PRACTICE TEST II ANSWER KEY

1. C	29. E	57. C	85. A
2. D	30. D	58. A	86. D
3. E	31. A	59. C	87. A
4. A	32. D	60. A	88. B
5. B	33. B	61. E	89. C
6. A	34. D	62. C	90. D
7. B	35. C	63. D	91. B
8. C	36. A	64. E	92. D
9. C	37. B	65. B	93. A
10. A	38. C	66. E	94. A
11. D	39. D	67. B	95. C
12. B	40. A	68. D	96. B
13. C	41. A	69. E	97. E
14. E	42. D	70. D	98. B
15. A	43. E	71. B	99. D
16. C	44. E	72. E	100. A
17. D	45. C	73. D	101. E
18. C	46. B	74. A	102. E
19. C	47. A	75. C	103. C
20. E	48. D	76. E	104. C
21. D	49. B	77. B	105. A
22. A	50. A	78. A	106. D
23. B	51. E	79. A	107. A
24. E	52. E	80. B	108. D
25. A	53. C	81. D	109. E
26. D	54. B	82. C	110. A
27. C	55. E	83. C	111. C
28. B	56. D	84. E	112. D

113. E	143. B	173. C	203. C
114. C	144. B	174. C	204. D
115. E	145. D	175. B	205. B
116. E	146. B	176. E	206. C
117. B	147. D	177. D	207. E
118. C	148. E	178. C	208. C
119. A	149. C	179. D	209. D
120. B	150. A	180. D	210. A
121. E	151. A	181. E	211. E
122. E	152. B	182. E	212. A
123. B	153. C	183. A	213. B
124. D	154. B	184. D	214. A
125. C	155. E	185. D	215. B
126. B	156. C	186. B	216. D
127. D	157. B	187. C	217. C
128. B	158. D	188. D	218. D
129. E	159. B	189. D	219. A
130. E	160. A	190. A	220. D
131. C	161. E	191. A	
132. A	162. A	192. B	
133. A	163. A	193. C	
134. B	164. C	194. E	
135. D	165. C	195. E	
136. D	166. E	196. C	
137. C	167. B	197. A	
138. A	168. D	198. B	
139. E	169. B	199. E	
140. A	170. C	200. E	
141. B	171. E	201. C	
142. E	172. B	202. A	

EXPLANATIONS TO PRACTICE TEST II

1. C

Remember, we're looking for the answer choice that cannot explain the attitude change, so let's begin by looking at the answer choices that *can* explain the attitude change. Choices (A) and (D) cluster because they are so closely linked. Group polarization refers to the tendency for group discussion to enhance the group's initial tendencies towards riskiness or caution. The risky shift can be considered a specific type of group polarization where group discussion enhances the group's initial tendencies towards riskiness. If Susan's classmates are more critical of the government than she is, it seems plausible that all the members of the group (including Susan) might become more critical of the present government as they discuss it. Regarding choice (E), it is possible that Susan will conform to her collegiate peer group. Finally, choice (B), the mere exposure effect, tells us that just by being exposed to a more critical opinion of the government, Susan could wind up favoring the more critical position. However, it is difficult to see how choice (C), social facilitation, could explain the attitude shift. Social facilitation has to do with the effect that the presence of others has on performance, and doesn't explain Susan's attitude shift.

2. D

Correctly answering question 2 required a knowledge of Freudian defense mechanisms. Projection occurs when a person attributes his forbidden feelings and thoughts to an external object or person. You might have been tempted by choice (B), but in displacement, pent-up feelings (often hostility) are discharged on objects and people less dangerous than those causing the feelings.

3. E

The question stem here refers to the standard learned helplessness scenario. At the beginning of a learned helplessness experiment, a dog is exposed to a series of shocks that the dog is powerless to control. After a series of uncontrollable shocks, the dog is placed in a situation where he can escape the shock after it begins by jumping to another area. However, the dog does not escape: it just whimpers and lies down.

4. A

The Whorfian hypothesis suggests that our perception of reality is determined by our language. To put this another way, it suggests that language largely determines the way in which we perceive the world. For instance, Whorf's hypothesis suggests that the more words our culture has to describe different types of snow, the better we will be at perceiving the difference between the different types of snow.

5. B

The air from the blow dryer is the unconditioned stimulus and the eye blink in response to it is the unconditioned response. People do not have to learn to blink in response to a puff of air on the eye: it just happens. In the question stem, we're told that an alarm clock ring preceded the puff of air. The alarm clock ring is the conditioned stimulus. Over time, the subjects began to blink in response to the alarm clock. The blinking in response to the alarm clock ring is the conditioned response: the subjects had to learn to do it; it didn't come naturally.

6. A

Systematic desensitization was developed by Joseph Wolpe. It was used to cure patients of their phobias without overwhelming them with fear. The first step in systematic desensitization is to construct an anxiety hierarchy. The client progresses through the anxiety hierarchy while deeply relaxed until, finally, the client can remain relaxed even when imagining the most anxiety-provoking situation in the hierarchy. Choice (B), Carl Rogers, is associated with client-centered therapy. Choice (C), Albert Ellis, is associated with the development of rational-emotive therapy. Choice (D), Richard Lazarus, divided coping styles into two types: problem-focused and emotion-focused. Finally, choice (E), Jacob Moreno, is associated with a form of group therapy called psychodrama, in which, as the name implies, patients act out their conflicts.

7. B

The availability heuristic comes in to play when we try to decide how likely something is. When we use this heuristic, we make our decisions based upon how easily similar instances can be imagined. Think about this a minute. What is more likely to make headlines: someone killed by asthma or someone killed by a tornado? Obviously, tornadoes make more news than asthma does, and therefore, instances of people being killed by tornadoes are likely to be more readily available in memory. Therefore, most people are likely to say that tornadoes kill more people than asthma.

8. C

This was a tricky question. It appears to require detailed knowledge about the WAIS (Wechsler Adult Intelligence Scale), but all you really need to know is that scores on the Wechsler are approximately normally distributed. Once you know this, the question becomes a fairly simple normal distribution/percentile question. The question stem asks for what percentile a score one standard deviation below the mean falls at. Therefore, we want to know what percentage of scores fall below a score one standard deviation below the mean. We know from the statistics chapter that 34 percent of the scores in a normal distribution will occur between the mean and one standard deviation below the mean. Therefore, to find out the percentage of scores occurring below one standard deviation below the mean, we can subtract 34 percent from 50 percent, which give us 16 percent. Therefore, a person whose IQ score is one standard deviation below the mean is at the 16th percentile, which means that 16 percent of the scores occur below his score.

9. C

Wernicke's aphasia impairs the ability to comprehend language. It is related to damage in the area of the brain known as Wernicke's area, which is what was probably damaged by the stroke. Wernicke's aphasia is usually contrasted with choice (D), Broca's aphasia, which impairs the ability to *produce* language. Aphagia is an eating disturbance, retrograde amnesia is a memory disturbance characterized by amnesia for events that occurred before the brain injury, and dyslexia is a reading disorder.

10. A

Freud proposed five stages of psychosexual development, covering the period from birth to adolescence. In contrast, Erikson proposed eight stages of psycho*social* development, covering the entire life span. However, the ages of Erikson's first five stages correspond roughly to the ages of Freud's stages. So,

since Freud's oral stage is his first stage, covering the first year or so of life, the correct answer choice is that stage of Erikson's that covers the first year or so of life, choice A.

11. D

The four basic schedules of reinforcement are fixed-ratio, variable-ratio, fixed-interval, and variable-interval schedules. In a fixed-ratio schedule, the animal only receives reinforcement after a fixed number of responses. In a variable-ratio schedule, the animal receives reinforcement after a varying number of responses. In a fixed-interval schedule, the animal will be reinforced on the first response after a fixed period of time has elapsed since the last reinforcement. Finally, on a variable-interval schedule, the animal will be reinforced for the first response made after a variable amount of time has elapsed since the last reinforcement. In the situation depicted in the question stem, the reinforcement is completing a sale. Salespeople don't get a sale at every house they visit, only the occasional house. Furthermore, they don't get the sale at every fifth house they visit or every twelfth house they visit: it varies. Therefore, the question stem describes a variable-ratio schedule. Variable-ratio schedules produce the most rapid response rate of the four schedules and produce behaviors very resistant to extinction. So these two effects of the variable-ratio schedule can explain why the salespeople in the question stem maintain high levels of perseverance.

12. B

Baumrind identified three styles of parenting: authoritarian, authoritative, and permissive. Authoritarian parents exert high control over their children and are somewhat emotionally cold and distant. They tend to be very inflexible and adhere rigidly to the rules. On the other hand, authoritative parents exert high control over their children but encourage their children and deal warmly with them. Permissive parents do not set guidelines and are unwilling to punish their children's wrong-doings. You might have been tempted by choice (A), but are three styles of group leadership identified by Lewin. Choice (C) consists of the three phases of moral development identified by Lawrence Kohlberg, while choice (D) consists of the three strategies identified by the personality theorist Karen Horney that people use in relationships with others. You most likely don't need to know about choice (E) for the GRE Psychology test, but these are three modes of experience proposed by Harry Stack Sullivan.

13. C

It makes sense that the more ambiguous the stimulus, the more likely it is that the subject will conform to group pressure. While Asch's experiment demonstrated that some people will conform to group pressure even when the stimuli are not at all ambiguous, ambiguous stimuli increase conformity. Choice (A) refers to the results of Milgram's experiments on obedience to authority. Since Milgram's classic experiment on obedience to authority did not concern perceptual judgments, choice (A) is incorrect.

14. E

Cognitive-structuralists stress that the child actively seeks to incorporate novel stimuli into pre-existing psychological constructs. In this way, the child expands these constructs, and increases her knowledge. Choice (A) is the view proposed by John Locke, that the neonate's mind is a *tabula rasa* upon which experience writes. Choice (B) is the view of the psychoanalytic school, especially its founder, Sigmund Freud. Choice (C) is also incorrect. The cognitive-structuralist orientation holds that psychological change takes place in stages and that there are indeed qualitative as well as quantitative differences between the psychological processes of children and adults. Finally, choice (D) is diametrically opposed to cognitive-structuralism.

15. A

There are three elements involved in balance theory: a subject, another person, and a thing, idea, or third person. The crux of balance theory is that a triad will be in balance if a person agrees with someone he likes or disagrees with someone he dislikes. Choices (B) and (C) are not balanced because in both choices, Jack is agreeing with someone he dislikes. Choice (D), while not clearly unbalanced (because we don't know whether Jack hates football, or tolerates it, or what) is also clearly not balanced, since only Jill likes football. Similarly, we don't have enough information to evaluate choice (E). It's possible that Jill also likes football and that Jack also likes baseball. Likewise, it's possible that Jill hates football and Jack hates baseball. However, choice (A) is clearly balanced, since Jack is agreeing with someone he likes.

16. C

Functional fixedness can be defined as the inability to use a familiar object in an unfamiliar way. If subjects have problems completing the task described in the question stem, it is likely due to an inability to conceive of using the hammer and nail as units of measurement.

17. D

Functional autonomy refers to the possibility that a given activity may become an end or goal in itself, regardless of its original reason for existence. For instance, as a youngster, someone may read because it's part of his homework or to please his parents. However, later on, the same person may read just for the sake of reading. Functional autonomy is a key part of Allport's personality theory. Striving for superiority is associated with Alfred Adler and moving away from others is associated with Karen Horney.

18. C

Diffusion of responsibility is a major factor affecting whether or not an individual bystander will help. Darley and Latané discovered that as the number of bystanders increases, the probability of any individual person helping decreases because it becomes less and less likely that the person will consider it to be his or her own responsibility. You might have been tempted by choice (B) since it too is related to helping behavior. However, a state of pluralistic ignorance is more likely to develop as the situation becomes more ambiguous.

19. C

Paradoxical sleep refers to REM sleep. During REM sleep, brain waves as recorded on an EEG look similar to alpha waves (which occur when we are awake) even though muscle tone remains relaxed. Choice (A) is incorrect. In fact, the EEG pattern during REM sleep is faster than would be expected. Choice (B) is also incorrect. The most difficult sleep stage to wake someone up from tends to be the REM stage. Choice (D) is also incorrect. REM sleep is vital for our functioning. In fact, after being deprived of REM sleep, organisms *do* compensate for the loss when they resume sleeping by spending a greater percentage of time in REM sleep. This phenomenon is known as "REM rebound." Finally, choice (E) is incorrect. As with all areas of human behavior, questions remain to be answered, but investigators are not completely unsure what transpires during this stage.

20. E

The primacy effect refers to better retrieval of items, in this case letters, from the beginning of a list. The primacy effect is usually contrasted with choice (C), the recency effect, which refers to better retrieval of words at the end of a list. Although it is true that both primacy and recency effects are generally in evidence, in the case presented in the question stem only the primacy effect occurred.

21. D

Assimilation and accommodation refer to the interaction between the child's schemata and information in the outside world. Assimilation is the process of making new information part of your existing schemata. Accommodation, in contrast, is what happens when the new information doesn't really fit into existing schemata, and you must change your schemata to conform with the new information. According to Piaget, intelligence (and indeed, all of cognition) develops due to the changing of these schemata through the processes of assimilation and accommodation. Regarding answer choice (B), the distinction between crystallized and fluid intelligence is associated with Cattell.

22. A

An afterimage is a visual sensation that appears after prolonged or intense exposure to a stimulus. If you stare at a stimulus and look at a blank wall, you see the afterimage. Emmert's law suggests that the farther away the object appears to be, the more the scaling device in the brain will compensate for its retinal size by enlarging our perception of the object. Emmert's law explains size constancy in the following manner. Suppose you first look at two identical objects: one four feet away from you and the other eight feet away from you. Now, the retinal size of the second object is half the size of the first object. Therefore, the scaling device in the brain will enlarge our perception of the second object so that we "see" it as being the same size as the nearer object. Emmert's law also works in the example in the question stem, but with a twist. As we move further away from the apparent object on the wall (the afterimage), the scaling device enlarges our perception to compensate for the usual decrease in the retinal size of the apparent object. However, because we're dealing with an afterimage, the retinal size of the image is fixed on the retina and the scaling device operates when it

doesn't have to. Therefore, as we move further away from the wall, the object appears to grow larger, and the correct answer is choice (A).

23. B

Concurrent validity is a type of criterion validity in which the criterion measure is obtained at about the same time as the test score. The developers of the MMPI wanted to make sure that the test was able to assess current personality. If the developers were concerned with predicting future personality organization (e.g., is it likely that this person will develop schizophrenia in the next five years?), then they would have constructed the test by correlating test scores with, for instance, the mental health of the test-takers five years later. They would then have been concerned with predictive validity.

24. E

The issue is how to group the individual elements of the figure. To make the explanation clearer, the figure is reproduced below, with the elements numbered.

Element number: 1 2 34 56 78 9

] [ ][ ][ ][ ]

As you go from left to right, if you group elements 1 and 2 together, elements 3 and 4 together, and so on, you are doing so because of proximity: you are grouping elements that are close together. If on the other hand, you group elements 2 and 3 together, elements 4 and 5 together, and so on, you are doing so because of closure: you are grouping elements whose contours form a rectangle. Therefore, the correct answer is choice (E) since it is probably about equally likely that elements in the figure would be grouped on the basis of proximity or closure. Similarity involves grouping elements that are similar to one another. In the figure, it is not likely that a person would group elements 1, 3, 5, 7, 9 and elements 2, 4, 6, and 8. Common fate refers to the tendency to group together elements that appear to be moving together. You might have been tempted by choice (D), but *prägnanz* is the general name for the result of the operation of all these Gestalt principles and refers to the notion that perceptual organization will always be as "good" (e.g., as regular, simple, symmetrical) as possible.

25. **A**

This is a good question for using a process of elimination strategy. First off, choice (C), the range, will be lower if generated from Group A. The range is the value of the lowest score subtracted from the value of the highest score. In both Group A and the entire distribution, the highest score is the same. However, the lowest score is lower for the entire distribution than for Group A. Therefore, the range will decrease if calculated using Group A scores alone. This information should also help to eliminate choice (D). For Group A, there is a restriction of range effect on the math scores. Therefore, one would expect that the correlation will be lower when calculated using only the data from Group A than when using the entire distribution. This leaves us with choices (A), (B), and (E). We might surmise that the standard deviation for Group A will be lower than the standard deviation for the entire distribution of scores, but there is really no way to make any kind of conclusion without having more information. You might have been tempted by choice (B), but, once again we don't have enough information to make a conclusion. For example, what if 10 students received 100, and the rest of the scores varied randomly between 0 and 95? In all likelihood, the mode of the entire distribution would be 100, and the mode of the Group A scores would also be 100. No increase there. In a different situation, it is possible that the 10 highest scores were all different. In that case, the scores from Group A wouldn't even have a mode, so we need more information before we can make a conclusion about the value of the mode. This leaves us with choice (A), which is the correct answer. The median divides the distribution in half, so that an equal number of scores is below the median as is above it. When looking at the entire distribution of scores, the median would be halfway between the 50th and 51st highest scores. When looking at Group A, the median would be between the 5th and 6th highest scores. Clearly, if no more that 20 scores can be the same, the median for Group A is going to be higher than the median for the entire distribution.

26. **D**

Dark adaptation refers to the fact that when you first enter a dark place after having been in a brighter place, you have problems seeing; however, as you stay in the dark place, you become adapted to it and become better able to see. The mechanism underlying dark adaptation is the regeneration of rhodopsin. Rhodopsin is the photopigment in the rods, the receptors in the retina that enable us to see in dim light. Rhodopsin is made up of a vitamin A derivative, called retinal; and a protein, called opsin. When a molecule of rhodopsin absorbs a photon of light, the pigment begins to decompose, or split, into retinal and opsin. Deprived of rhodopsin, the rods do not function well. After the splitting occurs, it takes time for the pigments to regenerate. As you sit in the darkness, the rhodopsin begins to regenerate, and you, therefore, begin to see better.

27. **C**

The law of effect states that behaviors followed by satisfiers will tend to be repeated while behaviors followed by annoyers will tend not to be repeated. Thorndike was the one who first formulated it. Answer choice (A), John Garcia, investigated biological constraints on classical conditioning, and more specifically, learned taste aversions. Answer choice (B) might have tempted you. It is true that Skinner is associated with operant conditioning and that operant conditioning is largely based on the law of effect. However, Skinner disagreed with the mentalistic focus of the law of effect. Skinner's version of the law of effect didn't mention "satisfiers" or "annoyers," but focused on the effect the consequence of the behavior had on the probability of the behavior being committed in the future. Answer choice (D), Edward Tolman, investigated cognitive maps, which are mental representations of physical spaces. Finally, answer choice (E), E. O. Wilson, is a proponent of sociobiology, a branch of science that investigates the effect various social behaviors have on fitness.

28. **B**

Bowlby's major contribution to developmental psychology is his work on attachment. Attachment is the bond between the child and the primary caregiver that is established early in the child's life. Knowing just this, you could have thought through the answer choices and reasoned out the correct one. Since we're dealing with the bond between children and parents, it seems obvious that choice (B) might be correct. Indeed, Bowlby's thoughts about attachment proceeded from his studies of children brought up in institutions such as orphanages.

29. **E**

This was a tricky question, but if you didn't know the correct answer outright, you could have reasoned it out by using what you already do know. First off, you could have immediately eliminated choices (C) and (D), since they are involved in olfaction and touch, respectively. This leaves you with three possible answers: choices (A), (B), and (E). If you remembered that transduction is the translation of physical energy to neural impulses, you could have ruled out choice (A), since the inferior colliculus is in the brain. The brain can't interpret sound energy, so the sound energy has to be transduced into neural impulses somewhere before the information enters the brain. That leaves us with choices (B) and (E). If you remembered that the pinna is the name for the fleshy part of the ear visible from the outside, you could have guessed that transduction doesn't occur there, especially since parts of the middle and inner ears *do* respond to physical energy. That leaves you with choice (E), which is indeed the correct answer. The Organ of Corti, composed of thousands of hair cells, rests on the basilar membrane. When the basilar membrane moves, it causes the hair cells to move and bump into the tectorial membrane above them. The bending of the hair cells is then transduced into neural impulses in some way not yet fully understood.

30. D

According to the James-Lange theory, the sequence underlying our subjective experience of emotion is as follows: First, an external stimulus (such as the sight of a car accident) activates a change in our physiological arousal. Next, we perceive our body's response (in this case, running away). Only then do we recognize our subjective experience of emotion—in this example, fear. Our experience of emotion thus occurs after we perceive our body's reaction to an external event. By the way, if you didn't remember the difference between the theories of emotion, you could have at eliminated choices (A) and (E) since neither are theories of emotion and guessed from the remaining three answer choices.

31. A

Primary process is the id's mode of response. Like the id itself, it does not take into account any consideration of reality. You may have been swayed by one of the other two answer choices related to Freudian theory, choices (D) and (E). However, as the name implies, primary process thought is primary and is neither dependent on the ego nor a response to superego demands. Although it is true that both the id and the superego are irrational, they have different goals and methods of

operation. The id, and therefore the primary process, operates on the basis of the pleasure principle, while the superego operates to try to obtain a moral ideal.

32. D

A standard deviation is a measure of variability. Hence, calculating a standard deviation would be most helpful when you are concerned with some question about variability. This points directly to answer choice (D). You could compute the standard deviation of daily corn prices during July and the standard deviation of daily wheat prices during July and whichever set of prices has the greater standard deviation had the greater amount of fluctuation that month.

33. B

Physical, objective properties describe the physical stimulus (e.g., the sound wave) itself. Psychological, subjective properties describe our experience of the stimulation. Frequency refers to the number of cycles per second of the sound wave, and is measured in Hertzes. Therefore, it is an objective, physical property of sound. Loudness, pitch, and timbre are all subjective, psychological dimensions of sound. Hue is a subjective dimension of vision related to wavelength, which is a physical property of light.

34. D

To use the Method of Loci, you associate what you have to memorize with some sequence of places with which you are familiar. You might have been extremely tempted by choice (C), because the phrase *cognitive mapping* does seem to fit the procedure described in the question stem. However, cognitive maps, studied by Edward Tolman, are mental representations of physical spaces—that is, mental representations of what is where. Tolman was able to show that rats were able to form cognitive maps of various mazes. You may also have been tempted by choices (A) or (B), because both have to do with memory. Choice (A), encoding specificity, refers to the finding that recall is best if the context at recall approximates the context during the original encoding. Finally, choice (B), chunking, refers to grouping single items into larger patterns. This is a very effective way of getting around the limited capacity of short-term memory, which, as Miller found, can only contain 7 ± 2 items.

35. C

To assess the reliability of a test using the split-half procedure, the test-developer asks a sample of people to take the test. After they take the test, the test items are divided into equivalent halves, and scores are calculated for each half, that is, each person receives two scores: one score indicating performance on one half of the test and one score indicating performance on the other half of the test. A correlation coefficient is then calculated between the test takers' scores on the one half and the test takers' scores on the other half. A high positive correlation coefficient indicates that the test is highly reliable.

36. A

A longitudinal study is one in which a group of subjects are studied repeatedly at different ages. In the example presented in the question stem, the gifted children are studied repeatedly throughout their lives. Longitudinal studies are usually contrasted with cross-sectional studies. In a cross-sectional study, each subject is only studied once and is studied at about the same time as the other subjects. So, if we were to give three groups of gifted children, ages 5, 10, and 15, some kind of test and then compare the different age groups, we'd be doing a cross-sectional study.

37. B

Helmholtz's theory of color vision, often called the trichromatic theory, argues that the retina contains three different types of color receptors (cones), which are differentially sensitive to different colors: one maximally to red, one to blue, and one to green. Hering, however, proposed a conflicting theory of color vision, which suggested that color perception is due to three types of color receptors: one stimulated by green and inhibited by red; one stimulated by yellow and inhibited by blue; and one which codes brightness. Therefore, Hering's theory was called opponent-process theory. You might have been tempted by choice (A). It is true that frequency theory challenged Helmholtz's place-resonance theory, but these are theories of pitch perception, not color vision.

38. C

The essential features of autism are lack of responsiveness to other people, gross impairment in communication skills, and bizarre responses to various aspects of the environment, with onset prior to three years of age. Children with autism will not cuddle or make eye contact, and tend to display little or no facial expression.

39. D

In the mid-1980s, McClelland and Rumelhart published a two-volume book about parallel distributed processing (abbreviated PDP). Up until that time, many accounts of human information processing assumed that the brain processed information serially—that it performed one stage of processing at a time. However, PDP starts with a different assumption: that human information processing is distributed across the brain and is done in a parallel fashion.

40. A

All of the answer choices are symptoms of schizophrenia. The key to this question was to remember that the primary symptom of catatonic schizophrenia is a disturbance in motor behavior. Most notably, there is an alternation between extreme withdrawal and extreme excitement. The withdrawal may be accompanied by no movement or the maintenance of a peculiar position for hours or even days on end. The excitement involves excessive movement that is apparently purposeless and not influenced by external stimuli.

41. A

The key assumption of cognitive dissonance is that when attitudes and behavior are incongruent, a state of tension exists. Let's look at how you could have approached this question if you didn't know the answer outright. Answer choice (B) should have leapt out at you as being obviously incorrect. A large part of the social psychology chapter dealt with attitude change, so it should be clear that attitudes are *not* permanent and unchanging. Choice (E) might also have jumped out at you. The idea that behavior can be modified is held by just about everyone mentioned in this book. Therefore, it is just too general to be the best answer choice. This leaves us with choices (A), (C), and (D). If you had a general idea of the dictionary definition of *dissonance* (discord or incongruity), you might have realized that the correct answer choice would have involved some sort of tension between two or more elements, and therefore might have selected choice (A), the correct answer choice.

42. D

Piaget divides cognitive development into four stages: the sensorimotor, preoperational, concrete operational, and formal operational stages. The sensorimotor stage lasts from birth to approximately 18 months. During the final substage of the sensorimotor period, we see the beginnings of true thought. This means that the child has now begun to acquire the ability to make internal representations and symbolizations of external objects and events. Once the child begins this type of thought, she enters the preoperational stage, which lasts from about 18 months to about 7 years of age.

43. E

In rational-emotive therapy, the therapist challenges any irrational beliefs that the client has, such as "I'm only a good person if everyone likes me." This therapy was developed by Albert Ellis. Choice (D), client-centered therapy, was developed by Carl Rogers and is almost a direct opposite of rational-emotive therapy. Rogers' therapy is nondirective, which means that the therapist does not really try to direct the course of the therapy and displays unconditional positive regard towards the client, regardless of what the client says.

44. E

The nondominant hemisphere (in most people, the right hemisphere) is more adept at spatial organization. Remember, the *Left* (dominant) hemisphere is associated with *Language* and *Logic*. This would have allowed you to eliminate choices (A), (C), and (D). Finally, since the dominant hemisphere is also associated with parts of that most *Logical* science, mathematics, choice (B) can be eliminated.

45. C

Interposition was one of the depth cues proposed by George Berkeley. While the images on the retina are two-dimensional, we perceive three dimensions. One explanation for this is that the image on the retina contains certain cues that indicate depth.

46. B

Bandura's studies of aggression suggested that the observation of aggressive responses can lead to aggressive behavior in children. In one of Bandura's experiments, children who watched adult models punch a "Bobo doll" (a large inflatable punching bag) were more apt to punch the doll themselves than children who had not watched the models punching the doll.

47. A

As discussed in the chapter on physiological psychology, both tricyclics and MAO inhibitors are used to treat depression. Both of these types of antidepressants facilitate the transmission of norepinephrine and serotonin, neurotransmitters implicated in depression. Choices (B), (C), and (D) are all used to treat schizophrenia. In fact, Thorazine and chlorpromazine both refer to the same drug (Thorazine is the trade name, chlorpromazine is the generic name). Choice (E), Ritalin, is a drug often used to treat attention-deficit/hyperactivity disorder.

48. D

A morpheme is the smallest unit of language that conveys a meaning. For instance, the word *talking* consists of two morphemes: *talk*, indicating action, and *ing*, indicating that the action takes place in the present. Choice (E) gives a definition of a phoneme, not a morpheme. So, for instance, two people may pronounce the *b* sound in two slightly different ways (e.g., at different pitches), yet we recognize both speech sounds as being a single sound.

49. B

Olds and Milner implanted electrodes in the septal region of rats' brains, and allowed rats to electrically stimulate their septal region (i.e., to send a small electric current to the septal region) at will. Olds and Milner discovered that the rats found such stimulation so pleasurable that they preferred it to eating, even after going 24 hours without food.

50. A

Almost without exception, children, including deaf children and those with mute parents, spontaneously begin to babble during their first year. Furthermore, infants are capable of producing all of the sounds in all the world's languages, even sounds not used in their native tongue.

51. E

The Ames room is a room that looks rectangular when viewed through the peephole provided. However, it really isn't rectangular. Because you are fooled into misperceiving the shape of the room, you think that the two rear corners of the room are equidistant from you, even though the left corner is actually farther away from you than the right corner. If a person inside the room were to walk from the left rear corner to the right rear corner while you were looking through the peephole, the size of that person's image on your retina would increase. However, because you perceive the two rear corners as equidistant from you, your brain ascribes this increase in retinal size to the only other thing that can affect retinal size, namely, the person's size. Therefore, you conclude that the person is getting bigger. So, the Ames room shows, in a very compelling way, the influence of apparent distance of the perception of size.

52. E

Galton was one of the first people to study individual differences. He was an important influence on James McKeen Cattell. Up until Cattell's time, most psychologists were interested only in finding commonalities amongst different people. Cattell, influenced by Galton, was one of the first psychologists to take seriously the notion that psychologists should study individual differences and it was this belief that fostered the whole mental testing movement in the United States.

53. C

Conservation refers to the understanding that the physical properties of an object (such as volume and numerosity) do not change if its appearance changes (providing, of course, that nothing is added or taken away). In the question stem, the child understands that when you pour milk from one glass into a glass of a different shape, the amount of milk you have does not change. Children in the preoperational stage of cognitive development, which lasts from about 18 months to 7 years, have not yet mastered conservation of volume. Children in the sensorimotor period, who are even younger than those in the preoperational period, do not conserve.

54. B

According to the classical conditioning account of phobias, the phobic patient is afraid of an originally neutral stimulus that became paired with a fear-inducing stimulus (the UCS). Thus, the neutral stimulus became a conditioned stimulus (CS) that elicits the conditioned response of fear. The key to the persistence of phobias is that people with phobias do all they can to avoid having to face the fear-inducing CS. According to the classical conditioning model, the way to get rid of the fear is to force the client to experience the CS without experiencing the associated UCS. One way to

do this is through flooding. In flooding, the therapist forces the client to directly experience the fear-inducing CS. Flooding is usually contrasted with implosion, in which the therapist forces the client to *imagine* the CS.

55. E

Before we look at answer choice (E), the correct answer, let's look at the incorrect answer choices. Choice (A) is true: Freudian therapy does tend to refer to "patients" while client-centered therapy uses the term *client*. However, the question stem asked for a *substantial* difference between the two therapies; while the client label may be more empowering, choice (A) is not the best answer choice. Choices (B) and (D) *do* refer to differences between Rogerian and Freudian therapy, but each case, the answer choice better describes Freudian therapy than client-centered therapy. Choice (C) is a distracter: all therapists, of whatever type, try to be observant. This leaves us with answer choice (E). Freudian therapists tend to believe that the roots of mental disorder lie within the recesses of childhood. Hence, the Freudian therapist considers it important to trace the patient's personality back to its earliest beginnings. On the other hand, the focus of the Rogerian therapist is more grounded in the present and in the present incongruity between the client's ideal self and her real self. Therefore, tracing the client's personality back to its beginnings is not the emphasis of the Rogerian therapist.

56. D

The dual-code hypothesis, proposed by Paivio, suggests that concrete information is encoded into memory both visually and verbally while abstract information is encoded into memory only verbally. Furthermore, Paivio found that the better the word is at evoking mental images, the better the recall would be. Hence, words high in imagery (such as *elephant*) are more likely to be recalled than words low in imagery (such as *virtue*). This gives us enough information to eliminate choices (B) and (C). Unlike abstract words, concrete words tend to be encoded both verbally *and* visually (i.e., as a mental image). Therefore, concrete words would, by definition, tend to be high in imagery. Therefore, concrete words would tend to be recalled better than abstract words, and choice (D) is correct. Choices (A) and (E) are the positions put forth by the levels-of-processing theory and the semantic feature-comparison model, respectively.

57. C

The tip-of-the-tongue phenomenon is that phenomenon where you feel like you're on the verge of remembering something, but continue to be unsuccessful doing so. This is a problem with recovering information already in memory, or retrieval. Choice (D), working memory, is another phrase for short-term memory. Most tip-of-the-tongue experiences occur trying to recall material in long-term memory, e.g., "What was the name of my 3rd grade teacher?"

58. A

This was another Piaget question, but this one required you to remember the difference between assimilation and accommodation. Assimilation is the process of making new information part of your existing schemata. Accommodation, in contrast, is what happens when the new information doesn't readily fit into existing schemata, and you must change the schemata to agree with the new information. In the question stem, the child is changing his behavior (and therefore, modifying his mental structures) to agree with the new information he obtained through the novel experience. Hence, the child is accommodating.

59. C

By now, the association between Bandura and social learning theory should be old hat to you. You may have been tempted by choice (D), since John Garcia *did* do research into the biological (instinctual) constraints on learning. However, Garcia's research was on learned taste aversions. The people who did the research on instinctual drift were Keller and Marion Breland.

60. A

Ebbinghaus used the method of savings to assess the amount of material retained from a prior learning task. Ebbinghaus would read through the items in a list of nonsense syllables, one at a time and in the order they appeared on the list. Then he would read and reread the list again in the same order until he could remember every item in the list in the correct order. After this, he distracted himself by trying to learn many other such lists. At various time intervals, he would return to his original list of nonsense syllables and measure how much of the list he remembered, rereading the original list until he again memorized it. He then compared the number of times he had to read the list in order to memorize it the first time with the number of times he

had to read the list in order to rememorize it. If he rememorized the list faster than he originally memorized it, Ebbinghaus concluded that he had saved information from his previous study of the list. Choices (B) and (D) may have been tempting since they are related to Ebbinghaus' work on memory and forgetting, but they both miss the mark here. Choice (B) describes *how* Ebbinghaus measured savings, not what he was trying to determine by measuring it, which is the concern of this question. Ebbinghaus' work on memory did utilize nonsense syllables, but choice (D), too, misses the point of the question. By the way, Zipf's law, choice (E), suggests that there is an inverse relationship between the length of a word and how often it is used.

61. E

The hypothalamus plays a vital role in eating and sexual activity. The two areas of the hypothalamus most commonly associated with eating are the ventromedial hypothalamus and the lateral hypothalamus. The part of the hypothalamus most commonly associated with sexual activity is the anterior hypothalamus. The thalamus is a relay station for incoming information from all the senses except for olfaction. The cerebral cortex is the outer surface of the brain. The amygdala is an important part of the limbic system and plays an important role in defensive and aggressive behaviors. The corpus callosum is a large collection of fibers that connects the left and right hemisphere and therefore helps the two hemispheres to communicate with each other.

62. C

The hippocampus plays a vital role in learning and memory processes, a point well worth remembering for the GRE Psychology test. Researchers originally discovered the connection between memory and the hippocampus the hard way. In an attempt to control severe epileptic seizures, parts of the temporal lobes including the amygdala and hippocampus were removed in a famous patient now known to the world as H.M. After surgery, H.M.'s intelligence was largely intact, but he suffered a drastic and irreversible loss of memory for anything new. This kind of memory loss is called anterograde amnesia. Choice (D), retrograde amnesia, refers to memory loss for events before trauma.

63. D

The agression scale has to be used to claim that Joe is twice as aggressive as Jim. This means that we are looking for a scale where multiplication is meaningful. Of the four basic scales we discussed in the chapter on tests and measurements, the *only* scale on which multiplication is meaningful is the ratio scale, which allows one to say that "the ratio of Joe's aggression to Jim's aggression is 2 to 1."

64. E

According to Fritz Heider, one of the founders of attribution theory, we are all naïve psychologists who attempt to discover causes and effects in events. Attribution refers to the process of finding a cause for behavior, be it someone else's behavior or your own. Making attributions about behavior, therefore, helps us to organize behavior and make it meaningful. Choice (A) actually refers to McGuire's inoculation theory.

65. B

The Type A personality is characterized by behavior that tends to be competitive and compulsive. The Type A person tends to be impulsive, impatient, and always seems to be in a hurry. You may have been tempted to choose answers (A) or (D). However, the obsessive-compulsive personality disorder is characterized by a preoccupation with orderliness, perfection, and control, and isn't associated with high competitiveness and impulsivity. Regarding choice (D), a Machiavellian personality is characterized by a tendency to be manipulative and deceitful. Finally, a person with an external locus of control is not likely to be a Type A personality. A person with an external locus of control tends to believe that outside events or chance control his destiny; Type A personalities are more likely to believe that they control their own destiny, that is, have an internal locus of control.

66. E

Both the method of introspection and the goal of analyzing consciousness into its elements are associated with structuralism, of which Titchener was the founder. You might have quickly eliminated choice (D), Hermann von Helmholtz, since he was not a psychologist. As a leading behaviorist, Watson, choice A, eschewed the method of introspection. This would have left you with choices (B), (C), and (E). While it is true that Sperling (choice (B)) studied cognition (specifically memory), his most famous study used a tachistoscope to present 3 by 3 arrays of letters to assess the capacity of visual sensory memory. Choice (C) is also incorrect. Although it is true that Wertheimer used himself (and Köhler and Koffka) to study the phi and other phenomena, his goal was not to analyze consciousness into its parts. In fact, the rallying cry of the Gestalt school, of which Wertheimer was a founder, was that the whole is something more than the sum of its parts.

67. B

Elizabeth Loftus has found that what we remember about what we have seen can be altered by presenting new information or by asking misleading questions. Loftus has studied the implications of her findings for eyewitness testimony. It is true that Bartlett studied how we use schemata to reconstruct information in memory, but he did not focus on eyewitness testimony as Loftus has done.

68. D

Syntax is concerned with the grammatical arrangement of words in sentences.

69. E

The cerebellum helps maintain posture and balance. It also coordinates body movements. Damage to the cerebellum causes clumsiness and loss of balance. Therefore, it is possible that a patient who walks with a jerky, uncoordinated motion has damage to the cerebellum. Let's look at the other answer choices. The hypothalamus serves many important homeostatic functions in the body and helps regulate eating, drinking, and sexual behavior. The thalamus serves as an important relay station for incoming sensory information, including all senses except for olfaction. The amygdala plays an important role in defensive and aggressive behaviors. Finally, the reticular activating system serves to regulate arousal and alertness.

70. D

Chlorpromazine is an anti-schizophrenic drug that alleviates some of the symptoms of schizophrenia. It does so by affecting the action of dopamine at the synapse. Choice (C), L-Dopa, also affects the dopaminergic system, but instead of decreasing activity, it increases activity in the dopaminergic system. It is used to treat it. Parkinson's disease, not schizophrenia. MAO inhibitors, choice (B), are used to alleviate depression. Choice (E), diazepam, is the generic name for Valium. It is a minor tranquilizer used to reduce anxiety. Finally, choice (A), diphenylhydantoin, is a drug used in the treatment of epilepsy.

71. B

In the Milgram experiment, every subject was willing to give painful electric shocks to the victim and many continued to do so up to and including the maximum voltage. This information eliminates choice (A). Choices (C), (D), and (E) can be clustered because they all relate the subjects' behavior to some aspect of the people involved in the experiment. If Milgram found that subject characteristics governed willingness to shock, the experiment probably wouldn't be as famous as it is, because one would expect that certain types of people would be more willing to administer shocks than others. However, Milgram found that it was the characteristics of the situation (most notably the perceived authority of the experimenter) that influenced willingness to shock. Therefore, choices (C), (D), and (E) can be ruled out as a group, leaving only the correct answer, choice (B).

72. E

The hypothetico-deductive method requires that scientists first define and formulate their hypotheses. Second, the scientists perform experiments under carefully controlled conditions to test their hypotheses. Finally, the scientists interpret the results of their experiments, and, if necessary, change their hypotheses. In this case, the Young-Helmholtz theory provided the hypothesis. When it became possible to do so, later researchers tested the hypothesis. It turned out that the hypothesis was largely correct. Although the hypothesis was formulated years before it could be directly tested, the sequence described in the question stem does illustrate the hypothetico-deductive method.

73. D

Both Berko and Chomsky stressed the necessity of some sort of innate process to drive language development. Berko gave young children nonsense words and asked them to supply their past tense. The fact that the children were able to do so, even though they had never heard the words before, provided some evidence that there must be an innate component to language development. Chomsky calls this innate component a language acquisition device (LAD). The LAD enables the child to abstract the rules of language from the

fragments of speech she hears. Choice (C) describes the viewpoint of Lev Vygotsky, while choices (B) and (E) are related to behaviorist attempts to explain language acquisition. Regarding choice (A), holophrases are one-word utterances made by children that stand for entire proposition; for instance, depending on the context, when the young child says "No," she might mean "No, I don't want that" or "No, don't take that away."

74. A

Symptoms of dissociative fugue include amnesia and a sudden, unexpected flight away from one's location of usual daily activities. A person in a fugue state will be confused over his identity, and may even assume a new identity. Choice (B), multiple personality disorder (now called dissociative identity disorder by the DSM-IV), is characterized by two or more personalities that recurrently take control of a person's behavior. There's no indication that control of Mr. L's behavior is being recurrently switched between two personalities. None of the remaining disorders are dissociative disorders. Obsessive-compulsive disorder and agoraphobia are both anxiety disorders and dysthymic disorder is a mood disorder.

75. C

Harlow studied baby Rhesus monkeys separated from their mothers. In his most famous experiment, he took newborn monkeys from their mothers and placed them in a cage with two so-called "surrogate mothers." One of these surrogate mothers was a wire cylinder with a feeding nipple attached. The other was a wood cylinder covered with terry cloth that did not provide food. Surprisingly, the monkeys overwhelmingly preferred to cling to the cloth mother. From this, Harlow concluded that what he called "contact comfort" was more essential in bond formation than providing for physical needs. The details of the experiment eliminate both choices (D) and (E) from contention. Choice (B) is also incorrect. A securely attached infant is, in fact, more likely to explore his environment when his mother is around because she provides a secure base from which to explore. Finally, choice (A) makes a distinction that is irrelevant to Harlow's experiment.

76. E

An avoidance–avoidance conflict is one in which the person has to choose between two options she'd rather avoid, that is, between two undesirable situations.

77. B

Korsakoff's syndrome is a disease often related to alcohol abuse. It produces anterograde amnesia (memory loss for anything new). Confabulation refers to the filling in of gaps in memory with distorted, fanciful material. It is a symptom of Korsakoff's syndrome. By the way, the official DSM-IV name for Korsakoff's syndrome is alcohol-induced persisting amnestic disorder (due to thiamine deficiency).

78. A

Both Weber and Fechner were important in the early history of psychophysics. Choice (C), S. S. Stevens, proposed his power law as an alternative to Fechner's psychophysical law. John Swets was one of the original developers of signal detection theory (in the mid-20th century), an important antecedent to psychophysics. The correct answer choice, Hermann von Helmholtz, was an important figure in the development of psychology, having proposed explanations for both color vision and pitch perception. However, he is not known as a psychophysicist. Therefore, the correct answer is choice (A).

79. A

Jung developed the idea of the collective unconscious. The collective unconscious contains the residue of the experiences of our earliest ancestors. It is based on our ancestral past and includes images that are a record of people's common experiences, such as having a mother and father. These images are referred to as archetypes. You may have been tempted to choose answer (B). Although it is true that Allport proposed the distinction between idiographic and nomothetic approaches to personality, Allport came down strongly in support of the idiographic approach to personality.

80. B

Retroactive inhibition is not directly related to psychotherapeutic technique. Retroactive inhibition, discussed in the chapter on cognitive psychology, is forgetting what you learned earlier as you learn something new. Don't confuse retroactive inhibition with reciprocal inhibition, which is directly related to systematic desensitization. Choices (A), (C), and (D) are all behavioral methods of dealing with phobias. Choice (E), transference, is a process that occurs during psychoanalysis when the patient applies to the therapist the attitudes and feelings that developed in the patient's relations with significant others in the past.

81. D

Iconic memory is another name for visual sensory memory. If you had never heard of iconic memory before, you could still have narrowed down the contending answer choices. If you remembered that working memory and short-term memory are synonymous, you could have eliminated choices (A) and (C), since both answer choices refer to the same thing. This leaves you with choices (B), (D), and (E). If you knew the general definition of *icon* (a picture or an image), you might have been able to guess that iconic memory would have something to do with vision and could have guessed choice (D).

82. C

According to the question stem, if less than a majority votes for the measure, the measure does not become law. However, once the affirmative vote is above 50 percent, it doesn't matter whether just 51 percent vote affirmatively or 99 percent vote affirmatively; either way, it becomes law. So, it's either all or nothing. Likewise, an action potential will only be fired if the incoming stimulation is above threshold. Furthermore, it doesn't matter how much above the threshold value the stimulation is: the axon fires at the same voltage, regardless of whether the stimulation is just above threshold or way above threshold. You might have been tempted by choice (B). However, recall from the chapter on physiological psychology that postsynaptic potentials (generally in the dendrite) are not governed by the all or nothing law. The intensity of the postsynaptic potential is proportional to the stimulation.

83. C

Predictive validity is a type of criterion validity in which the performance you are trying to predict occurs a relatively long time after the test administration. Here we're correlating GRE scores with later graduate school GPA. Therefore, we're dealing with predictive validity. If we were to correlate GRE scores with current *under*graduate GPAs, then we'd be dealing with concurrent validity. To measure content validity, you would assess the representativeness of the test and its coverage of the particular skill or knowledge area that it is supposed to measure. The remaining two answer choices are methods of assessing reliability. In the test-retest method, the same test is administered to the same group of people twice. The correlation between the scores on the two tests is then calculated. A high positive correlation indicates a high degree of reliability. In the split-half method, the test-takers only have to take one test each. After they take it, the test items are divided into equivalent halves and the scores on one half are correlated with the scores on the other half. Again, a high correlation coefficient indicates that the test is reliable.

84. E

Both Alfred Binet and David Wechsler were influential in the development of the intelligence test. In 1905, Binet collaborated with Theodore Simon and published the first modern intelligence test, known as the Binet-Simon test. Binet also introduced the concept of mental age. Wechsler developed three major IQ tests: the WPPSI, the WISC, and the WAIS. The Wechsler tests yield three deviation IQs: a verbal IQ, a performance IQ, and a full-scale IQ. So (E) is correct. Henry Murray is best known for his work developing the Thematic Apperception Test (abbreviated TAT). However, the TAT is a personality test, not an intelligence test. Alfred Adler is best known for his psychoanalytic studies of inferiority, superiority, and the influence of birth order. Erik Erikson is a developmental psychologist who developed a theory of psychosocial development that involved the resolution of a series of crises over the course of a lifetime. Kurt Lewin is best known for his development of field theory in social psychology.

85. A

Of the methods listed, the most successful treatment for phobia is systematic desensitization. In systematic desensitization, the goal is for the client to be relaxed when imagining the fearful situation. The first step in this therapy is to construct an anxiety hierarchy, a listing of the anxiety-eliciting situations to be used in the systematic desensitization ranked from low to high. While relaxed, the client is asked to imagine the situation on the list that evokes the least anxiety. If the client can stay relaxed while imagining the item, he moves on to the next item in the hierarchy. This process is repeated until the client can stay relaxed even when imagining the most anxiety-provoking item on the hierarchy.

86. D

Mental chronometry is the use of reaction time to study cognitive processing. By using a variety of experimental tasks, the experimenter can measure how much time it takes to perform various mental processes. If you were able to break down *chronometry* into its root words

chrono and *metry*, and realized that *chrono* had to do with time (as in *chronology*) you could have been able to choose the correct answer.

87. A

This question tests your knowledge of the duplexity theory of vision. Vision is based on the differential functioning of two types of photoreceptors: rods and cones. The correct answer is choice (A): we would expect that object discrimination will be worst in the fovea. A key phrase in the question stem is "under dim light." This means that the subject will be relying on his rods. If you didn't read the question carefully, you may have chosen choice (B) since the fovea, the highly concentrated region of cones near the center of the retina, is typically associated with high visual acuity. However, in dim light, our rods take over and we would see better when the visual image falls on the area of the retina where the rods are most highly concentrated; namely, the periphery. Our sight would be worst when the image of the object falls on the fovea since there are no rods in the fovea. The (C)-(D) cluster could have been quickly ruled out. Since the light is dim, the subject in the question stem will be relying on his rods, which leads to achromatic vision.

88. B

Gordon Allport distinguished between idiographic and nomothetic approaches to personality. The idiographic approach to studying personality focuses on individual case studies while the nomothetic approach focuses on groups of individuals and tries to find commonalities. The tricky part of this question is that two of the answer choices mention case studies. However, in answer choice (C), rather than study the uniqueness of the individual people, the psychologist combines the data to analyze a group, whereas in choice (B), the psychologist studies each individual personality structure. Choices (A), (C), and (E) are examples of studies utilizing a nomothetic approach to personality, while choice (D) is irrelevant to the nomothetic/idiographic distinction.

89. C

Retroactive inhibition occurs when you forget what you learned earlier as you learn something new. So in Condition I, the subject learns A, and then learns B. However, as the subject learns B, she forgets A. Therefore, when asked to do so, she cannot recall A.

This is retroactive inhibition. In proactive inhibition, choice (A), what you learned earlier interferes with what you try to learn later. Proactive inhibition would be implicated if a subject in Condition II could not recall B.

90. D

Vicarious learning is learning that takes place without the person's own behavior being reinforced or punished. In other words, it is learning that takes place by observing the consequences of other people's behaviors. Albert Bandura is the name most closely associated with vicarious learning.

91. B

Smell (olfaction) and taste interact and much of the perceived "taste" of food is actually due to smell.

92. D

Choices (C) and (E) might quickly have jumped out at you as being incorrect. Choice (C), the medulla oblongata, is responsible for regulating vital functions such as breathing, heartbeat, and blood pressure. Choice (E), the adrenal medulla, is a part of the endocrine system that manufactures and secretes adrenaline. This would leave you with choices (A), (B), and (D), all of which play vital roles in aggressive behavior. However, as discussed in the physiological psychology chapter, it is the septum that inhibits aggression. Damage to the septum leads to a form of sham rage, while damage to either the amygdala or the hypothalamus leads to a marked decrease in aggressive behavior. From these results, researchers have concluded that a normal, whole septum inhibits aggression; while a normal, whole amygdala and a normal, whole hypothalamus each act to promote aggression, and fighting behavior.

93. A

What the psychologist needs is an intelligence test suitable for children. We can, therefore, immediately eliminate choices (B) and (D), because they are personality tests, and choice (E), because it is not a test at all. (IRT is an abbreviation for item response theory, sometimes used in computerized adaptive testing to determine which items will be presented to which test-takers.) Choice (C), WAIS, is an acronym for Wechsler Adult Intelligence Scale. Therefore, the only choice remaining, choice (A), must be correct. And in fact, the Stanford-Binet Intelligence Test *is* used for children

94. A

Transference is a process that occurs during psychoanalysis when the patient applies to the therapist the attitudes and feelings that developed in the patient's relations with significant others in the past. In displacement, feelings are discharged on objects and people less dangerous than those causing the feelings.

95. C

The key to answering this question is to remember that fraternal twins arise from two different fertilized eggs. Hence, the genetic similarity between fraternal twins is no greater than that between ordinary sibling. If an ordinary sibling has a 50 percent chance of having the disease, a fraternal twin also has a 50 percent chance of getting the disease. Even if you did not know this, you might have immediately eliminated choices (D) and (E), since it is unlikely that a fraternal twin would have *less* of a chance of getting the disease than an ordinary sibling. Likewise, you might have eliminated choice (A). Choice (A) would be true if we were dealing with *identical* twins, who have 100 percent of their genes in common.

96. B

Schachter and Singer's experiment concerning cognitive influences on emotions is one of the classics in psychology. According to Schachter and Singer's two-factor theory of emotion, when physiological arousal occurs without any known cause, a person will search the environment for something to explain that arousal and thus give it emotional meaning. The subjects in the experiment were given injections of adrenaline, but were told that they were receiving vitamins. Injections of adrenaline normally increase physiological arousal, but only some of the subjects were told to expect increased heart rates, perspiration, etc. Following the injections, the subjects were asked to wait in a room with another "subject" (who was actually a confederate of the experimenter). With one group of subjects, the confederate acted silly and played with paper airplanes; with another group he acted irritable and angrily tore up a study questionnaire. Those subjects who weren't told in advance to expect changes in their physiological arousal ("uninformed subjects") reported feeling different emotions depending on whether the confederate had acted silly or angry. Subjects who were told to expect physiological arousal were not influenced by the confederate's antics in the waiting room.

97. E

Thomas Szasz argues that most of the mental disorders treated by clinicians are not really illnesses, but are instead traits or behaviors that differ from the cultural norm. Szasz further argues that labeling these people mentally ill is a way to force them to change and conform to the societal norm rather than dealing with the societal causes of their problems. Therefore, mental illness, according to Szasz, is largely a social and legal problem.

98. B

A Type II error occurs when a false null hypothesis is accepted. It is usually contrasted with choice (A), a Type I error. A Type I error occurs when an experimenter rejects a true null hypothesis. As to choice (C), because the experimenter accepted the null hypothesis, we can infer that her results were statistically *insignificant*. Although it is true that her results *should* have been statistically significant (because the null hypothesis is actually false), the researcher found them insignificant. As to choice (D), if we have a false null hypothesis, the way to minimize the chances of making a Type II error is to increase the chances of rejecting the null hypothesis. A way to do this is to make our criterion of significance bigger, say by increasing it from .05 to .10. Therefore, a Type II error cannot be due to a criterion of significance that is too large, but can be due to a criterion of significance that is too small. Finally, regarding choice (E), predictive validity is a characteristic of tests, not experiments.

99. D

To figure out the difference threshold for the 50 gram stimulus, we need to figure out the Weber fraction. We can do so using what we know about the 20 gram stimulus. To obtain the Weber fraction, you need to divide the difference threshold by the intensity level of the standard stimulus. For the 20 gram standard stimulus, the Weber fraction is 2 over 20, or $\frac{1}{10}$. This Weber fraction tells us that the difference threshold is one-tenth of the standard stimulus. In the case of a 50

gram standard stimulus, the difference threshold is one-tenth of 50, or 5 grams. Therefore, a 55 gram stimulus would feel just heavier than a 50 gram stimulus.

100. A

Bipolar disorder is a mood disorder formerly known as manic-depression. It is characterized by marked mood swings alternating between manic highs and depressive lows. Lithium is a notably effective mood stabilizer, eliminating 70 to 90 percent of symptoms associated with bipolar disorder.

101. E

In a cross-sectional study, subjects of different ages are used, each subject is only studied once, and everyone is studied at about the same time. The responses of the different age groups are then compared. Cross-sectional studies are usually contrasted with longitudinal studies, choice (A). In longitudinal studies, one group of subjects is studied repeatedly at different ages. The other answer choices are not specifically methods of studying development.

102. E

A sociobiological explanation for the evolution of dominance hierarchies would attempt to find a relationship between rank in the hierarchy and fitness. More specifically, a sociobiological explanation would tend to suggest that the more dominant the animal, the greater the fitness. Hence, the higher-ranked animals would be expected to have more offspring, and/or more relatives in general. The answer choice that would most clearly weaken this explanation would be choice (E), which suggests that the higher the rank, the lower the fitness. If it were true, choice (E) would refute the sociobiological explanation for the evolution of dominance hierarchies. Let's go through the other answer choices. Choice (A) doesn't necessarily weaken the sociobiological explanation. Remember, the key to fitness is not how long you live, but how often you reproduce. If lower-ranking males are indeed able to reproduce more because they live longer, the sociobiological explanation would be weakened. However, we're not given that information. Choice (B) might even strengthen the sociobiological explanation, if food is scarce. Choice (C) also tends to strengthen the sociobiological explanation since offspring of high-ranking parents would tend to be high-ranking themselves and therefore, might tend to have higher fitness. Finally, choice (D) concerns inclusive fitness. Recall that an individual's inclusive fitness is related to how many relatives they have. If the brothers of high-ranking males reproduce more than the brothers of the low-ranking males, the inclusive fitness of the high-ranking males will likely be higher than the inclusive fitness of the low-ranking males. Therefore, the only answer that necessarily weakens a sociobiological explanation for the evolution of dominance hierarchies is choice (E).

103. C

Reproductive isolating mechanisms are behaviors which prevent animals of one species from attempting to mate with animals of a closely related species. They work by providing an animal with a way of identifying others of its own species. They tend to evolve when the different species live in close proximity to each other. So, the correct answer choice has to have something to do with two different species living in close proximity to each other. This eliminates choices (D) and (E). Choice (B) is tempting, but reproductive isolating mechanisms serve to isolate different species, not different troops. This leaves choices (A) and (C), and in both of these answer choices, the different species are in close proximity to each other, but the two different species referred to in the respective answer choices are more closely related in choice (C) than in choice (A).

104. C

Anorexia nervosa is characterized by a refusal to maintain a minimal normal body weight. The person with anorexia nervosa also has a distorted body image, so that she believes she is overweight even when she is emaciated. There is also a type of anorexia nervosa where the anorexic person regularly engages in binge-eating and/or purging. Although bulimia nervosa also involves binge eating and excessive attempts to compensate for it (by purging, fasting, or excessive exercising), in bulimia nervosa the individual tends to maintain at least a minimally normal body weight.

105. A

Glial cells enclose individual axons in a protective sheath, which is called the myelin sheath. One purpose of the myelin sheath is to increase the conduction velocity in the axon (i.e., to increase the speed at which the axon potential travels). Knowing that the action potential travels faster in myelinated axons than in unmyelinated axons, you could have eliminated choices (C) and (E). The second thing you had to remember was the relationship between the width of the myelin sheath and the conduction velocity: the thicker the sheath, the faster the conduction. Therefore, action potentials will travel more quickly in thick myelinated fibers than in thin myelinated fibers. Don't be tempted into choosing (D) because the fiber is shorter. The question stem is not concerned with how long it takes to get from one end of the axon to the other, but with the speed of the action potential. Think of two cars: car 1 going from New York to Boston at 40 miles per hour and car 2 going from New York to Los Angeles at 60 miles per hour. Although car 1 will get to its destination before car 2 will, car 2 is nevertheless going faster than car 1.

106. D

Sperling devised a method called the partial-report procedure. Using this procedure, Sperling discovered that the capacity of sensory memory was about nine items. Choice (B) might have tempted you since researchers before Sperling believed they had discovered that the capacity of sensory memory was only about four items. However, Sperling showed that this was incorrect. You might have also been tempted by choice (C). Seven *is* an important number in memory research, but recall that this is the capacity for short-term memory, not sensory memory. To be more specific, George Miller found that short-term memory could contain 7 ± 2 chunks of information.

107. A

In a control group design, the control group and experimental group go through the same procedures, except for receiving different levels of the independent variable. So for instance, if the independent variable is the amount of a drug, the experimental group might receive five milligrams of the drug, while the control group would receive zero milligrams. Remember that the independent variable is the variable whose effect is being studied, while the dependent variable is the variable expected to change due to variations in the independent variable.

108. D

Both schizophrenia and Parkinson's disease are related to abnormalities in the dopaminergic system. The dopamine hypothesis of schizophrenia argues that the delusions, hallucinations, and agitation associated with schizophrenia arise from an oversensitivity to dopamine in the brain. Parkinson's disease is thought to result from a loss of dopamine-sensitive neurons in the basal ganglia. Alzheimer's disease is not linked to the activity of dopamine.

109. E

The dominant hemisphere controls the expression and comprehension of language. Choices (A), (B), and (C) are all better descriptions of the nondominant hemisphere. As to (D), the dominant and the nondominant hemispheres work together to process information. The importance of this coordination can be seen in the results of experiments performed on patients with so-called split-brains who have had the fibers that connect the two hemispheres severed, often to control epilepsy. These patients show striking deficits on certain experimental tasks.

110. A

Factor analysis attempts to account for the interrelationships found among variables by analyzing how groups of variables "hang together." Some investigators of intelligence have used factor analysis to analyze intelligence into its component parts. These investigators might administer a series of tests (called a test battery) designed to test specific attributes such as reasoning and arithmetic. They would then use factor analysis to try to determine the factors that underlie the differences between individuals. This would help them ascertain the component parts of intelligence. Spearman did use factor analysis and suggested that individual differences in intelligence were largely due to variations in the amount of a general factor which he called *g*, but Spearman's work is an example of what can be done with factor analysis and is not the statistical method itself.

111. C

To obtain a ratio IQ, you divide the child's mental age by her chronological age, and multiply the result by 100.

In this case, the mental age is 10.7 and her chronological age is 9.5. 10.7 divided by 9.5 is 1.13, so the child's ratio IQ is about 113. If you chose choice (E), you probably divided 10.7 into 9.5 instead. You can make sure you've divided the right way by looking at the mental and chronological age. If the mental age is greater than the chronological age, the ratio IQ must be above 100. If the mental age is less than the chronological age, the ratio IQ must be below 100.

112. D

The endorphins are natural pain killers produced in the brain. Broken into its root words, *endorphins* has the same ending as *morphine*, an artificial pain killer. If you also remembered that *endo-* means *within*, you could have figured out the answer.

113. E

GABA, the abbreviation for gamma-aminobutyric acid, produces inhibitory postsynaptic potentials. The other answer choices all produce excitatory postsynaptic potentials. Postsynaptic potentials are the tiny electrical charges that occur when the neurotransmitter binds to the receptor site on the postsynaptic dendrite. An excitatory postsynaptic potential makes it more likely the neuron will fire. An inhibitory postsynaptic potential makes it less likely the neuron will fire.

114. C

A supernormal stimulus is a stimulus which more often releases the fixed-action pattern than the stimulus found in nature. If the smaller egg was *not* a supernormal stimulus, the gull would have rolled her own egg back to the nest first. Answer choice (A) may be tempting because the smaller egg *is* a sign stimulus, but so is the larger egg. Answer choice (B), the innate releasing mechanism, is the mechanism that mediates between the sign stimulus and the fixed-action pattern. Answer choice (D), fixed-action pattern, describes the gull's egg-rolling behavior, but does not describe the egg. Answer choice (E) is an outlier and refers to behaviors which prevent animals of one species from attempting to mate with animals of a closely-related species.

115. E

The clinical method, sometimes called the case study method, can be used when developmental psychologists want to take a detailed look at the development of a very small number of individuals. Piaget made brilliant use of this method to find out why children at various stages of development behaved the way they did.

116. E

The baby duck's behavior is an example of imprinting. Imprinting can be defined as the rapid formation of an attachment bond between an organism and an object in the environment. When the ethologist Konrad Lorenz imitated the strut of a jackdaw, a young jackdaw became attached to him. The bird followed Lorenz about and even preferred the company of humans to members of its own species. Separation anxiety refers to the anxiety young children have when they are separated from the primary attachment figure (usually the mother). However, nothing is said about separation in the poem. Contact comfort is an important factor in developing the attachment bond, as Harlow discovered, but the best answer here is the definition of the attachment bond, not the reason it occurs.

117. B

DSM-IV is an abbreviation for *Diagnostic and Statistical Manual of Mental Disorders, Fourth Edition.* Published by the American Psychiatric Association in 1994, it is the most widely accepted system in the United States for the classification of mental disorders. DSM-IV's classification scheme is not based on the possible etiologies or treatments of the different disorders. Rather, it is based on an atheoretical description of the symptoms of the various disorders. A hallmark of the DSM is its system of multiaxial assessment. In this system, clients are assessed on five different domains of information, all of which may help the clinician plan treatment. On Axis I, the clinician lists the client's clinical disorders (e.g., schizophrenia or claustrophobia). Axis II records information on the client's personality disorders and/or any mental retardation that may exist. Axis III is used for recording any medical conditions that are potentially relevant for understanding or treating the client's mental disorder. Axis IV is used to indicate any psychosocial or environmental problems the client may have. Finally, Axis V indicates the clinician's judgment of the client's overall functioning. Regarding choice (E), the DSM-IV generally uses a categorical approach to the classification of mental disorders. A categorical approach attempts to place people in discrete categories (e.g., normal, paranoid schizophrenia, dissociative fugue, and so on) while a dimensional approach

attempts to describe behaviors on the basis of where they fall on certain continuous scales, or dimensions.

118. C

Both Horney and Adler emphasized the significance of social relationships in psychological development. Alfred Adler stressed the importance of the immediate social imperatives of family and society while Horney elucidated the strategies people use in relationships to overcome basic anxiety and attain a degree of security (i.e., moving toward people, moving against people, and moving away from people). This differentiates them from theorists such as Sigmund Freud and Carl Jung, who stressed the intrapsychic contributions to personality development.

119. A

The sleeper effect refers to the finding that, over time, an argument from a source low in credibility will become more credible while an argument from a source high in credibility will become less credible. In the question stem, the consumer magazine is the high credibility source while the president of the company is the low credibility source. Notice that the *before* and *immediately after* scores are identical for all the answer choics. What we want to focus on is the difference between the *immediately after* and *4 weeks after* columns. If the sleeper effect were true, we would expect that the agreement score with the low credibility source (Group A) will increase over those 4 weeks while the agreement score with the high credibility source (Group B) will decrease. The only answer choice where both groups show these trends is choice (A).

120. B

Choices (A), (C), (D), and (E) are all related to potentially reversible environmental factors. In choice (B), however, the brain is actually damaged, either through some genetic disorder or through physical injury. This is not easily surmountable, and can lead to very severe mental retardation.

121. E

The visual cliff has been used to study the development of depth perception. It is a table set up to create the illusion that the left half of the table is much lower then the right half, so that it looks like there is a cliff in the middle of it. There *is* a real cliff in the middle of the table since half of the table is actually about three feet higher than the other half; however, the entire table is covered by a level piece of clear glass: on the "shallow" side the glass is flush with the table while on the "deep" side, the glass is three feet higher than the table. The infant is placed on the shallow side while the child's mother stands on the floor by the apparently deeper side. To get to his mother, the infant has to crawl over the apparent cliff. If the infant is unwilling to do so, the experimenter infers that the infant is capable of perceiving depth.

122. E

The mere exposure effect states that repeated exposure to a stimulus increases one's liking of it. In terms of pictures of yourself, the mere exposure effect would suggest that you would prefer a mirror image of yourself, since that is the image of yourself you most often see. On the other hand, since you are used to seeing the *true* image of your friend, the mere exposure effect would suggest that you would prefer to look at the true image.

123. B

Multiple personality disorder is characterized by two or more personalities that recurrently take control of a person's behavior. DSM-IV now calls this disorder *dissociative identity disorder*. In dissociative disorders, the person avoids stress by dissociating from his or her own personal identity. You might have been tempted by choice (A), but, remember, multiple personality disorder and schizophrenia are not the same thing! Regarding choice (E), multiple personality disorder is not a personality disorder, but is rather classified in the Axis I category.

124. D

The zone of proximal development refers to the difference between the child's performance when given no help and the child's performance when given guidance by an adult or more talented peer. Choice (B) is a theory in social psychology that says people will try to align their attitudes and their behaviors to avoid dissonance. Choice (C) can also be eliminated, since Bandura's theory is more closely associated with learning theory. Choices (A) and (E) are both strong distracters, because Piaget and Binet are prominent cognitive and intelligence theorists. You would have to remember that neither Piaget's theory of conservation or Binet's concept of mental age are directly related to

whether or not a child is given help and guidance from an adult.

125. C

Social facilitation is the improvement of performance due to the mere presence of others. Here, the presence of others improves the athlete's race time. Social influence is one of the situational factors Latané and Darley hypothesized to explain when people will help a bystander.

126. B

In negative reinforcement, the probability that the desired response will be performed is increased by taking away or preventing something undesirable whenever the desired response is made. There are two types of negative reinforcement: escape and avoidance. In escape, the behavior removes something undesirable. In avoidance, the organism gets a warning that an aversive stimulus will occur soon, and the appropriate response avoids the aversive stimulus. The warning here is that without studying, the student will get a bad grade on the test, and the student studies in order to avoid the bad grade. Since avoidance is a type of negative reinforcement, choice (B) is the correct answer.

127. D

This is a pretty standard question that asks you differentiate between the various aspects of classical conditioning. The unconditioned stimulus is the electric shock. The shock automatically elicits the unconditioned response of foot withdrawal. Before each shock is presented, a green light is flashed. Eventually, through conditioning, the green light alone will be able to elicit the conditioned response of foot withdrawal. Therefore, the green light is the conditioned stimulus.

128. B

Correctly answering this question required knowledge of Robert Zajonc's approach to social facilitation. Social facilitation is the improvement of performance due to the mere presence of others. However, social facilitation doesn't always work. Sometimes the presence of others actually worsens performance. Zajonc argued that the presence of others increases arousal. The increase in arousal enhances the emission of dominant responses, responses that are stronger or more likely to be emitted. Knowing this, you could have eliminated choices (A), (C), and (D), leaving you with choices (B) and (E). The key to deciding between (B) and (E) is whether dominant responses are always correct. When we are just starting to learn something new (e.g., learning how to play a piano), the correct responses are not likely to be dominant since they are new . If you try to perform on a piano before you've really learned your stuff, you will likely find that the presence of others will make you play worse. Hence, in the presence of others, the performance of correct responses will only improve when they are the dominant responses.

129. E

Vicarious learning is learning that takes place without the person's own behavior being reinforced. In other words, it is learning that takes place by observing the consequences of other people's behaviors. Vicarious learning is an important part of Bandura's social learning theory. Choice (B), learning to learn, is a phrase to associate with Harry Harlow; it refers to the finding that as an animal gets more experienced at performing a particular task, it tends to get better and better at performing the task.

130. E

PKU, or phenylketonuria, is a degenerative disease of the nervous system that occurs when a child lacks the enzyme needed to digest phenylalanine, an amino acid found in milk and other foods. Today, infants are given an early test for PKU. With a strict diet low in phenylalanine, children with PKU are able to avoid the severe effects of the disease. It's less easy to avoid the severe effects of the other disorders, although environmental manipulation can, in some cases, help.

131. C

Feature detection involves breaking the incoming stimulus down into parts and analyzing the parts to see what features the stimulus possesses. From this analysis, we can determine what the stimulus is. This kind of processing, that begins by analyzing the stimulus, is bottom-up processing. Top-down processing, choice (A), stresses the role of expectations and other higher processes in stimulus recognition. In top-down processing, we start with the big picture. Choice (B), ROC, or receiver-operating-characteristic, curves are a part of *signal* detection theory, not *feature* detection. As for the answer choices that were probably easier to eliminate, transduction is the translation of physical energy into neural impulses and field dependence is a personality characteristic.

132. A

The key to answering this question correctly was remembering the memory aid for the effects of lesions in various areas of the hypothalamus. Hyperphagia is a condition where an animal consumes abnormally large amounts of food. So then, hyperphagia can be thought of as being *very hungry*, or VH: the initials for *ventromedial hypothalamus*. Aphagia is a condition where the animal does not eat. Aphagia can be thought of as *lacking hunger*, or LH, which are the initials for *lateral hypothalamus*. Note that these memory aids refer to the effects of lesions and not to the normal functioning of these areas. Don't confuse aphagia with aphasia, choice (B). Aphasia is an impairment in speech production and/or comprehension. Finally, adipsia, choice (E), is a condition where the animal does not drink any liquids. This condition is related to damage to the lateral hypothalamus, not the ventromedial hypothalamus.

133. A

Consistency theories hold to the assumption that we seek a consistent and coherent system of thoughts and beliefs. If a person hates cigarette smoking, but falls in love with a smoker, it would be an inconsistency. If he is aware of this inconsistency, then, according to consistency theories, he will try to resolve it. Inconsistencies are often resolved by changing attitudes. Two of the most well-known consistency theories are Heider's balance theory and Festinger's cognitive dissonance theory.

134. B

Before we discuss the correct choice, let's briefly discuss the incorrect answer choices. The limbic system *is* found in mammals and was actually the *second* part of the brain to evolve: the brainstem, consisting of the hindbrain and midbrain, was the first. The limbic system is not a part of the reticular activating system. Finally, lesions to the limbic system tend to impair memory and/or emotional expression, not sensorimotor processing. In fact, lesions to the part of the limbic system known as the septum can lead to aggressive, vicious behavior in response to stimuli that wouldn't ordinarily cause violent behavior. Therefore, the correct answer is choice (B).

135. D

According to Kurt Lewin, a personality can be divided dynamically into ever-changing regions. Each individual region contains an attitude towards something, e.g., one region might house your attitude towards your father while another might house your attitude about baseball. Boundaries between each region can either be fluid or rigid. Fluid boundaries indicate more differentiation and permeable connections. Differentiation refers to the ability to break up concepts into smaller concepts. Rigid boundaries on the other hand, indicate little differentiation and influence between systems and often indicate, for example, high stress situations or mental retardation.

136. D

Imprinting can be defined as the rapid formation of an attachment bond between an organism and an object in the environment. Many researchers who have studied imprinting consider it to have an innate component. Certainly, the fact that imprinting occurs so quickly and so early in life strongly suggests an innate component.

137. C

Dissonance occurs when one's attitudes and behaviors clash. The only answer choice where attitude and behavior clash is choice (C). Here the attitude *I don't really like her* clashes with the behavior *I spend time with her*. This clash is clearly dissonant, and Festinger would predict that if the person continues to spend time with her, his attitude is likely to change. None of the other answer choices are clearly dissonant.

138. A

Stranger anxiety, the name implies, is an intense fear of strangers. It reaches its peak as the attachment bond between the infant and the primary caregiver strengthens, sometime during the last third of the first year. Choice (B), the Moro reflex, occurs when an infant reacts to an abrupt movement of his head by flinging out his arms, extending his fingers, and then bringing his arms back to his body. The Moro reflex usually disappears after four months. Choice (C) is also incorrect. Children don't master conservation until the concrete operational period (about age seven). Abilities in the zone of proximal development are those abilities that are in the process of development but which are not yet fully developed. Children don't enter and exit this zone, abilities do. Regarding choice (E), the 10-month old infant is likely to be in the oral, not the anal, stage.

139. E

Females with only one X chromosome, that is, with an XO chromosome combination, have Turner's syndrome. Turner's syndrome results in a failure to develop secondary sex characteristics and in some cognitive impairment. Choice (B), Klinefelter's syndrome, appears in males who possess an extra X chromosome. These males would have an XXY configuration and are sterile and may be mentally retarded. Choice (C), Down's syndrome, is a form of severe mental retardation that results from having an extra 21st chromosome (technically called trisomy 21). Finally, PKU, choice (A), is a degenerative disease of the nervous system that occurs when a child lacks the enzyme needed to break down phenylalanine, an amino acid found in milk and other foods.

140. A

Neurosis is not a category of mental disorder in the DSM-IV. Neurosis is really a theoretical term used by Freud to denote certain intrapsychic conflicts between the id and the ego's and superego's prohibitions. Because the DSM-IV strives to be atheoretical, it does not include neurosis as a category of mental disorder. Choice (B) is incorrect because the hallmark of neurosis is not impaired reality testing, but anxiety. As to choice (C), the use of the term *neurosis* goes back about 100 years before Kraepelin. General paresis, choice (D), is a serious brain disease caused by untreated syphilis. Finally, Von Meduna used ECT (electroconvulsive therapy), choice (E), to treat schizophrenia, not neurosis.

141. B

The foot-in-the-door effect suggests that compliance with a small request increases the likelihood of compliance with a larger request. So here, the small request is to stay on the line and answer a few questions. If the foot-in-the-door effect holds true, the customers who comply with this small request will be more likely to comply with the larger request (changing their long-distance carrier). The foot-in-the-door effect is usually contrasted with the door-in-the-face effect. This effect is one in which people who refuse a large initial request are more likely to agree to a later smaller request.

142. E

State-dependent learning suggests that recall will be better if your psychological or physical state at the time of recall is the same as your state when you learned the material. State-dependent learning suggests, therefore, that John is more likely to remember the coworker's name when he is drunk than when he is sober.

143. B

Spearman proposed that there were two types of factors that affected performance on intelligence tests: a general factor, or *g*; and specific factors, or *s*. The general factor is largely responsible for a person's test score and greatly affects performance on all intellectual activities, but each individual activity also has an *s* factor associated with it. Spearman saw the *g* factor as being most important. You might have been tempted by choice (E), but L. L. Thurstone identified seven primary mental abilities, whose importance depended on the particular task. Binet and Wechsler, choices (C) and (D) respectively, both developed intelligence tests.

144. B

Witkin endeavored to draw a relationship between an individual's personality and the way she perceived the world. Witkin classified people according to their degree of field dependence. At one pole of the continuum is the capacity to make specific responses to perceived specific stimuli (field independence). At the other pole is a more diffuse response to a perceived mass of somewhat undifferentiated stimuli (field dependence). The origin of Witkin's theory is found in the rod and frame test of perception. Part of the apparatus is a square frame that can be oriented at various angles and another part is a rod suspended in the square frame that can also be oriented at various angles. The task is for the subject to orient the rod so that it is vertical. Field-dependent individuals will be unable to screen out the irrelevant information in the surrounding field, namely the orientation of the square, and will tend to orient the rod with respect to the square. Field-independent individuals, on the other hand, will generally be able to ignore the orientation of the square and will tend to orient the rod to the true vertical.

145. D

Jimmy generalized his bad experience from one particular boat (at summer camp) to all boats. This is an example of stimulus generalization. Answer choice (B), stimulus discrimination, is the flip side of stimulus generalization. We would have an example of stimulus discrimination if Jimmy had no problems riding the

ferry but still refused to ride in boats at summer camp. Flooding, answer choice (C), is a therapy for phobias that forces clients to confront, in real life, their fears. Forcing Jimmy to ride on the ferry would be an example of flooding.

146. B

Freud hypothesized five stages of psychosexual development. In order from first to last, they are oral, anal, phallic (Oedipal), latency, and genital.

147. D

A mental set is a tendency to keep repeating solutions that worked in other situations. The Luchins water-jar problem is used to assess the effect of mental sets on problem solving. The subject has to figure out how to obtain varying amounts of water (without using measuring cups) using jars of specified capacities. In one variation, all the problems can be solved using a rather complicated method, but the last problem can also be solved relatively simply. Most subjects will not even see the simple solution to the final problem, and will instead continue to use the relatively complicated method because of their mental set.

148. E

The population of interest is all the students at the university. Clearly, it would be impractical to use the whole population in this research, so instead, the researcher decides to use a subset of the population: a sample. Since the researcher in the question stem is selecting a sample, not a population, choice (D) is incorrect. To select her sample, she stands at the entrance of the performing arts building and selects only from students who enter that building. Therefore, students who do not have reason to enter that building on that day have a zero percent chance of being selected. Because the defining characteristic of a random sample is that every member of the population has an equal chance of being selected for the sample, choice (A) is not the correct answer. Furthermore, since the researcher is likely to pick mostly performing arts students, her sample will most likely not be representative of her population of interest. Therefore, choice (C) is not the correct answer. Finally, no mention is made in the question stem about any subject characteristic for the sample to be stratified on. Therefore, choice (B) is not the correct answer.

149. C

A correlation of +1.00 or −1.00 indicates a perfect correlation. That is, knowing the value of one variable allows you to predict with absolute certainty the corresponding value of the other variable. Therefore, choice (C) is correct and choice (E) is incorrect. demonstrates animals can not learn to perform any response: there are biological constraints on learning.

150. A

Petty and Cacioppo developed the elaboration likelihood model of persuasion. This model distinguishes between a central and a peripheral route to persuasion. If an issue is important or meaningful to us, it is related to the central route. If an issue is not important to us, we adopt a peripheral route. Not surprisingly, Petty and Cacioppo found that subjects follow a persuader's argument more attentively when dealing with central issues.

151. A

The prodromal phase refers to the period of poor adjustment that a patient goes through prior to being diagnosed with schizophrenia. This phase is followed by the active phase in which a patient exhibits the symptoms typical of schizophrenia. The length of the prodromal phase is fundamental to the distinction between process and reactive schizophrenia. A lengthy prodromal phase is indicative of process schizophrenia while a brief prodromal phase is associated with reactive schizophrenia.

152. B

Instinctual drift refers to the tendency of animals to return to innate behavioral propensities after they have been conditioned to behave in a different way. Therefore, it would be advisable to develop a training program that takes biological predispositions for certain behaviors into account. Choice (B) is a good paraphrase of this idea.

153. C

Arnold Gesell was an important force in early-to-mid 20th century developmental psychology. He believed that maturation (nature), and not the environment (nurture), was primary in development. None of the other answer choices held such an extreme maturationist viewpoint. In fact, choice (B), John Locke, took the opposite view and believed that the newborn was a blank slate (a *tabula rasa*) just waiting to be written on by experience.

154. B

The overjustification effect is an implication of self-perception theory. It states that if you reward people for something they already like doing, they may stop liking it. So for instance, the child in the question stem works in the garden. When she thinks about why she does it, she concludes that she gardens because she enjoys it. However, if her parents start paying her, she's liable to start thinking that she works in the garden not because she likes it, but because her parents pay her. Hence, she is likely to start thinking that she doesn't like it. The overjustification effect, therefore, strongly suggests that the parents ought not to pay their child for gardening, because doing so is liable to decrease her liking for gardening.

155. E

Dorothea Dix was a zealous advocate of treating the hospitalized mentally ill in a humane way. Her campaign was instrumental in improving the lives of the mentally ill in the United States.

156. C

The genotype is the genetic complement of an individual. The phenotype is the collection of expressed traits (in this case, we're talking about physical traits, not psychological traits). In this example, the fetus has one X chromosome and one Y chromosome, so it is genetically male: it has a masculine genotype. This immediately eliminates choices (A) and (D). In genetically male fetuses, certain genes on the Y chromosome initiate production of androgens not long after conception. Normal development of the testes and penis then proceeds. However, if the fetus does not produce androgens, development will follow the female pattern, regardless of chromosomal sex. Hence, the infant will have a feminine phenotype. A hermaphrodite, choice (E), has both ovarian and testicular tissue. Some of the cells in the hermaphrodite's body have two X chromosomes and some have an X and a Y chromosome. Therefore, you can't identify a true hermaphrodite's sex even on a genetic level.

157. B

Your strategy in this question should be to group answer choices into clusters. In this case, cluster (A)-(C)-(D) contains choices which sound more or less similar to the original sentence, but which have introduced changes in meaning. Common sense can eliminate choice (E). Recall that long-term memory is organized semantically rather than phonemically. Bartlett's reconstruction theory is also pertinent to this question. We remember the gist of something and we reconstruct the details around that. We're likely to change the wording so that the gist remains unaltered while substituting common words such as *bottle* for less common words like *flask*.

158. D

The lateral geniculate nucleus, located in the thalamus, is involved in vision. *Ablation* in neuropsychology means the removal or destruction of a part of the brain. You might have chosen (A) if you confused the lateral geniculate nucleus with the medial geniculate nucleus. The latter is also in the thalamus, but is involved in audition, not vision.

159. B

Heuristics are short-cuts and rules of thumb that humans (and computers) can use in making decisions. When heuristics are programmed into computer simulations of chess, the computer can use them to help decide on its next move. This allows the computer to make much faster decisions than when it uses the brute force method.

160. A

Reliability is based on a correlation between test scores. Therefore, a reliability of 0.00 indicates that the test is not at all reliable. The standard error of measurement is a measure of how much, on average, people's obtained scores vary from their "true scores." Reliability and the standard error of measurement are intricately related. Thus, if our test had a perfect reliability (+1.00), it would have a standard error of measurement of 0.00. The lower the reliability gets, the higher the standard error of measurement gets. Regarding choice (D), remember: high reliability is necessary but not sufficient for high validity. If a test has high reliability, it may be valid; but if a test has low reliability, it can not be valid.

161. E

Köhler believed that the chimp's behavior was insightful because the chimp used items in the environment in a novel way. Trial-and-error learning was Thorndike's explanation for how his cats escaped from their puzzle boxes. A fixed-action pattern is a stereotyped behavior that does not have to be learned by the animal and which is triggered by a sign stimulus. Classical conditioning, discovered by Pavlov, has to do with the pairing of a conditioned stimulus and an unconditioned stimulus so that, eventually, the conditioned stimulus comes to elicit a conditioned response. Instinctual drift refers to certain built-in, instinctual, ways of behaving which are able to override behaviors learned through operant conditioning. Instinctual drift is associated with the work of Keller and Marion Breland.

162. A

In a double-blind experiment, neither the subjects nor the researchers interacting with them know which groups received which level of the independent variable. Answer choice (C) describes a single-blind experiment. Answer choice (D) is incorrect because blinding has to do with the independent variable and not the dependent variable. The Hawthorne effect has to do with the effects of being observed. Double-blinding does not counteract the Hawthorne effect. Double-blinding does, however, minimize the possible effects of experimenter bias.

163. A

Primary prevention is concerned with changing conditions that cause mental disorders and also with establishing conditions that foster mental health, like a program to increase self esteem. Choice (B), secondary prevention, refers to attempts to reduce the impact or duration of a problem. Choice (C), tertiary prevention, is aimed at restoring someone to mental health after a breakdown has occurred.

164. C

The fundamental attribution error is the finding that observers tend to overestimate dispositional factors and underestimate situational factors when inferring the causes of other's behaviors. When John himself yells at the TV, he attributes his yelling to situational factors, yet when John sees Andrea yelling at the TV, he attributes her yelling to her personality.

165. C

Maslow proposed that needs were organized hierarchically. Thus, people would strive for the higher-level needs only when their lower-level needs were met. Maslow's lowest levels of needs are the physiological and safety needs: food, shelter, and so on. Following this are the belongingness and love needs. Above these are the esteem needs (approval and recognition), cognitive needs, aesthetic needs, and finally, the highest order of need: self-actualization. Self-actualization refers to the need to realize one's potential to the fullest. According to Maslow, self-actualized people are more likely than non-self-actualized people to have what he called peak experiences, profound and deeply moving experiences in a person's life that have important and lasting effects on the individual.

166. E

The Babinski reflex in infants consists of extending the toes when the sole of the foot is stimulated. The grasping reflex, choice (B), is sometimes called the palmar reflex, and choice (D) refers to the Moro reflex.

167. B

Frequency theory suggests that the basilar membrane vibrates as a whole in response to incoming stimulation, and that the rate of vibration equals the frequency of the stimulus. Further, this vibration rate is then directly translated into the appropriate number of neural impulses per second. The problem with this theory is that we know neurons cannot fire more than 1,000 times per second, due to their refractory period. However, since we can discriminate between frequencies higher than 1,000 Hz, there must be another mechanism involved in pitch perception. The solution, put forth by Wever and Bray, was that high rates of neural firing can be maintained if nerve fibers work together. This is the volley theory. By staggering their firing rates, neurons can code frequencies higher than 1,000 Hz. The volley principle uses the same basic idea as the frequency theory (that pitch is coded by the frequency of neural firing), just improves it a bit. Helmholtz's place-resonance theory, choice (A), says that pitch is coded not on the basis of the frequency of the vibration of the basilar membrane, but on which part of the basilar membrane vibrates; this theory stands in opposition to the frequency theory. The traveling wave theory, choice (C), suggests that the whole basilar membrane vibrates in response to the stimulus, and that frequency is coded based on the place of *maximal* displacement along the basilar membrane. The remaining two answers, choices (D) and (E), are concerned with vision and could thus have been eliminated from consideration fairly quickly.

168. D

When we're talking about investigating the effects social behaviors have on fitness, we're talking about sociobiology, and the founder of sociobiology was E. O. Wilson. Both John Garcia and Keller Breland would be more interested in the effect that inborn capacities and tendencies have on learning. Francis Galton was interested in the inheritance of various traits and was an advocate of eugenics. John Bowlby is associated with research on attachment.

169. B

Fluid intelligence is the ability to quickly grasp relationships in novel situations and make correct deductions from them. In contrast, crystallized intelligence is the ability to understand relationships or solve problems that depend on knowledge acquired as a result of schooling or other life experiences.

170. C

When a researcher randomly assigns subjects to groups, she can assume that subject variables, such as IQ, will randomize out, leaving the different groups with, on average, approximately the same IQ. Holding IQ relatively constant is another possible solution, as would be using a matched-subjects design, matching subjects on IQ. Adding IQ as another independent variable is another possible strategy. This strategy would allow the researcher to analyze the effect of IQ on her dependent variable, and would also allow her to see whether there is an interaction between IQ and her other independent variable. However, answer choice (C), running a double-blind experiment, would not help the researcher deal with the problem of varying IQs.

171. E

In a classic study, Lewin divided leadership styles into three types: autocratic, democratic, and laissez-faire. Lewin found that groups led by democratic leaders tended to be most satisfying and most cohesive. Choices (B) and (C) are two of the three styles of parenting described by Baumrind.

172. B

Gilligan's theory is centered around the idea that women adopt an interpersonal orientation that is neither more or less mature than the rule-bound, principle-bound thinking of men. Both Kohlberg and Gilligan use a progression of stages to describe moral development.

173. C

Follicle-stimulating hormone is secreted by the so-called "master gland": the pituitary gland. This hormone stimulates the growth of the ovarian follicle, a small protective sphere surrounding the ovum.

174. C

In the empirical criterion-keying approach to test development, items are not selected for inclusion in the test on the basis of some theory. Rather, items are selected on the basis of whether they differentiate between criterion groups. Here, the investigator wants to assess entrepreneurship, so he wants to use those items which best differentiate between those whose small businesses have succeeded and those whose small businesses have failed. Those items that successfully differentiate between the two groups are included in the final test; those that don't are discarded. You might have been fooled by choice (A), because the investigator is splitting his group of item testers into two halves.

175. B

For Bartlett, memory was a reconstructive process that acted on the memorized material on the basis of the person's schemata. Specifically, the better the material fit into the subjects' schemata, the better the material would be memorized. Obviously, a story from one's own culture is more likely to fit into pre-established schemata than a story from a strange and unfamiliar culture.

176. E

In a typical autoshaping experiment, a pigeon is placed in a Skinner box, but instead of performing operant conditioning, the experimenter performs classical conditioning. The unconditioned stimulus (UCS) is grain and the conditioned stimulus (CS) is a light shining on the key. Pigeons naturally peck at grain, so the pecking is the unconditioned response (UCR). After the CS and the UCS become associated, the light shining on the key is able to elicit a conditioned response (CR) of key pecking. This result was important because key pecking had generally been produced by operant conditioning. However, autoshaping showed that even key pecking has a classically-conditioned component. Regarding answer choice (A), autoshaping does not provide evidence that operant and classical conditioning work in similar ways—it just suggests that they interact. While conditioned suppression experiments (choice (B)) have shown that classically conditioned fear can suppress operantly conditioned responses, and this also suggests an interaction between classical and operant conditioning, autoshaping and conditioned suppression are two different phenomena. Avoidance (choice (C)) is a type of operant conditioning where the organism receives a warning of an imminent aversive stimulus and can avoid experiencing the aversive stimulus by making the appropriate response.

177. D

Categorical perception refers to the ability to ignore differences in sound that do not denote differences in meaning while attending to those differences in sound that do denote differences in meaning. In the question stem, the female and the male say "bit" differently. But that difference does not denote a difference in meaning, and the adult knows this. Furthermore, the adult also knows that the difference between the /b/ sound and the /p/ sound *does* denote a difference in meaning.

178. C

If the gene for blue eyes is recessive, then in order for a child to have blue eyes, she must have two blue-eye genes, one from each of her parents. Note that this does not mean that both parents must have blue eyes. It is possible that each parent might have one blue-eye gene and one brown-eye gene. Therefore, both parents would have brown eyes, since the gene for brown eyes would be dominant. Based on just this information, we know that choice (C) is the correct answer and that choices (A) and (D) must be wrong. Choice (E) is one possibility if the child has blue eyes, but it is also possible that one or both parents have two blue-eye genes.

179. D

Signal detection theory suggests that two factors enter into sensory decision-making: response bias and sensitivity. Response bias refers to the tendency of subjects to favor responding in a particular way due to nonsensory factors, such as beliefs or attitudes. Sensitivity refers to how well the subjects can sense the stimulus (in the situation presented in the question stem, sensitivity refers to how well the subjects can sense changes in the stimulus). Unlike the earlier psychophysics, signal detection theory gives us a way to measure both response bias and sensitivity.

180. D

The prisoner's dilemma is used to assess cooperation and competition. The Robber's Cave experiment is the name of an experiment Sherif performed to investigate intergroup cooperation and competition, but it is not generally used as a model for assessment.

181. E

When social pressure becomes so blatant that a person's sense of freedom is threatened, the person will tend to try to reassert her sense of freedom. This is reactance. In choice (E), the mother is threatening her child's sense of freedom (not that this is necessarily a bad thing, but that's besides the point). In response, the child reasserts her freedom by smoking. We don't know the toddler's response in (B), so we don't know if there is reactance there, and the other choices don't demonstrate the opposite reactions characteristic of this response.

182. E

Julian Rotter suggested that people tend to hold either an internal locus of control or an external locus of control. People who have an internal locus of control tend to believe that they control their own destinies. People who have an external locus of control, tend to believe that outside events or chance control their destinies. If Jenny has an external locus of control she might very well believe that her grade on the exam will be due to fate. So, Roman numeral III can provide an explanation for Jenny's behavior. Self-handicapping provides a way to protect one's self-image, especially when one's performance on a task is highly tied up with one's self-esteem. By giving oneself a ready excuse to fail, any failure can be attributed to the excuse (a situational attribution) rather than to some personal deficiency (a dispositional attribution). Therefore, Roman numeral option II belongs in the correct answer choice. So, since the correct answer choice must include both II and III, the correct answer must be choice (E). Regarding Roman numeral option I, self-monitoring refers to the degree to which you monitor your own behavior so that it conforms to the situation. High self-monitors care deeply about the impression they make

on others and constantly try to change their behavior to fit the situation. It is unclear how self-monitoring can explain Jenny's behavior, at least not without being given additional information.

183. A

The Premack principle states that more preferred behaviors can be used to reinforce less preferred behaviors. Here, the less preferred behavior is doing the homework and the more preferred behavior is going out to play.

184. D

The method of presenting different messages simultaneously to the two ears is called dichotic listening. When the subject is asked to repeat one of those messages as she hears it, it's called shadowing. Shadowing is used to study selective attention.

185. D

The depth-of-processing theory is another name for the levels-of-processing theory. According to this theory, there are three ways information can be processed: the first is physical, by focusing on its appearance and the size and shape of the letters; the second is acoustical, by focusing on the sound combinations the words have; the third is semantic, by focusing on the meaning of the words. The three ways demand different amounts of mental effort. The first way, the shallowest way, demands relatively little effort. The third way, the deepest way, demands a lot of effort. The deeper the processing, and thus, the greater the effort, the better your memory of the material. If you're thinking about how you can use each of the items in the list, you have to think about what the word means, and are at the deepest levels of precessing.

186. B

A stereotaxic instrument is a specialized clamp that holds the animal's head in place. It also helps the researcher implant electrodes at specified coordinates in the brain. This allows researchers to implant electrodes in areas of the brain they can't directly see.

187. C

ROC stands for Receiver-Operating Characteristic. ROC curves are employed by many users of signal detection theory to graphically summarize a subject's responses. You might have been tempted by choices (A) or (B), since they both have to do with psychophysics, but signal detection theory places little stock in the concept of a threshold.

188. D

The diathesis-stress model suggests that mental disorder is caused by excessive stress operating on a person who has a predisposition towards developing a specific mental disorder. The hypothesis presented in the question stem suggests that mood disorder is caused by excessive stress (a separation) operating on someone with a predisposition to mood disorder (the genetic disturbance).

189. D

When presented with a question asking you to choose the appropriate significance test, the first question to ask yourself is "what kind of data do we have?" What we want to know is whether these data are amounts or categories. In this instance, a subject is asked what his eye color is and what his political affiliation is. These are categories, not amounts. Therefore, we want to do a chi-square test. Choice (C), the goodness of fit test, is a special kind of chi-square test that you can use when data are classified on only one variable. However, here, data are classified on the basis of two variables: affiliation *and* eye color. Therefore, a goodness of fit test is not appropriate. Choices (A), (B), and (E) are all tests you can use when the data are amounts. The t-test is used when you have only two groups, while ANOVA must be used if you have more than two groups. Both the t-test and ANOVA are discussed further in the chapter on statistics. ANCOVA is similar to ANOVA, except that ANCOVA is able to statistically remove the effects of confounding variables.

190. A

The crucial distinction here is between critical periods and sensitive periods. A critical period is the only time in development when a particular environmental factor can have an effect on the development of a particular ability. A sensitive period is the time in development when a particular environmental factor has a maximal effect on the development of a particular ability. As we

have learned from Genie and other language-deprived children, children need to be exposed to language if language is to develop normally. If there were a critical period for language development, then exposure to language after a certain age would have no effect. If there were a sensitive period for language development, then exposure to language after a certain age would have some effect. Generally, this certain age for language development is seen as the onset of puberty. Genie was discovered after she had reached puberty. The fact that Genie was able to learn some language suggests that the idea of a sensitive period for language is correct and also argues strongly against the existence of a critical period for language.

191. A

Karl von Frisch discovered that honey bees were able to use special movement patterns, often called dances, to communicate to their fellow hive members the direction and distance of a food source. Indeed, this work was so startling that von Frisch won a Nobel Prize for it. The person who studied taste aversion in rats was John Garcia; the people who studied the misbehavior of raccoons were Keller and Marion Breland; Niko Tinbergen studied aggression in male sticklebacks; and, finally, both Tinbergen and Konrad Lorenz studied egg-rolling in gulls.

192. B

As the name implies, in electroconvulsive therapy (ECT) an electric current is passed through the patient's brain. Although originally developed to treat schizophrenia (unsuccessfully, by the way), ECT is now used mostly to treat serious depressions.

193. C

Metamemory refers to a person's ability to think about and monitor her own memory processes. The task of describing how the subject memorized the list of words is a metamemory task.

194. E

Question 194 required you to differentiate between several different projective tests (we can eliminate choices (B) and (C), which are personality inventories). The key to discriminating between the remaining choices is to keep in mind that the sound is ambiguous and is not meant to suggest anything specific to the subject. Both the Blacky pictures and the items on the

Thematic Apperception Test (TAT) are specific pictures of objects (e.g., a TAT item might show a boy staring at a violin). Therefore, they can be eliminated from contention. On the other hand, in the Rorschach test, the clients are given very ambiguous ink blots and are asked to describe what they see. Of the five answer choices, therefore, the Rorschach is most analogous to the situation presented in the question stem.

195. E

Latent learning is learning that is present but not visible. More specifically, latent learning is learning that is not revealed through behavior. If not all learning is revealed through behavior, then we need to make a distinction between learning and behavior. Since another word for behavior is *performance*, latent learning depends on there being a distinction between learning and performance.

196. C

In a cross-sectional study, different subjects are studied at different ages, and all these subjects are studied at about the same time. For example, if a researcher were interested in looking at the relationship between weight and age, she might take ten 5-year olds, ten 10-year olds, and ten 15-year olds, weigh them, and then compare the weights of the 5-year olds, 10-year olds, and 15-year olds. The crucial point is that each subject is measured only once. Hence, her study, a cross-sectional one, would be an example of a between-subjects design. The defining characteristic of a between-subjects design is that each subject is measured only once on the variable(s) of interest, so a cross-sectional study can be considered to be an example of a between-subjects design. An alternative to the cross-sectional design is the longitudinal design in which, to use our example, the researcher would select one group of subjects and study their changes in weight as they age. In fact, this is an example of a within-subjects design, so choices (A) and (D) are both incorrect. Choice (B) is also incorrect. It is possible that our researcher could have matched subjects on, say, the average weight of their parents, but matching is not necessary in a cross-sectional study. Finally, because the subjects in a cross-sectional design are not randomly assigned to the different groups by the experimenter, but are assigned to groups on the basis of age, a cross-sectional design cannot be a true experiment. Therefore, choice (E) is incorrect.

197. A

A basic assumption of social-exchange theory is that a person weighs the rewards and costs of interacting with another person. The more the rewards outweigh the costs, the greater the attraction to the other person will be. Equity theory proposes that we consider not only our own costs and rewards but also the costs and rewards of the other person. We prefer that our ratio of costs to rewards be the same as the other person's ratio. The gain-loss principle states that an evaluation that changes will have more impact than an evaluation that remains constant. The theory of need complementarity suggests that people choose relationships so that they mutually satisfy each other's needs. Social comparison theory suggests that affiliation is related to people's needs to evaluate their own opinions and abilities.

198. B

In bipolar disorder, there are instances of both depression and mania. In fact, the former name for bipolar disorder was manic-depression. You might have been tempted by choice (E). It is true that cyclothymic disorder is similar to bipolar disorder, but they are different disorders. In bipolar disorder, the mood swings tend to be more severe than in cyclothymic disorder. Bipolar disorder is better treated by lithium than by Valium (Valium is a minor tranquilizer used to reduce anxiety) and choice (C) is incorrect because bipolar disorder is not a schizophrenic disorder.

199. E

Walter Mischel states that human behavior is largely determined by the characteristics of the situation rather than by those of the person (i.e., by traits). Therefore, he would be likely to criticize trait theory (and has done so vigorously). Choice (A), Raymond Cattell, was a trait theorist so he would not be likely to criticize trait theory. Choice (B), William Sheldon, was technically a type theorist, but type theorists are very similar to trait theorists. Choice (C), Starke Hathaway, was one of the developers of the MMPI. Since the goal of the MMPI is to assess people's trait structures, Hathaway would certainly not argue against trait theory. Finally, choice (D), James McKeen Cattell, was an early psychologist who did much of his work before the development of modern trait theory. Cattell's two major contributions to psychology are that he focused on individual differences and that he helped introduce mental testing to the United States.

200. E

In a question of the "all of the following EXCEPT" format, we're looking for the answer choice that does not belong. In question 200, that's choice (E). The rod and frame apparatus has been used to study field dependence. All the other answer choices have been used to study perceptual development. The visual cliff, devised by Eleanor Gibson and Richard Walk, has been used to study the development of depth perception. Habituation and preferential looking allow researchers to infer whether or not their infant subjects perceive differences among stimuli. Finally, animal experiments have been used to shed additional light on the nature-nurture issue in perceptual development.

201. C

McGuire has demonstrated that people's beliefs can be inoculated against an attack of persuasive communication against those beliefs. McGuire tested inoculation theory by using what he called cultural truisms: beliefs that are seldom questioned. Since these beliefs are seldom questioned, they are very vulnerable to attack. According to McGuire, people can be psychologically inoculated against an oncoming attack by first exposing them to a weakened attack. These are known as refuted counter-arguments. In experimental tests, McGuire found that inoculation can be quite effective in increasing the resistance of cultural truisms to subsequent attacks.

202. A

An independent variable is the variable whose effect is being studied. The dependent variable is the variable presumably dependent on the independent variable. In other words, the dependent variable is the response that is expected to vary with changes in the independent variable. A *level* is a value that an independent variable has in a particular study. In the situation described in the question stem, the researcher is interested in the effect that the number of bystanders has on helping behavior. Therefore, there is one dependent variable: the helping behavior of the subjects. There is also one independent variable: number of bystanders. However, there are three levels of that independent variable: bystanders, bystanders, and bystanders.

203. C

"*Roy G. Biv*" is an acronym formed by taking the first letter of each of the seven rainbow colors (red, orange,

yellow, green, blue, indigo, violet). In general, it is easier to remember only one piece of information (Roy G. Biv) than seven.

204. D

An androgynous person has a high number of both masculine and feminine characteristics. Transsexual people, choice (A), are those who do not accept their anatomical gender and wish to have the characteristics of the opposite sex. Many transsexuals seek sex reassignment surgery. Bisexual people, choice (E), are those who are sexually attracted to both females and males.

205. B

All of the answer choices are archetypes proposed by Carl Jung. However, the correct answer is choice (B). Let's begin by looking at the wrong answer choices. The persona, choice (A), is a mask which is adopted by the person in response to the demands of social convention. The shadow, choice (D), consists of the animal instincts which humans inherited in their evolution from lower forms of life. The self, choice (E), represents the person's striving for unity. None of these are correct, so that leaves us with choices (B) and (C): the anima and animus, respectively. The anima is the feminine archetype in men while the animus is the masculine archetype in women.

206. C

Free association is the fundamental rule of psychoanalysis. In free association, a person says whatever comes to his mind regardless of how personal, painful, or seemingly irrelevant it may appear to be. The belief is that the free associations are not randomly presented but form a pattern of unconscious material which allows the analyst and patient together to reconstruct the original conflict.

207. E

Content validity refers to how well the test questions sample the different aspects of what the test is supposed to be measuring. Here, the instructor is concerned that the test adequately samples the material covered in the course. If it does, then the test has content validity. Concurrent validity, choice (A), is a type of criterion validity in which the criterion measure is obtained at approximately the same time as the test score. Discriminant validity, choice (B), is a type of construct validity that is concerned with whether performance on the test is *not* related to variables it should *not* be related to. The remaining two answer choices are methods of assessing reliability. Remember the difference between reliability and validity: reliability is concerned with how well the test measures whatever it is that it measures, while validity is concerned with how well the test measures what you want it to measure.

208. C

George Miller found that 7 (plus or minus 2) chunks of information can be stored in short-term memory. A chunk is a meaningful unit of information.

209. D Look at the figure below.

View of the brain from top

You'll notice that in both eyes, the image of the circle falls on the left half of the retina. The temporal fibers from the left eye stay on the left side of the brain, while the nasal fibers from the right eye cross over at the optic chiasm to the left side of the brain. Hence, it is the image of the circle that gets processed in the left visual cortex. If the left visual cortex is damaged, vision of objects whose images fall on the left half of each eye's retina is impaired and the correct answer is choice (D). Choices (A) and (B) are both incorrect as damage to the left visual cortex will impair vision in both eyes. Choice (C) is also incorrect, since damage to the left visual cortex will not impair vision for objects whose images fall on the right half of each eye's retina. Therefore, choice (E) is also incorrect.

210. A

In the context of animal behavior, altruism is usually defined as an action that increases the reproductive fitness of other members of the species while decreasing the reproductive fitness of the animal that performed the action. Classical Darwinian evolutionary theory tends to have a problem explaining altruism. The altruist, by definition, is decreasing his reproductive fitness. Therefore, altruism shouldn't occur. However, it does occur. Kin selection has been proposed in order to explain the existence of altruism. The theory of kin selection suggests that animals act to increase not their *reproductive* fitness, but their *inclusive* fitness. Inclusive fitness takes into account not only the number of offspring who survive to reproductive age, but also the number of other relatives who survive to reproductive age. This makes intuitive sense because animals share genes not only with their offspring, but with their other relatives (and remember that natural selection operates at the level of the gene).

211. E

The cerebral cortex is divided into two hemispheres. Each hemisphere is divided into four lobes: frontal, parietal, occipital, and temporal. Of these four, the parietal lobe is most involved in spatial processing. The lobe most associated with vision is the occipital lobe and the lobe most associated with audition (hearing) and receptive language (understanding spoken language) is the temporal lobe. Finally, the lobe most responsible for long-term planning is the frontal lobe.

212. A

A sign stimulus triggers a fixed-action pattern (abbreviated as FAP). Looking at the other answer choices, a releaser is a type of sign stimulus that triggers social behavior in other animals. A supernormal stimulus is a stimulus that more often triggers the FAP than the actual stimulus found in nature. A conditioned response (CR) is triggered by a conditioned stimulus (CS). The relationship between the CS and CR, unlike that between the sign stimulus and FAP, must be learned. Choice (E) might have tempted you. Although the animal has to learn neither the sign stimulus–FAP connection nor the UCS–UCR connection, an FAP tends to be more complex than a UCR. The FAP tends to be a whole pattern of action, such as a gull rolling an egg back to her nest, whereas the UCR tends to be a relatively simple reflex such as salivating or blinking a eye.

213. B

The halo effect is the tendency to use a general impression about another person to form judgments about specific qualities. So, when the individuals are identified as criminals, the subjects in the experiment used this information to help form their judgments of the individuals' attractiveness.

214. A

The autokinetic effect occurs in a dark room when all the subject can see is one spot of light (e.g., from a lighted cigarette) without any frame of reference. If the subject looks at this spot of light, it will appear to move erratically.

215. B

The key to correctly answering this question was to remember the difference between recall and recognition. In a recall memory task, the subject has to remember the correct response from scratch, whereas in a recognition memory task, the subject is given several possible responses and asked to choose which one is correct. In the question stem, the subjects are asked to memorize pictures. A week later, the subjects are presented with an assortment of pictures and asked to indicate the pictures they saw a week ago. This is, therefore, an example of recognition memory.

216. D

Let's look at each of the answer choices in turn—and remember, we're looking for the answer choice that is LEAST likely to be a plausible explanation. Choice (A), deindividuation, refers to a loss of self-awareness. Large crowds can lead to deindividuation and, as Zimbardo discovered, deindividuation can lead people to behave in ways they ordinarily wouldn't (such as being wild and impulsive). Choice (B), anonymity, can also lead to deindividuation, and being in a large crowd can give one a feeling of anonymity. Choice (C), diffusion of responsibility, can also have an effect here. The larger the crowd, the less likely that any individual person will feel responsible for the crowd's actions, and therefore, the more likely wild and impulsive behavior becomes. Group polarization, choice (E), refers to a tendency for group discussion to enhance the group's initial tendencies towards riskiness or caution. If members of the crowd initially have a moderate tendency to engage in wild and impulsive behavior, discussion amongst themselves could lead to an increased tendency towards wild and impulsive behavior. Finally, we come to answer choice (D). Functional autonomy is an important part of Allport's personality theory. It refers to the notion that a means to a goal may become a goal itself. It is hard to see how this can explain the correlation between the number of persons present and the likelihood of wild, impulsive behavior.

217. C

When George Kelly began to theorize about human personality, he set aside the more traditional concepts used to explain personality and suggested instead that people were intuitive scientists, who devise and test predictions about the behavior of significant people in their lives. Kelly suggested that the fundamental characteristic of human personality was that people need to know and to control their universe (i.e., the environment).

218. D

In the morning, you repeatedly try to use the phone. You repeatedly pick up the phone, hoping to hear the dial tone. In this case, hearing the dial tone is positive reinforcement. However, you never hear that dial tone, so your response of picking up the phone becomes extinguished and you stop picking up the phone. However, later on, after a period of not picking up the phone at all, you pick up the phone and try again. This is spontaneous recovery.

219. A

Maslow is the personality theorist who postulated a hierarchy of needs, with the highest need being self-actualization. Self-actualization refers to the need to realize one's potential to the fullest.

220. D

In a normal distribution, 48 percent of cases will fall between the mean and two standard deviations above the mean and 48 percent will fall between the mean and two standard deviations below the mean. Adding 48 percent and 48 percent gives you 96 percent. If you did not know the correct answer choice, you might have been able to rule out answer choice (E), because it would suggest that no observations can occur more than 2 standard deviations away from the mean, and that is not true.

For more information about how to score your practice test, go to gre.org and select Subject Tests.

Glossary

Ablation A surgically induced brain lesion.

Absolute refractory period The period that follows the onset of an action potential. During this period, a nerve impulse cannot be initiated.

Absolute threshold The minimum of stimulus energy needed to activate a sensory system.

Accommodation A principle of Piaget's theory of cognitive development. It occurs when cognitive structures are modified because new information or new experiences do not fit into existing cognitive structures.

Acetylcholine A neurotransmitter found in both central and peripheral nervous systems linked to Alzheimer's disease and used to transmit nerve impulses to the muscles.

Acrophobia An irrational fear of heights.

ACT model (Adaptive Control of Thought) A model that describes memory in terms of procedural and declarative memory.

Actor-observer effect The tendency of actors to see observer behavior as due to external factors (situational factors) and the tendency of observers to attribute actors' behaviors to internal characteristics (dispositional characteristics).

Adrenaline A hormone that increases energy available for "fight or flight" reactions (also known as epinephrine).

Afterimage A visual sensation that appears after prolonged or intense exposure to a stimulus.

Agnosia Impairments in perceptual recognition.

Agoraphobia An irrational fear of being in places or situations where escape might be difficult.

All-or-nothing law A law about nerve impulses stating that when depolarization reaches the critical threshold (−50 millivolts) the neuron is going to fire, each time, every time.

Alternate-form method In psychometrics, it is the method of using two or more different forms of a test to determine the reliability of a particular test.

Altruism A form of helping behavior where the animal's intent is to benefit other animals at some cost to itself.

Amnesia A dissociative disorder where individuals are unable to recall past experience, but this inability is not due to a neurological disorder.

Analogy of inoculation McGuire's analogy that people can be psychologically inoculated against the "attack" of persuasive communications by first exposing them to a weakened attack.

Analysis of Variance (ANOVA) A statistical method to compare the means of more than two groups by comparing the between-group variance to the within-group variance.

Anima (animus) An archetype from Jung's theory referring to the feminine behaviors in males, and the masculine behaviors in females.

Anorexia nervosa An eating disorder characterized by a refusal to maintain a minimal normal body weight.

Anterograde amnesia Memory loss for new information following brain injury.

Antisocial personality disorder A personality disorder characterized by a pattern of disregard for, and violation of, the rights of others.

Aphagia An impairment in the ability to eat.

Aphasias Language disorders, which are associated with Broca's and Wernicke's areas in the brain.

Apparent motion An illusion that occurs when two dots flashed in different locations on a screen seconds apart are perceived as one moving dot.

Apraxia An impairment in the organization of voluntary action.

Archetypes The building blocks for the collective unconscious referred to in Jung's theory of personality.

Assimilation A principle of Piaget's theory of cognitive development. It is the process of understanding new information in relation to prior knowledge, or existing schemata.

Association area Areas in the brain that integrate information from different cortical regions

Atkinson-Shiffin model A model of memory that involves three memory structures (sensory, short-term and long-term), and the processes that operate these memory structures.

Attachment bond Evidence of a preference for the primary caregiver and a wariness of strangers.

Attention-deficit/hyperactivity disorder (ADD/HD) A disorder characterized by developmentally atypical inattention and/or impulsivity-hyperactivity.

Attribution theory Fritz Heider's theory that people tend to infer the causes of other people's behavior as either dispositional (related to the individual) or situational (related to the environment).

Authoritarian parenting style A parenting style tending to use punitive control methods and lacking emotional warmth.

Authoritative parenting style A parenting style tending to have reasonably high demands for child compliance coupled with emotional warmth.

Autism A disorder whose essential features are lack of responsiveness to other people, gross impairment in communication skills, and behaviors and interests that are repetitive, inflexibly routined, and stereotyped.

Autokinetic effect An illusion that occurs when a spot of light appears to move erratically in a dark room, simply because there is no frame of reference.

Availability heuristic A decision-making short-cut that people tend to use when trying to decide how likely something is based upon how easily similar instances can be imagined.

Aversion therapy A behavioral therapy of pairing unpleasant stimuli with undesirable behavior.

Balance theory Fritz Heider's consistency theory that is concerned with balance and imbalance in the ways in which three elements are related

Behavioral contracts A therapeutic technique that is a negotiated agreement between two parties that explicitly stipulates the behavioral change that is desired and indicates consequences of certain acts.

Behavioral-stimulants A class of drugs that increase behavioral activity by increasing motor activity or by counteracting fatigue, and which are thought to stimulate receptors for dopamine, norepinephrine and serotonin.

Békésy's traveling wave theory Proposed by Von Békésy, the theory holds that high frequency sounds maximally vibrate the basilar membrane near the beginning of the cochlea close to the oval window and low frequencies maximally vibrate near the apex, or tip of the cochlea.

Between-subjects design An experimental design whereby each subject is exposed to only one level of each independent variable.

Binocular disparity (stereopsis) A cue for depth perception that depends on the fact that the distance between the eyes provides two slightly disparate views of the world that, when combined, give us a perception of depth.

Bipolar disorder A mood disorder characterized by both depression and mania.

Boomerang effect In theories of attitude persuasion, it is an attitude change in the opposite direction of the persuader's message.

Borderline personality disorder A personality disorder characterized by an instability in interpersonal behavior, mood and self-image that borders on psychosis.

Bottom-up processing (data-driven processing) Information processing that occurs when objects are recognized by the summation of the components of incoming stimulus to arrive at the whole pattern.

Brightness The subjective impression of the intensity of a light stimulus.

Brightness contrast In brightness perception, it refers to a when a particular luminance appears brighter when surrounded by a darker stimulus than when surrounded by a lighter stimulus.

Broca's aphasia Impairments in producing spoken language associated with lesions to Broca's area.

Bulimia nervosa An eating disorder that involves binge eating and excessive attempts to compensate for it by purging, fasting, or excessive exercising.

Bystander effect The reluctance of people to intervene to help others in emergency situations when other people also witness the situation.

Cannon-Bard theory A theory of emotions stating that awareness of emotions reflects our physiological arousal and our cognitive experience of emotion.

Case study An experimental method used in developmental psychology to take a very detailed look at development by studying a small number of individuals. This is also called the clinical method.

Centration A term from Piaget's theory, it is the tendency for preoperational children to be able to focus on only one aspect of a phenomenon.

Chi-square test A statistical method of testing for an association between two categorical variables. Specifically, it tests for the equality of two frequencies or proportions.

Chlorpromazine An antipsychotic drug thought to block receptor sites for dopamine, making it effective in treating the delusional thinking, hallucinations and agitation commonly associated with schizophrenia.

Circadian rhythms Internally generated rhythms that regulate our daily cycle of waking and sleeping, approximating a 24-hour cycle.

Classical conditioning Also known as respondent conditioning, it is a result of learning connections between different events.

Claustrophobia An irrational fear of closed places.

Client-centered therapy, person-centered therapy, non-directive therapy Carl Rogers' therapeutic technique that is based on the idea that clients have the freedom to control their own behavior, and that the client is able to reflect upon his or her problems, make choices and take positive action.

Clustering A technique to enhance memory by organizing items into conceptually-related categories

Cognitive dissonance theory Leon Festinger's consistency theory that people are motivated to reduce dissonant elements or add consonant elements to reduce tension.

Cognitive map A mental representation of a physical space.

Color constancy Refers to the fact that the perceived color of an object does not change when we change the wavelength of the light we see.

Compensation A defense mechanism whereby something is done to make up for something that is lacking.

Conception Takes place in the fallopian tubes where the ovum or egg cell is fertilized by the male sperm cell.

Conditioned response In classical conditioning, it is the learned response to a conditioned stimulus.

Conditioned stimulus In classical conditioning, it a neutral stimulus that has been paired with an unconditioned stimulus to elicit a conditioned response.

Confounding variables Unintended independent variables.

Connectionism Also called parallel distribution processing, it is a theory of information processing that is analogous to a complex neural network.

Consistency theories Theoretical perspectives from social psychology that hold that people prefer consistency between attitudes and behaviors, and that people will change or resist changing attitudes based upon this preference.

Construct validity A type of validity that refers to how well a test measures the intended theoretical construct.

Content validity A type of validity that refers to how well the content items of a test measure the particular skill or knowledge area that it is supposed to measure.

Control group design A technique of treating experimental and control groups equally in all respects, except that one group is exposed to the treatment in the experiment, and the other group is not exposed to the treatment.

Conversion disorders Disorders characterized by unexplained symptoms affecting voluntary motor or sensory functions. Conversion disorder used to be referred to as "hysteria."

Correlation coefficient A type of descriptive statistic that measures to what extent, if any, two variables are related.

Counterbalancing A method of controlling the potential effects of unintended independent variables (e.g., order effects) by making sure that the experimental and control groups are similar in all respects expect for in the independent variable being measured.

Countertransference In psychoanalysis, it occurs when the therapist experiences emotions in response to the patient's transference.

Criterion validity How well the test can predict an individual's performance on an established test of the same skill or knowledge area.

Cross-sectional studies An experimental method used in developmental psychology to compare different groups of individuals at different ages.

Crystallized intelligence Proposed by Raymond Cattell, it is a type of intelligence that uses knowledge acquired as a result of schooling or other life experiences.

Cynophobia A specific phobia referring to an irrational fear of dogs.

Decay theory A theory that holds that if the information in long-term memory is not used or rehearsed it will eventually be forgotten.

Declarative memory Sometimes called fact memory, it is memory for explicit information.

Defense mechanisms In Freud's structural dynamic model of personality, they are unconscious mechanisms that deny, falsify, or distort reality.

Delusions False beliefs, discordant with reality, that are maintained in spite of strong evidence to the contrary.

Demand characteristics Cues that suggest to subjects what the researcher expects from research participants.

Dementia praecox The word literally means "split mind," and was used to refer to what is now known as schizophrenia.

Dementias A neurological disorder characterized by a loss in intellectual functioning.

Dependent variable A measurement of the response that is expected to vary with differences in the independent variable

Depersonalization disorder A dissociative disorder that involves a sense of detachment from the self despite an intact sense of reality.

Depolarization The second stage in the firing cycle, occurs when the membrane's electrical charge decreases—anytime the membrane's voltage moves toward a neutral charge of 0 millivolts.

Descriptive statistics Statistics concerned with organizing, describing, quantifying, and summarizing a collection of actual observations.

Deviation quotients A deviation IQ score that tells us how far away a person's score is from the average score for that person's particular age group.

Diathesis-stress model A framework explaining the causes of mental disorders as an interaction between biological causal factors (a predisposition toward developing a specific mental disorder) and psychological causal factors (excessive stress).

Difference threshold The amount of difference that there must be between two stimuli before they are perceived to be different.

Diploid cells Cells that contain 23 pairs of chromosomes.

Discriminative stimulus In operant conditioning, it is a stimulus condition that indicates that the organism's behavior will have consequences.

Displacement A defense mechanism that refers to the pent-up feelings (often hostility) discharged on objects and people less dangerous than those objects or people causing the feelings.

Dissociative disorders Disorders characterized by an avoidance of stress by escaping from personality identity.

Dissociative fugue A dissociative disorder that involves amnesia plus a sudden, unexpected move away from one's home or location of usual daily activities.

Dissociative Identity Disorder A dissociative disorder characterized by two or more personalities that recurrently take control of a person's behavior (formerly Multiple Personality Disorder).

Dissonance theory The tendency to change thoughts or behavior in response to perceived inconsistencies.

Distal stimulus In perception, it is the actual object or event out there in the world, as opposed to its perceived image.

Domain-referenced testing Sometimes called criterion-referenced testing, it is concerned with the question of what the test taker knows about a specified content domain.

Dopamine hypothesis A biochemical explanation for schizophrenia suggesting that the delusions, hallucinations and agitation associated with schizophrenia arise from an excess of dopamine activity at certain sites in the brain.

Double-bind hypothesis A psychosocial theory of schizophrenia holding that people with schizophrenia received contradictory messages from primary caregivers during childhood, and that these contradictory messages led them to see their perceptions of reality as unreliable.

Double-blinding A research design that controls for the influence of the researcher and research participants since neither group knows which participants are in the control group and which participants are in the experimental group.

Down's syndrome A set of physiological conditions, including severe mental retardation, resulting from an extra 21st chromosome.

Duplexity, or duplicity theory of vision The theory holding that the retina contains two kinds of photoreceptors.

Echoic memory Auditory memory.

Ego psychology A branch of psychoanalytic theory that emphasizes the role of the ego as autonomous.

Eidetic memory Memory for images.

Elaborative rehearsal The process of organizing information and associating it with what you already know to get information into long-term memory.

Electroencephalograph (EEG) It records a gross average of the electrical activity in different parts of the brain.

Embryonic stage The third stage during prenatal development, it refers to the period during which the embryo increases in size dramatically, begins to develop a human appearance with limb motion, produces androgen in the testes of male embryos, and develops nerve cells in the spine.

Emmert's law A law describing the relationship between size constancy and apparent distance—the farther away the object appears to be, the more the scaling device in the brain will compensate for its retinal size by enlarging our perception of the object.

Empathy It is the ability to vicariously experience the emotions of another, and it is thought by some social psychologists to be a strong influence on helping behavior.

Encoding The process of putting new information into memory.

Encoding specificity theory A theory that recall is best if the context at recall approximates the context during the original encoding.

Endorphins Peptides that are natural pain killers produced in the brain.

Episodic memory A type of declarative memory, episodic memory refers to memories for particular events, or episodes, from personal experience.

Equity theory A theory stating that individuals strive for fairness and feel uncomfortable when there is a perception of a lack of fairness.

Eros In Freud's structural dynamic model of personality, it refers to the life instincts that serve the purpose of individual survival (hunger, thirst, and sex).

Ethology The study of animals in their natural environment.

Exchange theory The tendency to evaluate interactions and relationships in terms of relative costs and benefits.

External validity In research methodology, it refers to how generalizable the results of an experiment are.

Extinction In operant conditioning, it is when a conditioned stimulus is repeatedly not reinforced and as a result, the conditioned response is no longer produced as consistently.

Extirpation A process of removing various parts of the brain, and then observing the behavioral consequences.

Extrinsic motivation Behavior that is motivated by some external reward.

Face validity A type of validity that refers to whether test items *appear* to measure what they are supposed to measure.

Factor analysis A statistical technique using correlation coefficients to reduce a large number of variables to a few factors.

Fechner's law A law that expresses the relationship between the intensity of the sensation and the intensity of the stimulus, and states that sensation increases more slowly as intensity increases.

Fetal period The last stage of prenatal development, its onset is marked by the beginning of measurable electrical activity in the brain.

Fictional finalism A concept in Alfred Adler's theory of personality, it is the notion that an individual is motivated more by his or her expectations of the future based on a subjective or fictional estimate of life's values, than by past experiences.

Field independence-field dependence A personality style characterized by an ability/inability to distinguish experience from its context.

Fight or flight responses The emotional experience associated with the sympathetic nervous system and managed by the hypothalamus during high arousal.

Figure A concept in visual perception referring to the integrated visual experience that stands out at the center of attention.

Fixation From psychoanalytic theory, it is an inability to successfully proceed through a stage in development because of an overindulgence or frustration.

Fixed action pattern A behavior that is relatively stereotyped and appears to be species-typical.

Fixed-interval (FI) In operant conditioning, it is when behavior is reinforced on the first response after a fixed period of time has elapsed since the last reinforcement.

Fixed-ratio (FR) In operant conditioning, it is when behavior is reinforced after a fixed number of responses.

Flooding A behavioral modification technique used to treat anxiety disorders by exposing the client to the anxiety-producing stimulus.

Fluid intelligence Proposed by Raymond Cattell, it is a type of intelligence that has the ability to quickly grasp relationships in novel situations and make correct deductions from them (e.g., solving analogies).

Follicle stimulating hormone A hormone that is secreted by the pituitary gland to stimulate the growth of an ovarian follicle, which is a small protective sphere surrounding the egg or ovum.

Free association A psychoanalytic technique in which the client says whatever comes to his or her mind regardless of how personal, painful, or seemingly irrelevant it may appear to be so that the analyst and patient together can reconstruct the nature of the client's original conflict.

Frequency In sound perception, it is the number of sound wave cycles per second.

Frequency theory A theory suggesting that the basilar membrane of the ear vibrates as a whole, that the rate of vibration equals the frequency of the stimulus and that the vibration rate is directly translated into the appropriate number of neural impulses per second.

Functional autonomy A given activity or form of behavior may become an end or a goal in itself, regardless of its original reason for existence.

Functional fixedness An impediment to effective problem solving because of an inability to use a familiar object in an unfamiliar way.

Functionalism A system of thought in psychology that was concerned with studying how mental processes help individuals adapt to their environments.

Fundamental attribution error The tendency to attribute individual characteristics as causes of others' behaviors and situational characteristics to one's own behavior.

g Proposed by Charles Spearman, this is an individual difference in intelligence that refers to a general, unitary factor of intelligence.

GABA (gamma-aminobutyric acid) A neurotransmitter that produces inhibitory postsynaptic potentials and is thought to play an important role in stabilizing neural activity in the brain.

Garcia effect Named after researcher John Garcia, it is basically food aversion that occurs when people attribute illness to a particular food.

Gate theory of pain A theory that proposes that there is a special "gating" mechanism located in the spine that can turn pain signals on or off, thus affecting whether we perceive pain.

Generation-recognition model Model that proposes that recall tasks tap the same basic process of accessing information in memory as recognition tasks, but also require an additional processing step.

Genes Located on the chromosomes, they are the basic units of hereditary transmission.

Germinal period A period of rapid cell division during prenatal development that lasts approximately two weeks, and ends with the implantation of the cellular mass into the uterine wall.

Gonadoptropic hormones Hormones produced by the pituitary gland during puberty that activate a dramatic increase in the production of hormones by the testes or ovaries.

Ground A concept in visual perception that refers to the background against which the figures appear.

Group polarization A tendency for group discussion to enhance the group's initial tendencies towards riskiness or caution.

Groupthink A tendency of decision-making groups to strive for consensus at the expense of not considering discordant information.

Hallucinations Perceptions that are not due to external stimuli but have a compelling sense of reality.

Halo effect In social psychology, it is the tendency to generalize from one attribute or characteristic to a person's entire personality.

Haloperidol (Haldol) An antipsychotic drug thought to block receptor sites for dopamine, making it effective in treating the delusional thinking, hallucinations, and agitation commonly associated with schizophrenia.

Haploid cells Cells that contain 23 single chromosomes. The gametes (sperm and egg cells) are haploid.

Hawthorne effect The tendency of people to behave differently if they know that they are being observed.

Homeostasis A term referring to those self-regulatory processes that maintain a stable equilibrium.

Humanism A system of thought that arose in opposition to both psychoanalysis and behaviorism, and is characterized by a belief in the notion of free will and the idea that people should be considered as wholes rather than in terms of stimuli and responses (behaviorism) or instincts (psychoanalysis).

Hyperpolarization An increase in the membrane potential that decreases the possibility of generating a nerve impulse.

Hypochondriasis A disorder that causes an individual to be preoccupied with fears that he or she has a serious disease, based on a misinterpretation of one or more bodily signs or symptoms.

Hypothesis A tentative and testable explanation of the relationship between two or more variables.

Iconic memory Visual memory.

Id In Freud's structural dynamic model of personality, it is the source and the reservoir of all psychic energy.

Idiographic An approach to studying personality that focuses on individual case studies.

Illumination A physical, objective measurement that is simply the amount of light falling on a surface.

Illusory correlation An apparent correlation that is perceived, but does not really exist.

Imprinting An attachment bond between a organism and an object in the environment.

Independent variable The variable whose effect is being studied.

Induced motion An illusion of movement occurring when everything around the spot of light is moved.

Inferential statistics Statistics concerned with making an inference from the sample involved in the research to the population of interest in order to provide an estimate of popular characteristics.

Innate releasing mechanism (IRM) A mechanism in the animal's nervous system that serves to connect the stimulus with the right response.

Insomnia A disturbance affecting the ability to fall asleep and/or stay asleep.

Instincts In Freud's structural dynamic model of personality, these are inner representations of a psychological excitation or wish, and are the propelling aspects of Freud's dynamic theory of personality.

Intensity In sound perception, it is the amplitude or height of the air-pressure wave and it is related to loudness.

Interneurons Neurons located in the spinal cord that connect sensory neurons with motor neurons to form the reflex arc.

Interposition Also called overlap, it refers to the cue for depth perception when one object (A) covers or overlaps another object (B), and we see object (A) as being in front.

Interval scale A scale of measurement using actual numbers (not ranks).

Intrinsic motivation Motivation by some reward that is inherent to the task.

IQ A well-known measure of intelligence aptitude using an equation comparing mental age to chronological age.

Isomorphism A theory that suggests that there is a one-to-one correspondence between the object in the perceptual field and the pattern of stimulation in the brain.

James-Lange theory of emotions A theory that people become aware of their emotions after they notice their physiological reactions to some external event.

Just-world hypothesis The tendency to believe that the world is fair; that is, that people who are good are rewarded while people who are bad are punished.

Klinefelter's syndrome The possession of an extra X chromosome in males that leads to sterility and often to mental retardation.

Language acquisition device (LAD) Proposed by Noam Chomsky, this is an innate, biologically-based mechanism that helps us understand rule structures in language.

Lateral inhibition In visual perception, it is the process of inhibiting the response of adjacent retinal cells resulting in the sharpening and highlighting of the borders between dark and light areas.

Law of closure From Gestalt psychology, it is the tendency for people to perceive complete figures even when the actual figures are not complete.

Law of good continuation From Gestalt psychology, it is the tendency for elements appearing to follow in the same direction (such as a straight line or a simple curve) to be grouped together.

Law of *prägnanz* From Gestalt psychology, it is the tendency for perceptual organization to be as "good" —as regular, simple and symmetric—as possible.

Law of proximity From Gestalt psychology, it is the tendency for elements close to each other to be perceived as a unit.

Law of similarity From Gestalt psychology, it is the tendency for similar objects to be grouped together.

L-dopa A synthetic substance that increases dopamine levels in the brain and is used to treat motor disturbances in Parkinson's disease. When L-dopa leads to an oversupply of dopamine in the brain, it can produce psychotic symptoms in Parkinson's patients.

Levels-of-processing theory (depth-of-processing theory) Proposed by Craik and Lockart, the theory suggests that there is only one memory system, and that items entering the memory are analyzed in one of three stages: physical (visual), acoustical (sound), or semantic (meaning).

Libido From psychoanalytic theory, it refers to the life drive present at birth.

Lightness constancy Refers to the fact that, despite changes in the amount of light falling on an object (illumination), the apparent lightness of the object remains unchanged.

Linear perspective A cue for depth perception that refers to the perception of parallel lines converging in the distance.

Linguistic relativity hypothesis The theory proposing that our perception of reality is determined by the content of language. Also called the Whorfian hypothesis.

Lithium A drug used to treat bipolar disorder.

Long term memory The memory system that holds a permanent store of information.

Longitudinal studies An experimental method used in developmental psychology to compare the same group of individuals repeatedly over time.

Loudness The subjective experience of the magnitude or intensity of sound.

Luteinizing hormone A hormone associated with ovulation.

Maintenance rehearsal The process of rehearsing information so that items remain in short term memory for a longer duration than usual.

Major depressive disorder A mood disorder characterized by at least a two-week period during which there is a prominent and relatively persistent depressed mood, or loss of interest in all or almost all activities.

Mania A sympton of bipolar disorders, it is characterized by an abnormally elevated mood, accompanied by a speeding up of thought processes and activities and an abnormally decreased need for sleep.

MAO inhibitors Behavioral stimulants that reduce depression by inhibiting the action of an enzyme called MAO, which normally breaks down and deactivates norepinephrine and serotonin.

Matched-subjects design In research methodology, it is a technique of matching subjects on the basis of the variable that he or she wants to control.

Mean The numerical halfway point between the highest score and the lowest score, the arithmetic average.

Median The middle value when observations are ordered from least to most or from most to least.

Mental chronometry A cognitive psychology research method of measuring the time elapsed between a stimulus presentation and the subject's response to it.

Mere-exposure hypothesis The tendency for people to prefer things with which they are familiar.

Meta-analysis A statistical procedure that can be used to make conclusions on the basis of data from different studies.

Metacognition The ability to think about and monitor cognition.

Metamemory The ability to think about and monitor memory.

Method of savings A research technique for studying memory by measuring the amount of time it takes to learn material and comparing it to the amount of time it takes to relearn material later. The decrease in time represents an indication of original learning.

Methylphenidate A behavioral stimulant that increases alertness and decreases motor activity, and is used to treat hyperactive children who suffer from attention deficit disorder. Also known as Ritalin.

Mnemonic devices Techniques used to improve the likelihood that we will remember something.

Mode The value of the most frequent observation in a set of scores.

Modeling A therapeutic technique in which the client learns appropriate behavior through imitation of someone else.

Monoamine theory of depression A theory that holds that too much norepinephrine and serotonin leads to mania, while too little leads to depression. It is also sometimes called the catecholamine theory of depression.

Morphemes The smallest units of meaning in a language.

Motion aftereffect An illusion that occurs when you first view a moving pattern, such as stripes moving off to the right (or a waterfall), and then you view a spot of light—the spot of light will appear to move in the opposite direction.

Motion parallax A cue for depth perception that occurs during movement when objects that are closer move.

Motor neurons Neurons transmitting motor commands from the brain to the muscles along efferent fibers.

Narcissistic personality disorder A personality disorder characterized by a grandiose sense of self-importance or uniqueness, preoccupation with fantasies of success, an exhibitionistic need for constant admiration and attention, and characteristic disturbances in interpersonal relationships such as feelings of entitlement.

Negative reinforcement The probability that the desired response will be performed is increased by removing something undesirable whenever the desired response is made.

Neologisms Newly invented words.

Neurotransmitters Chemical substances that allow neurons to communicate with one another.

Nominal scale A scale of measurement (also called a categorical scale), that labels observations rather than quantifying observations.

Nomothetic An approach to personality that focuses on groups of individuals and tries to find the commonalities between individuals.

Nonequivalent group design An experimental design whereby the researcher doesn't use random assignment, so the control group is not necessarily equivalent to the experimental group.

Norepinephrine Also known as noradrenaline, it is involved in controlling alertness and wakefulness and is implicated in mood disorders such as depression and mania.

Normal distribution A distribution that is symmetrical and has its greatest frequency in the middle.

Norm-referenced testing Comparing the test-taker's performance to that test's norms that are derived from standardized samples.

Object permanence From Piaget's theory, it is the capacity for representational thought.

Obsessive compulsive disorder (OCD) A disorder characterized by repeated obsessions (persistent irrational thoughts) and/or compulsions (irrational and repetitive impulses to perform certain acts) that cause significant impairment in a person's life.

Operant conditioning Instrumental conditioning, reward learning, is based on learning the relationship between one's actions and their consequences.

Operational definitions Measurable definitions of variables in research.

Opiate receptors Receptor that respond to the body's own naturally produced pain killers (endorphins) as well as narcotics such as heroin and morphine.

Opponent-process theory of color vision Ewald Hering's theory that there are four primary colors in additive color mixing (red, blue, green and yellow), and that the primary colors are arranged in opposing pairs.

Order effects A problem in research design when the results of the study are attributed to the sequence of tasks in the experiment rather than to the independent variable.

Ordinal scale A scale of measurement using ranks rather than actual numbers.

Osmoreceptors Receptors in the hypothalamus that control the maintenance of water balance in the body.

Outliers Scores falling far outside the main cluster of scores.

Overjustification effect The tendency of people to stop liking something that they previously enjoyed because of receiving a reward for the behavior.

Paivio's dual-code hypothesis According to this theory, information can be stored (or encoded) in two ways: visually and verbally. Abstract information tends to be encoded verbally, whereas concrete information tends to be encoded visually (i.e., as an image) and verbally.

Paradoxical intervention A therapeutic technique that appears to contradict the therapeutic needs.

Parallel Distributed Processs (PDP) This theory holds that information processing is distributed across the brain (across nodes in a network) and is done in a parallel fashion.

Perceptual sets Expectations we have about perception due to past experiences.

Permissive parenting style A parenting style referring to the tendency to score very low on control/demand measures.

Persona An archetype from Jung's theory referring to a mask that is adopted by the person in response to the demands of social convention.

Personality disorders A pattern of behavior that is inflexible and maladapative, causing distress and/or impaired functioning in at least two of the following: cognition, emotions, interpersonal functioning or impulse control.

Phelogeny The term for evolutionary development in humans.

Phenothiazine Anti-psychotic drugs thought to block receptor sites for dopamine, making it effective in treating the delusional thinking, hallucinations and agitation commonly associated with schizophrenia.

Phenylketonuria (PKU) A degenerative disease of the nervous system occurring when a child lacks the enzyme needed to digest phenylalanine, an amino acid found in milk and other foods.

Phi phenomenon An illusion of movement that occurs when two dots flashed in different locations on a screen seconds apart are perceived as one moving dot.

Phobia An irrational fear of something that results in a compelling desire to avoid that thing.

Phonemes The smallest sound units of language.

Phrenology The study of the psychological functions of areas in the brain.

Physiological zero The temperature of the skin.

Pitch The subjective experience of the frequency of the sound.

Place theory Proposed by Helmhotlz and Young, the theory holds that each different pitch causes a different place on the basilar membrane of the ear to vibrate.

Placebo effect A therapeutic effect resulting from an inactive substance, such as a sugar pill.

Pleasure principle In Freud's structural dynamic model of personality, it is the id's operating principal, which is to immediately discharge any energy build-up.

Positive reinforcement Increasing the probability that a desired response will be performed by reinforcing (rewarding) that response when it does occur.

Predictive validity The use of some criterion scores obtained in advance, and validating them against scores obtained later.

Premack principle A more preferred activity can be used to reinforce a less preferred activity.

Preparedness In-born tendency to associate certain stimuli with certain consequences.

Primacy effect A social psychology term that refers to those occasions when first impressions are more important than subsequent impressions.

Primary circular reactions From Piaget's theory, it is reflex activities characteristic of behavior during the sensorimotor phase.

Primary prevention Efforts to correct the conditions that foster mental illness and establish the conditions that foster mental health.

Primary process In Freud's structural dynamic model of personality, it is the id's response to frustration— "obtain satisfaction now, not later."

Prisoner's dilemma A classic method of investigating people's choices to compete or cooperate using a hypothetical case where two men have been taken into custody, separated, and can choose either to confess or not to confess.

Proactive inhibition When what you learned earlier interferes with what you learn later.

Procedural memory Memory for how things are done.

Prodromal phase The phase before schizophrenia is actually diagnosed, characterized by poor adjustment.

Progesterone A hormone produced and secreted by the ovary to prepare the uterus for implantation of the fertilized egg.

Projection A defense mechanism that refers to when a person attributes his forbidden urges to others.

Projection area Areas in the brain receiving incoming sensory information or sending out motor-impulse commands.

Proprioception A general term for our sense of bodily position, including aspects of both the vestibular and kinesthetic senses.

Protection-motivation theory A social psychology theory proposing that an appeal to fear produces attitude change under particular conditions.

Proxemics The study of how individuals space themselves in relation to others.

Proximal stimulus In perception, it is the information our sensory receptors receive about the object.

Psychoanalysis An intensive, long-term treatment for uncovering repressed memories, motives, and conflicts stemming from problems in psychosexual development—the goal of therapy is to gain insight into the repressed material.

Psychodynamic, or psychoanalytic theory A system of thought that postulates the existence of unconscious internal states that motivate the overt actions of individuals and determine personality.

Psychopharmacology The science of how drugs affect behavior.

Psychophysics A branch of psychology concerned with measuring the relationship between physical stimuli and psychological responses to the stimuli.

Punishment The probability that a response will be made is decreased by giving the organism something undesirable whenever the response is made.

Range A descriptive statistic that measures the variability.

Ratio scale A scale of measurement using actual numbers where there is a true zero point that indicates the total absence of the quantity being measured.

Rational emotive behavioral therapy A therapeutic approach that focuses on changing irrational belief systems.

Rationalization A defense mechanism that refers to the process of developing socially acceptable explanations for inappropriate behavior or thoughts.

Reactance When social pressure to behave in a particular way becomes so blatant that the person's sense of freedom is threatened, the person will tend to act in a way to reassert that sense of freedom.

Reaction formation A defense mechanism that refers to when a repressed wish is warded off by its diametrical opposite.

Reality principle In Freud's structural dynamic model of personality, it is the ego's response to frustration that takes into account objective reality as it guides or inhibits the activity of the id and the id's pleasure principle.

Recency effect In social psychology, it refers to those occasions when the most recent information we have about an individual is most important in forming our impressions. In cognitive psychology, it is the tendency for items that are presented last to be remembered the best.

Reception The first step in all sensory information processing; each sensory system has receptors to react to the physical external energy.

Reciprocity hypothesis The hypothesis that we tend to like those who seem to like us, and dislike those who dislike us.

Refractory period The period following the firing of a neuron just before the neuron is able to fire again.

Regional cerebral blood flow (rcbf) A noninvasive procedure that detects broad patterns of neural activity based on increased blood flow to different parts of the brain.

Regression A defense mechanism that refers to a person who reverts to an earlier mode of satisfaction.

Relative refractory period The period following the absolute refractory period. During this time, the neuron will fire in response to a *strong* stimulus.

Relative size A cue for depth perception that occurs when as an object gets farther away and its image on the retina gets smaller. People can tell how far away something is relative to another object by comparing the size of the images on the retina with what is known about actual sizes.

Reliability The consistency and stability of a test measure.

REM Rapid Eye Movement sleep characterized by the presence of theta waves and the absence of delta waves. Dreams occur during REM sleep.

Representativeness heuristic A decision-making short-cut that people tend to use when trying to decide how likely something is by categorizing on the basis of whether it fits the prototypical, stereotypical or representative image of the category.

Repression A defense mechanism that refers to the unconscious forgetting of anxiety-producing memories.

Reproductive isolating mechanisms Behaviors that prevent animals of one species from attempting to mate with animals of a closely-related species.

Resistance An unwillingness or inability to relate to certain thoughts, motives or experiences, it is a major part of psychoanalysis.

Response bias The tendency for research participants to respond to sensory perception in a particular way, due to nonsensory factors.

Resting potential A slight electrical charge (-70 mV) stored inside the neuron's cell membrane—a charge just waiting to be transformed into a nerve impulse.

Retrieval Process of recovering stored material in memory.

Retroactive inhibition Learning something new that interferes with what was learned earlier.

Retrograde amnesia Memory loss for events that occurred before brain injury.

Rhodopsin The only photopigment in the rods, it is made up of a vitamin A derivative, called retinene, and a protein, called opsin.

Risky shift It refers to the finding that group decisions are riskier than the average of the individual choices (and, this average riskiness of the individual choices can be considered to be an estimate of the group's original riskiness).

Rods Located in the periphery of the retina, these are sensory receptors for vision that work best in reduced illumination, and only allow perception of achromatic colors, low sensitivity to detail and are not involved in color vision.

Role theory A theoretical perspective from social psychology that holds that people are aware of the social roles they are expected to fill, and behavior can be understood and attributed to the adoption of those social roles.

Sample In research design, it is a subset of the population.

Scatterplot A graphical representation of correlational data.

Schema (schemata) Conceptual frameworks used to organize knowledge.

Schizoid personality disorder A personality disorder characterized by a pervasive pattern of detachment from social relationships and a restricted range of emotional expression.

Schizophrenia A disorder characterized by any or all of the following symptoms: delusions, hallucinations, disorganized thought, inappropriate affect, and catatonic behavior.

Secondary process In Freud's structural dynamic model of personality, it is the ego's mode of functioning, which is to postpone the discharge of energy until the actual object that will satisfy the need has been discovered or produced.

Secondary sex characteristics Physical sex characteristics that do not appear until puberty—for females, enlarged breasts and widened hips, for males facial hair and deeper voices.

Sedative-hypnotic drugs A class of drugs that slow down the functioning of the central nervous system by facilitating the action of GABA.

Selective serotonin reuptake inhibitors (SSRI) Behavioral stimulants that reduce depression by blocking the reuptake of serotonin, and increases serotonin in the synapse.

Self-actualization From Abraham Maslow's theory, it is the need to realize one's fullest potential.

Self-awareness theory The theory that our behavior is influenced by an awareness of the self, and that there are certain situations that trigger a focus on ourselves (mirrors, cameras, recording devices).

Self-disclosure theory A theory that refers to those conditions that prohibit or facilitate the process of revealing personal or intimate aspects of oneself.

Self-perception theory Daryl Bem's theory that when attitudes about something are weak or ambiguous, people observe their own behavior and then attribute attitudes to themselves.

Semantic feature-comparison model The model, proposed by Smith, Shoben and Rips suggests that concepts are represented by sets of features, some of which are required for that concept, and some of which are typical of that concept.

Semantic memory A type of declarative memory, semantic memory has to do with remembering general knowledge, especially the meanings of words and concepts.

Semantics The meaning of words and sentences.

Sensory memory Part of the stage theory of memory that contains the fleeting impressions of sensory stimuli.

Sensory neurons Neurons that transmit sensory information to the spinal cord and then to the brain, through afferent fibers.

Sequential cohort studies An experimental method used in developmental psychology to study groups of subjects at different ages, repeatedly over time.

Serotonin A neurotransmitter loosely classified as a monoamine or biogenic-amine transmitter generally thought to play roles in regulating mood, eating, sleeping and arousal—an oversupply of serotonin is thought to produce manic states; an undersupply is thought to produce depression.

Shadow An archetype from Jung's theory referring to the animal instincts which humans inherited in their evolution from lower forms of life.

Shaping In operant conditioning, it is the process of reinforcing successive approximations of a desired behavior.

Short term memory A memory system that has a limited capacity (7 ± 2 items) and a relatively short duration (approx. 30 sec.).

Sign stimulus A feature of a stimulus that is sufficient to bring about a particular fixed-action pattern.

Signal detection theory A theory that suggests that non-sensory factors influence sensory perception.

Significance test A statistical technique used in inferential statistics to test the probability of an observed difference.

Single-blind experiment. A research design that controls for the influence of the research participants' expectations by not revealing whether participants are in the control group or in the experimental group.

Single-cell recording A method of study in sensory perception that records the response cell by placing a microelectrode in the cortex.

Size constancy When an object appears to retain its size despite the fact that its image on the retina has changed in size.

Sleep apnea A disorder characterized by an inability to breathe during sleep.

Social comparison theory Leon Festinger's theory that the tendency to evaluate the self in comparison to other people drives affiliation.

Social exchange theory The theory that we are motivated to affiliate with others based upon the rewards and costs of affiliation—the more the rewards outweigh the costs, the greater the attraction to the other person.

Social facilitation The idea that being in a group enhances performance.

Social influence The notion that the presence of other people affects an individual's judgment about an event.

Social learning theory According to the theory, behavior is learned through modeling (direct observation), or through reinforcement.

Social loafing A group phenomenon referring to the tendency for people to put forth less effort when part of a group effort than when acting individually.

Somatoform disorders Disorders that are characterized by the presence of physical symptoms not fully explained by a medical condition.

Split-half consistency Dividing a test into equal halves and correlating scores on one half with the scores on the other half.

Standard deviation A measure of the typical distance of scores from the mean.

Standard error of measurement (SEM) An index of how much, on average, we expect a person's observed score to vary from the score the person is capable of receiving based on actual ability.

State-dependent learning When recall is better if the psychological or physical state at the time of recall is the same as the state when original learning occurred.

Steven's power law A law that relates the intensity of the stimulus to the intensity of the sensation.

Storage Process of retaining the information in memory over time.

Strange situation A laboratory study designed to measure the quality of the caregiver-child attachment relationship.

Structuralism System of thought that refers to breaking consciousness down to its elements.

Sublimation A defense mechanism that refers to the process of transforming unacceptable urges into socially acceptable behaviors.

Subtractive color mixture Occurs when we mix pigments; yellow, blue and red are the primary colors.

Superego In Freud's structural dynamic model of personality, it strives for the ideal rather than the real and it is not directly in touch with reality.

Supernormal stimulus A stimulus that is more effective at triggering the fixed action pattern than the actual stimulus found in nature.

Suppression A defense mechanism that refers to a deliberate, conscious form of forgetting.

Synapse The tiny gap between neurons.

Syntax The grammatical arrangement of words in sentences.

Systematic desensitization A technique used to treat phobias by pairing the object of fear with relaxation.

Tabula rasa The idea that all knowledge is gained through experience.

Tardive dyskinesia Resting tremors and jerky motor movements caused by disruptions of dopamine transmission.

Temperament Individual differences thought to have a genetic basis, and thought to form the foundation of personality.

Test-retest method To estimate the inter-individual stability of test scores over time, the same test is administered to the same group of people twice.

Texture gradients A cue for depth perception that refers to the variations in perceived surface texture as a function of the distance from the observer—the more distant parts of a scene appear to have smaller, more densely packed elements, and sudden changes in texture generally signal either a change in distance or a change in direction.

Thanatos In Freud's structural dynamic model of personality, it refers to the death instincts that represent an unconscious wish for the ultimate absolute state of quiescence.

Collective unconscious From Carl Jung's personality theory, it is the idea that all humans share an unconscious, a residual of the experiences of our early ancestors.

Law of effect Proposed by E. L. Thorndike, the law holds that if a response is followed by an annoying consequence, the animal will be less likely to emit the same response in the future.

Law of specific nerve energies Proposed by Johannes Müller, this law states that each sensory nerve is excited by only one kind of energy (e.g., light or air vibrations), and that the brain interprets any stimulation of that nerve as being that kind of energy.

Method of loci A mnemonic device of associating information with some sequence of familiar places.

Theory of motivation A drive-reduction theory proposed by Clark Hull suggesting that the goal of behavior is to reduce biological drives—that is, behavioral reinforcement occurs whenever a biological drive is reduced.

Theory of multiple intelligences Howard Gardner's theory that there are 7 intelligence factors: linguistic ability, logical-mathematical ability, spatial ability, musical ability, bodily-kinesthetic ability, interpersonal ability, and intrapersonal ability.

Thorazine An antipsychotic drug thought to block receptor sites for dopamine, making it effective in treating the delusional thinking, hallucinations and agitation commonly associated with schizophrenia.

Timbre In sound perception, it is the tone quality—the aspect that distinguishes the sound of one instrument from another.

Tip-of-the-tongue phenomenon A problem with memory retrieval where some parts of the information are available to memory, but not enough for complete recall.

Token economies A technique used in behavior therapy to reinforce behavior by giving tokens (that can be cashed in for something desirable) for appropriate behavior.

Top-down processing (conceptually-driven processing) From object recognition theory, it refers to when people recognize objects by using conceptual processes such as memories and expectations about the whole object.

Tourette's disorder A disorder characterized by multiple motor tics (e.g., eye-blinking, skipping, deep knee bends) and one or more vocal tics (e.g., grunts, barks, sniffs, snorts, coughs, utterance of obscenities).

Transduction The second step in sensory information processing where physical energy is translated into neural impulses or action potentials.

Transference Involves the carrying over and applying to the therapist attitudes and feelings that developed in the patient's relations with significant others in the past.

Transformational grammar Rules that govern the ways in which changes in word order change meaning.

Triarchic theory Robert Sternberg's theory of intelligence that suggests that there are three aspects to intelligence: componential (e.g., performance on tests), experiential (creativity) and contextual (street smarts/business sense).

Tricyclic antidepressants Behavioral stimulants thought to reduce depression by facilitating the transmission of norepinephrine or serotonin at the synapse.

True experiments Research designs that use random assignment and manipulate the independent variable.

T-scores A test score that is converted to a normal distribution that has a mean of 50 and a standard deviation of 10.

T-tests A significance test used to compare the means of two groups.

Turner's syndrome Caused by the lack of one X chromosome in females, it results in a failure to develop secondary sex characteristics and cognitive impairment.

Two-factor theory of emotion A theory stating that the subjective experience of emotion is based on the interaction between changes in physiological arousal and cognitive interpretation of that arousal. In absence of any clear emotion-provoking stimulus, interpretation of physiological arousal depends on what is happening in the environment.

Two-point thresholds The minimum distance

necessary between two points of stimulation on the skin such that the points will be felt as two distinct stimuli.

Type I errors An error of mistakenly rejecting the null hypothesis. The likelihood of making a Type I error is the criterion of significance.

Type II errors An error of mistakenly failing to reject the null hypothesis.

Unconditioned response In classical conditioning, it is a response that occurs without any behavioral conditioning—like a reflex.

Unconditioned stimulus In classical conditioning, it is a stimulus that elicits an unconditioned response, without any behavioral conditioning.

Validity The extent to which a test actually measures what it is purports to measure.

Value hypothesis A hypothesis that suggests that the risky shift occurs in situations in which riskiness is culturally valued.

Variable A characteristic or property that varies in amount or kind, and can be measured (e.g., height, weight, mental abilities, physical abilities, personality characteristics, and so on).

Variable interval (VI) In operant conditioning, it is when behavior is reinforced at the first response made after a variable amount of time has elapsed since the last reinforcement.

Variable-ratio (VR) In operant conditioning, it is when behavior is reinforced after a varying number of responses.

Variance The square of the standard deviation, it is a description of how much each score varies from the mean.

Vestibular sense The sense of balance of our bodily position relative to gravity.

Visual agnosia An impairment in visual recognition whereby the person can see an object, but is unable to recognize what it is.

Weber's law A law stating that the change in stimulus intensity needed to produce a just noticeable difference, divided by the stimulus intensity of the standard stimulus is a constant.

Wernicke's aphasia Impairment in understanding spoken language associated with damage to Wernicke's area.

Yerkes-Dodson law A law stating that performance is worst at extremely low or extremely high levels of arousal, and optimal at some intermediate level.

Young-Helmhotz theory (trichromatic theory) A theory of color vision that suggests that the retina contains three different types of color receptors (cones), which are differentially sensitive to different red, blue or green, and all colors are produced by combined stimulation of these receptors.

Zone of proximal development It refers to those skills and abilities that have not yet fully developed but are in the process of development.

Z-score A score that represents how many standard deviations above or below the mean a score is.

Zygote A single, fertilized cell created during conception when the egg and sperm cells combine.

A SPECIAL NOTE FOR INTERNATIONAL STUDENTS

About a quarter million international students pursue advanced academic degrees at the master's or Ph.D. level at U.S. universities each year. This trend of pursuing higher education in the United States, particularly at the graduate level, is expected to continue. Business, management, engineering, and the physical and life sciences are popular areas of study for students coming to the United States from other countries. Along with these academic options, international students are also taking advantage of opportunities for research grants, teaching assistantships, and practical training or work experience in U.S. graduate departments.

If you are not from the United States, but are considering attending a graduate program at a university in the United States, here is what you'll need to get started.

- If English is not your first language, start there. You will probably need to take the Test of English as a Foreign Language (TOEFL) or show some other evidence that you're proficient in English prior to gaining admission to a graduate program. Graduate programs will vary on what is an acceptable TOEFL score. For degrees in business, journalism, management, or the humanities, a minimum TOEFL score of 600 (250 on the computer-based TOEFL) or better is expected. For the hard sciences and computer technology, a TOEFL score of 550 (213 on the computer-based TOEFL) is a common minimum requirement.

- You may also need to take the GRE® (Graduate Record Exam). The strategies in this book are designed to help you maximize your score on the computer-adaptive GRE exam. However, most sites outside the United States and Canada offer only the paper-and-pencil version of the GRE exam. For paper-and-pencil strategies, see Chapter 2.

- Since admission to many graduate programs is quite competitive, you may want to select three or four programs you would like to attend and complete applications for each program.

- Selecting the correct graduate school is very different from selecting a suitable undergraduate institution. You should research the qualifications and interests of faculty members teaching and doing research in your chosen field. Look for professors who share your specialty.

- You need to begin the application process at least a year in advance. Be aware that many programs offer only August or September start dates. Find out application deadlines and plan accordingly.

- Finally, you will need to obtain an 1–20 Certificate of Eligibility in order to obtain an F-1 Student Visa to study in the United States.

Kaplan English Programs*

If you need more help with the complex process of graduate school admissions, assistance preparing for the TOEFL or GRE, or help building your English language skills in general, you may be interested in Kaplan's programs for international students.

Kaplan English Programs were designed to help students and professionals from outside the United States meet their educational and career goals. At locations throughout the United States, international students take advantage of Kaplan's programs to help them improve their academic and conversational English skills, raise their scores on the TOEFL, GRE, and other standardized exams, and gain admission to the schools of their choice. Our staff and instructors give international students the individualized instruction they need to succeed. Here is a brief description of some of Kaplan's programs for international students:

General Intensive English

Kaplan's General Intensive English course is the fastest and most effective way for students to improve their English. This full-time program integrates the four key elements of language learning—listening, speaking, reading and writing. The challenging curriculum and intensive schedule are designed for both the general language learner and the academically bound student.

TOEFL and Academic English

Our world-famous TOEFL course prepares you for the TOEFL and also teaches you the academic language and skills needed to succeed in a university. Designed for high-intermediate to advanced-level English speakers, our course includes TOEFL-focused reading, writing, listening, speaking, vocabulary, and grammar instruction.

General English

Our General English course is a semi-intensive program designed for students who want to improve their listening and speaking skills without the time commitment of an intensive program. With morning class time and flexible computer lab hours throughout the week, our General English course is perfect for every schedule.

GRE for International Students

The GRE is required for admission to many graduate programs in the United States. Nearly one-half million people take the GRE each year. A high score can help you stand out from other test-takers. This course, designed especially for non-native English speakers, includes the skills you need to succeed on each section of the GRE, as well as access to Kaplan's exclusive computer-based practice materials and extra Verbal practice.

Other Kaplan Programs

Since 1938, more than 3 million students have come to Kaplan to advance their studies, prepare for entry to American universities, and further their careers. In addition to the above programs, Kaplan offers courses to prepare for the SAT, GMAT, LSAT, MCAT, DAT, USMLE, NCLEX, and other standardized exams at locations throughout the United States.

Applying to Kaplan English Programs

To get more information, or to apply for admission to any of Kaplan's programs for international students and professionals, contact us at:

Kaplan English Programs
700 South Flower, Suite 2900
Los Angeles, CA 90017, USA

Phone (if calling from within the United States): 800-818-9128
Phone (if calling from outside the United States): 213-452-5800
Fax: 213-892-1364
Website: **kaplanenglish.com**
Email: **world@kaplan.com**

* Kaplan is authorized under federal law to enroll nonimmigrant alien students.

Kaplan is accredited by ACCET (Accrediting Council for Continuing Education and Training).